My Sociology

My Sociology reconceptualizes introductory sociology for the changing demographics in today's higher education environment. Concise and student-focused, *My Sociology* captures students' attention with engaging stories and a focus on nondominant populations. Rather than introducing students to theory and history at the beginning of the text, the book integrates the necessary information throughout to keep students engaged.

Rosalind Gottfried, Brandeis University PhD, is a veteran community college teacher with 35 years of teaching experience. She also has a counseling degree and has worked in a variety of settings including criminal justice, domestic violence, foster care, mental health, and families. She is the proud single mother of two young adult daughters.

Here at last is something long needed: an introductory sociology text that skips the jargon and goes right to the concepts, that students can relate to, and addresses what is going on it capitalist societies today. Although the author tells the students that many of them will use this book in the only sociology course they will ever take, this book may inspire them to enroll in many more.

—**Yale Magrass**, Chancellor Professor of Sociology,
University of Massachusetts-Dartmouth

Rosalind's years in the classroom are evident in the practical explanations of sociology that combine theory, definitions, and student friendly examples to both show and tell what sociology is all about. I have been searching for years for an introductory sociology text that provides both the intellectual and the practical, the classic and the contemporary. This is that text.

—**Pamela Chao**, Professor, Sociology,
American River College

My Sociology

An Introduction for Today's Students

Rosalind Gottfried

Routledge
Taylor & Francis Group

NEW YORK AND LONDON

First published 2019
by Routledge
711 Third Avenue, New York, NY 10017

and by Routledge
2 Park Square, Milton Park, Abingdon, Oxon, OX14 4RN

Routledge is an imprint of the Taylor & Francis Group, an informa business

Library of Congress Cataloging-in-Publication Data

Names: Gottfried, Rosalind, author.
Title: My sociology : an introduction for today's students / Rosalind Gottfried.
Description: New York, NY : Routledge, 2019. | Includes index. |
Identifiers: LCCN 2018016695 (print) | LCCN 2018019646 (ebook) | ISBN 9781315402826 (Master) | ISBN 9781315402802 (ePub) | ISBN 9781315402819 (Pdf) | ISBN 9781315402796 (mobi) | ISBN 9781138224322 (pbk.) | ISBN 9781138224315 (hardcover)
Subjects: LCSH: Sociology.
Classification: LCC HM585 (ebook) | LCC HM585 .G68 2019 (print) | DDC 301--dc23
LC record available at https://lccn.loc.gov/2018016695
A catalog record for this title has been requested

ISBN: 978-1-138-22431-5 (hbk)
ISBN: 978-1-138-22432-2 (pbk)
ISBN: 978-1-315-40282-6 (ebk)

Typeset in Sabon LT Std
by Servis Filmsetting Ltd, Stockport, Cheshire

Visit the eResources at www.routledge.com/9781138224322

In honor of social activists, past, present, and future. Keep up the good fight.

Contents

Preface

My Sociology is the outcome of 35 years of teaching, mostly in the community college system. It is a response to students' suggestions that textbooks be more engaging, written in "plain English," and incorporate more nondominant perspectives. I developed this book with that mandate in mind. The focus is on current American issues in a global context. The book contains enough sociological theory to establish a foundation for those students who wish to take further courses.

When I think back on my doctoral work, I recall the struggle to make sociology work in the way I envisioned. In addition to conducting unstructured interviews with women respondents, I analyzed the characters women fiction writers were creating in their novels (this would be the late 1970s). My peers were highly critical regarding my use of fiction but I believe that novels reveal trends "pre-theoretically," and so I felt studying fiction would be enlightening. Some themes I discovered there emerged later in social science research. The three male professors on my committee eventually dropped their suggestion that I include quantitative data. To this day, I retain a skepticism regarding "factual" data derived from quantitative research though I acknowledge the value of solid efforts. I hope future sociologists will develop innovative research techniques to follow their instincts and challenge the status quo. All "science" requires heart as well as mind.

Rosalind Gottfried
Sacramento CA.
July 2018
Please send comments or questions to:
mysociologyauthor@gmail.com

Acknowledgements

I am grateful to Samantha Barbaro for her belief in this project and her efforts to bring it to fruition. I also thank Fred Coppersmith for his work in overseeing the production and review process. I thank Erik Zimmerman for his assistance, especially with the figures and permissions. I am grateful for the care and skill Barbara Spender brought to the task of copyediting the manuscript. I wish to thank all the reviewers for their helpful comments on multiple chapters, including:

Amber Blazek, Lone Star Community College
Ingrid Brown, Tulsa Community College
Thomas H. Cooper, Central Piedmont Community College
Gretchen DeHart, Community College of Vermont
Keri Diggins, Scottsdale Community College
Rod Golden, Mesa Community College
Paul Hanson, Cuyahoga Community College
Madison A. Hinton, Mississippi State University
William Hoffman, Houston Community College
Kimberly Lancaster, Coastal Carolina Community College
Crystal Lupo, Rutgers University
Jairo R Ledesma, Miami Dade College
Karen McCue, Central New Mexico Community College
Laurie Mengel, University of Hawaii at Hilo
Charles Miller, University of New Orleans
Donna Minnich, Northern Virginia Community College
Tom Quinn, University of Utah
Michelle A. Rush, Ivy Tech Community College
Dawn Tawwater, Austin Community College
Justin A. Thompson, Herkimer County Community College
P.J. Verrecchia, York College of Pennsylvania

This book is surely improved by these, and any deficiencies are mine.

I am especially grateful to Valerie Gnassounou, Founder/Director/Choreographer of the Yameci Dance Company, for contributing the cover photography. I appreciate the support of Holly Korda and Nancy Greenberg Concool, especially in their encouragement during the early phase of the project. I thank Alisa Rosenhaus for her support, especially in the final stages of the project. Allan Weissman read multiple chapters, providing insightful comments, for which I am very grateful. Aubrey Joy has been a continual, vital support of my work, family, and personal life.

Finally, I want to thank my students who have provided feedback. This list represents formal critiques students submitted but many others provided feedback, sometimes inadvertently. I am particularly moved by the students who asked where they could purchase the book, not knowing that I had written the manuscript. That provided me with some incentive when my confidence was wavering.

Student reviewers: Kathy Nguyen, Trellin McCoy, Maryann Tran, Miriam Ruiz, Hannah Estensen, Micaela Kautz, Hiep Nguyen.

CHAPTER 1

Society and Sociology

WHAT YOU WILL READ ABOUT IN THIS CHAPTER:

- **Sociology** is defined as the study of human behavior focusing on social forces. Sociology is distinct from other fields in the social and behavioral sciences in its emphasis on external forces affecting the individual. These perceptions become internalized and inform values, behaviors, attitudes, and habits and consequently feel "natural" or inevitable, though they are the result of human creation. Sociology utilizes the concepts of **social roles**, **institutions**, and **structure** as well as **socialization** and **cultural symbols**, in explaining this process. **Micro-level** analysis concerns daily interaction while **macro-level** analysis concentrates on the interdependency of social institutions. Examples of how these analyses are utilized are presented in the chapter.

- The development of societies, from hunting and gathering to post-industrial and global, is illustrated by how it affects the organization and efforts of societies to sustain themselves.

- Major historical perspectives in sociology are noted. Auguste Comte and Harriet Martineau will be introduced as figures inspiring the classical French sociological theorist, **Emile Durkheim**. His sociological approach to the study of suicide, and his methodology based in hard "facts," is presented. His influence in the development of **functionalist theory** in sociology is established.

- **Karl Marx's** theories regarding the *bourgeoisie*, as owners of production, and their exploitation of the workers, referred to as the *proletariat*, is introduced. Marxist theory suggests that major social institutions, such as the government, education, and even the family, support the powerful interests of the bourgeoisie. Marxist theory, with its emphasis on the protection of the interests of those who have resources, privilege, and power, is seen in contemporary **conflict theories**.

- The German sociologist **Max Weber** is known especially for his study of the relationship between religions, economies, and social structures. His methodology, based in the concept of *verstehen*, roughly translated as understanding or "to make meaning of," illustrates how broadly held religious and cultural ideas affect daily behaviors. This approach, with its central theme of symbolic and shared cultural meanings, influenced the American school of **symbolic interaction**. Symbolic interaction theory has, as its central theme, the idea that society is smoothly sustained as a result of shared meanings expressed in symbolic communication.

- The influential American theorist, **C. Wright Mills**, is best known for his concept of the **sociological imagination**, suggesting that sociological analysis best hits its mark by focusing on the interdependence of individual biography and historical context. Mills asserted that the individual cannot be understood unless the cultural referents are considered.

- Two other important figures in the early history of American sociology will also be introduced. W.E.B. Du Bois, a sociologist who addressed issues of race and other salient social issues, was the first African American to earn a doctoral degree at Harvard University. Jane Addams, a founding figure in American sociology and social work, was an activist who fought for issues of equality and civil rights. She was co-winner of the 1931 Nobel Peace Prize.

Introduction

Imagine a son is born to an impoverished family in an inner-city neighborhood. This boy is so smart that his nursery school teachers and peers refer to him as "the professor." His single, African American, working mother provides a loving environment and encourages him to excel in school and in character development. Even at a young age, her sensitive son is eager to earn money to help ease her circumstances.

He is also supported by his father and grandparents, who live in the same neighborhood. His father is a community icon; friendly and social, he visits with people all day long, allowing his son to proudly tag along. He contributes to his son's education by frequently testing his academic skills.

When the boy is seven years old the father is arrested, and convicted, on a double murder charge. The son grieves for his father and, as an adolescent, works diligently to free him. The father is ultimately incarcerated for life, in spite of the son's temporarily successful efforts to re-open the case. Despite his persistent grief over the loss of his father, the son wins a scholarship to a private academy and ultimately to four years at Yale University. He majors in molecular biophysics and biochemistry and excels, receiving nearly straight As.

The boy has a group of close childhood friends who remain a vital part of his life. His Yale friendships are limited and casual. Upon graduation, he pursues his dream to travel and then, after a period of indecision, takes a job at his old high school where he works for several years. After that he works as a baggage handler at the nearby airport. In 2011, he finally makes plans to apply to graduate schools, but is shot in a drug deal one mile from his childhood home.

The young man never stopped dealing drugs, mostly marijuana, at college and afterwards. In the last year of his life he became involved with individuals he knew were particularly dangerous but he felt he needed their help to move some product. He was killed in a drug-related incident.

This is the *true* story of *The Short and Tragic Life of Robert Peace* (Hobbs 2014). The telling of the story raises many questions. If not for his untimely death, would he finally have applied to graduate school? Why was he unable to establish a career in the field of study he showed remarkable aptitude for? Did going back to his neighborhood represent a "failure"? What forces were at work in his return to his old neighborhood? Why were other people, from similar circumstances, able to successfully change their circumstances? Was his *character* weak? What he psychologically *damaged*? Were the *ties* to home too compelling to resist? Perhaps these questions ultimately are unanswerable but this book will address some means for analyzing contributing forces. At the end of the chapter we will review the case of Robert Peace with a sociological eye.

What Is Sociology?

There is no easy or simple statement defining *sociology*. To say that "*Sociology* is the study of *society*" does not adequately explain it to the introductory student. The definition requires more specifications. Sociology illuminates human behaviors by focusing on the *social forces* that shape the individual's behavior in society. These are external forces which exert unavoidable impact on a person's life and prospects. These include the region, neighborhood, sex, race, religion, and ethnicity of a person as well as the social class and composition of their family. Sociology also offers a way to study how the structural organization of the society addresses the needs of the population for food, clothing, shelter, and security.

Society is another vague concept commonly utilized though difficult to adequately define. Our working definition of society concerns shared *social institutions and social relations, land, and government*. Societies also typically possess defining cultural aspects though the nature and adherence to these can vary among groups within the society. Nevertheless, if a person hears *The United States of America*, she or he can identify certain features of that society and can locate it on a map. Residents and citizens of the US are subject to the laws and institutions of the "society," usually readily identifiable. Common elements of language and artifacts, such as the American flag or a stop sign on a road, are generally universally understood within the society. Special practices of a particular group, in language or customs, such as *Ramadan, quinceaneras,* or *bar mitzvahs,* are vital to specific group identity and are not shared by all societal members. Today we also experience a *global society*, where the interdependence of nations is seen in politics, commerce, human migration, and mass communication and creating more commonalities between cultures.

Box 1.1 – Sociology Terms

Sociology is the study of human interaction at the *social* level. This refers to the social institutions, social roles, and social forces which shape society and social behaviors. Sociology can be thought of in terms of a telephoto lens which sometimes profiles the individual but also permits a wide-angle view focusing on other elements in the frame as seen in family, neighborhood, and general environment.

Second, sociology employs the *scientific method*. Sociologists support assertions about people and social life by investigating how it is lived. Other commentators, such as novelists, playwrights, and comedians are keen observers but they are not sociologists because their observations are largely based on subjective (personal) insights rather than objective principles of science.

Society refers to the social structure and social relations which unify a collection of people by providing a common identity, a body of laws, and a dominant culture. For example, most people have a shared concept of what the term *the American Dream* refers to.

Global society refers to elements of business, culture, and commerce which are interdependent and felt across national boundaries creating more commonalities than in previous eras. The internet, for example, has constricted the world in that communication can be accomplished virtually instantaneously anywhere it is available, and its reach is in perpetual extension.

Social forces are aspects of the social environment that influence a person's experiences and perspectives. They are conceptual but have "real-life" impact. Most notable among these are a person's social class, race, and sex. Additional influences emanate from the family structure, immigrant status, geographic region, and neighborhood.

The Social Construction of Reality is a theory which maintains that social forces feel fixed and exert pressure on people since they become internalized and compelling. The view highlights that social institutions are human creations and they therefore can also be subjected to changes.

Social customs and practices exert influence which becomes part of the social forces impacting daily life. The collective adherence to particular practices is entrenched in the society and can feel obligatory or coercive. At the same time, these external influences become internalized and consequently feel as if they are chosen, comprising a complementary relationship between the social order and an individual's "free will." This approach to sociology is labeled *the Social Construction of Reality* (Berger and Luckmann 1966). The theory reminds us that what feels like external mandate originates with people's activities and, once internalized, can be resisted or modified. *Sociology* studies the social nature of the human animal, with a particular eye towards elaborating its components and viewing it critically. In this context, critical does not mean "negatively" but refers to suspending what we think we know and examining social phenomena with a fresh perspective.

The technology available to a society is a major element in determining how people live. Today's computer, smart phones, and social media have had far reaching repercussions for just about everyone; a "tweeting" president was unthinkable just a few years ago. An example of changing behavioral norms can be seen in commonly acceptable practices such as texting to others while physically visiting with friends or family, or sitting in sociology class. The extensive use of technology changes the way people relate in daily, face to face interactions. Whatever your feelings regarding this trend, it is pervasive. People feel free, or even under obligation, to post frequent updates of their daily activities on social networks no matter how mundane or personal the activity. The expectation is that the recipients will respond to these updates immediately, or risk being socially sanctioned. The concept of privacy has changed, with regard to both the types of information shared and the number of people who are expected to care. Though some of these new trends can be experienced as enhancing a feeling of connection, they can also quickly spill into feelings of isolation or exclusion.

Sociology offers explanations of social phenomena, both those deeply entrenched and those newly emerging. The smart phone, for example, has led to new social developments such as cyber bullying; sexting; the formation of *community* based on specific interests (rather than proximity); and the creation of spontaneous mass events such as flash mobs. Sociology probes the consequences of social and technological innovations on both the individual and culture. The relationship is reciprocal, changes in the individual will influence social life and changes made in the social realm will impact the individual. We may not like to admit it but many choices we make, such as the type of clothing we prefer to wear or the way we carry the objects we need in daily life, are influenced by marketing decisions made by executives and specialists whose business it is to establish these tastes in the consuming public. This inter-relationship between product and social life is an essential element of the American capitalistic economy.

Finally, established organizations fulfilling social needs are referred to as *social institutions*, and their study is fundamental to the purpose of sociology. Studies at this level would examine the relationships between the economy, education, family, childrearing, religion, politics, media, health, science, and the military. All the social institutions make up the *social structure*, or the general organization of a society. Changes in one institution can force modifications in another. These structural elements in society shape personal experience. For example, consider what happens to a family when the economy tanks. If the family breadwinner loses a job, or suffers decreases in hours or pay, the family can lose their house; older children may have to drop out of college; younger children may be unsupervised during the day; and the stress can lead to marital separation and/or health issues. All of these trends can occur as a consequence of one person's unemployment, though downward economic trends generally impact many people and have multiple social ramifications.

How Can We Understand the Social Structure of the US Today?

Box 1.2 – Societal Terms

Community refers to those people who comprise a group whose members share social or cultural affinities, and frequently serve as resources for each other. Community formerly implied proximity but today communities are just as likely to exist virtually. For example, a local girls and boys club is a neighborhood association, while video game players comprise a virtual community.

Social institutions are components of the social structure. They shape the ways the population meets basic needs to sustain the society. These include reproduction and childrearing (family), education, exchange of goods (economy), and protection against outside groups or threats (polity), and some view of meaning beyond the individual (religion). These social institutions, in establishing the means to sustain the society, also provide ideal guidelines for behavior. For example, historically, marriage in the US was expressed as a long-term union between two heterosexual adults; though other relationships occurred outside of legal marriage, they were not regarded as acceptable until recently.

Social structure is the skeletal organization of society. Patterns of interaction emerge based upon the relationships between major social institutions in society. The social institutions are considered to be complementary; each supports the sustenance of the others and of society as a whole.

Social roles refer to recognized behaviors that support social interactions. Examples of social roles include student, spouse, parent, worker, church member. Once a person's behaviors are seen through an established social context, we know what to expect of the interaction.

Social Structural Forms in Human Societies

Social structures were relatively uncomplicated, for most of human history. The most common structural arrangement in human society, enduring for tens of thousands of years, was characteristic of *hunting and gathering* societies in which the division of labor required few differentiated social institutions. Social institutions incorporate **social roles** which influence a person's identity and indicate information about how a person spends her or his time. A person can possess multiple **social roles** such as parent, partner, worker, church member, team member, volunteer, and student in any combination. In hunting and gathering societies, work and family roles incorporated **social roles** largely stemming from factors of age and sex. For example, women typically gathered nuts, fruits, and berries which sustained daily life, especially in the absence of seasonal sources of food such as meat. Women cared for the young while young adult men hunted and protected the group. The society operated as a single unit with a relaxed pace and a short work week, perhaps about 35 hours. Daily activity varied and leisure time allowed sociability and development of crafts (Harari 2015).

Some ten thousand years ago, the *agricultural revolution* made it possible for people to produce food surplus by cultivating plant and animal life, and thus societies became sedentary. Harari (2015) suggests that life actually became more unpleasant in agricultural societies, as diets likely were monotonous and the mineral depletion of soil would eventually lead to crop failure. The ability to produce extra food nevertheless allowed for larger groups but the average individual likely had a tougher life and faced a greater risk of starvation and disease. The hard work of the farmers and shepherds led to the inception of an elite group with access to luxuries and leisure. The evolution of social class hierarchies is initiated in this era of human history.

The *industrial revolution*, originating more than 250 years ago, ultimately permitted the work of food production to be limited to a small group of laborers while the majority of workers toiled through long days in factories. The mechanization of production allowed for widely available cheaper products, accomplished by conditions of employment characterized by long days and dangerous machinery. New societal relations emerged as people moved to the cities to get work, most essentially that work now occurred away from the home rather than on a family farm. The tenuous nature of farm life was exchanged for jobs which frequently led to more imminent ill health, injury, and death. During this period, social inequality grew and social problems, many stemming from the separation of work and home, plagued family and community life. Many of today's typical complaints—from idle and delinquent youths to women-headed households—stem from this period

Figure 1.1 For most of the history of human beings, societies were small groups dependent on hunting and gathering. According to historians, life was pretty leisurely and pleasant, most of the time, with about 35 hours a week devoted to maintaining the group's basic needs. How do you imagine the rest of the time was spent? What would be the drawbacks in such a nomadic existence? Source: Anton_Ivanov / Shutterstock.com

Figure 1.2 In a post-industrial society, most workers are in service or information occupations. Here is an image of a packing warehouse, which represents the type of work typical of industrial/manufacturing societies Source: wellphoto / Shutterstock.com

of industrialization. A small portion of the society, factory owners and aristocrats, enjoyed the fruits of others' labors and lived an idle lifestyle devoted to consumption, pleasure, and leisure.

Today the US is considered a *post-industrial* society, initially characterized by the economic growth and well-paid jobs characteristic of the immediate post-World War II era. Most of the workforce is now involved in providing services and information. Everything from food service and custodial work to teaching and sales, and professional services such as legal or medical work, is incorporated into this category. While some highly skilled technical and professional work is well paid, much skilled labor has become automated or relocated "offshore" to other countries, resulting in pervasive economic inequality (see Chapter 5). Many workers find themselves in low-paid occupations requiring minimal training. Un- and semi-skilled laborers earn wages too low to bring them out of poverty, resulting in a transition from a viable working class to chronic poverty. A smaller group of technically advanced workers and managers emerges as a well-paid elite possessing benefits such as healthcare, leave time, retirement contributions, and stock options (see Chapter 5). The average American's standard of living has been compromised due to the economic globalization of the post-industrial era and accelerated by changing government policies favoring world trade and compromising wages and programs for workers.

> **Box 1.3 – Social Structures in Human History**
>
> The vast majority of human history was characterized by **hunting and gathering** societies, in which work was devoted to procuring food and shelter. The division of labor was limited to designations based upon age and sex.
>
> **Agricultural** societies developed about ten thousand years ago, and were characterized by cultivating plant and animal life which allowed the group to become sedentary and larger. Diets were limited and crops were vulnerable to failure, due to soil depletion. The size and stability of the society allowed for the development of a limited social hierarchy.
>
> The **industrial revolution**, originating roughly 250 years ago, permitted food production to be limited to a small group of laborers while the majority of workers were involved in the manufacture of goods in factories. This ushered in an era of separation between work and domestic life and shifted some responsibilities, formerly belonging to the family, to other social institutions. Social class divisions become more pronounced in industrial society with a significant portion of the group involved with production of goods.
>
> **Post-industrial** societies refer to countries where the majority of the population is involved in providing information and services. This has allowed for more equality between the sexes but has developed into greater disparities between elite professional and technical workers, on the one hand, and lower level service providers, on the other.

The Hunger Games Trilogy (Collins 2008, 2009, 2010): A Social Structure of Complete Institutional Control

The *Hunger Games* trilogy is a chilling sociological representation of how a society might look when an isolated, centralized government controls the conditions of each individual living in the society. In these books, the inhabitants have no choices with respect to their work, diet, freedom of movement, or any personal rights. Daily life is tightly controlled and monitored. In the first volume, we are introduced to a North American society partitioned into twelve districts which exist in a virtual communications vacuum and each is forced to accomplish a specific task, such as food production or mining. In contrast, in the Capital district, where the corrupt government is situated, a population of overfed, overindulged, and bored residents enjoys the fruits of the other districts' labors. They are desperate for entertainment and ultimately obtain some relief as a result of the "hunger games," a heavily orchestrated competition featuring one female and male adolescent from each district who will fight to the death until there is only one remaining person who "wins." The residents of the capital are lured into the games by the ability to help competitors with care packages they design from watching the competition at home.

Katniss is the female from District 12 and the heroine of the trilogy. She volunteers to go to the games when her younger sister is selected by lottery in her first eligible year. She and her confidante, and district male co-competitor, Peeta, trick the President into allowing a double winner earning themselves a lifelong enemy in the humiliated leader. Katniss and Peeta captivate the capital's audience with their bravery and intensely romantic love story, initially fabricated to win the allegiance and support of the audience.

The games were created as punishment for a subdued rebellion and to remind the fans of the power of the government. The arena, where the games occur, is a constructed "set" where all the action is monitored and manipulated. The games are embellished with pre-game festivities of pageantry orchestrated for the entertainment of the elite Capital residents. For the district residents, they are life and death, not only for the participants but for the winner's district which will be granted additional "privileges" such as more food rations. The districts' residents are under constant surveillance and are intimidated into avoiding any action that might be viewed unfavorably by the Capital. Access to any real information, about the other districts or the central government, is virtually nonexistent. When Katniss first arrives in the Capital, she is oblivious as to the conditions there or the extent of the control of the players. (Later in the series, an underground resistance is revealed.)

District life is harsh and seemingly hopeless. The residents of each district are permitted only narrowly defined activities. There are no individual freedoms and the desperately poor population has virtually no means to achieving better circumstances. People are under constant scrutiny and the penalty for breaking a rule would be separation from the community into robot-like servitude in the Capital. The citizens of the districts are unaware that there is a 13th district which is home to a rebellion; they have been led to believe that District 13 was destroyed. Secretly, some people from each district, who have some role in the games, are aligned with the rebels from District 13. They ultimately rescue an injured Katniss and bring her to District 13 but not before she completely loses a sense of who, among her support group, is trustworthy.

The rebels convince Katniss to travel to the districts for recruitment to the revolutionary cause. She wears a *mockingjay* pin which becomes a symbol of the rebellion. Eventually, the Capital is conquered and Katniss kills the President, a job she won by agreeing to be the face of the revolution. In the end, after years of ambivalence, Katniss marries her confidante and has a family though she resists doing so since she fears what could potentially befall them.

The trilogy creates a fully integrated system of *dystopian* institutions supporting the corrupt central authority. It is especially interesting, sociologically, for the ways in which it manipulates the population, largely through orchestrated media and desperate poverty. Ultimately, the story ends with hope, the revolution succeeds, and life continues under a fledgling though imperfect democracy. The struggle to form a new society takes time to develop and necessitates an armed rebellion. The new world is not everything that Katniss had hoped for but she hesitantly puts her faith in it.

Why are these books of interest to sociologists? The books are an indictment of authoritarian regimes; a total disregard for the environment; information and mind control; and the darker side of *human nature*, which the books imply exists in all people. Ultimately, the trilogy stands as a testament to human resilience. The strength of the story lies in the familiarity of some of the trends in the society portrayed. The evolution does not come "cheaply," main characters in the novels, including both active rebels and "innocents," ultimately are sacrificed to the cause, raising the question of at what point conditions would make the sustaining of life untenable (The Artifice).

Social Institutions

The term *social institution* refers to the patterned ways in which a society addresses basic human needs. The social institutions make up the *social structure*, or the general organization of a society, characterized today by many specialized institutions, often with complicated interdependencies. The *basic* institutions of society are the economy, the polity (government), the family, education, and religion. All developed societies contain some form of these. Sports, entertainment, healthcare, media, science, technology, and the military also comprise essential social institutions since each represents a significant contribution to the economy and can easily be recognized by specific uniforms, logos, music, names, and/or language.

In examining the social institutions, sociologists look beyond stated intentions and investigate the actual impact of policies and practices. The social institutions shape all aspects of civil and legal life, so sociologists are especially interested in seeing what underlies any stated goals and mechanisms they express. The government, for example, is often represented as the mechanism for protecting the rights and interests of its citizens, though "it frequently fails" to protect some groups and perpetrates harm. Many policies, regulations, laws, and judicial decisions favor business and finance, representing the interests of a small, elite societal group. The *Citizens United* Supreme Court ruling (2009) which effectively provides for corporations and unions to fund political campaigns with no limitations through money spent on ads and other campaign supports, illustrating the bias of the system. Although money donated directly to a candidate is still capped, this ruling effectively provides for "independent" entities such as corporations and unions, to exert virtually limitless political influence. The Court's ruling mandated that the first amendment's guarantee of free speech extends to formal organizations. The minority's opinion maintained an interpretation of the first amendment's free speech provision as pertaining to individuals and suggested that allowing unlimited spending for corporate and union interests violates fundamental democratic principles since the larger entities have enormous resources at their disposal, capable of drowning out the voices of the citizenship (Bentley). Nevertheless, *Citizens United* prevailed and attempts to reverse it have been unsuccessful.

Another example of government policy favoring business interests can be seen in the failure to charge a regular "sales tax" on financial transactions such as the purchase of stocks, bonds, or other financial products. These are tax free while the more universal sales of commodities such as clothes, cars, alcohol, and restaurant services are taxed at an increasingly higher rate. The financial burden represented by these taxes consumes a significantly greater portion of average and low annual incomes. It is estimated that extending the sales tax to financial products would bring an additional 100 billion dollars a year in revenue (Baker 2016).

Systemically, the US exhibits unfair policies not only with regard to taxation but also to labor. Most Americans work, and a large group work at low wage jobs that barely bring the workers out of official poverty. Yet, the safety net for the more vulnerable segments of the population falls short of the protections offered in other post-industrial societies. American employers, and government, fail to guarantee paid family leaves for parenting or family illness; do not provide for paid vacations which are as long as six to eight weeks in Europe; offer fewer paid holidays than the average 12 days in other countries; fail to guarantee healthcare; and do not offer free or low-cost higher education. The US never has had programs as generous as in Europe, but the past 35 years have seen a reduction in the minimal aid offered (see Chapter 5).

Since the events of 9/11, the US government has been seen as stripping citizens' rights in the name of "national security." The potential threats to the security of the nation, with regard to potential terrorist events, have been used to curtail the freedoms and civil rights of citizens and residents. People are more vulnerable today to government intrusion, particularly if they belong to a group that is deemed "suspicious" in any way. Some commentators suggest we are at risk of repeating past history, such as when the government interned anyone of Japanese descent during World War II, effectively seizing many of the group's assets (Nelson 2017). Many Muslims fear being publicly identified as such and are even reluctant to wear the hijab in public. Additionally, some politicians are calling for closing our borders to refugees from the Syrian war, or anyone who looks or seems remotely Islamic.

Even an institution addressing elements of personal life is affected by public policies. The small, typical, modern nuclear family, frequently with only three to five members, has been viewed as isolating the family unit. Dependence on low-wage jobs to survive, sometimes leading to excessively long days or work weeks, or to maintaining a job where the worker is exposed to toxins or other abusive conditions, is characteristic of the lives of low wage earners. Workers fearing unemployment sometimes relocate to secure a job, even if it means leaving extended family or a closely knit community. Although not all families conform to this model, economic necessity and legal biases contribute to the poor work situation of many wage earners who endure adverse effects on their family life. Increasingly, single and married young adults are living with parents, often as a result of financial stressors, delaying their full entry into adult roles (Fry 2016).

Keep in mind that social institutions describe the *norms* that are promoted as desirable but they do not necessarily represent "real" life. The legal aspects of family life are slower to change than personal behaviors and the delay can be detrimental to the well-being of individuals. Conforming to acceptable standards confers legitimacy and ease of access to certain civil rights. Consider the issue of cohabitation. Today the majority of married couples cohabit prior to marriage though most will either marry, or dissolve the relationship, within a couple of years. To some extent, cohabitation has lost the stigma associated with it but many still desire the designation of "legal spouse." This desire is equally strong among gay couples, legally able to marry according to federal law since 2015 (Chappell 2015). What does marriage confer regarding social status? One element is some clarification of the implied relationship. When a couple says they are married, we have a relatively clear view of the nature of the relationship. The couple also gains legal rights involving government agencies in taxation, immigration, property, and inheritance. The culture recognizes marriage as a (relatively) permanent union and as one that usually gains religious support, as well. This "normalization" is reflected in our language. If I present someone as my *spouse*, most people recognize the general type of relationship indicated, even considering personal variations. If I attend a social event with my *cohabiting partner*, how will I make the introduction? I can choose from such designations as *Friend, Roommate, Significant Other, Better Half*, etc. but the variety and choice of words does not communicate the relationship with the same ease and clarity as *spouse*. This immediate association imparts legitimacy and recognition which eases a social situation. Complying with the expectations of established social institutions implies a sense of belonging and acceptance. Marriage maintains a strong symbolic meaning for many people.

Religion, as a major institution, underscores common values contributing to social cohesion but it also reveals divisive cultural elements, as can be seen in hate crimes and intolerance towards non-Christian groups. Religion is the institution which provides solace and meaning to individuals though sociologically it is studied more for what it contributes to the fabric of society than for the content of its theology. Religion frequently acts as a behavioral and ethical guiding force, creating a sense of community and purpose, both within the individual and for the group. Americans are more apt to describe themselves as religious than people in other developed countries. Twenty percent of recent survey respondents checked *nonaffiliated* as their chosen church, indicating an increase in the portion of society who lack membership in any particular church or religious group (Masci and Lipka 2016). This is a shift away from collective worship, suggesting more personalized ties to religion. This lack of institutional affiliation is considered more characteristic of the millennial generation (born between 1982 and 2000) and is the subject of speculation regarding its impact on society.

Social institutions often demonstrate coordination, as in the case of federal tax exemptions granted to churches and religiously based organization. Some religiously oriented agencies provide community social services such as food banks, daycares, substance abuse treatments, homeless shelters, and other support services. In fact, many Republican politicians favor supporting "faith-based" community agencies, in

Figure 1.3 It is sometimes difficult to acknowledge behaviors that don't agree with personal or religious values
Source: a katz / Shutterstock.com

lieu of government agencies, as a means to reduce public expenditures to the poor. Such a policy is contested by more "liberal" politicians, who more ardently support the safety net and fear the mingling of Church and state.

Education represents the fifth basic social institution in society. Acculturation, socialization, literacy, skills building, vocational training, generation of new knowledge, peer relations, consumerism, and social mobility are all "tasks" attributed to the education system. There is little agreement, even between "experts" regarding the best educational practices. Most Americans support public education and feel that obtaining a good education is a basic right. We do not always follow our beliefs with our purses, since education budgets suffer severe cuts during recessions and have yet to recover from the "great recession of 2008." The American public-school system has persistently exhibited inequalities due to race, ethnicity, gender, and social class divides. The *Common Core* curriculum was developed to improve the quality and standardization of the K-12 system though it has generated a great deal of conflict among both parents and educators. The possession of a college degree, especially to secure decent employment, is more essential than in previous eras. The high cost of a college education, even in public institutions and controlling for inflation, has accelerated in recent decades (see Chapter 11).

Study of the social institutions can illuminate much of the actual lived existence of citizens. One major contribution of sociology is to probe beyond the stated mandates of the institutions shaping society to analyze their full impact. The examples above, derived from basic elements of the social organization of contemporary life, are an introduction to the more detailed analyses that will appear in chapters addressing more specific topics. Students are encouraged to think about how laws, policies, regulations, and social habits affect both personal and collective life. Many students are aware of "sociological" revelations as a result of their own experiences. Sociology will aid in providing a framework for understanding these more systematically.

How Does Globalization Impact Society Today?

Life, in contemporary societies, is no longer restricted to elements generated from within national borders. *Globalization* refers to a situation where the economies of nations exhibit an *inter*dependence due largely to the policies and business interests of advanced capitalist economies. Trade, production, and labor policies affect where commerce occurs and how much it costs. Social and cultural domination through media, such as television, film, fashion, and music also travels between nations and contributes to the homogenization of cultural forces, reducing the uniqueness of specific cultures. *Transnational corporations*, headquartered in a specific country, typically have sales forces, holdings, and production in multiple countries and may own a wide range of enterprises unrelated to their primary products. It is not surprising to see American corporations opening retail outlets in relatively remote areas. McDonald's, for example, has over 36,000 outlets in over 100 countries (Rosenberg 2017). The Nestlé corporation, which has worldwide distribution and is headquartered in Switzerland, is responsible for many more products than those generally associated with the Nestlé label. Examples of their brand include *Purina* pet food, *Nespresso* coffee products, *Haagen Dazs* ice cream products, *Lean Cuisine*, *Stouffers*, *Perrier*, *S- Pellegrino*, and *Gerber's* baby food.

Box 1.4 – Globalization Terms

Globalization occurs when the economies of nations are interdependent, frequently resulting in the domination of advanced capitalist economies over those of developing nations.

Transnational corporations, headquartered in a specific country, typically have sales forces, holdings, and production in multiple countries owning a wide range of enterprises, not necessarily related to each other.

Developing nations are countries which are in the process of expanding their industrial base as they shed their agricultural roots. They frequently feature *export processing zones*, or areas where manufacturing is centered. These zones promote industry by providing incentives such as tariff reductions, tax relief, and lax labor regulations.

Developed nations are characterized by high per capita incomes, high levels of technology and automation.

Brexit refers to the 2016 referendum in which United Kingdom voters elected to separate from the *European Union*, which includes 28 member countries.

Globalization is frequently associated with an improved standard of living in *developing countries*. Developing countries include nations increasing their industrial base but still transitioning from an agricultural system. The standard of living, generally measured by per capita income, is lower than in developed countries. Whether the average worker's standard of living has improved, along with the expansion of industry, is debatable. Many nations fall into this category; a few examples would be Mexico, China, Brazil, Bangladesh, Turkey, and India. Developing countries frequently have *export processing zones*, where production is centered. These areas are provided with government incentives such as tax relief or tariff reductions and lax labor regulations to increase their allure to corporate executives. Often the workers have no protective legislation and can be required to work long days under poor conditions. The work environment can lead to health hazards, injury, or even death but many people work there since there are few competing opportunities. In these countries, farming has become impossible due to poverty wages, the poor quality of the depleted soil, or the corporate purchase of farm land. Some commentators suggest the newly available low-wage factory jobs are preferable to the destitution of subsistence farming. Research shows mixed outcomes. There is evidence that globalization has increased inequality within a country but not necessarily increased poverty. Some data suggest that factory work creates and encourages child labor while others indicate that if family income rises, and the children's income is no longer required for subsistence, school attendance increases (Pavcnik 2009; Bardhan 2006). Though the consequences of globalization for a country's residents are unclear, its profitability to the corporate bottom line is undeniable.

Developed countries are characterized by a high industrial base, technological advancement, and solid per capita income. Globalization has increased the affluence of the educated and, in conjunction with automation, decreased the standard of living and wages of the working class. The developed world includes Europe, US, Canada, Australia, Japan, and South Africa, among others. In a 2016 United Kingdom (UK) referendum, referred to as *Brexit*, the British voted 52 percent to 48 percent to separate from the European Union (EU), which has 28 member countries. The outcome was surprising and many observers, including many among the British population, failed to foresee it. This stunning result has been explained as a partial response to dissatisfactions arising from globalization. Since the 1989 breakup of the Soviet bloc, globalization has become increasingly significant to the world economy and trade, impacting the internal conditions of many countries. Frustration with trade agreements, immigration, and declining standards of living contribute to the disaffection seen in the *Brexit* vote and incite the desire for more local control of the economy and related policies. The immigrant population is seen as depressing wages by taking jobs with wages unacceptable to the British. Working-class Britain, with high unemployment rates, has suffered losses in well-paid jobs, labor protections, and reduced welfare programs. Globalization is viewed as benefitting the few at great expense to most citizens. Especially disaffected segments of the population include people over 60, working-class people with no university education, low-income citizens, and economically depressed regions (McGill 2016). The older group, identifying more as "English" rather than "British," presumably felt a loss of identity and status, being subsumed into the EU. The university-educated population, enjoying expanded work opportunities across the continent, showed more favorable attitudes towards the EU. The final vote reflected differences in education, social class, age, and immigrant status, issues which are also currently rife in American politics. As British journalist Larry Elliott explained, "Now we have Britain's rejection of the EU. This was more than a protest against the career opportunities that never knock and the affordable homes that never get built. It was a protest against the economic model that has been in place for the past three decades" (Elliott 2016).

How Are Sociological Concepts Applied to the Study of Society?

Study of the relationships between social institutions constitutes what sociologists call *macro-level* sociology where the focus is on how changes in one exert consequences for another. For example, in response to the "great recession," states and municipalities reduced budgets with consequent cutbacks to the public schools. Reduced education budgets led to larger classes, fewer teachers, and curricular cuts. These losses had a detrimental effect on the quality of education, especially in the lower income communities where parents were less likely to fill in resource gaps. Myriad ramifications spread throughout higher education, as well. On the one hand, enrollments went up in community colleges, where the fees are more accessible than in four-year institutions. The lack of paid employment also leads to greater participation in education, not only because of freed time but also to gain new skills for employment opportunities. At the same time, higher enrollments, combined with reduced budgets, make it more difficult to enroll in required classes due to reduced course offerings. These trends often lead to more years needed to attain educational goals, delaying a person's return to the job market. The consequences of the strains in the systems, emanating from economic forces, eventually impact individuals but viewing them on the institutional scale comprises a macro-level analysis since the focus is generalizable to many:

Reduced budgets = Fewer courses, teacher layoffs, expanded enrollment time

Institutional trends ultimately impact individuals, which can be analyzed as well, but macro analysis focuses on institutional factors. In a macro analysis, it is not necessary to study individuals, the analysis can proceed from data which describes group trends. We can project the impact on individuals but studying the life experiences of individuals is referred to as *micro-level* analysis. A micro analysis, regarding the impact of a recession on individuals, might look at how the stress of reduced personal income, losses of roles such as breadwinner, and time spent improving work skills creates stress affecting physical and mental health, family life, and overall life satisfaction. In a micro analysis, the researcher will directly reach out to individuals to find out if they have made behavioral changes as a result of the recession. They may not ask this question directly, but ask about education, family, and work histories modifications and see if they show any relationship to the changes in the economy.

Box 1.5 – Levels of Analysis

Micro analysis and *macro analysis* are the categories which describe the *levels* at which sociologists conduct studies. A micro-level analysis concerns the day to day, usually face to face, personal level of analysis. Macro analysis concerns the relationship between social institutions. Although the repercussions of macro-level analysis are felt by individuals, the analysis is institutional, usually linking changes in one institution to consequences in another. For example, studying the classroom at the **micro level** might entail examining the type, content, and frequency of interactions between students and between students and the teacher. Are there frequent interactions? Are they informal or formal? Do they tend to be student to student or student to teacher, or both?

A **macro-level** study might focus on the relationship between class size or graduation rates and how they are impacted by budgetary limitations. In a recession, for example, states cut their education budgets and this can result in the hiring of fewer teachers, increases in class sizes, and less personalized attention. Weak students are more likely to go unnoticed, or unsupported, when such changes occur.

Micro and macro refer to the **level of analysis** and not to the number of people studied. Studying 25 classrooms, if the classroom interaction is the subject of study, constitutes a micro analysis. Macro analysis generally refers to systemic inter-relationships in that the analysis can be based on statistical trends rather than personal cases.

Micro analysis is frequently interactional, utilizing the concept of **social roles**. **Social roles** are the normative patterns of behaviors associated with particular activities. For example, the student role has many obligations that are recognized by the student, teacher, and society. We expect students to read and write assignments, show up to class with appropriate behaviors, take exams, and pass the class. The student role also carries non-classroom identifying factors such as clothing and appearance; students usually wear jeans and t-shirts or sweatshirts, carry back packs, and engage in social activities typical of their group. Increasingly, the use of cell phones, particularly texting while in class, is also part of the student motif. Each college campus may express unique variations characteristic of their own campus culture but, for the most part, the behaviors and obligations of the students, faculty, and staff are mutually understood. Without such an understanding, the classroom would be a much more disagreeable place, as may be experienced when someone fails to observe proper behaviors. What behaviors, in students or teachers, might prompt a complaint to the administration? Have you ever read your student handbook? Virtually every campus has one which lists the consequences of violating essential codes of conduct, from classroom behaviors to academic dishonesty. All of these rules, and their repercussions, are micro-level sociological analyses.

It must be emphasized that the difference between macro and micro levels of analysis is not one of size or number of people studied but of the *level* at which they are studied. The macro level concentrates on relations between institutional developments, such as recessions and transitions in political parties. The micro level concerns how people behave in concrete situations. A common mistake that students make is to say that studying one classroom is micro sociology and that the study of multiple classrooms, or multiple schools, is macro sociology. This is incorrect. Micro sociology would be to study the *interaction in* the classroom, for example, by investigating the differences in lecture-based classrooms versus experiential-based classrooms. Macro analysis, in contrast, would consider the ramifications of budgetary change on education, the classrooms, or student enrollments in general. It is the **level** at which the analysis occurs that is significant in describing the study. The distinction in levels is essential to sociology since connecting macro- and micro-level analyses contributes to understanding the complexities of social life.

Many believe that life in our society is fast and highly pressured. We take on multiple **social roles** and this can lead to feelings of fragmentation and stress. A 24-hour day is not sufficient when, for example, students with jobs and families must meet all their school, work, and family responsibilities. Consequently, some people suggest we have more stressful lives than in previous generations or in other societies. The comparison to other social structures, such as in agricultural societies, veils the different types of stress in each. The varied roles we play have to do with the nature of industrial society, and the existence of separate spheres of work, family, and education absent in agricultural societies. We may worry about bills, exams, children, or responding to emails but we are not worrying about a crop failure which would result in no income or food. Some of our perceived stressors are in our control. Our young generation, post-millennial, is growing up never having known a time without smart phones and instant access to technology, affecting family and social life, and many other factors (see Chapters 2 and 4). It might be beneficial to set aside cell-phone-free times at home, in order to enhance family relationships and reduce stress. In order to reduce the pressures associated with the work place some are prohibiting access to work emails outside of the regular workday.

Because we have so many roles to play, we often feel stretched to the point of ineffectiveness. Sociologists speak of *role conflicts* due to the number of roles we inhabit. A role conflict ensues when the demands of one role make it impossible to perform another role. Imagine you are on your way out the door to class and the daycare calls you to pick up your sick child. What will you do about the exam scheduled for that day? Alternatively, your job demands that you stay late to deal with a sale crowd but the daycare is closing in 15 minutes. All of us commonly experience such conflicts, although some of us have more resources available to address these problems. A single, working parent who also attends college, for example, will be especially susceptible to role conflict.

Box 1.6 – Social Roles and Social Statuses

Role conflict refers to the difficulty a person has fulfilling a role due to the demands of another role. Examples of role conflicts would be if your child is sick and you have to miss an exam. Another situation of role conflict would be if you are asked to stay late at work and cannot pick up your child at school. Much contemporary stress emanates from the responsibilities of multiple roles.

A *social status* refers to a position a person holds and it is different from a social role because a person can have a status without the role. Conversely, a person can have a role without the status. For example, a person can be legally married but not living with the spouse and not playing that role. A person can also play the role of spouse without the legal status, as in the case of cohabitation.

An *ascribed* status refers to one that is "given" to a person without any effort on their part. If you were born into royalty or leadership, in a society where these titles were inherited, this would constitute an ascribed status.

An *achieved status* is one that a person has earned, such as "college graduate."

A *master status* is a position that is salient, because it is presumed to be the core *social* identification of the person. This status may not be essential to the person's *self-definition* but it is one which carries social significance. For example, a convict is primarily seen as a "con" even after they are no longer under the supervision of the criminal justice system. In the US, physical disability often is seen as a master status. Master statuses can also be positive, as when the President of the US is still allowed the title even when no longer holding the office.

Sociologists also utilize the concept of *social status*, which refers to a *position* a person occupies. A status may, or may not, have an accompanying **social role**. For example, a person can have a parental status but not play the role if, for example, the child lives with someone else. Some social statuses, such as *prince* or *chief*, are inherited or *ascribed*. Some, such as college graduate, are earned or *achieved*. On a social level, we are sometimes defined primarily in relation to one particular status. This is referred to as a *master status*, in that this one particular characteristic is the primary social filter through which an individual is viewed. The master status may feel inconsequential to the person inhabiting it; the designation reflects the weight the society attributes to it. A convict may be viewed, first and foremost as a felon, even if the offense was a decade ago and the person has been out of the prison system for years. This status follows the person and makes it difficult to find a job. The social view regarding a status reveals much about what is valued in society. A person who is physically "different" may be seen primarily as "disabled" though their self-concept may not reflect such a view at all. During the impeachment proceedings of Bill Clinton, one article noted that his lawyer gave an eloquent speech from his wheelchair in the Senate chambers. Why mention his wheelchair? His speech was completely independent of his physical condition. One news report, of a hijacked plane, stated that some of the passengers were Americans, some were Panamanians, and some were women! As if being a woman precludes having a nationality!

Figure 1.4 Disability is often treated as a master status. This individual is unlikely to be referred to simply as one of the runners
Source: mezzotint / Shutterstock.com

A master status often carries a negative stigma but it can be positive. Once a person is President of the US, for example, she or he is always entitled to be addressed as "President." Many physicians or professors utilize the title of "Dr" even in a social setting where their professional credentials are irrelevant. Similarly, in a report of a car accident, the injured person might be identified as an honor student, which is irrelevant to the incident being reported.

What Is Distinctive About the Sociological Approach?

As a student, you will likely study more than one social science. Social sciences generally include the fields of anthropology, economics, political science, geography, and sometimes psychology. Psychology, in some institutions, is grouped with biology under a category such as "behavioral sciences." Modern psychology is more dependent on physical measures than in previous periods and behaviors labeled as psychological are increasingly associated with neurological and biochemical elements. The changes are due, in part, to advanced technologies in MRIs, CT scans, and other mechanisms producing neurological data.

Each of the social science disciplines defines its domain as *human behavior* but each has a particular *perspective* or approach. Some differences between these disciplines do represent distinctive viewpoints in *what* is studied or *how* it is studied but sometimes it is just a matter of the researcher's affiliation. Cultural anthropology and sociology, for example, can produce research that is virtually indistinguishable in its approach. Researchers in both fields study homelessness, urban street life, gang affiliations, family life, and many other topics, frequently with little variation. Techniques brought to the research are sometimes more characteristic of one discipline over another. Anthropologists have been more likely to study the artifacts, or products, of a society for what they can reveal, even digging through people's garbage. Sociologists have been more likely to use quantifiable data resulting in graphs and charts. Sociologists have diagrammed the social networks among friends attending the same school to see, for example, who appears in multiple networks suggesting social leadership.

Since sociology is the study of *society*, a common error occurs when someone states that psychology studies the individual while sociology studies the group. This distinction has been uttered in both psychology and sociology courses but it is misleading and simplistic since psychologists do study groups and sociologists sometimes study individuals. A statement differentiating the two disciplines, on the basis of *who* they study, obscures the unique approach of each discipline. It would be more correct to say that psychologists focus on the subjective elements of experience and on biochemical processes in the brain. Sociologists pay more attention to objective measures or social forces, originating outside of the individual, but influencing the individual's actions and thoughts.

A couple of examples can illustrate the differences. A topic which has garnered much societal attention is the increase in births to unwed mothers. The percentage of births to unmarried women was 40 percent in 2014, the first slight decline from 41 percent in 2008. These figures more than double the rate seen in 1980, when unmarried births accounted for 18 percent of all births (Livingston and Brown 2014). A sociologist, in considering why any particular woman is among this cohort of unmarried mothers, is likely to consider the state of the economy, religious affiliation, employment status, education, and other social elements which have been shown to affect birthrates and marital status. As we will see in Chapter 10, educated women comprise a very small percentage (6 percent) of these unmarried births. The economic background of a woman influences the age and marital status of motherhood. The recent slight decrease in unwed births has been attributed to assumed greater work opportunities in the post-recession economy (Livingston and Brown 2014).

A psychologist investigating the same subject would more likely focus on the family composition, dynamics, and situation of the family a young woman grew up in. Personal experiences affecting the individual's development would be an integral part of this examination. The researcher might analyze, for example, the role the woman played in the family: Was she the caretaker of younger siblings? Was she the peace maker? Were her parents married? Does she perceive multiple options for her future, outside of childbearing? How did these affect her experiences; they can contribute to early motherhood or to a choosing to be "child-free." The psychologist, like the sociologist, is also trying to explain the behavior of women who have children outside of marriage. Researchers in each discipline will select specific factors to focus on though there is often some overlap. Both psychologists and sociologists are likely to consider the job prospects and financial status of the woman, though sociologists tend to do it in a more general way while psychologists focus on the specifics; is the economy tanking or is this person jobless with few skills? These are frequently inter-related but illustrate a different concentration.

A second example of how different social scientists study an issue concerns the large proportion of incarcerated African American men. A sociologist will generally consider such factors as the experiences African American men have had with law enforcement personnel; residence in an economically depressed neighborhood; attendance in a low-performing school; unfair laws and practices governing sentencing; and the difficulty of gaining employment once released from prison. Sociological research has turned up some evidence which disputes commonly held assumptions. For example, research reveals that African American men are **less** involved in drug use than White males though they are much more likely to be arrested and serve time for drug-related crimes (see Chapter 6).

A psychologist, in studying incarceration, might focus on an individual and his personality development, substance abuse, family interactions, and mental health status. A cultural anthropologist might focus on the cultural symbolism of crime and punishment and the cultural attitude towards rehabilitation. Of course, all these elements contribute to any individual's probable risk for incarceration and again we can see that the boundaries between the studies of the sociologist and the psychologist overlap. Most sociologists would not only focus on the discriminatory practices of law enforcement and the prison system but also would view the changing perspectives on rehabilitation over the past 35–40 years (see Chapter 6). Each discipline is likely to highlight different aspects of the person and environment and no discipline's viewpoint will completely explain both the social and cultural trends and the personal experiences of individuals.

Other disciplines define more specific areas of research than the general fields of psychology, sociology, and cultural anthropology. Economists focus on factors which influence the distribution of goods and services. Political scientists explore the nature of government and its various forms. History, more commonly considered a humanity than a social science, examines changes over time in human communities.

Figure 1.5 Much attention has been directed, in recent years, to the excessive incarceration—both in terms of numbers of people and length of sentences—leveled at African American males, frequently for minor offenses
Source: sakhorn / Shutterstock.com

Who Was Significant in Establishing Sociology?

The French theorist, **Auguste Comte** (1798–1857), is credited with coining the term *sociology* in 1838. He believed that applying the scientific method to social life would identify interactional patterns which would allow for the prediction of future trends, just as it does in the physical sciences. Comte was especially interested in investigating societal forces which promoted social stability or change. He believed that the revelations of sociology could be utilized to better society. Comte is considered an igniter of sociological insight and inspiration but his contributions to the field are considered limited in scope (Crossman 2017).

Harriet Martineau (1802–1876) was a British writer who translated Comte's works into English but who received no acknowledgement in the field until the last few decades. It is likely that this was due to sexism, especially since much of her work foreshadowed that of scholars who later were credited with major contributions to the field. Martineau was self-taught and considered herself a political economist though her writing had a sociological perspective. She earned a living as a journalist, speech writer, and novelist as well as a scholar. She addressed social issues, in her fictional and journalistic works, because she felt these would be the most accessible to the greatest number of people. Martineau covered a lot of territory in her life. She analyzed the impact of industrialization and capitalism and advocated an empirical, scientific approach. She investigated American society and was an early proponent of equality in race, sex, and class. She was an activist for women's rights and supported women's suffrage. She also made financial contributions to the US abolitionists. Due to personal experiences during a long illness, she was an early critic of the doctor/patient dynamic of authority and submission and was severely criticized by the medical establishment. Later in her life, she turned to atheism and suggested that humanity was becoming more "rational" and established religions were evolving as less rigid (Cole 2014).

French sociologist **Emile Durkheim** (1858–1917) is considered a founding theorist in the field. Durkheim's father was a rabbi, as was his paternal grandfather and great grandfather. It was initially assumed that Emile Durkheim would take up the family profession but, as a young man, he broke with the religion. Still, as the son of a traditional, orthodox Jewish family he was heavily influenced by his religious training and the rampant anti-Semitism of the day. Some of the areas he studied intensively included sociology of religion, sociology of education, social solidarity, collective conscience, and the development of beliefs and values in a society. Durkheim made essential contributions to the substance of sociological study, studying topics that previously had been considered individual or personal issues. He also elaborated methodological innovations to mold sociology as a "true" science (Crossman 2017).

Box 1.7 – Early Figures in Sociology

Auguste Comte coined the term *sociology*, representing a science of society. He proposed that the scientific method can be applied to social phenomena, identifying patterns and predicting future outcomes, as it does in the physical and natural sciences. Comte was interested in the social forces affecting social stability and change.

Harriet Martineau was a successful journalist, speech writer, novelist, and scholar. She was a prolific writer with both academic and popular influence. She was progressive in her support of equal rights in the areas of race, class and sex. A contemporary of Comte's, she also translated his work. Her influence on sociology was largely overlooked until recent decades.

One of Durkheim's most influential books was *Suicide* (1897/2012). In this treatise, Durkheim advanced the radical idea that the extremely personal act of suicide actually had its roots in the **social** environment. More specifically, he suggested that suicide was related to a person's level of **social integration** into the society. This dynamic was proposed as explaining both those very separated from society as well as those enmeshed. He described **anomic** suicide, literally "without order," as an explanation for suicide when a person experiences a **lack of belonging,** as in conditions of joblessness or social isolation. This can occur when a person has no family or community ties, as is the case for unmarried people and those lacking a job. He also looked at the role of the community, particularly in religion, in supporting a person's sense of integration in society. In contrast, he also maintained that a very strong tie to a **social role**, indicating extreme social integration, can lead to suicide when the **social role** a person inhabits **requires** the individual to kill her or himself. Examples of this type of suicide can be found in kamikaze pilots or in *suttee*, a Hindu practice requiring a woman to throw herself on her husband's funeral pyre in order to ascend to the afterlife with him. Durkheim categorized these as **altruistic** suicides.

Durkheim's explanations of suicide moved it from the personal to the social realm. At the time, most people attributed suicide to religious possession or to "madness," which was considered an inherited characteristic. To investigate his theory, Durkheim obtained data from the Census Bureaus in major European cities, for people whose cause of death was listed as suicide. For every recorded suicide, he viewed the person's marital status, parental status, employment status, home ownership status, and religious affiliation. He believed these elements were windows into the world of the individual and would indicate how much they felt a part of the society. He showed that these characteristics had predictive value in suicide. Contemporary research investigating the social aspects of suicide supports Durkheim's earlier work. A recent study of 35,000 male health professionals, over a 24-year period, utilized a social integration index scale which included factors similar to those employed by Durkheim. The researchers found that men scoring high on measures of social integration were less likely to commit suicide. Factors such as marital status, frequent attendance at religious services, and participating in a large social network emerged as mitigating factors in determining the risk of suicide (Tsai et al. 2014). Durkheim, as it turns out, was advanced for his time in suggesting the social dimensions of suicide risks. Research data today indicates the impact of characteristics such as sex, sexual orientation, employment, social networks, and economics on suicide risk.

Recently, much attention has been focused on the suicide rate of military veterans, linking it to social factors as well. One study of over a million US military veterans, who served from 2001–2007, shows that their suicide risks were the highest three years after discharge and that they were slightly *higher* among veterans who did *not* deploy to active warfronts. This suggests that there is some consequence of the military experience, aside from being in combat, which is stressful. Enlisted men have twice the suicide rate of officers and military men are three times more likely than military women to commit suicide. Women with military service are twice as likely as non-military women to commit suicide. Though mental health factors can contribute to suicide potential, some have linked the suicide rate to the weak economy at the time of the veterans' return, and consequent feelings of displacement (Zarembo 2015).

Durkheim's approach to research was also innovative. For his *Suicide* study, he did not talk to a single person. It was not that he was uninterested in people's lives or motives, he just didn't think people were a reliable source in explaining their behavior! Durkheim's research process, elaborated in **The Rules of Sociological Method** (1895/2014; Lukes 1982), suggests that sociological research must be derived from *social facts*, defined as tangible aspects of behaviors which can be measured. From the Census Bureau data on suicide, he analyzed the factors present in suicide victims which could be measured and used to predict who would be at risk. This ability to predict events, culled from actual research, is a basic goal of science.

In further elaboration of his methods, he asserted that no behavior can be explained by a constant. In other words, a behavior common to more than one group cannot be the explanation for differences which exist between the groups. So, for example, he found that Catholics had a lower rate of suicide then Jews or Protestants. Can you guess why? Many students suggest it is because the Catholic Church sees suicide as a sin. This is a reasonable guess though it is incorrect because Judaism and Protestantism also see suicide as a sin and therefore this cannot be used to explain differences between the groups. Recall that Durkheim's theory addresses issues of social integration. What Durkheim believed is that the Catholic Church offered more of a community context than the other groups studied, especially in that it requires confession and communion. In this way the community involvement was different among Catholics, explaining their lower rates when all three groups shared prohibitions against suicide. The lower suicide rate in the Catholic community cannot be due to something which also exists in the other faiths; the cause had to lie elsewhere. Durkheim utilized his theoretical premise regarding community intensity to infer causation from the data. Catholics, he proposed, had less suicide due to stronger group ties which acted as "protection" against suicide.

Durkheim's work became the foundation for the approach to studying sociology which is known as *functionalism* or *structural functionalism*. This perspective focuses on the assumption that a society maintains a basic *stasis*, or *equilibrium* due to a consensus regarding social beliefs and practices. *Functionalists* believe that if something exists in society, it must be there because it adds to the integrity and cohesiveness of society. A social element may not look, at first glance, as if it is actually functional but it can still be so. Remember that this view is looking at the societal implications of a factor, not the individual consequences. For example, unemployment is certainly not "functional" for an individual but it can be functional for the society. In a classic article, the sociologist Herbert Gans (1971) suggested this very idea—that poverty is functional for society. Gans suggests that poverty conditions allow for a pool of workers who will take unpleasant jobs at low wages; rent substandard apartments in depressed neighborhoods; buy used or obsolete products; provide middle-class incomes for people whose job is to help the poor; provide cheap domestic services for more affluent people; absorb the costs of "progress" seen in urban renewal (gentrification); and maintain the political domination of those in power since the poor are less likely to vote and to have a voice. Poor neighborhoods are more vulnerable to bad practices leading to environmental jeopardy since the government, and businesses, see them as unlikely to resist things such as chemical dumping, other waste disposal, or polluting factories. Gans demonstrates that poverty is good for society, though it affects different groups to a greater or lesser extent. For the most part, however, functionalists don't separate the population in their analyses; they just see trends and practices as operating for the stability and "good" of society.

Another tenet of *structural functionalism* focuses on the fact that the structures in society are determined by functionality. For example, they suggest the smaller nuclear family, with just parents and children, evolved in the era of industrialization because it was more expedient for getting workers to go where there was work to be done. It was desirable to limit the number of children since they no longer produced family income and represented significant costs for the family. Additionally, American functionalists believed that the division of labor of the post-World War II family, where the working- and middle-class husband/breadwinner was able to support the wife/homemaker, was functional for harmony in the family since it avoided career competition and freed the husband to work unencumbered by domestic concerns.

Figure 1.6 Increased diversity can lead to inclusion or competition. Conflict theorists see competition while functionalists see accommodation
Source: Rawpixel.com / Shutterstock.com

Though these ideals were not available to all groups, they dominated the cultural landscape, and still do for some, even if many families cannot attain the ideal. The functionalists never paused to ask if this was hurting anyone because they came from a perspective imagining a greater good for society in which everyone was presumed to have an equal investment.

Functionalist theory is still employed today but it is limited by its presumption that there is cohesion and consensus in the institutions and practices of society. It rarely acknowledges the conflicts that can arise from the particulars of different situations. Schools, for example, represent different opportunities for various groups but they keep many young people occupied, and at least physically segregated, during the school day. The functionalists see society as greater than its parts and they believe that society exerts influence over its members.

Conflict theory takes an opposing view to functionalism. It starts with the premise that the central sociological question concerns who is gaining an advantage and at what cost to others. The conflict perspective suggests that a small group of people maintain power in society by controlling the economy, government, media and, in fact, all the social institutions and even what constitutes knowledge. Conflict theory was inspired by **Karl Marx,** though there are multiple theorists whose subsequent work has extended his views.

Box 1.8 – Classical Sociological Theories

Emile Durkheim was a French sociologist, considered a founding theorist of sociology. Durkheim's sociology focused on the integration of the social institutions of society especially with regard to their tendency to maintain stability. He analyzed the act of suicide as a response to issues of social integration, most often as a feeling of separation. Durkheim's methodology of research relied upon *social facts*, or elements of society which were tangible and could be measured. This focus was considered an *objective*, *empirical* approach to sociology.

Functionalism is the school of thought which stems from Durkheim's work. It emphasizes the balance of the social institutions and the reciprocal adjustments among the institutions to support the maintenance of society. Functionalist theory assumes elements of the social structure exist because they are functional, and that is why the perspective is sometimes called *structural functionalism*. This approach applies to the greater society, not necessarily to each individual within it. Functionalism suggests, for example, that poverty is functional for society though not for the individual.

Conflict theory suggests that there is constant state of tension in society due to the economic and institutional control of powerful groups whose interests dominate society. Unlike the functionalists, they do not see an overall complementary functioning of social institutions but a coercive dynamic where the interests of the powerful are promoted, compromising the well-being of the majority of the population. This would be especially true with regard to government, business, and education.

Karl Marx was a German-born theorist who spent much of his adult life in England. His studies focused on the social structure, especially the economy. He viewed the relationships of production as key to social relations and social institutions. He studied the increasingly disparate circumstances of the *proletariat*, or workers who sold their labor for wages, and the *bourgeoisie* who owned the factories and profited from exploiting the workers. Marx suggested that workers were maintained on subsistence wages and perpetually exhausted from long hours and poor conditions. These workers were alienated by their mechanized work and easily replaced. The profit generated by their work went straight into the pockets of the owners. Marx believed that all the major social institutions supported the bourgeoisie. Today's protests against the extreme inequality of the ultra-wealthy "1 percent" compared to the rest of the society would not surprise Marx.

Max Weber was a German intellectual who is considered to be another founding theorist of sociology. He was especially interested in studying the relationship of religion to the social structure and *ethos* of a society. He also investigated forces of economics, social class, and bureaucracy. Weber's methodology concerned *Verstehen*, which means "understanding" or how meaning is created. His methods have been associated with formulating a *subjective* understanding of behavior which was still empirically based in scientific principles but does not depend on statistical data.

Weber's theories and writings inspired *symbolic interaction theory*. Unlike the previous two theoretical perspectives, symbolic interactionism originated in the US. This theory focuses on the nature of *symbols*, defined as figures which represent something else, and their significance in social interactions. All human language is symbolic as are many objects and gestures. Think, for example, of an up-raised fist, a flag, or a wedding band.

Marx's (1818–1883) analysis of society stems from analyzing the structure of the economy. He proposed a growing division, in industrial society, between the *bourgeoisie* and the *proletariat*. The bourgeoisie are the capitalists or the owners of production. The proletariat are the workers who sell their labor for wages barely sufficient to sustain life. Marx believed that the social institutions in society supported this dynamic and protected the interests of the bourgeoisie. In the Marxian view, laws and regulations might appear neutral, or even favorable to the workers, but they actually support the sustained domination of the elite. Marx suggested that the excessive exploitation of the masses would eventually lead to revolt which would transform society to a collectivist system protecting the well-being of the masses (Crossman 2017). The sweeping changes he predicted failed to materialize but his cautionary analysis, regarding the length the elite will go to further their interests, remains essentially relevant.

Today's conflict theorists take their lead from Marx but modify his views. Most of them do not limit their analysis to the simple relations of production with just two social classes. Advanced capitalism is more complicated since some people who do not "own" corporations either manage them or command high wages for contributing specialized technological skills. Frequently, these higher-level workers own a small piece of the pie, through stock shares, though they do not qualify as bourgeoisie in the way that Marx described. Contemporary conflict theorists broaden the analysis of a controlling elite by addressing the exploitation of all nondominant groups. Resistance to such powerful group interests occurs only when it becomes too obvious, as it did during the bank and corporate "bail out" of the 2008 recession. Another example is seen in the 2017 attempt to "repeal and replace" the *Affordable Care Act* (see Chapter 9).

Max Weber (1864–1920) was a German scholar who influenced the development of sociology. Like Durkheim, he was an early proponent of the scientific approach to the study of society. In contrast to Durkheim, he was very interested in how people understood society and constructed meaning, though he also felt that direct questioning of people was not a reliable research method. His methodology utilized the concept of *Verstehen*, a German word meaning "understanding." Weber chose to support his investigations by scrutinizing influential works of the day, such as treatises by Protestant reformers, and assessing the ways in which they guided social behaviors and values. His most influential book, in the US, was *The Protestant Ethic and the Spirit of Capitalism*. The clue to his theory is in the title in that ethics is usually applied to civic society and spirit to religion, though he exchanges their placement in his title. He is telling the reader that there is something within the Protestant perspective which supports capitalism and even contains a religious appeal. The

Figure 1.7 The US, as a country of immigrants, has always had to respond to newly arrived groups, but there are many other groups which fight for inclusion today who are not newly arrived but newly recognized
Source: Juan Camilo Bernal / Shutterstock.com

Protestant emphasis on duty and discipline, coupled with the belief in the doctrine of predestination, were both elements of reform which supported capitalism. Hard work and the reinvestment of profit, rather than its use for leisure and pleasure, supported the growth of business. Belief in the doctrine of predestination also contributed to the spread of capitalism because many people came to believe that prosperity in life was an indication of God's favor and the ultimate reward of Heaven. Although this argument might seem abstract, Weber utilizes the words of reformers such as John Calvin, and Martin Luther, to make his points. Weber wrote extensively about the economy, religion, social class, urbanization, and bureaucracy. Weber was a co-founder of the German Sociological Association (1909) and, later in his life, became active in progressive political causes (Crossman 2017).

Box 1.9 – American Figures in Sociology

G.H. Mead developed a social psychology based on how children interpret and incorporate the things they learn from the family. Personal identity is thus established by understanding the values and meaning of the social group, mediated through the family. His work inspired the development of symbolic interaction theory.

Erving Goffman was an American sociologist who specialized in micro-level analyses and developed the contemporary symbolic interaction perspective. His theories are referred to as the *dramaturgical* approach because he drew comparisons between the way people play social roles in society to the way actors play roles on the stage. In each case, he asserted, there are principal actors, supporting actors, stage settings, props, costumes, and a script. There are also front-stage areas, where the performance takes place, and back-stage spaces where the preparation or relaxation for the roles take place.

C. Wright Mills was an American sociologist who focused on the manifestations of power in society. He saw sociology as a mechanism for social criticism and activism. He wrote several important books but his most enduring contribution remains his treatise on *The Sociological Imagination* in which he laid out his vision for what sociology could accomplish. He believed that the individual's biography, and the history of a society, were inter-related and neither could be sufficiently understood without the other. The richness of sociology depended on understanding the differences, and interplay, of *personal troubles* and *public issues*.

Jane Addams is best known as the co-founder of Chicago's Hull House, the first settlement house. Hull House operated like today's social service agencies to help people, largely drawn from recent migrants and immigrants, to adapt to the city. Housing, employment, language classes, healthcare, and other support services were her focus in settling new arrivals. She championed many social causes including pacifism, women's rights, and civil rights. She worked with national organizations addressing these issues and is considered to be a founding figure in the field of social work. She was co-recipient of the Nobel Peace Prize in 1931.

W.E.B. Du Bois was the first African American to receive a doctorate from Harvard University. He wrote extensively on the topic of racial equality and published the first sociological analysis of an African American community. He fought for peace and race equality. In one of his best known essays, *The Soul of Black Folk* (1903), he explained the dual consciousness of African American community life in White America, an essay which many see as relevant today.

Weber's work influenced the development of *symbolic interaction* theory, which has its origins in the US. *Symbols* are physical or written signs that stand for something else. All human language is symbolic as are the American flag, wedding rings, and religious emblems. Language, for example, permits unequivocal understanding. If a group of people is asked to vacate the building, they understand the intention of the speaker. For the most part, people cooperate with these shared definitions and that permits social life to be sustained with relative equanimity. Resisting the "rules" of interaction can lead to conflict and difficulties, so most people conform. Recently, the National Football League (NFL) player, Colin Kaepernick, deliberately refused to stand for the national anthem, preferring to kneel in order to draw attention to the persistent oppression of African Americans, and other people of color, in the US. He knew that there would be negative reactions to this act but his goal was to promote awareness of a situation he was unwilling to tolerate. Some people reacted by accusing him of being unpatriotic by showing disrespect for the anthem but he felt he was exercising his civil duty to resist discrimination. His contention that people of color were being oppressed challenged the common belief that racism was no longer significant in American life. Challenging people's core beliefs can create discomfort but Kaepernick's aim was to do just that in the hope that it would incite reflection regarding race in America. With his act, subsequently followed by similar efforts among other players and teams, he successfully promoted greater discussion of racial issues.

Weber influenced the American social philosopher G. Herbert Mead (1863–1931), who was instrumental in establishing the symbolic interactionist perspective. Mead developed a social psychology based on how children interpret and incorporate the things they learn from the family. Personal identity is thus established by understanding the values and meaning of the social group, mediated through the family (see Chapter 4). The American sociologist, **Erving Goffman** (1922–1982), extended this approach by conducting extensive studies of social roles and micro-level analyses of daily life. Goffman took a *dramaturgical* approach, drawing an analogy between theater and the enactment of social roles. As in live theater, Goffman suggests that social interaction proceeds with the actors, the setting, the props, costumes, and the script contributing to the performance. Goffman advanced many observations about behavior based on his approach. He also declared that social life has a *front stage* and *back stage* for every role. The front stage is where the public performance takes place, as when a student behaves with interest during class time. The back stage reveals the true feelings of the performer, as when a student fails to complete homework assignments or even open the book outside of class time. Back-stage behavior is private and so it does not "spoil" the performance. Goffman explained how performing a role can simultaneously represent conformity as well as role distance. An example would be the tendency for adolescents to roll their eyes when they do not want to hear what an adult is saying, even if they do as they are told. Another example would be when a person, whose work requires a uniform, gets a tattoo in order to retain some personal element of identification while still conforming to the demands of the workforce. Non-verbal communication also conveys much information which can strongly support or undercut our role "performance." A person's posture can indicate interest, or lack of it, during a job interview which can result in the person winning or losing the job, regardless of how they answer questions. The overt performance of a role frequently does not provide the whole story. Goffman suggests that the self-concept is more than just the sum of a person's social roles (Crossman 2017; see Chapter 4).

C.W. Mills (1916–1962), another influential American theorist, was more focused on macro-level analysis. Mills was especially interested in the nature of power in society, developing a conflict theory orientation. He considered himself a social reformer, believing that sociological insight could, and should, be utilized to create social changes. Mills sought to elaborate the inter-connections between industry, business, and government to expose the ways in which these groups impacted people's lives. He believed that the practices of this *power elite* needed to be challenged so that society could be more fair and equal (Crossman 2017).

Mills' writing regarding *the promise* of sociology was presented in his book *The Sociological Imagination* (1959). It is his most enduring contribution to American sociology. Mills believed that sociologists should study how historical changes impact daily life by contextualizing personal experiences. He believed that sociology provided an understanding of the *reciprocal* relationship between history and biography and that human nature is not stable but defined by time and place. His approach is best explained by providing an example. Recent history has seen the worst recession since the post-Depression era. Many people lost jobs and/or homes. This phenomenon occurred across social classes and occupations though individuals in lower and moderate-income areas were especially vulnerable. Personal income declined, either through job

Figure 1.8 Mills is considered responsible for elaborating the unique approach sociology offers in gaining understanding of social life

Source: wallnarez / Shutterstock.com

loss or reduced hours. Many people suffered financial setbacks caused by structural changes in the workforce, such as automation, and financial policies which favored investors. Biography had to be understood in the context of this history. Mills called this personal suffering as the consequence of social changes a *public issue*, since the *cause*, and thus the solution, was in the *social structure*. In contrast, a *personal trouble* refers to a problem where the cause lies in the individual, as when a person is fired for poor work habits. Mills promoted social reform as the remedy for public issues whereas the remedy for personal troubles lies in the development of better work habits.

Mills extended this concept to suggest that human nature was expressed variously by what a society would support. The lives of Barack Obama and Hillary Clinton, for example, illustrate this point. Obama would not have been elected without the preceding civil rights movement. Clinton would not have been a Yale-educated attorney, Senator, Secretary of State and presidential candidate without the modern women's movement. The accomplishments of these people rested on historical events. Their personal characteristics were expressed only in terms of what the society was "ready" for. Mills believed that the historical era not only influenced the details of a person's life but influenced the very notion of what is considered "natural" to humans. Consequently, the dynamic of the personal and the historical cannot be seen as distinct but as interactive and both must be incorporated into sociological analyses.

Another American social activist who influenced sociology was **Jane Addams** (1860–1935). Addams is best known as the co-founder of Hull House in Chicago (1889). Hull House was a *settlement house* which operated, as many nonprofit organizations do today, to provide services to poor and immigrant populations. Hull House addressed issues of housing, employment, education, and health especially among migrant and immigrant populations. Addams was committed to supporting marginalized groups and dedicated her life to improving their circumstances. She was a pacifist, feminist, and anti-racist activist. She was heavily involved with national organizations for peace, suffrage, social work, and civil rights. In 1931, she was the co-recipient of the *Nobel Peace Prize* for her efforts in these areas (Biography).

W.E.B. Du Bois (1868–1963) was the first African American to earn a PhD from Harvard University. Du Bois was a prolific writer and dedicated activist though much of his work was overlooked until the last couple of decades. He fought for peace and racial equality and was a founding member of the *National Association for the Advancement of Colored People* (NAACP). He was dedicated to sociological analysis and wrote the first treatise on an African American community, *The Philadelphia Negro: A Social Study* (1899). In sociology, he is most remembered for his collection of essays, *The Soul of Black Folks* (1903), where he described the *double consciousness* of the Black experience in America. This concept refers to the necessity to adopt two identities, one for dealing with White America and one for interacting within the African American community (Wormser). This double consciousness still pervades the writing of many African American writers as well as authors from other nondominant groups.

Sociology continues to provide insight into contemporary issues though frequently it reflects the work and experiences of the dominant group. Today's membership in

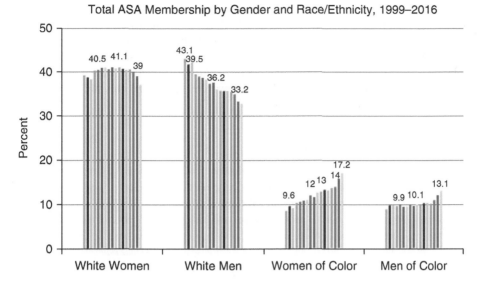

Total ASA Membership by Gender and Race/Ethnicity, 1999–2016

Figure 1.9 The ASA membership is still predominantly White. Would sociology be different if more sociologists were from non-White groups? Does the ASA represent the majority of practicing sociologists? Source: ASA member data. Tabulation by ASA Research Department. Updated 12/5/16

the major professional organization, The *American Sociological Association* (ASA Membership 2016), is still disproportionately White, with White women currently exceeding the portion of White men. People of color, especially males, remain under-represented. Although "objective" science would suggest that anyone can study any group or topic, it is likely that new theories and emphases will emerge as more nondominant researchers conduct original research. In fact, it is essential that sociology incorporate more researchers from nondominant groups or it runs the risk of insularity.

In summary, let's return to the case of Robert Peace. Looking at Peace's life through a sociological lens explains some things and fails at others. Sociology provides some insight into the difficulties a person growing up in a poor neighborhood would face in dealing with people from wealthier families and schools. Different life environments and the consequent feeling of isolation and marginality probably contributed to Peace's feelings of distance from his more privileged peers. He may also have experienced ambivalence, or disloyalty, to having "left behind" his old friends and neighborhood. People experiencing such shift often express feelings of displacement (Lubrano 2004). Peace also responded dramatically to the loss of his father and his permanent incarceration. Understanding issues of race, income, family composition, neighborhood, and privilege can provide insight into Peace's mindset. It is easy to imagine that Peace experienced a life without a safe harbor, a place where he just could develop a persona compensating for the tenuousness of his early experiences.

At the same time sociology fails to explain why others from his community who had an opportunity to attend universities and professional schools were able to make a successful transition. His abilities and talents were virtually limitless. Was the tragic outcome of his persistent drug selling a psychological weakness in him? Did his failure to pursue his graduate plans indicate an absence of personal grit or determination? Was his emotional loyalty to old friends too strong an emotional pull for him to feel that he had left them behind? Were his sociability and emotional needs unfulfilled by the new acquaintances who felt too "other" from him? These latter questions might more accurately be assessed by a psychologist, since sociologists can provide explanations of social factors contributing to trends affecting individual outcomes but are less likely to be able to definitively analyze the outcome for any particular individual.

Key Terms

Sociology   Society   Social Forces   Social Institutions   Social Construction of Reality
Community   Social Structure   Social Roles   Hunting and Gathering Societies
Agricultural Societies   Industrial Societies   Post-industrial Societies   "Nons"
Globalization   Transnational Corporation   Export Processing Zones   Developing Nations
Developed Nations   Brexit   Macro- and Micro-Level Analyses   Role Conflicts   Social Status:
Ascribed, Achieved, and Master   Auguste Comte   Harriet Martineau   Emile Durkheim
Structural Functionalism   Karl Marx   Conflict Theory   Max Weber   Verstehen
Symbolic Interaction   G.H. Mead   Erving Goffman   C.W. Mills   Jane Addams   W.E.B. Du Bois

Concept Review

What Is Sociology?

The simplest way to define sociology is to say that it explains the **structure** of society and the **social forces** which shape a person's **social roles**. Significant factors include social class, race, sex, and immigration status. Each of these impacts a wide range of life circumstances from physical and mental health, to education and occupational attainment, to the likelihood of marriage. Sociology establishes its base of knowledge through the practice of **science**, which distinguishes sociologists from other societal observers such as novelists, journalists, playwrights, and philosophers.

What Is the Social Structure?

The **social institutions** make up the **social structure** of the society which determines how life is lived in the society. All sociologists agree that there are five basic institutions: the family, the polity, the economy, religion, and education. Many sociologists would add the military, healthcare, sports, entertainment, the media, and science due to the large role each plays in the economy. Analysis of the inter-relationship of these institutions refers to a **macro level** of analysis, as when, for example, an economic recession significantly impacts education budgets.

Social institutions also define **social roles** and confer legitimacy on people's behaviors. Behaviors occur outside of acceptable institutional forms but are usually unacknowledged or devalued. Institutional changes are affected by outlying behaviors but it takes time for the laws to catch up to common practices to create institutional changes. The establishment of **social roles** provides for some shared standards of behavior which guide social interactions. Study at this level of sociology, generally focusing on face to face interaction, is referred to as *micro-level* analysis as, for example, when it is considered rude to answer a cell phone call while on a date.

What Type of Society Is the US?

For most of human history, societies have been organized by the tasks of *hunting and gathering*, where roles were determined by age and sex. Some 10,000 years ago, *agricultural* developments permitted larger groups of people to settle down and become *sedentary*. *Industrialization* followed, where manufacturing was the prime activity for most people. In the post-World War II era, developed societies (US, Japan, Canada, and most of Europe) became *post-industrial* with the majority of workers currently employed in service and information occupations while manufacturing, for the most part, occurs "offshore." Countries producing goods for the post-industrial societies generally are referred to as "*developing*" since their industrial base is still in the process of growth. *Globalization* refers to the interdependence of national economies, markets, and culture. The internet and social media have shaped the forces of globalization and homogenized many elements of culture.

How Did Sociology Begin?

Early theorists promoted the use of scientific methodology to investigate social conditions. Auguste Comte and Harriet Martineau represent two of the figures whose works influenced the founding theorists. Many early sociologists were proponents of social activism. As sociology developed into the twentieth century, many sociologists promoted "objective" sociology, moving from social activism to favor a more neutral, academically oriented form of study.

Emile Durkheim, Karl Marx, and Max Weber are considered the European originators of modern sociological theories. These early theorists' ideas represent the "classical" sociological perspectives: structural functionalism, conflict theory, and symbolic interaction. There are other theories today but the classical theories are considered the starting point of sociological theory. In the US, early figures in sociology included C.W. Mills, Jane Addams, and W.E.B. Du Bois. All three of these American figures promoted awareness of power and privilege in the areas of social class, race, or immigrant status.

Review Questions

1. What is *sociology*? Be specific. Make sure to give a definition that will distinguish it from other disciplines. What type of explanations is it likely to provide?
2. Apply a sociological analysis to an issue of interest to you. What elements of your approach illustrate a sociological perspective? How would you analyze the same topic from a different perspective?
3. Explain Emile Durkheim's theory of suicide. How are the concepts of *anomic* and *altruistic* suicide related? Do you think this interpretation of suicide is accurate? Evaluate the theory from your own viewpoint.
4. Compare and contrast structural functionalism and conflict theory. Can they each be applied at both the macro and micro levels? Which approach do you like better? Why?
5. What is *the sociological imagination*? Be sure to address issues of history, biography, personal troubles, and public issues. How can this approach help you to understand something in your family and/or community?
6. What do you think about the fate of Robert Peace? Why did he return to his neighborhood after he graduated college? Could it have turned out differently? What, if anything, could have prevented his eventual violent death?
7. How do you think that increased diversity among sociologists will change the field? Explain.

References

The Artifice. *The Political Message of the Hunger Games.* Retrieved from https://the-artifice.com/the-hunger-games-political-message/.

ASA Membership (December 5, 2016) Retrieved from http://www.asanet.org/research-and-publications/research-sociology/trends/total-asa-membership-gender-and-raceethnicity.

Baker, D. The Blog. (May 31, 2016) The Elites and the Rise of Donald Trump. The *Huffington Post.*

Bardhan, P. (March 26, 2006) *Does Globalization Help or Hurt the World's Poor? Overview/Globalization and Poverty.* Retrieved from https://www.scientificamerican.com/article/does-globalization-help-o-2006-04/.

Bentley, N. *What is Citizens United? An Introduction.* Retrieved from http://reclaimdemocracy.org/who-are-citizens-united/.

Berger, P. and Luckmann, T. (1966) *The Social Construction of Reality.* New York: Random House, Inc.

Biography. *Jane Addams Biography.* Retrieved from http://www.biography.com/people/jane-addams-9176298#early-life.

Chappell, B. (June 26, 2015) *Supreme Court Declares Same-sex Marriage Legal in all 50 States.* National Public Radio.

Cole, N. (June 10, 2014) *Harriet Martineau: A Brief Biography and Intellectual History.* Retrieved from https://www.thoughtco.com/harriet-martineau-3026476.

Collins, S. (2008) *The Hunger Games*. New York: Scholastic, Inc.

Collins, S. (2009) *Catching Fire*. New York: Scholastic, Inc.

Collins, S. (2010) *Mockingjay*. New York: Scholastic, Inc.

Crossman, A. (March 2, 2017) *Famous Sociologists*. Retrieved from https://www.thoughtco.com/famous-sociologists-3026648.

Du Bois, W.E.B. (1899) *The Philadelphia Negro: A Social Study*. Philadelphia: The University of Pennsylvania Press.

Du Bois, W.E.B. (1903) *The Souls of Black Folk; Essays and Sketches*. Chicago: A.C. McClurg & Co.

Durkheim, E. (1895/2012) *Suicide: A Study in Sociology*. New York: Free Press.

Durkheim, E., Lukes, S., Halls, W.D. (2014) *The Rules of Sociological Method: and Selected Texts on Sociology and its Method*. New York: Free Press.

Elliott, L. (June 26, 2016) Brexit Is a Rejection of Globalization. Retrieved from https://www.theguardian.com/business/2016/jun/26/brexit-is-the-rejection-of-globalisation.

Fry, R. (May 24, 2016) *For First Time in Modern Era, Living with Parents Edges Out Other Living Arrangements for 18- to 34-Year-Olds*. Pew Research Center. Retrieved from http://www.pewsocialtrends.org/2016/05/24/for-first-time-in-modern-era-living-with-parents-edges-out-other-living-arrangements-for-18-to-34-year-olds/

Gans, Herbert J. (July-August 1971) The Uses of Poverty: The Poor Pay All. *Social Policy*, 2, 2, 20–24. http://eric.ed.gov/?id=EJ042380

Harari, Y. (2015) *Sapiens: A Brief History of Humankind*. New York: HarperCollins Publishers.

Hobbs, J. (2014) *The Short and Tragic Life of Robert Peace: A Brilliant Young Man Who Left Newark for the Ivy League*. New York: Scribner.

Livingston, G., Brown, A. (August 13, 2014) *Birth Rate for Unmarried Women Declining for the First Time in Decades*. Pew Research Center.

Lubrano, A. (2004) *Limbo: Blue-Collar Roots, White-Collar Dreams*. N.J.: John Wiley & Sons.

Lukes, S. (1982) *The Rules of Sociological Method and Selected Texts on Sociology and Its Method*. New York: The Free Press.

Masci, D., Lipka, M. (January 21, 2016) *Americans May Be Getting Less Religious, but Feelings of Spirituality Are on the Rise*. Pew Research Center.

Nava, G. author/producer. (2002–2003) *American Family: Journey of Dreams*. PBS series.

McGill, A. (June 25, 2016) Who Voted for the Brexit? Retrieved from http://www.theatlantic.com/international/archive/2016/06/brexit-vote-statistics-united-kingdom-european-union/488780/.

Mills, C. Wright. (1959) *The Sociological Imagination*. New York: Oxford University Press.

Nelson, A. (February 2, 2017). A Lesson from America's Japanese Internment Camps. *Aljazeera*. Retrieved from http://www.aljazeera.com/indepth/features/2017/02/lesson-america-japanese-internment-camps-170206134742135.html

Nestle Good Food, Good Life. Retrieved from http://www.nestleusa.com/brands.

Pavcnik, N. (April 28, 2009) *How Has Globalization Benefited the Poor?* Retrieved from http://insights.som.yale.edu/insights/how-has-globalization-benefited-the-poor.

Rosenberg, M. (March 3, 2017) *Number of McDonald's Restaurants Worldwide. How Many McDonald's Restaurants Exist Worldwide?* Retrieved from https://www.statista.com/statistics/219454/mcdonalds-restaurants-worldwide/.

Supreme Court of the United States. (October term 2009) *Citizens United v. Federal Election Commission.* Retrieved from www.supremecourt.gov/opinions.

Tsai, A. Lucas, M., Sania A, Kim, D., Kawachi, I. (2014) Detailed Study Confirms High Suicide Rate Among Recent Veterans. *Ann Intern Med.*; 161(2): 85–95. doi:10.7326/M13-1291. Retrieved from http://annals.org/article.aspx?articleid=1887025.

Wormser, R. *Jim Crow Stories. W.E.B. Du Bois.* WNET. PBS. Retrieved from http://www.pbs.org/wnet/jimcrow/stories_people_dubois.html.

Zarembo, A. (January 14, 2015) Detailed Study Confirms High Suicide Rate Among Recent Veterans. *LA Times*, http://www.latimes.com/nation/la-na-veteran-suicide-20150115-story.html.

CHAPTER 2

Cultures in America

WHAT YOU WILL READ ABOUT IN THIS CHAPTER:

- **Culture** is comprised of **learned behavior and beliefs** in all aspects of human life. Because every culture transmits these to its members, from birth, behaviors and values feel "natural" even though they are human products. Living cultures change with societal developments, responding to changes in immigration, technology, and government. Social changes can be reflected in language, which is specific to a culture. Culture incorporates material and nonmaterial aspects though it often takes time for these to be in sync.

- Technological developments pervade every aspect of contemporary society. The power of the **social media** is the newest major factor affecting social life. The internet and satellite technology have made news and information available in "real time," influencing the quality and timeliness of "news."

- The **dominant group** refers to the Anglo White culture. More specifically, it references the experiences of White, Protestant, affluent, males. The standards of the dominant group establish those of "*the culture*" and are falsely promoted as universal. Media, news, arts, and entertainment disproportionately reflect the experiences of the dominant group and are controlled by it.

- American culture is characterized by materialism, often as a measure of personal "success." American culture embraces the entrepreneurial spirit, both in terms of business enterprises and in celebrating personal characteristics associated with the *American Dream*. The notion that anyone is "free" to accomplish limitless achievements and material success is an integral part of the cultural ideal so that anyone who resists any part of this ideal faces potential marginalization.

- Culture is not lived in the same way by all group members. A person's position in a society can influence their connection with the dominant culture, resulting in feelings of incorporation or alienation from the cultural mandates. **Nondominant** groups are evaluated on the standards set by the dominant group and any modifications of behavior or attitude can result in viewing nondominant members as inferior or deficient. Nondominant groups frequently are designated by a hyphenated label, such as Mexican-American or Gay-American, implying that they are not fully American.

- The perspective of **post-modern theories** incorporates the concept that universality of culture is a myth and analyzes the experiences of residents as variable. They suggest that the ideas promoted as objective knowledge require "deconstruction" from their unacknowledged but persistent biases, reflecting dominant group experiences. In sociological terminology, nondominant groups are frequently given the status of a **subculture** membership, which implies differences leading to devaluation of the group. Some sociologists promote eliminating that term, in favor of utilizing the term "culture" and recognizing multiple American cultures.

- Culture is composed of many descriptive elements, such as **values**, **norms**, **laws**, **folkways**, **taboos**, **mores**, **sanctions**, **and stigma**.

Introduction

Historian Yuval Noah Harari explains the distinguishing features of the human animal. We are an "open" species capable of many different social arrangements, diets, and creative outlets. In contrast to other animals, we possess only one imperative, the need to assure survival. Because humans have no specific mechanism driving the path to survival, except the human brain, we construct culture as a means to compensate for biologically specific drives such as which animal to eat or where and when we must mate. Humans cannot live in isolation as a matter of survival. The human infant has an extended period of dependency and, for most of human history, living alone would not have allowed for adequate resources to sustain life.

> This fact [human infant dependency] has contributed greatly to both humankind's extraordinary social abilities and to its unique social problems. Lone mothers could hardly forage enough food for their offspring and themselves with needy children in tow. Raising children required constant help from other family members and neighbours. It takes a tribe to raise a human. Evolution thus favoured those capable of forming strong social ties. In addition, since humans are born underdeveloped, they can be educated and socialised to a far greater extent than any other animal ... Humans emerge from the womb like molten glass from a furnace. They can be spun, stretched and shaped with a surprising degree of freedom. This is why today we can educate our children to become Christian or Buddhist, capitalist or socialist, warlike or peace-loving.
>
> (Harari 2015)

The significance of this local interdependence is receding in the twenty-first century, as we are now dependent on producers of food and other goods which are spread all over the world. Consequently, we are increasingly aware of the connections established by the global economy and less likely to honor the significance of the local community. We are increasingly unlikely to know our neighbors, or any details of their lives while, at the same time, experiencing a false familiarity with a celebrity we "follow" on social media, tweeting to hundreds, if not thousands, of others. Culture supports the human capacity to adapt to the environment which, for most of history, meant relating to people living in close physical proximity, likely within the same group. Today's influx of information regarding people we are unlikely ever to meet is of questionable value to adapting to our actual life needs. The mythological notions we attribute to others' lifestyles may tell us something about cultural aspirations but it also provides for unrealistic comparisons. No cultural element is inherently of higher value than any other, except that the group promoting it believes it to be so.

Cultural habits support a way of life that is peculiarly *American*, and may not "translate" to values in other cultures. American materialism, as a measure of success, has come to imply that those without it have deficient personality characteristics or values. American individualism, suggesting the salience of individual desires over family or community, has undermined a social institution which formerly offered extensive financial, social, and emotional support as well as logistical aid, such as providing multiple caretakers to raise children. While some families sustain these qualities, they do so against the ideal that the individual should maximize their freedoms to fulfill themselves, as in who they marry, where they live, what jobs to pursue.

Ideal cultural tendencies are shown in variable behaviors in different cultures and even the same outward appearances do not always indicate culturally consistent attitudes. For example, in January 1990, McDonald's built its first Russian restaurant in the heart of Moscow. There were several hurdles to jump in order to get this project underway. Logistically, there were bureaucratic and infrastructural requirements which appeared insurmountable. However, according to Russians who worked there at the time (Spiegel and Rosin 2016), the most significant impediment was *cultural*; Russians simply did not smile unless they were greeting a person who was a genuine intimate:

> To create a viable McDonald's in Russia, McDonald's had to reach deep into the heart of Russians themselves and change their very souls. In the homeland of Dostoyevsky, of Stravinsky, McDonald's had to convince its employees to be cheerful.
>
> (Spiegel and Rosin 2016)

Casual cheerfulness was not an element of the culture and even raised suspicion. To staff the McDonald's with employees exemplifying the corporate mandate of friendliness, the corporate trainers provided videos breaking down the elements of American cheerfulness so that Russians could mimic it. Corporate executives articulated some concern, regarding the stress this would cause the employees, because it was so oppositional to cultural habits. A bigger fear was that the patrons, unaccustomed to such outgoing behavior, would feel uncomfortable and avoid the store. To the relief of the corporate development department, the Russians took to the McDonald's approach and viewed the restaurants as a place where they could sit and relax.

Fears that the smiling friendliness might be taken negatively have some basis in fact. Associations surrounding the expression of friendliness are culturally specific. Research from the *Smiling Report* (Obrazkova 2015), a 2015 survey of the international confederation of mystery shoppers, shows that the US is thirteenth in smiling and Russia is now fifteenth. The results in this report represent a big shift in Russian culture, but what does it actually signify? In an interview with a Russian McDonald's worker, training for the first stores, he admitted that though he learned to smile habitually, he began to feel alienated from his fellow, unsmiling citizens and dreamed of moving to the US, where he felt people would be more welcoming and were truly more approachable. Most Americans promote cheerfulness and don't hesitate to tell a glum-looking person, particularly if female, to "smile!" However, when the worker moved to the US, after two years of working at the Russian McDonald's, he was disappointed to discover the American friendliness represented by the smile actually was shallow and impersonal. He gained an appreciation for "earning" the smile of his Russian associates. Superficial cheeriness can have other

Figure 2.1 Culture affects common behaviors; in the Soviet Union McDonald's workers were taught to be friendly and to smile
Source: OlegDoroshin / Shutterstock.com

disappointing effects. Research shows that forced smiling, when it fails to reflect a person's inner emotional state, actually can be bad for a person's health. There is a health cost to the dissonance between a person's outward appearance and internal mental state. It can lead to alcohol use and disconnection from one's own emotions, resulting in other problems such as depression. Additionally, there is no evidence that smiling changes the bottom line in retail.

How Do Sociologists Understand Culture?

Culture is a powerful force shaping not only social life but underlying beliefs regarding basic human nature. Cultural presumptions can play a role even in areas considered predetermined by genetics and biology; our beliefs can even impact our health and aging process (Northrup 2015). Culturally determined behaviors influence everything from how we wake up in the morning to what values we hold, so their specific content is not inevitable. Culture is *constructed* through human activity, and passed from one generation to the next, so that it appears immutable. All human cultures communicate through *language*. *Languages* are symbolic systems composed of elements which stand for something else and are social in nature because they facilitate shared understanding. The words "husband" and "wife" usually create an automatic association to the spousal roles, presumed to belong to heterosexual couples, and most people will readily understand the roles they depict. But English is a living language and the terms husband or wife can also refer to legal spouses in gay relationships. This indicates both the social nature of language, the ability to readily make an association, and the changing nature of language, since the use of husband or wife no longer definitively refers only to heterosexual couples. Marriages today can have two husbands or two wives. Some categorical labels apply to concepts changing so quickly they have become points of contention, particularly by those who feel oppressed by the language. After concerted criticism, *Facebook* provided for 58 options for identification of a person's gender and, after further criticism, allowed for any variation to be filled in by the user (Associated Press 2015). Because of societal changes, new words emerge all the time. Words and phrases like "google it," "facetime," "twitter," and "emoji" did not exist until recently.

Box 2.1 – Culture

Culture refers to all the distinguishing elements of a society; it is learned and passed down from one generation to another. Culture is always in flux, especially with regard to the use of new technologies which can change the way people work, live, and interact. Language is a major element of culture and is a "living" factor, subject to modifications as new words emerge all the time. Words and phrases like "google it," "facetime," "twitter," and "emoji" did not exist until recently.

Language is an essential component of human society. It is symbolic, or representational, and provides for common understanding and ease of communication. The words "husband" and "wife" usually create an automatic association to the spousal roles in heterosexual couples. But English is a living language and the terms husband or wife can also refer to legal spouses in gay relationships. This indicates both the social nature of language, the ability to readily make an association, and the changing nature of language, since the use of husband or wife no longer definitively refers only to heterosexual couples.

Each language contains its own syntax, making for a unique and complete system. Languages can be written or oral, or both. The question as to whether language shapes thought in a deterministic and limiting fashion is one which is consistently debated. The *Sapir–Whorf hypothesis*, formulated by two twentieth-century theorists, promotes the idea that language shapes reality. This has been variably argued as too deterministic while others have read it as more relativistic. Theorists have debated how much language influences perceptions of reality and disagree regarding the relative presence of universality and uniqueness in languages. Concepts of time, for example, vary greatly from culture to culture and are reflected in the utilization of various verb forms in referencing past events. In some languages, verb choices are utilized depending upon whether the person speaking witnessed the event or is simply reporting it from another source (LSA, n.d.). Languages also vary with references to spatial relations, with some using environmental fixed points, such as "northwest" as a reference while others use the language of the body, as in front/back and right/left (LSA, n.d.). *American Sign Language* (ASL) is different from other forms of English and is considered a separate language, with its distinctive syntax, grammar, and vocabulary. Many people in the deaf community are against the use of technology to facilitate hearing since they feel that ASL is an integral, defining feature of deaf culture (Startasl n.d.).

Language permits cultures to operate through intersubjective fictions, referring to stories regarding essential elements of the group's history and beliefs. For most of history, these intersubjective webs were specific to small groups and were extended to larger, but still limited groups, in the agricultural revolution. Today, with the assistance of technology to retain more information than possible with the human brain, we have created the possibility of infinite intersubjective networks (Harari 2017). *Technology*, defined as "The application of knowledge, techniques, and tools to adapt and control physical environments and material resources to satisfy wants and needs" (*Sociology Dictionary*, n.d.), establishes the parameters of culture by what is made possible and by how it is regulated. It includes everything from flush toilets and modern plumbing, to computers and cell phones, to automation and farming techniques and just about anything else humans invent in the belief that it will serve some positive outcome.

Box 2.2 – Technology

Technology refers to knowledge, tools, and machines which allow people to build new approaches and skills to accomplish goals. Technology also creates new "needs," as when people "need" a new cell phone or the latest tablet. Technology incorporates machines and artifacts from modern plumbing to computers, to robotics and automation.

Because culture feels so "natural," the disconcerting aspects of arriving in a new culture can cause disorientation and even intense discomfort. Lillian Faderman's study, *I Begin My Life All Over* (1998), highlights such experiences in members of the Fresno CA Hmong community. With the help of a local community member, Faderman studied the lives and families of the immigrant community. The book frequently provides first-person accounts, allowing the reader to feel the experiences of the respondents. Many of the Hmong had been situated in rural Laos, prior to emigrating, and supplied assistance to the US government and military during the Vietnam War. The Hmong were an insular community, maintaining their own language and communities rather than integrating into Laotian society. Hmong life was accomplished without any of the conveniences associated with modernity, such as running water, electricity, plumbing, or mechanical transportation. One woman, who escaped the country by running through the jungle with her five children, speaks to the confusion she felt when told to board an airplane:

I could not tell the inside of a building from the inside of an airplane. So when we were coming to America, I didn't know if I was sitting in a house or an airplane or where. I couldn't tell the difference—the inside of a house was like the inside of an airplane, and the inside of the airplane was like the inside of house. We got on, we got off, and I just sat and sat.

Another respondent similarly describes her disorientation towards conveniences most Americans take for granted:

> We were so scared when we first got here because there was so much food everywhere, and lights, and TV—I had never seen television my whole life. We came and there was TV—and I saw cartoons on TV. I thought that was weird. I go, "Weird!" They fed us, and then they taught us how to use the stove, refrigerator, everything they thought we should know. Then they went home. I was there watching them teach my parents. Then, after they left, we tried to turn off the light—and we didn't know how to do it! So, we just kept the light on all day and all night because we didn't know how to turn the switch off.

The technology and cultural systems of modern US life were alienating and even frightening because they were completely unfamiliar; the people literally did not know what to make of the world they had entered, or even how to engage with it. Faderman reveals how the integration of the *shaman* faith into all the facets of Hmong life provided cultural continuity for the community. Shamanism is a set of integrated beliefs characteristic of the group's religious/spiritual system, and it also plays a more pervasive role by conferring meanings which affect social interactions and personal identity. Hmong who assimilate into American culture and adopt Christianity lose this core element of Hmong culture and threaten the continuity of the culture. Without the Shamanistic underpinnings of the culture, what would be "Hmong" about the Hmong? Faderman speculates that the disappearance of Shamanism can lead to the eventual destruction of the Hmong culture (107). The case of the Hmong is particularly dramatic, with respect to the vital differences between their culture and modern America. The question of how to address the tension between maintaining traditional cultural references and embracing modern American ones is universal among all immigrant groups. Issues of assimilation become even more pronounced in the life choices of Americanized offspring, particularly with regard to the choice of marital partners. Various groups of US immigrants have retained varied levels of their home cultures, either by design or default, and maintain different levels of traditional practices (see Chapters 7, 14).

For the Fresno Hmong, westernization of the younger generation created volatile tensions between generations. Gender roles, even among the adult immigrants, were stretched by the experience of American life and created discord. The immigrant women had somewhat of an easier time adjusting to life in the US than the men. The men sustained a greater status loss since their traditions mandated that the husband's family was much closer, socially and emotionally, to the couple than the wife's (referred to as *patrilineal*). In the US, the couple's familial intimacy was enhanced by whose family members resided here, rather than by traditional priorities associated with the husband's family. Women had more positive experiences because they were more likely to gain status and freedoms while the men frequently were stripped of the breadwinner role, as well as losing other community roles. The women were more likely to possess skills from home which were transferable to the new setting. Women's aptitude in embroidery, for example, was far more valuable

Figure 2.2 A Hmong market in Missoula Montana, where many Hmong relocated. Other significant Hmong communities developed in Fresno and Merced CA, and the Central valley of CA where farming is still common. Wisconsin, California, and Minnesota are states with the most Hmong
Source: StephenSlocomb / istockphoto.com

on the American market than the men's farming skills. Traditionally oriented immigrant men were more vulnerable to unemployment, and to losses of status with respect to wives and children, as their authority and respect could be challenged in a way not permissible in their traditional environment. Loss of the roles of breadwinner and authority figure, in the worst cases, led to *sudden death syndrome* where men would die in their sleep

Figure 2.3 Susan B Anthony Elementary School, Sacramento CA. Hmong immersion school
Source: Sacramento City Unified School District

without any apparent organic cause. These inexplicable deaths ultimately were attributed to men's suffering from "cultural depression."

What Constitutes Culture?

Without culture to provide order and sense, we might feel immobilized by the seemingly limitless daily options. Without cultural habits, we would have to expend more time and thought on automatic activities structuring daily life, such as what to do when we wake up and how to organize our day. "Vacations" and "retirement" are celebrated as a time characterized by more freedom of choice, and lack of routine.

Consequently, some people need a prolonged period of adjustment for these breaks because they are so unaccustomed to them. Even the very concept of a vacation, however, is a cultural construct. A vacation is supposed to be "relaxing" and "fun," a time for physical, mental, and spiritual renewal. But, it was not always like that. The Puritan roots of American culture promoted work, six long days a week, and worship on the seventh. When vacations were initiated, in the early nineteenth century, they were a privilege of the elite. Eventually, they became a break for the middle class but, for some, retained a religious element; many vacation resorts were religiously based in order to protect people from the "temptations of idleness." Today Americans view vacations largely as a source of entertainment or self-improvement, though some people find vacations and free time problematic. Time off from work can feel oppositional to the American ethos of hard work and stoicism promoted by the Puritan ethos. It has been remarked that Americans only take a break so they can get back to work refreshed. By contrast, Europeans are more likely to perceive work as necessary to secure the means to vacation (Norris and Siegel 2009).

Box 2.3 – Aspects of Culture

Material culture refers to the tangible objects in a culture. These include such things as shelters, arts, musical instruments, clothing, appliances, or tools.

Non-material culture refers to the intangible aspects of a culture such as values, beliefs, customs, and etiquette. Everything from democratic principles to table manners qualifies as non-material culture.

Popular culture refers to elements widely disseminated and consumed by many citizens and generally readily identifiable. Popular culture is frequently associated with popular movies, music, fashion, art, print media, and cyber products. Social media have made access to popular culture immediately available in real time.

Material culture is the core element of culture. The food we eat and the technology we utilize contribute to the shape of a culture. Cultural roles, mediated by the family, often are steeped in tradition and seem intransigent.

Cultural Challenge and Gender Roles

The 2016 documentary, *The Eagle Huntress* (Bell 2016), shows how deeply entrenched social roles can be modified with support from those who carry some cultural clout. The movie follows the story of a young girl who dreams of being an eagle hunter, a role exclusively inhabited by males and passed down in families. Eagles are integral to the traditional Kazakh and Kyrgyz societies. Eagles work closely with their trainers to hunt small game for food and fur skins, which provide protection against the harsh winters of the Mongolian steppe, where temperatures can reach 40 degrees below zero. Aisholpan, a 13-year-old girl, desperately wanted to learn to be an eagle hunter, to carry on the tradition of 12 generations of award-winning masters in her familial lineage. The documentary shows community elders asserting that a girl cannot hunt but Aisholpan's determined father chooses to train her as he would a son, and passes his skills to her. The training is arduous and the girl's mother becomes effectively isolated from her daughter as a result of the intensity of the relationship between master and student, father and daughter. The mother agrees to this withdrawal from the traditional mother/daughter closeness, to support her daughter's aspirations.

To achieve a master status as an eagle hunter, hunter and bird virtually become one entity. To begin the journey, every hunter must first trap a baby eagle to train. We see Aisholpan traversing a steep, frigid, snowy mountain to search for a partner. To catch the eagle, she must rappel from a steep cliff, with the help of her father. She experiences successive stumbles but ultimately captures a beautiful bird. She will train this eagle, which can dive at speeds of up to 190 miles per hour, to ready herself for *The Golden Eagle Festival* competition. In this contest the candidates must achieve several difficult tasks. The hunter competes by accomplishing a smooth flight of the bird from a high distant cliff to her hand, by calling commands with her voice. The competitor is judged on the quality of her equipment and costume as well as by her hunting skills.

Aisholpan is crowned the champion at age 13, the youngest competitor and the only female. Nevertheless, in all the interviews with male elders, there is adamant denial of female capabilities to excel at hunting. The real test, they assert, will come when Aisholpan lands her first fox in the harsh winter landscape. The first day out, and on the third attempt, she joyously succeeds, to the surprise of the community. She has proved herself to be an expert hunter, and at a very young age. Most important, Aisholpan sustains the proud family tradition of expert eagle hunting and is destined to perpetuate it, to the delight of her family (Bell 2016). The traditions of the hunt, crucial to the well-being of the group and central to the culture, have been challenged and now cannot be restricted to men, though the females are not yet easily accepted. Living cultures can undergo change in their basic structures, but it takes time and the investment of members in high standing who support the change can be central in promoting it.

Aisholpan was unwavering in her commitment and withstood extreme conditions, and stigma, to achieve her goal. Similarly, cultural expansion occurs in the US only through concerted efforts and some risk. As can be seen in examples such as the fight for the legalization of gay marriage and the inclusion of sex reassignment surgery as a covered medically necessary procedure, old assumptions and laws can be challenged and changed, even against a backdrop of antipathy.

Since the *industrial era*, technology has been a driving force behind cultural
and attitudinal changes. Technological advances today occur exponentially but
attitudes and laws supporting these can often be delayed. This gap has been referred
to as *cultural lag* where people are hostile or reluctant to integrate social changes.
Technology can be a double-edged sword; it can enhance the quality of life but it
can also endanger the well-being of the population or the planet (see Chapter 14).
Advances in technology have changed our diets as well as our manner of food
production. "Progress" often exhibits mixed results. We are both better nourished and
obese, as a result of changes in food production. Our work environments, in fact our
whole economy, is configured by technological shifts which impact the availability
of jobs. Automation has resulted in greater production, cheaper goods, and modern
conveniences, on the positive side. In contrast, an increasing portion of jobs have
become obsolete, automated, or relocated overseas, leading to unemployment and
low wages among the less skilled workers and contributing to many Americans
feeling left behind (see Chapters 5 and 12). Offshore manufacturing by American
corporations is a result of technology, improvements in transportation, available
cheap labor, and trade policies making it more expedient than domestic production.
The more favorable conditions instituted in less developed countries, often through
governmental negotiations, have contributed to the globalization of economies.

The use of newer technologies has changed the nature of social interactions.
We have gone from "communities" based on proximity to ones based on common
interests and *networking*. We may know more through the tweeting of a stranger
than from the person who lives next door. Today, two thirds of the population own a
smart phone (Smith 2015) and nearly two thirds of the population use social media,
including 90 percent of Americans 18–29 years of age (Beck 2015). Technology is
deeply embedded in daily routine, also with debatable results. "Connection" by cell
phone is so pervasive it might better be described as being tethered, especially among
youth. Face to face interaction, minus cell phone monitoring, seems a lost art. As
a result, the frequency and content of actual physical social interactions have been
modified, containing less intimate conversation than in the past (Turkle 2015). Our
social customs have changed; instead of meeting for coffee we might just "*Facebook*"
or send a text. We can access other people from anywhere, while doing almost
anything. In fact, 19 percent of people have dropped their cell phone in the toilet,
at least once, and between 38 and 75 percent use their smart phone while sitting on
the toilet (Rivers 2016). Ninety percent of 18- to 29-year-old youths sleep with their
smart phone and one in three people state that they would rather give up sex than
their phones (Blodget 2012). In another report, 71 percent of respondents admitted
to sleeping with, or next to, their phones and 44 percent said they could not go a day
without their phone (Ma 2015). Fifty-five percent of people reported texting during
meal time (Ma 2015). The decline of face to face interaction is not only socially
regrettable but dangerous to our mental health since conversation between physically
present people has been shown to have emotional and physical benefits (Turkle 2015;
Fredrickson 2013).

Constant monitoring of activities with social media can dilute the immediacy
of live action compromising human compassion. Activities occurring in real time

can seem unreal, or like entertainment. On 9/11, many viewers were transfixed by the images of the collapsing towers, which were played frequently throughout the day. Today, a person can choose to receive immediate notification of political, international, or social events as they occur. The ability to document events as they unfold has become integral to demands to monitor the behaviors of police officers involved in arrests which turn violent. The use of these records in determining culpability is highly controversial. The potential dilemmas around social media are stunning, raising legal questions, as when an 18-year-old engaged in live streaming the rape of her 17-year-old friend. To many people this was an abhorrent development. She claimed that she was recording it to stop the crime though she made no attempts to do so. She was ultimately charged with multiple felonies and the prosecutor believes that she persisted in recording the rape due to the number of "likes" she was receiving (Shahani 2016). Although this case may be extreme, it does demonstrate how technology can make people feel removed from real events and basic civil obligations to help others. A more superficial example of the exaggerated importance attributed to social media concerns a recent report of the social activities of young, privileged urban professionals: "For them, taking photos and videos for *Instagram* and *Snapchat* is not a way to memorialize a night out. It's the night's main event" (Rosman 2016).

How prevalent is social media participation, considering all technologies? A study on youth and social media habits surveyed 1060 pairs of youths and parents, 614 from White families, 101 from non-Hispanic Black families, and 236 from Hispanic families, in the fall of 2014 and winter of 2015 (Lenhart 2015). The report shows high rates of usage, with 92 percent of the youths reporting being online daily, 24 percent almost constantly, 56 percent several times a day, 12 percent once a day,

Figure 2.4 Social media use is so pervasive that snapping pictures of the group to post on social media sites has even become the focal point of social interaction
Source: William Perugini/ Shutterstock.com

6 percent weekly, and 2 percent less often. Nearly three quarters have a smart phone or access to one. The type of instrument preferred by different groups varies, with African Americans the most likely to have a smart phone (85 percent), followed by Whites and Hispanics (71 percent each). Mobile devices are the major means of accessing the internet. *Facebook* is still the most utilized site, with 71 percent of teens using it. Next popular among teens is *Instagram* with 50 percent usage, and 40 percent visiting *Snapchat*. There is a correlation between household income and what app teens utilize to access social media. Lower income teens (household incomes less than $50,000) are more likely to use *Facebook* while more affluent teens (household incomes of over $75,000) are more likely to use *Snapchat* and *Twitter*. Overall, girls use social media more than boys but boys are more likely to own a gaming console and play video games. Hispanics and African Americans have less access to desktop computers and are more likely to rely on text messaging phone apps (Beck 2015).

Is all this use of technology making us "smarter" or contributing to skills development? Currently, there seems to be some support for the contention that internet use reduces memory; it was found that millennials have worse working memories than seniors (Gregoire 2015). The skills involved refer to the ability to move information into long-term memory. Reliance on the internet to retrieve information, as needed, appears to be impeding the ability to remember it. Research evidence also indicates that people exhibit less empathy as a result of technology use and that "cognitive control," the ability to choose what to think about, is also decreasing. By contrast, healthy brain development and plasticity depend on the ability to fully focus which requires concentration uninterrupted by technological distraction (Gregoire 2015). Intensive focus additionally promotes deep thinking.

The prevalence of all the technology is not only failing to make young people smarter, it is interfering with the ability of students to discern "real" news from fake reports. In a large, year-long project published by Stanford University researchers in 2016, students in middle schools, high schools, and colleges in 12 states were studied to discern their ability to evaluate information culled from a variety of sources (Domonoske 2016). The respondents showed a consistent inability to distinguish real and fake news; sponsored content from factual articles; and neutral vs. biased sources. More than 80 percent of middle school students could not identify any difference in paid articles of sponsored content and "news" articles. High school students were likely to accept the accuracy of a photograph of weirdly formed flowers, allegedly impacted by nuclear fallout, though the photo appeared without attribution. Only 25 percent recognized a blue checkmark verifying a story on *Facebook*, while 30 percent argued a fake account was "more trustworthy" than a real one. Most college students did not recognize that a tweet from *MoveOn* was potentially biased. The tweet quoted a professional polling source but only a few recognized this and more than one half did not contemplate following the link to the source. When Stanford students were given two articles to read from pediatric medical associations, more than one half failed to distinguish between the article published by a mainstream group and the other written by a small fringe organization. The fringe group members represented a segment, splintered from the larger group, because they opposed gay parenting; linked homosexuality to pedophilia; and supported other views which led to their classification as a hate group. More than half the students actually identified the article by the fringe groups as "more reliable" even though they preferred the other article. This trend suggests an increasing tendency to accept false information without question and to trust unreliable sources. The internet entices users to accept everyone's contribution equally, effectively leveling the influence of experts. The researchers were so shocked at the analysis of the 7800 responses, they admitted to fearing for the future of democracy (Domonoske 2016).

To moderate the influence of informational resources, some schools utilize internet filters which direct students to legitimate sources. Educators are challenging the wisdom of providing this service as it fails to inform the students to make their own assessments of news and information sources. To address the need to develop such a skill, one organization, *News Literacy Project*, was formed by an *LA Times* reporter to guide students to be smarter consumers. The project is endorsed by 33 additional news venues. In May 2016, the organization released a program, *Checkology Virtual Classroom*, to help students evaluate sources (Turner 2016).

American Core Values

Core cultural values serve as a source of identity for the group's members. When asked, most students articulate material success, family, religion, freedom, and education as central features of life. Although there are variations among groups, most people consider basic values to include freedom of speech, religion, and movement within society; equal rights and opportunities; strong family ties; a solid work ethic; and the ability to attain a good standard of living. Almost all Americans manifest a belief in religion, though not necessarily in the same one. However, the *nature* of religiosity is shifting today, since 22.8 percent of the population is *non-affiliated*, most of this group indicating religious beliefs but a lack of identification with any particular denomination. Seven percent of the *non-affiliated* report being agnostic or atheist (America's Changing Religious Landscape 2015). Researchers refer to this group variously as "*nons*" or "*nones*." This phenomenon represents a growth in Americans considering themselves "spiritual" rather than religious (Lipka and Gecewicz 2017). It also illustrates one core value of American society, individual freedoms which are guaranteed in the *Bill of Rights*. The institutionalization of free speech makes it possible for any individual to voice any perspective, even those which are extremely offensive to others. Americans value "American ingenuity" which has been credited with the development of many business ideas and inventions, including the harnessing of natural resources for human improvement. Americans are proud of being inventive and resourceful. This attitude was evidenced in Barack Obama's campaign slogan, "Yes, we can," a phrase originating in the farmworkers' movement (see Chapter 12).

Even categorizations we presume are fixed actually are influenced by cultural perception. Although there is a physical reality to the biology of sex, the historian Yuval Noah Harari succinctly shows (2015) that the categories of woman and man are **not** uniform but are *culturally construed*. The disparate "natures" and roles attributed to each sex are not defined consistently across cultures. For example, the right to the legal recognition of a woman as a separate and fully human actor has been culturally defined (149). It took American women over 150 years to win the right to vote. Harari maintains that though the concepts of woman and man are culturally specific (152–159), post-industrial society has evolved so that, based on technological developments, anyone can accomplish anything which needs to be done. Consequently, some commentators suggest the need for gender differentiation is no longer apparent and that gender roles will disappear. Some writers believe that pregnancy and childbirth will become possible for men and in laboratories (Melchior 2017).

Social science perspectives contain presumptions, with regard to the development of humans and society, which are seen as objective or scientific but which have been transformed over decades and centuries. Eighteenth-and nineteenth-century European social science theorists held an evolutionary approach to the development of "civilization," in which the earliest cultures were viewed as the simplest and the modern ones, the scientists' own, as possessing higher levels of sophistication and advancement. This assumption negated the richness of earlier cultures, which were very complex. With the rise of western civilizations, particularly in the industrial era, there was a belief in the inherent goodness of technological and scientific "progress." These developments were presumed to provide universally beneficial effects. Social scientists, and others, believed in the achievement of ever higher standards of life for everyone, with no negative fallout. Today this notion seems naïve, at best. While some cultures have evolved to formerly unimaginably high levels of material life, others suffer economic exploitation, political domination, and the persistence of curable disease. Within cultures, similar disparities also can be seen. Today most of us recognize the grave jeopardy our scientific "progress" has wrought on our global environment, even leading to predictions of its ultimate collapse. Our underlying beliefs in "science" and "progress" are gaining critical examination even as many of us, ironically, believe the key to sustaining the planet also lies in scientifically based interventions.

How Is American Culture Constructed?

Is there a unified American culture which applies to everyone? When we speak of American culture, do we all mean the same thing and share it in the same ways? When we define ourselves as "American" we are claiming some national identity that suggests some commonalities. What would these be? Americans enjoy a relatively high level of personal freedoms, standard of living, and material comfort compared to most other nations, though these are not evenly distributed in the population. Consequently, it would be foolish to say we all experience "American life" in equivalent fashion, though many of us take for granted some basic elements of life which are rare in other countries, such as food, shelter, water, and medicine. We do not all live with the same advantages in our neighborhoods, schools, families, and states. Still, diverse people proudly claim the title of *American*. The defining feature may reside in the powerful image of the *American Dream*, and all it signifies. Though it may not be true in every detail that "anyone can grow up to be president," it loosely translates into a belief that a person is limited only by her or his imagination. Most Americans can define

elements of this dream, though we will see (in Chapter 5) that it is further out of
reach than in the past or than most people believe. Americans' belief in the "rags to
riches" stories is a mainstay of popular culture. The concept of the self-made man (and
initially it applied only to men), enhanced the idea that inequality could be eliminated
by will and hard work. Horatio Alger, the nineteenth-century writer who made this
idea popular, also promoted the notion of honor and good morals in hard-working
heroes. Unfortunately, some of these ideals have been compromised and the fable
has also fostered the idea that poor people are just not motivated or hard working,
implying that character flaws are at the heart of their problems. Today, the Horatio
Alger stories still promote hope in many poorer Americans (Smith and Gillett 2015)
and even influence citizens' voting habits, attitudes towards immigration, the *Occupy*
movement, and the *Tea party* (Ghosh 2013).

Box 2.4 – American Culture

American culture incorporates values, attitudes, and behaviors. Basic values
likely to be elaborated by Americans include freedom of speech, religion,
and both physical and social movement within society; equal rights and
opportunities; strong family ties; a solid work ethic; and the ability to attain
a good standard of living. The American Dream incorporates the idea that
hard work and self-discipline will win the individual material success and full
membership in American society.

Easy access to securing basic needs is another taken-for-granted aspect of
American life. Many Americans don't worry about the loss of running water, indoor
plumbing, electricity, and internet availability, although there are areas where their
consistent availability is not assured. We love our cars and utilize our automobiles
far more than people in most comparable nations, where public transportation
generally is cheaper and more convenient. Bicycle lanes are also more prevalent in
other countries, though there is an active movement to make US city roads more bike
friendly. Frequently, we hop in our cars to do errands, visit friends, and commute to
school or work even when these destinations are accessible by foot or bicycle. The
relative cheapness of gas, particularly in comparison with the European countries
which have heavier gasoline taxes and more environmental protections, affords most
of us little reason to question our daily dependence on the automobile.

Many Americans count on the competitive market to assure us of consumer
"rights." We can make consumer choices, whether that be where to shop or what
to buy but we can be pretty assured that there will be a place we can go, with
inventory we can select from, for just about any need, as long as we have money
or credit. This assumption of access to basic needs is enjoyed by many in America
though it is not universal and, in spite of claims otherwise, the portion of people
struggling to meet these needs is growing (see Chapter 5). Nevertheless, the
"American way" ethos is to provide choice, even if the choices are produced by
different companies, with different brand names, but actually represent the same

product. We can go to a supermarket and find an entire aisle of cold cereals, all essentially the same. The absurdity of American commercialism is depicted in the movie *The Hurt Locker* (Bigelow 2008), when a soldier returning from the Iraq war appears overwhelmed by the bright, colorful packages of cereal seemingly

Figure 2.5 Americans are apt to take for granted access to automobiles, either for easy transportation to work or for recreational purposes. America has had a love affair with the automobile, and is more dependent on it, than other developed countries Source: Natalia Bratslavsky / Shutterstock. com

Figure 2.6 We expect fully stocked grocery stores, even as we are confronted by consumer "choices" controlled by major corporations offering their versions of the same products Source: Sergey Ryzhov / Shutterstock.com

assaulting his sensibilities. The scene communicates his visceral sense of displacement and the unreality of daily life, presumably against the backdrop of the war he just survived. Some theorists suggest that many aspects of society, from commercialism to what constitutes news, actually are constructed to distract us from the "real" problems facing us (Glassner 1999). Which cereal to choose is an easier task than determining which wire will defuse a bomb, the soldier's military job, or why we are at war with Iraq.

Whose Culture Is It?

The promotion of a universal American culture masks the reality that references to "the" culture frequently reflect the interests of an elite group of people who represent the *dominant group*. The "Occupy Wall Street" movement, with its protests against the 1 percent, has drawn attention to the economic control that a small portion of society wields over the majority, but their influence is not limited to the financial realm. This group can be described as White, male, affluent, and Anglo-Saxon Protestant. Much of the power of this group is cloaked in policies and practices that appear neutral and supported by law. Until very recently, no person outside of this group held a position of power or leadership, and currently the number of "outsiders" is very limited.

The dissemination of the White, male norm as universal persists largely unexamined. Alternative images, perspectives, or practices typically are explained as anomalous or dismissed. With respect to sociology, the dominant group is referred to as the *majority group* but this terminology sometimes leads to misinterpretation since the majority group can frequently be numerically in the minority. Majority, in this context, refers to power not numbers. *Minority group* refers to *marginalized* groups; or groups who deviate, in some aspect, from the dominant group. Even if these groups reach parity with the dominant group, they will retain minority status since they remain less represented in positions of power or authority. Minority, in this context, is a term of status not numbers. These groups will be referred to as nondominant in order to avoid the association of "less than" the word minority implies. The dominant standard is the source of assessment and anyone falling outside the parameters is subjected to scrutiny and very likely marginalized. Nondominant groups frequently are judged with more exacting standards and any modification from the dominant practices is viewed negatively. The process of portraying the cultural standards of the dominant group as "universal" and "correct" is referred to as *hegemony*.

Box 2.5 – Dominant Group

The dominant group refers to the narrow segment of society which controls resources and has the power to form political and economic policy. This group also exerts influence in what knowledge is valued and what constitutes acceptable standards of behavior. The US dominant group is White, Anglo-Saxon, Protestant, affluent, and male. With respect to sociology, the dominant group is referred to as the *majority group* but this terminology sometimes leads to misinterpretation since the majority group can frequently be numerically in the minority. *Minority group* refers to **marginalized** groups; or groups who deviate, in some aspect, from the dominant group. These groups will be referred to as **nondominant** in order to avoid the association of "less than" the word minority implies.

Hegemony refers to the ways in which the dominant group imposes its dominance and standards onto other groups in society such that everyone is measured, explicitly and implicitly, by the standards of the dominant group. Practices, beliefs, or lifestyles which differ from the standards of the dominant group are devalued, or made invisible, as are the groups and people who exhibit them. Consequently, it appears that there is consensus, even when there is not.

Hegemony creates an association between the dominant group and the label of "American." If you are reading an article about an American who accidentally drowned in the Caribbean, who would you picture? Most people will imagine a White American and, depending on the context, a male or female. White is the American "default" option (see Chapter 7). Unless otherwise specified, American translates into "Euro-American." In fact, White will only lose its dominant designation when it, too, is qualified, as in "White American," or Euro-American. The description of a person who has a nondominant status usually includes the adjective describing the nondominant status as opposed to the dominant group whose categorization is usually simply "American." If a White male is charged with a crime, the news headline does not say "A White male was indicted for …" but if a woman or a racial minority is charged, likely the report would say so, as in "A woman was arrested last night for …" or "An African American youth was …" *Nondominant* status suggests someone who is not considered a fully legitimate group member, as if an African American male is not fully a man, or a woman not completely a human on par with a man.

The "hyphenated" terminologies currently utilized indicate that this dynamic persists. Consider the terms African American, Muslim American, Native American, Chinese American, Japanese American. Each of these has the connotation of not being *a real* "American," even if the person is a fifth-generation American. These qualified titles are not only applied to people but to cultural endeavors. Consider the following: African American literature, Native American literature, women's literature, southern literature, Black musicians, Indian actor, woman comedian, woman governor, gay novelist, etc. Each of these designations suggests that these people are somehow not "real" writers, actors, comedians, or politicians. The implication is that they do not reflect the universally human experience but represent experiences specific to their group members. It bears repeating that the dominant group is also a special interest group; it possesses no special claim to universality. The recognition that different groups experience "reality" uniquely has led to the development of *post-modern* theories in sociology. In this group of theories, sociologists have promoted the *deconstruction* of what we believe we know, since "knowledge" has been constituted from privilege. Post-modern theory suggests that there is no "objective" reality but rather multiple realities which rely upon specific perspectives or situations which characterize a person or group. The post-modern point of view contextualizes knowledge, perspective, habit. In social science, the post-modernist theories highlight the role of the economy and its promulgation of a *culture of consumption* as a central force in cultural development.

> ## Box 2.6 – Post-modernism
>
> *Post-modernism* is the perspective which recognizes that there are multiple realities and that a person's experiences are shaped by their positions in the culture. Ideas which previously have been considered "objective" fact are seen as specific to a particular perspective. This concept challenges the dominant group, which generally maintains the notion that its values and behaviors are universal and neutral. For this reason, post-modernism promotes the need to "deconstruct" what we think we know, in order to highlight the biased view of an imagined *objective* reality. The popular culture and media often promote the biases of the dominant group.

According to university professor and former Labor Secretary Robert Reich (2016), the dominant group has rigged the system, from corporate law, to market regulations, to Constitutional law. Even when it comes to our "inalienable" rights, Reich cautions we should ask "Whose freedom of speech" is protected? White men have held the exclusive right to define the government, the law, the television industry, the news media, politics, opinion, standards of art, literature, music, and etiquette. Any alternative style, or content, is seen as substandard rather than simply representing a different approach. A Black, or female, or gay entertainer is often seen as just that—a person who does not represent the general public but only the one segment the person represents. This translates into their being seen as limited in appeal and substance and otherwise as less talented and worthy than—White, male—entertainers who allegedly have universal appeal. As a result, the entertainment industry, for example, is afraid to make a movie or television show where marginalized groups are not acting "marginal." It is presumed that there is no interest in "marginal" types just doing "normal" things, and consequently executive producers fear that no one would be interested in these performances (Thorp 2016). People from marginalized groups struggle to avoid being placed in this role of limited appeal. In the 2008 election of Barack Obama conscious efforts were made to sell him as a Black candidate for "America" rather than as a candidate for Black America, indicating that he could have universal appeal rather than representing only his own group.

White control of power in politics, the economy, and culture persists. A brief summary of the demographics of power makes the point. White men comprise 31 percent of the population and about 70 percent of Congress. Women are 18.5 percent of Congress and minorities are 15.5 percent, with some overlap.

Interestingly, it is easy to find data on the portion of women and minorities in social institutions, but rare to see the portion of White males starkly stated (National Journal 2014). In a demographic report regarding the 114th Congress, under the heading of "Gender and Ethnicity," the portion of members who were female, African American, Latino, Asian American, American Indian, foreign born, or had military service were all reported. There were no categorical data provided for males or Caucasians (Manning 2016). Another article reported the Congress as 80 percent male, 80 percent White, 92 percent Christian but failed to report the total of "White males" (Bump 2015). The media demonstrate a reluctance to draw attention to the preponderance of White males and a cultural tendency only to make a count of minorities so that we can look at our "improved" rates of minority involvement, which are still *disproportionately* low.

A look at business tells a similar story. In 2014, there were only 23 women CEOs in the Fortune 500 companies (the largest American corporations), six African Americans, ten Latinos and ten Asian Americans. Directors of Fortune 500 companies were 74.4 percent White males with 13.3 percent White females. The statistics were 5.3 percent African American males and 1.5 percent African American females. Of the Latinos, 2.4 percent were male and .7 percent female. Asian American males comprised 2 percent of the Boards; Asian American females comprised .4 percent (Domhoff 2013). Interestingly, African American women are much more likely than their male counterparts to obtain college and graduate degrees and yet a lot less likely to rise in the corporate ranks, indicating the persistence and strength of sexism.

Media Hegemony

Perhaps nothing is as prominent in perpetuating dominance as the media and entertainment. The representation of women and minorities, in both news media and entertainment, reveals deeply entrenched stereotypical practices. Male reporters still dominate the bylines in the ten top US newspapers, at 63 percent, and they typically are the major writers of the "hard" news of politics, business and finance. Women are more likely to be relegated to soft news such as culture, education, lifestyle, and health. Male hegemony in opinion and commentary, represents the starkest disparity with male to female ratios of 2:1 at the *Wall Street Journal*; more than 3:1 at the *Washington Post*; and 5:1 at the *New York Times* (Mundy 2014).

> In 2014, all minority groups accounted for 22.4 percent of television journalists, 13 percent of radio journalists, and 13.34 percent of journalists at daily newspapers. Pretty pathetic, considering the fact that minorities make up 37.4 percent of the U.S. population. But walk into most major newsrooms in the U.S. and you'll be overwhelmed by the whiteness and maleness of the editorial staff.
>
> (White 2015)

Staffing patterns reveal discrimination but obtaining a first job can be even more difficult. Minority journalism graduates were 17 percent less likely than their White counterparts to find a job in their field (White 2015).

Are the Media Biased in News Reporting?

There are charges, from both the liberal and the conservative segments of society, that the media are biased towards the other group. Extensive research shows that news reporting is more often balanced and that accusations of bias are unfounded (Kramer 2016; Farhi 2012). Accusations regarding bias in the 2016 election were leveled by all parties, especially by the Trump campaign. But, as the story unfolded, the most pervasive unfairness emerged as the bias against Democratic candidate Bernie Sanders. In an extensive review of 200 editorials and op ed pieces in the *Washington Post*, one of the most respected news outlets in the country, Thomas Frank asserts that the *Post* published negatively toned articles against Sanders at a rate of 5:1, while such articles about Hillary Clinton were much less common, at a rate of 1:1. Frank suggests that the Democratic Party machinery defines party positions and does not tolerate diversion from these (Frank 2016). After the election, the Democratic Party was shown to have taken dramatic and consistent steps to ensure the candidacy of Hillary Clinton over Bernie Sanders, ultimately leading to the resignation of the Democratic National Committee Chairwoman, Debbie Wasserman Schultz (Gearan et al. 2016).

The wrath directed towards Sanders, according to Frank, stems from the fact that Sanders seriously challenged basic tenets of the Democratic Party platform which were standard fare and largely unexamined by the party machinery. The Party's interests reflect those of Wall Street, free trade, globalization, technology workers, and the white-collar middle class while Sanders was clearly anti-bank and anti-capitalist. The *Post* writers represent the privileged who come from high socio-economic backgrounds and possess elite educations. They share a peer group with the Democratic Party, comprised of the elite from Wall Street, academia, healthcare, and Silicon Valley. Frank suggests that this allegiance contributed to the *Post* writers' predilection to see "something deeply threatening about Sanders and his political views" (Frank 2016).

Incendiary headlines characterized the articles regarding Sanders in the early stages of the campaign leading to the Iowa Caucuses, perhaps in reaction to the recognition that Sanders actually could have posed a threat to a Clinton candidacy. Some examples were: *Nominating Sanders Would Be Insane* (1/27/16); *A Campaign Full of Fiction* (1/28/16); and *The Real Problem with Mr. Sanders* (1/29/16). An editorial, from January 29, 2016, forecast that a Sanders nomination would leave the Democrats open to disaster (Frank 2016).

Sanders was consistently criticized for his alleged lack of explicit programs to attack the deficit and other causes he championed. He was criticized for "pandering" to the working class by promoting universal healthcare and free college tuition. Frank states: "The paper hit every possible anti-Sanders note, from the driest kind of math-based policy reproach to the lowest sort of nerd-shaming—from his inexcusable failure to embrace taxes on soda pop to his awkward gesticulating during a debate with Hillary Clinton." In a similar vein, one editorial asserted that Sanders was an "unacceptable leader" with "simple sounding solutions" (Frank 2016).

There were a scattering of *Post* articles in support of Sanders but "coincidentally" the paper terminated their author, Harold Meyerson, in December 2015, for the stated reason that he failed to attract readers. Meyerson was a proponent of German manufacturing and its pro-worker conditions and was a Sanders supporter. Frank suggests that Meyerson was terminated for being at odds with the paper's bias. Another source of Sanders support was a strong editorial, on May 26, 2016, by the economist and Columbia University professor Jeffrey Sachs. Sachs asserted that charges regarding the infeasibility of Sanders' positions failed to take into account the sweeping legislative proposals he established to promote their viability. Nevertheless, eleven days after Sachs' statement, the *Post* declared Hillary Clinton the preemptive nominee of the Democratic Party.

Frank's analysis of the *Post* campaign is of special significance to understanding sociology in that it is illustrative of a *conflict theory* view of the consolidation of elite power against the majority of the population. Frank maintains that the media, in this case the *Post*, has the power to designate certain ideas "inadmissible." Consequently, the paper is part of a "machinery by which the boundaries of the Washington consensus are enforced." Frank substantiates this claim by extending his analysis of remarks against Sanders, to the examination of *Post* statements regarding the general nature of political reform. He asserts that the paper promoted "incremental changes," reflected in the Clinton campaign, as the only justifiable means of transformation, even in opposition to historical occurrences which would suggest otherwise. The paper's opinion pieces consistently advanced the ideas of compromise and increment, charging that "sweeping change is structurally impossible," and aligning that view with Sanders. Frank suggests that the danger inherent in this type of coverage is the power of the press to make its declarations the "truth" (Frank 2016).

The lack of representation of nondominant participants is not limited to "hard" news but is prevalent in the entertainment field, as well. The year 2014 was celebrated as a year of great achievement for women in television, yet Scovell (2015) points out that the level of achievement that year just brings the figures to the 1990 level previously acclaimed as a "Golden Year" for women's achievement. Women's appearances in television expanded from 1990 to 1997 and then contracted until 2014, which was heralded as a new high. In fact, Scovell calls it an actual "catching up." Women's "unprecedented participation" is actually decreasing since women were 29 percent of television writers and 15.1 percent of executive producers in 2013–2014, the latter being down from 18.6 percent two years earlier. Women comprise only 18 percent of late night writers. In 2016 women accounted for 17 percent of all directors, writers, producers, executive producers, and cinematographers in the top grossing 250 films. This is a decrease of 2 percent from 2015 and equal to the 1998 figures. Women were 7 percent of directors and 3 percent of composers (Lauzen 2016).

The representation of racial and ethnic minority group writers is proportionately very low. The figure for minority television writers was 13.7 percent in 2013–2014, down from 15.6 percent two years prior, and represented only 3.5 percent of late night writing staff. Yet, the total national minority population is 40 percent. In broadcast television, minorities are under-represented by 6:1. Through the twenty-first century, the television trend in minority representation has been one of decline, with a marginal increase in 2015. Additionally, the majority of minority roles are restricted to ones depicting experiences specific to minorities (Julious 2015).

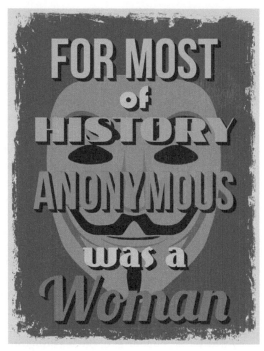

Figure 2.7 Nondominant groups have had their work ignored by established venues and have had to fight for public recognition. This statement was a popular feminist adage, especially in the 1960s and 1970s
Source: sibgat / Shutterstock.com

For several years, media attention has focused on the lack of African Americans nominated for Academy Awards, especially in all the acting categories, where no African Americans were nominated in the four major acting categories in 2015 or 2016 (Kilday 2016). This led to a boycott and a campaign, #OscarsSoWhite, to draw attention to the dismal showing of diversity in Hollywood (McNamara 2016). The Annenberg School of Communications and Journalism (Deggans 2016) highlighted the dominance of male, White characters in television and movies produced between September 2014 and August 2015. People of color comprise 40 percent of the population but were only 28 percent of speaking roles on TV in the time period studied. There were no Asians in half of the programs and in one fifth there were no Blacks. With regard to the division of the sexes in television, women made up only one third of speaking roles though women are slightly more than 50 percent of the population. When women characters are present, the depiction frequently is a sexualized one or one that focuses on their attractiveness. The LGBT community, with very few exceptions, was absent altogether. An assessment of 109 movies revealed only 7 percent accurately reflected the American population and only 3 percent had women directors (Deggans 2016). Hollywood executives believe that nondominant-led films run counter to audience taste and are therefore reluctant to move beyond the

Figure 2.8 Kendrick Lamar at the Grammy Awards ceremony in LA February 15, 2016 in which Mr. Lamar is highlighting the incarceration of African Americans (see Chapter 6) Source: Robyn Beck / Getty Images.

usual genres for fear they will not sell. It is a baseless concern since so-called "Black films" and "women's films" have proven lucrative and are crucial to the full cultural integration of these groups.

In contrast to the Academy Awards program, the 2016 Grammy show made headlines for its bold portrayal of today's Black America. The African American rapper, Kendrick Lamar, performed a song to call attention to the mass incarceration of African Americans by posing as a member of a chain gang with his band playing from inside jail cells (Zeitchik 2016).

The cultural representation of nondominant groups suffers from the absence of authentic voices of its members. Countless products created in nondominant groups are lost to history. It has been difficult, if not impossible, for members of these

Figure 2.9 The Dinner Party
Source: Photo: Donald Woodman. Work of Art: Judy Chicago. Megan Schultz (assistant to Judy Chicago)/ Wikimedia Commons

groups to get material published, shown, or produced. Some people succeeded by using initials for first names or names that were neutral with respect to sex, race, and ethnicity. Works identified as originating in a nondominant group are often evaluated as substandard in some way, or as anomalous examples not likely to recur. Even the works of established and well-regarded artists or experts are questioned if they depart, in any way, from acceptable form. This can be seen in the controversy surrounding Maya Angelou's poem (1993), created to celebrate

President Clinton's first inaugural ceremony. "On the Pulse of Morning" incited debate regarding the standard of the work or even if it qualified as "poetry." A similar controversy erupted, with articles disputing the artistic merit of Judy Chicago's exhibit, *The Dinner Party* (1974–1979), which incorporated weaving and Japanese enamel painting, historically associated as women's "crafts." Because Chicago drew on the historically female crafts, reviewers questioned whether the exhibit constituted a work of art. These two women have achieved the highest regard in their fields but since their conceptualizations differed from the prevailing standards, their creditability and accomplishments were considered suspect.

Excerpt from "On The Pulse of Morning"

Delicate and strangely made proud,
Yet thrusting perpetually under siege.
Your armed struggles for profit
Have left collars of waste upon
My shore, currents of debris upon my breast.
Yet today I call you to my riverside,
If you will study war no more. Come,
Clad in peace, and I will sing the songs
The Creator gave to me when I and the
Tree and the rock were one.
Before cynicism was a bloody sear across your
Brow and when you yet knew you still
Knew nothing.
The River sang and sings on.

(Angelou 1993)

Suppression of additional aspects of nondominant American daily life are also seen in history and literature. Understanding of the lived experience of slavery is persistently distorted since slaves were not legally allowed to read and write, and most of the written accounts are by non-slaves. One exception is a recently published novel (2002) credited to a North Carolina plantation slave, titled *The Bondwoman's Narrative*, by Hannah Crafts.

Another example of lack of expression of "lived" life can be seen in the 2015 film, *Carol*, about a married woman in the 1950s who risks everything, including rights to her daughter, to engage in a lesbian affair. Based on the novel, *The Price of Salt* (Highsmith 1952/2004), this movie depicts the tragic loneliness of women who do not conform to social expectations. Though attitudes towards lesbianism have changed, at least for some portion of the population, women still suffer from being judged for behaviors deemed inappropriate to the traditional female gender role. Women who choose to defy conventions are not only shunned and stigmatized but vulnerable to being legally judged as unfit mothers and deprived of rights to their children.

What Sociological Concepts are Used to Analyze Cultures?

Ethnocentrism is the term that describes the tendency of a group to judge other groups by its standards. Implicitly, or explicitly, the other groups are assumed to be aberrant or deficient. Some people might feel it is inappropriate for Muslims to wear a headscarf, or *hijab*, to school or work. This view is discriminatory in that the hijab is a part of a traditional religious observation. To deny a person the ability to wear the hijab is tantamount to telling them they cannot express their identity and it also exhibits denigration of the culture. The increasing fears accompanying public identification as Muslim have caused some women to remove the hijab even at the risk of feeling that they have abandoned a custom with personal meaning. Hijab removal constitutes a violation of religious practice which alienates a woman from herself and her community (Rojas 2016). In a more dramatic move, five towns in France banned the *burkini*, a full body bathing suit. The ban was supported by the Prime Minister who claimed that the burkini represented "the enslavement of women" (Rubin 2016). Such a move shows a blatant disregard for the value of modesty embedded in Muslim culture.

The obverse concept to ethnocentrism is ***cultural relativism***. This refers to understanding a cultural reference in the context of that culture. For example, Faderman recognizes the integral role of Shamanism in Hmong culture and suggests that its elimination, especially by adoption of Christianity, would violate the culture. Shamanism is not limited to religious practices but includes a way of relating to the entire human environment and is incorporated in the healing arts. To impose western medicine on Hmong individuals as the right way to offer treatment is potentially damaging and lacking in cultural sensitivity. It has been shown that utilizing non-western forms of treatment improves a patient's well-being, even if western treatment

Figure 2.10 Muslim women are fearful of wearing the hijab in public but the omission of this garment would alienate them from their community and their religious beliefs
Source: Creative Family / Shutterstock.com

is also utilized. To dismiss the Shamanistic practice as "nonsense" is ethnocentric and punitive.

Box 2.7 – Cultural Perspectives

Ethnocentrism refers to the evaluation of other cultures by the standards of a person's own culture. The *hijab,* or headscarf, is an essential garment for some observant Muslim women, and is indicative of their religious observation. Because of threats of violence and discrimination, some women are reluctant to wear the hijab in public. This animosity towards women who simply are observing their cultural traditions, is evidence of ethnocentrism.

A *subculture* refers to a group within a dominant culture that has specific characteristics which distinguish it from other segments of society but does not oppose major aspects of the dominant culture. Groups that qualify as subcultures often form along socio-demographic characteristics such as race, religion, ethnicity, age, or locale. *Subcultures* can also develop in accordance to shared interests such as hip-hop music, surfing, gaming, or robotics. Subcultural groups contain language, activities, or beliefs which are not part of the dominant culture. Some sociologists recommend avoiding this term since "sub," referring to underneath, often connotes less value.

Cultural relativism is a concept which represents an opposing view to ethnocentrism. It suggests that any cultural element must be considered within the context of that culture. Recognition of the vital role Shamanism plays in Hmong culture, and incorporating its practices into healthcare for the Hmong community, represents cultural relativism.

Cultural assimilation refers to how much a nondominant group chooses, or feels coerced into adopting the values and manner of the dominant group. Nondominant group members may reserve various customs and language for use only among their group.

Cultural assimilation refers to the extent to which a group incorporates the practices of a culture they have entered. Virtually all nondominant groups participate in the dominant culture to some extent, just by participating in social institutions. Every person must consider how, and to what extent, to maintain their original culture. To navigate a comfortable inter-cultural existence is difficult, at best, and many people within nondominant groups disagree on the "correct" level of assimilation. Within the deaf community, for example, the decision to utilize procedures to obtain partial hearing is a source of community divisiveness since some see it as an admission that deaf culture is "illegitimate," while others support its use as practical. Many people in the community believe that deaf life represents a separate culture and to force some participants to bridge the hearing world is to violate that culture and to insinuate that deafness is a disability, rather than a different way of being in the world, as deaf culture would suggest.

The deaf community constitutes what sociologists refer to as a *subculture*; a group which participates in "American society" but incorporates some characteristics, practices, or beliefs which separate them from the "main" culture. The deaf community practices its own form of language and this shapes the culture of the group with some aspects absent in hearing America. Subcultures often form along demographic variations in race, ethnicity, sexuality, religion, age, and other social characteristics. They can also be generated from interests or activities such as sports, music, dance, gaming, etc. These "subcultural" groups are referred to as distinct from others, as in a "southern writer" or "Black musician," as described in the case of hegemony discussed above.

Sociologists have developed a variety of terms to describe cultural elements. These are *values, norms, folkways, laws, sanctions, mores, taboos, and stigma*. Values refer to cultural attitudes or goals defined as desirable. These are ideals which are *generally* sought rather than pertaining to any particular behavior or role. Examples of American values would include rights to personal freedoms, to vote, to pursue education, and to participate in civic life. Theoretically, all members of the society are entitled to these elements.

Box 2.8 – Elements of Culture

Values are the basic ideals in a society, such as ideas of right and wrong; beauty; morality; and life goals.

Norms are specific behaviors associated with social roles. Examples would be student, parent, church member, spouse, neighbor.

Laws are norms which have been codified and given the support of the government. Breaking a law usually is more serious than violating a norm.

Sanctions are consequences for behaviors. Sanctions can be positive or negative and formal or informal. Breaking a norm may result in an *informal sanction*, such as peer isolation. Conforming to expectations can also result in positive sanctions, such as popularity. *Formal sanctions*, associated with written codes, generally result in expressly stated consequences, such as being charged with a crime or earning an honor.

Folkways are habits of people which are largely automatic for people in the culture, for example, saying "excuse me" or "pardon me" if you bump into someone. Greeting a person with a handshake is also a folkway.

Mores (pronounced more-rays) refer to values that are so basic to a society that most people would not dream of breaking them; examples would be incest, pedophilia, polygamy.

Taboos are prohibited behaviors and can be seen as transgressions of mores. A person should not commit incest, child molestation, or marry a relative.

Stigma is the negative evaluation of a person resulting from violation of socially prescribed behaviors.

One example of a basic American value is the desirability of home ownership. There are banking practices guiding the qualification for a home loan. An article regarding legal charges against the practices of a bank in New York's Chinatown highlights the variable ways ethnic communities support the goal of home ownership (Fan 2015) and highlight how ethnocentrism is perpetuated in "normal" business practices. In the traditional Chinese community, family is highly valued, as is owning a home in which to raise a family. Home owning typically is seen as a precondition for starting a family. A home represents security and stability. Due to this goal of home ownership, and family support for obtaining it, 65 percent of the Chinese American population are home owners though their path to financing the purchase may seem unorthodox. Many US Chinese workers engage primarily in a cash economy and in many traditional Chinese families, the extended family network members will contribute to a young couple's down payment on a house to make it affordable. On a traditional mortgage application, such a purchasing couple may appear as a poor risk since they lack declared savings to secure the loan. In the traditional Chinese community, the extended network contributing cash to obtain the home would not be listed as purchasers on the loan. One established Chinatown community bank, *Abacus,* in New York City, was investigated for fraud due to its "unorthodox" processing of loan applications. The bank was owned by a local Chinese American who understood the neighborhood and the nontraditional ways in which a couple paid for a home. The bank ultimately was found to be "not guilty," though its process of granting loans was not "by the book." Analysis of the 4390 mortgages the bank held in 2009, showed that only 16 were in trouble, a figure considerably lower than the US national average (Fan 2015).

This unorthodox banking process illustrates a bank's relationship to its community and the value to be gained from smaller banks with community roots. The terms utilized by sociologists can be applied to explain why there was a legal challenge to the bank's practices. The overall *value* of home owning and family life was enacted in ways that pertained to the specific *norms*, or patterns of behaviors, in the community. Because nonmainstream practices were incorporated into the bank's loan program, the bank drew the attention of the regulatory commissions, and was the object of a formal investigation. *Laws* are norms, or patterned practices which have been codified and given the support of the government, and reflect the biases of the privileged who make them. As such, violation of the law can result in *formal sanctions*, such as fines and incarceration. Generally, deviation from acceptable legal practices can result in these formal sanctions but the local community bank was able to provide evidence of its calculated risk analysis. The example suggests why "one size fits all" laws and procedures can be seen as inherently biased. The case provides an example of how some nondominant groups within American society actually adhere to basic values in the culture, such as home ownership, and manifest them in ways that are culturally specific but that work for the community and the national economy. The acceptance of this culturally specific practice can be understood in terms of the concept of *cultural relativism.*

Folkways refer to behaviors so habitual that most people do not even think about them but perform them almost mindlessly. Saying "excuse me" or "pardon me" when

Figure 2.11 A bank in
Chinatown, NY. Local
banks integrate community
values in considering loan
applications
Source: Spondylolithesis /
istockphoto.com

bumping into another person is one example of a folkway. Another would be greeting
a person with a handshake, rather than a bow or kisses, as occurs in other cultures.
The Chinese banking example is one which shows the way that informal practices
can be incorporated into more formal institutional ones. Folkways develop over time,
and generally require some period of adjustment. It might once have been considered
rude to ignore others while socializing with them in a public setting but today it is
commonly acceptable for people to read text messages, or view images on *Snapchat*
or *Instagram,* even while participating in a social activity. Young people have become
so dependent on their technology that one movie theater company is considering
allowing texting so that it can leverage the patronage of the millennials (Montagne
2016).

The behaviors of millennials around technology are modifying many practices
which might formerly have been considered offensive. Youth's reliance on quick and
short communication, as in the abbreviated language of text messages, tweets, and
the use of emojis, has resulted in a documented reduction of the average attention
span from 12 seconds in 2000 to 8 seconds in 2015. The popular television series,
Downton Abbey, featured very rapid cuts from scene to scene (Egan 2016) as a
nod to these new norms. Even the Bible has been "translated" into emoji symbols
(Cuthbertson 2016).

Dependence on technology starts early in life. It has been suggested that the
reduction in "real play" in preschool, where children are free to interact with
others and learn social and emotional skills, is detrimental to the psychological
and emotional development of children. When children are interacting in play, with
peers, they learn to adjust their behaviors to get along and not stand apart from the
group (Turner 2016a). A person who is viewed as too "different" can suffer social

isolation. *Stigmas*, negative evaluations by others which follow a person through life, can affect adult life satisfaction and goal attainment. This highlights the long-term damage, sustained in childhood, from behaviors such as bullying. The ability of sociologists to highlight these concerns can enhance critical evaluation of our values and norms.

The concepts of *mores and taboos* are less vulnerable to change. *Mores* (pronounced more-rays) refer to values that are so basic to a society that most people would not dream of breaking them; examples would be incest, pedophilia, or polygamy. These behaviors are so sacrosanct (appearing to have religious support) that they are unlikely to be successfully challenged. *Taboos*, which represent behaviors to be avoided, support the significance of mores. For example, there are prohibitions against having sex with relatives, marrying relatives, eating human flesh, and other behaviors generally considered abhorrent. These elements of cultures vary between societies, and within societies, as well. The key to attaining diversity and cultural affirmation lies in the ability of people to understand the meanings of various behaviors in a cultural context.

Key Terms

Culture   Language   Technology   Material Culture   Non-material Culture   Popular Culture   American Culture   Dominant Group   Hegemony   Post-modernism   Ethnocentrism   Subculture   Cultural Relativism   Cultural Assimilation   Values, Norms, Folkways, Laws, Sanctions   Mores   Taboos   Stigma

Concept Review

What Is Culture?

Culture describes the shape of society and the lives within it. It incorporates all the material and nonmaterial aspects of collective life. Symbolic communication, through language, represents the social nature of culture. Culture can be experienced as "natural" but it is a product of human construction and can be modified, a situation that is reflected in the addition of new vocabulary. The *American Dream* represents a defining feature of the ideal American culture, signifying material success through individual effort and discipline. There are a limited number of universal features of American culture which can be exhibited in the material and nonmaterial features of American life. One factor in the fabric of American culture is the persistent presence of many cultures which claim membership.

The elements of a culture are modified by the available technology. Developments in technology are today occurring at an exceptionally fast pace, resulting in a lag between their advancements and the social integration of their consequences. Today's culture, dependent on computers and the internet, would have been unimaginable even a few decades ago. Social media plays a central part in the dissemination of contemporary popular culture, which provides some common reference for all societal members. The *American Dream* represents a defining feature of the ideal American culture, signifying material success through individual effort and discipline.

What Does It Mean to Recognize a Dominant Group in Society?

Cultural elements are frequently assumed to be universal but in truth they reflect the beliefs and experiences of the dominant group. In the US, culture mirrors the White, male, affluent, Anglo-Saxon, Protestant experience. Individuals from other groups may feel somewhat removed from the *dominant* culture though they need to be schooled in it for purposes of adaptation to the social environment. *Nondominant* group members are vulnerable to marginalization, often expressed as representing a subgroup. Marginalized group members are subjected to modifications in their identification which constitute a lesser "American" status, as occurs with the terms African American, Muslim American, or Mexican American. This diminished status can be seen when works of art or literature are referred to as by a "southern novelist," "African American poet," "woman writer," or "Muslim designer." The implicit message is that these works are not universally applicable, like the work of White, male figures, but apply only to the specific group represented by the actor/writer.

Postmodern thought reflects the notion that there is no perspective or set of experiences which is universal to all societal members but there is rather a quality of life which is modified by the subcultural identifications a person possesses. The *hegemonic* forces of the dominant group can obscure the consequences of a person's differential experiences of American culture.

What Are the Elements of Culture?

Culture can be analyzed in terms of its elements. *Values* are general guiding principles in society while *norms* refer to behaviors associated with particular social roles. *Laws* are norms which have been codified and given the authority of the government. *Folkways* refer to habits of social interaction less significant than norms. *Sanctions* are consequences, both positive and negative, for conforming or failing to conform. *Stigma* is a negative evaluation or label which, once applied to a person, generally exerts a persistent effect. *Mores* refer to behaviors which are considered inviolate and *taboos* are specific proscribed behaviors. The analysis of these social attributes can reveal information about the culture.

Review Questions

1. How significant is the impact of culture on the human being's development? Give two examples of the way in which culture affects social life and behavior.
2. Provide two examples of the effect of technology on social relations. Be specific to studies reported in the chapter.
3. What values, if any, are characteristic of an American, incorporating all members? How have the experiences of particular groups modified their American identity?
4. Would you agree that consumerism is an integral value of American society? Explain your response by providing examples.
5. Who does the dominant group refer to and how is the concept linked to post-modernism?
6. What is hegemony? Describe two areas of society in which it occurs.
7. How is American defined and what is the "hyphenated experience"? Discuss a personal experience relating to this topic.
8. Have you expressed *ethnocentric* views or behaviors? Explain your response by providing examples.
9. Have you utilized the concept of *cultural relativism*? If so, how?
10. What *norms* do you experience in your home and community which might be specific to your group identification?

References

Angelou, M. (January 20, 1993) "On the Pulse of Morning." Read at the Inauguration of President Clinton. Retrieved from http://poetry.eserver.org/angelou.html

Associated Press. (February 26, 2015) When 58 Choices Aren't Enough: Facebook Launches 'Fill in the Blank' Option for Users. *Daily Mail*. Retrieved from http://www.dailymail.co.uk/sciencetech/article-2970681/Facebook-adds-new-gender-option-users-blank.html

Beck, M. (October 9, 2015) Pew Survey: Nearly Two-Thirds Of All Americans Use Social Media. Marketing Land. Retrieved from http://marketingland.com/pew-survey-nearly-two-thirds-of-all-americans-use-social-media-146026

Bell, O. (Dir.) (2016) *The Eagle Huntress* A Sony Pictures Classics Release. Retrieved from http://sonyclassics.com/theeaglehuntress/

Bigelow, K. (Dir.) (2008) *The Hurt Locker*. Voltage Pictures.

Blodget, H. (November 21, 2012) 90% of 18–29 Year-olds Sleep with their Smartphones. *Business Insider*. Retrieved from http://www.businessinsider.com/90-of-18-29-year-olds-sleep-with-their-smartphones-2012-11

Bump, P. (January 5, 2015) The New Congress is 80 Percent White, 80 Percent Male and 92 Percent Christian. *The Washington Post*. Retrieved from https://www.washingtonpost.com/news/the-fix/wp/2015/01/05/the-new-congress-is-80-percent-white-80-percent-male-and-92-percent-christian/?utm_term=.0a0e4e836744

ChemKnitsBlog2 (February 13, 2017) Horatio Alger: The Myth of the American Dream. *Letterpile*. Retrieved from https://letterpile.com/books/horatio-alger

Chicago, J. (1974–1979) The Dinner Party. Art Work. On permanent display at the Elizabeth A. Sackler Center for Feminist Art at the Brooklyn Museum, Retrieved from http://www.judychicago.com/gallery/the-dinner-party/dp-artwork/

Crafts, H., Gates Jr., H.L. (2002) *The Bondwoman's Narrative*. NY: Warner Books.

Cuthbertson, A. (February 6, 2016) Bible Translated into Emoji as 'scripture 4 millennials'. *Newsweek*. Retrieved from http://www.newsweek.com/emoji-bible-translation-millennials-465687

Deggans, E. (November 22, 2016) After Rough Starts, These Fall TV Shows Have Found Their Legs. All Things Considered. *NPR*. Retrieved from http://www.npr.org/2016/11/22/503052604/after-rough-starts-these-fall-tv-shows-have-found-their-legs

Domhoff, W.G. (2013) Wealth, Income, and Power. *Who Rules America?* Retrieved from http://www2.ucsc.edu/whorulesamerica/power/wealth.html

Domonoske, C. (November 23, 2016) Students Have 'Dismaying' Inability to Tell Fake News from Real, Study Finds. *NPR.org*. Retrieved from http://www.npr.org/sections/thetwo-way/2016/11/23/503129818/study-finds-students-have-dismaying-inability-to-tell-fake-news-from-real

Egan, T. (January 22, 2016) The Eight-Second Attention Span. *The New York Times*. Retrieved from https://www.nytimes.com/2016/01/22/opinion/the-eight-second-attention-span.html

Faderman, L. with Xiong, G. (1998) *I Begin My Life All Over: The Hmong and the American Immigrant Experience*. Boston: Beacon Press.

Fan, J. (October 12, 2015) The Accused. *The New Yorker*. Retrieved from http://www.newyorker.com/magazine/2015/10/12/the-accused-jiayang-fan

Farhi, P. (April 27, 2012) How Biased Are the Media, Really? *The Washington Post*. Retrieved from https://www.washingtonpost.com/lifestyle/style/how-biased-is-the-media-really/2012/04/27/gIQA9jYLmT_story.html?utm_term=.de4272e9cabe

Frank, T. (November 2016) Swat Team. *Harper's Magazine*. Retrieved from https://harpers.org/archive/2016/11/swat-team-2/7/

Fredrickson, B. (2013) *Love 2.0: Finding Happiness and Health in Moments of Connection*. New York: Hudson Street Press.

Gearan, A., Rucker, P., Phillip, A. (July 24, 2016) DNC Chairwoman Will Resign in Aftermath of Committee Email Controversy. *The Washington Post*. Retrieved from https://www.washingtonpost.com/politics/hacked-emails-cast-doubt-on-hopes-for-party-unity-at-democratic-convention/2016/07/24/a446c260-51a9-11e6-b7de-dfe509430c39_story.html?utm_term=.9dd88400cee7

Ghosh, C. (2013) *The Politics of the American Dream: Democratic Inclusion in Contemporary American Political Culture*. Palgrave Macmillan.

Glassner, B. (1999) *The Culture of Fear: Why Americans Are Afraid of the Wrong Things*. New York: Basic Books.

Gregoire, C. (October 9, 2015) The Internet May Be Changing Your Brain In Ways You've Never Imagined. *Huffpost*. Retrieved from http://www.huffingtonpost.com/entry/internet-changing-brain-nicholas-carr_us_5614037de4b0368a1a613e96

Harari, Y. (2015) *Sapiens: A Brief History of Humankind*. New York: HarperCollins Publishers.

Harari, Y. (2017) *Homos Deus: A Brief History of Tomorrow*. New York: HarperCollins Publishers.

Highsmith, P. (1952/2004) *The Price of Salt*. New York: W.W. Norton and Company.

Julious, B. (March 25, 2015) Hollywood 'Race Casting': What the Industry Is Getting Wrong about Diversity. *The Guardian*. Retrieved from https://www.theguardian.com/tv-and-radio/tvandradioblog/2015/mar/25/deadlines-race-casting-article-tvs-diversity-wrong

Kilday, G. (January 14, 2016) Oscar Nominees Include Zero Nonwhite Actors. *The Hollywood Reporter*. Retrieved from http://www.hollywoodreporter.com/news/oscar-nominees-include-zero-nonwhite-855751

Kramer, M. (October 24, 2016) Is Media Bias Really Rampant? Ask the Man Who Studies it for a Living. *Poynter*. Retrieved from https://www.poynter.org/2016/is-media-bias-really-rampant-ask-the-man-who-studies-it-for-a-living/435840/

Lauzen, M. (2016) *Research*. Center for the Study of Women in Television & Film. Retrieved from http://womenintvfilm.sdsu.edu/research

Lenhart, A. (April 9, 2015) Teens, Social Media and Technology Overview. Pew Research Center. Retrieved from http://www.pewinternet.org/2015/04/09/methods-teens-tech/

Lipka, M., Gecewicz, C. (September 6, 2017) More Americans Now Say They're Spiritual but Not Religious. Pew Research Center. Retrieved from http://www.pewresearch.org/fact-tank/2017/09/06/more-americans-now-say-theyre-spiritual-but-not-religious/

LSA. (n.d.) *Language and Thought*. Linguistic Society of America. Retrieved from https://www.linguisticsociety.org/resource/language-and-thought

Ma, A. (June 29, 2015) A Sad Number Of Americans Sleep With Their Smartphone In Their Hand. *Huffpost*. Retrieved from http://www.huffingtonpost.com/2015/06/29/smartphone-behavior-2015_n_7690448.html

Manning, E.J. (December 5, 2016) *Membership of the 114th Congress: A Profile*. Retrieved from https://fas.org/sgp/crs/misc/R43869.pdf

McNamara, M. (January 19, 2016) Critics Notebook: Why the #OscarsSoWhite Fuss Matters. *Los Angeles Times*. Retrieved from http://www.latimes.com/entertainment/tv/showtracker/la-et-st-0119-why-the-oscarssowhite-fuss-matters-20160119-column.html

Melchior, J.K. (January 1, 2017) 'Pregnancy Without Women' Discussion Creates Rift Between Feminists and Trans Scholars. *Heatstreet*. Retrieved from https://heatst.com/culture-wars/pregnancy-without-women-discussion-creates-rift-between-feminist-trans-scholars/

Montagne, R. (April 15, 2016) Should Movie Theaters Allow Texting? *Morning Edition*. NPR. Retrieved from http://www.npr.org/2016/04/15/474325016/should-movie-theaters-allow-texting

Mundy, L. (April 26, 2014) The Media Has a Woman Problem. *The New York Times*. Retrieved from https://www.nytimes.com/2014/04/27/opinion/sunday/the-media-has-a-woman-problem.html

National Journal (January 31, 2014) White Men Are Everywhere. *National Journal.* Retrieved from http://www.nationaljournal.com/politics/2014/01/31/white-men-are-everywhere

Norris, M., Siegel, R. (hosts) (June 17, 2009) The History of the Vacation Examined. *All Things Considered.* NPR. Retrieved from http://www.npr.org/templates/story/story.php?storyId=105545388

Northrup, C. (February 28, 2015) *PBS Television Special.* Retrieved from http://www.drnorthrup.com/press/dr-northrups-new-pbs-special-2015/

Obrazkova, M. (April 7, 2015) Russian Store Assistants Smiling More, Says Customer Service Report. *Russia Beyond the Headlines.* Retrieved from http://www.smilingreport.com/press/2015/2015-04-07_RussiaBeyondHeadlines.pdf

Pew Research Center (2015, May 12) *New Pew Research Center Study Examines America's Changing Religious Landscape.*

Rivers, A. (April 7, 2016) How Many People Check Their Smartphone in the Bathroom? *The Marketing Scope.* Retrieved from https://www.themarketingscope.com/how-many-people-check-their-smartphone-in-the-bathroom/

Rojas, L.B. (January 9, 2016) California Muslim Women Reconsider Wearing Hijab 7 Over Safety Concerns. *KPCC.* Retrieved from https://ww2.kqed.org/news/2016/01/09/california-muslim-women-reconsider-wearing-hijab-over-safety-concerns/

Rosman, K. (April 6, 2016) Move Over, Rat Pack and Brat Pack: Here Comes the Snap Pack. *Nytimes.com.* Retrieved from http://www.nytimes.com/2016/04/07/fashion/rat-pack-brat-pack-snapchat.html?contentCollection=weekendreads&action=click&pgtype=Homepage&clickSource=story-heading&module=c-column-middle-span-region&region=c-column-middle-span-region&WT.nav=c-column-middle-span-region

Rubin, A. (August 17, 2016) Fighting for 'the soul of France,' More Towns Ban a Bathing Suit: the Burkini. *The New York Times.* Retrieved from https://www.nytimes.com/2016/08/18/world/europe/fighting-for-the-soul-of-france-more-towns-ban-a-bathing-suit-the-burkini.html

Scovell, N. (September 12, 2015) The 'Golden Age for Women in TV' Is Actually a Rerun. *The New York Times.* Retrieved from https://www.nytimes.com/2015/09/13/opinion/sunday/the-golden-age-for-women-in-tv-is-actually-a-rerun.html

Shahani, A. (April 19, 2016) Live-Streaming of Alleged Rape Shows Challenges of Flagging Video In Real Time. *NPR.org.* Retrieved from http://www.npr.org/sections/alltechconsidered/2016/04/19/474783485/live-streaming-of-alleged-rape-shows-challenges-of-flagging-video-in-real-time

Smith, A. (April 1, 2015) *U.S. Smartphone Use in 2015.* Pew Research Center: Internet, Science & Tech. Retrieved from http://www.pewinternet.org/2015/04/01/us-smartphone-use-in-2015/

Smith J., Gillett, R. (August 3, 2015) 17 Billionaires Who Were Once Dirt Poor. *Business Insider.* Retrieved from http://www.businessinsider.com/17-billionaires-who-were-once-dirt-poor?op=1#ixzz3hwsarwRM

Sociology Dictionary (n.d.) *Technology.* Retrieved from http://sociologydictionary.org/?s=technology

Spiegel, A., Rosin, H. (June 17, 2016) *Invisibilia*. NPR. Retrieved from http://www.npr.org/2016/06/17/482443233/listen-to-the-episode

Startasl (n.d.) *Deaf Culture*. Retrieved from https://www.startasl.com/deaf-culture_html

Thorp, B. (February 19, 2016) What Does the Academy Value in a Black Performance? *Nytimes.com*. Retrieved from http://www.nytimes.com/2016/02/21/movies/what-does-the-academy-value-in-a-black-performance.html?hp&action=click&pgtype=Homepage&clickSource=story-heading&module=photo-spot-region&region=top-news&WT.nav=top-news

Turkle, S. (2015) *Reclaiming Conversation: The Power of Talk in a Digital Age*. New York: Penguin Books.

Turner, C. (December 22, 2016) The Classroom Where Fake News Fails. *NPR.org*. Retrieved from http://www.npr.org/sections/ed/2016/12/22/505432340/the-classroom-where-fake-news-fails

Turner, C. (February 9, 2016a) What Kids Need from Grown-Ups (But Aren't Getting). *NPR.org*. Retrieved from http://www.npr.org/sections/ed/2016/02/09/465557430/what-kids-need-from-grown-ups-but-arent-getting

White, G.B. (July 24, 2015) Where Are All the Minority Journalists? *The Atlantic*. Retrieved from https://www.theatlantic.com/business/archive/2015/07/minorities-in-journalism/399461/.

Zeitchik, S. (February 16, 2016) On Issue of Race, Grammys Leap Past the Oscars, Then Stumble. *Los Angeles Times*. Retrieved from http://www.latimes.com/entertainment/tv/showtracker/la-et-mn-grammys-awards-kendrick-lamar-oscars-so-white-20160216-story.html

CHAPTER 3

Doing Sociological Research

WHAT YOU WILL READ ABOUT IN THIS CHAPTER:

- The *research process*, characteristic of all scientific investigations, is presented. *Theory*, is a general, abstracted statement regarding the relationship of social elements. A theory helps the researcher define the research topic and choose an approach to its study. Theories are *operationalized*, meaning that they are transformed into measurable objects or specific representations of a concept. Once measurable criteria have been identified, the researcher can state *hypotheses*, or specific relationships between measures elaborated. The development of hypotheses allows for theories to be tested *empirically*, and typically the results are published in an academic journal reviewed by peers in the field. Other researchers can then repeat and build upon the research, refining theories and developing new ones. This process of building upon research, as a collective process between scientists, is the essence of the research process.

- Ideally, social scientific research is *neutral* in that neither its topics, design, nor its conclusions should reflect the values of the researcher, subjects, or culture. In reality, the process is never completely free from values since subject matter selected by social scientists reflects current issues of concern in the culture, and are reflected in the research design.

- Research can be accomplished through *qualitative* or *quantitative* methods. The former contains "softer" types of research, based upon verbalization, observation, and interpretation. This type of research allows for more in-depth and flexible study though it can be time consuming, expensive, and have limited respondents. Quantitative methods entail collecting information which is in numerical form, or can easily be made into numerical form. Quantitative research can be quicker, cheaper, and include a larger sample, particularly due to the use of statistical analysis that is possible with computers. The type of research method chosen often depends on what type of information the researcher seeks.

- Specific techniques of research, such as *surveys*, *interviews*, *field research*, *ethnographies*, *content* and *secondary analysis*, and *experiments*, are reviewed with attention to the strengths and weaknesses of each. Ethical issues are often part of research with human subjects and require the researcher to follow specific guidelines.

- A brief review of descriptive *data* reporting is presented. Elementary statistical concepts, such as *averages* and *correlations*, are explained.

Introduction

It is important to have a basic understanding of how sociologists do their research. Knowledge of the elements of basic research allows for assessing the credibility of the information presented. The research process is complex, so we will focus on some examples to show how it is done. The first research task addresses choosing a "topic," *what* to research. The topic has to be specifically elaborated or the research will be compromised. For example, simply stating "divorce" is too broad; there are too many aspects of the issue which could be investigated and they need to be narrowed. The researcher's intent must be clear. Potential issues for divorce studies encompass causes of divorce; financial consequences of divorce; child custody issues; post-divorce adjustment of the adults and/or children; or remarriage issues. The designated research question will determine *how* to approach the study. Is the intent exploratory, such as investigating how a person feels after a year about the decision to divorce? Or, more "objective": for instance, how many people share child custody or remarry? *Who* to choose for the study is also an important decision because the pool of research subjects chosen can enhance the information gathered or render it virtually meaningless. If the research is to investigate child custody arrangements, for example, the researcher will need to avoid the inclusion of couples with no children, since they would dilute the results.

How Do Sociologists Conduct Research?

Typically, the easiest way to focus on a research topic is by posing a question, for example: Do millennials' plans for adult life differ significantly from those their parents made at similar ages? The next step is to *review the literature* on the topic. This ensures that the researcher knows what already has been established in the field and consequently can develop a project that will extend or qualify this knowledge. A starting point is the generation of a **theory**—an abstracted idea which usually draws a relationship between two phenomena. The theory regarding millennial life may be that they are more nontraditional than their parents, perhaps exhibiting different values in making lifestyle choices. The guiding principle can be explored through behavioral measures, such as whether millennials are less likely to choose the suburbs over large cities; less likely to have children; more likely to marry later in life; or more likely to choose to be single than their parental generation. A researcher may also want to know how these priorities are conceived by the subjects. Perhaps millennials choose the city over suburbs because of the greater availability of public transportation, corresponding to their high prioritization of environmental protections and the reduction of gasoline use. The theory represents an association between personal values and behavior, so each dimension will need to be included in the research model.

Box 3.1 – The Research Process

The *research process* utilizes scientific methods of study to establish information pertaining to sociological analyses. *Theory* provides an initial framework for organizing information and perspectives on a topic. Theories are abstract, broadly stated ideas which must be transformed into measurable behaviors or measures which can be directly studied. Once measurable criteria have been identified, the researcher can state **hypotheses**, or specific relationships between the defined elements.

To conduct an actual study, the researcher will have to define "real-world" elements representing aspects elaborated in the theory. This is called *operationalizing* the concepts. Typically, a set of *hypotheses* are developed in order to make specific statements relating to factors included in the study. In this example, the researcher will have to define what is meant by the key terms of *millennials, lifestyle, personal values,* and *environmental concerns.* The *millennials* generally are designated as people born between 1982 and 2000. They can be compared to the generation of baby boomers, born between 1946 and 1964. *Lifestyle* choices can be enumerated in many ways and can include such things as participating in cultural events; choosing to marry; choosing to remain childfree; and preferring apartment life to having a house. *Environmental concerns* can incorporate depending on public transportation and choosing not to own a car; using public transportation and limiting automobile use; or choosing to live close to a job to reduce commuting time. *Personal values* can be considered in choices to maximize leisure time; have ready access to cultural activities; live close to friends; and similar concerns.

After a research project has been completed, the researcher will evaluate the findings to establish whether the theory was corroborated. If it does not seem to be, the researcher must carefully evaluate the process to analyze whether the theory was faulty or the project failed to adequately investigate the theory. The research must be examined for its validity and reliability. *Validity* refers to whether a measure is actually accounting for what is stated. Consider Durkheim's study, *Suicide*, from Chapter 1. Durkheim, for example, utilized marital status, religious status, employment status, parental status, and home ownership to measure levels of *social integration.* Since these dimensions seemed influential in the lives of his subjects, he concluded that social integration did impact a person's risk of suicide, suggesting his theory was accurate. But what if he had failed to show a correlation between these factors and incidents of suicide? Would that indicate that his theory regarding the greater suicide risk of socially isolated individuals was inaccurate? Maybe, but it might have been that the measures he chose to assess social isolation actually failed to do so. For example, social isolation might have been more a factor of subjective feelings of loneliness rather than of the external factors he obtained through the Census Bureau data.

Reliability refers to the question of whether a research measure can produce the same results over time. If the characteristics Durkheim used to assess suicide risks were reliable, then they would be so with different samples, or with similar groups over time. If they accomplish this, they are considered reliable measures. If his entire study can be successfully repeated, especially by other researchers following his process, it is considered to have achieved *replication* which enhances the likelihood that the scientific community will support the study. A study which cannot be replicated is viewed as scientifically invalid.

The researcher will then publish the study, usually in an academic journal. Academic journals are peer reviewed, indicating that other experts in the field support the research project and feel that it should be part of the material in the field relating to the topic. This does not necessarily suggest that the reviewers agree with the findings but it does indicate that the research is considered to have achieved scientifically valid status.

The Research Process Summary

Formulate a Topic
Review the Literature
Theory Building
Develop Hypotheses
Choose A Method
Design and Execute the Study
Analyze the Data
Re-consider Theory and Project Design
Publish the Results

Choosing a Research Issue

Sociologists believe that research should be "value neutral." This extends to the topics chosen for study, the way the study is conducted, and the conclusions reached. Social scientists are obligated to report their findings and to analyze the ramifications of these, in terms of past, present, and future research. The application of their conclusions to programs and/or policies is not part of the research process, though other people can refer to the research when promoting social action or political positions. Research, however, is not impartial, even with the best of intentions to remain neutral. Topics chosen for study, and the manner in which they are studied, reflect contemporary concerns. Social trends can be present for decades prior to their being defined as an "issue"; they become the subject of research when there is community concern regarding them. This idea can be illustrated by looking at the developments in family research, especially with regard to single parent households and divorce. Prior to the rising divorce rate of the post-World War II era, parents were more likely to be single due to the death of one parent, but this was not considered a topic for research or a "social problem," since it was common and "natural" for some parents' deaths to precede the adulthood of younger children, especially in large families. Beginning in the post-war era, the divorce rate was on the rise, peaking around 1980, before exhibiting a gradual decline. This increase, accelerating with the decades, led to many new situations and questions regarding the effects of divorce on children, adults, and family life: What causes people to divorce? Why was the rate lower prior to WWII? Who is at risk of divorce? What happens to children after divorce? Do women and men respond to divorce in the same ways? How are issues of child custody and support resolved? Is divorce preferable, especially for the children's development, to life in a family with marital discord? Do divorced women and men remarry at the same rates? Do people have children in second marriages? Are second marriages at greater risk of divorce? Is the millennial divorce rate seemingly similar to that of the baby boomers?

We know the answers to some of these questions, but only because certain issues were selected for study while others were bypassed. There are myriad reasons why World War II initiated changes in divorce rates. Quick marriages, characteristic of war time, certainly contributed but changes in social roles during, and following, the war likely had a more significant impact. Many women entered the paid labor force during the war and this created a shift in women's roles, even though the war was initially followed by a return to traditional gender roles for many working- and middle-class women. The expansion of higher education for women, occurring in the 1950s and 1960s, led to women examining the nature of gender roles. Consequently, women began to desire to use their education, either delaying marriage and/or childbearing, leading to instability in the expectations individuals brought to marriage and family life. By 1980, the divorce rate reached its peak and it has been on a steady, gradual decline since. Marriage today might incorporate more awareness of the roles desired in marriages, and this may play a part in a decision to marry. Other variables impacting today's divorce rates concern later age of marriage and the lack of marriage among people without college degrees (see Chapter 10). This is why today's marriages end in divorce at a lower rate than in the previous generation. Another research question might involve at what point in the marriage a person is likely to divorce. Maybe people divorce when the kids grow up; maybe it is the result of a "seven-year itch." In any case, comparisons *between* generations, and studies of developments over the *life span of a single generation*, can each illuminate factors affecting divorce.

Another example of elements impacting the research process concerns the type and presentation of data utilized. The data on marriages and divorces can be misleading, even when it seems statistical or factual. Sometimes writers give the divorce rate as the proportion of divorces to marriages in any given year, which tells only the relative occurrences of each for that year; it denotes nothing regarding the success rate of marriages over time. Another common divorce measure is reported as the number of divorces per 1000 adults over the age of 15, often referred to as the *crude divorce rate,* which fails to provide information regarding any clarifying elements such as age of marriage or divorce; presence of children; longevity of the marriage, etc.

In contrast, a more accurate measure of divorce trends can be accomplished through a *cohort* study. Cohort refers to a group of people who share some characteristic. In this type of study, a researcher can choose to identify couples who married in the same year and conduct a *longitudinal* study, where the same group is studied over time. The years at which the cohort is most at risk can be determined and compared to cohorts from other times or parts of the country. Research has shown, for example, that the divorce rate for people who married in the 1990s is significantly lower than that of people who married in previous post-World War decades. Sociologists predict the rate will further decrease for those married in the 2000s and thereafter (Miller 2014).

Family researchers are also likely to be concerned with the impact of divorce on children. Research in this area began in the 1970s and generally limited its focus to comparisons of the children of divorce with children from intact marriages. It assumed *a priori* (beforehand, without investigating this assumption) that the significant factors in the achievements of children of divorce depended specifically on that status. Studies typically failed to consider other significant factors such as household composition; the quality of involvement of the non-custodial parent; the parenting style of the parents; the support of other relatives; or single parenting as the result of death of a spouse. These early studies also neglected to utilize a group of children from dysfunctional married families to form a base for comparison. The research sample also generally represented Anglo American families. Research accomplished with African American families usually looked simply at single parent households, not those resulting from divorce. The research presumed single parenting to be prevalent in African American families and failed to analyze the families with respect to comparable African American married parents or to families, for example, with grandparents or aunts and uncles present. The research, in all groups, omitted any recognition of unmarried "spouses"; unofficial "step parents"; or any other adults in the household. At the time, these concerns were not incorporated into the research designs:

> The manner of writing is a reminder that the research was conducted by a particular human subject (or subjects) in particular social contexts. Thus this structure invites readers to be active participants in the interpretation not only of the ethnography but also of the author's interpretation itself. In these ways, readers are reminded (sometimes despite the author) that position, perspective, and context are always involved in the production of knowledge.
>
> (Holmes 2013)

The research trends reflected biases concerning the prevalence and causes of divorce and presumed that children's life outcomes were primarily determined by parental marital status. If the variables selected to study are limited in scope, they will certainly not shed any light on the full dimensions of the questions investigated. This can lead to inaccurate conclusions which may support theoretical assumptions without recognizing their limitations. Today the research is broader, for example, comparing the children of married parents, divorced parents, and married couples with high levels of hostility. The research is also more likely to incorporate non-marital issues such as parenting style; the engagement levels of each parent; socio-economic status; and other related issues. Investigation occurs on many issues ranging from the offspring's school achievements to relationship histories.

Choosing a Research Method

A researcher must first consider whether a *quantitative* or *qualitative* approach to a topic is appropriate to their research question. If a researcher's interest is on issues of motivation, attitudes, or sensitive behavioral topics, or is generally exploratory in nature, then a *qualitative* study would probably be more expedient. In a **qualitative** project, the researcher generally probes for understanding trends more than establishing them. The research is generally conducted by analyzing communication between people, either through interaction, observation, or print.

In *quantitative* studies, the researcher collects a lot of statistical data, generally from a large group of subjects. Quantitative data is more typically gathered from surveys or collected data which already exists from sources such as government agencies or social service providers. Quantitative research data can be collected at one point in time, allowing for a comparison of many different groups. The research also can follow the same groups over time, or compare them to similar groups from different time periods to extend the analysis beyond one defined time period, occurring among one finite group. To develop a quantitative project, the researcher generally has sufficient information on the topic to predict the type of things they want to ask and the likely responses their interests will elicit. Additionally, the information might be relatively simple in that it is descriptive, regarding general behavioral trends such as age of marriage or the numbers of miles in a daily work commute.

> ## Box 3.2 – Evaluating the Research Process
>
> *Validity* refers to whether a measure is assessing what it purports to be investigating. For example, did Durkheim's use of marital, parental, employment, and religious statuses actually measure social integration. *Reliability* is the concept that states a measure is reliable if it can produce the same result consistently. If Durkheim's measures were only accurate in some cities, then they would not be considered reliable. If an entire study can be successfully repeated, with the same group over time, with different groups, or by other researchers, then it has established what is referred to as *replication*.

Sociologists usually choose from *surveys, interviews, field research, experiments, content analysis, and secondary analysis* when developing a research project. The researcher must also consider the targeted subject pool because mistaken selections can render a project useless. For example, if I want to study the best time of day to offer general education classes at a particular college, I want to question a sample which proportionately includes day and night students; women and men; parents and nonparents; people with cars and those depending on public transportation; and any other dimension which potentially can affect the optimal timing to meet student need.

Surveys

Surveys are frequently utilized in sociological research. Their chief advantage is their ability to inexpensively reach a large number of respondents to gain information on a specific topic. *Survey* research asks focused questions, generally with forced responses, to compile information. A *sample* is chosen to represent the entire *population* which could be included in the study. The sample is a smaller group than the population,

Figure 3.1 Survey research can be very informative but there are risks, especially with choosing the appropriate respondents and asking the "right" questions in a useful format
Source: Fran / Cartoon Stock

87% OF THE 56% WHO COMPLETED MORE THAN 23% OF THE SURVEY THOUGHT IT WAS A WASTE OF TIME

selected with care to accurately represent all significant dimensions of the population. Difficulties with survey research concern selecting a research sample which accurately represents the group. The other typical challenge lies in creating good survey questions to accurately obtain the desired information. Since surveys usually are constructed in multiple choice fashion, with a list of responses to choose from, a researcher must also be able to anticipate the likely responses. Surveys are useful for establishing descriptive characteristics of a cohort and investigating relationships, referred to as *correlations*, between them.

A recent survey studied 1800 youths aged 18–30, and was conducted monthly for a period of six months from July to December 2016. The respondents were African American, Latino/a, White, and Asian American (GenForward 2016). Investigated topics included issues relating to the presidential campaign and election; economic comfort and prediction of financial well-being in the future; and general attitudes regarding race, gender, voting, immigration, and gun control. The research was conducted by responses to specific questions obtained through phone calls to home and cell phones. Below is a summary of responses to issues regarding race and sex discrimination at work. What do they reveal? The articulation of research findings must be stated with care so as to avoid making claims beyond those supported by the data. From the data below, it can be seen that racial discrimination was felt to be more prevalent than sex discrimination. African Americans reported greater feelings of racial discrimination than other nondominant groups. African Americans were as likely to feel discrimination in job seeking as they were once they were in a job. The other nondominant groups also showed consistency between discrimination in job seeking and when occupying a job. African American women and men were equally likely to report gender discrimination in the workplace though disparities in reports

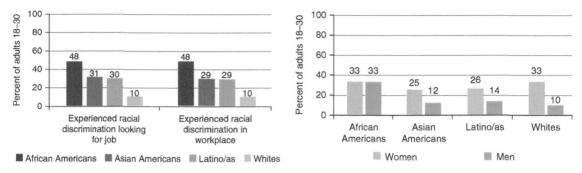

Figure 3.2 Perception of discrimination by race and gender among young adults
Source: Adapted from Gen Forward Survey, November 2016

of gender discrimination were seen in all other groups. The largest difference between reported gender discrimination was identified as between White women and men.

Note the language used in the research reported above. The respondents addressed perceptions and self-reported attitudes regarding discrimination. It cannot be asserted, from this research, whether discrimination is "objectively" occurring or how it is being measured or perceived. This would take additional questions and, most likely, some observation to check whether respondents' perceptions had a demonstrative reference. Other ways to assess these perceptions would be to interview bosses, read work evaluations, and interview co-workers. All that can be said from the present work is that African Americans are more likely to *perceive* racial discrimination than other racial groups and that White women are as likely as African Americans, of both sexes, to report gender discrimination. What do these responses imply? It is difficult to say. We can infer that race discrimination is more salient than sex discrimination for African Americans but appears to be more of a feature of work life among the women of other racial groups. More investigation would be needed to refine these interpretations. The data also do not show any comparison to other points in time or whether they are sensitive to the particular work setting a person inhabits. The researchers, in this study, consciously sought to incorporate a significant portion of young people of color, since research studies typically underrepresent these groups.

Box 3.3 – Quantitative and Qualitative Research

In *qualitative research* the researcher generally probes for understanding trends more than establishing them. The research is generally conducted by analyzing communication between people, either through interaction, observation, or print. These studies focus on verbal and physical communication and are likely to contain interviews, observation, field research, and detailed analysis of popular culture. Because these processes are cumbersome, this research tends to be conducted with limited numbers of subjects.

Quantitative research utilizes statistical analyses. These are accomplished through survey research or other data collected by organizations in their routine processes. Quantitative research, in its simplest form, generates descriptive information regarding the characteristics of a population. Surveys are especially convenient for providing quick access to specific information about a large number of people.

Correlations

Correlations are relationships between two characteristics, or *variables*, to be studied. They can be *positive* or *negative* (also referred to as *inverse*). These terms apply to the *direction* of the relationship, not its strength. The strength of the relationship is represented by a statistical value or number associated with the correlation, where 1.0 would be a perfect correlation. Almost nothing in human life is 100 percent correlated. A *positive correlation* is shown in the statement that the more calories a person consumes, the more likely they are to gain weight. A .6 correlation for this factor indicates a fairly strong relationship. It is also accurate that when a person increases their aerobic exercise, it is reflected in weight loss. This relationship may be as significant to caloric intake but is written as -.6 since the two variables are flowing in opposing directions, representing a *negative correlation*. As exercise goes up, weight goes down. In this example, increases in the intake of calories, and increases in aerobic exercise, each have an equivalent impact on weight. Correlations do *not* indicate a causal relationship, though they might. Further research would have to be undertaken to make such a claim. For example, maybe neither of these factors is causing weight fluctuations; a person's weight might actually be determined by medication or genetics. A *spurious correlation* is the term applied to two variables which appear related but actually are either completely independent or caused by a third factor.

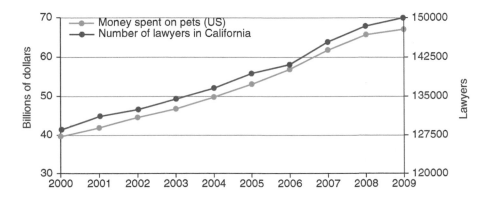

Figure 3.3 Adapted from GenForward Survey, November 2016 Source: https:// cdn1.vox-cdn.com/ assets/4442425/ Screenshot_ 2014-05-12_ 12.45.09.png

Interview Research

Interviews can be similar to surveys if they ask specific questions and record answers. This type of interview is called "structured," while some interview research is considered unstructured, allowing for a freer-flowing feeling in the interaction. In this type of interview, all the respondents address the same topics but the order can be changed and follow-up questions can be easily incorporated. The advantage of this type of interview is that the researcher can probe for deeper meanings, motivations, and nuances. This type of study, with more personable interaction, can have both a positive and negative impact on the research. On the plus side, the interviewer can establish rapport and obtain information that would not have been anticipated or that might have been withheld. On the other hand, the interviewer can risk bias by her or his verbal, or nonverbal, responses. Unstructured interviews are typically audio recorded and transcribed, which takes time and can be costly.

Box 3.4 – Interviews

Interviews are person-to-person interactions which can be structured or unstructured. In the former case, questions are specifically formulated and asked in the same way to multiple subjects, though they can incorporate open-ended questions. An unstructured interview is more like an informal conversation where the researcher will ask about particular areas of interest but will do so in a varied manner. This process allows for a more "natural" flow between the investigator and the respondent. The small samples generally characteristic of these studies present problems with generalizing the findings to other similar groups.

Samples are usually small and, as a consequence, it may be difficult to make the case that the research is valid for similar cases. This research is especially applicable with sensitive or tricky topics, such as household division of labor, where respondents can misrepresent the actual time each partner spends on housework, intentionally or not. Interviews, frequently accompanied with observation, can illuminate intricacies unlikely to be revealed in survey research. For example, one study which incorporated open interviews (Klein et al. 2013) showed that couples' interactions around household work had an impact, beyond the equitable distribution of household tasks, affecting the overall quality of the relationship. The researcher suggested that working together affected the couples' sense of well-being and intimacy, contributing to enhanced trust and equality.

Box 3.5 – Surveys

Survey research asks specific questions, generally with selected responses, and is frequently utilized with large groups to gain information on a specific topic. A **sample** is chosen to represent the entire **population** which could be included in the study. The sample is a smaller group, selected with care to accurately represent all significant dimensions of the population.

Correlations refer to the relationship between two characteristics, or *variables,* being studied. A **positive correlation** indicates that the two measures are moving in the same direction. A **negative**, *or inverse*, **correlation** indicates that two factors are moving in opposing directions. The variables are moving in opposite directions but the relationship is still significant. The direction of the relationship does not indicate its *strength*; a positive and negative correlation can represent measures of equivalent significance, as indicated by the number associated with them, as for example, .6 or -.6, for positive and negative measures respectively; the sign indicates the *direction* of the relationship. A **spurious correlation** refers to two measures which appear related but likely are not. They might just represent completely independent occurrences or there might be an intervening condition affecting each.

Field Research

Interviews and field research can be paired or accomplished separately. Field research is conducted in "real-life" situations. There are several research decisions which must be made in conducting field research. A researcher may decide to simply observe a situation or to become a participant/observer. Sometimes the situation limits this choice, as for example, in observing actions in a daycare center. A researcher could become a temporary teacher, but the responsibilities of that position would likely make the systematic observation of the children difficult and there would be more risk of bias. Observation, ideally through a two-way mirror, likely would be the preferred method. Research institutions frequently offer opportunities to make direct observations of preschools. In order to study children, in any setting, a researcher is required to obtain the written permission of the parent or guardian.

The researcher engaged in field research also must address the issue of being revealed or unrevealed. In *Gang Leader for a Day*, sociologist Sudhir Venkatesh (2008) writes about his long-term relationship with JT, a gang leader in a large and notoriously violent housing project in Chicago. Through his friendship with JT, Venkatesh gained quicker and deeper access to the gang activities than he otherwise would have been able to access though, he later realized, it alienated him from other factions in the projects who were not affiliated with JT. Venkatesh calls himself a "rogue sociologist" because he was not exclusively an "objective" observer but sometimes participated in gang-related activities. Such behavior opens the researcher to questions regarding bias as well as failure to observe the ethical codes mandating non-intervention. Venkatesh also was not entirely honest with JT, allowing him to believe he was the main object of the study, rather than the gang, and that may be why he so readily agreed to help. Venkatesh did not correct JT's perception because he felt that JT's commitment to the project was invaluable. During their long relationship, Venkatesh also was aware of personal imbalances as a result of his role as a graduate student, which ultimately would lead him to depart for an academic job while JT would remain behind, subjected to any consequences of the research.

These considerations highlight the difficulties inherent in field research. Human connections permitted by field work are fertile ground for research but also likely to be ripe for violation of subjects. Venkatesh believes his research achieved the understanding of intricacies and complexities of gang functioning which otherwise never could have been discovered by social scientists. He was convinced that he learned much regarding the social structural foundations of gang behavior, with all its positive and negative community impacts. Yet, the intensive immersion, in just one setting, can lead to questions regarding just how characteristic these rules and roles might be in other settings.

Venkatesh performed a participant observation field study which is similar to an *ethnography*, more commonly executed by cultural anthropologists. In ethnographic studies, the researcher utilizes participant observation to study an entire culture, generally by immersion in it as a participant. Nevertheless, the ethnographer is expected to retain some distance to preserve their neutrality and to leave the culture untouched by their research, a nearly impossible guideline. Obtaining such an insider's view is understood to facilitate a more authentic sense of the culture (Hoey n.d.). This type of project is seen in Angela Garcia's study *The Pastoral Clinic: Addiction and Dispossession along the Rio Grande* (2010). Garcia, at the request of the agency's executive director, participated in the program by working at the rural detoxification facility being studied. Through her job, and extensive interactions with two mother/daughter pairs of addicts, Garcia developed an analysis which moves beyond simply interpreting the "drug culture," to comprehending the intricate web of familial dynamics sustaining intergenerational transmission of drug use. She discovered that obligations to deceased members, coupled with the displacement of Hispanic cultural experiences of those living in rural New Mexico, suppresses "normal" familial and social interactions. She shows how dispossession of the land leads to chronic depression and mourning whereby heroin use becomes a means to cultural sustenance, even as it incites personal destruction. Garcia demonstrates how heroin has become an integral part of communal life in response to specific cultural issues rather than to a generic "drug culture" (Bartlett 2011). This study exemplifies the greatest potential of ethnographic research to reveal cultural nuances which would otherwise be missed and thereby avoiding simplistic, stereotypical explanations. The richness of ethnographic research sustains its practice and is justification for the risks of misrepresentation or intrusion. As in other types of field research, a potential drawback addresses whether the conclusions extend to similar cases. The drug clinic in Espanola, for example, was not just a rural clinic but one in a specific valley of northern New Mexico, reflecting a history constrained by the specific groups residing there at the time. The researcher would need to justify the validity of extending the findings to other contexts.

Content and Secondary Analysis

A *content analysis* "decodes" elements of a product to examine particular features. A study regarding the persistent negative portrayals of Bernie Sanders in the *Washington Post* opinion pieces, exemplifies this method (see Chapter 2). Content analysis is especially useful in determining biases which may be difficult to unearth. It has been applied to gender roles in books, movies, and television. The content of these media has also been examined in relationship to racial and ethnic stereotypes (see Chapter 7). This research, if well-constructed, can be crucial to understanding the role of cultural artifacts in maintaining prejudice and discrimination. It must be done precisely, and meticulously, to be sure that bias is not interjected into the process.

Content analysis can also be categorized as one form of secondary analysis. *Secondary analysis* refers to research performed on material originally collected for other purposes. For example, Durkheim utilized Census Bureau data to conduct research on suicide and demographic characteristics. Weber utilized published historical documents to develop his theories. Case studies of individuals, collected for purposes other than the research, can also provide research data, though the researcher will need to obtain permission. Examples of these might include records from health clinics or from Individual Education Plans (IEPs) for special needs students. Significant information can be drawn from such sources even though, or especially because, they were not constructed specifically for research purposes.

Experiments

Classical experimental research, in which a scientist creates *equivalent groups* and manipulates one dimension designated as the *experimental condition,* are rarely done in sociology. Equivalent groups are sets of people who are demographically interchangeable; each group represents the same range and portions on established criteria for the study. If each group can be seen as the equivalent of the other, then the conditions of one group can be manipulated to become the *experimental group* while the other remains stable and is the *control group*. An example of this type of research would be the studies the federal *Food and Drug Administration* does in testing new drugs where two groups of people with the same illness, controlled for multiple variables of disease severity, duration, and previous treatment will be followed over time. The experimental groups will be given a newly developed drug, or treatment, while the control group will receive a placebo (sugar pill) or no treatment at all. In this research, it is expected that the outcome will be affected only by the experimental condition since the other factors will remain constant. Usually, neither the researcher nor the subjects know who is in the experimental group. This is referred to as a *double-blind* study because bias, in the researcher and subject, is eliminated.

These studies are hard to accomplish in sociology because factors contributing to human behaviors are too varied to adequately control for equivalent groups. Imagine a relatively simple research question, concerning the comparison of teaching introductory sociology with lecture or discussion-based classrooms. To simplify the research design, the same instructor can be used in each setting, during the same semester. "Success" will simply be measured by the final grades in each class. Superficially, only one aspect—teaching method—is being manipulated but imagine how many things can confound the outcome: there are issues regarding the time of day of the class; the number of semester class meetings; the duration of the class meetings; the qualities and preparation of the students in each class; the textbook's content and form; the tests and assignments; and the teacher's enthusiasm for each method. Suppose the same teacher was teaching two classes solely by lectures and two by means of structured discussions. It would still be difficult to make any assertion that one method was the *cause* of any differences in average final grades. Any number of factors could vary among the student groups. One class might be better prepared or have students with greater interest in the subject; one class might be right after lunch, generally acknowledged as a biologically "slow" time of day; the tests might be biased since research suggests multiple choice exams favor the lecture method; the teacher might show different levels of enthusiasm, either due to the method or to the students in a particular classroom; there might be differences resulting from a format of 50 minutes three times a week versus 75 minutes twice a week; and on and on. These complications are why classical experiments are rarely done in social science unless the project concerns a simple response to a specific stimulus.

Sociologists using experimental techniques are likely to do so in a laboratory setting, where all the elements are controlled by the researcher. In what is now considered a "classic" social science experiment, Stanley Milgram (1963) set out to study how far people would go in obedience to an authority figure. His research was inspired by the testimonies of war criminals during the Nuremberg trials of the post-war period, declaring that they were "just following directions" (McLeod 2007). Milgram wanted to see how likely it was for people to follow instructions, even if they ran counter to personal conscience. Milgram set up an experiment, purporting to be studying learning styles, where a *teacher* would practice word pairs with a *learner*. The learner actually was working with the experimenter, while the designated "teacher" was the blind subject of the experiment. The learner would respond to word pairs by providing an incorrect response to the word presented. The teacher was to give an electric shock to the learner whenever a wrong answer was given, and told to increase the voltage for every wrong answer given. The voltage started at 15 volts and advanced, by 30 settings, to 450. The teacher was given a sample shock, at the beginning of the session, to get a sense of what it entailed and to make the situation seem "real." In fact, the shock plate actually was shut off during the experiment and the alleged learner was in a different room from the teacher in order to control for unity in the responses, which were pre-recorded. Responses changed to match the increments in the voltage, so that all subjects heard the same vocal responses at the same levels of shock. As the voltage increased, the alleged subject would sound distressed and then apparently pass out. Sixty-five percent of the exclusively male subjects continued to shock the ultimately unresponsive "subject" to the 450-volt level. Sometimes the "teacher" would resist, but a scientist would emerge and say "You must continue," and many did, in spite of apparent discomfort. Modifications in the design, where the research was moved to a storefront in a working-class town, resulted in decreased obedience with compliance at 47.5 percent. When the "teacher" had to place the learner's hand on a shock plate, obedience dropped to 30 percent. The least likely case facilitating obedience (at 20 percent), was when the researcher provided guidance from another room, never making physical contact, as in the original study, by entering the room to issue orders.

This research contained many aspects which would today make it unlikely to pass an ethics board. The subjects faced situations which failed to control for their safety and informed consent. Violations included the fact that the subjects were not told the "real" subject, obedience to authority, examined in this study. The shocks were potentially harmful, even if not "real." Protecting the subject from distress was not a factor in the study's design. Some critics feel the *debriefing*, following the study, was not adequate to resolve any mental stress stemming from the experiment. Milgram justified his experimental design by asserting that stating the real nature of the study would have affected the responses. He felt that his design was necessary to test his thesis. His experiment controlled the elements of the research in a manner he believed approximated real-life situations. Critics maintain that, since the research was done in a university setting, the subjects did not take it as "real" and probably didn't believe they actually had inflicted damage on the alleged subjects. One article supporting Milgram's research examines the massacre of hundreds of innocent villagers during the Vietnam War, suggesting it illustrates Milgram's design (Kelman and Hamilton 1989). Lab experiments tend to be relatively sparse since the validity of the transfer from the lab to real life, as well as the potential for ethical issues, make them less efficacious than other types of research.

Animal Research Investigating Mental Processes

Though rarely done in sociology, experimental research studies accomplish astounding findings with respect to animals and evidence of their possessing abilities previously thought to belong only to humans. The following example demonstrates how meticulous attention to research design can yield impressive glimpses into animal cognition. Research conducted at the *Dolphin Research Institute* in the Florida Keys considered whether dolphins can discern "less" in ordinal math recognition. Specifically, dolphins were trained to look at two boards with dots painted on them and, upon a signal from trainers, indicate "which is less?" The dolphins would select which board contained fewer dots. To control for bias, neither the trainer signaling the dolphins, nor the two associates holding the boards, knew which board had less. Also, to control for the difference between discerning numbers, rather than area covered by the dots, the dots had varied diameters. In the vast majority of cases, the dolphins were able to correctly identify the board with "less," even when the size of the dots was expanded to cover more space. Although this is animal research, it is instructive regarding the care given to the research design and to the illumination of cognitive abilities in dolphins. The project was reported in a journal of the *American Psychological Association* (Adelson 2005).

Figure 3.4 Dolphins have been extensively studied by scientists due to their remarkable intelligence and communication skills
Source: Angelo Vianello / Shutterstock.com

Ethics in Research

Any research involving human subjects must adhere to a code of ethics established by the American Sociological Association. This code assures subjects basic protections and respect. Subjects involved in research must be informed of the true intent of the research; be assured of confidentiality and anonymity; and be protected from harm. Researchers must avoid intrusion; observe regulations of informed consent; provide fair compensation when warranted; and inform the subjects of all research findings and any limitations of access to research data or notes (Ethical Guidelines 2014). There are many situations when researchers can violate these basic guidelines. Consider Venkatesh's gang research. Some people believe Venkatesh behaved unethically because of how close he became to JT, especially since his relationship was initiated for research purposes. Some critics felt that his intimacy with JT was self-serving and exploitive. Other criticism addressed Venkatesh's actions while engaged with the gang, where he occasionally became an active participant rather than simply an observer (Grimes 2008).

In another research setting, dubbed the *Love Lab*, at the University of Washington, John Gottman, and co-researcher Robert Levenson, spent decades studying marriage with special focus on what characteristics contribute to a happy marriage. Gottman would give married couples topics to discuss and watch their conversations. By looking for particular styles of interaction (see Chapter 10), Gottman claimed he could tell, with an accuracy of close to 100 percent, which married couples were likely to divorce (Gottman and Gottman 2013). Research ethics mandate that the well-being of the subjects should be protected. Critics of Gottman's research suggested that he should intervene to help the subjects assessed as being at risk of divorce, rather than simply identify them. He embraced this criticism and offered the subjects "debriefing" sessions where he suggested ways they could improve communication. These interventions are incorporated into his training programs promoting skills for marital success (Gottman Couples & Marital Therapy, n.d.).

Sometimes researcher violations are fairly explicit. One example of such violation can be seen in the behavior of Erich Goode. Goode, in several different settings, engaged in sexual relationships with his research subjects. Goode did research in the areas of drug use and admitted to engaging in sexual relationships with women in three research projects. He believes that these relationships could have influenced his conclusions, interfering with his objectivity as well as violating a vulnerable population (Goode 1999). Specifically, Goode admitted engaging in sexual relationships during his research on obesity and stigma, creating a dynamic of exploitation. He claimed that engaging in sexual intimacy provided him access to deeper emotional rapport with his subjects. Although this may be an accurate perception, it does not allow his participants to make an informed decision regarding their involvement and strips them of basic human volition (Goode 1999).

Data Reporting

When sociologists obtain data, they initially perform simple descriptive statistical analyses. An example of this type of research can be seen in a recent study, reported in the *New York Times*, on the distance American adults live from their mothers. The article (Bui and Miller 2015) reports that "The Typical American Lives only 18 miles from Mom." The authors show that 50 percent of Americans live 18 miles or less from their mothers. They further show that only 5 percent live more than 1418 miles from mom, while 20 percent live more than 370 miles from mom. They depict these trends in a graph showing the percentiles of miles away from mom.

The graph shows *percentile*, which is a comparative measure providing *relative ranking*, referred to as *ordinal data*. In this example, the number of miles a person resides from their mother is presented. The **95th percentile** indicates that only 5 percent of the sample surpasses the others on this measure; a figure of 95 percentile indicates a rank in the top 5 percent. The percentile value gives you a comparison relative to the rest of the group. Find the number on the graph that indicates how far from mom the 20 percent who are most distant starts at (the figure is 370, or the point on the graph of 80 *percentile*). Percent, in contrast to percentile, indicates a portion of the whole. What *percentage* of people lives an average of five miles from mom? Four out of every ten people studied (40 percent) live five miles from mom (not shown on graph).

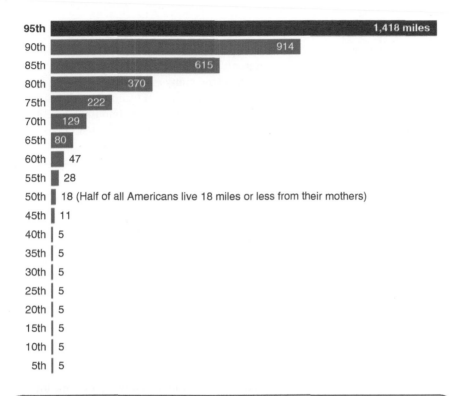

Figure 3.5 Distance from mom by percentile Source: Adapted from "Staying Close," in *The New York Times*, data from The Health and Retirement Study, 2008

Box 3.6 – Qualitative and Field Methods

Field research is done in the actual setting a researcher seeks to investigate. This type of research can elicit material that would otherwise be difficult to obtain. Researchers must decide whether to be revealed or anonymous and whether to simply observe or to participate, as well. Field research can be time consuming and the applicability of the findings to similar settings is not assured.

Ethnographies are a type of field research where the researcher is immersed in a setting as an active participant immersed in the culture.

A *content analysis* "decodes" elements of a product to study particular features. Examples might be studying the gender roles of characters in children's books or the images of non-white persons utilized in textbooks.

Secondary analysis refers to research performed on data originally collected for other purposes. For example, Durkheim drew data from the Census Bureaus of European cities to analyze data obtained for his research on suicide.

Classical experiments refer to research where a scientist creates *equivalent groups* and manipulates one dimension, designated as the *experimental condition*, and compares this group to a control group. Equivalent groups are sets of people who are demographically interchangeable, representing the same criteria for selection to the study. One intervention is introduced for the experimental group only. Group differences are then evaluated as being due to the experimental condition. Sociologists rarely employ such experiments because human beings have too many elements to establish truly equivalent groups. When sociologists use experimental techniques, they are more likely to do so in a *laboratory setting* where all experimental elements are controlled by the researcher. With such a setting, the researcher hopes to create a controlled environment reflecting a "real-life" situation.

Simple descriptive data can provide some basic information but it is important to understand what it says and what it does not. When we say the average American lives no more than 18 miles from their mothers we are, in this data, using **median** as the average. That refers to the exact middle value, referring to the actual midpoint of the designated group. The median figure indicates that half of the designated group lives between 0 and 18 miles. This is distinct from the **mean**, which is the mathematical model in which the numbers of miles distant from mom, for everyone in the study, are added up and divided by the number of responses. So, the **mean**, in this study, would be a larger number because the small portion of people who are very distant from their mothers would inflate the "average." When there are large values, in this case with respect to what is being measured (miles) and in the number of units being measured (US families), most researchers prefer the median to the mean. Use of the median reduces the likelihood of contamination by extreme low or high results and it is a more manageable statistic to determine. Statistics on the "average" household income, for example, are usually provided by the median rather than the mean. This is due to the large number of American households and the fact that incomes are generally tens of thousands of dollars.

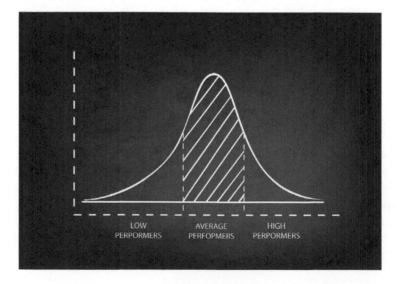

Figure 3.6 In "normal distribution," commonly referred to as a bell curve, the mean, median, and mode would all be the same figure
Source: Iamnee / Shutterstock.com

The mode is another measure of central tendencies, or what is commonly referred to as an *average*. The mode refers to the value which occurs most frequently in data. It can be the most misleading because if the data show information for 100 people, and five people have the same score, it does not reveal anything about the other 95 people. The exception to this would be in the case of a **normal distribution**, or what is commonly referred to as a **bell-shaped curve**.

A normal distribution represents the way data would be distributed if the sample group reflected a very large population. The above image shows that when the population is represented by a bell curve, only 2.14 percent of the population fall at the extremes. The vast majority of cases will fall in the center region. If a researcher were to graph the average height of the adult population, the figures would fall into the pattern of a bell curve, with very few people at either end, representing extremely short or tall cases. When testing companies produce exams, such as the SAT test, they develop a standardized test by giving it repeatedly until a large group of students score in the shape of a bell curve.

The next step in utilizing descriptive statistics would be to examine the data and try to explain the trends it illustrates. The researchers, in the study of distance from mothers, were surprised to find that 50 percent of American adults live within 18 miles of their mothers. Culture critics complain that family life is deteriorating and family members are dispersed around the country. Often it is implied or assumed, in the media, that people live far from their families. This is more likely to be accurate for the highly educated professional class who relocate for employment opportunities but it is not typical of people with lower incomes, who represent a much larger portion of the population. Middle-class, moderately educated professionals (e.g. teachers and nurses) are more likely than graduate educated or high-income professionals to live near their mothers. People with less income tend to need more "in person" help with familial obligations such as childcare and/or elder care since they are less likely to have the means to pay for these services. There also are ethnic differences in family life. Euro-American families, for example, are more likely to provide financial aid, while Mexican American families are more likely to provide in-person care. Geographic differences also exist. Families live closer together in the northeast and south. This can be attributed to more geographically spread out residential patterns in the west and mountain regions, as well as to cultural differences (Bui and Miller 2015).

Box 3.7 – Descriptive Statistics

Percent figures represent the **portion** of a whole. If a student correctly answers 80 questions out of 100, the score would be 80 percent. Percentile is an ordinal or comparative measure, while the percent is an absolute measure. If the student's score of 80 percent is designated as being in the 95th *percentile*, this indicates that the student's grade surpasses 95 percent of the other scores, or alternatively, that only 5 percent bettered that student's score.

There are three terms which designate averages, or what is referred to as **measures of central tendency**. The **mean** is a *mathematical* average; the **median** is the *mid-point* of data; and the **mode** is the value which occurs *most frequently*. If a group of 100 students took a test the mean would be determined by adding all the scores and dividing them by the number 100, the number of cases. The median would be the middle point; if the scores are listed in order, in this example, it would be the score between the 50th and 51st grades. The mode would be the score that occurs the most frequently, which tells nothing about the other scores, unless the data represents a bell curve.

A **bell curve** is referred to as a **normal distribution**. This is a statistical description of data which reflects the distribution of a trait in the population. If a sample is sufficiently large, the characteristic being investigated will describe a curve that is symmetrical and looks like a bell. In a "normal distribution," the mean, median, and mode would all be the same value. Characteristics such as the height of the population, if all adults were included, would fall into a bell curve, with the greatest portion of the population clustered in the middle and very few at the edges, who are either very short or very tall.

Other descriptive data show, also in contrast to popular media stereotyping, that the majority of families are not only geographically close but emotionally and financially interdependent, and visit with each other frequently. Geographic distance does not necessarily imply lack of contact, as can be seen by examining basic data on airline flights. Airline industry data show that three in four domestic trips are for leisure purposes and some of that is surely for family visits (On Average... n.d.). Almost 900 million people flew through US airports in 2015 (Peltier 2016). Although this figure accounts for all flights, the majority represents domestic travel (no specific data on purpose, other than the designation of "leisure," is available).

Analyzing data is more complicated than gaining descriptive profiles. There are several interpretations with regard to the relatively rare trend of living more distantly from the parental generation. What is characteristic of those who move further away from their parents? Highly educated people have more money to buy services, such as help with childcare, than those whose education is lower (Gerstel and Sarkisian 2010). High-level professionals may need to go to larger cities to find employment suitable to their training. This would be especially true if the individual is married to another professional and the couple is seeking two jobs. Married people, in general, are also more likely to move further from mom. This can be due to job requirements or to the social and emotional support available from a spouse. Other factors influencing family dynamics are cultural. African Americans remain geographically closer to their families, even among the more educated.

It is also essential to note, in the study reported above, that the sample is comprised largely of baby boomers (born between 1946 and 1964) and it may be that these trends are specific to this generation. Subsequent generations may demonstrate different trends due to factors such as the changing economy; the increasing expense of housing; the rising cost of higher education; immigrant status; greater longevity in the parental generation; and other demographic shifts. This demonstrates that showing trends at one point in time may not be indicative of trends at other times. It also shows how one simply constructed study can open a topic to additional research questions.

A simple study, concerning geographic distance between generations, can stimulate interest in multiple areas for future study. Questions about the level of *internal migration* (movement of residents within the US), which has been decreasing in the last 30 years, can be studied to see if the pattern persists (Molloy et al. 2011). The trend is accurate across all social classes and raises the question of what is contributing to its downturn. The researchers say that this trend is NOT explained by fluctuations in housing prices and the overall economy. Not counting college attendance or military service, the Pew Research Center currently reports that 37 percent of US residents never leave their hometown and 57 percent never move out of their home state (Cohn and Morin 2008). This move towards greater familial proximity is not as pervasive in comparable European countries. What might account for this difference? European culture provides some hints. Europeans traditionally favor living closer to relatives and so may never have gotten to the same portion of families living distantly as seen in the US. European countries also have populations exhibiting less dependency on automobile travel and more use of public transportation, making consistent long-distance travel less convenient. Perhaps most significant is the greater likelihood of government aid in European countries, which can support family continuity by providing financial and housing subsidies to young couples.

Research data should be taken as an indicator of social trends, not as the "last word." Research must be evaluated for design with a critical eye, to establish any errors of omission or commission. Scientific research is based on a principle of accumulation where research is subjected to *replication* before it is established as part of the accepted knowledge in a field. Researchers need to question both personal and expert assumptions to protect against bias which can make them overlook important findings which contradict accepted knowledge. Some of the most important scientific discoveries stem from accidents or research "failures" because the outcomes did not support researchers' expectations. Penicillin, for example, was discovered when laboratory neglect caused a mold, known as *Penicillium notatum*, to inhibit the growth of bacteria in petri dishes containing the highly contagious bacteria *Staphylococcus*. The bacteriologist, Dr. Alexander Fleming, enlisted the aid of another scientist, pathologist Dr. Howard Florey, who not only supervised a large lab of researchers but was adept at gaining funding to conduct his research. It was through his efforts that scientists successfully cultivated more mold to test whether its application could inhibit the spread of the bacteria. The realization that this technique could be harnessed to stop infections gave birth to modern-day antibiotics. Although Dr. Fleming is generally credited with the discovery of antibiotics, it is likely that they never would have been developed without the business acumen and diligence of the researchers in Dr. Florey's lab. This situation reveals the very essence of good science, based on replication, collaboration, and the will to commit expenditures to the enterprise (Markel 2013).

Accuracy in Reporting Data

Statistics can be manipulated in many ways, so attention to detail in evaluating research is essential. For example, I might say that the males taking my sociology class achieve final grades significantly higher than the females, where the average final score for men is 89 percent but only 68 percent for women. Such reporting can lead to the idea that men are better students, or at least better at sociology, than women. But what happens if I tell you that there were three men in my class and 45 women? Is it "fair" to provide percentages without reporting the sample size in each group? What if I told you that 20 percent (about eight females) received scores in the 90s and six did not finish the course, consequently receiving a failing grade? How would these scores affect the averages? More complete information would foster a much different interpretation.

Attention must be paid to other dimensions of a research project than the reported statistics. I might tell you, for example, that I had two groups of students taking an introductory sociology course and one group had much higher test scores than the other, even though the course was taught by the same person, with the same textbook, and the same exams. But what if I told you that one course was with students attending a four-year university and one was filled with high school freshmen? These groups might be expected to perform differently. Of course, a good research report would elaborate the composition of each group, but often when a study is taken from academic reports and presented in popular media, the details can be compromised, leading to the dissemination of "misinformation."

Care must be given to the wording of a reported outcome because a small change can completely transform meaning. Are the following statements conveying the same information? "**Every year** since 1950, the number of American children gunned down has **doubled.**" Compare that statement to: "The number of American children killed each year by guns has **doubled since** 1950" (Best 2015; emphasis added). The research in this report covered 1950 to 1995. In the phrasing of the first sentence, this would amount to 35 trillion deaths in the 45 years covered, by doubling the number every year for the period. In the second statement, the author states that child gunshot deaths doubled over the **period** of 45 years, not per year. We are still not clear whether this accounts for the growth in population and is reporting proportionately, or whether it is just a doubling of the absolute number of deaths. Other difficulties with this reported statement would include the lack of the data source; the definition of a child; and the meaning of "killed by gunshots"— is that homicide, suicide, and accident (Best 2015)?

The solution to the problem of bad statistics is not to ignore all statistics, or to assume that every number is false. Some statistics are bad, but others are pretty good, and we need statistics—good statistics—to talk sensibly about social problems. The solution, then, is not to give up on statistics, but to become better judges of the numbers we encounter. We need to think critically about statistics.

(Best 2015)

Stunning statistics become widely quoted in media, perpetuating skewed views of reality transformed into accepted "fact." This manipulation is reflected in the recent attention paid to "alternative" facts. False "truths" are easily established by publishing "misinformation" and presenting it as objective or mathematical reality. Any data can be "rewritten" to skew the meaning—even in portraying something as half empty or half full. Is it partly cloudy or partly sunny? What is the "real" difference? Critical questions, regarding research and reports derived from it, require consideration: where the research was conducted; how was the sample selected; were consistent measures utilized in assessing the topic; were the findings replicated; were the measures valid? A reader needs to be able to answer these questions in order to reach an informed opinion.

Key Terms

*Theory   Hypothesis   Qualitative and Quantitative Research   Validity   Reliability
Replicability   Surveys   Correlations   Interviews   Field Research   Ethnographies
Content Analysis   Secondary Analysis   Experiments   Research Ethics   Descriptive Data
Reporting   Percentile   Measures of Central Tendency   Mean   Median   Mode*

Concept Review

How Do Sociologists Study Society?

Sociological research is based on scientific methods. Researchers must identify topics and then follow an established process to conduct research. Research is initiated by a broadly based proposition or **theory**, suggesting a relationship between two phenomena. These are transformed into measurable elements and a set of hypotheses is developed to test them. Research protocols enhance objectivity and provide guidelines for establishing the credibility of research outcomes, but no social science research successfully attains complete neutrality.

What Types of Research Are Commonly Utilized?

Sociologists must decide whether a **quantitative** or **qualitative** study is warranted. The research approach will impact the quality of the information gathered. Quantitative research yields statistical data which is primarily descriptive while a qualitative project generally is more interpretive. Each method contains strengths and weaknesses which must be considered when designing a research project. **Surveys** are commonly utilized in sociology because they can reach a large sample and are relatively inexpensive. They yield quantitative data. Qualitative methods include *interviews*, *field research*, *content and secondary analysis*, and *experiments*. Research is scrutinized for standards relating to *validity, reliability, and replication*.

What Issues Emerge in Sociological Research?

Data reporting and analysis must be critically analyzed to ensure that the research is accurately assessed for what it reveals, and for its limitations, regarding subject matter and the extension to other groups or time periods. Ethical considerations, especially with field research and experiments, must be addressed to protect the well-being and anonymity of human subjects.

Review Questions

1. What was Durkheim's theory of suicide (Chapter 1) and what method did he use to conduct his research on the topic? Why did he select that method? (Hint: a theory is an abstract concept, distinct from hypotheses.)
2. What measures did Durkheim use to operationalize his theory? Do you think these were valid, or accurate, measures of social integration?
3. How far does the average American adult live from mom? What type of statistics were used in establishing the average distance? What factors contributed to the distances between parents and child(ren)?
4. What does the term validity refer to and why is it important? Provide an example of a study and discuss what aspect of research needs to be analyzed for its validity.
5. Can social science research be neutral? What issues emerge with respect to neutrality?
6. What are the three types of correlations? Provide an example of one of them.
7. What are the advantages and disadvantages of survey research?
8. What topic might you pick to do a field project on? What factors would lead you to make this project a field project?
9. Why don't sociologists typically use experimental methods in designing research? Provide an example of the difficulties involved with experimental research.
10. What do you think about the Milgram study? Was it conducted ethically? Does it have a relationship to "real" life? Would you want to be a research subject in it? Why or why not?
11. What is the bell curve? What happens with the mean, median, and mode in a bell curve? Why?

References

Adelson, R. (September, 2005) Marine Mammals Master Math. *APA Monitor*. Retrieved from http://www.apa.org/monitor/sep05/marine.aspx

Bartlett, N. (October 5, 2011) *Angela Garcia's The Pastoral Clinic. Somatosphere.* Retrieved from http://somatosphere.net/2011/10/angela-garcias-the-pastoral-clinic. html

Best, J. (2015) Telling the Truth about Damned Lies and Statistics. In Massey, G. (ed.) (2015) 8th edn. *Readings in sociology.* New York: W.W. Norton & Company, Inc.

Bui, Q., Miller, C. (2015, December 23). The Typical American Lives Only 18 Miles from Mom. *The New York Times.* Retrieved from https://www.nytimes.com/interactive/2015/12/24/upshot/24up-family.html?_r=0

Cohn, D., Morin, R. (December 17, 2008) Who Moves? Who Stays Put? Where's Home? Pew Research Center. Retrieved from http://www.pewsocialtrends. org/2008/12/17/who-moves-who-stays-put-wheres-home/

Ethical Guidelines for Good Research Practice. (December 15, 2014) Association of Social Anthropologists of the UK and Commonwealth. Retrieved from https:// www.theasa.org/ethics/guidelines.shtml

Garcia, A. (2010) *The Pastoral Clinic: Addiction and Dispossession along the Rio Grande.* Berkeley: University of California Press.

GenForward (October, 2016) Discrimination and Advantage. Retrieved from http:// genforwardsurvey.com/assets/uploads/2016/11/Discrimination-and-Advantage-1. pdf

Gerstel, N. and Sarkisian, N. (2010) Marriage Reduces Social Ties. In Barbara Risman (ed.) *Families as They Really Are.* New York: W.W. Norton & Company, Inc.

Goode, E. (1999) Sex with Informants as Deviant Behavior: An Account and Commentary. *Deviant Behavior,* 20(4), 301–324. doi:10.1080/016396299266416

Gottman Couples & Marital Therapy (n.d.) Couplestraininginstitute.com. Retrieved from http://couplestraininginstitute.com/gottman-couples-and-marital-therapy/

Gottman, M.J., Gottman. S.J. (2013) *The Empirical Basis of Gottman Couples Therapy.* [PDF File]. Retrieved from https://www.gottman.com/wp-content/uploads/ EmpiricalBasis-Update3.pdf

Grimes, W. (January 16, 2008) If You Want to Observe 'Em, Join 'Em. *The New York Times.* Retrieved from http://www.nytimes.com/2008/01/16/books/16grimes.html

Hoey, B. (n.d.) *What Is Ethnography?* Retrieved from http://brianhoey.com/research/ ethnography/.

Holmes, S. (2013) *Fresh Fruit, Broken Bones: Migrant Farmworkers in the United States.* Berkeley CA: University of California Press.

Kelman, H.C., Hamilton, V.L. (1989) *My Lai Massacre: A Military Crime of Obedience.* New Haven: Yale University Press.

Klein, W., Izquierdo, C., Bradbury, T.N. (2013) Housework. In Ochs, E., Kremer-Sadlik, T. (2013) *Fast-forward family.* Berkeley, CA: University of California Press.

Markel, H. (September 27, 2013) The Real Story behind Penicillin. *PBS Newshour.* Retrieved from http://www.pbs.org/newshour/rundown/the-real-story-behind-the-worlds-first-antibiotic/

McLeod, S. (2007) The Milgram Experiment. *Simply Psychology.* Retrieved from https://simplypsychology.org/milgram.html

Milgram, S. (1963) Behavioral study of obedience. *Journal of Abnormal and Social Psychology*, 67, 371–378.

Miller, C.C. (December 2, 2014) The Divorce Surge Is Over, but the Myth Lives On. *The New York Times*. Retrieved from https://www.nytimes.com/2014/12/02/upshot/the-divorce-surge-is-over-but-the-myth-lives-on.html

Molloy, R., Smith, L.C., Wozniak. A. (May, 2011) *Internal Migration in the United States*. [PDF File]. Retrieved from www.federalreserve.gov/pubs/feds/2011/201130/201130pap.pdf

On Average, How Many People Fly in the US Every Day? (n.d.) *Quora*. Retrieved from https://www.quora.com/On-average-how-many-people-fly-in-the-US-every-day

Peltier, D. (March 24, 2016) The U.S. Set a New Record for Airline Passengers in 2015. *Skift*. Retrieved from https://skift.com/2016/03/24/the-u-s-set-a-new-record-for-airline-passengers-in-2015/

Venkatesh, S. (2008) *Gang Leader for a Day: A Rogue Sociologist Takes to the Streets*. London: Penguin Books Ltd.

Socialization and Social Groups

- **Socialization** is the process of learning the social roles and values of a society. **Primary socialization** refers to the initial phase of instruction which most people learn at home, from the family. Although some of the learning takes place through the articulation of desired behaviors and attitudes, the child learns a great deal through imitation and observation, which frequently occurs without conscious acknowledgement. In both these modes, children learn much about social class, race, and gender. Socialization continues to develop in relation to peers, media, schools, and religion. Human development continues through adulthood, as people experience different life events.

- Psychologists focus on how the person develops a secure sense of self and the ability to behave autonomously. **Attachment theory** suggests that the quality of the relationship with the parent(s) sets the stage for the success of adult relationships. **Agency** refers to the quality of taking responsibility for life's choices and activities.

- The **nature/nurture debate**, regarding the relative influence of biology and environment, has been an issue in the social sciences for over a century. The twentieth century began with a belief in the salience of biology and transitioned to the primacy of the environment in the mid-century. Today, most biological and social scientists would see the argument as obsolete since biology and environment are now recognized as interdependent, evidencing reciprocal influences.

- Both psychologists and sociologists have proffered views of how a baby develops into a "person." The development of the "social self" by groups typifies the symbolic interaction perspective, initially developed by sociologist **George H. Mead.** The psychoanalytic perspective of personality, developed by **Sigmund Freud**, dominated psychology for much of the twentieth century and remains influential today, often as a point of contention.

- Theories regarding the development of morality, developed in the later twentieth century, have generated much debate. The work of **Lawrence Kohlberg** is presented as establishing the role of abstract ideas in the development of morality and is contrasted to the work of **Carol Gilligan**, who suggests that the traditional gender roles embrace distinctly different perspectives where females are guided by relational issues and that the belief that women are "less moral" reflects the sexism of the culture.

- The decrease in the competencies of **soft skills** in social interactions is presented with an emphasis on the effects of the use of social media and texting. The conditions which require the relatively rare need for **resocialization**, or undergoing a second primary socialization, are presented.

- **Erik Erikson's** extension of psychological development over the life cycle is discussed, especially in relationship to increases in longevity.

- **Primary and secondary groups** are defined and differentiated from **aggregates. Formal organizations** are introduced and explained in terms of their bureaucratic structure. The effects of group dynamics on the individual are discussed.

Introduction

Socialization refers to the process where a child learns the social roles and values of a society. The family a person is born into is the initial, and most significant, socializing force. Evidence from cases of extreme childhood isolation show that a child who is denied human contact, beyond subsistence levels, will fail to fully develop human qualities (Davis 1940; Pines 1981). The child may fail to speak and will be at risk of being unable to control bodily functions, eat solid food or feed themselves, and be severely undersized, often referred to as "failure to thrive." A child faced with severe deprivations will never fully recover these qualities, even with professional intervention. A child raised in a large orphanage, with insufficient staffing, is more likely to be undersized and show some level of cognitive and emotional impairment as a consequence of lack of physical nurturance. Isolation and neglect can have a devastating impact on the development of a human baby.

How Do People Learn Culture?

The family provides the initial environment for the child, physically and psychologically. It provides instruction, deliberate and unintended, which has a lifelong impact on the child. The family, as a cultural filter, communicates a life perspective. Initial socialization, addressing the acquisition of language and basic behaviors and values, is referred to as *primary socialization*. As a person matures, the lessons learned at home can be modified or even rejected but they usually retain some influence. A person may choose different life courses from their parents but these frequently are in reaction to parental influences. Preparation for specific roles such as employee, college student, or spouse are referred to as *secondary socialization*. This occurs through observation, training, and selection of particular models. *Anticipatory socialization* suggests that children learn many behaviors which are not immediately incorporated into their lives but set the stage for future roles. A child learns much of a future parenting role from watching their family members. Parents may read to a child to prepare for a future student role. Many people will attest to how difficult it is to "unlearn" assumptions and behaviors absorbed as a child. This can affect, among other things, conceptualizations of gender roles; attitudes towards other races and religions; and political views.

Box 4.1 – Socialization

Socialization refers to the process by which a person learns social roles and values.

Attachment theory, developed by the British psychoanalyst John Bowlby, emphasizes the quality of the infant's attachment to the parent(s) in determining the outcome of adult relationships.

Primary socialization refers to the basic elements of a culture, including social roles, manners, and values. *Secondary* socialization applies to learning specific roles such as student, spouse, worker, or retiree. **Anticipatory socialization** suggests that children learn many behaviors which are not immediately incorporated into their lives but set the stage for future roles.

Family members' influence is enduring even after they are no longer present. Parental and sibling influences are absorbed from the moment of birth, and possibly pre-natally. Admittedly, there are many individual factors which affect a person's life, as is evident from disparate developments of children from the same family. However, the family is predictive of trends in educational attainment, occupation, political views, religion, and lifestyle. Research evidence supports *attachment theory*, developed by the British psychoanalyst John Bowlby, suggesting that the quality of the attachments experienced in infancy exerts an intensive impact on relationships throughout adulthood (Murphy 2017). Poverty can also have long-ranging ramifications, affecting both physical and mental health. Even with loving parents, there is substantial evidence that the stressors related to poverty impact a child's ability to concentrate and learn and that deficiencies developed early in life can plague a child into adolescence and adulthood. Children experiencing severe poverty, in preschool and in the primary grades, suffer the worst impact of poverty on later achievement (BMJ 2011; Ostrow 2013).

One misinformed sociological theory, with origins in the 1960s, suggests that children of lower-income parents are likely to be poor because they learn values that perpetuate the cycle of poverty. This idea is dangerous because it suggests that values, not stress, low wages, and insufficient resources, are the most significant factor in success (Rank 2013). This is an individually based theory which blames those subjected to impoverished conditions for deficiencies produced by economic, social, and environmental factors. Such a view falsely places the locus of change in the individual, rather than in the social structure. In spite of the persistence of stereotypic views of the impoverished, the *values* of poor Americans are consonant with those of other social classes. In contrast, research provides evidence that wealthier people are less generous than those with limited resources. Wealthy people actually are less likely than middle-class persons to give an equitable portion of their income to charities (Daniels 2014; Savchuk 2014). Sociological study of personal development challenges us to question our assumptions regarding factors contributing to "character"; personal development is heavily influenced by factors affecting people such as poverty, racism, and gender discrimination (see Chapters 5, 6, and 7).

The study of how various social forces affect individual development is the subject of *social psychology*; a discipline which is listed as a specialization in both sociology and psychology. One core element of this field addresses how much of an individual's personality is predetermined by biology rather than environmental elements. *Nature* refers to attributes given at birth through biological elements of chromosomes, hormones, and biochemistry. *Nurture* refers to what is learned through the family and social environment. Over the past 150 years the dominant viewpoint has gone back and forth between biological and social determinism.

In the second half of the nineteenth century into the early part of the twentieth century, nature was considered the essential factor; a person's nature was considered immutable, established by traits inherited from the parents. By the mid twentieth century, the influence of behaviorist theories promoted the salience of the environment. *Behaviorism* suggests that behavior can be molded largely through the reinforcement of desirable behaviors.

The debate has shifted, more recently, in large part due to the innovations of technology leading to greater information regarding the brain and neuropsychology. Biology has regained some primacy in explaining human behavior but through a much more complex process of *interaction* with environmental forces. Biochemical responses are shown to be the basis of much behavior and to be vulnerable to alterations through experience. The newer approaches do not view nature and nurture as an *either/or* proposition but as an *either/and* one. Today most behavioral scientists will agree that biology and experience are not independent phenomena. A person's biology will impact behavior and the ensuing experiences can modify the biochemistry and neural pathways of the brain. This has been discovered through the use of brain imaging with MRIs and other technology not previously available. In earlier eras, it was virtually impossible to study the brain because a researcher was not going to open the skull in order to conduct such a study. New developments in surgical techniques allow for brain operations with conscious patients, which show how stimulating specific parts of the brain affects particular nerves and bodily responses. These developments have led to new treatments for disorders such as severe epilepsy, as well as providing new insights regarding the shape and function of the brain. Neuropsychology, which incorporates these investigations, is a rich and largely unexplored field with the potential to reveal answers to questions previously impossible to resolve. It is an inviting field for anyone interested in biology and psychology.

> ## Box 4.2 – Social Psychology
>
> *Social psychology* is the study of the processes surrounding socialization. Both psychologists and sociologists can be social psychologists and each group recognizes it as a specialization within their fields.
>
> *Nature* refers to the ways in which behaviors are influenced by biology, including genetics, brain chemistry, and hormones.
>
> *Nurture* is the belief in the person's environment and experiences shaping the *personality*.
>
> The relative impact of each has been studied, and contested, for over 150 years. Today the debate is almost irrelevant since nature and nurture are not considered distinct phenomena; a person's brain physiology and hormones can impact behavior and behavior can alter the brain.

Childrearing

Many people assume that certain behaviors regarding childrearing are universal. It is true that babies spend a lot of time being fed, held, soothed, supervised, and interacted with but the manner, and relative time spent in these activities varies quite a bit. J.C. Niala writes of her experiences in choosing to raise her baby with the best practices available to her. She felt the pull between the cultural practices of her native Kenya and the "expert" knowledge she learned as a person educated in the UK; she decided to return to Kenya to become a mother there because she was drawn to what she knew of that cultural tradition. She had read that African babies cry less and she set out to investigate the validity of this claim. She ultimately followed her grandmother's approach to childrearing and rejected all she learned from the western experts. She discovered that African-raised babies are attached to the mother's body all day and so well clothed that no skin is exposed to the elements, and she felt that was a good practice. She followed the African practice of breast-feeding her daughter on demand. When she felt compelled to introduce baby rice, as recommended in western practice, she noticed that her daughter's desire to nurse was returning to the rate of a newborn, rather than decreasing as it "should" when solid food is introduced. Her grandmother advised her to follow the baby's lead, and she did, nursing for both food and comfort. Western advice warns against letting the baby nurse too much or doing so only for soothing. She felt that following a schedule interrupted her responses to her child's needs.

Debates concerning feeding a baby on schedule versus by demand have flourished in the US since 1946, when Dr. Spock's babycare "Bible" first appeared. Although other theorists have authored babycare books, Spock's approach is still influential and his book remains in print. Dr. Spock promoted a compromise view, with some scheduling and some responsiveness to the baby's demands. Prior to that time, some parents put their children on a rigid schedule, an idea which is still favored by some parents and authorities (WebMD 2008; BabyCenter 2016). Critics suggest that scheduling is for the parents and detrimental to the children.

Niala also chose to sleep with her baby. "Co-sleeping" is frequently followed unquestioned in other cultures and the suggestion of separating the baby from the mother, for any length of time, is unthinkable. In the US, debates regarding the benefits of sleeping with babies and toddlers are another source of contention, with some experts adamantly against it. Some American pediatricians warn against the potential to suffocate a sleeping baby and consequently oppose bed sharing (Bed-Sharing n.d.). Sleeping with older babies and toddlers is not advised by many western "child experts" because it is believed that, to enhance a child's emotional security and self-reliance, the child should learn early to self-soothe and be independent. A contrasting view, more characteristic of non-western cultures but adopted by some Americans, suggests that keeping a young child close at night ensures a deeply rooted sense of security and safety; promotes better interpersonal skills; and will transfer to confidence, independence, and exploration as the child matures (Editors of *Child* magazine 2015).

After her investigations, Niala chose the traditional Kenyan practices in her belief that they provide the best parenting practices leading to the most happy, adjusted babies. She believes that because Kenyans are in constant contact with the baby, the children cry only when there is something "horribly wrong" (Niala 2010).

The western world, in contrast, has treated childrearing like a "condition" to be supervised by experts, negating the influence of parental intuition and common sense, and creating intensive anxiety regarding doing it "right":

> Children strain our everyday lives ... but also deepen them. 'All joy and no fun' is how a friend with two young kids described it ...
>
> 'Parenting' may have become its own activity (its own profession, so to speak), but its goals are far from clear. Children are no longer economic assets, so the only way to balance the books is to assume they are *future* assets, which requires an awful lot of investment, not to mention faith. Because children are now deemed emotionally precious, today's parents are also charged with the *psychological* well-being of their sons and daughters, which on the face of it may seem like a laudable goal. But it's a murky one, and not necessarily realistic: building confidence in children is not the same as teaching them to read or to change a tire on our car.
>
> (Senior 2014)

Varied childrearing in other countries illustrates how culturally specific practices can be. Some examples violate basic tenets of standard American procedures. In Norway, children are typically raised in an enforced uniformity, with one-year-olds attending state-sponsored, affordable daycare all day. They are also left outside to nap in their strollers, even in sub-zero weather. Vietnamese parents potty train children at nine months and even teach the child to urinate at the sound of a whistle. The Kisii of Kenya do not look into the baby's eyes as that is viewed as giving them power and it is felt that the baby should not have any. As a result, the babies exhibit less attention-seeking behaviors. Danish parents leave children at the curb while they shop. Unattended strollers are a common sight on city streets. In New Zealand, French Polynesia and other Polynesian Islands, as soon as a baby can walk it is left in the care of other preschoolers who learn to calm the babies. The toddlers, in these cultures, appear self-reliant. In Tokyo, children as young as four ride the subway alone and commonly do so at age seven. Spanish and Argentine children stay up late, till around 10 pm, in order to participate in the social life of the family. Aka Pygmy dads play the same roles as mothers in a fluidity of roles where each parent is equally likely to hunt or to take care of the children. Finally, the French expect their children to eat as adults and to like what they eat. They do not make special concessions to

Figure 4.1 Much of what we assume is "natural" in human development is actually culturally specific. Some families see no problem with having their children sleep in their bed, and in some cultures is it unthinkable to have a child sleep alone. In modern western traditions, most psychologists and pediatricians advise parents to have their children begin early to go to sleep on their own, suggesting it enhances the ability to comfort oneself and develop autonomy. Other people disagree, suggesting that sleeping with children facilitates a sense of security which can later lead to greater self-reliance
Source: wavebreakmedia / Shutterstock.com

their children, nor do children get any snack food to tide them over to the next meal (Lodish 2014).

A general psychological perspective, social learning theory, utilizes elements of behaviorist principles of reinforcement while incorporating the child as a much more active participant. In this theory, the child's environment is considered, along with the importance of imitating people who the child perceives as similar. The theory has been utilized to explain, for example, how children learn appropriate gender roles as a consequence of negative reactions received for inappropriate behaviors and kudos for behaving in accordance with social expectations. They not only are subject to parental responses but they can see what is considered appropriate, at home, school, and in the media, and these observations play a cognitive role in how they think about gender and behavior (Bandura 1977).

Human beings also develop "agency." This concept refers to the ability of a person to develop a sense of individuality as an independent actor. A person makes choices in the development of autonomy, acting with personal values and preferences, impacted by the social environment and personal experiences. A person's biological predispositions, as well as social and cultural situation, contribute to the sense of agency expressed. This can change with time and situation so that is it largely fluid. The development of the individual reflects the quality of personal relationships, as well as interpretations stemming from social factors such as gender, race, and personal histories. This concept is important in understanding socialization and identity because it indicates that the person can also choose to make psychological and behavioral changes, and these can be supported by professional help (Frie 2008).

> **Box 4.3 – Psychological Theories**
>
> **Behaviorism** is a psychological theory based on conditioning and reinforcement in promoting desired behavioral changes. This approach has been criticized as limited to the external aspects of behavior while ignoring internal or deeper behavioral motivations.
>
> **Social learning theory** is based in behavioral principles of conditioning but incorporates the ability of the individual to choose to adopt observed behaviors based, in part, on the received reinforcement.
>
> **Agency** refers to the perceived human capacity to actively develop a personal identity.

Sociological Approach to Personal Development

George Herbert Mead was the most influential sociologist in social psychology. His perspective emphasized the social components in the development of a *self-concept*. Mead used the terminology of the *self*, in his work, to distinguish it from *personality* which he viewed as more of a psychological formulation. The books credited to him were not actually written by him but by his students, after his death, from course notes and papers. This accounts for the lack of detail in some of his theories.

Mead believed that it is only through social interactions that an individual develops a sense of identity or *self* (Mead 1934). He suggested a child's initial learning is through interactions with particular people in the environment, primarily the parents. He referred to these as *significant others*. Children, he proposed, mimic what they see around them, long before they can actually understand what the behaviors represent. Though the results can be comical, Mead believed that this penchant for mimicry actually incorporated significant learning. In *taking the roles of others* Mead suggested that the child was learning about appropriate behavior. A child may dress up like her mother and pretend to go to work. This would indicate some understanding of the existence of work. Although a young child may have no idea of what the mother does at work, there is a budding awareness of the obligation. As the child develops, a more comprehensive understanding will develop through interaction with family, peers, school, and media.

Eventually a child learns that parents represent the community's social and behavioral mandates. Mead referred to the subsequent incorporation of societal expectations and rules as the *generalized other*. The child learns, through language and symbols, what is important and how to discern it. In *organized games*, Mead identified the mechanisms for navigating the larger world. In a game, the child must understand an entire set of roles and rules in order to cooperatively accomplish a successfully played game. The same principle applies to living in society. He utilized the game of baseball as a metaphor for this development.

When a child understands her or his placement in a system, Mead suggests the child has developed a sense of self, with the capacity for self objectification. Think, for example, of preparing for a date. Suppose you want to look sexy and alluring. You will look at yourself in a mirror and think about how you would appear to someone else. When you do this, you are treating yourself as an object, as something outside of yourself. Then you can make adjustments in your appearance to arrive at your desired effect. Mead suggested that this ability is necessary for successful social interactions, as well as for solidifying an identity or self-concept. The American theorist, Charles Horton Cooley, agreed with Mead's perspective and labeled this process of self-objectification the *looking glass self* (Cooley 1998; Isaksen 2013). With this concept, Cooley describes how a person, looking in a mirror, is seeing more than her or himself; the mirror image is also being appraised for how it might appeal to others. The subject in the mirror can make adjustments to accommodate the anticipated responses of others. In preparing for a job interview, a person can modify her or his appearance to look appropriately "professional." In this way, the "social self" demonstrates a constant monitoring of self and society.

Mead believed that people had two facets to self-concept, which he labeled the "I" and the "Me." The "I" represents the more subjective, intuitive, and creative aspect of the self which thinks "outside the box." The "Me" refers to all the expectations the person incorporates, through socialization, regarding desirable behaviors. Mead believed that people possessed the ability to critically examine learned responses in order to modify, or even reject, them. This was the source of behavioral innovation in his theoretical framework. He believed that an "I"-dominated person would behave differently than a "Me"-dominated person, selecting a different way to enact a role and preferring some roles over others. For example, a teacher who is "I" dominated would be more creative in the classroom, rather than following explicit curricular guidelines, while a "Me"-dominated person would be unlikely to deviate from these. Similarly, a scientist would choose different scientific roles if "I" or "Me" dominated. In the former case, the person might be a theorist, while in the latter case they might conduct meticulously detailed laboratory research. Similarly, an "I" person might choose to be an artist or an entrepreneur while a "Me" person might be a bureaucrat or a soldier. These differences are not absolute; for example, a high-ranking military officer likely can be more effective if "I" dominated.

The recognition of the dynamic ability of the person to create a "self" underlies the social behaviorist perception of a basic symmetry between the individual and society. Mead and Cooley are credited with establishing the groundwork of *symbolic interaction theory*, which emphasizes the ability of symbols to provide a common understanding of social rules of behavior. Because societal members learn the social expectations of a situation, most of the time action will occur accordingly. For example, classroom activities are able to proceed because there is basically a shared agreement of the process to be followed. A teacher can monopolize the "air space" but most students would be upset by a student doing so, unless it was a special assignment. This perspective shows how most social encounters proceed with relative ease, even with incorporating practices for addressing conflict.

Mead's pioneering work was further developed by the Canadian-born, American professor *Erving Goffman* (1922–1982). Goffman developed a dramaturgical approach to micro-sociology, emphasizing the parallels between theater performance and social life. In each the action depends on having the "right" actors, supporting cast, props, sets, and scripts. Goffman (1959) suggested that people create an impression of who they want to be by carefully constructing their part. He called this *impression management*. Much of the time, social interaction unfolds without major crises. The symbolic interactionists emphasize the availability of shared meanings through symbols in making this possible. A person can further support the role presentation through body language, vocal tone, or facial expression. Because much of this nonverbal behavior is generally stronger than words, and frequently not consciously controlled, these behaviors can also weaken a performance by failing to provide a convincing performance. An example would be if a person acts as if she or he wants a job but yawns or slouches during the interview.

Box 4.4 – Symbolic Interaction Theorists

George Herbert Mead (1863–1931) was a social philosopher who created the theories which represent *symbolic interactionism*, the "self" as a product of the social process. Initially, the family contributes to the developing self but, with maturity, the child recognizes that the family also represents larger societal values. Mead believed that the development of a "self" was dependent on its formation through social interactions.

Charles Horton Cooley (1864–1929) was an American sociologist most known for his work on social interaction and primary groups. He developed the concept of *the looking glass self*, establishing that the development of a sense of self is dependent on the ability to see oneself as we imagine others see us. In this process, the person is consistently adjusting behaviors to meet the expectations of social interactions.

Symbolic interaction emphasizes the ability of symbols to provide a common understanding of social rules of behavior, allowing for social interactions to unfold without major challenges. Shared meanings, made possible by common symbolic learning, facilitate this process. Even dissension in social interactions can be communicated by mutually understood signals.

Erving Goffman (1922–1982) developed a *dramaturgical* approach to micro-sociology emphasizing the parallels between theater performance and social life. In each the action depends on having the "right" actors, supporting cast, props, sets, and scripts.

Psychoanalytic Approach to Personal Development

The theories of **Sigmund Freud,** the creator of psychoanalysis, present a very different perspective from the sociological construction of the self. For Freud, human development occurs in *reaction* to the social world, and demonstrates an unhappy alliance between the individual and society. Freud was a physician, clinician, and

Figure 4.2 When we look in the mirror, we can adjust the image to what we wish to present; Cooley called this the looking glass self. When we dress for a job interview, we can contemplate how to present a professional image. Likewise, when we dress for social occasions we may look at ourselves and imagine how we will appear to others and dress accordingly
Source: Marco Rosario Venturini Autieri / istockphoto.com

prolific writer. His theories cover a lot of territory, from how civilization is possible to why people have trouble in relationships. His writings contain contradictory elements and have been the subject of much debate. Unlike the sociological theorists, he believed that personality was rooted in biology. He asserted that all human organisms are born with a biological imperative to pursue pleasure and avoid pain. He viewed this "pleasure principle" as the *id*, the motivating force underlying human behavior. Freud's impact on sociology concerns his central belief that the individual's pursuit of pleasure is constrained by social convention. The tension between human impulses and cultural constraints is considered the foundation of culture and individual personality. Much of this develops on an **unconscious** level, defined as the psychological consequences of interactions which are unknowable to the person. A person's feeling about society, and other people, is dependent on these unconscious forces.

To gain acceptance in society, this pleasure-seeking individual will suppress her or his unacceptable impulses by what Freud called *sublimation*, creating instead art, law, business, and scholarship. Freud believed that pleasure impulses become expressed in culturally acceptable form, as in heterosexual monogamy. For men this proceeded through their occupations while for women, sublimation occurs in accepting the roles of childrearing and homemaking. In fact, Freud actually suggests that women have a retarding effect on culture due to their concerns for the safety of children and home (Freud 1955). Freud is often perceived as misogynistic (woman hating) and anti-gay because of his theoretical orientation.

Daily social interaction is made possible by the development of the *ego*, the part of the psyche the individual uses to navigate social interactions. The baby must take an active role with caretakers to fill its needs for warmth, stimulation, food, and other essential life elements, defining what Freud called the *reality principle*. These behavioral skills are part of the conscious activities of the person. In the developing dynamic between infant and mother, ideally, the child experiences adequate care and develops a positive relationship with the social world. Failure to achieve sustained satisfaction of basic needs will result in a weak ego and create difficulties for the individual throughout life. Freud believed that unsatisfactory patterns of behavior were doomed to be repeated, due to their unconscious roots. Because of this, they only can be modified through psychoanalytic therapy.

Box 4.5 – Sigmund Freud

Freud (1856–1939) was an Austrian-born physician who developed the theory and practice of *psychoanalysis*. Freud developed his theories of the *id, ego, and superego* to explain how human beings channeled biological impulses into socially acceptable forms to create complex cultures. He explained that the psychical development of the person occurs largely on an *unconscious* level, referring to all the psychological reactions a person incorporates without her or his awareness.

For Freud, the human psyche is composed of three parts: the **id**, the **ego**, and the **superego**. The id represents the biological impulses of the human being to pursue pleasure and avoid pain. The ego is the element of individual's personality which engages in social interaction to get its *idinal* impulses met; it develops as soon as the baby interacts with other people to meet its needs. The superego develops later, at around age five, and represents the development of mechanisms which constrain the individual from unacceptable behaviors.

Freud recognized the **preconscious** level of experience, as well. This refers to aspects of the personality, or behaviors, which can be explained but are not immediately apparent. These can provide some insight into a person's motivations but still fail to modify the essential unconscious forces impacting a person's experiences. At around the age of five, a person develops a *superego*, roughly described as guilt or, more accurately, an amorphous anxiety. The superego acts to inhibit the person from committing "anti-social" or disruptive acts and consequently is a central idea to Freud's concept of the maintenance of a civil society.

The Formation of the Freudian Superego

Personality is formed by moving through what Freud called the psychosexual stages of development. These stages are sequential and failure to accomplish any of the psychological tasks associated with them will result in personality difficulties. Each stage refers to what is the focus of the child's pleasure seeking. The stages are the oral stage (0–18 months); the anal stage (18 months–3 years); the phallic phase (3–6 years); the latent stage (6–puberty); and the genital stage (adolescence to adulthood)* (Heffner n.d.).

The **superego**, so essential to the maintenance of society, is established during the phallic phase which focuses on the consolidation of gender identity. Early in this phase, the anatomical and social differentiation of girls and boys is recognized as permanent. This is the beginning of gender identity, characterized by the adoption of a distinct gender role. Later in the phase, the child acquires a *psychological* gender through identification with the same sex parent. For girls, the identification takes place through the close relationship with the mother/caretaker. For boys, Freud suggests identification shifts to the father whose role lacks clarity, since fathers were largely absent from the daily life of the household. Freud developed his concept of the **Oedipus Complex** to explain how the boy psychologically transfers his affiliation to the father. In the Oedipus myth, it is foretold that the baby Oedipus will grow up to kill his father and marry his mother. In order to avoid this fate, the king and queen order the child killed but he is saved and raised in another kingdom. Later, Oedipus becomes aware of the prophecy and, in order to escape this destiny, runs away from the kingdom. Paradoxically, on his journey he kills his biological father and marries his mother. After he has had children with his mother/wife, his transgression is revealed and he blinds himself so that he will never have to sicken himself by seeing his own shameful image.

Freud used this myth to illuminate the psychological process contributing to gender identification. He maintained that boys covet the mother but understand that sexual feelings toward the mother are unacceptable. The boy learns to manage these feelings by transferring this desire to identification with the father. The son believes that if he becomes like his father he can obtain a woman like his mother, so he must learn to be like his father. Additionally, he can vicariously experience the mother through this identification. This is how the child embraces his gender identity.

The girl undergoes a similar process, resulting in the resolution of the **Electra Complex**, based on an obverse myth in which the girl aids in avenging and resolving issues relating to her father, through killing her mother. The unconscious desires a child experiences for the parent of the other sex are the source of feelings of guilt and shame which must be suppressed. The urges leading to engaging with the parent are presumed to be transferred to acceptable objects. In this way, the child learns appropriate gender roles and prepares for "normal" heterosexual life. In working through this process, the child learns to subdue feelings of guilt and anxiety and to channel sexual urges towards "permissible" persons. By accomplishing this, extreme anxiety can be managed, appropriate behaviors reinforced, and cultural advancement can be promoted. The superego is the psychical product of this development and, according to Freud, stronger in males. It acts as a safeguard against "bad" behaviors and the accompanying psychological distress they cause. Males, Freud asserted, are dominated by the fear of castration which keeps them strictly in line. Girls, he suggested, perceive themselves as "already castrated" so they do not fear castration (Chodorow 1978). The declaration of the stronger superego in boys, and its alleged origins, have been the subject of intensive debate.

*Definitions regarding the ages of Freud's psychosexual stages can vary by up to a year.

The Development of Morality

Lawrence Kohlberg (1927–1987) was a Harvard research psychologist who is considered one of the leading theorists addressing issues of moral development. Kohlberg (1981) researched moral decision making with boys aged 10–16, utilizing stories with moral dilemmas and analyzing the ways in which the research subjects resolved the dilemmas. He elaborated three levels of development. The first, pre-conventional (ages seven to ten), describes simple dichotomies of "good" or "bad" behaviors, with good behavior resulting in avoiding punishment. The conventional level, which extends into adulthood, is explained by motivations to achieve social acceptance through conformity. The post-conventional level expressed the highest development. In this level, Kohlberg declared that boys utilize ideas that are abstract such as social contracts, individual rights, and social justice. Not many adults actually reach this level, according to Kohlberg, and he suggests that boys are more morally "advanced" than girls, who generally don't express the thinking which typifies the post-conventional level. His work was criticized for being *androcentric* (pertaining only to men), and using poor methodology, containing theoretical decision-making topics inappropriate to the life experiences of his respondents. His sample represented only a small group leading to questions regarding its generalizability (Darley and Shultz 1990).

Box 4.6 – Moral Development

Lawrence Kohlberg (1927–1987) was a Harvard psychologist known especially for his studies in moral development. He suggested that, in the most advanced stage of moral thinking, a person invokes abstract reasoning and relies on concepts such as justice and fairness in making moral judgements. He made the claim that males are more likely to express an abstracted, complex level of reasoning.

Carol Gilligan (1936–) is a psychologist who advanced a critical analysis of Kohlberg's formulations as androcentric and methodologically weak. Her research suggests that when women attain highly developed moral reasoning the content prioritizes relational concerns rather than abstract principles.

Carol Gilligan (1982) challenged Kohlberg's formulations, establishing her perspective that girls are not morally less developed than boys but likely to couch moral issues in a different light. Because women are more attuned to relationship issues, she suggested these would be reflected in their moral decision making rather than the invoking of abstract ideals. She suggests that "female" characteristic morality depends on promoting the optimal outcome for all involved and that this chief concern is reflected in post-conventional levels of moral development. She utilized story-telling scenarios but also included interviews with women who had made actual life decisions to have an abortion. She not only reformulated the content of the three levels of moral reasoning but was critical of the inherent flaw of studying only males and then measuring the behaviors of females against those results. This type of androcentric research was the standard for most social scientific research until the last few decades. Much of the standard "knowledge" in the social sciences is actually specific to one group, White males, but never identified as such. It was just taken for granted that whatever was "discovered" applied to everyone. This research serves mostly to convey the difficulties with defining a concept itself laden with judgement, such as morality, and the biases created by the historical context. Neither perspective is inherently "correct" and neither is confined to a specific gender. Morality, as with all complicated analyses, likely draws from myriad elements.

What Issues Occur with Socialization?

Forces impacting socialization include the family, peers, school, media, and religion. Cross influences occur between these sectors since none operates in a cultural vacuum. Parents feel that social media have exacerbated the pressures of the peer group which operates outside of their awareness. Teachers feel that parents are so stressed by work demands that the quality of their childrearing suffers. Religion, some believe, has lost much of its ability to provide a moral compass, or behavior references, particularly since Church affiliation is at an all-time low. Face-to-face communication skills are suffering, especially among the younger millennials, who have grown up with pervasive social media use.

Studies attest to the benefits of personal, physical interaction (see Chapter 2) but people are spending less time engaging in this as a result of increased use of social media and the internet, both at work and in personal life. *Soft skills*, such as how to read people's body language; how to dress appropriately; and even how to initiate a conversation, have suffered. Non-verbal communication, a powerful component in communication, is shielded when social media is utilized. First impressions are predictive of relationship outcomes and are an especially influential element of dating and employment searches. Essential elements of nonverbal impressions include focusing on the person you are addressing, making good eye contact; vocal tone; body posture; limited movement; and relaxed appearance (Bragg 2002). These help to convey important information regarding a person's personality, confidence, and competency which is influential in all social settings and particularly in job interviews. A person should also be mindful of qualities of interactional assertiveness since its evaluation often varies by gender. In a job interview, a person strives to convey enthusiasm and competency and trustworthiness. A person's emotional state should be consonant with nonverbal cues (Whitbourne 2016). Cultural and gender variations should be honored in all interactions, so it is essential to be aware of these. Nondominant group individuals pay particular attention to presenting a professional appearance in clothing, demeanor, hair, and accessories in the belief that they will be especially singled out for scrutiny (Goldsby, personal communication). Refinement of these skills is considered compromised by less practice in face-to-face relationships. In as much as positive feedback feeds confidence, the loss of these interactions can be seen to have a snowball effect on self-perception which is then transferred to new situations.

> ## Box 4.7 – Soft Skills
>
> **Soft skills** refer to interpersonal skills such as conversational skills, body language, attire, gender and cultural sensitivities, and other interactional dynamics which frequently are not directly taught.

Due to pervasive deficiencies, some workplaces are incorporating these skills in their training and budgets. A recent report highlighted a program to enhance the conversational skills of Spokane WA sheriff's department officers. A sergeant in the training division of the department noticed that young officers were having trouble engaging with the public. Older officers frequently complained about the lack of skills in the youngest officers. Utilizing training initially developed for the military, the officers were coached regarding their gestures, smiles, and eye contact. In the training, they had to approach people at malls and bus stations and practice initiating casual conversation. The deputies appeared to take the training seriously, and earnestly engaged in the activity and the follow-up feedback from the training officer, with positive results (Kaste 2017). Not all observers credit the use of social media as the primary cause for communication deficiencies but there is a consensus regarding their influence. Some feel the deficiencies are due to heavy reliance on social media but other commentators think that there is a more pervasive cultural problem, affecting older people as well (Kaste 2017). Due to the increased awareness of the dynamics of police encounters, and the potential for escalation in hostile exchanges, the ability to approach the public with sensitivity seems more essential than ever.

A person's entry into new roles frequently requires learning new sets of behaviors, many of which are not overtly stated. A new school, job, relationship, community or life stage can bring new challenges. Most of these fall under the category of anticipatory socialization and do not require the unlearning of previously learned elements of socialization. In the rare cases when a new primary socialization is required, sociologists have described a process of *resocialization* (Goffman 1961). In this process, a person must develop a whole new set of norms, values, symbols, and even language. Examples of non-medical life events requiring resocialization typically result from institutional sources. Entering or leaving the military, the clergy, the hospital, or prison are common instances of resocialization. Immigrating to a new culture is another situation which often entails resocialization. In the movie, *The Shawshank Redemption* (Darabont 1994), as the prison "librarian" is released from a 40-year imprisonment, he emerges into a world which is totally foreign to him. The city is buzzing with activity and unfamiliar elements. He works as a "bagger" in a supermarket and, as such, is a "nonentity." People barely acknowledge him as he packages their purchases. In prison, he had been a "veteran" with access to information useful to others. He enjoyed an elevated status; in short, he was "somebody." As a result of displacement, coupled with a change from an elite status to anonymity, he kills himself. When a person undergoes fundamental challenges to attributes central to self-identity, suicide risk rises. Recall the displaced Hmong men, from Chapter 2, who experienced "the sudden death syndrome."

> ## Box 4.8 – Resocialization
>
> *Resocialization* occurs when a person must undergo a new primary socialization. People moving in or out of institutional settings, such as the military or prison, are the most likely to experience resocialization. Immigrants are also another group likely to have to relearn basic life skills appropriate to their new setting, as well as a new language.

Boot Camp and Resocialization

In basic military training, the goal is to "break down" new enlistees and recreate them into "soldiers." Marine training is the longest, and most arduous, boot camp in the American military services. "Those who prevail after 12 demanding weeks will emerge completely transformed, prepared to defend our country and each other" (US Marine Corps n.d.). Every aspect of the day is controlled by the training so that behaviors are uniform, among all participants, and no time is left unfilled. The recruit will learn essential military skills, as well as being schooled in how to respond to authority figures and peers. The 12 weeks of training are highly choreographed, from the first step, where recruits literally place their feet in yellow footprints initiating the entry into training, to the Emblem Ceremony, where each candidate is officially conferred the title of "Marine." The loss of personal identity is substituted with the allegiance to the group and the organization.

Every element of the training period is contrived to support this goal. The training begins with the issuing of gear, medical exams, strength tests and an explanation of the *Uniform Code of Military Justice*. The training is geared "to instill order and attention to detail" in the recruits (U.S. Marine Corp n.d., week 1). Drill instructors "work relentlessly to bring out the warrior in every recruit." The recruits learn to shoot and to regard their weapons as an extension of their physical boundaries: "A Rifleman has complete control over their rifle and their body at all times." The recruits must learn to work as a team and to undergo grueling training missions, in small groups, where they must function as one person with no one left behind. In the last week, before graduation, the Marines will undergo a continuous 54 hours of physical and mental challenges with little food and rest. At the end of the basic training, each individual emerges as a *new* person: "From the day a recruit sets foot on the yellow footprints, he or she begins to learn what it means to be ready at all times, under any circumstances, to challenge an opposition and overcome any enemy force. They are taught to work as a team and always look out for their fellow marine" (US Marine Corps 2016). Their allegiance is always to "the few," referring to all Marines as both an entity and fellow soldiers.

Marines describe their experience as one of brotherhood and family. This substitutes for any previous family, or for the lack of one. As with induction into the military, discharge from the service can initiate a crisis of identity and loss which is a vulnerable time for the former soldier. Many soldiers have vast difficulties adjusting to this change, with 20 veterans committing suicide every day. Re-entry into civilian life represents a resocialization experience, replete with all its risks. As a result of the distress many military personnel feel in readjusting to termination of their military service, there is a movement to create a "reverse boot camp" to help soldiers adjust to the resumption of civilian life (The Return Boot Camp 2017).

Figure 4.3 Boot camp training is arduous and emphasizes becoming one with all the other soldiers. This is an example of resocialization, the process where a person's "self" is transformed to a new one which fits the group. This represents a reformation of primary socialization, an experience most of us will not ever undergo. A soldier may undergo another resocialization when leaving the military Source: Lorado / istockphoto.com

Adult Development and the Life Cycle

For much of the modern history of psychology, it was believed that essential aspects of socialization, and "personality development," occurred only through adolescence. Erik Erikson (1902–1994), challenged that notion by his suggestion that there are predictable stages of psychological mastery that extend into adulthood and characterize the process of dying. Erikson suggested that these psychological phases were predictable and universal. He divided adulthood into three stages—early, middle, and late adulthood, and elaborated specific tasks in each.

Box 4.9 – Erik Erikson

Erikson was a Neo-Freudian psychoanalyst. He is known especially for his suggestion that psychological development does not end upon entry into adulthood but continues throughout life. He elaborated specific psychological tasks in a person's early, middle, and late adulthood. His work was the impetus for studies in life-cycle research, including death and dying, which began in the late 1960s and continue today.

As a result of his pioneering work, life-cycle research has proliferated since the 1960s. Much of the initial research was conducted only on men. It was presumed that women's development would mimic men's but this assumption was questioned

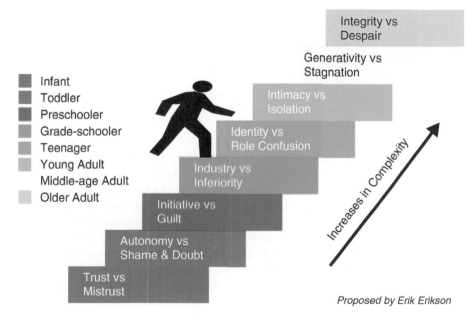

Stages of Psychosocial Development

Infant
Toddler
Preschooler
Grade-schooler
Teenager
Young Adult
Middle-age Adult
Older Adult

Integrity vs Despair

Generativity vs Stagnation

Intimacy vs Isolation

Identity vs Role Confusion

Industry vs Inferiority

Initiative vs Guilt

Autonomy vs Shame & Doubt

Trust vs Mistrust

Increases in Complexity

Proposed by Erik Erikson

Figure 4.4 Erik Erikson extended the psychological tasks beyond adolescence to old age. After his pioneering theories of adult socialization, researchers took up the task of investigating how adults change throughout adulthood, adding more detail to his broad stages of adult socialization

AGING PEOPLE # 2

Figure 4.5 Research suggests that life-cycle development follows predictable stages which are universal. We like to think of ourselves as unique individuals but there are predictable phases of development during which we contemplate many similar feelings, regardless of the specific details of our lives. One significant question, posed by life-cycle research, concerns whether women and men experience adult life stages differently. Although there are likely many similarities, women's typically salient role in childrearing may alter some aspects of the process of adult development
Source: Natalia Hubbert / Shutterstock.com

and researchers set out to determine whether women's life-cycle stages followed the same patterns as men's (Levinson and Levinson 1997). Although aging is a universal process, there are some notable differences between women and men. Women's life courses are more likely to have periods of major childrearing responsibility which interrupt, or even end, career paths. In the recent past, women's careers generally were presumed to be secondary to men's, with women expected to subordinate their desires to their spouse's. Departures from this dynamic were considered exceptional. There is some evidence that gender roles have altered this dynamic (see Chapters 7 and 10) but these modifications are by no means ubiquitous. Perhaps the next few decades will see more convergence between the sexes as women need to provide financial family support and men move to share more of the childrearing responsibilities.

Recent decades have witnessed greater testimony regarding cultural variations in life-cycle research, challenging the assumption of universality. Latina author Sandra Cisneros reveals aspects of her life in relationship to sex and ethnicity:

I was obliged to live at home as an undergraduate, unlike my brothers, because I was a girl. The struggle for a Mexican-American woman is one of you get married and that's the way you leave home or you get kicked out of home because you've done some sort of sexual transgression—you know, you've had a baby or you come out and say you're gay. But I used the winch of poetry. I said that I needed a place of my own to write, which was true. But I also wanted to have freedom to lead my life and to fall in love and to do things I couldn't do under my father's roof.

The hardest part was I didn't like living alone (laughter). I was afraid at night. There were sounds in the walls and sometimes a bug. And I doubted

Figure 4.6 Latina author Sandra Cisneros
Source: Gage Skidmore / Wikimedia Commons

every day, did I really want to live like this? Is this how writers live? Here I was, cold in a flat that was cold with a heater only in the kitchen and writing by a small, clamp-on architect's lamp. And I would just tape things by other women artists like Mary Cassatt—I can live alone and I love to work. And I—that was my mantra for those years. I would just say, yeah, I can live alone and I love to work. And then I would cry.

Now I add a third one, now that I'm 61, and that is learn how to be alone. It's OK to be by yourself. You do not have to be a unit. You do not have to be a father or a mother. And sometimes it's impossible to be that as an artist 'cause you can hardly make enough money to take care of you. We become artists because we're lonely. Then we have to be alone to create the art. And then finally, at my stage of my life, I like being alone and prefer my own company.

I always tell the young men and women you have to control one [thing], your money. If your money's coming from a source other than from your own earnings then that other person's going to tell you how to lead your life. So you have to control your own money so that you can control your destino, your own destiny. And for women—and men—control your fertility because that can throw you off your track from your brilliant career.

(Cisneros, in Martin 2016)

As the population ages, more questions are emerging regarding the nature of aging, with respect to physical and cultural presumptions. Much attention is focused on studying mental acuity in the aging process. Contemporary research reveals ways to reduce mental deterioration, suggesting that the brain can create some "cognitive reserve." Research shows that a person can enhance this status by achieving a college education, working at a complex job, and staying active in old age. People who have only a high school education can reach the same levels of acuity by doing puzzles, attending lectures, reading and writing letters (Hagerty 2016). The brain can be exercised to guard against memory loss and to sustain mental acuity. One study found that one third of people whose autopsies indicated Alzheimer's disease actually showed no symptoms (Hagerty 2016).

Older people can also significantly lower the risk of dementia by sustaining mental exercise and social engagement. This would include reading, social visits, activities such as walking and movies, and other "excursions." Learning a new skill also helps to promote memory, even more than maintaining a difficult activity; the challenge of learning something new promotes neuroplasticity and can even stimulate new brain cell growth. Research on friendship, showing that friends increase a person's lifespan, represents another innovation in the study of aging. People without social connections show a significantly elevated risk of death. In her book, *Life Reimagined*, Barbara Bradley Hagerty (2016) states:

> Now I know that *losing* friends can be lethal. Feeling lonely and isolated, no matter what your age, will shorten your life as much as smoking fifteen cigarettes a day. It destroys your body as effectively as alcoholism. It is twice as lethal as obesity. Maintaining relationships with friends, family, or work colleagues increases your odds of survival by 50%.

Loneliness increases the body's inflammation response which weakens the effectiveness of the immune system. It also compromises the body's ability to fight viruses and to produce antibodies. This body of research is just taking shape, with more attention likely to be focused on family and social aspects of illness, especially the increasing portion of aging citizens.

A long-term study of longevity, initiated in 1921 and spanning 80 years, found that some popular assumptions regarding aging are false. Multiple generations of researchers were involved in culling the data and conducting follow-ups. The research subjects represented over 1500 San Francisco youths, born in 1921, who were considered very bright and selected in order to study people who might become intellectual leaders. While it is true that healthy people are happier and happy people are healthier, the mutuality of these factors is more complex than previously contemplated (Friedman and Martin n.d.). Researchers found that factors regarding social connection, personality, and lifestyle were significant. Genetics accounts for only about one third of factors contributing to longevity. The assumption that a cheerful, optimistic outlook in people exhibiting the attitude that things will go well would improve longevity is noted by the research. Because they fail to accurately weigh the risks, such people are more prone to negative behaviors such as smoking and excessive drinking. The researchers suggest that some worrying is productive in that it promotes planning and persistence, attention to social relationships, and greater accomplishment at work. These attributes appear to be significant in the achievement of longevity. Because a strong social network emerges as especially significant, widows generally outlive widowers because they tend to maintain stronger networks. Physical activity is beneficial but only if it is enjoyed and not felt as obligatory.

Some unanticipated outcomes were revealed from the Longevity project. Elevated male happiness in married couples predicted the health and well-being of both spouses. "Neurotic" widowers outlived other widowers because they took better care of themselves (Bouton 2011). The single most influential personality trait to emerge, forecasting longevity, was conscientiousness. This tendency begins in childhood, where the trait is expressed in terms of good organizational skills and mild obsessiveness. Conscientiousness leads to healthier lifestyles characterized by more doctor visits; greater adherence to instructions from professionals; increased seatbelt use; avoidance of alcohol and smoking; and generally healthier relationships.

This group also is less prone to disease, including those lacking association with bad habits (Bouton 2011). As more people live into their 80s, and beyond, more medical, psychological, and social research will likely be done to extend the knowledge of what enhances well-being among the elderly.

Social Groups

A *social group* refers to two or more people who have sustained contact and a shared purpose or identity. Sociologists differentiate primary and secondary groups. *Primary groups* are small groups, characterized by frequent, personal interactions. These groups are generally long term and involve the whole person, typically containing an affective element. The family is the prototypical primary group but close friendship groups also qualify. A *secondary group* is larger, typically has a purpose, and can be time limited. Interaction is generally restricted to a specific goal and participants are less likely to know personal information about group members. For most people, Church membership, for example, would indicate secondary group membership though a person may identify a primary group within the Church. A group is juxtaposed to an *aggregate*, which amounts to a collection of people, with no common purpose and no shared identity, who are unlikely to be together again (sociologydictionary.org). Think of people shopping at a sale, waiting at a bus stop, or attending a concert. While it is true that they may be doing the same thing, they are not actually doing it together.

Box 4.10 – Social Groups

A *social group* is two or more people who have sustained contact and a shared purpose or identity.

A *primary group* is a small group with intimate relationships and frequent interactions.

A *secondary group* is a larger group characterized by a specific purpose. Interaction is generally limited to achieving the group's goals; participants have limited knowledge regarding members' personal lives.

An *aggregate* is a collection of people who are doing something in common but not really together. Examples would be people waiting at bus stop, shopping at the mall, or attending a concert.

A *dyad*, the smallest social group, contains two people and is vulnerable to dissolution.

A *triad* is a group of three and is unstable due to the possibility of shifting alliances, with two persons against one.

Expressive and instrumental leadership. Groups frequently contain leaders who may be responsible for the emotional well-being of the groups' member—the expressive leader—or for focusing the group to be "on task"—instrumental leadership.

> *Leadership styles* can be *democratic, laissez-faire, or authoritarian.*
> *Democratic* leaders ensure all members have a chance to participate. *Laissez-faire* leaders generally let the group process unfold with its spontaneous dynamic. *Authoritarian* leaders take control, delegating tasks, and managing the process.

Group sizes range from *dyads* to extremely large groups. A dyad, a group of two, is the most intimate, and the most vulnerable, since it dissolves if one person leaves. A *triad* is a group of three and it can be unstable because there is always the possibility of one person feeling excluded. The dynamics can shift, at any time, leaving each person vulnerable to the feeling of being the "outsider." Due to its instability, the triad can contain dramatic elements as with the prototypical love triangle. Consequently, it is wise to have four people when contemplating renting an apartment or traveling with friends. It is unclear at what scale a small group no longer functions well as a single entity, and it may depend on what aspect of group dynamics is under investigation—emotional, decision making, stability—but typically the limit is considered to be between five and seven people. When a group gets larger it breaks into several smaller groups.

Most people experience multiple types of secondary groups—from work groups, to classrooms, to membership in organizations focusing on a special interest or hobby. Secondary groups exhibit a variety of functions, each requiring different types of leadership, generally referred to as expressive and instrumental. The *expressive leader* takes on the task of making sure that everyone feels comfortable and included in the group. The *instrumental leader* generally keeps a group on task. Typically, these leaders are not the same person and not every group has each type of leader. A support group, such as *Overeaters Anonymous*, may just have an expressive leader since the task of the group is sharing experiences and feelings. A small work group, under an impending deadline, may have only an instrumental leader who makes sure that the task is completed on time. If a group will be engaging in sustained interaction, it likely will have two leaders because an instrumental leader might find it difficult to also take care of emotional needs in the group and ignoring these could risk the efficacy of the group. Similarly, the expressive leader might find their goals to be antithetical to those of the instrumental leader. Leadership can facilitate group process or, in some cases, complicate it but most groups will have leaders, either by designation or default.

Various *leadership styles* emerge in groups typically in response to the purpose of the group and, secondarily, to the leader's role. A *democratic* leader makes sure to include everyone in the process and ensures that all participants have a voice. This would be especially crucial in a self-help or therapy group setting and in cooperative group settings, where the leaders have an expressive function. A *laissez-faire* leader typically allows the group process to unfold with little intervention. An example of this might be the meeting of a club or loosely organized social group. This style might be employed by either an expressive or an instrumental leader but runs the risk of not accomplishing the leader's goals or satisfying all the members. Finally, an *authoritarian* leader role is assumed when one person seizes control, delegating tasks and process. This is more likely to be characteristic of a group with a task and members who have specific roles and skills, governed by an instrumental leader.

Group behaviors can become routinized, through habit and personal affiliation, and consequently less "successful." Research has identified a phenomenon called *groupthink* (Janis 1972, 1989), in which group loyalty or group "culture' overtakes the group and limits its effectiveness. In this situation, the allegiance to habitual behaviors can result in fossilized patterns of action and interaction which exclude innovation. When alternative behaviors are suggested, they may not receive any real consideration, frequently because no one wants to feel antagonistic towards the group or remote from it. The decision of John F. Kennedy to invade Cuba, in the *Bay of Pigs* (1961), has been attributed to groupthink regarding the group's belief of an imminent military threat. George W. Bush's invasion of Iraq (2003), based on the inner circle's belief in a nonexistent stockpile of weapons of mass destruction, was never challenged for its accuracy and was subsequently attributed to the dynamic of *groupthink* (Levine 2004). Groupthink can be circumvented by the presence of one group member willing to play the devil's advocate. If no one is able to play that role an outsider can be brought in to lead the group in investigating alternatives to their habitual behaviors. This is frequently the purpose of consultants who are not normally constrained by group loyalties or history.

Box 4.11 – Groupthink

Groupthink refers to the situation where group loyalty and habit restrict flexibility in the group, leading to routinization of process and outcome. To preserve the stability of a group, participants will discount new ideas and ways of doing things, even if they believe them to be better. Examples would include such events as the Bay of Pigs (1961) and the invasion of Iraq (2003).

A *reference group* provides a model for behavior and attitudes a person aspires to. An example would be when a young person attends the college of a favorite professional athlete in the hope of following in her or his footsteps.

On an individual level, a person may identify a *reference group*. A reference group represents a group whose members serve as role models. A person's identified reference group is not necessarily a physical one. Occupational, personal, or financial goals can be the target behavior sought in a reference group. A person aspiring to a career in professional dance, for example, may read about the lives of successful professional dancers and see what they were accomplishing at various times in their careers. These people can become models to emulate and can also provide normative information regarding preparation and characteristics typical of the group. This would be especially helpful if a person is unlikely to actually know such a figure. A personal role model may be emulated for any number of characteristics besides occupation. Today, with the internet, people frequently aspire to the lifestyles or goals of people they normally would never meet in their "real" lives.

Box 4.12 – Formal Organization

A *formal organization* is a large, highly structured secondary group with a specific purpose. Examples of these would include a college, the military, or a corporation.

Formal organizations possess a **bureaucratic** structure, characterized by a hierarchical division of labor, written rules and regulations, a specialized workforce based on credentials, and impersonality.

Contemporary life is complex, where the many roles a person plays will necessitate movement in a variety of settings. Most of us will spend a great deal of time in *formal organizations*; large secondary groups which have a specific purpose and are highly structured. Examples of these would include a college, the military, or a corporation. Many of these organizations contain a bureaucratic structure. A *bureaucracy* is a formal organization characterized by a hierarchical structure, a division of labor based on specialization, written rules and regulations, impersonality, and credentialism. Today, it is common to see bureaucracies as difficult to navigate but when Max Weber first studied bureaucracy, he considered it a beneficial innovation. He predicted that bureaucracies would be more efficient, judicious, and avoid nepotism (Gerth and Mills 1946). Although this is partly accurate, each aspect of bureaucracy can create new problems resulting from the large size and the varied tasks it is assuming. Upper management, for example, can be isolated and ignorant with regard to the conditions of the rank and file. Expertise and specialization can lead to rigidity so that prospective employees, who could be assets, are not considered for jobs they could perform well. A problem with a customer or client may fail to be resolved since employee specialization can lead to no one feeling competent or responsible for the problem. Red tape can be so overwhelming that business or money is lost. After getting the "run around" a person might just give up. The impersonality can be so pervasive that any individual dealing with the organization can feel invisible.

Some believe that bureaucracies have become too unwieldy and that power is limited to a small group of leaders who have a vested interest in retaining it (Michels 1949/1911). Recent media attention has been focused on the lack of diversity in corporate leadership, especially with regard to race and gender. This has been particularly pronounced in the tech field which has some of the lowest rates of women and persons of color in leadership and as employees. The question of how to address the issue of diversity, as well as bridging the divide between management and other employees, has become not only a matter of equity but of profitability. In work settings, *quality circles* provide an opportunity for managers and workers to engage in problem solving together. Some theorists have promoted the idea of *shared governance*, where workers and management discuss issues in the workplace and cooperate in finding solutions. This approach is generally found in education, government agencies, and medical settings. Each of these models involves sustained communication between "rank and file" and managers with the goal of achieving greater worker satisfaction and enhanced productivity.

As consumers, most of us have felt some frustration in dealing with bureaucracies whether within government agencies, service organizations, or businesses. At the same time, if they were to disappear, daily life would become more cumbersome. Today's bureaucracies have been greatly enhanced by technological innovations, which allow for much personal business to be conducted remotely, significantly cutting the time it takes to pay bills or shop. Some employees can now work remotely, in home offices, thereby reducing commuting time and supporting environmental conservation. Bureaucratic structures in large formal organizations present both positive and negative attributes and appear to be a permanent feature of daily life.

Key Terms

Socialization   Attachment Theory   Agency   Social Psychology   Nature/Nurture   G.H. Mead   Significant and Generalized Other   Sigmund Freud   Id   Ego   Superego   Conscious   Pre-conscious   Unconscious   Lawrence Kohlberg   Carol Gilligan   Soft Skills   Resocialization   Life Cycle   Social Group   Primary and Secondary Groups   Dyad   Triad   Aggregate   Groupthink   Formal Organization   Bureaucracy

Concept Review

How Do People Learn the Culture?

Socialization is the process of learning social behaviors and values characteristic of society. For decades, social scientists have debated the relative contribution of biology and culture to this process. Today, the argument is largely irrelevant because it has been established that behavior is an interaction between biology and experience, and consequently should be considered as either/and rather than either/or.

The sociologist, G.H. Mead, and the founder of psychoanalysis, Sigmund Freud, present very different views on how a human being becomes socialized. Mead emphasizes the development of the self as formed by the society, dependent on the social processes of group life. Since social forces form the person, there is a complementary fit between the individual and society. Freud suggests that the development of the individual is rooted in the biological drive to achieve pleasure and the societal mandate to control these impulses, highlighting the tension between the individual and the society. **Social psychology**, the sub-specialty studying issues of self and society, bridges the disciplines of sociology and psychology and is considered a subfield of each.

What Constitute Elements of Moral Development?

Lawrence Kohlberg and Carol Gilligan each investigated how children develop moral reasoning. Kohlberg suggests that the most advanced moral thinking utilizes abstract concepts such as justice and fairness, more characteristic of male thinking. Gilligan disagrees, suggesting that moral development reflects the deeper concerns associated with typical social roles. Since women have been more invested in emotional life and social networking, she suggests that female morality is rooted in protecting relational well-being. She challenged Kohlberg's assertion that more men demonstrate higher levels of moral development, indicating that women's concerns are based in a different context, but can be every bit as complex as male reasoning.

What Special Issues Emerge in the Area of Socialization?

Nonverbal communication is a powerful force in communication and frequently impacts social interaction. Because of its significance, and the increasing utilization of social media which minimizes "in person" interactions, some observers have highlighted a critical weakness in young people's ability to deal with face-to-face relationships, both among peers and at work. These include deficiencies in regard to eye contact, body posture, conversational tone, clothing and any other nuanced feature of interaction. These aspects of behavior were not previously considered a subject requiring special instruction, as they are in some institutions today.

Most people can build on the foundation of their primary socialization but small sectors of society will require **resocialization** into a second primary socialization. This need is generally restricted to people undergoing major institutional transitions, such as imprisonment or release from prison; induction or release from the military; and immigration.

How Do People Change Over the Life cycle?

Erik Erikson, a Neo-Freudian psychologist, was the first theorist to maintain that people undergo psychological development well into adulthood. His theory elaborates predictable stages of development, with particular psychological tasks, through old age. Since his pioneering theories, much research has been conducted regarding the content of adult development. His presumption that developmental changes are universal is being scrutinized with regard to experiences affected by race, gender, social class, parental status, and employment opportunities. Currently, as the aging population represents a growing segment of society, more research is being conducted on the physical, social, familial, and emotional issues associated with aging.

What Is the Nature of Social Groups?

Social groups take many forms and sizes, from **dyads** to **formal organizations**. The size and purpose of a group will affect the quality and mode of interaction. Groups experience different leadership roles and various approaches to leadership style, largely dependent on the purpose of the group. Some groups are vulnerable to **groupthink**, a process where a group becomes so habituated to its routines that it stagnates. This can lead to inefficiencies or malfunctioning. **Bureaucratic** organizational elements, developed to be more efficient and equitable, can also have a negative impact in operating dysfunctions. Rigidity in leadership, rules, skills specialization, communication, and impersonality can contribute to frustration or failure.

Review Questions

1. What is the contemporary understanding of the roles of *nature and nurture*? Explain how it differs from earlier conceptions.

2. How does Mead view the development of the self? Be sure to explain his use of the concepts of *play* and the *game* in the achievement of selfhood as well as the roles of the "I" and the "Me."

3. How does Freud use the concepts of the *id, ego, and superego* in personality development? What is the role of the *unconscious*?

4. How is Carol Gilligan responsible for understanding moral development in a *different voice*? Which theorist did she critique and on what basis?

5. Do you believe that females and males exhibit different types of morality? Justify your response with examples.

6. What is *resocialization?* Provide an example.

7. What innovation did Erik Erikson make to Freudian theory? When does a person become an adult? Or old?

8. What stage, according to Erikson's stages, would you place yourself in? What factors contributed to your choice?

9. Why is the "love triangle" such a dramatic form?

10. What is *groupthink*? How does it impact the group and can it be avoided?

11. Do you see bureaucracies as "good" or "bad"?

References

Baby Center. (2016) The Basics of Baby Schedules: Why, When and How to Start a Routine. https://www.babycenter.com/0_the-basics-of-baby-schedules-why-when-and-how-to-start-a-rou_3658352.bc

Bandura, A. (1977) *Social Learning Theory*. Englewood Cliffs, NJ: Prentice Hall.

Bed-Sharing. (n.d.) Retrieved from http://kidshealth.org/en/parents/cosleeping.html

Bouton, K. (April 18, 2011) Eighty Years Along, a Longevity Study Still Has Ground to Cover. *The New York Times*. Retrieved from http://www.nytimes.com/2011/04/19/science/19longevity.html

BMJ—British Medical Journal (April 29, 2011) Long-term Poverty but Not Family Instability Affects Children's Cognitive Development, Study Finds. *ScienceDaily*. Retrieved November 4, 2017 from www.sciencedaily.com/releases/2011/04/110420184437.htm

Bragg, T. (May 13, 2002) Body Language Affects First Impressions. *Bizjournals.com*. Retrieved from https://www.bizjournals.com/louisville/stories/2002/05/13/editorial2.html?page=all

Chodorow, N. (1978) *The Reproduction of Mothering: Psychoanalysis and the Sociology of Gender*. Berkeley and LA: University of California Press.

Cooley, C.H. (1998) *On Self and Social Organization*. Chicago: University of Chicago Press.

Daniels, A. (October 5, 2014) As Wealthy Give Smaller Share of Income to Charity, Middle Class Digs Deeper. *The Chronicle of Philanthropy*. Retrieved from https://www.philanthropy.com/article/As-Wealthy-Give-Smaller-Share/152481.

Darabont, F. (dir.). (1994) *The Shawshank Redemption* [Motion Picture]. USA: Castle Rock Entertainment. Retrieved from http://www.imdb.com/title/tt0111161/

Darley, J.M., Schultz, T. (1990) Moral Rules: Their Content and Acquisition. *Annual Review of Psychology*, 41: 525–556.

Davis, K. (1940) Extreme Social Isolation of a Child. *American Journal of Sociology*. 45(4): 554–565.

The Editors of *Child* magazine. (June 11, 2015) The Pros and Cons of the Family Bed. Retrieved from http://www.parents.com/baby/sleep/co-sleeping/the-family-bed/

Freud, S. (1955) *Civilization and its Discontents*. London UK: Hogarth Press.

Frie, R. (ed.) (2008) *Psychological Agency: Theory, Practice, and Culture*. Cambridge, MA: MIT Press.

Friedman, H.S., Martin, L.R. (n.d.) The Longevity Project. Retrieved from http://www.howardsfriedman.com/longevityproject/introtext.html

Gerth, H.H., Mills, C.W. (1946) *Max Weber: Essays in Sociology*. New York: Oxford University Press.

Gilligan, C. (1982) *In a Different Voice: Psychological Theory and Women's Development*. Cambridge, MA: Harvard University Press.

Goffman, E. (1959) *The Presentation of Self in Everyday Life*. New York: Anchor Books.

Goffman, E. (1961) *Asylums: Essays on the Social Situation of Mental Patients and Other Inmates*. Chicago: Aldine.

Goldsby, S. (n.d.) Clinical Psychologist and Licensed Social Worker. Personal communication.

Hagerty, B.B. (2016) *Life Reimagined: The Science, Art, and Opportunity of Midlife*. New York: Riverhead Books.

Heffner, C.L. (n.d.) Chapter 3: Section 4: Freud's Stages of Psychosexual Development. In *Psychology 101*. Retrieved from AllPsych Online.

Isaksen, J.V. (May 27, 2013) The Looking Glass Self: How Our Self-image Is Shaped by Society. *Popular Social Science*. Retrieved from http://www.popularsocialscience.com/2013/05/27/the-looking-glass-self-how-our-self-image-is-shaped-by-society/.

Janis, I. (1972) *Victims of Groupthink*. Boston, MA: Houghton Mifflin.

Janis, I. (1989) *Crucial Decisions: Leadership in Policymaking and Crisis Management*. New York: Free Press.

Kaste, M. (January 12, 2017). In Social Media Age, Young Cops Get Trained for Real-life Conversation. Retrieved from http://www.npr.org/sections/alltechconsidered/2017/01/12/509444309/in-social-media-age-young-cops-get-trained-for-real-life-conversation

Kohlberg, L. (1981) *The Philosophy of Moral Development: Moral Stages and the Idea of Justice, vol. 1: Essays on Moral Development*. San Francisco: Harper and Row.

Levine, D.I. (February 5, 2004) *The Wheels of Washington / Groupthink and Iraq*. *SFGate*. Retrieved from http://www.sfgate.com/opinion/openforum/article/The-Wheels-of-Washington-Groupthink-and-Iraq-2825247.php

Levinson, D.J., Levinson, J.D. (1997) *The Seasons of a Woman's Life*. New York: Ballantine Books.

Lodish, E. (August 25, 2014) 9 Incredible Lessons in Parenting from Around the World. Retrieved from https://www.pri.org/stories/2014-08-11/9-incredible-lessons-parenting-around-world

Martin, R. (Host). (August 14, 2016) *Wisdom from YA Authors on Leaving Home*: Sandra Cisneros [Radio broadcast episode]. Retrieved from http://www.npr.org/2016/08/14/489964114/ya-author-wisdom-sandra-cisneros

Mead, G.H. (1934) *Mind, Self, and Society*, Morris, C. (ed.) Chicago: University of Chicago Press.

Michels, R. (1949) *Political Parties*. Glencoe, IL: The Free Press, (orig. pub. 1911).

Murphy, K. (January 7, 2017) Yes, It's Your Parents' Fault. *The New York Times*. Retrieved from https://www.nytimes.com/2017/01/07/opinion/sunday/yes-its-your-parents-fault.html?ref=opinion&_r=1

Niala, J.C. (December 31, 2010) *Why African Babies Don't Cry*. Retrieved from http://www.incultureparent.com/2010/12/why-african-babies-dont-cry/

Ostrow, N. (October 21, 2013) Stress of Childhood Poverty May Have Long Effect on the Brain. *Bloomberg*. Retrieved from https://www.bloomberg.com/news/articles/2013-10-21/stress-of-childhood-poverty-may-have-long-effect-on-brain

Pines, M. (September, 1981) The Civilizing of Genie. *Psychology Today*: 28–34.

Rank, M. (November 2, 2013) Poverty in America Is Mainstream. *The New York Times*. Retrieved from https://opinionator.blogs.nytimes.com/2013/11/02/poverty-in-america-is-mainstream/.

The Return Boot Camp. (2017) Retrieved from https://www.change.org/p/the-return-boot-camp

Savchuk, K. (October 6, 2014) Wealthy Americans Are Giving Less of Their Incomes to Charity, While Poor Are Donating More. *Forbes Magazine*. Retrieved from https://www.forbes.com/sites/katiasavchuk/2014/10/06/wealthy-americans-are-giving-less-of-their-incomes-to-charity-while-poor-are-donating-more/#4ef0693b1264.

Senior, J. (2014) *All Joy and No Fun*. New York: Harper Collins Publisher.

US Marine Corps. (n.d.) *Recruit Training*. Retrieved from http://www.marines.com/becoming-a-marine/recruit-training/-/twelve-weeks/week/1

US Marine Corps. (November 7, 2016) *United States Marines Corps*. Retrieved from http://www.marines.com/news/-/news-story/detail/news_07nov16_fighting-spirit-lives-within-every-marine

WebMD. (2008) *Should You Feed Your Baby on Demand or on a Schedule?* Retrieved from https://www.webmd.com/parenting/baby/features/your-babys-feeding-on-demand-or-on-schedule

Whitbourne, S.K. (November 18, 2016) 5 Ways Our Body Language Speaks Loud and Clear. *Psychology Today*. Retrieved from https://www.psychologytoday.com/blog/fulfillment-any-age/201610/5-ways-our-body-language-speaks-loud-and-clear

CHAPTER 5

Social Class, Inequality, and Poverty

WHAT YOU WILL READ ABOUT IN THIS CHAPTER:

- There are three crucial themes to understanding *social class*. The first is that the post-World War II era represents two distinct periods. In the immediate post-war decades, prosperity was fairly widespread, with all segments of the population sustaining income gains. But beginning in the 1980s, only the top income earners made significant gains, while most of the population suffered decreasing or stagnating wages. Secondly, the *middle class is shrinking*, in that it is both smaller and less well-off than in the past. Finally, the group living in poverty is expanding, with increased segments of the population qualifying as **officially poor** and **"working" poor**.

- It is difficult to define social class because the measure is not a simple one based solely on income. Access to benefits such as healthcare, retirement, sick leave, and job security contribute to social class, as does educational attainment and occupation. **Max Weber** elaborated an analysis of social class based on multiple measures incorporating wealth, power, and prestige. **Gilbert and Kahl** work in this tradition and elaborate six social classes. **Karl Marx** believed social class was contingent on a person's location in production, with most employed as wage workers. **Erik Olin Wright** has updated the Marxist view to incorporate four social classes characteristic of advanced capitalism. **Social mobility**, generally associated with upward class mobility, has been on the decline in recent decades.

- Wages, in the past four decades, have declined in "real" terms, referring to the purchasing power of wages in constant dollars. The federal minimum wage was worth more in the 1970s than it is today. Women are over-represented in low wage jobs. **Technology** and **automation** account for more job loss than **outsourcing** and **offshore production**. The tax structure favors business and wealth, with fewer tax burdens than in other groups and in previous eras.

- The **federal poverty level** is determined by a formula, dating from 1960, where the food budget of a family is multiplied by three, since government economists believed that impoverished families spent one third of their budget on food. Economists now believe this conception to be outdated due to costs of housing, daycare, and healthcare. To apply this idea today, economists suggest a food budget multiplied by a factor of five. If the official federal poverty level is doubled, to account for an actual minimal standard of living, one third of the population would qualify.

- **The New Deal**, established under F.D. Roosevelt, was the first federal legislation to address the needs of the poor. It established the **welfare program** *Aid to Dependent Children* which remained intact from the 1930s until its reform under President Clinton in 1996. The new program, *The Personal Responsibility and Work Opportunity Act*, has several elements resulting in fewer people qualifying for aid, though it has not reduced the portion of the impoverished. Other programs, such as *supplemental food programs*, are more accessible to the poor. The **Social Security** mandates protecting families from aging, death, and disability also stem from New Deal legislation. **Medicare** and **Medicaid** (1966), providing government healthcare support for the poor and elderly, originate in the administration of President Lyndon Johnson.

- **Food insecurity**, or lack of sufficient food to support nutrition, is more widespread than is commonly understood, affecting about one in seven Americans. Lack of nutrition, and life stressors, impact the development of children and can have long-term effects on adult life.

Introduction

There are three inter-related trends regarding social class and the economy which will be elaborated in this chapter. The **first** is that the US economy has demonstrated two distinct periods since 1945. The first occurs in the decades following WWII and the second begins with the Reagan administration and extends to the present. The first era witnessed a widespread prosperity, with income gains across all segments of society. Subsequently, Changes brought by automation, offshore production, and information technology contribute to a shrinking middle class, increases in a segment referred to as the *working poor*, and a decrease in upward mobility. At the same time, the 1 percent have enjoyed explosive gains in wealth.

Second, middle-class America has changed in at least two ways. Fewer households qualify as middle class by any measure utilized. Additionally, those who claim middle-class status are not as well off as previous generations considered middle class. Today's median wages translate into less buying power than in the past. Assets distinguishing the middle class, such as education savings for children, reserve emergency funds, retirement benefits, and decent healthcare are dissipating and the middle class is increasingly living paycheck to paycheck, a characteristic formerly associated with the working class.

Third, poverty affects a large segment of society, as much as 40 percent, depending on the measurement used. Poverty is a result of structural economic changes resulting in poorly paid unskilled and semi-skilled work and wages that fail to keep pace with a minimal standard of living. Today, many of the poor are full-time workers. Decreasing and stagnating wages, and the diminished purchasing power of the minimum wage, have contributed to the impoverishment of the working poor.

What Defines the Social Classes?

This may seem like a straightforward question but there is nothing simple about social class. Social class is partially about money and income but the full picture is more encompassing. *Social stratification* refers to the separation of people into layers, hierarchical in social status, with differential access to resources and opportunities. Other factors contribute to social class identification, including neighborhood, social capital, language, family status, and education. Occupation, leisure activities, personal priorities, and aspirations also are components of class. Contrary to stereotypes about the poor, virtually all Americans share a work ethic, and the dream of seeing their kids do better than themselves, though access to resources varies by background. Many younger children are unaware of social stratification because neighbors seemed to be "just like them." As a young person experiences a wider social environment, often after elementary school, recognition of social class differences emerges.

There are identifiable attributes associated with social class, though they are becoming less distinct. One standard social class typology distinguishes the following classes: the capitalist class; the upper middle class; the middle class; the working class; the working poor, and the underclass (Gilbert 2015). The *capitalist class* refers to the "1 percent," who are investors and the very wealthy, whether by inheritance or entrepreneurship. The *upper middle class* refers to people with highly valued professional expertise, generally in management and professions such as physician, attorney, engineer, computer software. This group is relatively small, estimated as about 14 percent of the population. *Middle class* refers to a category with jobs that generally require a college degree, are salaried, and the workers have some control over their time. Examples would be lower level managers, teachers, and skilled craftsman. Some theorists suggest that, since this group has become less well off than in past decades, they classify them as *lower middle class*. Estimates of this group vary but usually hover between 30–35 percent. Typically, middle-class jobs provide paid leave, holidays, healthcare and some form of retirement contribution by the employer, though these have been significantly reduced in recent years or are at risk of being so in the future. The "middle" middle class seems to be hollowing out, with the greater portion swelling the lower ranks. The *working class* refers to people who work for hourly wages in skilled or semi-skilled labor. The work time in this group is usually rigidly controlled by the clock, with workers receiving an hourly wage. These jobs frequently have limited benefits with regard to sick time, paid vacation, health benefits and retirement plans. The *working poor*, variably estimated as between 15 and 35 percent of the population, work full time and make between 100 and 150 percent of the official poverty level. They are lower paid retail workers, service workers, and manual laborers. The *underclass* refers to those who live in poverty; they may not work, or work temporary or casual labor in the *contingent labor force*; or live on assistance. They average about 13–15 percent of the population.

Most Americans define themselves as *middle class*, as being "neither rich nor poor." In fact, the middle class is shrinking. Economists tend to inflate this portion of society by designating it as those who make between one half and twice the *median* income (Robert Reich in Kornbluth 2013) or as two thirds to twice median income (Elkins 2017). In 2016, the national median income, according to the Pew Research Center, was $55,775 (Elkins 2017). Although the upper figure might permit a middle-class lifestyle, the lower figure ($27,500 to $37,400) does not. The range shifts for different states but it seems evident that the middle class, as defined by the "experts," is falsely construed. The official poverty level accounts for about 15 percent of the population, but if waged workers whose income exceeds official poverty levels, but fails to meet their needs are included, the rate is as high as 40 percent of the population.

> **Box 5.1 – Social Class**
>
> *Social class* refers to the grouping of people by access to resources including money, opportunity, power, and social status. Social class is not only about access to resources but carries assumptions regarding lifestyle, education, and habits. The American middle class is shrinking with regard to both its size and assets.
>
> *Social stratification* refers to the separation of people into layers, hierarchical in social status, with differential access to resources and opportunities.
>
> *Gilbert* (2015) presents a model based on Max Weber's schema, which today address factors of income, education, technical expertise, time management, and employee benefits. They divide the social classes into the capitalist, upper middle, middle, working, working poor, and underclass.
>
> *Erik Olin Wright*, whose classification is in the Marxist tradition, elaborates four social classes: the capitalists; the managerial class; the small business class, and the working class. Wright focuses more on relationships to production, including not only ownership but management, supervision, and autonomy.

Many Americans claim "middle-class" status, but what do they mean by that? The concept of *middle class* implies access to enough resources to feel secure. Home ownership is a crucial component in that it provides for stability in the community, particularly when the majority of the neighborhood is comprised of owner-occupied homes. The middle-class neighborhood is considered as providing a good public education. Neighborhood safety is assumed, largely devoid of fears of assault or property crime. The family would have some discretionary income remaining after basic bills are accounted for. Discretionary funds can be set aside as savings, college fees, vacation funds, home improvement, etc. The existence of discretionary income,

U.S. Average Income, 2014

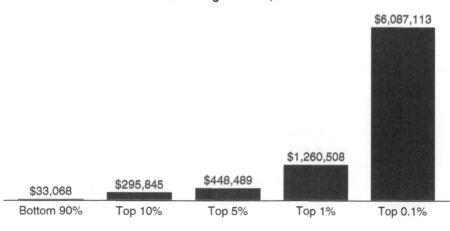

Figure 5.1 Income gains have gone to the top US earners, resulting in stagnant incomes in much of the lower groups Source: Institute for Policy Studies, http://inequality.org/wp-content/uploads/2014/10/Figure-1-e1455723650211.png

as with the employment benefits mentioned above, has eroded in the past 35 years, and particularly in the last ten. Realistically, how much income is required to attain a middle-class lifestyle? It is difficult to state, especially as it changes by locale, but the lower end would likely be at the national median household income 50–55K (Martin 2016) and could extend to twice that amount.

How Do Sociologists Explain Social Class?

Social class is not just about money; some *"working-class"* people, such as those who are unionized laborers, have higher incomes than *"middle-class"* people such as school teachers. The classical sociologist, **Max Weber**, viewed social class as a combination of ***wealth, prestige, and power***. His theory offers an explanation regarding the middle-class identification of persons who are not making much money, and the lack of middle-class identification in some workers who are. *Wealth* translates into income and financial assets. *Prestige* refers to the value placed on a person by society and to the type of work accomplished. Physical labor is generally devalued in comparison to "mental" labor. Examples of high prestige would be a clergyman, a physician, a judge. *Power* is the wherewithal to accomplish whatever goal is set. Supervisors and managers, as well as politicians and judges, can exert power over others. Together these contribute to social class identity, explaining why a clergyman can be poor but "middle class," and a unionized electrician can be financially better off and "working class." If Weber was writing today, rather than a century ago, he likely would have added educational attainment to this mix. In his era, only the privileged attended college.

Karl Marx's theory of social class also impacts contemporary sociology. He suggested the capitalist class structure was constricting and ultimately would evolve into just two social classes, the ***bourgeoisie***, or the capitalist class of people who owned production (factories) and the ***proletariat***, the designation for the people who sell their labor for wages. Marx suggested that the worker was exploited, earning subsistence wages while producing huge company profits. He also suggested that wages were not sufficient to attain all the necessities of life, keeping the worker shackled to the job. Consequently, the proletariat were indebted to the capitalist because they had no financial reserves allowing them to seek other employment, further providing for the likelihood of depressed wages. Workers might be indebted to the company if they lived in company housing or shopped at company stores, as was common in earlier stages of capitalism.

Box 5.2 – Classical Theories of Social Class

Max Weber's theory of social class utilizes multiple criteria. Weber incorporated **wealth, prestige, and power** to determine a person's class status. If Weber was alive today, it is likely he would have incorporated education in his schema, but education opportunities were largely limited to the elite in his lifetime.

Karl Marx's theory of class derived from the economic structure. He delineated two major classes, the *bourgeoisie*, who owned the means of production, and the *proletariat* who sold their labor for subsistence wages. Marx believed that the bourgeoisie would become increasingly oppressive and the proletariat ever more alienated or detached from their labor, and that this conflict would lead the proletariat to agitate for social change.

Marx also discussed the *alienation of labor*, suggesting that the worker becomes an extension of a machine, resulting in a disassociation from the product. In contrast, the craftsmen of earlier times took pride in the process and products of labor. Industrialization, particularly as controlled by capitalism, sacrificed the humanity of the proletariat. Marx extended his economic analysis by suggesting that the major societal institutions promoted the interests of the bourgeoisie. In the Marxist perspective, systemic changes in the economy would incite changes in other areas of social life. He predicted that the workers would seize control and restructure resources and power.

Today, many theorists readily point out that Marx was "wrong." Industrialized societies did not separate into two distinct classes with abject poverty on the one hand and extreme wealth on the other. Marx failed to foresee the diversity of educated and skilled workers with well-paying jobs. A person flipping hamburgers, cleaning offices, or working as an aide in a hospital is providing "wage labor," as is the college president, government manager, judge, lawyer, insurance salesperson. These two sets of employees, however, have different wages, benefits, autonomy, and security. Some managers and executives also may have a stake in "ownership" through stock options. The most highly rewarded employees do not share interests identical to the capitalist class but neither do they align themselves with hourly workers. Maybe Marx's most enduring analytic contribution was his insight into the alliance of societies' institutions with the interests of the "1 percent."

Erik Olin Wright, a contemporary social theorist, has spent much of his career updating Marx's theories and is referred to as a *neo-Marxist*. Following Marx's perspective, he sorts people into these classes based on ownership of production and on the relationship to labor, with reference to whether a person can purchase labor, supervise workers, or sell her or his labor. He describes four social classes (Wright 1979): the *working class, the small business class, the managerial class*, and the *capitalists*.

In Wright's schema, the *working class* is the largest class, composed of blue-collar skilled and semi-skilled workers and white-collar workers who are non-managerial, non-owners, and have little or no power in the workplace. The salaried portion of this group is also referred to as the *"new middle class"* because they are less well off than the earlier generation of *"middle class."* The *small business class* refers to people with small businesses who may employ a few workers but, mostly, this class is made up of owners/workers. This includes people who have their own professional practices, such as lawyers or doctors. The income within this group can vary from just making it to "making it." This group contains those with an entrepreneurial spirit who seek independence. The *managerial class* are executives who work for corporations and technically are "workers" but have a lot of control in production, though they are unlikely to set goals or the course of the large corporations; they oversee it. The *capitalist class* is the owning class; the "1 percent." They own and control the boards of the major corporations which drive the economy. They are a tightly knit group, with members who sit on multiple corporate boards (Domhoff 2013). This group also determines much of the information disseminated nationally since only six corporations are responsible for 90 percent of the media (Lutz 2012). Many people believe that the news and media are neutral agencies but this assumption is far from true. It is difficult to find "independent" news sources, though they do exist. "News" is portrayed as "objective," unless noted as an opinion piece, but it rarely is neutral (Fox 2017).

American culture also contains a perspective, one that can be characterized as assuming a middle-class ethos, defining the American *norm*. This undercuts the experiences of many "real" Americans. Across the social class spectrum, the population seeks the "American Dream," without the recognition that differences in resources to obtain it persist. The presumption that poorer people are vastly different in attitudes and behaviors is not substantiated by research (Rank 2013). The different circumstances of poor people are not to be found in "bad values" but in scarce *opportunity structures*. *Social mobility* refers to the likelihood that a person will live an adult life in a social class different from their parents, and for multiple generations this was a valid claim, but the upward mobility characterizing the baby boom generation is largely unavailable to their offspring, predicted to be the first generation to experience significant downward mobility. Our social mobility today is also less likely than in comparable European countries (Stiglitz 2013a). Americans cling to the American ideals, overestimating the likelihood of social mobility; the lowest groups show the strongest optimism (Kraus et al. 2015). Fifty-eight percent of Americans born in the lowest quintile will move out of that category. Only 6 percent will move to the top fifth (Stiglitz 2013), while 30 percent will move to the top three quintiles (Kraus et al. 2015). People in ethnic minorities are more unrealistic, regarding potential upward mobility, than European Americans (Kraus et al. 2015). The millennials are not only predicted to experience the most *downward mobility* of any post-World War II generation, in that they are less well off than their parents were at their age, but are also predicted to remain so throughout their lives (Goodman 2015; Pew Research Center 2014).

Much of the time, the effect of social class identity is largely unconscious until some status change brings it to the forefront. The nature of class identity is difficult to articulate because it is largely unexamined. A change in social class status feels disruptive or alienating. This is true whether the mobility is up or down. Alfred Lubrano published a book regarding the difficulties with upward mobility.

> ## Box 5.3 – Social Mobility
>
> **Social mobility** refers to the likelihood that a person will exceed their parents' social class. Social mobility generally is spoken about in terms of upward mobility, which typified the baby boomers of the post-WWII era. The millennial generation is failing to achieve the income characteristic of their parents as young adults, and is predicted to sustain this **downward mobility** through their lifetimes.
>
> **Social capital** refers to the ability of a person to navigate society smoothly. This would include understanding informal rules of the culture and the ability to access resources, such as social networks, internships, and scholarships. The educated, higher social classes typically possess greater access to social capital, perpetuating their advantages.
>
> **Cultural capital** refers to familiarity with all the aspects of life which contribute to status, such as clothing, mannerisms, posture, etiquette, language and other symbolic elements. Most learning in these areas, for the more privileged, is by imitation and familiarity.

Straddlers: Alfred Lubrano

In **Limbo**, Lubrano (2004) identifies deeply conflictual responses to changes in social class status. Lubrano's one hundred research subjects grew up in poor or working-class environments, moving into the professional and upper middle classes as adults. In their interviews, many respondents described feeling alienated from neighbors and colleagues. They also described feeling separate from "home" when visiting family and old friends. They expressed feeling in a state of *"limbo,"* where they hovered between worlds and belonged in none.

Dissociation from relatives and old friends as a consequence of social mobility was first documented in a classic sociological study, *The Hidden Injuries of Class* (Cobb and Sennett 1972). That study documented the sadness in Boston families where working-class parents worked extra hours, making many personal and familial sacrifices to send their kids to elite colleges, only to find that they sometimes facilitated the distancing of their offspring. Frequently they experienced a double familial loss—fathers often worked long hours, or second jobs, and so missed much of their children's childhood. A second wave of loss occurred when the adult child seemed transported to another world, making bridging the cultures strained, often from both generations.

Lubrano chronicles a similar loss suffered by both the parental generation and their offspring. A professional work life creates demands disparate from those of the working class. Lubrano suggests that to succeed for the professional requires more than the acquisition of skills and competency. Professional employment proceeds through soft skills for which middle-class children are primed in a way that working-class kids are not. It is not that the *straddlers* can't learn these rules, it is more that they run counter to the way the straddlers were raised. The straddlers attest to being mystified by the interactive rituals of the workplace, experiencing them as dishonest or consuming too much time which could have yielded more tangible outcomes. The formerly working-class professionals prefer to address work issues in direct conversation, rather than thinking through presentational strategies and appealing to intra-group dynamics. They experience *the emperor without clothes* phenomenon where no one wants to offend the ruler by pointing out his actual appearance. Lubrano suggests there is a better fit between middle-class childrearing practices and the culture of work, a game playing the *straddlers* were initially unaware of. Sociologists have referred to this situation as a difference in **social and cultural capital**. Social capital refers to this ability to rely on social networks and relationships to gain access to resources, particularly in relationship to obtaining entry into jobs and other groups which can help a person advance. Cultural capital refers to familiarity with all the aspects of life which contribute to status, such as clothing, mannerisms, posture, etiquette, language and other symbolic elements. Most learning in these areas, for the more privileged, is by imitation and familiarity (Bourdieu 1973; 1986).

Lubrano suggests that his working-class respondents long to return "home" but find that such visits frequently prove unrewarding. They have difficulty articulating their dilemma. Lubrano formulates it as: "Can a white-collar person do that—return to his blue-collar beginnings and live a new kind of life? For some *straddlers*, the middle class gets to be a burden, its rituals and requirements forever foreign" (Lubrano 2004). These dynamics are not prohibitive, many of the people studied thrive in their new worlds while maintaining ties to their origins but Lubrano suggests that a significant portion feel persistent discomfort, which is likely to diminish somewhat in the next generation.

America is a segregated society. Segregation is usually automatically associated with racial issues but social class separation is just as pervasive. Both affluent and poor Americans are residentially segregated from middle America. Though most people are aware of poor neighborhoods, often associated with slums and the inner city, few are equally conscious of the extent to which the wealthy segregate themselves; 30 percent of Americans live in exclusively high-income areas. The top 20 percent of households also exhibit distinctive patterns in family structure, education, cultural capital, lifestyle, and voting. "Affluent" households are 20 percent of the population and account for 30 percent of voters, so they exert more political influence than other groups. Poor people are the least likely to vote and the most likely to be ineligible to vote. Education, not surprisingly, is correlated with the income of households. In 2013, 83 percent of heads of household, in the top quintile, had at least a college degree compared with 65 percent for the fourth and third quintiles and

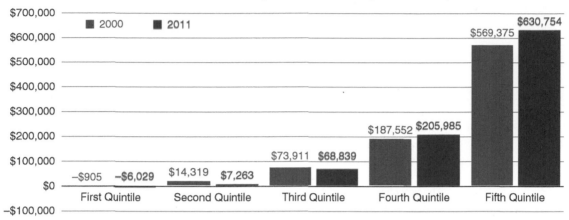

33 percent for the bottom two (Edsall 2016). Education, however, does not guarantee a high income, though coming from an affluent family usually provides sources of cushioning.

Affluence and Privilege

In a recent article, Neil Gabler writes autobiographically of *The Secret Shame of the Middle-Class Americans* (Gabler 2016). He confesses to being one of the 47 percent of Americans, highlighted in a recent report (Federal Reserve 2015), who would have difficulty raising 400 dollars for an emergency expense. He admits he hides his financial fragility from his friends and colleagues, "passing" as an affluent middle-class intellectual.

> I am nowhere near rich, but I have typically made a solid middle- or even, at times, upper-middle-class income, which is about all a writer can expect, even a writer who also teaches and lectures and writes television scripts, as I do. And you certainly wouldn't know it to talk to me, because the last thing I would ever do—until now—is admit to financial insecurity or, as I think of it, "financial impotence," because it has many of the characteristics of sexual impotence, not least of which is the desperate need to mask it and pretend everything is going swimmingly. In truth, it may be more embarrassing than sexual impotence…. America is a country, as Donald Trump has reminded us, of winners and losers, alphas and weaklings. To struggle financially is a source of shame, a daily humiliation—even a form of social suicide. Silence is the only protection.
>
> (Gabler 2016)

Figure 5.2 Most of the gains in wealth have been concentrated in the upper quintiles; middle-class wealth often is reflected in the value of the family home
Source: Institute for Policy Studies. Source: http://inequality. org/wp-content/ uploads/2014/10/17.- Median-Household- Networth- 2-e1455659585183.png. Adapted from Distribution of Household Wealth in the US: 2000 to 2011, US Census Bureau, August 2014

A graduate-degreed author of privileged background, he admits to making lifestyle choices without regard to financial stability. He recognizes that his choices to be a freelance writer, a parent, a suburban homeowner, and to provide expensive educational opportunities for his two children are possible because he could draw upon the resources of his affluent parents. His career was characterized by lean years punctuated with a few flush ones, but none in which he saved very much. When he and his wife decided to move to the NYC suburbs to raise their kids, she quit her lucrative executive job and never was able to re-establish it. His parents paid most of the expenses for his daughters' elite higher education with the savings that he otherwise would have inherited at their deaths. His daughters are now degreed professionals, one a licensed social worker and the other a physician. His privileged background allowed him to gamble on success, as an independent writer, in a way that individuals from families lacking such resources would likely be more reluctant to risk.

Gabler suggests that his disregard for the financial risks he took stemmed from the sense of security and confidence, as well as material aid, he took from his privileged upbringing. This byproduct of privilege is rarely credited because it is largely unrecognized. Gabler continues to work as a freelancer at the same pay rate he has had for the past 20 years. He points out that he is not alone in this stagnation; many people in the middle class have had no, or little, net income gain. He cites research showing that it would take an average family $130,000 to live the imagined *American Dream*, whereas average household income is about half of that (Gabler 2016).

What Significance Is There in the Rise in Social Inequality in Recent Decades?

The stark reality of the class structure is that inequality is more extreme today than in any other time since just before the stock market crash of 1929. The clichés that "the rich are getting richer" and "the poor are getting poorer," are true and the middle class is joining the poor in its decline. Most of the income gain in the past 30 years is restricted to the top "1 percent" of the population, and even more concentrated in the top one quarter of the "1 percent" (Kahn 2013). In contrast, in the years between the 1950s and 1980, all the US income *quintiles* made significant gains of equivalent proportions. Another way to express this dominance is to say that the top 1 percent of American households take home 22 percent of the national income (Stiglitz 2013b). The prosperity of the American population has truly become skewed. If the well-being of the population is viewed in terms of *Gross Domestic Product* (GDP) per person, a measure often utilized to indicate the general health of the economy, a troubling trend emerges. Though the economic impact of the 1930s depression was more severe than the recent recession, the recovery from the depression was quicker and more robust. Twelve years after the recession (in 2019), the GDP per person rate is projected to be less than that seen in the mid-1940s (Leonhardt 2017a).

> ## Box 5.4 – Income Inequality
>
> ***Income inequality*** refers to the skewed distribution of income among the population. ***Quintile*** refers to the division of the population into five groups of 20 percent each. Income gains, in recent decades, have been confined to the top quintile, especially the top 1 percent. Past decades, especially between the 1940s and 1980, witnessed equivalent gains among all the quintiles.
>
> ***Constant dollars*** refer to figures given for different years as if they were earned in the same year. For example, when the 1973 minimum wage was $1.65 it was worth more than the $7.25 minimum wage of 2015, so in constant dollars it would amount to $8.81.

Figure 5.3 Income disparities have grown in recent decades
Source: http://www.census.gov/hhes/www/income/data/historical/household/

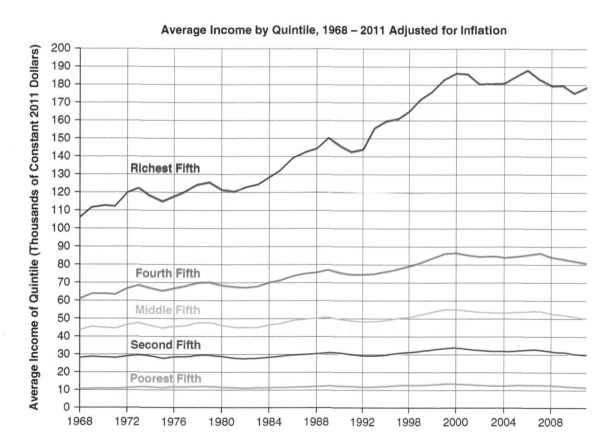

Average Income by Quintile, 1968 – 2011 Adjusted for Inflation

The minimum federal wage, controlled for inflation, has declined from its highest point in 1968 (Dube 2013). The federal minimum wage of $7.25 would need to be $10.78 to reach the buying power of the 1968 wage. Currently, the buying power of the minimum wage is down one third from its highest point. For the typical male worker, who earns something beyond the minimum wage, the average income today is also lower than in 1968 (Stiglitz 2013). One half of US jobs pay less than $34,000 per year and one quarter pay less than $23,000, though each figure exceeds the minimum wage (Edelman 2012). Wages in the bottom 50 percent of the population have been stagnant since 1973. This is particularly highlighted when considering net pay. A few decades ago, middle-class take-home pay was increasing more rapidly than among the wealthy, at 2 percent annually, resulting in doubling the income in a 34-year period. Now only the very affluent, the top 1/40 of the population, are receiving commensurate increases. The compensation disparity between the average worker and the corporate executive has increased dramatically. In 1965 the average salary of the typical company executive was *20 times* that of the average worker. By 2013 the comparable executive's figure was *296 times* the average worker's wage (Krugman 2013). Unionization is one factor which contributed to higher wages in the past, particularly in the private sector. By 2016, unionization was at an all-time low, with only 6.4 percent of workers in the private sector belonging to a union, while the comparable figure in the public sector was 34.4 percent (BLS 2017). These factors contribute to the widening gap between the rich and poor. Gains in productivity have been shared only among the wealthy while the wages, and tax burdens, of the working and middle classes rise. Tax policies favoring the affluent, a weak public education system, weakened labor representation, and corporate consolidation promise a continuance of this trend, unless significant legislation and policy reform is made (Leonhardt 2017).

Decreasing wages are highlighted by a 2016 report on US manufacturing jobs. In 2013, one third of all private nonfarming jobs created were in manufacturing. While manufacturing production used to pay a middle-class wage, the current wage figure is 7.7 percent less than the median wage (Edsall 2016). In 2013, the average manufacturing wage was $15.66 an hour, although 25 percent of this group earned $11.90 or less. The workers studied included some who were directly hired by manufacturers as well as personnel hired by staffing agencies. No one who did not work at least 10 hours a week in the 27 weeks prior to the study was included. The researchers determined that from 2009 to 2013, the government spent 10.2 billion dollars in safety net supports for this group of workers, including expenditures in the *Supplemental Nutrition Assistance Program* (SNAP), the federal *Earned Income Tax Program* (EITC), "welfare" *Temporary Assistance to Needy Families* (TANF), and healthcare (see below). Thirty-four percent of all the workers studied were enrolled in more than one program. Fifty percent of the workers hired through staffing agencies relied on social programs, comparable to the figure seen among the generally lower paid fast food workers. The researchers determined that this reliance on government subsidies was due more to low wages than to fewer hours (Edsall 2016). Although manufacturing might have been a remedy for poverty in past decades, it no longer is. In order to accomplish a standard of living comparable to that of the

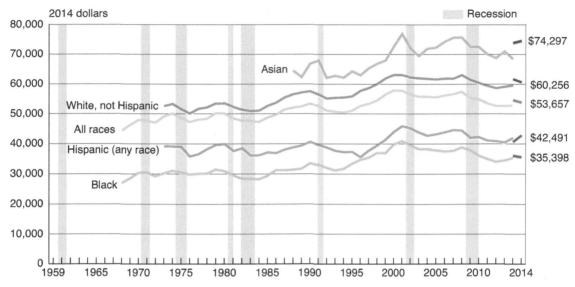

Note: The 2013 data reflect the implementation of the redesigned income questions. Median household income data are not available prior to 1967. For more information on confidentiality protection, sampling error, nonsampling error, and definitions, see <ftp://ftp2.census.gov/programs-surveys/cps/techdocs/cpsmar15.pdf>.

Source: US Census Bureau, Current Population Survey, 1968 to 2015 Annual Social and Economic Supplements.

post-WWII manufacturing workers, an increase in the number of jobs will have to be accompanied by corresponding legislation to raise minimum wages and to decrease the cost of living, particularly in housing and healthcare.

Figure 5.4 Income inequality by race and ethnicity is still significant Source: US Census Bureau, Current Population Survey, 1968 to 2015 Annual Social and Economic Supplements.

Students Lead a Successful Fight for an Increased Minimum Wage

Students in a San Jose State sociology class (a course on "social action") led the way to a 2012 ballot initiative increasing the city's minimum wage. The students wanted to establish a "*living wage*," one which reflects the actual pay needed to reach basic life needs. At first no civic organization the students contacted would support their efforts but they persisted, refusing to be discouraged by the disinterest shown by the organizations contacted. Many of the students were working 30 hours a week, while enrolled full-time in school, and struggling to make ends meet. The students raised $6000 to pay for a survey of San Jose voters and found that 70 percent of those respondents, regardless of their incomes, supported increasing the wages. Armed with their research, the students appealed for help to the *South Bay Labor Council*, which previously had turned them down. Their compelling data prompted the council to support the ballot effort. The council enlisted the aid of labor unions to further fund the effort and get the issue on the ballot. Sufficient money was raised and the issue went to the voters. The students triumphed, the minimum wage was raised to 10 dollars an hour, and future raises were tied to the consumer price index, so that a rise in the cost of living would be matched with an adjustment to the minimum wage (G. Thompson 2012). This stunning effort by the students demonstrates what concerted efforts can accomplish if a group is willing to stick it out, even in the face of opposition. Rather than becoming discouraged by the lack of response in any labor or civic organization, the students persisted, raising the money for the seed research and ultimately achieving success. Such grassroots efforts have become more essential in an era where Congressional action is functionally frozen.

The spike in inequality can be viewed by the specific data illustrating the decline in middle-class well-being. Today's average middle-class household income is equal to that achieved in 1989 (US Dept of Labor n.d.) but even this statement is misleading because this level is maintained only through the additional wages of a second adult, usually a woman. Even if the minimum wage was increased, the lower wage earners' incomes would improve but not at the same rate of income gains among the top 10 percent (Scheiber 2015). At the lowest income levels, the burden on women is particularly dramatic. Women are more likely than men to work minimum wages jobs and also more likely to be raising a family on these wages (Krogstad 2014). The lack of public policy for childcare and paid family leave severely impacts poor families. The US is the only country of 41 nations studied that lacks parental leave (Livingston 2016). In a UNICEF report considering the well-being of children in rich countries, the US ranked 26 of 29 countries studied (UNICEF 2013). Poor American children are likely to experience inconsistencies in childcare, healthcare, education, residence, and family composition.

Bigger Paychecks, But Little Change in Purchasing Power

Average hourly wages, seasonally adjusted

Figure 5.5 Although incomes may seem to have risen, their purchasing value has not significantly increased in the past five decades
Source: "For most workers, real wages have barely budged for decades", Pew Research Center, Washington, DC (October 9, 2014) http:// www.pewresearch.org/ fact-tank/2014/10/09/ for-most-workers-real-wages-have-barely-budged-for-decades/

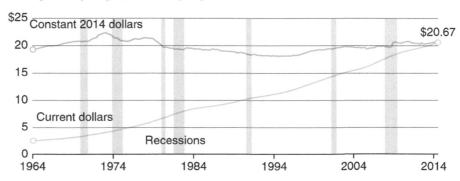

Note: Date for producttion and non-supervisory employees on private non-farm payrolls.
Source: Bureau of Labor Statistics.

The quality of life of the poor is exacerbated by the cost of housing, especially if the family experiences the loss of the family home. Lower income groups with any assets are likely to have these invested in their home and consequently have no resources for emergencies or retirement. Three in ten *nonelderly* have no retirement savings or pension. Three in ten also go without medical care for lack of money (Krugman 2015). Seventy-five percent of the US population cannot cover their bills for six months and student debt averaged $33,300 in 2015 (Krugman 2015). For today's millennial generation, the average young person with a high school diploma will earn only 62 percent of the average earnings of a person with a college degree (Pew Research Center 2014). The student in possession of a degree is also a lot less likely to suffer unemployment, even during recessionary years, though education does not guarantee financial security. Even with clear financial advantages to college graduates, the costs are sometimes prohibitive. Students are accruing significant debt and sometimes not completing a degree, resulting in the burden of loan payments while failing to achieve an adequate income.

Box 5.5 – Wages and Wealth

Minimum wage refers to the lowest legal hourly rate a person can be paid. There is a federal minimum wage but states can make their rate higher and so can a city; it just cannot be lower than the federal standard. More than half the states have a higher minimum wage than the federal level.

Living wage refers to the hourly rate a person needs to earn to meet *basic* expenses. Obama raised the minimum wage to $10.10 for federal workers to establish a living wage. Many experts suggest that $15.00 an hour is a more realistic figure.

Wealth is total assets minus debt. Household wealth has decreased significantly in the post-recession years and varies by racial groups, largely due to the impact of intergenerational well-being. When a family is middle class, or above, it can help young people to establish themselves in adulthood by reducing student debt or helping with a home purchase. Home ownership enhances the well-being of family in multiple ways, providing more stability and access to better resources.

Inequality stands out even more when considering inter-generational well-being. *Wealth* refers to a person's assets minus any debt. The wealth gap between social classes, and between racial and ethnic groups, is substantial. A person has a greater chance of accruing assets if they can start saving, and making financial investments, earlier in life. For example, if a young couple can get help with a down payment on a home they will gain multiple benefits. Home ownership brings tax breaks, a more stable community with better services, and the ability to save. Home ownership is increasingly out of the reach of the working class which, in the decades following WWII, had been equally as likely as the middle class to buy a home. The costs of buying a house are steeper for lower income people since they generally acquire loans with additional initiation costs, higher interest rates, and balloon payments. Non-dominant group workers often have been completely shut out of loan programs, such as Federal Housing Authority (FHA) and the Veterans' Administration (VA). African Americans are targeted for subprime loans and are more likely to have borrowed on their homes and to have lost them. African American households have fewer cash reserves than comparable White households (Cohen 2015; Kiel 2016). Similar patterns hold for Latino families.

Wealth reflects entrenched inequities with regard to race and ethnicity. The net worth of all American families averages $66,000 which is 6 percent less than in 1989 (Stiglitz 2013a). The current figure is down from $126,400 in 2007 (Stiglitz 2013). Median wealth declined by 40 percent in three years during the recession, largely due to real estate losses (Stiglitz 2013b). Total wealth for nonWhite groups ranges from 9 to 12 percent of White wealth, depending on the study. Hispanic wealth declined by 72 percent between 2007 and 2013; the decline for Black households between 1992 and 2013 was 56 percent (Cohen 2015). Americans work about the same number of hours as 25 years ago though income, controlled for inflation, has not risen. By contrast, in European nations, people's wealth has improved and the number of leisure hours also has increased. Steep increases in the cost of medical expenses, college, and housing represent areas contributing to the decline of the middle class.

It is essential to recognize the growing inequality because it poses a threat to the well-being of society. When, for example, a neighborhood undergoes a substantial rate of foreclosures, the consequences reverberate throughout the community. Empty homes signify less revenue for education and infrastructure. The deterioration of the neighborhood leads to a reduction in services and abandoned neighborhoods further reduce the value of the real estate; the community becomes less stable. Stressful environmental factors, including extra parental hours at work, poor diets, frequent moves, exposure to toxins, and poor sleep, negatively impact children's school performance. A thriving middle class contributes to stronger communities which are better equipped to support individual achievements.

Social policies and practices increase inequality. As we have seen, the falling value of the minimum wage, along with the increased costs of housing, higher education, and healthcare contribute to the growing instability of the working poor. But other policies, mostly in the finance field, are less visible and just as essential in robbing the poor of stability and the potential for mobility. The tax structure favors the wealthy. Income from financial investments such as stocks, real estate, or inheritance is taxed differently than income from wages. This is why Warren Buffet famously asserted that his secretary pays considerably more taxes than he does, as a billionaire. Although Obama did raise the tax rate on the wealthy, from 36 to 39 percent, many of the wealthy have mechanisms shielding their taxable income. Even if they did pay the full 39 percent, this is far below the 90 percent tax on the wealthy in the Eisenhower era (1950s) and the 75 percent of the Nixon era (1970s) (Kornbluth 2013). Contributions to Social Security (SSA), often referred to as "the payroll tax," are progressive but are particularly burdensome to the lower earners

Figure 5.6 The recession was accompanied by the loss of many family homes, which are a significant element in the wealth of the middle class, and which leads to the deterioration of neighborhoods
Source: rSnapShotPhotos / Shutterstock.com

since contributions top out at incomes of $118,500. Only about 15 percent of the population reaches beyond that figure. President Trump passed significant tax reforms in December 2017, effective for 2018. These included a permanent reduction of corporate taxation from 35% to 21%. Personal taxes, expiring in 2025, have been reduced for all income groups. The 39% rate for the highest group, under Obama's policies, has been reduced to 37% by Trump (Amadeo 2018).

Corporate taxation today is minimal. The portion of federal revenues from corporations has been at 10 percent since the 1980s, down from 28 percent in the 1950s. Corporate taxes on profit are low, 12.1 percent in 2011, compared to an average of 25.6 percent from 1987 to 2008. In the 1970s the comparable figure was 33 percent, down from 49 percent in the 1950s (Kornbluth 2013). As a result, a greater portion of the federal tax revenue is generated from personal income taxes, which places a much heavier burden on the shoulders of the middle class; the middle class is paying more than in previous eras, both in terms of the portion of their income going to federal taxes and of the portion of total revenues they are carrying.

Nevertheless, personal income tax is not the greatest source of diminished reserves for the poorer and lower middle class. Most people pay state, county, and city taxes. These vary by place of residence but can be a significant burden. If, for example, everyone is assessed 9 percent sales tax on purchases, such a fee is going to have more impact on low-income households than affluent ones. Additionally, other forms of taxation affect daily life, such as taxes on cigarettes, liquor, and gasoline. Moreover, the poorer credit rating assigned to many struggling Americans results in higher interest rates on credit cards, mortgages, and other loans. A person without credit cards is vulnerable to exploitative lending practices such as payday loans, which can ultimately cost a person several times more than the initial loan amount (Edsall 2013).

Box 5.6 – The Tax Structure

The **tax structure** refers to all the ways the government collects revenues. With regard to **personal income taxes**, there are federal taxes and most states collect an additional state tax. Wages are taxed for social security contributions up to $118,500, often referred to as "the payroll tax." There are also local taxes collected by the counties and municipalities which can be in the form of property taxes, bonds, and surcharges on consumer items and services. Tax fees are contained in the prices of gas, liquor, cigarettes, airline tickets, or hotel stays.

Corporate tax refers to assessments leveled on businesses though many companies can claim a variety of tax breaks to reduce their payments. Taxation on business profits is at a record low.

How Is Poverty Defined and Addressed in the US?

The official federal poverty level was established by a formula initiated in 1960. This formula was devised by government economists who estimated that a poor family spent about one third of its income on food. Consequently, the Department of Agriculture established a family food budget and multiplied it by three to arrive at the official federal poverty level. In 2016, it was $24,300 for a family of four (Federal Poverty Level n.d.). Today most economists agree if such a formula was to be employed, it should be multiplied by a factor of five, due to the high cost of today's housing. This would bring the poverty threshold to about $40,000 for a family of four, which would significantly increase the official poverty count. About 13.5 percent of the population is designated as officially poor, though the figure varies annually (see Figure 5.7). Using the current poverty standard, 104 million people, or one third of the population, live in households making less than two times the poverty level. Twenty and a half million people live on **less** than one half of the poverty level (Edelman 2012).

The official definition of the **working poor**, as a measure of impoverishment, is defined as people who work at least half of a year but remain under the official poverty level. In 2014, the working poor represented 6.3 percent of the labor force and 51.8 percent of working adults fell below the poverty level (*Who Are the Working Poor in America?* n.d.; Reich 2015). Slightly over 25 percent of the working poor worked for 50 weeks of the year. Senator Elizabeth Warren addresses the fears typical of hard-working lower income earners:

But I'm worried. I'm worried that my story is locked in the past, worried that opportunity is slipping away for people who work hard and play by the rules. I mean look around — Americans bust their tails, some working two or three jobs, but wages stay flat. Meanwhile, the basic costs of making it from month to month keep going up. Housing, health care, child care — costs are out of sight. Young people are getting crushed by student loans. Working people are in debt. Seniors can't stretch a Social Security check to cover the basics.

And here's the thing. America isn't going broke. The stock market is breaking records. Corporate profits are at all-time highs. CEOs make tens of millions of dollars. There is lots of wealth in America but it isn't trickling down to hard-working families like yours. Does anyone here have a problem with that? Well I do, too. People get it. The system is rigged. It's true.

(Drabold 2016)

The impoverishment of the remaining working adults, lacking full-time employment, is attributed to stagnant wages and insufficient hours. Another income group that struggles to make ends meet is the **nearly poor**, defined as making between the poverty rate and 150 percent of the poverty rate. This group, for the most part, is ineligible for most subsidies but often finds itself lacking in basic necessities such as food, housing, healthcare, and medicine.

Figure 5.7 The pre-recessionary levels of poverty have not yet been fully recovered
Source: Adapted from US Census Bureau, Current Population Survey, 1960 to 2016 Annual Social and Economic Supplements

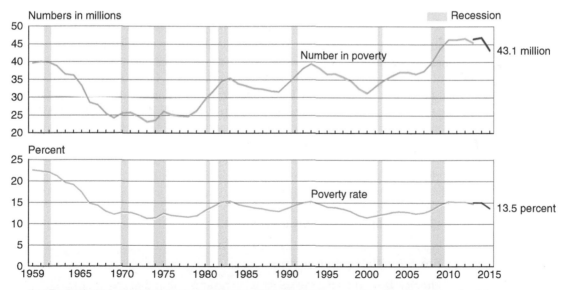

Note: The data for 2013 and beyond reflect the implementation of the redesigned income questions. The data points are placed at the midpoints of the respective years. For information on confidentiality protection, sampling error, nonsampling error, and definitions, see <www2.census.gov/programs-surveys/cps/techdocs/cpsmar16.pdf>.

Source: US Census Bureau, Current Population Survey, 1960 to 2016 Annual Social and Economic Supplements.

> **Box 5.7 – Poverty Definitions**
>
> Those designated as **the poor** have incomes falling below the official federal poverty level, ranging from 13.5–15 percent in recent years. The **working poor** are people who work a substantial part of the year but are officially poor. The **nearly poor** are people who make between 100 and 150 percent of the official poverty level but are NOT counted in the official poverty rate. An accurate measure of poverty would include all these designations and would amount to 33–40 percent of the population, depending on the sources utilized.

The Development of Poverty and Social Security Programs

The *Great Depression* is remembered as an era of massive suffering, plummeting a large portion of the population into poverty and unemployment. Hunger, homelessness, and lack of employment fostered feelings of hopelessness. What support was there for such people? Tent cities appeared and became known as "Hoovervilles," in reference to the lack of government aid from President Hoover's administration. Hoover declared that "prosperity would return" and "there'd be a chicken in every pot." With this perspective, he justified the lack of government aid for the unemployed. For the many unemployed, the statement was galling; how were they to live in the interim, even if Hoover's policy was sound? There were no government-sponsored relief programs until several years after the onset of the Great Depression. What aid existed was in the form of private charities in religious and community-based organizations which were uncoordinated and erratic.

The suffering citizens elected Franklin D. Roosevelt (FDR) in 1932, with his promise of **the New Deal**. The *"New Deal"* was innovative in that, for the first time, the federal government provided aid to the poor and unemployed. The policy contained two approaches to the widespread destitution. First, the government put people directly to work by funding projects supporting education and the infrastructure. Programs like the *Worker Progress Administration* (WPA) made dams, roads, bridges, schools, parks, and other civic improvements by hiring workers at government expense. These workers were not employed by established government agencies but were paid by the government to work on special projects. The hired workers were White men; many of these projects excluded African Americans and other nonWhite groups, as well as women. Other *New Deal* projects placed artists and writers in community jobs and schools, and included some women. These employment opportunities were temporary.

> **Box 5.8 – Welfare Programs**
>
> *The New Deal* was a package of social programs enacted in response to the Great Depression by the Franklin D. Roosevelt administration. The *New Deal* included employment programs where people were paid by the government to improve the infrastructure and education. Additionally, artists and

writers were supported to work in community projects. The *Social Security Administration* (SSA) was initiated to help with economic hardships relating to disability, death, aging, and unemployment. The *New Deal* also implemented a *welfare* program for the indigent, called **Aid to Dependent Children (ADC)**. Government agencies were developed to provide regulation of banking, home buying, and labor.

ADC offered minimal cash assistance to indigent parents but, as the title indicated, the target group was children. The program was renamed **Aid to Families with Dependent Children (AFDC)** in the Johnson administration, to highlight the need to aid whole families.

The **Social Security Act of 1935** (SSA) is another innovation dating to the era of Franklin D. Roosevelt. Citizens were now eligible for pensions, survivor benefits, unemployment insurance and disability insurance as well as the welfare program.

The AFDC program was replaced by President Clinton's administration, through legislation called **The Personal Responsibility and Work Opportunity Reconciliation Act of 1996**. This program was the first major reform in 60 years and consisted of block grants to states where the programs became known as **Temporary Assistance to Needy Families (TANF)**. TANF allowed the states discretion in tailoring programs to fit states' needs but federal guidelines established a five-year lifetime limit on eligibility and required the recipient to be in a work or work readiness program. The program articulated two goals, one to reduce the welfare rolls and the second to reduce poverty. Only the first goal was realized.

A second set of *New Deal* innovations established the *Social Security Act of 1935* (SSA). Citizens were now eligible for pensions, survivor benefits, unemployment insurance, disability insurance, and programs for *Aid to Dependent Children* (ADC, known as *welfare*). These programs were essential in providing some safety net though the relief was not immediate. The *New Deal*, radical for its innovation in aid, actually represented a compromise program. Conservatives were not happy with any government intervention and the liberals believed the programs did not go far enough. The *New Deal* incorporated policies allowing for collective bargaining, unionization, and agricultural regulations and subsidies from the government. The *New Deal*, however, did not provide the same standards of government support available in comparably developed countries and perpetuated the vulnerability of large sectors of the population. It also failed to contain any healthcare legislation, which had been a part of the original program. *Medicaid* and *Medicare* (1965) were created during the Johnson administration and the *Affordable Care Act* (2010), further expanding access to health insurance, was passed in the Obama administration.

Other factors contributing to the prosperity of the immediate post-World War II era were made possible through the low cost of housing, relatively high wages, and programs which offered support to returning military personnel. White men with jobs, both working class and middle class, were able to buy homes through the veterans' mortgage lending programs and to attend college with benefits awarded in the GI Bill. Suburban developments flourished and families, both working class and middle class, flocked to them and enjoyed a comfortable lifestyle. Suburban life, with its affordable housing, allowed for the support of stay at home moms. Fathers commuted to cities on highways constructed with government subsidies. The suburban lifestyle became a mainstay of the culture, often depicted in newspapers, television, magazines, and advertisements, and presumed almost universal. The poverty of rural areas and inner cities receded from national consciousness. The publication of Michael Harrington's *The Other America* (1962) exposed the poverty amidst the affluence so many believed ubiquitous. Presidents Kennedy and Johnson waged the "war on poverty" to alleviate this shameful condition. The years immediately following the "war on poverty" did alleviate some poverty but its successes were not sustained (Matthews 2014). The specific individuals living in poverty are fluid but the portion is fairly constant. This suggests that the structure of the economy depends on sustaining an impoverished group of people. This would seem to contradict common sense but poverty can be lucrative for society, providing a source of cheap labor and people who are too busy working to pose a substantial threat to the power structure.

The minimal aid provided by the New Deal's ***welfare program*** remained virtually intact for 60 years. Its philosophic origins were inspired by the English *Poor Laws of 1601*. These maintained that a person receiving government "relief" should be worse off than the most poorly paid worker. In this way, the system always promoted work over aid. The original welfare program of the *New Deal* was called *Aid to Dependent Children (ADC)*. President Johnson renamed it *Aid to Families with Dependent Children (AFDC)* but the actual program remained intact. It represented an income qualifying program serving indigent parents, most of whom were single. In 1996, President Clinton made the first distinct reform in the welfare system when he passed *The Personal Responsibility and Work Opportunity Reconciliation Act*, known in the states as *Temporary Assistance to Needy Families* (TANF). As the name indicates, the program emphasizes the temporary status of aid and it mandates that recipients be in a work program, or a "work readiness" program, in order to qualify for the program. It also contains a two-year limit in the

Figure 5.8 Famous image of an impoverished Native American mother during the Depression, by Dorothea Lange
Source: wantanddo / Shutterstock.com

duration of aid and a lifetime limit of five years. If a recipient has an additional child while on aid there will be no additional cash value added.

> ## Box 5.9 – Food Insecurity
>
> **Food insecurity** is when a person does not have an adequate supply of nutritious food. It is estimated that some 15 percent, or 50 million people, in the US experience food insecurity, including 17 million children. The **Supplemental Nutrition Assistance Program (SNAP)**, sometimes referred to as "Electronic Benefit Transfer" (EBT), is available to lower income families not qualifying as officially poor. It was expanded during the recession, but sustained Congressional cutbacks and eligibility restrictions in 2013.
>
> **Food deserts** refer to areas where access to fresh produce is limited or nonexistent. Typically, food deserts are found in the inner cities and in rural areas.

Clinton's program had two goals, one was to reduce the welfare rolls and the other was to reduce poverty. The program did decrease the number of welfare recipients but failed to reduce poverty. Research shows that only 27 percent of kids in poor families receive aid while, prior to the reform, the comparable figure was 67 percent (Edelman 2012; Abramsky 2013). In any case, the purchasing value of the welfare allotments has been steadily declining for the past four decades, dating to before the Clinton reform (Abramsky 2013). To be eligible for TANF, a household has to be under the federal poverty level.

There are many misconceptions regarding both the recipients and the programs in TANF. Most people are on it only for a short time and generally have sustained an emergency, such as the loss of a job or partner. Only a minority of recipients stay on welfare long term and the vast majority, some 91 percent, who receive government benefits of one type or another, are elderly, disabled, or working (Cheese 2013). Most households receiving aid are similar to other lower income populations in the US in that they are working and exhibit behaviors, attitudes, and values consistent with middle-class America (Cheese 2013; Rank 2013; Hays 2003). There are fewer welfare recipients on drugs than in the general population (Cheese 2013). For many other aid programs providing daycare vouchers, food subsidies, healthcare or healthcare subsidies, and housing supports, states can set their own standards.

Many parents on welfare struggle to improve their situations. Under the AFDC program, a student could attend college and achieve a four-year degree. In contrast, TANF provides only short-term work readiness programs and the vast majority of participants end up in low-level, dead-end jobs. This indicates why the welfare reform was unsuccessful in actually reducing the poverty of enrolled families. Helping a person to gain significant education or skills, made possible under the earlier programs, pays off in the long term. A parent with more resources will provide a better environment for the child(ren), impacting their daily life and adult success.

Programs with a long-term vision exist today but are increasingly limited because they require larger expenditures. Generally, they represent local attempts to construct more comprehensive programs. These have been shown to pay for themselves many times over in financial stability for the recipients, and in achievement and adult income of their offspring. One such program, called *Parents as Scholars*, in the state of Maine, supports poor parents to attend college and provides a campus job. Although the program has helped single parents achieve economic security, the state legislature is moving to discontinue the program (Riordan 2014). Many local programs are restricted to the short term, due to lack of a sustained source of revenue.

The availability of government funds for higher education for welfare recipients is desirable since educating young adults increases wages and employment, delays childbearing, and decreases entry into the adult criminal justice system. Demographic shift, in the young adult population, hints at why more aid can ultimately lead to less people needing aid. Twenty-six percent of undergraduates are parents and they are more likely to be attending community colleges. Obtaining a two-year degree is helpful but the long-term benefits associated with a four-year degree are much greater (Freeman 2015). A woman with a college degree will make more money over her lifetime (1 million to 1.5 million more), resulting in significant gains in income taxes, home ownership, and the purchase of consumer goods. These all contribute to securing a better outcome for her children. TANF money for higher education is limited. Aid for full-time college students has been reduced from 649,000 persons, just before the 1996 reform, to 35,000 currently. Writer Larkin Warren (2012), describes her unsuccessful attempt to stay in college as a single parent with basic federal education grants, work study jobs, and section 8 housing. Having worked through her savings, she eventually applied for the AFDC program and finished college. She has had a successful writing career and wonders what would have happened if she had not received welfare to finish her education. This success should be replicated since 80 percent of single headed households are headed by women and 40 percent of these are poor (Freeman 2015). The greater likelihood of poverty among women and their children has been referred to as the *feminization of poverty* (US Census Bureau 2014) and college represents good odds against impoverishment.

Education is not the only area where welfare funds are deficiently geared to where they could be most helpful. Detail regarding the TANF policies and resource allocation provides examples of funds used for purposes other than aiding the needy families. TANF block grants to states permit the states to allocate the monies in any way they see fit to meet the bill's four purposes. Purpose 1 is to "provide assistance to needy families"; Purpose 2 is to end the dependency of needy parents on government benefits; and Purposes 3 and 4 are to prevent and reduce unmarried births and to promote two-parent families. Under Clinton's reform bill, 16.5 billion dollars are distributed to the states. The program amount has not changed over the past 20 years. One quarter of the TANF money is spent on cash assistance and another quarter is committed to work supports such as job training and childcare. Fewer than 23 of 100 poor families receive cash assistance. State policies can vary greatly. Only 9 percent of families in Oklahoma, or one in seven poor families, receive any cash assistance while other states, like CA, NY, and Nevada, use 30 percent of their TANF budgets for cash assistance (Clark 2016).

The remaining 50 percent of TANF allotments are devoted to Purposes 3 and 4 in any way the state mandates. Frequently programs funding promoting marriage before childrearing are free to people with other resources. Oklahoma, for example, funds marital preparatory classes examining the "love style" of engaged and newly married couples. Participation in the program subsidizes fees paid for the marriage license. Participants are middle class. In Michigan, TANF allots money for scholarships to private colleges for families earning up to 250,000 dollars. In Pennsylvania, TANF funds pregnancy crisis centers which counsel against abortion. Indiana funds "Women's Care Centers" which will not provide any information on abortions. These agencies do not answer any questions regarding abortions or provide referrals for such information. In fact, it is against the law for federal money to be implicated in the referral or performance of abortions, although the Centers attract women with brochures broadly establishing they will be with a woman "before, during, and after her decision" (Clark 2016; 2016a).

With cash assistance increasingly stingy, and difficult to obtain, other programs offering support services to low-income families become more crucial. **Food insecurity**, or the lack of a secure food supply, affects 50 million Americans annually, including 17 million children. One in two children will suffer food insecurity at some point before they reach adulthood (Jacobson and Silverbush 2012; Rank 2013). The ***Supplemental Nutrition Assistance Program (SNAP)***, is one of the few programs where aid is available to people with incomes over the poverty level. There is a formula for pro-rating the amount received, based on household income and size. *SNAP* recipients grew from 26.3 to 46 million people between 2007 and 2012. The *SNAP* allotment was reduced, in 2013, and multiple states are re-establishing a work requirement of at least 20 hours to qualify (USDA 2013). *SNAP* allots $1.50 per meal, per person (Cheese 2013). Food aid was insufficient to the need during the recession as can be seen in the utilization of food banks which increased by 73 percent (Abramsky 2013; Jacobson and Silverbush 2012). Food banks fill a nutritional void:

> My name is Kwateca Riviore. I use the food bank when I need it. You know, they give you canned goods, fresh vegetables, fruit. You know, and that stuff is expensive. It makes me sad, because I could easily go to McDonald's and probably get a meal for my kid for five bucks, but is it healthy? What are the effects he's going to have digesting that type of food all the time? So I really need this food bank towards the end of the month when I'm running low. I can come here and then go home and prepare my kids a nice, healthy meal.
>
> I do work, but you know, my utility bill this month is $300. My job, I only get paid $10 an hour. I have a family that consists of six people, so you know, it's hard. A lot of things are expensive. When you come here, you feed your belly. You can feed your brain with books. You know, they have different resources as far as jobs. You know, low-cost, medical. It's a food bank, but you get so much more than just a meal. You get hope.

When I came here, I was stressed out, you know? When I leave here, my problems, they don't disappear, but I feel like I can make it through. You know? So, when I get paid on my next paycheck, I don't have to worry about is me and my kids going to go hungry? You know, am I going to be able to make it? Are they going to have a healthy meal? When I come here, that need is met, so I appreciate it a lot.

(Riviore 2015)

Another program to aid children relies on the federally funded subsidized lunch programs. Speculation that hungry children were avoiding the program, due to a reluctance to be identified as needing a "free lunch," resulted in the elimination of proving "need." All children are currently provided with a free lunch and there are no separate lines or tickets in the cafeteria. Many low-income children also receive breakfast at school and some localities have instituted programs to distribute food during school breaks to sustain adequate nutrition.

Poorer people are also more likely to live in food deserts. **Food deserts** are areas where the accessibility to fresh produce is rare or nonexistent. Inner-city neighborhoods often depend on small, independent markets and convenience stores which carry little, if any, fresh produce. Rural areas also lack fresh produce due to distance and lack of population density. Some government and nonprofit agencies fund programs to enhance access to farmers' market produce. Programs to address food waste also can provide increased resources. Forty percent of US food is thrown out. The average family wastes 1500 dollars' worth of food each year. Twenty-five percent of all the water used in food production is also wasted (Baxter 2016).

Another contributing factor to the failure of program access, even with qualifying eligibility, stems from poor management. One example concerned a NYC program to promote housing stability by providing five years of rent vouchers. The guiding principle was that by guaranteeing five years of subsidies, landlords would be more likely to enroll in the program. But the program failed due to the landlords' reluctance to accept the vouchers as a consequence of an earlier program which had no such guarantee and which left the landlords with nonpaying tenants (Kahn 2015).

Figure 5.9 San Francisco bus stop (2016)
Source: Photography by Rosalind Gottfried

What Are the Consequences of Poverty in Daily Life?

Government poverty aid generally is reserved for crisis intervention and takes a short-term approach. People can, however, require support during transitional periods but programs generally cease as soon a person's income surpasses the cutoff, even by a dollar; some people even have to return aid received before paperwork could be processed. Any small change in circumstances requires paperwork and benefit adjustments. One family describes their experience:

> The dollar pay raise had knocked us off housing benefits; we went from $612 rent to $1,030 rent. Knocked off food stamps, so we didn't get any food assistance. We had no Medicaid, because the dollar pay raise knocked us off that.
>
> (Abramsky 2013)

The government supports many white-collar jobs to provide services to the poor and these workers enjoy a secure income, often with government benefits. The system dissuades aid recipients from making changes which would eliminate benefits and reduce their standard of living. Another problematic aspect of government aid can be seen in lack of agency coordination. The fragmentation of US services to the poor results in more persistent poverty, since those in need are not aware of all the programs and/or are put off by the cumbersome processes of application and usage. Programs such as food stamps, housing, employment aid, and welfare have different regulations and may be applied differentially depending on a person's family status and other factors. In the documentary, *A Place at the Table* (Jacobson and Silverbush 2012), the example of the welfare recipient, Barbie, is presented. A single mother, who finally obtains a job, Barbie believes she will improve her family's quality of life and be a good role model for her children. Her optimism and happiness, however, are short-lived. In her new job, she makes just enough money to be disqualified from receiving food stamps and she is dismayed when, by the month's end, she is shown searching for food in her empty refrigerator.

Lack of support for parents can have sustained impacts on their children. One seemingly minor setback can have a snowball effect. Poverty and violence contribute to lower levels of both physical and mental health. Poor youths are two times as likely as their peers to be diagnosed as depressed and 55 percent of babies raised in poverty have depressed mothers (Kristof 2015). Exposure to parasitic infection, more common in the poor, results in cognitive and mental health challenges, and the poor have little access to services. Stressors of poverty consistently elevate cortisol levels (a stress hormone), which affects behavior and cognitive development (Kristof 2015). Additionally, poverty has biological implications beyond mental health, notably brain alterations with lifelong repercussions (Kristof and WuDunn 2014; Kristof 2015).

Lack of affordable housing is one of the most severe challenges facing low-income households, particularly in major urban areas where the housing supply is scarce and the costs prohibitive for poorer households. What government programs exist often have low inventory, long waiting lists, and policies more beneficial to landlords than to tenants. In his book, *Evicted*, Desmond (2016) explains these elements:

> For many landlords, it was cheaper to deal with the expense of eviction than to maintain their properties; it was possible to skimp on maintenance if tenants were perpetually behind; and many poor tenants would be perpetually behind because their rent was too high.
>
> Money judgements [for damages to properties] accrued interest at an annual rate that would be the envy of any financial portfolio: 12 percent. For the chronically and desperately poor whose credit was already wrecked, a docketed judgment was just another shove deeper into the pit. But for the tenant who went on to land a decent job or marry and then take another tentative step forward, applying for student loans or purchasing a first home—for the tenant, it was a real barrier on the already difficult road to self-reliance and security.
>
> (Desmond 2016)

Housing instability, with its consequent impact on discontinuity in education and contributions to stress, also inhibits the healthy development of children.

Evidence suggests that assuring a family's income does change the way a family lives and plans for the future. In an experiment with the Eastern Band of Cherokees in North Carolina, every family was guaranteed a portion of casino profits. By 2001, five years into the program, payments were $6000 per person annually. Research on the consequence of the payouts found that four years of supplemental income yielded marked improvement among families who no longer qualified as poor. Behavioral problems declined by 40 percent, attaining the same level as seen in kids whose families never had been poor. The research also showed that improvement applied specifically to children designated as poor; children who had not previously qualified as poor showed no changes. The poorest children underwent the most dramatic improvement in well-being. Minor crimes decreased and on-time high school graduation increased. By 2006, the payment had grown to $9000 a year. Sustained research showed that the younger the children were when the payments began, the better the child's mental health in early adulthood. The researchers concluded that beyond access to obvious physical benefits, the money seemed to improve the quality of the parenting (Velasquez-Manoff 2014).

Securing basic necessities is even more difficult for poor young people when they cannot find a job; there is virtually no aid for single nonparents beyond *SNAP*. Public service programs such as *"Americorps"* are great opportunities to gain work experience, while providing community services. Upon completion, *Americorps* "grads" are awarded education grants to pay for tuition or student loans, but too often students with the fewest resources are unable to participate since during the program the "volunteers" are provided a stipend rather than a salary, requiring the recipient to live on a subminimum wage. Poorer students who give a year of service to *Americorps* struggle financially, both during the year and afterward:

I manage, but it's rough, and it would be a lot rougher without that $89 in food – that goes a long way. That's usually my entire food budget for the month. I have a very small savings account, but I couldn't even pay a month's worth of expenses with it. When I finish my service with AmeriCorps, I will go back to my parents' house while I look for a real job, hopefully with more success now that I have this experience under my belt. I'm lucky to have the help that I do from my parents, and without it, I don't know how I'd manage after I finish my service here. And I did what I was "supposed" to do – went to college, did well, looked for the job people assured me I'd be able to find upon finishing. And now, I'm glad to be serving the community and all, but I wish that doing so didn't leave me in such a rough position financially.

(Nolan 2015)

How can poverty be better addressed? A veteran poverty worker, Mauricio Lim Miller, was approached by former mayor Jerry Brown of Oakland CA who, frustrated by the weak efforts of the "war on poverty," asked Miller how to best address poverty. After reviewing his 30 years in social services, Miller asserted that the poor did not need "aid" or services from "professionals," concluding that "a paternalistic conceit has hindered the development of poor families" (Bornstein 2017). He suggested that the optimal approach was to support the community's strengths and ask them what works. Poorer people actually are more likely to value the support of their social network and are more attuned to interpersonal relations (Goleman 2013). His program, *Family Independence Initiative,* offers no services or advice but supports participants' social networks and offers small stipends for tracking and reporting personal behaviors. Program participants, comprised of 2000 families across the country, have made gains in income, education, and mutual

Figure 5.10 City Year participants, an AmeriCorps program
Source: Photography by Rosalind Gottfried

assistance. Their lending circles have circulated about two million dollars in local loans (Bornstein 2017).

Other sources of guidance in curtailing poverty can be gleaned from other developed countries which provide services without the layers of application and programs typifying US programs. They simply provide an income subsidy to attain a minimal standard of living, already advanced by universal, comprehensive healthcare. After accounting for aid adjustments, the US poverty rate is assessed as twice that characteristic of European countries (Rank 2013). Poverty rates have largely been unchanged, more than 50 years after the "war on poverty" (Rank 2013; Lowrey 2014). The lack of guaranteed programs, such as exist in Europe, is tied to the American attitude that poverty results from stereotypic ideas that the poor lack discipline and a strong work ethos (Egan 2013). The negative stereotyping of poor people allows other groups to withhold empathy and aid (Goleman 2013; Kristof 2015).

The recent fiasco with the water supply in Flint Michigan is a good example of negligence and disdain for the well-being of marginalized groups. To save money, the city management substituted the water supply from Lake Huron's Detroit water district with water from the dirty Flint River. This change, initiated in 2014, revealed immediate problems. Immediately, residents of Flint were told to boil water to eliminate e. coli (Hulett 2015) but officials failed to shield the residents from the dangers of lead exposure. Residents had been reporting skin lesions, hair loss, high lead blood levels, vision and memory impairment, depression and anxiety, and brain damage (Ganim and Tran 2016). The effect of the lead poisoning on the children will lead to permanent impairments costing untold amounts of misery and financial burdens. Perhaps the worst aspect of this catastrophe is the fact that it could have

Figure 5.11 Homelessness is a big problem which is difficult to measure. This image shows a homeless woman in NYC Source: chameleonseye/ istockphoto.com

been avoided altogether. Flint's 100,000 largely Black population was disregarded for a year and a half after the evidence of danger already had surfaced (Carmody 2016). In fact, as of February 1, 2016, the population of Flint was still being billed between 120 and 150 dollars for their bad water (Kennedy 2016). The pipes could have been cheaply fixed prior to starting the diversion, but officials declined to implement the alteration (Canepari 2016). The "bad" behavior in this case was not among the poor but among those in power.

To effectively fix poverty, and its accompanying disadvantages, gaps in opportunity structures will have to be addressed, and these are most efficiently met when they are accomplished early in life. Intervention, through home health visits during pregnancy and in the early years, can be a significant determinant of adult success. Early intervention impacts physical development and emotional attachment, leading to gains in educational attainment, decreased delinquency, and reduced adult criminality. Children whose mothers had home health aide visits show fewer cases of abuse and fewer arrests in teen years. Their mothers also experienced fewer subsequent births and less time on welfare. For every dollar invested in early invention, an estimated $5.70 in benefits can be saved (Kristof and WuDunn 2014). In viewing the persistent portion of impoverished Americans, it becomes clear that the will to make programmatic and budgetary changes is necessary to effect real change, but the country has been moving in the opposite direction (Khan 2013; Kristof 2014).

Key Terms

Social Class   Gilbert and Kahl   Erik Olin Wright   Max Weber: Wealth, Prestige, and Power Karl Marx: Bourgeoisie, Proletariat   Social Mobility   Wealth   Poverty   Working Poor Nearly Poor   Hoovervilles   The New Deal   Welfare   AFDC   TANF   Food Insecurity   SNAP Food Desert

Concept Review

How Can the Current Economic Structure of American Society Be Understood?

There are three elements that are key to understanding the economics of today's society. The first is the severe inequality which characterizes the very wealthy, compared to the remaining 99 percent of the population. The gap in income is the largest since the Great Depression. Second, the middle class is constricting, both in terms of the portion who qualify as middle class and with regard to their relative affluence, compared to the middle class of previous eras. Finally, the portion of the nation qualifying as impoverished has not changed much since the "War on Poverty" waged in the 1960s.

How Is Social Class Defined?

There is no specific definition of social class. The definition of middle class typically has a lower limit reflecting about two thirds of the median household income. This figure, generally established as about $36,000–40,000 of annual income, would not support financial security, home buying, savings, vacations, or funding children's higher education—characteristic components of a middle-class lifestyle.

The official government poverty level is also unrealistically low, leaving some people struggling for daily survival and excluding some people from government benefits altogether because they are ostensibly over the poverty limit. The percentage of those considered officially poor remains stable, around 15 percent. Over half of the population will experience poverty at some point in life.

What Is the Structure of Wealth and Poverty in the US?

The US is characterized by greater income inequality than at any other time since 1929. In the period since the 1980s, social mobility has become less likely than at any time since World War II and is less likely than in comparable European countries. Income gains are exclusive to the very top earners in the US, while the middle range is undergoing stagnation and the lower income groups actually are experiencing wage losses. The costs of housing, higher education, and healthcare are contributing to the decreasing standard of living in the struggling middle class. Manufacturing jobs are disappearing, largely through automation and outsourcing, and the remaining opportunities do not pay as well as they did in the several decades following WWII. Banking and tax practices favor the wealthy. The de-regulation of the financial institutions has led to exploitative lending practices and huge financial gains for a small elite segment of investors.

How Is Poverty Experienced?

Poverty is actually a "norm" in society, since so many people will experience it. Poverty results in reduced circumstances in terms of educational attainment, health and well-being, employment status, exposure to toxins, food insecurity, and homelessness. There is virtually no area of life that escapes the consequences of poverty. Women, children, and racial and ethnic minorities are at increased risk of poverty.

How Has the US Addressed the Needs of the Impoverished?

Our safety net, established in the Depression and augmented in the 1960s' "War on Poverty," is not as generous or comprehensive as in other developed countries. The US safety net has saved people from the most dire effects of poverty but it has not offered a path to changing their circumstances. Contrary to stereotypes of the poor, most people who struggle financially possess the same characteristics and goals as those who live more comfortably. The majority of the poor and near poor are working poor.

We have the resources to eradicate poverty though there is little change in its prevalence. President Clinton's welfare reform (1996) significantly reduced the welfare rolls while failing to reduce poverty. Enhanced early childhood interventions have been shown to be effective in producing better outcomes in adulthood, especially with respect to educational attainment, employment, health, and avoiding the criminal justice system. Such programs are rare and limited in scope, largely because of their upfront costs. Policy in the US generally does not consider the long-term impact of failure to fund the widening opportunity gap.

Review Questions

1. Explain the two different periods since WWII with regard to wages, work, and inequality (address all three components).
2. What defines middle class and what changes are currently occurring in the middle class?
3. What is poverty? How is the federal poverty level determined? What portion of the population qualifies as poor?
4. Who are the "near poor"? The "working poor"? What part of the population qualifies in these categories?
5. How would you describe your social class as a child? Currently? In the future?
6. What is TANF and when, and why, was it developed? What other federal programs exist?
7. Do "welfare" programs vary from state to state?
8. How has the tax structure, corporate and personal, changed in recent decades? Be specific.
9. How should the poverty level be determined and what should it be (for a family of four)?
10. Why is home ownership such an important element of middle-class life?
11. How would you identify a person's social class? Do people with similar incomes typically identify as being in the same social class?

References

Abramsky, S. (2013) *The American Way of Poverty*. New York: Nation Books.

Amadeo, K. (May 30, 2018). Trump's Tax Plan and How it Affects You. *The Balance*. Retrieved from https://www.thebalance.com/trump-s-tax-plan-how-it-affects-you-4113968

Baxter, A. (April 20, 2016) *The Economics of Wasting Food*. Retrieved from https://www.marketplace.org/2016/04/19/world/food-waste

BLS. Bureau of Labor Statistics. (January 26, 2017) Union members—2016. Retrieved from https://www.bls.gov/news.release/pdf/union2.pdf

Bornstein, D. (August 15, 2017) When Families Lead Themselves Out of Poverty. *The New York Times*. Retrieved from https://www.nytimes.com/2017/08/15/opinion/poverty-family-independence-initiative.html

Bourdieu, P. (1973) Cultural Reproduction and Social Reproduction. In Richard Brown (ed.) *Knowledge, Education, and Social Change: Papers in the Sociology of Education*. London: Tavistock: 71–112.

Bourdieu, P. (1986) The Forms of Capital. In John G Richardson (ed.) *Handbook of Theory and Research for the Sociology of Education*. New York: Greenwood Press: 241–258.

Canepari, Z. (May/June, 2016) Flint and America's Corroded Trust. *Mother Jones*. Retrieved from http://www.motherjones.com/environment/2016/04/flint-water-lead-crisis-snyder-mad-max/

Carmody, S. (December 14, 2016) A Year Later Unfiltered Tap Water Still Unsafe to Drink. *Morning Edition*. NPR. Retrieved from http://www.npr.

org/2016/12/14/505478931/a-year-later-unfiltered-flint-tap-water-is-still-unsafe-to-drink

Cheese, J. (June 6, 2013) The 4 Types of People on Welfare Nobody Talks About. *Cracked*. Retrieved from http://www.cracked.com/blog/the-4-types-people-welfare-nobody-talks-about/

Clark, K. (2016) You'd Be Surprised by How "Welfare" Money Is Spent in Some States. *Slate Magazine*. Retrieved from http://www.slate.com/articles/news_and_politics/moneybox/2016/06/_welfare_money_often_isn_t_spent_on_welfare.html

Clark, K. (June 2, 2016a) "Oh My God—We're on Welfare?!" *Slate* and *Marketplace*. Retrieved from http://www.slate.com/articles/news_and_politics/moneybox/2016/06/_welfare_money_often_isn_t_spent_on_welfare.html

Clark, K., Esch, C. (June 23, 2016) S01-5: Pregnant? We Can Help. Retrieved from http://www.marketplace.org/2016/06/22/wealth-poverty/uncertain-hour/s01-5-pregnant-we-can-help

Cobb, J. and Sennett, R. (1972) *The Hidden Injuries of Class*. New York: W.W. Norton and Company 1993.

Cohen, P. (August 17, 2015) Racial Wealth Gap Persists Despite Degree, Study Says. *The New York Times*. Retrieved from https://www.nytimes.com/2015/08/17/business/racial-wealth-gap-persists-despite-degree-study-says.html

Desilver, D. (October 9, 2014) For Most Workers, Real Wages Have Barely Budged for Decades. Pew Research Center. Retrieved from http://www.pewresearch.org/fact-tank/2014/10/09/for-most-workers-real-wages-have-barely-budged-for-decades/

Desmond, M. (2016) *Evicted: Poverty and Profit in the American City*. New York: Crown Publishing Group.

Domhoff, W.G. (2013) Wealth, Income, and Power. *Who Rules America?* Retrieved from http://www2.ucsc.edu/whorulesamerica/power/wealth.html

Drabold, W. (July 25, 2016) Read Elizabeth Warren's Anti-Trump Speech at the Democratic Convention. *Time.com*. Retrieved from http://time.com/4421731/democratic-convention-elizabeth-warren-transcript-speech/

Dube, A. (November 30, 2013) The Minimum We Can Do. *The New York Times*. Retrieved from https://opinionator.blogs.nytimes.com/2013/11/30/the-minimum-we-can-do/

Edelman, P. (July 29, 2012) Poverty in America: Why Can't We End it? *The New York Times*. Retrieved from http://www.nytimes.com/2012/07/29/opinion/sunday/why-cant-we-end-poverty-in-america.html

Edsall, T. (September 17, 2013) Making Money Off the Poor. *The New York Times*. Retrieved from https://opinionator.blogs.nytimes.com/2013/09/17/making-money-off-the-poor/

Edsall, T. (April 27, 2016) How the Other Fifth Lives. *Nytimes.com*. Retrieved from http://www.nytimes.com/2016/04/27/opinion/campaign-stops/how-the-other-fifth-lives.html?action=click&pgtype=Homepage&clickSource=story-heading&module=opinion-c-col-left-region&region=opinion-c-col-left-region&WT.nav=opinion-c-col-left-region&_r=0

Egan, T. (December 20, 2013) Good Poor, Bad Poor. *The New York Times*. Retrieved from http://www.nytimes.com/2013/12/20/opinion/egan-good-poor-bad-poor.html?rref=collection%2Fcolumn%2Ftimothy-egan

Elkins, K. (March 13, 2017) Here's How Much You Have to Earn to be Considered Middle Class. *CNBC*. Retrieved from http://www.cnbc.com/2017/03/13/heres-how-much-you-have-to-earn-to-be-considered-middle-class.html

Federal Poverty Level (FPL). (n.d.) HealthCare.gov. Retrieved from https://www.healthcare.gov/glossary/federal-poverty-level-FPL/

Federal Reserve. (May, 2015) *Report on the Economic Well-being of U.S. Household in 2014*. [PDF File]. Retrieved from https://www.federalreserve.gov/econresdata/2014-report-economic-well-being-us-households-201505.pdf

Fox, G. (February 17, 2017) 10+ Independent Online News Sources and Why America Needs More of Them. Retrieved from https://soapboxie.com/social-issues/A-Real-Need-for-the-Real-News

Freeman, A. (August 18, 2015) Single Moms and Welfare Woes: A Higher-Education Dilemma. *The Atlantic*. Retrieved from https://www.theatlantic.com/education/archive/2015/08/why-single-moms-struggle-with-college/401582/

Gabler, N. (May, 2016) The Secret Shame of Middle-Class Americans Living Paycheck to Paycheck. *The Atlantic*. Retrieved from http://www.theatlantic.com/magazine/archive/2016/05/my-secret-shame/476415/

Ganim, S., Tran, L. (January 11, 2016) How Tap Water Became Toxic in Flint, Michigan. *CNN*. Retrieved from http://www.cnn.com/2016/01/11/health/toxic-tap-water-flint-michigan/index.html

Gilbert, D.L. (2015) *The American Class Structure in an Age of Growing Inequality*, 9th edn. Thousand Oaks, CA: Sage Publications, Inc.

Goleman, D. (October 5, 2013) Rich People Just Care Less. *The New York Times*. Retrieved from https://opinionator.blogs.nytimes.com/2013/10/05/rich-people-just-care-less/

Goodman, M.L. (May 27, 2015) Millennial College Graduates: Young, Educated, Jobless. *Newsweek*. Retrieved from http://www.newsweek.com/2015/06/05/millennial-college-graduates-young-educated-jobless-335821.html

Harrington, M. (1962) *The Other America*. New York: Touchstone.

Hays, S. (2003) *Flat Broke with Children: Women in the Age of Welfare Reform*. New York: Oxford University Press.

Hulett, S. (September 29, 2015) High Lead Levels in Michigan Kids After City Changes Water Source. *All Things Considered*. NPR. Retrieved from http://www.npr.org/2015/09/29/444497051/high-lead-levels-in-michigan-kids-after-city-switches-water-source

Jacobson, K., Silverbush, L. (2012) *A Place at the Table*. Video.

Kahn, C. (host). (December 27, 2013) New York City's Homeless Are Finding Voucher Program Void. *WFAE. NPR*. http://wfae.org/post/new-york-citys-homeless-are-finding-voucher-program-void

Kennedy, M. (April 20, 2016) Lead-laced Water in Flint: A Step-by-step Look at the Makings of a Crisis. *NPR*. Retrieved from https://www.npr.org/sections/thetwo-way/2016/04/20/465545378/lead-laced-water-in-flint-a-step-by-step-look-at-the-makings-of-a-crisis

Khan, S. (December 14, 2013) We Are Not All in this Together. *The New York Times*. Retrieved from https://opinionator.blogs.nytimes.com/2013/12/14/we-are-not-all-in-this-together/

Kiel, P. (January 3, 2016) Debt and the Racial Wealth Gap. *The New York Times*. Retrieved from https://www.nytimes.com/2016/01/03/opinion/debt-and-the-racial-wealth-gap.html

Kornbluth, J. (dir.) (2013) *Inequality for All*. Distributed by RADiUS-TWC.

Kraus, M., Davidai, S., Nussbaum, A.D. (May 1, 2015) American Dream? Or Mirage? *The New York Times*. Retrieved from https://www.nytimes.com/2015/05/03/opinion/sunday/american-dream-or-mirage.html

Kristof, N. (February 22, 2014) When Even the Starting Line Is Out of Reach. *The New York Times*. Retrieved from https://www.nytimes.com/2014/02/23/opinion/sunday/kristof-when-even-the-starting-line-is-out-of-reach.html

Kristof, N. (June 14, 2015) It's Not Just About Bad Choices. *The New York Times*. Retrieved from https://www.nytimes.com/2015/06/14/opinion/sunday/nicholas-kristof-its-not-just-about-bad-choices.html?rref=collection%2Fcolumn%2Fnicholas-kristof

Kristof, N., WuDunn, S. (September 14, 2014) The Way to Beat Poverty. *The New York Times*. Retrieved from https://www.nytimes.com/2014/09/14/opinion/sunday/nicholas-kristof-the-way-to-beat-poverty.html

Krogstad, J.M. (May 5, 2014) More Women than Men Earn the Federal Minimum Wage. Pew Research Center. Retrieved from http://www.pewresearch.org/fact-tank/2014/05/05/more-women-than-men-earn-the-federal-minimum-wage/

Krugman, P. (December 15, 2013) Why Inequality Matters. *The New York Times*. Retrieved from http://www.nytimes.com/2013/12/16/opinion/krugman-why-inequality-matters.html

Krugman, P. (May 29, 2015) The Insecure American. *The New York Times*. Retrieved from https://www.nytimes.com/2015/05/29/opinion/paul-krugman-the-insecure-american.html

Leonhardt, D. (August 7, 2017) Our Broken Economy, in One Simple Chart. *The New York Times*. Retrieved from https://www.nytimes.com/interactive/2017/08/07/opinion/leonhardt-income-inequality.html

Leonhardt, D. (October 12, 2017a) We're About to Fall Behind the Great Depression. *The New York Times*. Retrieved from https://www.nytimes.com/2017/10/12/opinion/great-depression-recession.html

Livingston, G. (September 26, 2016) Among 41 Nations, U.S. Is the Outlier When it Comes to Paid Parental Leave. Pew Research Center. Retrieved from http://www.pewresearch.org/fact-tank/2016/09/26/u-s-lacks-mandated-paid-parental-leave/

Lowrey, A. (January 4, 2014) 50 Years Later, War on Poverty Is a Mixed Bag. *The New York Times*. Retrieved from https://www.nytimes.com/2014/01/05/business/50-years-later-war-on-poverty-is-a-mixed-bag.html?_r=0

Lubrano, A. (2004) *Limbo: Blue-Collar Roots, White-Collar Dreams*. NJ: John Wiley & Sons.

Lutz, A. (June 14, 2012) These 6 Corporations Control 90% Of the Media in America. *Business Insider*. Retrieved from http://www.businessinsider.com/these-6-corporations-control-90-of-the-media-in-america-2012-6

Martin, R. (host). (April 10, 2016) Hanging On: A Pressured Middle Class in Economic Recovery. *NPR.org*. Retrieved from http://www.npr.org/2016/04/10/473702974/hanging-on-a-pressured-middle-class-in-economic-recovery

Matthews, D. (January 8, 2014) Everything You Need to Know About the War on Poverty. *The Washington Post*. Retrieved from https://www.washingtonpost.com/news/wonk/wp/2014/01/08/everything-you-need-to-know-about-the-war-on-poverty/

Nolan, H. (April 21, 2015) True Stories of Life on the Dole: Poverty from State to State. *Gawker*. Retrieved from http://gawker.com/true-stories-of-life-on-the-dole-poverty-from-state-to-1698532894

Pew Research Center. (February 11, 2014) *The Rising Cost of Not Going to College*. Retrieved from http://www.pewsocialtrends.org/2014/02/11/the-rising-cost-of-not-going-to-college/

Proctor, D.B, Semega, L.J., Kollar, A.M. (September, 2016) *Income and Poverty in the United States*. [PDF File]. Retrieved from https://www.census.gov/content/dam/Census/library/publications/2016/demo/p60-256.pdf

Rank, M. (November 2, 2013) Poverty in American Is Mainstream. *The New York Times*. Retrieved from https://opinionator.blogs.nytimes.com/2013/11/02/poverty-in-america-is-mainstream/

Reich, R. (2015) *Saving Capitalism: For the Many, Not the Few*. New York: Penguin Random House LLC.

Riordan, R. (November 20, 2014) I Got Help and a College Degree with State Support. Now, I'm Off the Welfare Rolls. *The Bangor Daily News*. Retrieved from http://bangordailynews.com/2014/11/20/opinion/contributors/i-got-help-and-a-college-degree-with-state-support-now-im-off-the-welfare-rolls/

Riviore, K. (2015) Hiddenhungerstorybooth. *Capital Public Radio*. Retrieved from http://www.hiddenhungerstorybooth.com/kwateca

Scheiber, N. (July 27, 2015) Raising Floor for Minimum Wage Pushes Economy into the Unknown. *The New York Times*. Retrieved from http://www.nytimes.com/2015/07/27/business/economy/scale-of-minimum-wagerise-has-experts-guessing-at-effect.html.

Stiglitz, J. (February 16, 2013) Equal Opportunity, Our National Myth. *The New York Times*. Retrieved from https://opinionator.blogs.nytimes.com/2013/02/16/equal-opportunity-our-national-myth/

Stiglitz, J. (January 19, 2013a) Inequality Is Holding Back the Recovery. *The New York Times*. Retrieved from https://opinionator.blogs.nytimes.com/2013/01/19/inequality-is-holding-back-the-recovery/

Stiglitz, J. (December 21, 2013b) In No One We Trust. *The New York Times*. Retrieved from https://opinionator.blogs.nytimes.com/2013/12/21/in-no-one-we-trust/

Thompson, D. (May 10, 2012) Unpaid Internships: Bad for Students, Bad for Workers, Bad for Society. *The Atlantic*. Retrieved 11 April 2017, from https://www.theatlantic.com/business/archive/2012/05/unpaid-internships-bad-for-students-bad-for-workers-bad-for-society/256958/

Thompson, G. (November 28, 2012) How Students in San Jose Raised the Minimum Wage. *The Nation*. Retrieved from https://www.thenation.com/article/how-students-san-jose-raised-minimum-wage/

UNICEF (2013) Child Well-being in Rich Countries: A Comparative Overview.

USDA. (2013) *SNAP Food Security In-depth Interview Study*. Retrieved from https://www.fns.usda.gov/sites/default/files/SNAPFoodSec.pdf

US Census Bureau. (2014) *Income and Poverty in the U.S.: 2013*. Retrieved from http://www.census.gov/content/dam/Census/library/publications/2014/demo/p60-249.pdf.

US Dept of Labor (n.d.) Women's Bureau. Issue Brief. Women's Earnings and the Wage Gap. Retrieved from https://www.dol.gov/wb/resources/Womens_Earnings_and_the_Wage_Gap_17.pdf

Velasquez-Manoff, M. (January 18, 2014) What Happens When the Poor Receive a Stipend? *The New York Times*. Retrieved from https://opinionator.blogs.nytimes.com/2014/01/18/what-happens-when-the-poor-receive-a-stipend/?_r=0

Warren, E. (July 25, 2016) Democratic Convention Speech. *Time.com*. Retrieved from http://time.com/4421731/democratic-convention-elizabeth-warren-transcript-speech/

Warren, L. (September 23, 2012) I Was a Welfare Mother. *The New York Times*. Retrieved from http://www.nytimes.com/2012/09/23/opinion/sunday/taking-responsibility-on-welfare.html

Who Are the Working Poor in America? (n.d.). Retrieved from http://poverty.ucdavis.edu/faq/who-are-working-poor-america

Wright, E.O. (1979) *Class Structure and Income Determination*. New York: Academic Press.

CHAPTER 6

Deviance, Substance Abuse, and Incarceration

WHAT YOU WILL READ ABOUT IN THIS CHAPTER:

- No act is inherently deviant, as the concept is formed by cultural context. The nature of **deviance** is complicated by issues of who is committing the behavior, who is observing it, and who has the power to respond to it. Most sociologists are interested in researching the causes and effects of deviance. Labeling theory suggests that the social label of deviance can explain why some people develop persistent deviant behaviors. Other major sociological theories illuminate various aspects of deviance, such as why some people are more at risk for deviant behavior; why some people are more likely to commit crimes; and how the very designation of "crime" is not a value-neutral concept. Some sociologists turn the question around, asking why so many people conform, generally arguing that they do so because it is too socially costly not to.

- **Substance abuse** is prevalent in the US and refers to all substances, legal and illegal, from cigarettes to alcohol to prescription drugs to illegal drugs. Abuse involving legal substances is more prevalent that the use of illegal ones, though the term is more frequently associated with illegal substances. Some states have legalized marijuana and many states are considering legalization or de-criminalization. The potential physical harm of a substance is unrelated to the legal status of the substance. Alcohol is the most commonly used substance. Opioid use has been on the rise, often initiated by the use of prescription painkillers.

- Crimes are typically viewed in terms of "**street crimes**," and property crimes though **"white-collar" crimes** actually impact more people and cost society more money. Typically, white-collar criminals are less likely to be charged, convicted, and incarcerated.

- The **criminal justice system** refers to all law enforcement agencies, courts, and correctional agencies. The US has the highest rate of incarceration of ANY country in the world. The prison population is disproportionately people of color, though there is no evidence that their crime rate is higher than the White rate. The system is biased in multiple ways and there is a reform movement to reduce the classification of some offenses from felonies to misdemeanors and to reduce prison time.

- The **prison system** primarily serves a custodial purpose as there has been a movement away from **rehabilitation**. Currently, there is renewed attention to creating accessible substance abuse programs, as well as education and job training opportunities. A status of *convict* can lock a person into a life without hope, resulting in chronic unemployment and disenfranchisement. Some states are repealing laws which permanently bar ex-felons from voting.

- The *Black Lives Matter* movement has brought national attention to the issues of racial profiling and the need to examine the racial trends with regard to traffic stops, searches, aggressive physical restraint, and deadly force by law enforcement. The trends of mass incarceration have decimated the African American community, enhancing the likelihood of absent and unemployable men. Incarceration of women has contributed to an increased number of children being raised without any parent in the home resulting in the placement of children in non-family environments.

Introduction

Open any sociology textbook to the chapter on deviance and the typical definition will read that *deviance* is when a person, by virtue of attitudes, beliefs, or behaviors, violates basic norms in the society. But this begs the question, whose norms are the reference point and do all people suffer similar scrutiny? Sociologists have developed many theories to explain deviance. Perhaps they identify with the "deviant" label since the *norm* for college professors tends to be liberal and sociologists are more likely to be liberal than professors in other fields, indicating they are at the high end of "normal," and not representative of the general population (Klein 2015). One potential sociology graduate student at an elite East Coast university chose another field of study fearing a "deviant" label due to her previous job at a conservative research institution (Goodnow 2017). This "deviant" student situation demonstrates the problem with defining deviance since the behavioral point of reference is always contextual. In a graduate sociology program, a person of conservative political or personal values most likely would be considered "deviant" as a consequence of contradicting the prevailing ethos. In another context, perhaps among a conference for the *Young Republicans National Federation*, this student would represent the norm.

What Is Deviance?

Anything can be potentially deviant depending on who is doing it, who is observing it, and who has the power to respond to it. When this author was working at a large urban detention center as a psych counselor, she was called to see a man being booked into the jail on minor misdemeanor charges. What were his crimes? He was hugging a tree, with his pants down but retaining his underwear. Is that a crime? He was not indecently exposed. Why was he booked into the jail? This man had the misfortune of having been caught hugging someone else's tree in a middle-class neighborhood. He was booked on charges of *criminal trespassing* and *public nuisance*. Do you think he would have been arrested had he been "communing with nature" on his own property? How about if he had been in a park in an inner-city neighborhood? On a public golf course?

> ### Box 6.1 – Deviance
>
> *Deviance* is commonly defined as the violation of social norms in attitudes, beliefs, or values. This view presumes a uniformity of norms and ignores the power differences in both the actor and observer. Deviance is *socially constructed*; no behavior is inherently or universally undesirable. Conceptions of deviant behavior vary not only between groups in a society but over time. Both legal and illegal acts can constitute a deviant behavior.
>
> *Crime* refers to acts which break *laws*, which are codified norms given legitimation by government statute. Most illegal acts are considered deviant,

but not universally. The consumption of marijuana is an example of a behavior that is illegal in most states, but not considered negatively by some portions of the population.

Another murky example occurred when a full-term pregnant woman was refused an alcoholic drink, with dinner, and harassed by the serving staff who provided her a label regarding the potential harm of alcohol on fetal development. The woman had not consumed alcohol earlier in her pregnancy, but she was past her due date and wanted a drink with her meal. There is no evidence that a small amount of alcohol is harmful at the end of pregnancy though it is potentially harmful to fetal development, particularly in the first trimester. The customer complained to the management and the two servers were fired. Who was deviant, the pregnant diner or the staff (London 1991)? Since this case, which received national media attention, more attention has been given to policies regarding whether an establishment can deny a pregnant woman entry and/or service. Policies and laws vary by locality but all outlets serving alcohol must post warnings regarding the potentially harmful effects of alcohol consumption during pregnancy. Laws are persistently challenged, and controversy persists. A 2016 ruling in New York City mandates that it is illegal to deny a woman a drink simply because she is pregnant (Peltz 2016).

What Are the Major Perspectives in the Study of Deviance?

There are many legal behaviors which commonly occur but are considered deviant by many people. A sample list would include bullying, atheism, religions which are

Figure 6.1 Who defines deviance and are the standards equally applied to all populations? Source: Ljupco Smokovski / Shutterstock.com

not monotheistic, single parenting, choosing to be child-free, cigarette smoking, vegan diets, rudeness, using the cell phone while on a date, and hitting a child. Virtually no behavior is inherently deviant. Anyone of the behaviors just listed could be viewed as deviant, or not, depending on the social group and context. Changing attitudes towards cigarette smoking provides a good example of rapid change towards a behavior. In a relatively brief period, it went from being seen as acceptable to being scorned, and subsequently prohibited by law in public places. In the decades of the 1940s–1970s people openly smoked in movie theaters, airplanes, and even grocery stores. Societal behaviors around smoking were much more permissive than today, and laws much less likely to be enforced. Children often were dispensed to purchase cigarettes for their parents, despite laws making it unlawful to sell cigarettes to minors. A reverse process is provided by tattoos, which went from being informally restricted to specific populations, such as prisoners or navy personnel, to being largely acceptable in the general adult population. It is fairly common for younger adults, and women, to have tattoos. Many people see tattoos as desirable, particularly if done in "good taste," which is a concept also dependent on group definitions.

When a behavior breaks the law, rather than just a norm, the deviance is designated as a *crime*. The consequences of law breaking will vary depending on the circumstances. Emile Durkheim suggested that deviance and crime are "normal" societal traits which help to define the limits of acceptable behavior. The desire to feel integrated with the community is seen as sufficient motivation for conformity, allowing for the smooth running of society. The concept of *social control* stems from this perspective, alluding to all the mechanisms which act upon a person to avoid deviance and crime. *Internal* social control forces include individual conscience, desire for social acceptance, pleasing others, and the development of self-esteem. *External* social control mechanisms are socially imposed by carrying direct consequences. Examples include receiving a failing grade for poor school work; expulsion from school for cheating or plagiarism; or arrest for breaking the law.

Most of us break rules, and even laws, but the majority of the time we do not get caught or see ourselves as "bad," preferring to justify our behaviors in ways which are "acceptable": "Yes officer, I was speeding but I was late for work …" or "Yes, I did 'borrow' some of my paper from my friend but my child was sick and I had no daycare." Defining these situations as temporary, or circumstantial, allows a person to maintain a positive sense of self. People can resist feelings of deviance, usually until they are seen as deviant or criminal by others.

One of the most utilized sociological theories is *labeling theory*, which emphasizes the power of societal responses to place a label on someone and to modify the view of that person in terms of the label. Many of us have committed a deviant, or illegal, act and yet do not see ourselves as deviant or criminal. Committing an initial act of deviance is called *primary deviance*. Being labeled increases the likelihood that a person will repeat the behavior, referred to as *secondary deviance*. As a result of the label, and the subsequent expectations which accompany it, the person will identify with the label and incorporate it in their self-concept. In a classic study illustrating the power of labels, Rosenhan (1973) had graduate students present themselves at mental hospitals as suffering symptoms of schizophrenia. Eight students, with a total of twelve hospital admissions, were admitted every time they approached a facility. Once admitted, the students behaved "normally," interacting as they would in any other situation. In no case did any therapist or staff member identify these students as "fakes"; the only people to do so were other patients.

Rosenhan suggests this study demonstrates the power of labels in several ways. Once a student "patient" was labeled as "ill," all daily behaviors were interpreted as expressions of the diagnosed illness, even if the actual behavior was neutral. The pseudopatients were discharged only when believed to be "in remission." Rosenhan concludes that the lack of accurate assessment was a result of the investment the staff had in their medical expertise. The "real" patients, who lived with the pseudopatients, and observed them with less bias, were more likely to accurately assess their behaviors, accusing them of not being "crazy" at all. Rosenhan did not see any significant differences between private and public hospitals, which was another area of research interest. In a later variation of the study, Rosenhan contacted mental institutions telling them that he would be sending pseudopatients. He wanted to see if this error worked in reverse. It did! Staff reported having received one of these "fakes," though Rosenhan never actually sent them any.

Some people may actively resist the acceptance of a label, sometimes redefining a behavior as not deviant. This has been called *tertiary deviance* (Kitsuse 1980). Mental illness, some disability justice proponents suggest, is a means of establishing social control over people whose behaviors are uncomfortable to others. They see no positive outcome for labeling people as "ill." Critics of the diagnosing of mental illnesses suggest the concept of "pathology" allows the medical establishment to marginalize certain people by defining their behaviors as requiring a "fix." However, on an institutional level, a label can sometimes provide services a person would otherwise be denied, such as special education resources or social security disability eligibility. Labels can be either helpful or hurtful and so sociologists suggest assessing their impact on the individual and society before invoking them.

"Cool" or "Autistic"? A Different Kind of Cool

You give a label to someone so you can treat them differently and that label will be with that person forever. We like labels because it is easier for us to compartmentalize. When we have a label, we don't have to think about it, we can apply the stereotype to them.

(Gallagher 2010)

Actor, writer, comedian Jack Gallagher created a play, *A Different Kind of Cool*, about his delightful son Liam. Gallagher defines *cool* as the confidence of uniqueness, free of guile and born out of a commitment not to be concerned with the appraisal of others. Liam was *cool*, in Gallagher's schema, maybe different than other people's *cools*, but still very *cool*. Liam's charming personality showed rare intelligence and an unusually high ability to focus. Liam also showed quirky behaviors such as an intolerance of loud noises, difficulty making friends, and a fondness for jumping up and down. Initially, Gallagher just defined these as part of Liam's uniqueness but they ultimately led to a diagnosis of *autism*, a label laden with the stigma of pathology. Gallagher, and his wife, initially resisted testing the child in favor of just letting him be who he was. But by second grade, Liam's teacher was unwilling to maintain him in class without an aide and, in order to acquire an aide, the school district required a qualifying diagnosis. The psychologist pronounced the child "charming, interesting, and very healthy" and also exhibiting "behavioral characteristics consistent with the diagnosis of autism." Consequently, the school district was required to provide supportive services and Liam was able to stay in his classroom. The parents remained ambivalent regarding the diagnosis.

'"Saying it out loud is like someone kicked you in the stomach because it is terrible to think there is something wrong with your kid" (Gallagher 2010).

Gallagher describes the anguish regarding the pigeonholing of his child even as he recognized the institutional policies which made it necessary. He admits to feelings of parental guilt, reflecting cultural norms to blame "bad" behaviors on parents. He wonders if he did something wrong, or neglected to do something right, thereby contributing to his son's status. He speaks of feeling helpless and that he failed his child by having his "cool" redefined as "illness" or deviance. He fears that the wonderfully unique person of Liam will be dismissed by his being assigned the *autistic* label.

Gallagher initially tried to "fix" his child so as to save him from the fate of the label. He decided, in the end, that the hard push to "normalize" Liam was more for himself than for the benefit of his son. He regrets that he allowed social pressures to push him to mold Liam into the "perfect" son, since it masked the reality that Liam was perfect as he was. He recognized that even with the label of "autism," his son had not changed. He had his "cool" son, albeit maybe a "different kind of cool." Gallagher embraced his love and relationship with Liam, as with his older son, Declan. Gallagher's play reminds us that a person is the same individual, with or without a label, and that the job of a parent is to facilitate the development of the child, however that plays out.

The power of labeling can be implemented to promote positive behavioral change. In their classic study *Pygmalion in the Classroom*, Rosenthal and Jacobson (1968) told teachers that certain students were predicted, based on testing from the previous year, to have a learning growth spurt. In fact, there were no such test results but the researchers found that all the selected students accomplished significant academic growth during the year. They interpreted this as a consequence of greater attention and higher expectations placed on these children. The students had no knowledge of the experiment; they simply responded to the dynamics in their classroom. The study suggests how labeling, formally or informally, can induce positive behavioral changes. It shows how positive reinforcement, such as praise, can be more forceful than negative reinforcement, as in criticism or loss of privileges.

Another labeling study illustrates how informal labeling can result in stigmatizing a whole group, while elevating one that exhibits the same behaviors. Chambliss (1973) followed two groups of high school youths, one informally labeled the "*Saints*" and the other the "*Roughnecks*." These two groups of boys held very different reputations in their high school. The "Saints" were the "good" boys; they were athletes, student leaders, and did well in school. The "Roughnecks" had a reputation for fighting, hostility, receiving poor grades, and getting into trouble. Chambliss discovered that the groups' delinquent activities outside school were not significantly different but that the *Roughnecks* were more likely to be caught and sanctioned. None of the *Saints* were ever arrested though the *Roughnecks* frequently were in trouble with the law. The *Roughnecks* were hostile and challenging when interacting with authority figures. The *Saints* were polite and played a deferential role when dealing with the system. When the Saints were apprehended by the police, for example, they voiced regret, promising to do better, and their parents backed them up. These responses reflect interactions characteristically witnessed by each group's members as a result of their neighborhood environment. Each group's members emulated behaviors familiar to them, and therefore "earned" their labels. The labeling of the boys also led to their behaviors being assessed differentially. The *Saints* missed more school than the *Roughnecks* because they were less likely to be held accountable for truancy. They would get each other "legitimately" excused from class by forging notes for each other. Bad behaviors in the *Saints* tended to be excused by circumstances while the same behaviors in the *Roughnecks* were attributed to character flaws or low aptitudes.

The only demographic difference between these groups was social class. The *Saints* were from middle-class families where *social and cultural capital* permitted them to manipulate the perceptions people held towards them in ways unavailable to the *Roughnecks*. The *Saints* had learned positive means of manipulating people and situations by adopting the manner of their parents when dealing with institutional authority. They understood how to work the system rather than be worked by the system, as was more characteristic of the upbringing of the *Roughnecks*. The unofficial labels associated with each group of boys reflected these differences. The biggest handicap experienced by the *Roughnecks* was associational.

No theory of deviance can explain the causes and consequences of all deviance. *Labeling theory* is particularly good at explaining why some people are likely to repeat deviance and incorporate it into their self-concept. Most of us have witnessed this theory as applied to daily life. Imagine a child who misbehaves in class and so, whenever anything "bad" occurs, is immediately blamed, even when innocent. Consequently, the child feels little motivation to behave and so embraces the behaviors attributed to her. This is the aspect of labeling theory that leads to a *"self-fulfilling prophecy,"* referring to the tendency of a person to play to the audience's expectations, eventually succumbing to the persona suggested by the label. Labeling illuminates how a deviant "career" develops, though it fails to explain the cause of the initial acts of deviance (Becker 1963).

Labeling theory is a symbolic interactionist theory since it focuses on the interpretation of social roles and expectations. *Differential association theory* is another symbolic interactionist explanation of deviance. This theory states that a person is more likely to imitate behaviors if they are occurring in significant people in the environment. Consider, for example, that the best predictor of cigarette smoking, and substance abuse, is the presence of the behavior in a family member.

An Example of Differential Association Theory

I witnessed a sad example of *differential association theory* while working in a large urban detention center. I was called to see a young man whose fingers were immobilized in a strange muscular contraction, and whose jaw was locked out of joint so he could not speak well. First, we dealt with this physical ailment, which actually was "psycho-generative," meaning there was no organic cause for the physical symptoms. The physical ailments were a consequence of a visit from his mother and sister and his feelings of shame at being in jail on felony charges. This young man, just turned 22, was a very personable, polite, and pleasant individual; he had held the same job for four years and his employers were willing to write a letter in support of his character and to employ him again. As I spoke with this man, I discovered that all of his male relatives—father, grandfather, uncles, cousins—were heroin addicts and that his own crimes resulted from the need to get money to buy drugs, a habit he had begun about nine months prior to his arrest. What was of special interest was that he had not tried the drugs until he was 21. He also declared his intention to never use drugs again, since he did not like where it landed him. Given his family history, it was surprising that he had stayed relatively clean for so many years. This illustrates *differential association theory* in that his consistent exposure to the behaviors of drug users can predictably be expected to promote imitation. In this case, the young man's personal characteristics led him to ultimately reject the perpetuation of the behaviors.

(*My Sociology*, Author)

Differential association theory (Sutherland 1939) explains persistent deviance but it also offers some rationale for why some people are more likely to initiate "deviant" behaviors; in the example above, the young man's "deviance" occurred when he was "clean." This theory addresses issues of the environment and of learning. We tend to think of many deviant behaviors, such as drugs, alcohol, criminality, as "inherited," and they can be, but less by genetics than through social learning. We should also remember that "good" habits, such as the importance of reading, studying, and voting also are "inherited" by absorbing environmental habits. Children often mimic behaviors, even before they actually understand them. When behaviors pervade a person's milieu, the likelihood of imitation increases. The sociologist Akers (1998) combines the idea of differential association with learning theory, highlighting how the behaviors of significant people often are imitated by their followers and reinforced by the role model. The imitation initiates the behaviors and the reinforcement sustains it, illustrating a combination of social and psychological elements. All behaviors, those considered acceptable as well as those thought to be deviant, are typically learned in the same manner.

Structural strain theory is an approach to deviance that explains deviance as stemming from the principle that opportunity structures in society are not universally available. The theory, developed by the American sociologist Robert Merton (1968), suggests that though most people in society hold the same life goals, some people have more access to legitimate ways of achieving them. If a person wants financial success, and has the means, she or he will attend college and professional school. In Merton's schema, these people are *conformists*, possessing both the societal goals and the means to achieve them. Some people feel they have no access to achieving success through conventional means and seek alternative routes. A person who attends a poorly functioning school perceives little chance of "making it" professionally. An example of this can be seen in Sudhir Venkatesh's study (2008) of public housing gangs in Chicago. In over seven years of field research, Venkatesh was closely involved in working with J.T., the leader of a gang in the *Robert Taylor* public housing projects (now closed). Venkatesh remarks that J.T. had a college degree but felt, as a young African American man in the 1980s, that he would not get far in corporate America. Back in the projects he knew, J.T. perceived the chance to be a leader and entrepreneur. This example typifies the thinking of the *innovator* in Merton's schema; a person with conventional goals but who utilizes unconventional means of obtaining them. The *innovator* schema explains why some people "choose" to be deviant.

Box 6.2 – Sociological Theories of Deviance

Sociologists differentiate **primary deviance**, referring to initial rule breaking. **Secondary deviance** refers to repetitive deviance, often resulting in the labeling of the actor. **Tertiary deviance** refers to the tendency of some people to resist a deviant identity by redefining the behavior as nondeviant or by resisting the label.

Labeling theory is a symbolic, interaction-based theory which is best at explaining **secondary deviance**. This theory focuses on social dynamics which result in an official or informal label influencing the perceptions of the individual. The person is seen through the lens of the label and may respond by living up to the label. This reciprocity creates persistent deviant behavior.

A **self-fulfilling prophecy** refers to the tendency of a person, once labeled, to behave in accordance to the label. This is part of the process of building a deviant identity.

Differential association theory suggests that when the significant people in an individual's environment are doing something the behavior is likely to be adopted. Witnessing particular behaviors is a stronger influence than verbal instruction. A child whose parents use alcohol, cigarettes, or drugs is more likely to exhibit these behaviors even if the parents tell them not to.

Structural strain theory looks at the desirable goals of society and suggests that deviance can occur when there is tension between desired goals and a person's means to accomplish them. If a person does not perceive a legitimate opportunity to accomplish acceptable goals, another route which may lead to "deviant" behaviors can be substituted in a process of *innovation*. This perspective is useful in explaining why people with few educational and occupational opportunities, turn to criminal activities. Other disparities between means and goals can lead to what Robert Merton called *retreatism, ritualism, or rebellion.*

Conflict theories focus on the economic and political aspects of deviance and crime. One aspect of the theory suggests that financial stressors cause deviance and criminality, especially minor crimes such as petty larceny and drug abuse. Conflict theorists also suggest that what is considered crime is itself a political act. The privileged group defines behavior, and makes the laws, and can manipulate the cultural views and practices surrounding deviance and crime. "Crime" is more readily associated with street crimes such as robbery and battery than with white-collar crimes such as fraud, embezzlement, and insider trading, though these latter crimes are costlier to society.

Social control theory addresses the issue of why so many people conform, rather than why people deviate. It suggests that most want to "belong" so deviance becomes riskier with maturity, since a person stands to lose status, jobs, family, and property.

The conformist and the innovator are two common behavioral paths, though Merton accounts for other variations deriving from this theory linking goals and opportunity structures. In each of these situations, Merton draws a relationship between societal values and means of access to achieve these. This theory addresses issues of personal motivation and opportunity structures. This view stems from structural functional theory since it highlights the opportunity structure of society and cultural values which can contribute, or threaten, stability. Merton identifies three additional modes of cultural adaptation. Some people, according to this perspective, adopt the expected paths in life, but are not particularly motivated to excel or accomplish something "big." They go through life on automatic, towing the line but deriving little pleasure from it. Merton suggested this group is characterized by *ritualism*; just going through life to meet basic life needs. This group behaves

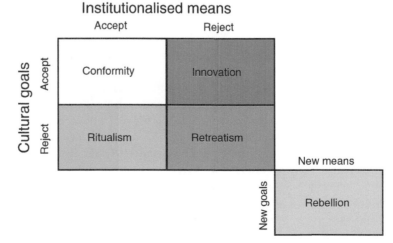

Robert K. Merton's Deviance Typology

Figure 6.2 Chart depicting Merton's Structural Strain Theory

with relative passivity as they perform "normal" roles. *Retreatism,* represents a more extreme path, with incumbents rejecting both the goals and practices in society. An example of this type of deviance can be seen in a person who joins a religious cult, choosing to live communally and rejecting individualistic and acquisitive behaviors embraced in the larger culture. A final group embraces *rebellion*, operating outside of the established social institutions to become activists, seeking alternative social, political, or personal practices. Groups embracing polyamory, by living with multiple significant life partners, would show this type of "deviance" by agitating for changes in the nation's tax, education, and insurance practices which would facilitate this choice.

Conflict theories of deviance and crime generally rely on two basic themes, reflecting a departure from symbolic interactionist and structural functionalist approaches. The first aspect relies on simple economics; some people steal or cheat because they need to in order to survive. If a person's income is not enough to meet basic bills, it becomes necessary to do something to supplement it. Such a shortfall can result in the illegal sale of drugs, dishonesty in the workplace, or misrepresenting information on taxes or applications for government services. These acts usually amount to petty fraud, with relatively small sums involved. This type of crime often receives the most media attention, deflecting attention from other types of crime. People in more powerful positions defraud the system in many ways, amounting to greater financial loss, but often under-reported in the media. These practices include behaviors such as dishonest accounting techniques; overbilling the government for services provided; misrepresenting information on taxes; or other misleading business practices, as seen more recently in the *Panama Papers* scandal which brought down government leaders by exposing the extensive wealth sheltered, legally and illegally, in offshore banking (Lipton and Creswell 2016; Calamur 2016; Harding 2016).

Not only are the crimes of the more privileged likely to cost the society more, the conflict view maintains that they are unlikely even to be viewed as crimes, remaining uninvestigated and uncharged. The following comments were made by an African American man, Brian Banks, who served five years for a false rape conviction. The statement is in response to a sentence of only six months, in a county facility, for Brock Turner, a White Stanford University athlete convicted on three felony charges for the rape of an unconscious woman. The juxtaposition of these two cases illuminates the irrationality and *institutional discrimination* of the criminal justice system:

I would say it's a case of privilege. It seems like the judge based his decision on lifestyle. He's lived such a good life and has never experienced anything serious in his life that would prepare him for prison. He was sheltered so much he wouldn't be able to survive prison. What about the kid who has nothing, he struggles to eat, struggles to get a fair education? What about the kid who has no choice who he is born to and has drug-addicted parents or a non-parent household? Where is the consideration for them when they commit a crime?

> I wasn't physically raped, but I was raped in a sense of my freedom … I was kidnapped, taken against my will, placed in a box for five years and two months. I was denied all human rights. When I screamed and pleaded and begged, it fell on deaf ears. It's a different form of being assaulted and taken advantage of. I know what she [Turner's raped woman] is going through.
>
> (Banks, in Myers 2016)

Brian Banks lost his college scholarship, and a chance for the NFL, when he was falsely accused at age 16 of the rape of a 15-year-old girl. After spending one year in juvenile hall waiting for his case to come up, his attorney negotiated him 90 days of observation in a state prison and probation, pronouncing it "a better option … than a young black kid facing an all-white jury." Nevertheless, the judge sentenced him to six years (Myers 2016).

Dan Turner, Brock Turner's father, made these public comments and pleaded for leniency in the sentencing of his son:

> These verdicts have broken him and shattered our family in so many ways. His life will never be the one he dreamed about and worked so hard to achieve. That is a steep price to pay for 20 minutes of action out of 20 plus years of life.
>
> (Myers 2016)

Another example of discrimination can be seen in the varying perceptions of criminal behaviors when high-level professionals are involved. Corporate executives who let a defective product go on the market rarely are seen as a "criminal" or as "deviant." Failing "O" rings in space shuttles, unsafe baby car seats, automobiles

Figure 6.3 Sexual assault is estimated to impact as many as one in four college students. The conviction of Brock Turner gained national attention as a result of the lenient sentence of six months imposed on the young, White, male Stanford student athlete who raped an unconscious woman Source: Avivi Aharon / Shutterstock.com

with potentially lethal defects, and faulty crib construction are a few examples of the marketing of hazardous products. In a calculated way, corporate executives prefer to do a "cost benefit" analysis which leads them to choose to chance litigating a few cases rather than taking pre-emptive action to fix products, industrial processes, or employment practices. When we think of assault, most people imagine personal cases of battery rather than corporate endangerment, but which type is responsible for more harm? The real sources threatening life and well-being frequently are veiled while the whole notion of *crime* is skewed by cultural biases (Glassner 1999).

Theories of deviance commonly address the origins and persistence of deviance. *Social control theory* reverses the process by asking why so many people conform, at least on the surface. Inspired by Durkheim, this view establishes that most of us desire to feel socially acceptable and are afraid to deviate because we might lose our status, property, family, or freedom. These fears keep our behavior in check, acting as a social control mechanism. In this view, the deviant actor would be someone who has "nothing to lose," because they have not accomplished those aspects of life which would render them "successful." This theory explains why there are not more people who are considered deviant or criminal. This view also incorporates the perspective that young people will outgrow their "delinquency." Theoretically, as people age, they have more to lose and so become more cautious and conforming.

How Prevalent Is Substance Abuse in the US?

Substance abuse refers to the use of psychoactive substances to the point where they are dangerous or mind altering. Any substance that influences affect or cognition is considered a psychoactive substance, including alcohol. When the use of a substance becomes a priority in life, interfering with other life obligations, it is considered abuse (WHO n.d.). The phrase "substance abuse" is commonly associated with illicit drug use, though abuse of legal drugs is more prevalent. Drug abuse costs society 700 billion dollars a year, with the biggest portions coming from tobacco, alcohol, and drugs, in that order (NIDA n.d.). The full cost of substance abuse incorporates losses due to illness, missed wages, drug treatment, and other related costs.

Box 6.3 – Substance Abuse

Substance abuse refers to the abuse of chemical substances which alter behavior. Substance abuse is most closely associated with illegal substances but the abuse of legal substances such as tobacco, alcohol, and prescription drugs surpasses the rate of illegal drug use. The legal status of a substance is unrelated to the relative danger of the substance. Tobacco and alcohol are two of the most harmful substances.

The severity of the harm caused by a particular substance does not explain societal attitudes towards that substance. Laws governing substances were initially the domain of localities and states. Public perceptions regarding threats to personal

Figure 6.4 Compre-
hensive cost of substance
abuse
Source: https://www.
drugabuse.gov/related-
topics/trends-statistics

	Health Care Costs	Overall Costs
Tobacco	$130 Billion	$295 Billion
Alcohol	$25 Billion	$224 Billion
Illicit Drugs	$11 Billion	$193 Billion

health, or societal welfare, depend upon who is using the substance and the desire
to control or vilify a particular group. A brief history of regulations concerning
opiates and marijuana illustrates this point. The movement against opiate drugs was
fueled by anti-Chinese sentiment. The first mandate against opiates occurred in San
Francisco in 1875, prohibiting smoking in opium dens. By 1890 Congress passed an
act taxing morphine and opium. Laws restricting the uses and sale of narcotics were
initiated at the federal level in 1909, with the banning of nonmedical use of opiates.
Later these laws were extended to the 1924 law making heroin illegal for any use,
including medical uses (NAABT n.d.).

In a similar vein, anti-marijuana laws were initially motivated by sentiments
against Mexican immigrants and Mexican Americans, though in some states they
were also a reaction to use by Mormons (Utah) and Black jazz musicians (the
northeast). Various states outlawed the use of marijuana between 1913 and 1937,
when the federal government began to tax marijuana (Guither n.d.; Schaffer Library
n.d.). In the 1950s, several laws were passed mandating minimum sentences for
drug use, including marijuana. These sentencing guidelines were repealed in the
1970s and, more recently, some states are moving to decriminalize possession of
small amounts of marijuana, and to reduce penalties, while others are legalizing it
(Frontline n.d.).

Alcohol is the most commonly used substance in America. It became illegal to
manufacture, sell, or transport in 1919 as a result of the 18th amendment to the US
Constitution. Since laws governing substances previously were made at the state or
local levels, the outlawing of alcohol required an amendment to the Constitution,
as did its repeal with the 21st Constitutional amendment in 1933. What inspired
the temperance movement? There are various explanations but they also represent
sentiments unrelated to the actual harmfulness of the substance. For religious
advocates of temperance, alcohol was "sinful." Additionally, some women agitated
for prohibition because they believed that alcohol was drawing men, and their
wages, from the family and enhancing the likelihood of physical abuse, neglect, and
impoverishment of women and children. Did prohibition reduce alcohol abuse?
It is actually unclear and debate regarding the impact of prohibition persists. One
position is that it cut consumption by about a third (Moore 1989) while others
suggest that alcohol use was declining in the years before the amendment passed
but worsened by 1926, well before its repeal (Drug Library n.d.). The repeal is
most often attributed to the increase in black market activity and organized crime
resulting from prohibition.

The physical harm posed by various drugs often is misunderstood. By almost any measure utilized, alcohol is as dangerous as any other drug, legal and otherwise, and more harmful on many measures (Watt n.d.; Drugs That Cause the Most Harm n.d.). Withdrawal from alcohol, which is a chemical sedative, can cause health problems such as heart arrhythmia and kidney or liver dysfunctions. Physical withdrawal from alcohol can be lethal and should be initiated with medical supervision (Rettner 2011). Withdrawal from Benzodiazepines (tranquilizing drugs such as Valium or Librium), can also be deadly though fatalities are relatively rare. In contrast, withdrawal from opiates is generally not lethal, though it is advisable to seek supervision (Jaffe 2010).

Alcohol, though commonly used, is not abused by most of its consumers. Thirty percent of Americans don't drink at all and 30 percent consume less than one drink per week. A person who drinks a glass of wine daily would be in the top 30 percent of consumers while the individual with two drinks a day would be in the top 20 percent (Ingraham 2014). The top 10 percent of drinkers are responsible for more than one half of the annual alcohol consumption, which amounts to the equivalence of ten drinks per day. Americans spend 1 dollar of every 100 dollars on alcohol (Vo 2012). In 2010 the alcohol beverage industry contributed 400 billion dollars to the economy, including 90 billion in wages from 3.9 million jobs (Distilled Spirits Council n.d.).

One highly contested issue with regard to alcohol use concerns setting the legal age for drinking. During the 1970s, many states lowered the drinking age to 18. The lower age limit significantly increased traffic accidents involving alcohol in the 18–21-year-old group. *Mothers Against Drunk Driving* (MADD) was founded in 1980 and actively lobbied for increasing the legal age to buy alcohol. Since the federal government cannot legislate a national drinking age, Congress passed

Figure 6.5 For many, especially young adults, socializing often occurs with alcohol consumption Source: Monkey Business Images / Shutterstock.com

laws, between 1984–1995, reducing the apportionment of highway moneys to any state which permitted those under the age of 21 to purchase or possess alcohol (Koroknay-Palicz n.d.). By 1995 all the states, and DC, had raised the drinking age to 21 (Griggs 2014).

Underage drinking remains high and issues relating to alcohol are prominent in the age group 15–24. Young people reflect cultural views regarding the role of alcohol in socializing, in that binge drinking often is viewed as "normal" behavior (Andersen 2015). One influential voice, in the appeal to lower the age to 18, has its source in college presidents who say that raising the drinking age to 21 actually encourages binge drinking while lowering it reduces binging and allows for more supervised consumption. Over 100 college presidents signed an initiative to get the drinking age lowered. They cited research which reveals that 40 percent of college students exhibit at least one symptom of alcohol abuse or dependence (Pope 2008).

Changing cultural attitudes might be the most expedient reform in addressing alcohol use. Although there are multiple sources showing that automobile accidents increase with lowered drinking ages, there are experts who feel appropriate use of alcohol would best be facilitated by its incorporation into family events. This view reflects that idea that the taboo around alcohol is more significant than the age of drinking. In most European countries, the drinking age is 18, and some even allow 16-year-old youths to use beer and wine. Dwight B. Heath, an anthropologist at Brown University, supports this view by suggesting that parents should allow their young children wine with meals so as to totally de-mystify the issue of alcohol (Griggs 2014).

While youth experimentation with substances is fairly common, habitual use is not. Alcohol use in youths is showing a slight decline, down to 41 percent who used alcohol in the past 12 months (2014) from 43 percent in previous years. Research shows that 70 percent of high school students try alcohol by the senior year of high school and one half will try an illicit drug; 40 percent have smoked cigarettes; and 20 percent have utilized legal drugs for nonmedical uses (NIDA 2016). Regular use of alcohol in youths is around 11.6 percent, while regular use of illicit drugs is 8.8 percent. Ten percent of substance-abusing adolescents will develop clinical substance abuse disorders as adults. These youths, a relatively small number, are unlikely to receive treatment. In 2013, only 9.1 percent of adolescents who needed substance abuse treatment received it.

What are the causes of substance use? It is suggested that social learning, from family, peers and the community can promote the use of substances. It also seems that when youths are feeling disassociated from social bonds they are more likely to develop substance abuse problems (OJJDP 2015). Each of these theories explains some of the factors contributing to adolescent alcohol use. If a young person is in an environment that supports substance abuse, the situation would correspond to the *differential association theory* of deviance while the lack of bonds can be related to *social control theory* and to Durkheim's perspective on social integration. Both of these approaches highlight the importance of addressing cultural issues, not only relating to attitudes towards alcohol and drugs but to the connection, or lack of it, we experience in our daily lives.

In recent years, much media attention has been devoted to the spread of heroin use. It is believed that the heroin epidemic emerged from legal use of opioids and the dependency that develops when primary care doctors provide prescription refills (Seelye 2016). Persistent use, after medical need, is partially due to its ready availability and relative cheapness, and also to its infiltration of White, suburban and rural areas (Montagne 2015; Block 2016; Noah 2016). There have been consistent reports regarding increases in deaths from heroin and the lack of beds for treatment (Szabo 2015). Addiction can go unnoticed for significant periods of time. Only 13 percent of workplace drug tests screen for prescription painkillers. The higher a person's professional status, the longer it generally takes for the addiction to be addressed. Addiction is costly to employers. In 2007, for example, substance abuse related expenditures amounted to 25 billion dollars (Noguchi 2016). Costs of addiction can be attributed to healthcare costs, absences from work, and workman's compensation claims.

Different forms of opioids are gaining popularity. Fentanyl is a powerful opioid painkiller which garnered much attention when the death of the musician Prince was attributed to it (BBC 2016). It is cheaper to make than heroin and more easily results in an overdose. Taken singly, or mixed with heroin, it was recently called a threat to "health and public safety" by the US Drug and Enforcement Administration (DEA 2015). Between 2005 and 2007, more than 1000 US deaths were caused by fentanyl-heroin overdoses, according to the Drug Enforcement Administration. Seizures of drugs containing the painkiller jumped from 942 to 3334 between 2013 and 2014 (Whitehead 2015). Fentanyl is lucrative, with one kilogram earning 1 million dollars, as opposed to only $80,000 from the same amount of heroin (Whitehead 2015).

The nonmedical use of non-opioid prescription drugs is also increasing. For example, Adderall, a common drug used in the treatment of Attention Deficit Hyperactivity Disorder, has seen nonmedical use increases of 67 percent in the five years between 2006 and 2011. It is sought after as a means to boost mental acuity but it can carry side effects of anxiety, agitation, and insomnia, as well as increased blood pressure (NCADD 2016). Young people often obtain Adderall from siblings or friends with prescriptions, and it has been sold on campuses for 25 dollars a pill (Sherman, n.d.). A google search regarding the sale of Adderall on campuses yielded 227,000 hits, some focusing on trends in particular schools, as well as articles containing information regarding other drugs for sale on campuses.

Deaths from legal substances surpass deaths from illegal substances, even excluding people who are using the legal drugs without prescriptions. Eleven percent of the American population uses anti-depressants and this figure is considered an underestimate. The US accounts for 60 percent of the world's use of psychotropic drugs and yet several studies show that many of these drugs perform no better than placebos (sugar pills) (Dubner 2016). Not only is their therapeutic value questionable but they can lead to negative side effects including violence and suicide (Shilhavy 2017). Prescriptions for psychotropic drugs are the biggest money maker in pharmaceuticals, which is considered the largest special interest lobby, with annual expenditures of 244 million dollars.

Figure 6.6 Addiction to drugs, legal and illegal, robs people of their freedoms
Source: Lightspring / Shutterstock.com

The ultimate societal cost of substance abuse is virtually impossible to calculate. There is fallout in lost work, health problems, injuries and accidents; parental neglect and abuse; cognitive impairment; and lack of treatment options. Many people "self-medicate" with alcohol or other drugs for underlying issues such as depression, anxiety, and feelings of hopelessness. If more money was spent on promoting mental health initiatives, especially in the community, some of this substance dependency could be reduced. Exercise promotes physical health by increasing cardio-vascular function and decreasing susceptibility to Type 2 diabetes, but it also has a significant impact on mental health. Exercise has been shown to impact mood, anxiety, ADHD, PTSD, stress, and to modify the bio-chemistry of the brain (Weir 2011). In spite of the benefits of physical activity, it is frequently cut from school programs in times of budgetary reductions and accessing private gyms can be very costly. Walking, which is great exercise, is free and generally easily accessible for most people but frequently is not integrated into our lifestyles. The benefits of face to face interactions also have a positive impact on mental well-being though they, too, seem on the decline (Dunn and Norton 2014). Reducing the likelihood of the development of a drug habit is more productive than addressing substance abuse once it has occurred. Cultural modifications represent the most fertile road to solving substance use problems. Any other solution represents a "band aid" in that it fails to address the root of the problem and yields only temporary, if any, efficacy.

It is suggested that legalizing substances may help in decreasing some of the associated problems of their uses. There is a tendency to draw a distinction between marijuana, on the one hand, and other illegal drugs, which are considered much more dangerous. After the 2016 election, seven states and the District of Columbia allowed legalized recreational use of marijuana while a total of 24 states have legalized some form of use (Rowley 2015). Marijuana represents the largest cash crop in the US, valued at 35.8 billion dollars (Gettman 2006). Taxes from marijuana could support a lot of improvement in education, the infrastructure, or arts. Resistance to legalization often addresses questions of safety, especially with potential threats to driving and brain impairment. Death from marijuana is exceedingly rare but there remains much debate regarding the safety of the drug with respect to behavior and general health. Some researchers suggest little negative impact from marijuana and, when compared to the consequences of alcohol use, they suggest it is much safer (Ingraham 2015).

Issues surrounding the legalization of "hard" drugs are more controversial and frequently focus on expenses associated with law enforcement. Arguments supporting the legalization of all drugs generally relate to the safety gained by controlling their use. It is estimated that the sale of such drugs would generate $85 billion in revenue. Legalizing drugs would significantly reduce costs related to the criminal justice system and potentially make financial sense in other ways, such as protecting the employment of users. Legalizing drugs is unlikely to significantly change the proportion of the population using them but it can improve the health of users, control the quality and content of the product, and generate revenues instead of stretching public budgets (Miron 2014). Some opponents of legalization suggest changing the legal status is regarded as condoning the behavior but there is little evidence to support that contention. Research in countries where drugs have been decriminalized or legalized, when matched with corresponding increases in treatment, show decreases in drug use and increases in safety and health elements (Drug Policy Alliance 2015; Kain 2011).

Cigarette smoking is the substance causing the most harm to general health. Smoking can be considered the most lethal drug available. Nearly 60 million Americans smoke cigarettes and another 23 million use some other form of tobacco. One half of smokers will die from a smoking-related illness and it is considered the leading cause of preventable deaths, followed closely by obesity (American Cancer Society n.d.). The powerful tobacco lobbies, both in farming and sales, are credited with societal tolerance for the continued legality of the products.

New research in neuroscience sheds light on the etiology (origins) and nature of addiction. Szalavitz (2016) suggests that two approaches have dominated the understanding of addiction. Generally, it is viewed either as a progressive "disease" over which a person has no control, or it is considered as a "moral" issue where the flaw lies in the individual's psychological constitution. Szalavitz suggests that modern science provides a third explanation. This theory depends on brain physiology showing that addiction releases dopamine in regions that control for comfort, safety, and love. Szalavitz suggests that social issues drive the initial use of substances which lead to a physical reliance. Her theory is that addiction is a coping mechanism which is linked to core human drives to belong, feel secure, and survive. Addiction becomes a "maladaptive way of coping," which is best addressed by empathy and love rather than punishment. In this view, a more compassionate approach to treatment, as opposed to punishment, is predicted to have more success. She notes that one half of all addiction ends by age 30 (excluding cigarette smoking), substantiating the idea that full attainment of brain maturation leads to an increased sense of safety, love, and belonging. Addiction, as a learned pattern of adjustment, can be unlearned and healthier behaviors substituted.

How Is Crime Reported?

It is difficult to assess the extent of crime since the reporting mechanisms are flawed and varied. Inconsistencies occur with respect to statutes, police discretion, identification of the offender, and plea bargains. The *National Institute of Justice* (NIJ n.d.) suggests that the most significant deterrent to crime is the certainty of being caught. The possibility of imprisonment does not act as a deterrent, nor does extending the sentence. Consequently, the best deterrent is an effective police force. There is some evidence that bolstering the police force's presence contributes about a 5 percent decrease in crime. Additionally, the use of computer programs to track crime patterns, initiated in the 1990s, has been an effective aid to reducing crime (Chettiar 2015).

Box 6.4 – Types of Crimes

Victimless crimes are those which present no apparent damage to persons or property although they affect many people, frequently vulnerable segments of the society, and result in heavy financial losses. Behaviors such as driving under the influence, prostitution, and gambling are a few examples of behaviors included in this category.

Street crimes are the crimes most people associate with the word "crime"; including assault, rape, murder, robbery, arson, burglary, larceny theft, and motor vehicle theft. These categories of *crimes against the person* and *property crimes* are reported in Part 1 of the UCR Offense Definitions 2017.

White-collar crime refers to breaking laws in financial and business transactions resulting in embezzlement, insider trading, and illegal practices associated with businesses and professions. Because many of the perpetrators commit their crimes while acting in a professional capacity, they are much less likely to be identified, charged, or sentenced to incarceration even when guilt is determined.

Victimless Crimes

Victimless crimes are commonly defined as illegal acts in which no one suffers apparent pain or injury:

> "Victimless" crimes are those that violate the ordered functioning of society in general, as opposed to those that directly harm individuals. A wide range of

crimes have been talked about at one time or another as 'victimless,' including such varied offenses as: failing to wear a seatbelt or a helmet, possession or use of illegal substances, gambling, driving while intoxicated or while texting, illegal possession of a firearm, leaving the scene of an accident, bigamy, charging an excessive interest rate, and ticket scalping.

(NCVLI n.d.)

This definition disregards harm done to vulnerable segments of the population. Think of prostitution; pornography; driving while intoxicated; the lotteries; failure to recognize the minimum wage or to pay overtime wages; ticket scalping; and payday loans. These are not accurately described as "victimless." Frequently, when an arrest is made, it bypasses the persons who manage and profit from the activities. Many of these activities generate significant profit. Prostitution and pornography, for example, typically punish the worker but not the customer. Deporting undocumented farm and service workers generally leaves a middleman/procurer of laborers untouched. Farmers can sustain their enterprises by paying low wages. Driving under the influence fails to address the huge revenues generated by advertising and lobbying. Pornography produces 10–12 billion dollars in revenues in the US (NBC 2015). Lotteries, gaming, and casinos prey on the poor who hope to dig themselves out of a hole though they are much more likely to be digging themselves into one; Americans spent 70 billion dollars on lottery tickets in 2014 (Thompson 2015). Payday loans and title loans, and other mechanisms of quick cash, prey upon the impoverished and charge exorbitant interest rates. In 2015, there were 15,766 payday stores in 36 states generating 3.6 billion dollars in fees. Compare that to the 1.31 billion dollars in profit earned from the 14,350 McDonalds stores in the US in the same year, and it is evident how much money is made from the desperate circumstances of the poor to survive to the next paycheck (CFPB 2016). How much money is lost to workers, and gained in corporate profit, by paying sub-minimum wages or by coercing workers to clock out and still work (see Chapter 12)?

Street Crimes

What we commonly think of as *crime*, and what is generally reported daily in the news, is a particular segment of "street crime," referred to as the "crime index." The data is culled from the FBI's *Uniform Crime Report* of over 18,000 jurisdictions, including local, state, federal, and tribal agencies and pertaining to eight crime categories perceived as personally threatening:

In Part I, the **UCR** indexes reported incidents in two categories: violent and property crimes. Aggravated assault, forcible rape, murder, and robbery are classified as violent while arson, burglary, larceny-theft, and motor vehicle theft are classified as property crimes.

(UCR Offense Definitions 2017)

Many people implicitly limit associations of crime with these categories, ignoring the higher incidence, and costs, associated with white-collar crime.

White-collar Crime

White-collar crime includes practices which have a negative effect on individuals or businesses but definitions vary considerably. Some unethical practices are not actually illegal. There are forms of "insider trading," for example, which are widely practiced and permitted by law (Keefe 2015). The prevalence of white-collar crime is high; one in four Americans will fall prey to these offenses, costing 400 billion dollars a year (Keefe 2015).

Will You Be Affected by White-collar Crime?

- It is estimated that one out of every four households will become the victim of a white-collar crime at some point.
- A majority of people in a recent survey (70 percent) believed that white-collar crime contributed to the great recession of 2008–2009.
- More than 88 percent of white-collar crime incidents are never reported to law enforcement agencies, although about half of all incidents are reported to someone, such as a supervisor.
- Seventeen percent of individual respondents in this survey reported experiencing at least one form of white-collar crime.
- When white-collar crime is committed against someone in the same household, the police reporting rate is just 11.7 percent.

(Brandongaille 2017)

These trends support conflict theory which suggests that what is defined as crime, and who is perceived as criminal, reflect the interests of the privileged class. Guilty verdicts resulting from prosecutions of white-collar crime are usually settled by fines and restitution; prison time is rare. Expenditures relating to white-collar crime are underestimated. The average "take" in an armed bank robbery is reported as $3137 while the average white-collar internet crime yield is as large as $500,000. White-collar fines are minuscule compared to overall profit gained; perhaps equaling about one day's worth of income (Brandongaille 2017; Reich 2015). Not all white-collar crime is financial. Fifty thousand people will die annually from occupational hazards deaths which could have been prevented (Brandongaille 2017). OSHA puts the death rate lower, but death and disease from exposure, overtime, chemical poisoning, and pollutants generally are not considered in crime data. OSHA data is specific to accidents on the job due to construction or machinery (OSHA n.d.). The US continues to use chemicals banned in other countries (Grossman 2014; Kollipara 2015; International Laws n.d.).

What Constitutes the Criminal Justice System?

The *criminal justice system* refers to three components governing the administration of crime and punishment. These are law enforcement, the courts, and corrections. Each of these three elements represents countless jurisdictions in local, state, and federal agencies. The total cost of the system is over $270 billion (White House 2016). Keep in mind that the above figures do NOT count the collateral expenses to the community in unemployment, lost education, and family disruption.

Law enforcement refers to all the agencies—local, state, and federal—that exercise authority and control over the population. These include local and state police forces and federal agencies such as the United States Marshals Service (USMS), the Federal Bureau of Investigation (FBI), the Drug Enforcement Administration (DEA), the Bureau of Alcohol, Tobacco, Firearms and Explosives (ATF), Federal Bureau of Prisons (BOP), plus others. Each agency is governed by specific rules and laws.

The American *court system* occurs at multiple levels but can be seen as two distinct systems, federal and state/local. The *juvenile justice system* operates independently of the adult system. Generally, the federal courts deal with federal laws, interstate issues, and issues addressing the US Constitution. State and local courts respond to incidences of civil and criminal acts covered by state and local laws. These would include such matters as family court, contract law, and most crimes which are not committed on federal land or between states (Federal Crimes n.d.; Federal vs State Courts n.d.). There are 30 million cases filed in state courts and one million in federal courts annually (Federal vs State Courts n.d.). The vast majority of cases, up to 97 percent, are plea bargained (Mangino 2014). A *plea bargain* generally means that a person pleads guilty to multiple crimes, or a lesser crime than originally charged, resulting in less time served and avoiding a trial (Plea Bargains n.d.).

The system of *corrections* includes probation and parole; local jails and county detention centers; state prisons and federal prisons. Jurisdiction depends on the nature of the specific charges and on the history of the offender. *Misdemeanors* are violations which are considered minor, such as petty theft, traffic violations, and simple assault. Driving under the influence is classified as a misdemeanor and treated as a local offense. Misdemeanor convictions, or admissions of guilt, generally require short-term sentences in local facilities and/or a fine. *Felonies* are more serious and cause more damage to people or property. Burglaries, robberies, battery, and rape would fall into this category. Typically, they result in a state prison sentence. Federal prisons are reserved for people who are convicted of transgressions against federal laws. Any act which takes place across states is generally a federal violation as is any activity relating to a federal agency, such as the post office or the Internal Revenue Service.

Box 6.5 – Criminal Justice System

The criminal justice system is composed of three parts; law enforcement, courts, and correctional institutions. Together these three entities address issues of crime and punishment. These agencies command heavy government budgets and evidence many biases and "irrational" or inconsistent mandates. *Misdemeanors* are relatively minor crimes such as petty theft and simple assault. *Felonies* are more serious offenses such as burglary, robbery, and battery.

Probation refers to sentencing where a person is supervised outside of detention, or given a shorter time in prison, coupled with a probationary period.

Parole is when a prisoner is released before the sentence is fulfilled and supervised for a period of time.

Recidivism refers to prisoners who return to the system with additional offenses. The recidivism rate in the US is substantial but varies by study and type of offense.

The rate of US incarceration is massive. At the end of 2014 there were 1,561,500 inmates in state and federal prisons and the vast majority were there for more than one year. Women represented 104,300, or fewer than 10 percent, of these inmates (Carson 2015). Jails, which represent city and county facilities, generally house people waiting adjudication of felony charges and people serving short sentences of under a year for lesser crimes. In 2013 there were 12 million admissions to jails and 730,000 people were incarcerated there. Another 4,708,100, or 1 in 52 adults were under the supervision of the community in probation or parole. *Probation* can be in lieu of incarceration or it can represent a split sentence with some jail time and some time under community supervision. *Parole* is when an inmate gains early

Figure 6.7 The US incarcerates more people, per capita, than any other country in the world and a disproportionate amount of these are people of color
Source: sirtravelalot / Shutterstock.com

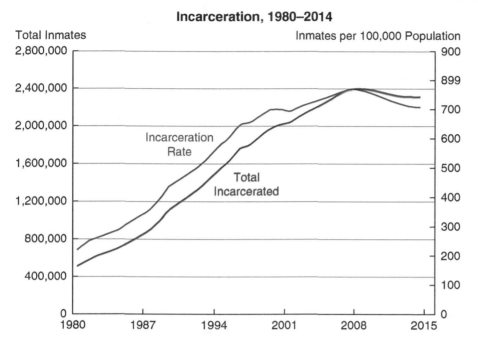

Incarceration, 1980–2014

Total Inmates

Inmates per 100,000 Population

Incarceration Rate

Total Incarcerated

Figure 6.8 Rates of incarceration 1980–2014 Source: https://www. whitehouse.gov/ sites/whitehouse. gov/files/documents/ CEA%2BCriminal% 2BJustice% 2BReport.pdf. Adapted from Bureau of Justice Statistics, CEA Calculations

release into the community and is supervised for a period of time. *Recidivism* rates, indicating the return of inmates to the system, vary greatly from study to study, from 40 percent to 67 percent (Gilligan 2012; Otis 2014). Calculation of recidivism rates is influenced by sentencing policies; severity of offense; community corrections; length of parole; and a jurisdiction's response to violations of parole. They also vary depending on the locality and the crime. For example, 82.1 percent of property crime offenders will have a recurrence, while 71.3 percent of violent criminals will reoffend (NIJ 2014). With regard to state offenses, Oregon has the lowest rate, at 22.8 percent, and Wyoming also has a low rate of 24.8 percent. The highest rates occur in California, at 57.8 percent, and Minnesota with 61.2 percent. Some states, such as California, require parole for all relased prisoners, typically for three years. As a result, they are under supervision and can be more easily exposed if violating the terms of release. Some states, such as Oregon, utilize prison as a last resort (Urahn 2011). All of these varying factors contribute to the wide range of reported recidivism.

Over the past 25 years, the violent crime rate in the US declined steadily although there is no agreement regarding the explanation for the trend. The increased rate of incarceration is thought to have had little effect on the reduced rates. The murder rate suddenly spiked in 2015, the year after a White police officer shot an unarmed African American teenager in Ferguson Missouri. Some experts attribute the spike in the murder rate to the "Ferguson effect," referring to less aggressive policing after the public outcry when the officer was acquitted of criminal charges. Other experts assert that there was no systemic fallout from the case. The Chicago superintendent of police feels that lax gun control laws are a contributing factor (Davey and Smith 2015; Kaste 2016). The Brennancenter research suggests that spikes in the most troubled cities have inflated the overall statistic:

> Final data confirm that three cities (Baltimore, Chicago, and Washington, D.C.) account for more than half (244) of the national increase in murders. While this suggests cause for concern in some cities, murder rates vary widely from year to year, and there is little evidence of a national coming wave in violent crime. These serious increases seem to be localized, rather than part of a national pandemic, suggesting that *community conditions* remain the major factor. Notably, these three cities all seem to have *falling populations, higher poverty rates, and higher unemployment than the national average.* This implies that economic deterioration of these cities could be a contributor to murder increases.
>
> (Brennancenter 2016, italics added)

The efficacy of the corrections system, measured against the system's articulated goals, is ambiguous. The 1970s initiated a period of decreased attention to rehabilitation with a reduction in work, education, and other programs that could have enhanced successful re-entry of inmates. Inmates have lower rates of high school completion than the general population. In 1994, reflecting a harsher perspective on offenders, the government eliminated the eligibility of prisoners to use Pell grants to obtain college classes. Research shows that the loss of Pell grant eligibility resulted in significant declines in education programs. Evidence shows that one dollar spent on prison education saves four to five dollars in re-incarceration costs (Munguia 2015). More education leads to employment and, when full-time employment is available, recidivism rates decrease. Released prisoners with full-time jobs are less likely to re-offend or to use publicly funded aid programs, saving 2.7 billion dollars annually. Employed convicts pay taxes and set an example for family and community members. A pilot program with Cornell University and two nearby prisons was successful in helping the prisoners receive college credit and degrees from the local community college. Well-constructed programs, often resisted as expensive, ultimately save public money (Skorton and Altschuler 2013; Noguchi 2017). Incarceration does not reduce crime and may actually promote it. Improving high school completion, and providing better social support services, particularly for the poor, would dramatically decrease the crime rate and improve conditions in high-crime cities. A large portion of the funds dedicated to the criminal justice system would be more "cost effective" utilized in education and prevention.

What Is Mass Incarceration?

One undisputed trend in criminal justice is the increased rate of incarceration initiated in 1980 and supported by the Reagan administration. The US has 5 percent of the world's population and 25 percent of the world's inmates. This amounts to 2.3 million incarcerated people. We incarcerate more people, per capita, than *any*

Figure 6.9 Sacramento CA billboard
Source: Photography by Rosalind Gottfried

other country in the world. The leaps in incarceration between the 1980s and 2010 can be linked directly to policies implemented by government agencies, ranging from the office of the President of the US, in the courts, and through corrections agencies. The prison system cost 80 billion dollars, in 2010, and more than 90 percent of that cost comes from state and local facilities (Kearney 2014).

Drug-related crimes and other minor offenses are the cause of much of the expansion in the prison population. The vast majority of convicted drug offenders are petty dealers with little control over distribution. This trend has had a particularly devastating impact on the African American community. As attorney Michelle Alexander argues in *The New Jim Crow* (2010), the mass incarceration of drug-related offenders not only has swelled the ranks of the prisons, it also has monopolized the budgets of multiple federal and state law enforcement agencies, jails, and prisons. The declaration of the "war on drugs" actually predates the epidemic and targeted the African American population. *Racial profiling* generated an association between drugs and African Americans that is *not* substantiated by data. Alexander offers evidence that the

Figure 6.10 Many people have come to believe that the African American community is a target for law enforcement. Do you agree?
Source: Rena Schild / Shutterstock.com

prevalence of drug use and sales is higher in the White community and yet 75 percent of the prison population is Black or Latino. She establishes that between the 1980s and 2000 the incarceration level increased 26 times for African Americans, and 22 times for Latinos, compared to that of the White population (Alexander 2010). Native Americans are also more likely than White people to be incarcerated for the same offenses and are more likely to have longer sentences for the same crimes. Native Americans are over-represented in incarceration in 18 states (Broze 2016). Additionally, powder cocaine offenses, more common for Whites, were given less time, 100:1, than possession of crack cocaine, though the Obama administration reduced the difference to 18:1 in 2010.

The increased incarceration, and the national focus on "law and order," has come to be associated with the perpetual targeting of the African American population. According to Alexander, these trends are more a reflection of racism than of crime rates. She suggests that in an era of integration, replacing the legal discrimination of the *Jim Crow* south, the topic of race is couched in allegedly race neutral terms of "law and order." The emphasis on "law and order" is a response to the challenges of the post-civil rights era, where "criminals" who pose a threat can be segregated. But, she suggests, the term *criminal* is code for African American. Supporting law and order translates into maintaining the African American male population as chronically poor, unemployable, and disenfranchised. This contention is supported by the media, which depict the problems of African American males as resulting from personal flaws rather than as a consequence of discrimination in policing, corrections, and poor urban conditions (Alexander 2010). The imposition of punitive government policies post 1980, such as prohibiting anyone with convict status from eligibility for many federal programs; evicting tenants from public housing for suspected drug-related activities; mandatory sentences for drug possession; and three strikes legislation, remain largely unacknowledged in the general population and popular media. Vitriolic attacks on "welfare queens" represent the criminalized view of African American women, further marginalizing the community and perpetuating negative stereotypes (White House 2016). This dynamic locks poor communities of color into permanent second-class citizenship.

The communities most affected by incarceration are the ones with the most constrained voice. In many states, felons' right to vote is completely denied, or at least delayed, even after the person is no longer in the criminal justice system. Over six million ex-felons cannot vote though voting rights, either upon prison release or completion of parole and probation, have been reinstated in some states. Presently, three states permanently disenfranchise convicts and six more do so for some felons (ACLU n.d.). Only two states have no restrictions; altogether 20 states have reduced restrictions. In April 2016, the governor of Virginia used his executive power to overturn a provision in the State constitution disenfranchising former felons. His mandate allows a person the right to vote upon the completion of parole and probation. This change in the law will create 200,000 new eligible voters, half of whom are African American. Several other states have passed laws reinstating voting rights to former felons, only to have them overturned, or restricted, by subsequent administrations (Stolberg and Eckholm 2016).

> ## Box 6.6 – Mass Incarceration
>
> *Mass incarceration* refers to the fact that the US accounts for 5 percent of the world's population, and 25 percent of the world's prison inmates; the highest rate of incarceration of ANY country in the world. Americans incarcerate more people for minor offenses, drug offenses, and nonviolent acts than any other country. The consequences of mass incarceration are especially pronounced among people of color, particularly African Americans, Native Americans, and Latinos.
>
> *The New Jim Crow*, a book by attorney Michelle Alexander, argues that the "war on drugs," coupled with the political focus on "law and order," amounts to a race neutral attack on the Black community. The African American population, and other marginalized communities, contain an underclass characterized by poverty, chronic unemployability, and disenfranchisement. The rate of incarceration, between the 1980s and 2000 increased by a factor of 26 for African Americans and 22 for Latinos, resulting in a prison population that is 75 percent Black and Latino. Indigenous people are also over-represented in the prison population. Alexander contends that convict status locks the person into secondary citizenship, devoid of many of the rights and privileges of full citizenship.

Integration back into the community is a stepping stone to decreasing recidivism. Many current prisoners can safely be returned to communities where they can thrive with supportive programs (Alexander 2010). To arrive at incarceration levels comparable to the 1970s, 80 percent of current inmates would need to be released. There are multiple means available to accomplish this goal. Sentencing practices can be modified; prison and re-entry programs reinvented; and drug treatment made more available. Alexander asserts that society has a common interest in making these changes since the whole society pays a price for the removal of 1.5 million Black men from the community (Wolfers et al. 2015).

Some progress has occurred. The past few years have seen a partial reversal regarding extensive sentences for drug offenders, partially due to experts' critiques and to law enforcement leadership. Over 100 leading police administrators gathered in the fall of 2015 and agreed that incarceration was not making anyone safer and was detrimental to society. They suggested that the criminal justice system should be reserved for serious and violent offenders. Increased attention to the unaddressed and underfunded issues of substance abuse was recommended (Johnson 2015). Under new federal laws, nonviolent drug offenders will be eligible for early release. Six thousand became eligible after the law passed in November 2015; the average time spent in prison for this nonviolent group was eight and a half years. Altogether 46,000 will be in this early release program. State and local jurisdictions also appear to be reconsidering sentencing trends (Apuzzo 2014). Additionally, the Chicago superintendent of police, Garry McCarthy (2015), cited data showing that more gun control laws, and the repeal of harsh drug sentences, successfully reduced incarceration and murders in New York, and aided gun seizures. He suggested that illegal gun possession is a gateway crime to committing murder and points to the need for stricter gun control laws. He attributed the higher murder rate in Chicago to gun control laws where carrying a loaded illegal gun is not seen as a violent offense for sentencing purposes (Montagne 2015).

Are Prison Inmates Protected by the Bill of Rights?

Death row inmate (sentence converted to life without parole) Mumia Abu Jamal speaking to journalist Amy Goodman about a 2014 Pennsylvania law limiting the speech of convicts and former convicts denying him free speech:

> It was a guard. I was talking to you. I believe it was '96, or around that time. We were having a *discussion*. It was live. And all of a sudden, the phone went dead. I couldn't believe what I was looking at. You know, I was like, "Hello, Amy? Hello?" because it just didn't make sense, to me, that he did that. He did that. But, of course, that was shortly after the publication of *Live from Death Row*, and the Department of Corrections sanctioned me, gave me a write-up, and we went to court about it. The case is preserved as *Abu-Jamal v. Price*. In that ruling, the Third Circuit of the United States Court of Appeals said I have a constitutional right to write. If I have a constitutional right to write under the First Amendment, then don't I have a constitutional right to read writings.
>
> (Abu-Jamal in Goodman 2014)

What Issues Emerge in Law Enforcement?

Recent events have focused media attention on the issues of injury and death to Black men by law enforcement personnel. Disproportionate violence, also prevalent among male Native Americans and Latinos, and to the women in all three groups, pervades the histories of these communities but national awareness has been promoted by a few prominent cases. The attention given to the death of Eric Garner as a result of being placed in a chokehold provides a prime example of how modifications in laws could have protected him, at least theoretically.

Garner might be alive today if the earlier case of *The City of LA v. Lyons* (1983) had been decided in favor of Lyons. The case was filed by Adolph Lyons, an African American man stopped for a broken tail light. Lyons had lowered his arms, because he was experiencing pain from their position; and subsequently was put into a chokehold though he posed no viable threat. He passed out and awoke to find himself having urinated, defecated, and spit up blood and dirt. He suffered sustained effects of unconsciousness and of a damaged larynx. His legal case addressed his fear of again being put into a chokehold since the police department had a tendency to use the

Figure 6.11 Eric Garner
Source: New York Daily News / Getty Images

chokehold even in non-threatening situations. Upon investigation, it was discovered that 16 men had died from chokeholds in Los Angeles, 12 of them African Americans (Alexander 2010). The District Court had imposed an injunction on chokeholds when there was no immediate threat of death or serious bodily injury. The Supreme Court admitted that chokeholds were used when there was no evidence of the threat of violence or bodily harm; that officers had insufficient training in the technique; and that they held a high risk of injury but the Court nevertheless overturned the injunction, by a 5:4 decision. The court's rationale rested on the argument that Lyons could not prove that he would again be at risk (Millhiser 2014). In writing for the dissenting position, Thurgood Marshall declared:

The Court today holds that a federal court is without power to enjoin the enforcement of the city's policy, no matter how flagrantly unconstitutional it may be … Since no one can show that he will be choked in the future, no one—not even a person who, like Lyons, has almost been choked to death—has standing to challenge the continuation of the policy.

(Millhiser 2014)

The use of chokeholds remains controversial. In 1993, the New York Police Department was banned from utilizing chokeholds yet there were 219 complaints against officers in 2013–2014.

The tragic deaths of Eric Garner, Trayvon Martin, Tamir Rice, Freddie Gray, Walter Scott, Michael Brown, Alto Sterling, and Philando Castile, to name only a few, highlight laws, police tactics, and court procedures which require reform. A Pew Research study indicates wide disparities in perception of police abuse since 80 percent of Black people, compared with 37 percent of White people, believe that the death of Michael Brown, in the Ferguson case involved a race issue (LaMar 2014).

A small group of officers are responsible for the majority of excessive force cases. However, data regarding officer shootings, in cases of unjustifiable use of force, are unreliable and likely under-reported due to reluctance to report incidents and the voluntary nature of the FBI's crime data collecting methods. One report establishes that Black men are 21 times more likely to be shot by police than their White counterparts. Research also shows that police are more likely to use force in high-crime areas independent of suspect behaviors and other controlling factors (Wihbey and Kille 2016). Similarly, it has been shown that Blacks are three times more likely than Whites to be searched but less likely to be found possessing drugs or guns. Differential racial rates of searches have been identified in every state and consistently show *less* contraband among the Black suspects (Guo 2015).

Unreasonable searches can almost be considered inevitable, since law enforcement entities profit from the pursuit of suspected drug offenders. *Civil forfeiture* is a practice whereby law enforcement personnel can remove property from any person who is *suspected* of criminal involvement. The police can keep or sell these possessions, even if the stop fails to lead to arrest or conviction. A person can try to regain the confiscated property but most people do not since the process is cumbersome and expensive (ACLUa n.d.). Even in states where the practice of civil forfeiture has been made illegal, the behavior persists because it is lucrative, adding hundreds of millions of dollars to local budgets. Some jurisdictions which have outlawed the practice actually persist in including it in their budget proposals (Kaste 2016).

How Are Communities Affected by Mass Incarceration?

African American communities are missing significant portions of their male population. The repercussions of male incarceration are vast since single-parent households experience more vulnerability in housing, education, health, and stability (Tierney 2013). For every 100 Black women living in the community, aged 25–54, there are 83 Black men. This is due to incarceration and early death. More than one in every six Black men in this age group is "disappeared" from life. One in 12 Black men in this age group is in prison, compared with one in 60 nonBlack men. The comparable figure for Black women is one in 100 and for nonBlack women one in 500. Ferguson has 60 Black men for every 100 Black women. Early death from heart disease, respiratory disease, accidents and homicide also contributes to the unbalanced ratio. The male/female gap emerges only after childhood and it is implicated in the low marriage rate and high rate of unwed births in the communities. This phenomenon has been referred to as the "*secondary prisonization*" of women (Alexander 2010).

Many African American women do not expect to count on a man to help them with the family, at least financially. By the age of 18, one in four Black children will experience the imprisonment of a parent. Many of the imprisoned men experienced an incarcerated father (Roberts 2012). Children rarely are able to keep in contact with their incarcerated parent, especially since state prisons tend to be located in more isolated areas and are difficult to travel to by public transportation. The cost of travel can be prohibitive, not to mention the lost wages for missed work. Contact by telephone is also impaired. Companies with prison contracts make extra money for prisoners calling out, especially from collect calls, and while some jurisdictions have passed regulations making this illegal many more have not. The Federal Communications Commission has been working to put caps on commissions made from interstate phone calls (Philip 2015; Katzenstein and Waller 2015; Rose 2015).

The well-being of the African American community has suffered since the 1990s though the data might not accurately represent the loss of the incarcerated population since it reflects the higher status of those remaining in the community (Wolfers et. al. 2015). Group gains in wages, education, employment, and voting do not include the portion of men incarcerated. Former prisoners face many obstacles upon release, especially in housing and employment. Shrinking pools of semi and unskilled labor, along with discrimination, make it difficult to accomplish a successful re-entry. Until recently, the ramifications of the prison experience were accompanied by a community reticence since no one wanted to publicly claim the loss of their males to prison (Alexander 2010). The increased willingness to address these community trends is expressed in the *Black Lives Matter* movement. The movement represents a desire for greater societal awareness of the injuries to the African American community resulting from law enforcement and incarceration. Movement adherents highlight the need for *systemic* reform with suggestions such as community-based policing; use of body cameras; changing laws such as "stand your ground"; and policy changes with regard to officer employment, education, and pay (Craven and Reilly 2015; Hawkins 2016; Our Demands n.d.).

Box 6.7 – Community and the Black Lives Matter Movement

Secondary prisonization refers to the community fallout resulting from the incarceration of men. Women and children often pay the price, in terms of lost income and familial quality, when a man is in prison. Additionally, when women are incarcerated, their children frequently are placed in some type of non-relative care since they are likely to be the sole custodial parent.

Black Lives Matter refers to the social activism associated with the African American community to draw attention to the high rate of death, especially of young Black males, at the hands of the law enforcement community. The movement's wider goal is to draw attention to the general societal disregard for the plight of African Americans, and males in particular, in the major institutions of the criminal justice system. Although this situation is not a new development, it only recently garnered widespread attention in the media.

Another area of concern stems from the recent incidents of mass shooting. The tragedy at Sandy Hook Elementary (2012); the movie theater shooting in Aurora, Colorado (2012); the Charleston SC church mass murders (2015); the San Bernardino County offices shooting (2105); the Orlando CA nightclub tragedy (2016); the Las Vegas shooting; and the Sutherland Springs Church shooting have raised issues regarding gun control laws. In spite of testimony by victims' relatives,

Figure 6.12 Black Lives Matter is a movement drawing attention to the brutality of the police against the Black community
Source: a katz / Shutterstock.com

and data corroborating its effectiveness, Congress has been unsuccessful in passing any restrictive legislation. In a poll conducted shortly after the Orlando attack, CNN reported that 92 percent of Americans supported expanded background checks; 85 percent agreed with prohibiting people on terror lists from gun purchases; 87 percent would ban convicted felons and people with histories of mental illness from purchasing guns; and 55 percent supported tougher gun control laws regarding the purchase of assault rifles and high-capacity ammunition clips. In spite of these data, five years after Sandy Hook, even with persistent episodes of mass murders, Congress has failed to pass proposed gun control measures (LoBianco et al. n.d.; Agiesta and LoBianco 2016; Phillips 2016).

Opponents of gun control maintain that evidence suggests that gun control laws would not reduce gun violence. Sentiments regarding the second amendment remain deeply entrenched and also are credited with the reluctance to pass more stringent laws (Stray 2013). The "gun culture" is highly engrained and unlikely to be weakened solely from legal injunctions. The US has a very high rate of gun ownership and exhibits higher rates of violent crimes and homicides than other industrialized nations. The US also has an elevated suicide rate in comparison to similar countries, and half of these deaths occur with a firearm. If guns were not accessible, some of these suicides might be prevented but their removal is unlikely to be included in any proposed measures.

Americans possess 310 million guns, representing 40 percent of households, which suggests that implementing stricter measures in gun control won't affect the prevalence of possession. Currently, there is insufficient information to show whether background checks and weapons bans would contribute to lowering the violent crime rate. There also is disagreement on whether laws, such as "right to carry,"

Figure 6.13 Flag with the names of the victims of the Sandy Hook shooting
Source: Ron Frank / Shutterstock.com

affect gun violence. There are no regulations regarding private gun sales. There is no consensus on what would reduce gun violence since research indicates that stiffer sentences for firearm offenses; gun buy backs; and safe storage laws are ineffective in reducing gun violence. Some research suggests that community elements, not directly related to gun control, would be more effective in reducing gun violence. Proposals to reduce gun violence include innovative probationary strategies and more policing, combined with community-based positions in leadership, law enforcement, and policy (Stray 2013).

Research indicates that mass murderers exhibit similar patterns of need to control others as seen in domestic violence. These experts believe that *mass terrorism* and *intimate terrorism* reflect the same dynamic. In both situations, the perpetrator feels violated either in a personal relationship or by authority figures and societal trends. Ninety-eight percent of mass shooters are men; these "injured" parties are usually heterosexual men who feel that their dominance is threatened (Taub 2016; Kluger 2014). Improved mental health services could reduce the access to guns by providing

---

Box 6.8 – Mass Terrorism

Mass terrorism refers to the mass shootings committed by US citizens or permanent residents. Perpetrators generally feel a sense of personal violation and are viewed as gaining a sense of control by their violent intimidation and dominance of their targets. These dynamics are similar to those seen in domestic violence.

lists of individuals who are ineligible to qualify for weapon purchases. Coupled with better background checks, these lists can impact access to semi-automatic weapons, like those used in recent mass shootings. It is unlikely that this would eliminate mass shootings, since it is virtually impossible to isolate the individual who is at risk of committing these acts, but it can reduce the dissemination of such weapons (Berreby 2016; Resnick and Zarracina 2016). The best means to reduce these tragic events lie in the provision of preventive measures.

Women and Incarceration

The population of incarcerated women increased by nearly 800 percent between 1980 and 2014. There were 1.2 million women in the criminal justice system in 2014. The growth rate in women prisoners surpassed the men's. Women in state facilities are more likely than incarcerated men to be in detention for drug or property offenses. African American women are two times as likely as White women to be in the system while the corresponding figure for Hispanic women is 1.2 times (The Sentencing Project 2015). Black women are disproportionately incarcerated since they represent 13 percent of the US female population and 30 percent of the incarcerated female population. Hispanic women are 11 percent of the general population and 16 percent of the incarcerated women (Marusic 2015).

More than 60 percent of women prisoners have children under 18 years old. The imprisonment of women presents some special problems because they are more likely to be the sole, or primary, caretakers of their children; their children are more likely to end up in foster care than when the father is incarcerated. It is very difficult for women to regain custody of their children after prison, due to their exclusion from welfare benefits and the stigma of "convict" when applying for jobs. Histories of physical or sexual assault characterize 60 percent of the female prison population. They are also more likely than incarcerated men to be ill and less likely to receive services. Incarcerated women face multiple health conditions commonly including sexually transmitted infections, HIV, hepatitis C, hypertension, and diabetes (English 2015). Three fourths of women in state prisons show symptoms of mental health problems and typically do not receive any counseling while in confinement. Incarcerated women are more likely to be overweight, and to gain weight, even with relatively short sentences. Exercise programs have been initiated to help with health and depression. Attention to diet has not been prioritized in corrections agencies (English 2015).

Pregnancy increases a woman's vulnerability since women have been physically restrained while giving birth in prison (Marusic 2015). A drug-dependent pregnant woman whose newborn will have to undergo withdrawal is "guilty" of "fetal assault," in at least three states. Pregnant women fear permanent loss of their child and are reluctant to draw attention to their substance abuse by seeking help. Women who overcome the fear of criminal charges and seek drug treatment find there is a scarcity of beds and they are exposed to the authorities (Yu and Shapiro 2015). "Neonatal Abstinence Syndrome" doubled between 2009 and 2012 and more states are considering making it a crime. If women can get drug treatment and supportive programming they have a better chance of staying in the community. Programs providing work training and assistance in job placement have helped women to successfully return to the community (Aubrey 2016).

Juveniles

Two in 1000 juveniles are in the juvenile justice system. There are many detrimental long-term effects associated with juvenile detention. Gender and racial bias pervade the system. African American youths are six times more likely than White youths to serve time for committing identical offenses (Alexander 2010). Girls comprise 14.3 percent of incarcerated youths. Girls have a higher portion of *status offenses,* behaviors which are only illegal for juveniles; and technical violations, such as truancy, running away, and lack of obedience to authority (The Sentencing Project 2015). Most girls in the system have suffered physical or sexual abuse (90 percent); mental health issues (80 percent); and they have a suicide rate four times that of the general population. Girls are placed in solitary confinement for minor behaviors or for no reason at all. While in detention, girls have been subjected to punitive punishments for petty transgressions such as hugging, singing, or picking flowers, or talking back (Levintova 2016). They also commonly experience sexual assaults perpetrated by staff and peers (Marusic 2015).

Thirty-seven percent of youths in detention have committed violent offenses while 24 percent commit property offenses. Seventy percent of youths are in public facilities which cost $88,000 per inmate (Kearney and Harris 2014). Many more juvenile offenders never enter the juvenile justice system because they are undetected or diverted to other programs. In every state, there are some provisions for juveniles to be tried as adults, though circumstances vary by state. Of those who do enter the juvenile system, even serious offenders rarely make an adult career out of crime though they are more at risk than a juvenile with no history. Juveniles committing murder were at their lowest in 2010 than at any time since 1980. Juveniles are most likely to commit violent crimes in after school hours on school days (OJJDP 2014).

Private Jails

Private, for-profit jails emerged in recent years partly to determine whether incarceration could be achieved more cheaply and partly to alleviate the overcrowding of public facilities. Privately contracted facilities account for 6 percent of state prisons, 16 percent of federal facilities, and some local jails. They have not been shown to decrease costs and more likely represent increased expenditures. Private facilities have been shown to have poor conditions and more incidences of violence (ACLUc; Bauer 2016). Private prisons have fewer inmate support programs and their employees receive less training and less pay, and supervise more inmates, than those in the public sphere. The federal government, in 2016, announced the phasing out of private prisons (Margulies 2016). It seems probable that other sectors of the system will follow.

Death Penalty

Controversial issues surrounding the death penalty address its constitutionality with regard to its existence and to the manner of its implementation. In 1972, the US Supreme Court halted executions, declaring the death penalty to be "cruel and unusual punishment" but the suspension was rescinded in 1976 (ACLUb). Some states chose to abolish it while others have instituted a moratorium. Thirty-one states have the death penalty but most executions are confined to a few states, with 89 percent occurring in Texas, Missouri, Florida, and Oklahoma (Ehrenfreund 2014; Amnesty International 2015). In 2005, the US Supreme Court prohibited the death penalty for minors (Lane 2005). The efficacy of the drugs utilized in lethal injections is questionable, with some evidence that the victim suffers a painful death. In 2015 the US Supreme Court upheld the legality of lethal injection with the controversial drug midazolam (DPIC n.d.). The death penalty has been completely eliminated in the European Union, and the EU refuses to supply the US with drugs for lethal injection (Gibson and Lain 2014).

There is no evidence that the death penalty acts as a deterrent. There are worrisome trends regarding the implementation of the death penalty. The death penalty, when utilized, is unfairly applied on the basis of poverty, race of the victim, and locale. People of color are more likely than White people to be given the death penalty even when convicted of the same crimes. There also is the potential for false convictions. Between 1973 and 2015, 152 death row inmates were exonerated before the death sentence was carried out. There were two documented cases of innocent people who were put to death (Editorial Board 2015). Yet a majority of Americans support the death penalty, viewing it as a "just penalty" (ACLUb). If no consensus can be reached outlawing the death penalty for moral reasons, its exorbitant costs, making it much more expensive than life without parole, could justify its discontinuance. Money currently diverted to death penalty cases could be better utilized to support backlogged courts and the reinstatement of laid off police (Dieter 1994).

Key Terms

Deviance   Crime   Social Control   Labeling Theory   Secondary Deviance
Tertiary Deviance   Self-Fulfilling Prophecy   Social Capital   Differential Association Theory
Structural Strain Theory   Conflict Theory   Social Control Theory   Substance Abuse
Victimless Crime   Street Crime   The Uniform Crime Report   White-Collar Crime   Criminal
Justice System   Probation   Parole   Law Enforcement   Court Systems   Misdemeanor
Felony   Plea Bargains   Recidivism   Corrections   Mass Incarcerations   Racial Profiling
Civil Forfeiture   Secondary Prisonization   Black Lives Matter   Domestic Terrorism   Status
Offenses   Private Jails   Death Penalty

Concept Review

What Is Deviance?

Deviance frequently is defined as behaviors and attitudes which contradict the norms of society. This view is simplistic since it does not elaborate the power relations implicit in the assigning of "**normative**" behavior or in the selection of people identified as "deviant." Many people who commit "deviant" or "criminal" acts manage to escape being socially identified as such and do not carry the stigma or consequences others suffer. No behavior is inherently deviant, but deviance is defined by the social context. Some behaviors are deviant but not illegal, though most illegal acts are labeled as deviant.

How Do Sociologists Study Deviance and Crime?

Sociologists present a variety of theories to explain why people are likely to be involved in deviance or crime. Many of these focus on the social responses surrounding a person or event or on the cultural context of the actor. These are explained in **labeling theory**, **differential association theory**, and **structural strain** theory. Labeling emphasizes the view others hold toward the actor. Differential association highlights the influence of the acts of significant people on the behaviors of an individual. Structural strain theory illuminates the effect of opportunity structures on a person's path. The presence of **social control mechanisms**, which highlight the desire of people to feel a sense of belonging to the group, emphasizes the internal and external forces which inhibit deviance and crime. This theory focuses on the question of why people choose conformity, rather than why some people are deviant as in the other theories. The **conflict** perspective deviates from the others by focusing on the economic system and its influence on crime as necessary for survival. It also promotes the idea that how we define crime is anything but "objective," and is actually based on the interests of the powerful, especially since focusing on the "criminal element" deflects attention from the elite's transgressions.

How Prevalent Is Substance Abuse in the US?

Substance abuse, including the use of tobacco and alcohol, is so prevalent that it might accurately be considered a cultural norm. Dependency on psychoactive substances accounts for many expenditures in healthcare, law enforcement, and corrections as well as lost wages and productivity. The legal status of substances has more to do with perception and history than with the actual dangers posed by the substance. Alcohol is the most commonly utilized substance and is often considered the drug with the greatest impairment to health, along with tobacco. Overall, legal substances carry a greater cost, especially in the areas of healthcare and employment-related losses, than illegal substances.

How Is Crime Defined?

In the US, crimes are differentiated by location and severity. There are crimes on the federal level and on the state/local level. **Misdemeanors** are more minor offenses which are generally resolved with fines and/or terms in local jails. **Felonies** are more serious offenses which carry longer sentences served in the state or federal prison system. Many associate "the crime rate" with "crimes against the person" (such as assault and battery) and property crimes, which make up only one part of the *Uniform Crime Report*.

Probation and *parole* are elements of the system which supervise offenders before or after, or in lieu of, incarceration. The period of the 1980s to the 2010s saw a movement away from rehabilitation and training for re-entry after prison which is only beginning to be addressed.

White-collar crime, or crimes committed in a professional capacity, frequently are not commonly expressed as illegal or deviant. White-collar criminal acts are less likely than "street crimes" to be charged, convicted, and sentenced to detention. White-collar crimes are costlier than crimes against the person or property crimes.

What Is the Criminal Justice System?

The criminal justice system refers to the federal, state, and local agencies that oversee the apprehension, charging, and dispensation of persons involved in committing crimes. Practices are susceptible to changes in cultural sentiment and policies. Since the 1980s, there has been a significant increase in the rate of incarceration. The US per capita incarceration rate is the highest in the world.

What Is Mass Incarceration?

Mass incarceration refers to the large portion of the population that has been under the jurisdiction of the criminal justice system and which disproportionately affects the African American population, the Latino population, and the Indigenous population. These groups are more likely to be involved in the system though there is evidence that they actually commit less crime, proportionately, than White people. Some theorists believe that the mass incarceration, and the "criminalizing" of the African American population is a mechanism of social control utilized to strip marginalized groups of civil rights under the guise of promoting public safety. This process has the effect of perpetuating the segregation associated with the *Jim Crow* laws while de-racializing the trend. Mass incarceration is considered a result of the "war on drugs" and the movement to protect "law and order," a veiled attack on communities of color. Mass incarceration has contributed to the dissolution of community and family life and perpetuated cycles of disadvantage in education, employment, and political involvement.

What Special Issues Emerge in the Criminal Justice System?

The incarceration of women presents special problems, most notably in terms of the loss of child custody. Other issues arising in the criminal justice system have to do with the incarceration of juveniles, which also is substantial. Many juvenile offenders have suffered physical, sexual, and mental abuse and neglect which might be addressed compassionately by more extensive support services in mental health, substance abuse, education, and job training.

Private jails have become a significant feature of the criminal justice system and have proven to be more expensive than public facilities and more dangerous to inmates. The federal government is phasing out private facilities and other jurisdictions will likely follow suit.

Finally, the death penalty, reinstated in the US in 1976 after a four-year hiatus, has been shown to have no value in deterring crime and to be costlier than life imprisonment. If the elimination of the death penalty does not occur for moral, religious, or civic reasons, its exorbitant financial costs can justify its elimination.

Review Questions

1. How do sociologists define deviance? How do you think deviance should be determined? Is deviant behavior always undesirable?
2. Discuss three theoretical approaches to deviance and elaborate the advantages and disadvantages of each perspective.
3. Apply a sociological analysis to a topic which might be considered deviant. Why did you choose it? How are you approaching it? What would a critic say about your view?
4. What is substance abuse and how big a problem is it? What are the differences between legal and illegal substances?
5. How would you explain the high use of substances in American society? How would you address the problem?
6. Do you think marijuana should be legal? What do you think about the legalization of other drugs which are currently illegal?
7. Should tobacco products be illegal? How did you arrive at your answer?
8. What constitutes the crime rate? What is white-collar crime? Who are considered to be "criminal" in the US?
9. What is mass incarceration and how does Michelle Alexander analyze it? What groups are more likely to be incarcerated? Why?
10. Do you think prison sentences should apply to all types of crime? Explain.
11. Do you think imprisonment is effective in deterring crime? Should there be a greater emphasis on rehabilitation or prevention?
12. Should male and female offenders be treated similarly when in custody?
13. Should juveniles be incarcerated? If so, under what circumstances? Should girls be detained for behavioral transgressions?
14. Do you support the death penalty? Explain your position.

References

Abu-Jamal, M., Goode, A. (2014) VIDEO: Extended Interview with Mumia Abu-Jamal on New Pennsylvania Law Restricting Prisoners' Speech. [Video File] Retrieved from http://www.democracynow.org/2014/10/24/video_extended_interview_with_mumia_abu

ACLU. (n.d.) State Criminal Re-enfranchisement Laws (Map). *American Civil Liberties Union.* Retrieved from https://www.aclu.org/map/state-criminal-re-enfranchisement-laws-map

ACLUa. (n.d.) Asset Forfeiture Abuse. *American Civil Liberties Union.* Retrieved from https://www.aclu.org/issues/criminal-law-reform/reforming-police-practices/asset-forfeiture-abuse

ACLUb. (n.d.) The Case Against the Death Penalty. *American Civil Liberties Union.* Retrieved from https://www.aclu.org/case-against-death-penalty

ACLUc. (n.d.) Private Prisons. *American Civil Liberties Union.* Retrieved from https://www.aclu.org/issues/mass-incarceration/privatization-criminal-justice/private-prisons

Agiesta, J., LoBianco, T. (June 20, 2016) Poll: Gun Control Support Spikes after Shooting. *CNN*. Retrieved from http://edition.cnn.com/2016/06/20/politics/cnn-gun-poll/index.html

Akers, R.L. (1998) *Social Learning and Social Structure: A General Theory of Crime and Deviance*. Boston: Northeastern University Press.

Alexander, M. (2010) *The New Jim Crow: Mass Incarceration in the Age of Color Blindness*. New York: The New Press.

American Cancer Society. (n.d.) Tobacco: The True Cost of Smoking. *American Cancer Society Infographics*. Retrieved from https://www.cancer.org/research/infographics-gallery/tobacco-related-healthcare-costs.html

Amnesty International. (March 31, 2015) Death Sentences and Executions 2014. *Amnesty International USA*. Retrieved from http://www.amnestyusa.org/research/reports/death-sentences-and-executions-2014?page=2

Andersen, A. (April 24, 2015) Bay Area Binge Drinking on the Rise. *KRON4*. Retrieved from http://kron4.com/2015/04/24/bay-area-binge-drinking-on-the-rise/

Apuzzo, A. (July 18, 2014) New Rule Permits Early Release for Thousands of Drug Offenders. *The New York Times*. Retrieved from https://www.nytimes.com/2014/07/19/us/new-rule-permits-early-release-for-thousands-of-drug-offenders.html?_r=0

Aubrey, A. (April 15, 2016) This Bakery Offers A Second Chance For Women After Prison. *NPR.org*. Retrieved from http://www.npr.org/sections/thesalt/2016/04/15/469942932/this-bakery-offers-a-second-chance-for-women-after-prison

Bauer, S. (2016) Private Prisons Are Shrouded in Secrecy. I Took a Job as a Guard to Get Inside—Then Things Got Crazy. Mother Jones. Retrieved from http://www.motherjones.com/politics/2016/06/cca-private-prisons-corrections-corporation-inmates-investigation-bauer

BBC. (June 3, 2016) *BBC Newsbeat*. Retrieved from http://www.bbc.co.uk/newsbeat/article/36443377/it-led-to-princes-death-but-what-is-the-prescription-medication-fentanyl

Becker, H.S. (1963) *Outsiders: Studies in the Sociology of Deviance*. New York: Free Press.

Berreby, D. (2016) Why We Can Predict a Lot About the Next Mass Shooting—But Never Enough to Prevent It. *Big Think*. Retrieved from http://bigthink.com/Mind-Matters/why-we-can-predict-a-lot-about-the-next-mass-shooting-but-never-enough-to-prevent-it

Block, M. (March 12, 2016) A Small Town Wonders What to Do When Heroin Is Everywhere. *Morning Edition, NPR*. Retrieved from http://www.npr.org/sections/health-shots/2016/03/12/469954366/a-small-town-wonders-what-to-do-when-heroin-is-everywhere?ft=nprml&f=7Board, E. T. (2015, April 13).

Brandongaille. (May 20, 2017) 35 Surprising White Collar Crime Statistics. *Brandongaille.com*. Retrieved from http://brandongaille.com/34-surprising-white-collar-crimes-statistics/

Brennancenter (January, 2016) Final 2015 Crime Stats: Claims of Rising Crime Overblown, Evidence Shows. *Brennancenter.org*. Retrieved from https://www.

brennancenter.org/press-release/final-2015-crime-stats-claims-rising-crime-overblown-evidence-shows

Broze, D. (2016) Report: Native Americans Account for Disproportionate Amount of Prison Population. *MintPress News*. Retrieved from http://www.brookings.edu/~/media/research/files/papers/2014/05/01%20crime%20facts/v8_thp_10crimefacts.pdf

Calamur, K. (April 4, 2016) The Names in the Panama Papers. *The Atlantic*. Retrieved from https://www.theatlantic.com/international/archive/2016/04/panama-papers-names/476688/

Carson, E.A. (September 17, 2015) Bureau of Justice Statistics (BJS)— Prisoners in 2014. *Bjs.gov*. Retrieved from https://www.bjs.gov/index.cfm?ty=pbdetail&iid=5387

CFPB. Consumer Financial Protection Bureau. (June 2, 2016) *Payday Loans, Auto Title Loans, and High-cost Installment Loans: Highlights from CFPB Research* [PDF File]. Retrieved from http://files.consumerfinance.gov/f/documents/Payday_Loans_Highlights_From_CFPB_Research.pdf

Chambliss, W.J. (November–December, 1973) The Saints and the Roughnecks. *Society* 11(1): 24–31. Retrieved from https://eric.ed.gov/?id=EJ088754

Chettiar, I. (February 11, 2015) CompStat Is Controversial, But It Works. *The Atlantic*. Retrieved from http://www.theatlantic.com/national/archive/2015/02/more-police-managed-more-effectively-really-can-reduce-crime/385390/

Craven, J., Reilly, J.R. (August 24, 2015) Here's What Black Lives Matter Activists Want Politicians to Do about Police Violence. *The Huffington Post*. Retrieved from http://www.huffingtonpost.com/entry/black-lives-matter-policy-demands_us_55d7392ae4b0a40aa3aa9443

DEA. (March 18, 2015) *DEA Issues Nationwide Alert on Fentanyl as Threat to Health and Public Safety*. Retrieved from https://www.dea.gov/divisions/hq/2015/hq031815.shtml

Davey, M., Smith, M. (August 31, 2015) Murder Rates Rising Sharply in Many U.S. Cities. *Nytimes.com*. Retrieved from https://www.nytimes.com/2015/09/01/us/murder-rates-rising-sharply-in-many-us-cities.html

Dieter, C.R. (1994) *Millions Misspent: What Politicians Don't Say About the High Costs of the Death Penalty. Death Penalty Information Center*. Retrieved from https://deathpenaltyinfo.org/millions-misspent

Distilled Spirits Council. (n.d.) Economic Contributions of the Distilled Spirits Industry *DISCUS. Discus.org*. Retrieved from http://www.discus.org/economics/

DPIC. (n.d.) *Death Penalty Information Center*. Retrieved from https://deathpenaltyinfo.org/lethal-injection-constitutional-issue

Drug Library. (n.d.) Did Alcohol Prohibition Reduce Alcohol Consumption and Crime? *Druglibrary.org*. Retrieved from http://www.druglibrary.org/prohibitionresults.htm

Drug Policy Alliance (February, 2015) *Drug Decriminalization in Portugal: A Health-Centered Approach*. [PDF File]. Retrieved from https://www.drugpolicy.org/sites/default/files/DPA_Fact_Sheet_Portugal_Decriminalization_Feb2015.pdf

Drugs that cause the most harm. (n.d.) *The Economist Online*. Retrieved from https://www.economist.com/blogs/dailychart/2010/11/drugs_cause_most_harm

Dubner, S. (December 7, 2016) Bad Medicine Part 2 Drug Trials and Tribulations. *Freakonomics Radio*. Retrieved from http://freakonomics.com/podcast/bad-medicine-part-2-drug-trials-and-tribulations/

Dunn, E.W., Norton, M. (April 26, 2014) Hello, Stranger. *NYTimes.com*. Retrieved from https://www.nytimes.com/2014/04/26/opinion/sunday/hello-stranger.html

Editorial Board. (April 13, 2015) 152 Innocents Marked for Death. *The New York Times*. Retrieved from https://www.nytimes.com/2015/04/13/opinion/152-innocents-marked-for-death.html?_r=0

Ehrenfreund, M. (April 30, 2014) There's Still No Evidence that Executions Deter Criminals. *The Washington Post*. Retrieved from https://www.washingtonpost.com/news/wonk/wp/2014/04/30/theres-still-no-evidence-that-executions-deter-criminals/

English, T. (October 11, 2015) Biking Behind Bars: Female Inmates Battle Weight Gain. *NPR.org*. Retrieved from http://www.npr.org/sections/health-shots/2015/10/11/444526183/biking-behind-bars-female-inmates-battle-weight-gain

Federal Crimes. (n.d.) *Justia.com*. Retrieved from https://www.justia.com/criminal/offenses/other-crimes/federal-crimes/

Federal vs. State Courts – Key Differences (n.d.). *Findlaw*. Retrieved from http://litigation.findlaw.com/legal-system/federal-vs-state-courts-key-differences.html

Frontline. Marijuana Timeline. (n.d.) *PBS*. Retrieved from http://www.pbs.org/wgbh/pages/frontline/shows/dope/etc/cron.html

Gallagher, J. (2010) *A Different Kind of Cool*. Directed by Busfield, B. Couplabob Productions, Inc.

Gettman, J. (2006) Marijuana Production: Comparison with Other Cash Crops. *Drugscience.org*. Retrieved from http://www.drugscience.org/Archive/bcr2/cashcrops.html

Gibson, J., Lain, B.C. (May 5, 2014) Europe Taught America How to End the Death Penalty. Now Maybe it Finally Will. *The Guardian*. Retrieved from https://www.theguardian.com/commentisfree/2014/may/05/america-end-death-penalty-finally

Gilligan, J. (December 9, 2012) Punishment Fails. Rehabilitation Works. *Nytimes.com*. Retrieved from http://www.nytimes.com/roomfordebate/2012/12/18/prison-could-be-productive/punishment-fails-rehabilitation-works

Glassner, B. (1999) *The Culture of Fear: Why Americans Are Afraid of the Wrong Things*. New York: Basic Books.

Goodman, A. (October 24, 2014) Video: Extended Interview with Mumia Abu-Jamal on New Pennsylvania Law Restricting Prisoners' Speech. *Democracy Now*. Retrieved from https://www.democracynow.org/2014/10/24/video_extended_interview_with_mumia_abu

Goodnow, N. (July 7, 2017). Will Your Sociology Professors Talk behind Your Back if You're Conservative? They Just Might. *National Review*. Retrieved from http://www.aei.org/publication/will-your-sociology-professors-talk-behind-your-back-if-youre-conservative-they-just-might/

Griggs, B. (July 16, 2014) Should the U.S. Lower its Drinking Age? *CNN*. Retrieved from http://www.cnn.com/2014/07/16/us/legal-drinking-age/index.html

Grossman, E. (June 9, 2014) Banned in Europe, Safe in the US. *Ensia*. Retrieved from https://ensia.com/features/banned-in-europe-safe-in-the-u-s/

Guither, P. (n.d.) Why Is Marijuana Illegal? *Drug WarRant.com*. Retrieved from https://www.naabt.org/index.cfm

Guo, J. (October 27, 2015) Police Are Searching Black Drivers More Often, but Finding More Illegal Stuff with White Drivers. *Washington Post*. Retrieved from https://www.washingtonpost.com/news/wonk/wp/2015/10/27/police-are-searching-black-drivers-more-often-but-finding-more-illegal-stuff-with-white-drivers-2/

Harding, L. (April 5, 2016) What Are the Panama Papers? A Guide to History's Biggest Data Leak. *The Guardian*. Retrieved from https://www.theguardian.com/news/2016/apr/03/what-you-need-to-know-about-the-panama-papers

Hawkins, G. (March 2, 2016) Black Lives Matter is Opportunity to Seek Real Remedies. *Delmarva Daily Times*. Retrieved from http://www.delmarvanow.com/story/opinion/2016/02/28/black-lives-matter-opportunity/81008646/

Henrichson, C., Rinaldi, J., Delaney, R. (May, 2015) *The Price of Jails: Measuring the Taxpayer Cost of Local Incarceration*. [PDF File]. Retrieved from http://www.vera.org/sites/default/files/resources/downloads/price-of-jails.pdf

Ingraham, C. (September 25, 2014) Think You Drink a Lot? This Chart Will Tell You. *Washington Post*. Retrieved from https://www.washingtonpost.com/news/wonk/wp/2014/09/25/think-you-drink-a-lot-this-chart-will-tell-you/

Ingraham, C. (February 23, 2015) Marijuana May Be Even Safer than Previously Thought, Researchers Say. *Washington Post*. Retrieved from https://www.washingtonpost.com/news/wonk/wp/2015/02/23/marijuana-may-be-even-safer-than-previously-thought-researchers-say/?utm_term=.9debe947da83

International Laws. (n.d.). *Campaign for Safe Cosmetics*. Retrieved from http://www.safecosmetics.org/get-the-facts/regulations/international-laws/

Jaffe, A. (January 13, 2010) Alcohol, Benzos, and Opiates—Withdrawal That Might Kill You. *Psychology Today*. Retrieved from https://www.psychologytoday.com/blog/all-about-addiction/201001/alcohol-benzos-and-opiates-withdrawal-might-kill-you

Johnson, C. (October 21, 2015) More than 100 Police Chiefs and Prosecutors Unite to Cut Prison Population. *NPR.org*. Retrieved from http://www.npr.org/sections/itsallpolitics/2015/10/21/450302932/more-than-100-police-chiefs-and-prosecutors-unite-to-cut-prison-population

Kain, E. (July 5, 2011) Ten Years After Decriminalization, Drug Abuse Down by Half in Portugal. *Forbes.com*. Retrieved from http://www.forbes.com/sites/erikkain/2011/07/05/ten-years-after-decriminalization-drug-abuse-down-by-half-in-portugal/#3c857c385ac2

Kaste, M. (June 15, 2015) Murder Rate Spike Could Be 'Ferguson Effect,' DOJ Study Says. *Npr.org*. Retrieved from http://www.npr.org/2016/06/15/482123552/murder-rate-spike-attributed-to-ferguson-effect-doj-study-says

Kaste, M. (June 7, 2016) New Mexico Ended Civil Asset Forfeiture. Why then Is It Still Happening? *NPR.org*. Retrieved from http://www.npr.org/2016/06/07/481058641/new-mexico-ended-civil-asset-forfeiture-why-then-is-it-still-happening

Katzenstein, F.M., Waller, M. (October 26, 2015) Phone Calls Won't Cost Up to $14 a Minute Anymore but Here's How Prisoners' Families Are Still Being Fleeced.

Washington Post. Retrieved from https://www.washingtonpost.com/news/monkey-cage/wp/2015/10/26/phone-calls-wont-cost-up-to-14-a-minute-anymore-but-heres-how-prisoners-families-are-still-being-fleeced/

Kearney, M. (November 22, 2014) The Economic Challenges of Crime and Incarceration in the U.S. *Brookings.* Retrieved from https://www.brookings.edu/opinions/the-economic-challenges-of-crime-incarceration-in-the-united-states/

Kearney, M., Harris, H.B. (May 1, 2014) 10 Economic Facts about Crime and Incarceration. *Brookings.* Retrieved from https://www.brookings.edu/research/ten-economic-facts-about-crime-and-incarceration-in-the-united-states/

Keefe, R.P. (October 27, 2015) Making Insider Trading Legal. *The New Yorker.* Retrieved from http://www.newyorker.com/business/currency/making-insider-trading-legal

Kitsuse, J.I. (1980) Coming Out all Over: Deviance and the Politics of Social Problems. *Social Problems* 28: 1–13.

Klein, P. (July 23, 2015) Why Do Sociologists Lean Left—Really Left? *Organizations and Markets.* Retrieved from https://organizationsandmarkets.com/2006/07/23/why-do-sociologists-lean-left-really-left/

Kluger, J. (May 25, 2014) Why Mass Killers Are Always Male. *Time.com.* Retrieved from http://time.com/114128/elliott-rodgers-ucsb-santa-barbara-shooter/

Kollipara, P. (March 19, 2015) The Bizarre Way the U.S. Regulates Chemicals—Letting them on the Market First, then Maybe Studying Them. *Washington Post.* Retrieved from https://www.washingtonpost.com/news/energy-environment/wp/2015/03/19/our-broken-congresss-latest-effort-to-fix-our-broken-toxic-chemicals-law/

Koroknay-Palicz, A. (n.d.) Legislative Analysis of the National Minimum Drinking Age Act – National Youth Rights Association. *National Youth Rights Association.* Retrieved from http://www.youthrights.org/research/library/legislative-analysis-of-the-national-minimum-drinking-age-act/

LaMar, S. (August 14, 2014) Smart Talk: African-Americans Treated Differently by Law Enforcement? *Witf.org.* Retrieved from http://www.witf.org/smart-talk/2014/08/smart-talk-african-americans-treated-differently-by-law-enforcement.php

Lane, C. (March 2, 2005) 5–4 Supreme Court Abolishes Juvenile Executions. *Washingtonpost.com.* Retrieved from http://www.washingtonpost.com/wp-dyn/articles/A62584-2005Mar1.html

Levintova, H. (2016) Thousands of Girls Are Locked Up for Talking Back or Staying Out Late. *Mother Jones.* Retrieved from http://www.motherjones.com/politics/2016/09/girls-juvenile-justice-status-offenses

Lipton, E., Creswell, J. (June 5, 2016) Panama Papers Show How Rich United States Clients Hid Millions. *Nytimes.com.* Retrieved from https://www.nytimes.com/2016/06/06/us/panama-papers.html?_r=1

LoBianco, T., Walsh, D., Klein, B., Raju, M. (n.d.) Senate Rejects Series of Gun Measures. *CNN.* Retrieved from http://www.cnn.com/2016/06/20/politics/senate-gun-votes-congress/index.html

London, R. (March 30, 1991) 2 Waiters Lose Jobs for Liquor Warning to Woman. *Nytimes.com*. Retrieved from http://www.nytimes.com/1991/03/30/us/2-waiters-lose-jobs-for-liquor-warning-to-woman.html

Mangino, T.M. (January 7, 2014) How Plea Bargains Are Making Jury Trials Obsolete. *The Crime Report*. Retrieved from https://thecrimereport.org/2014/01/07/2014-01-how-plea-bargains-are-making-jury-trials-obsolete/

Margulies, J. (August 24, 2016) This Is the Real Reason Private Prisons Should Be Outlawed. *Time.com*. Retrieved from http://time.com/4461791/private-prisons-department-of-justice/

Marusic, K. (January 4, 2015) 13 Seriously F--ked Up Things About Women and Girls in Prison. *MTV News*. Retrieved from http://www.mtv.com/news/2119680/13-seriously-f-cked-up-things-about-women-and-girls-in-prison/

McCarthy, G. (October 21, 2015) Law Enforcement Veteran: Locking Up Minor Drug Offenders Makes Us Less Safe. *NPR.org*. Retrieved from http://www.npr.org/2015/10/21/450464658/law-enforcement-veteran-locking-up-minor-drug-offenders-makes-us-less-safe

Merton, R.K. (1968) *Social Theory and Social Structure*. (Enlarged edition). New York: Free Press.

Millhiser, I. (December 5, 2014) How the Supreme Court Helped Make it Possible for Police To Kill by Chokehold. *ThinkProgress*. Retrieved from https://thinkprogress.org/how-the-supreme-court-helped-make-it-possible-for-police-to-kill-by-chokehold-d9f17a773190

Miron, J. (July 28, 2014) Why All Drugs Should Be Legal. (Yes, Even Heroin.). *Theweek.com*. Retrieved from http://theweek.com/articles/445005/why-all-drugs-should-legal-yes-even-heroin

Montagne, R. (host). (October 21, 2015) Law Enforcement Veteran: Locking Up Minor Drug Offenders Makes Us Less Safe. *Morning Edition, NPR*. Retrieved from http://www.npr.org/2015/10/21/450464658/law-enforcement-veteran-locking-up-minor-drug-offenders-makes-us-less-safe

Moore, M.H. (October 16, 1989) Actually, Prohibition Was a Success. *NYtimes.com*. Retrieved from http://www.nytimes.com/1989/10/16/opinion/actually-prohibition-was-a-success.html

Munguia, H. (July 31, 2015) Helping Inmates Pay for College Could Dramatically Reduce Incarceration. *FiveThirtyEight*. Retrieved from https://fivethirtyeight.com/datalab/obama-pell-grants-prisons/

Myers, G. (June 6, 2016) Wrongfully Convicted Brian Banks Disgusted by Brock Turner Ruling. *NY Daily News*. Retrieved from http://www.nydailynews.com/sports/football/wrongfully-convicted-brian-banks-disgusted-brock-turner-ruling-article-1.2663595

NAABT. The National Alliance of Advocates for Buprenorphine Treatment. (n.d.) *Laws*. Retrieved from https://www.naabt.org/index.cfm

NBC. (January 20, 2015) Things Are Looking Up in America's Porn Industry. *CNBC.com*. Retrieved from http://www.nbcnews.com/business/business-news/things-are-looking-americas-porn-industry-n289431

NCADD. (February 23, 2016) Nonmedical Use of Adderall on the Rise Among Young Adults—*NCADD Blog Roll*. *Ncadd.org*. Retrieved from https://www.ncadd.org/blogs/in-the-news/nonmedical-use-of-adderall-on-the-rise-among-young-adults

NCVLI. Protecting the Victims of "Victimless" Crimes. (n.d.) *Law.lclark.edu*. Retrieved from https://law.lclark.edu/live/files/15461-protecting-the-victims-of-victimless-crime-sep

NIDA. (n.d.) *Trends and Statistics*. Retrieved from https://www.drugabuse.gov/related-topics/trends-statistics

NIDA. National Institute on Drug Abuse. (December 13, 2016) *Monitoring the Future Survey: High School and Youth Trends*. Retrieved from https://www.drugabuse.gov/publications/drugfacts/monitoring-future-survey-high-school-youth-trends

NIJ. National Institute of Justice. Five Things About Deterrence. (n.d.) *National Institute of Justice*. Retrieved from http://nij.gov/five-things/pages/deterrence.aspx

NIJ. National Institute of Justice. (June 17, 2014) Recidivism. *National Institute of Justice*. Retrieved from https://www.nij.gov/topics/corrections/recidivism/Pages/welcome.aspx

Noah, T. (June 21, 2016) *The Daily Show*. Comedy Central.

Noguchi, Y. (January 20, 2016) Opioid Abuse Takes a Toll on Workers and their Employers. *Morning Edition*. *NPR*. Retrieved from http://www.npr.org/sections/health-shots/2016/01/20/462922517/opioid-abuse-takes-a-toll-on-workers-and-their-employers

Noguchi, Y. (March 27, 2017) College Classes in Maximum Security: 'It Give You Meaning'. *All Things Considered*. Retrieved from http://www.npr.org/2017/03/27/518135204/college-classes-in-maximum-security-it-gives-you-meaning?utm_source=npr_newsletter&utm_medium=email&utm_content=20170402&utm_campaign=bestofnpr&utm_term=nprnews

OJJDP. (December, 2014) *Juvenile Offenders and Victims: 2014 Report*. Retrieved from https://www.ojjdp.gov/ojstatbb/nr2014/downloads/NR2014.pdf

OJJDP. (March, 2015) Alcohol and Drug Prevention Treatment/Therapy. *OJJDP*. Retrieved from https://www.ojjdp.gov/mpg/litreviews/Alcohol_and_Drug_Therapy_Education.pdf

OSHA. (n.d.) Occupational Safety and Health Administration. *U.S. Department of Labor*. Retrieved from https://www.osha.gov/oshstats/commonstats.html

Otis, G.A. (November 26, 2014) Ex-cons Returning to N.Y. Prisons for New Felonies Hits All Time Low: Data. *Daily News*. Retrieved from http://www.nydailynews.com/new-york/nyc-crime/returnees-ny-prisons-hits-time-data-article-1.2025646

Our Demands. (n.d.) *Black Lives Matter*. Retrieved from http://blacklivesmatter.tumblr.com/demands

Peltz, J. (May 6, 2016) A Pregnant Woman Walks into a Bar: You Must Serve Her in NYC. *The Big Story*. Retrieved from http://bigstory.ap.org/article/00f36eefd6d74852b7165cdea0334068/agency-bars-cant-ban-pregnant-women-or-refuse-them-drinks

Philip, A. (April 28, 2015) Phone Call Rates Squeeze Inmate Families, Boost State Prison Revenues. *Cronkite News*. Retrieved from http://cronkitenewsonline.com/2015/04/phone-call-rates-squeeze-inmate-families-boost-state-prison-revenues/

Phillips, A. (June 20, 2016) The Senate Voted on 4 Popular Gun Control Proposals Monday. Here's Why None of them Passed. *The Washington Post*. Retrieved from https://www.washingtonpost.com/news/the-fix/wp/2016/06/20/the-senate-will-vote-on-4-gun-control-proposals-monday-heres-everything-you-need-to-know/

Plea Bargains: In Depth. (n.d.) *Findlaw*. Retrieved from http://criminal.findlaw.com/criminal-procedure/plea-bargains-in-depth.html

Pope, J. (September 18, 2008) College Presidents Want Lower Drinking Age, *USATODAY.com*. Retrieved from http://usatoday30.usatoday.com/news/education/2008-08-18-college-drinking_N.htm

Reich, R. (2015) *Saving Capitalism: For the Many, Not the Few*. New York: Penguin Random House LLC.

Resnick, B., Zarracina, J. (June 15, 2016) This Cartoon Explains Why Predicting a Mass Shooting Is Impossible. *Vox*. Retrieved from http://www.vox.com/2016/6/15/11934794/cartoon-predicting-a-mass-shooting-mathematically-impossible

Rettner, R. (July 29, 2011) Can You Die from Alcohol Withdrawal? *livescience.com*. Retrieved from https://www.livescience.com/15300-alcohol-withdrawal-death.html

Roberts, S. (October 27, 2012) How Prisoners Make Us Look Good. *Nytimes.com*. Retrieved from http://www.nytimes.com/2012/10/28/sunday-review/how-prisoners-make-data-look-good.html

Rose, J. (October 21, 2015) FCC Moves to Cut High Cost of Prisoners' Calls. *NPR.org*. Retrieved from http://www.npr.org/2015/10/21/450464766/fcc-moves-to-cut-high-cost-of-prisoners-calls

Rosenhan, D.L. (1973) *On Being Sane in Insane Places*. Retrieved from http://www.bonkersinstitute.org/rosenhan.html

Rosenthal, R., Jacobson, L. (September, 1968) Pygmalion in the Classroom. *The Urban Review* 3(1): 16–20. Retrieved from https://link.springer.com/article/10.1007%2FBF02322211?LI=true

Rowley, L. (October 6, 2015) Where Is Marijuana Legal in the United States? List of Recreational and Medicinal States. *Mic.com*. Retrieved from https://mic.com/articles/126303/where-is-marijuana-legal-in-the-united-states-list-of-recreational-and-medicinal-states#.WNr657QI3

Schaffer library of drug policy (n.d.) *When and Why Was Marijuana Outlawed?* Retrieved from http://www.druglibrary.org/Schaffer/library/mj_outlawed.htm

Seelye, K. (March 6, 2016) Heroin Epidemic Increasingly Seeps into Public View. *Nytimes.com*. Retrieved from http://www.nytimes.com/2016/03/07/us/heroin-epidemic-increasingly-seeps-into-public-view.html?hp&action=click&pgtype=Homepage&clickSource=story-heading&module=second-column-region&region=top-news&WT.nav=top-news

Sherman, C. (n.d.) The (new) Big Drugs on Campus. *ADDitude Magazine*. Retrieved from http://www.additudemag.com/adhd/article/861.html

Shilhavy, B. (July 25, 2017) Legal Drugs vs Illegal Drugs: Are We Fighting the Right War? *Health Impact News*. Retrieved from http://healthimpactnews.com/2012/legal-drugs-vs-illegal-drugs-are-we-fighting-the-right-war/

Skorton, D., Altschuler, G. (March 25, 2013) College Behind Bars: How Educating Prisoners Pays Off. *Forbes.com*. Retrieved from https://www.forbes.com/sites/collegeprose/2013/03/25/college-behind-bars-how-educating-prisoners-pays-off/#649f37427077

Stolberg, S.G., Eckholm, E. (April 22, 2016) Virginia Governor Restores Voting Rights to Felons. *NY Times*. Retrieved from https://www.nytimes.com/2016/04/23/us/governor-terry-mcauliffe-virginia-voting-rights-convicted-felons.html

Stray, J. (February 4, 2013) Gun Violence in America: The 13 Key Questions (With 13 Concise Answers). *The Atlantic*. Retrieved from https://www.theatlantic.com/national/archive/2013/02/gun-violence-in-america-the-13-key-questions-with-13-concise-answers/272727/

Sutherland, Edwin H. (1939) *Principles of Criminology*. Philadelphia: Lippincott.

Szabo, L. (May 24, 2015) Addiction Treatment Shortage. *USA Today*. Retrieved from https://www.usatoday.com/story/news/2015/05/24/addiction-treatment-shortage/27181773/

Szalavitz, M. (June 25, 2016) Can You Get Over an Addiction? *Nytimes.com*. Retrieved from http://www.nytimes.com/2016/06/26/opinion/sunday/can-you-get-over-an-addiction.html?mwrsm=Email&_r=0

Taub, A. (June 15, 2016) Control and Fear: What Mass Killings and Domestic Violence Have in Common. *Nytimes.com*. Retrieved from https://www.nytimes.com/2016/06/16/world/americas/control-and-fear-what-mass-killings-and-domestic-violence-have-in-common.html?hp&action=click&pgtype=Homepage&clickSource=story-heading&module=a-lede-package-region&region=top-news&WT.nav=top-news

The Sentencing Project. (November, 2015) *Incarcerated Women and Girls* [PDF File]. Retrieved from http://www.sentencingproject.org/wp-content/uploads/2016/02/Incarcerated-Women-and-Girls.pdf

The White House. (April 23, 2016) *Economic Perspectives on Incarceration and the Criminal Justice System* [PDF File]. Retrieved from https://obamawhitehouse.archives.gov/sites/default/files/page/files/20160423_cea_incarceration_criminal_justice.pdf

Thompson, D. (May 11, 2015) Lotteries: America's $70 Billion Shame. *The Atlantic*. Retrieved from http://www.theatlantic.com/business/archive/2015/05/lotteries-americas-70-billion-shame/392870/

Tierney, J. (February 18, 2013) Prison and the Poverty Trap. *The New York Times*. Retrieved from http://www.nytimes.com/2013/02/19/science/long-prison-terms-eyed-as-contributing-to-poverty.html?pagewanted=all).

UCR Offense Definitions. (January 26, 2017) *Uniform Crime Reporting Statistics*. Retrieved from http://www.ucrdatatool.gov/offenses.cfm

Urahn, S.K. (April, 2011) The State of Recidivism: The Revolving Door of America's Prisons. *The Pew Center on the States*. Retrieved from http://www.michigan.gov/documents/corrections/Pew_Report_State_of_Recidivism_350337_7.pdf

Venkatesh, S. (2008) *Gang Leader for a Day*. New York: Penguin Group.

Victimless Crimes. (n.d.) *TheFreeDictionary.com*. Retrieved from http://legal-dictionary.thefreedictionary.com/Victimless+Crimes

Vo, L.T. (June 20, 2012) What America Spends on Booze. *NPR.org*. Retrieved from http://www.npr.org/sections/money/2012/06/19/155366716/what-america-spends-on-booze

Watt, A. (n.d.) According to Scientists This is the Most Dangerous Drug in the World. *Unilad*. Retrieved from https://www.unilad.co.uk/drugs/according-to-scientists-this-is-the-most-dangerous-drug-in-the-world/

Weir, K. (December, 2011) The Exercise Effect. *APA Monitor on Psychology 42* (11). Retrieved from http://www.apa.org/monitor/2011/12/exercise.aspx

Whitehead N. (August 8, 2015) How the Prescription Painkiller Fentanyl Became a Street Drug. *NPR*. Retrieved from https://www.mprnews.org/story/2015/08/26/npr-fentanyl-street-drug

WHO World Health Organization. (n.d.) *Health Topics. Substance Abuse*. Retrieved from http://www.who.int/topics/substance_abuse/en/).

Wihbey, J., Kille, W.L. (July 28, 2016) Excessive or Reasonable Force by Police? Research on Law Enforcement and Racial Conflict. *Journalistsresource.org*. Retrieved from https://journalistsresource.org/studies/government/criminal-justice/police-reasonable-force-brutality-race-research-review-statistics

Wolfers J., Leonhardt, D., Quealy, K. (April 20, 2015) 1.5 Million Missing Black Men. *New York Times*. Retrieved from https://www.nytimes.com/interactive/2015/04/20/upshot/missing-black-men.html?_r=0

Yu, M., Shapiro, A. (November 18, 2015) Drug Treatment Slots Are Scarce for Pregnant Women. *NPR.org*. Retrieved from http://www.npr.org/sections/health-shots/2015/11/18/455924258/in-tennessee-giving-birth-to-a-drug-addicted-baby-can-be-a-crime

CHAPTER 7

Genders in Society

WHAT YOU WILL READ ABOUT IN THIS CHAPTER:

- Basic gender concepts are introduced with emphasis on the concept of **intersectionality**, which refers to the idea that though all people within a sex share some commonalities, gender is experienced differentially with respect to **race**, **ethnicity**, **social class**, and **sexualities**.

- Particular terms are defined, such as **sex**, **gender**, **intersexed**, **transgender**, **cisgender**, **genderqueer**, **gender binary**, **metrosexual**. Gender is a discrete concept from sexual orientation though the two categories often are misconstrued as interdependent.

- **Sexism** is a system of privilege based on sex. The manifestations of **patriarchy** are explored, particularly in relationship to the cultural impositions of male experience and their role in **misogyny**.

- Biological differences in gender are explored in relation to the effects of **brain physiology** and **biochemistry**.

- The processes of **gender socialization**, beginning with the differentiation of gender colors and toys, and extending into areas of social media, mass media, and games, are elaborated. **Lookism**, or the extreme attention to body image, especially for girls, will be considered as having enormous influence on self-image and achievement.

- Differential experiences in **education** are reviewed, especially in terms of the impact of Title IX guaranteeing women equal access to education programming and funding.

- Analysis of **occupational segregation** and **pay equity**, along with issues of **sex discrimination** and **sexual harassment**, are essential in understanding the status of women.

- **Violence against women** is explored with regard to language, domestic life, and **reproductive rights**.

- Comparisons of **sociological perspectives**, particularly in terms of their explanations of the role of gender in family and society, are presented.

Introduction

From the onset, it must be emphasized that gender is experienced differently by individuals based on their gender identification, or lack of it. Though all women share some social realities the experience of womanhood is not universal across races, ethnicities, religion, region, and immigration status. These varied experiences of women are referred to as *intersectionality*. Multiple oppressions are not simply a matter of addition but of complexities. Intersectionality refers to the experiences of persons in all the nondominant categories of race, ethnicity, abilities, sexual orientation, sex, and gender identity. People, and groups, face discrimination in both the power structures of the country and in personal experiences and identity. Law professor Kimberle Crenshaw coined the term to explain why Black feminism posed a critique of anti-discrimination laws declaring them insufficient to address the realities of African American women. The power structures oppress African American women in a way that separates their experiences from that of other women and from African American males. The laws protecting "minorities" fail to incorporate these overlapping layers of oppression and, consequently, fail to address the legal rights of the group. This is accurate for any persons, or groups, embodying multiple subjugated statuses. Because of the institutionalized systems of oppression, existing frameworks even inhibit the awareness of intersectionality. The focus on the school to prison pipeline, for example, generally excludes Black girls even as it recognizes the problem that exists for African American males and other non-Anglo males. Crenshaw describes the experiences of Black women as "being invisible in plain sight" (Adewumni 2014). Any effort to address these issues must necessarily address the power structures affecting groups with multiple oppressions (Crenshaw 2015; Adewumni 2014; Morris 2016).

> Without an **intersectional** lens, our movements cannot be truly anti-oppressive because it is not, in fact, possible to tease apart the oppressions that people are experiencing. Racism for women of color cannot be separated from their gendered oppression. A Trans person with a disability cannot choose which part of their identity is most in need of liberation.
>
> (Uwujaron and Utt 2015)

Box 7.1 – Intersectionality

Intersectionality refers to the experiences of persons in all the nondominant categories of race, ethnicity, abilities, sexual orientation, sex, and gender identification. People, and groups, face discrimination in both the power structures of the country and in personal experiences and identity. The laws protecting "minorities" fail to incorporate these overlapping layers of oppression and, consequently, fail to address the legal rights of the group. This is accurate for any persons, or groups, embodying multiple subjugated statuses. Because of the institutionalized systems of oppression, existing frameworks even inhibit the awareness of intersectionality.

What Are Some of the Gendered Experiences in Nondominant Groups?

African American women, for example, are subject to injurious racial assumptions, particularly with regard to body image and sexuality. Pressures to be a traditional stay at home mother were not prevalent since, historically, there was a greater tendency to play multiple and core community roles as worker, parent, and activist. This is not to say that

Figure 7.1 A Zuni woman or man? The question is not really relevant since the Zuni recognized more categories than "male" and "female." This person is not referred to as of either sex but simply as "two spirited." The concept of two distinct, often conceptualized genders as opposing, is associated with the western world and is gaining significant opposition in the twenty-first century. Some critics support the concept of multiple genders, others promote the idea that gender is fluid over time and content, and still others with respect reject the need for gender classifications altogether Source: US National Archives and Records Administration

men were absent, as has been frequently misconceived, but to understand that women were vitally present in, and outside of, the domestic realm (Jardine and Dallalfar 2012). African American men have suffered stereotypic labels as threatening, criminal, and uncommitted to family (Alexander 2010).

Gender issues in Native American cultures are varied, so it is difficult to make generalizations as there are hundreds of Indigenous cultures in North America, misunderstood and contaminated by European intrusion and bias. Some evidence suggests that even in patriarchal-oriented Indigenous cultures there actually was more egalitarianism than in the European schema, and some of the cultures demonstrated a *matrilineal* history:

Men were generally responsible for hunting, warfare, and interacting with outsiders, therefore they had more visible, public roles. Women, on the other hand, managed the internal operations of the community. They usually owned the family's housing and household goods, engaged in agricultural food production and gathering of foodstuffs, and reared the children.

Because women's activities were central to the community's welfare, they also held important political, social, and economic power. In many North American societies, clan membership and material goods descended through women. For example, the Five (later Six) Nations of the Iroquois Confederation all practiced matrilineal descent. Clan matrons selected men to serve as their chiefs, and they deposed chiefs with whom they were dissatisfied. Women's life-giving roles also played a part in their political and social authority. In Native American creation stories, it was often the woman who created life, through giving birth to children, or through the use of their own bodies to create the earth, from which plants and animals emerged.

(Pearson, n.d.)

Some Native American cultures recognize more than two genders, or no gender, and value all of these roles. Individuals in these roles are awarded an elevated status and consulted when community conflicts emerge. The term used for these persons is *"two spirit."*

Box 7.2 – Two Spirit

Two spirit derives from *Indigenous* cultures, in which variations on a binary conceptualization of gender were acceptable. A person also can choose to live with no particular gender identity and can develop a partnership with a member of any sex, or live without a partner.

Figure 7.2 The Quinceanera celebration marks the Latina's transformation from girl to woman; one aspect of the ceremony entails the young woman exchanging her flat shoes for heels
Source: istockphoto.com

Asian American women also have been subjected to racial stereotypes and misconceptions. The diversity of experiences in Asian communities makes it difficult to designate a generic "Asian" experience. Common stereotypes applied to the pan-Asian category, include docility, sexual slavery, rigid familial patriarchies, and more recently *tiger moms* who relentlessly push their children to achieve the highest educational accomplishments. Men have been portrayed as rigid, reserved, and authoritative.

Latino cultures also are diverse though they share some similarities with regard to traditional *machismo*, emphasizing the patriarchal authority of the male and the domesticity of the female. Women inhabit roles responsible for the home and the emotional life of the family. The family is salient and often is a primary consideration for its members so the contributions of women are highly valued, albeit in a somewhat subordinated position to the male (Galanti 2003). In the Mexican culture, the Quinceanera, derived from Catholic traditions, is a large and formal celebration of a daughter's fifteenth birthday. Traditionally, it marked her entry into the adult life of the community and her readiness to find a mate. Today, it retains many of the traditions of this coming of age theme, as when, for instance, the girl's flat shoes are ceremoniously replaced with heels. Families generally provide a lavish party, with cake, music, dancing, and rituals involving family and community members (Quinceanera n.d.).

What Terms Are Utilized in the Areas of Sex and Gender and What Do They Mean?

The term *sex* refers to biological differences between females and males. These are more complicated than consideration of the sex chromosomes. Biological differences occur in hormones, brain, and body development. Most of us are accustomed to thinking of sex in *binary* terms, as two distinct categories. Biologically speaking, most people are male or female but at least 1 percent of the population is not. The fetus is initially **undifferentiated** until around the sixth week of gestation when the sex organs develop. The fetal brain undergoes sex differentiation, due to hormonal surges, at around six months. The small undifferentiated portion of the population is referred to as *intersexed*. An *intersex* person can possess anatomical elements associated with each sex, have ambiguous physical attributes, or physical attributes which do not match internal organs. There are several biological conditions which can lead to this lack of clarity. Intersex activists promote allowing the person to choose how they wish to identify. Historically, children have been assigned to one or the other sex but in recent decades the recommendation has been to let children define themselves as whichever sex they choose or to elect no sex categorization (Intersex n.d.).

Box 7.3 – Sexes

The term *sex* refers to biological differences between females and males. These are more complicated than the presence of the pair of sex chromosomes. Biological differences also occur in hormones, brain, and body anatomy.

Intersex(ed) refers to people who do not completely fall into one of the categories recognized as either sex. A person can possess anatomical elements associated with each sex; have ambiguous physical attributes; or physical attributes which do not match internal organs. Intersex activists promote allowing the person to choose how they wish to identify, or to elect no sex categorization.

The term **gender** is a cultural construct which has been utilized to delineate the social roles and personality characteristics associated with a person's sex (APA n.d.). A person can be identified as more *masculine* or *feminine*, each aligned with the biological group associated with the label. Alternatively, a person could identify as androgynous, exhibiting characteristics associated with both genders. Currently, this binary schema is considered outdated and preference is given to the recognition of *gender as a continuum* with the possibility of changing gender identities over time and varying in content. The term *cisgender* has been utilized to describe a person whose gender identity follows traditional cultural constructs. Such a person can identify themselves as *cisgendered*; *cisgendered male*; *cisgendered female*; or simply as *cis* (Brydum 2015). The *cis* designation arose to challenge the presumption that everyone conforms to the dominant social expectations and to highlight the ensuing oppression of individuals who choose alternative views. The term cisgender was officially added to the Oxford English Dictionary in 2015.

Transgender refers to a person whose identification deviates from the dominant schema. Some transgendered people support a binary construct but identify with the sex that is not their apparent, biologically given one. A chromosomal male may identify as female, referred to as a *transwoman,* while the obverse is referred to as a *transman,* and

Figure 7.3 Two transwoman friends Source: JohnnyGreig / istockphoto.com

either may be designated simply as *trans*. Research shows that a transwoman's brain is formed as a woman's brain deviating from the characteristics associated with biological males (Nutt 2015). Many transgendered people embrace the gender binary, declaring they are in the "wrong" body, and they want to feel "right." Such a situation was seen in Bruce Jenner's very public transformation into Caitlyn Jenner.

People who identify as **"trans"** frequently choose to present themselves as the sex they prefer. A person's gender identification manifests as early as two years of age. Nicole, a transwoman, born an identical male twin, reportedly told her father "Daddy, I hate my penis," before her third birthday (Nutt 2015). As early as she could show a preference, Nicole identified as female and behaved accordingly. Interestingly, the children in her neighborhood fully accepted her. One friend remarked "I know that boys have penises and girls don't, but Wyatt [renamed Nicole] is a girl, and she just happens to have a penis" (Nutt 2015). When children show a strong transgendered preference, and are allowed to honor it, the mental and emotional traumas associated with being transgendered disappear. A supportive family is essential in easing the problems associated with transgender status. Many of the complications associated with transgender stem from feeling socially and psychologically dishonest if forced into cisgendered roles.

Box 7.4 – Genders

Gender refers to the social roles and personal characteristics of an individual and is considered a cultural construct. Historical gender categorization has been limited to two genders, designated feminine or masculine, each aligned with the biological groups associated with it. Current critiques of this binary suggest that gender is neither prescribed by biology nor an either/or phenomenon. Critics suggest that genders are best conceived as a continuum which can express fluidity in time or content. Some people reject the concept of gender, choosing to be referred to with gender-neutral terms.

Cisgender refers to people whose sex corresponds to the gender typically associated with it. A female who identifies with the female gender role can be called *cisgendered*; *cisgendered female*; or simply *cis*. Corresponding appellations can be applied to the male. Such a designation is considered necessary to draw attention to the presumption of traditional gender identities.

Transgender refers to a person whose sex and gender do not match the cultural designations. A woman who feels as if "she" is a man is transgendered as is a man who feels "himself" to be a woman. These are people who feel themselves to be "in the wrong body." Transgendered people can simply live as the other sex, without medical intervention, or they can undergo hormone therapy and/or sex reassignment surgery. A woman who transitions is referred to as a *transman* while the man changing to a female is called a *transwoman*. Either can also simply be referred to as *trans*.

Genderqueer has several meanings. Queer can refer to a person who rejects the gender binary altogether. Alternatively, it views gender as fluid in time or content. *Genderqueer* persons reject the masculine and feminine pronouns preferring the more neutral "they" or the more innovative "ze" or "hir." They feel that gendered pronouns give false validity to the social structures which impose the gender binary.

Sexual orientation refers to who is designated as an object of sexual desire. Sexual orientation, like gender, has been associated with a binary of either heterosexuality or homosexuality. Such a schema imposes a **heteronormative** framework where heterosexual norms are disseminated as the only "acceptable" choice, reflected in the laws and policies of the country. Sexual orientation, like gender, is best viewed as a continuum.

The recognition of the involuntary condition of transgender is spreading. Currently, nine states no longer exclude gender reassignment surgery from *Medicaid* eligibility (2014) and *Medicare* now covers the surgery. One third of Fortune 500 companies also provide for transgender health benefits (Transgender Law Center n.d.). Transgender rights, however, are not universal. While some states have incorporated progressive attitudes into law to protect transgender rights, other states have passed restrictive legislation. Currently, North Carolina, Mississippi, and Tennessee are among the states that have laws discriminating against transgendered people by stating, for example, that a person can only use the bathroom their biology appears to indicate. In April of 2016, upon the passage of restrictive laws in North Carolina, superstar Bruce Springsteen canceled a concert scheduled for Greensboro, NC and refunded ticket prices. Other artists and groups also have chosen to boycott states with restrictive legislation. In May of 2016, the Obama administration, through the Department of Education, issued guidelines making it mandatory for schools to allow students to use the bathroom and locker area of the sex they identified with. By July of 2016, 23 states filed suit against the federal government in protest of this mandate (Caitlin 2016). Early in 2017, President Trump rescinded rules allowing for transgender students to use the bathroom of their chosen gender (Peters et al. 2017).

A more radical gender critique is reflected in the concept of *genderqueer*. This term refers to a person who does not accept the gender binary, choosing to identify as no gender, or as gender fluid, characterized as embracing shifting gender identifications (APA n.d.). Activists have protested cultural mandates limiting gender identifications. In response to criticism regarding a limited view of gender fluidity, *Facebook* provided for 58 gender options and, in response to accusations of persistent lack of inclusiveness, now allows for a "custom" gender option where a person can write a personal gender description (RT News 2015). To reflect this rejection of gender oppression, *genderqueer* individuals prefer a gender-neutral pronoun such as *they*, *ze*, or *hir* (Urban Dictionary). The American Dialectic Society designated "they," as a singular pronoun, as the 2015 "word of the year" (Marquis 2015). Some people are critical of this usage, saying that it is confusing due to its use as a plural pronoun. But linguists assert that *they* was used in a singular capacity 600 years ago until that designation was transformed into the generic "he" (Nunberg 2016).

Sexual orientation refers to sexual attraction, or who is designated as an object of sexual desire. A person's sexual orientation does not imply anything regarding gender identity. Sexual orientation also has been associated with a binary of either heterosexuality or homosexuality. Such a schema imposes a *heteronormative* framework where heterosexual norms are disseminated as the only "acceptable" choice, reflected in the laws and policies of the country. Sexual orientation, like gender, is best viewed as a continuum. There are as many as 16 categorizations

Figure 7.4 Genderqueer is a term indicating rejection of the gender binary
Source: Creatista / Shutterstock.com

of sexual orientation (TrentAndLuke 2015). Here is a partial list taken from SexInfo Online (n.d.):

- Heterosexual: a person who is sexually attracted to those of a gender other than what is defined as their own
- Homosexual: a person attracted to other people defined as in the same gender as themselves
- Bisexual: a person attracted to members of their own sex as well as of "other" sexes
- Pansexual: a person attracted to people of all genders or sex identification and therefore inclusive of intersex, transgender, and genderqueer
- Asexual: a person with little or absent sexual desire
- Demisexual: a person who feels sexually attracted only to people with whom they have an emotional connection or bond
- Queer: often viewed as an "umbrella" category including any designation other than normative heterosexuality.

Individuals with unconventional gender identities or sexual orientations are subject to discrimination in education, media, work, pay, housing, culture, and social life. Increasingly, they are being seen as in need of protective measures similar to those enacted to attain civil rights for racial and ethnic minorities and women (see Chapter 15).

What Is Sexism?

Sexism is best defined as a system which privileges one sex over the others. In American society this refers to the systemic male privilege institutionalized in the patriarchy. *Patriarchy* results in all things associated with men and masculinity becoming more highly valued while anything pertaining to women is either devalued or invisible. Women are hurt by sexism in access to power, money, and opportunities but also because any character trait, personality trait, or activity associated with women, and femininity, is denigrated. *Misogyny*, the hatred of women, can be viewed as the flip side of patriarchy. Anything associated with women, and the feminine, is devalued. Some theorists suggest that boys learn misogyny as a "normal" aspect of male socialization because so much of what is taught as appropriate masculinity explicitly, or implicitly, denigrates behaviors and characteristics associated with women.

Men are also hurt by the patriarchy, especially with regard to their traditional role as primary breadwinner and the lack of social and emotional development associated with traditional masculinity. The costs of dominance to their physical and psychical well-being is largely unappreciated. Although women can perceive men in stereotypic terms, this is not sexism in the same way that pervades the patriarchy's treatment of women since women do not have the power to subjugate men. Cultural discrimination, such as racism or sexism, is best described as a product of *prejudice and power,* incorporating both attitude and privilege. Although the dynamic of sexism pertains more to women, rigid gender role conceptions ultimately impede self-actualization in both sexes, leading some people to prefer to approach gender issues in terms of *human rights* rather than *women's rights*.

Misogyny and Menstruation

A good example of the entrenched **misogyny**, or disdain for women, is humorously exposed in Gloria Steinem's essay, *If Men Could Menstruate* (1978). She suggests that if men menstruated it would be seen as having sacred qualities, men would boast of their heightened sensibilities while menstruating and brag about the quality of their periods:

> Male human beings have built whole cultures around the idea that penis-envy is "natural" to women—though having such an unprotected organ might be said to make men vulnerable, and the power to give birth makes womb-envy at least as logical. In short, the characteristics of the powerful, whatever they may be, are thought to be better than the characteristics of the powerless—and logic has nothing to do with it. What would happen, for instance, if suddenly, magically, men could menstruate and women could not? The answer is clear—menstruation would become an enviable, boast-worthy, masculine event: Men would brag about how long and how much. Boys would mark the onset of menses, that longed-for proof of manhood, with religious ritual and stag parties. Congress would fund a National Institute of Dysmenorrhea to help stamp out monthly discomforts. Sanitary supplies would be federally funded and free.

In contrast, menstruation has led men to challenge the capabilities of women at "that time of the month," and to support many presumptions regarding female "moodiness." Steinem suggests that the same biological process would be assessed completely differently if experienced by the dominant group (Steinem 1978).

Box 7.5 – Patriarchy

Patriarchy refers to the domination of men in the social institutions as well as the higher valuation of all things associated with men and masculinity. Men are over-represented in positions of power, receive higher salaries, and are promoted more rapidly and ultimately to higher positions than women. Men also establish the standards of excellence in culture, including in arts, entertainment, science, politics, and scholarship.

Misogyny, the hatred of women, can be viewed as the flip side of patriarchy. Anything associated with women, and the feminine, is devalued. Some theorists suggest that boys learn misogyny as a "normal" aspect of male socialization because so much of what is taught as appropriate masculinity explicitly, or implicitly, denigrates behaviors and characteristics associated with women.

History is also distorted as a result of women's invisibility. Steinem provides an example of this phenomenon when she learned, while conferring with a woman leader regarding the Indian independence movement, that Gandhi's nonviolent strategies for social change were adapted from observing women organizing against *suttee* (the practice requiring Hindu widows to immolate themselves on the funeral pyre of their husbands) and agitating for universal suffrage. Their struggle was "missing" from the histories Steinem knew (Steinem 2015).

Language is itself a mechanism of social control and ideology. Uwujaren, a Nigerian-American author, addresses transforming the values embedded in patriarchy by changing our language. She suggests that such modifications are not simply a matter of "political correctness," but are necessary to challenge dominant views:

> The English language normalizes and validates heterosexuality, whiteness, maleness, and ability so ubiquitously that people forget that *it reifies these things* [makes a concept appear as an objective reality]. The foundation of the English language was built by white men, and its continued evolution has been largely directed by that same group of people. In other words, what looks like catering to marginalized people is actually decentering a white, male perspective of humankind.
>
> (Uwujaren 2014)

The male mind has shaped the structures, laws, cultural, intellectual, and artistic standards of the western nations. Women's contributions, developed outside of public recognition, are frequently suppressed, stolen, or devalued. When women's endeavors are known, they have been measured and judged by standards set by Anglo, male "experts." Credit for the ethos of the American Constitution is attributed exclusively to the "Founding Fathers" though it was modeled after the Iroquois Confederacy, the oldest known democracy in the world, which Benjamin Franklin read and cited. This information is omitted from historical accounts of US history (Steinem 2015).

Not all of the male gender norm is expressly taught or articulated as anti-woman. A significant feature of male socialization in a patriarchal culture concerns *proscribed* elements from which men are restricted. Male socialization contains many negative mandates, chiefly comprised of things females do. Boys are taught *not* to "throw like a girl," "cry like a girl," "dress like a girl," or "be a girly boy"; show emotions or vulnerability; or show weakness of any type. "Masculinity" is a learned trait incorporating a putative attitude towards females and a disdain for all behaviors associated with the feminine, inherently misogynistic even if unintentionally. Genuine intimacy is difficult to maintain when one group subjugates another. It is no mystery that misogyny persists, in spite of efforts to eradicate some of its forms. As long as male socialization characteristically incorporates negative elements, the devaluation of women and the feminine is likely to be sustained, to the detriment of the well-being of all persons regardless of gender identifications.

Are Women and Men Biologically Different?

Biology is a complex interaction of brain physiology and biochemistry, genetics, hormones, and environment. Studies in these areas are the "new frontier" of science and health and especially of gender studies. Recent technological innovations allow the discovery of new knowledge regarding the structure and neurology of the brain. Comprehensive brain studies found that the few structural sex differences were minimal and that the overlap between the sexes was far greater than differences between them. A larger left **hippocampus** in the male, possibly associated with better capacity for memory, is not more significant than differences within a sex:

> Researchers studying the brain may not need to compare males and females when analyzing their data. For another, she says, the extreme variability of human brains undermines the justifications for single-sex education based on innate differences between males and females, and perhaps even our definitions of gender as a social category.
>
> (Jarrett 2015)

Other gender brain research has shown greater levels of within-brain-hemisphere connection for men and greater between-hemisphere connections for women, though these do not seem apparent until about age 14 years. Some studies, relating brain structure to tests of cognitive abilities, show some sex differences which are present at all ages. These found that men are better at spatial and motor tasks while women excel at nonverbal reasoning and in recognizing emotions. These differences in brain connectivity were also noted in the resting state of the brain. Again, the impact of these differences may ultimately be relatively insignificant in group averages. On the whole, cognitive patterns between the sexes were judged to be "more alike than different" (Jarrett 2015).

How Is Gender Learned?

Controversies surrounding the consequences of differential gendered treatment of children persist. Whether existing gender differences are due to biology or socialization remains the subject of intensive debate. What is uncontested is that adult interactions, based on the perceived sex of a baby, begin at birth, if not before. Color preferences associated with sex in children's clothing, diapers, blankets, and toys are historically recent, dating only to the 1990s. In the early twentieth century both boys and girls initially wore white gowns, which could be easily cleaned with bleach. Boys and girls both wore skirts until boys transitioned to trousers around the age of seven. In 1927 clothing changed and so did color mandates, but not in accordance with today's norms. In 1927, *Time* magazine published a color chart with boys dressed in pink and girls in blue (Maglaty 2011). Pink was associated with power and with a fiery temperament, attributed to boys. Girls were presumed to be delicate and dainty and possessing purity and goodness, reflected by the color blue.

In the 1940s, manufacturers and retailers initiated color differentiation in children's clothing, with arbitrary designations. In the 1960s, the activist movement for equal rights for women promoted gender neutrality in clothing colors which was dominant until around 1985. Since that time diapers, clothing, nursery accoutrements, and toys have been gender stereotyped with girls in pink and boys in blue (Maglaty 2011). There is no evidence, however, that girls prefer pink any more than boys do; evidence of preference does not appear until about the age of 2.5 years (LoBue and DeLoache 2011), suggesting the impact of socialization pressures (Hammond 2014). Once a child's gender is demarcated, disparate social experiences occur:

> One study shows that women treated the exact same babies differently *depending on whether they were dressed in pink or blue*. If the clothes were blue they assumed it was a boy, played more physical games with them and encouraged them to play with a squeaky hammer, whereas they would gently soothe the baby dressed in pink and choose a doll for them to play with (Hammond 2014). Girls and boys both prefer playing with dolls, before gender appropriate learning kicks in and then boys deny the appeal of dolls. Around two and a half boys also develop an aversion to pink which is around the same time girls develop a preference for it.
>
> (LoBue and DeLoache 2011)

Colors are not neutral elements of a child's environment. Color affects feelings and behaviors and can have an independent effect on personal development (Van Edwards 2013). Red and orange are associated with warm feelings and with actually making people feel warmer, while blue and green have the opposite affect (Augustin 2015). Yellow, for example, is a color that incites excitement and can contribute to sleeplessness. For that reason, it is not advised to use yellow, considered gender neutral, for a baby's room. It also has been noted to enhance the appetite, so many people will paint their kitchens yellow though it generally is an unpopular choice for other rooms (Augustin 2015).

Gender-appropriate behaviors are reinforced from the moment of birth, intentionally as well as thoughtlessly. Gender persists as a significant factor in how a parent raises a child (Lindsey 2011), and often people believe that gender is inherent in our biology, but much of our associations with gender actually are learned:

> If we do something over and over again, it becomes normal. If we see the same thing over and over again, it becomes normal. If only boys are made class monitor, then at some point we will all think, even if unconsciously, that a class monitor has to be a boy. If we keep seeing only men as heads of corporations, it starts to seem 'natural' that only men should be heads of corporations.
>
> (Adiche 2012)

Figure 7.5 Children emulate what they see around them from a very early age
Source: Halfpoint / Shutterstock.com

The same baby will be described differently, based on whether the child is seen as a girl or boy. Differences persist, for most people, unless there is a concerted effort to resist them. Although there is some movement towards treating each sex similarly, there remains much stereotyping in the media, the home, and school despite efforts to avoid it. Gender prescriptions are still strongly reinforced and failure to embody them results in stigma, if not outright hostility. Recent legal and policy changes notwithstanding, the bulk of the social institutions in society promote a gendered world for our youth.

Toys are gender specific, either by type of toy or in their colors. "Girl" toys still emphasize the *soft skills*, such as nurturance and domesticity while "boy" toys continue to promote manipulative mechanics and problem solving. Children adhere to gender-specific behaviors they have learned will gain parental approval. Children, by the age of three, already know that fathers will disapprove more if boys play with girl toys than if girls take on boys' activities (Lindsey 2011).

A study of google searches (news.com.au 2014) identified significant differences in parental concerns regarding sons and daughters. Braininess is emphasized for boys while weight is the focus for girls. Parents were two and a half times more likely to search "Is my son gifted?" than the same query for a daughter, even though girls have larger vocabularies and speak in more complex sentences earlier than boys. Girls also are 11 percent more likely to be in gifted programs. Google searches regarding whether a child was overweight were 17:10 for girls to boys, even though boys actually are 9 percent more likely to be overweight. Though these findings reflect parental concerns, rather than rigorous scientific research, the investigation highlights the typical concerns of parents. The emphasis on "braininess" is ironic when contrasted with the significantly greater portion of females attaining college and advanced degrees.

There is evidence that parents set the behavioral bar higher for girls. One study involved the reporting of whether two tossed coins matched. The researchers found that when parents are together, with no child present, they report matches about 40 percent of the time, an approximate 15 percent rate of cheating since chance would yield a rate of 25 percent. The researchers then had parents paired with their children and discovered that they did not "cheat" with daughters but did so with their sons. The researchers interpreted this as a greater reluctance to model dishonest behavior to girls. Other research supports the contention that girls are expected, and therefore taught, higher ethical standards. Research also indicates that parents will cheat when alone if they believe their children will benefit by it, suggesting that "we can tell ourselves that lying and cheating are really forms of love and altruism" (Vedantam 2016).

Girls focus on their appearances to a greater extent than boys. Girls and women spend a fortune on cosmetics. Cosmetic expenditures were 55 billion dollars in 2014 (Rawes 2014). Cosmetic purchases can pose a drain on personal finances but, even more essentially, they impact physical health. Substantial research suggests that cosmetics have a detrimental effect on health and contribute to hormone difficulties and diseases such as cancer and obesity (EWG 2008). Recent research reveals that switching the brands of cosmetics of adolescent girls resulted in a drop in four body chemicals that are known to be hormone disrupters. In three days of substitution, the percentage of these chemicals as measured in urine samples, dropped by 25–45 percent. These chemicals are implicated in obesity, cancer, asthma, and other health conditions (Aliferis 2016).

Girls are more likely to develop eating disorders. Twenty-five percent of college-aged girls report binging and purging. One half of teenaged girls, and one third of teenaged boys, have engaged in unhealthy habits in order to control their weight. Tragically, eating disorders are the leading cause of death from mental illnesses (ANAD n.d.). "*Lookism*," defined as the focus on desirable physical attributes, promotes rigid standards. The prototype for women is tall, leggy, very thin, with high cheekbones and full lips. This image persists despite several advertising campaigns developed to challenge these restrictions and enlarge the concepts of beauty and attractiveness (Waxman 2015). Some countries have instituted laws limiting how thin models can be due to their negative impact on girls' and women's health and self-concepts (Persad 2015; Frost 2015). Body image and self-concept are experienced variously among different populations of women. African American images of the female body ideal are more curvaceous (Nelson 2009).

Box 7.6 – Lookism

Lookism refers to the imposition of a certain "look" considered desirable. The dominant cultural image for women has been White, tall, long-limbed, thin, with prominent cheekbones and full lips. This image pervades the culture and has become prevalent in nondominant groups although some, most notably African Americans, enjoy a wider range of desirable body types.

Research shows that boys are paying more attention to their body image, size, and appearance. Male action hero figures have become increasingly muscled so that no man, not even the famed baseball player Mark McGuire, would actually have the biceps represented in today's GI Joe dolls (Katz 2013). The rate of increase of male plastic surgery is a stunning 43 percent (Harper 2015) and has been on the rise for several decades.

How Has Social Media Impacted Socialization?

Research and commentaries attest to the enormous pressures the social media exert on adolescents. While it is certainly true that peer pressure was a factor in earlier generations, the ubiquitous use of social media exacerbates peer influence. Evidence says the pressures are more severe for girls. A large study of eighth grade social media usage indicated that more than one third check social media 25 times a day, without posting themselves. The heaviest users check the media 100 times a day, including during class time. Some students reported taking "tons" of selfies until a perfect image "suitable" for publishing is accomplished. Perhaps the most poignant finding was that the media highlighted differences between high-status students and socially "awkward" ones. The popular crowd's elevated status was reinforced along with the sense of exclusion and isolation in the more anxious and vulnerable individuals. One third of the research respondents admitted to deliberately posting to encourage feelings of exclusion and one half attested to feeling excluded. The hurt feelings were not limited to low-status groups; even popular kids admitted to feeling bad when seeing pictures of their close friends at gatherings they were not attending (Underwood and Faris 2015).

The book *American Girls: Social Media and the Secret Lives of Teenagers* (Sales 2016) analyzes the effects of social media in teenaged girls. Sales found that cyberbullying was easily more salient in the lives of girls than boys. Girls are more susceptible to the use of media for promoting visual images and social acceptability. Sexualized postings appear as a common means of gaining approval:

> I talked to an 18-year-old girl who is talking about looking at Tinder with her older brother and ... she said she was struck by the way in which the boys and men's pictures were very different than the girls'. Guys tend to have a picture like, I don't know, they're standing on a mountain looking like they've climbed the mountain, or they're holding a big fish or they're doing something manly, or in their car ... But the girls' pictures ... tend to be very different; they tend to be a lot more sexualized.
>
> (Sales 2016)

Girls are more likely to make and lose friends on the internet. Sixty-three percent of girls and 53 percent of boys unfriended or unfollowed former friends. Girls were a lot more likely to delete or to block pictures (Groden 2015). The prevalence of suicidal ideation and attempts, even resulting in posts where girls were encouraged to kill themselves, has been attributed to the uses of social media (Mehta 2016).

The constant attachment to technology has been dated as originating around 1983, with the appearance of the term *24/7*. Pervasive night-time use of social media

Figure 7.6 Social media leads to increased pressures often resulting in feelings of exclusion or isolation, even among the more popular students Source: SpeedKingz / Shutterstock.com

has been implicated in sleep disturbances and increased mood disorders; one fifth of young people report waking up during the night to check social media. Girls report seeking comfort from the media rather than from their parents (Udorie 2015). Ironically, use of social media is actually associated with anxiety and depression. Poorer mental health is linked to obesity, which has been shown to be a contributing factor in lower grades (Gardner 2012).

Video gaming is an activity which appears more prevalent in boys, 84 percent of whom said they played online and in person. Women comprise about 48 percent of gamers if all types of games are taken into consideration. If only *hardcore* games are considered, men predominate (Gittleson 2014; Zorrilla n.d.). Video game participation is utilized to enhance conversation among boys (Groden 2015). One significant aspect of video games is the preponderance of male images and the stereotypic images of females. Males are more likely than females to be primary characters and heroes. Women characters have been a consistent 15 percent of the total from the 1990s to 2014 (Gittleson 2014). In the 25 top-selling games, only 4 percent of the main characters are women. Women characters are generally portrayed either as the *damsel in distress* or the *ultimate warrior*. In a review of video game research, male characters are more "playable," meaning that they express *agency*, or will, as part of their character. When women are primary characters they are frequently paired with a male character who is more active and who protects and guides them. The females amount to little more than a "sidekick" (Zorrilla n.d.). In games characterized as utilizing "realistic" imagery, women are depicted with smaller chests and bigger waists and hips than in other games (Zorrilla n.d.).

Is Athletic Participation Important for Girls?

The passage of *Title IX* of the Civil Rights Act (1972) made it illegal to fail to provide equal funding, based on sex, for any public-school program receiving federal money. Although Title IX extends to issues around assault, discrimination, harassment, admission, employment, and stereotyping in education (www.justice.gov), its most immediate impact was seen in equalizing sports programs. At the time of the Act's passage, there were 30,000 female NCAA sports participants, compared to 170,000 males. This disparity carries significant repercussions since participation in sports contributes to academic success, college attendance and completion, greater participation in male-dominated occupations, and higher wages (Wong 2015). Equally important are the less "objective" benefits of sports participation. Girls' participation in high school sports leads to a reduction in pregnancies, greater confidence, higher self-esteem, decreases in depression, better body image, and enhanced psychological well-being (Women's Sports Foundation 2016). Program inequities pervade the schools. Many female students are denied access to sports programs, despite the passage of Title IX. Schools with a 90 percent minority population are significantly less likely to provide sports opportunities to women and show a larger gender gap in sports availability than schools with more White students. Overall, however, more than one quarter of American high schools reflect a considerable gender gap in sports (Wong 2015).

> ### Box 7.7 – Title IX
>
> **Title IX** of the Civil Rights Act (1972) requires that institutions of public education, or those receiving public monies, must not discriminate on the basis of sex. This has had particular impact in the area of sports.

Figure 7.7 Competitive sports improve the health, mental health, social skills, grades, and graduation rates of females
Source: vivalapenler / istockphoto.com

Many controversies have emerged regarding the ramifications of Title IX legislation. Some of these include the alleged disadvantage to male athletes; greater levels of bodily injuries to women; and reductions in the numbers of female coaches as men move into coaching the more prestigious teams. However, the allegation that women's gains have caused discrimination against men in sports is unfounded. Although women's participation in sports has increased more than men's, men are still disproportionately overrepresented in high school and college sports. Men also receive more scholarship money than women do (Schulte 2013). Title IX was passed to help females gain *equal* access, if the total athletic budgets do not expand then equity requires sharing the existing resources equally, which is not commonly occurring.

Do Television and Movie Industries Perpetuate Gender Stereotyping?

In a word, yes. There are fewer women in front, and behind, the camera and the gender pay gap is expansive. To get a crude assessment of the status of gender in movies, cartoonist Alison Bechdel created the *Bechdel test*. The simple test challenges viewers to find movies in which there are 1) At least two named women characters; 2) who talk to each other; 3) about something other than men. Although a negative test result does not necessarily amount to the absence of powerful or strong female characters, there are a surprisingly high number of movies which fail the test. Producers fear "chick flicks" are not lucrative, though movies that passed the test yielded greater profits than those that did not. One study of 1615 movies, released between 1990 and 2013 (Vagianos 2014) revealed the average cost of movies which passed the test was 35 percent lower than for movies which did not. Low-budget films featuring women have a significant audience and therefore are better money makers. High-budget action films might reach a wider audience but the profit margin is smaller. Why, then, are women-oriented movies relatively scarce? Hollywood often is blind sighted by its own prejudices. Terry McMillan's novel turned film, *Waiting to Exhale* (1992), was the first major motion picture to feature four Black women as stars and to show the movie industry that such a movie could be beneficial to the "bottom line." The movie was the ninth highest gross box office of the top 100 films of that year. Very few movies featuring Black women leads have followed and none have focused on women's friendships (Davis 2015). Since this study, a movie (*Girls' Trip* 2017) has presented a strong, mutually supportive portrayal of long-term friendship between four African American women friends, accompanied by Hollywood's preference for providing entertainment through escapades replete with dance, silliness, and male intrigues (Lee 2017).

Discriminatory portrayals of female stories begin early. Many children watch at least one DVD a day. Predictably, characters are largely gendered stereotyped. In G, PG, and PG 13 movies, females are commonly shown in traditional roles and as hypersexualized. Over one half of the female characters were shown in nurturing capacities. In terms of sexuality, in one large study of characters females were five times more likely than men to be wearing revealing clothes, often exposing exceptionally thin figures. Females were also three times more likely to have distorted bodies, such as unrealistically small waists. Caricatured images were stronger and more prevalent in animated films than in live action G rated movies (Smith n.d.).

In a study of 15 lead female characters in popular G rated movies, almost all were especially valued for their appearance. The desire for love was emphasized, even when the characters possessed additional aspirations. Love was depicted as unidimensional. The surprise in these movies was that the role of damsel in distress was not as apparent as might be predicted (Smith n.d.).

Gender differences in pay pervade the film industry. Despite the fact that women stars produce a great profit for the movie industry, Jennifer Lawrence, the world's highest paid actress, recently highlighted the financial exploitation of women in film (Lawrence 2015). In this article, she revealed that her three male co-stars in *American Hustle* each negotiated himself a higher salary than she received. She acknowledges that women's fear of appearing "troublesome" contributes to anxiety about making demands. She admitted to greater concern with seeming affable, leading to less reticence apparently absent in men (Sollosi 2015). A lot of money is at stake; the average top-earning Hollywood female makes 40 cents to the male dollar (Woodruff 2015). Other entertainment industry data show that women's salaries peak at age 34 and then steadily decline, whereas men's salaries peak at 51 and remain steady (Vagianos 2014). In the top 100 movies of 2014, only 1.9 percent had women with directing credit, 11.2 percent with writing credit, and 18.9 percent with producer credit (Pomerantz 2015). Female directing credits in the top 250 films of the year remained the same in 2012 as they were in 1998. In behind the scenes jobs, excluding directing, women experienced a 1 percent increase in that time span (Woodruff 2015).

Perhaps more psychologically devastating than pay is the lack of roles. In the top 100 movies of 2014, only 28.1 percent had female characters, only 21 leads or co-leads were women, and none of them were over 45. This was worse than the previous year and a drop of 5 percent from 2008. Female nudity was present in 26.4 percent of the characters, compared to 9.1 percent for men. Sexy attire was seen on 27.9 percent of the female characters and only 8 percent of the men. Contributions to the production process also reflect women's relative absence. Older women are virtually invisible in movies. In a 2016 interview Sally Field remarked:

> I've spent my whole life in [entertainment] and the frustration of [lack of roles for women] and the way I've dealt with it is just to keep my head down, and the minute I started railing it and wanting to jump up and down, I found it just wasted energy and it hurt my feelings, and I had to just find the work where it was and not spend the time going [grumbling].
>
> I remember once, long ago, Diane Keaton one time in some publication complained and said "This is outrageous, look at how much product there are for men and look at what there are for women," and everybody rose up and called her a whiner. I will never, ever forget it. And I remember in my, oh so not brave way, I tucked myself under and said, "OK, I guess we won't be speaking up, will we?" Instead of standing up, as young women are doing today and saying, "Wait a minute, wait one minute folks," but I think the conversation about women is aided by the fact that it's a diversity issue altogether and that

helps that it isn't just women. If it were just women, I honestly don't think people would be paying that much attention still.

(Field in Garcia-Navarro 2016)

Older Women in Entertainment

Older women are exceptionally maligned in the media. Invisible at best, they are frequently portrayed as feeble or silly. A few new efforts to counter this trend can be seen in recent efforts, though some caricaturing persists. In the Netflix series *Grace and Frankie* (IMDb n.d.), starring Jane Fonda and Lily Tomlin, two 70-year-old women redefine themselves when their husbands, law partners for 40 years, declare they have been engaged in a 20-year affair and now intend to live together. The show is not without its stereotypes; Grace is an uptight, snobby "Protestant" type and Tomlin a ditzy, dope-smoking, hippy artist who raised one Black and one White son, both adopted, in a Jewish household. On the positive side, the series (scheduled for a fourth season in 2017) celebrates the ability of women to support each other and even grow to respect each other's differences. The show was inspired by the real-life friendship of the female leads.

In the 2015 movie *Grandma* (IMDb 2015), Tomlin plays a grandmother who is helping her teenaged grand-daughter get money for an abortion. Tomlin is portrayed as non-judgemental, empathic, and trustworthy. The granddaughter avoids turning to her mother for help because she fears the mother will be too emotional, judgemental, and unsupportive, a depiction which hints at the typical mother/daughter dynamic as fraught with boundary issues. The grandmother is seen both as a more accepting character and as "once removed" from the intensity of the mother/daughter dynamic. Tomlin is sought out as the better candidate to provide aid without judgement or emotion. Nevertheless, Tomlin is caricatured as eccentric, having divested herself of all credit cards in order to avoid unnecessary spending, and possessing no emergency reserve. Currently, she is grieving the loss of a long-term woman partner. The movie follows the Tomlin character as she spends the day seeking help from various friends and an ex-husband, revisiting her past. The grand-daughter tags along and is surprised to learn of the existence of an ex-husband. Although Tomlin earnestly tries to help, it is difficult to imagine a teenager traipsing after her grandmother, all day long, on the same day she is planning to undergo an abortion. The distressed grand-daughter remains relatively calm, unemotional, and ultimately unbelievable. When the day proves unfruitful, the mother, who has financial resources, comes through for her daughter showing compassion and concern. The daughter sees that her mother can be trusted to provide the support appropriate to the situation. The movie relies on the improbable "gimmick" of the Tomlin character's trip down memory lane, suggesting the inability of Hollywood to simply portray relationships between women. Not surprisingly, the script was written by a male.

What Gender Differences Are There in the Education System?

Girls and boys show different levels of achievement in school but these appear to be more a factor of teacher interaction, peer group pressure, and learning styles than innate differences in ability. Evidence suggests that teachers treat girls and boys differently in that they tend to give boys lower grades unless the boys show pronounced positive attitudes towards school (Christakis 2013). Boys get a small grade boost just for good behavior. Boys experience more school failure, more suspension and expulsion, lower graduation rates, lower college admission rates, and lower college graduation rates (Christakis 2013; Kohn 2002).

Girls outperform boys at all school levels, from elementary school to graduate programs (Lohmann 2014). Girls dominate in the Advanced Placement (college level) courses, even in math and science. Girls account for up to three quarters of the leadership positions in school settings (Kohn 2002). Although girls are more likely to pursue a bachelor's degree, boys outperform them on standardized tests, prompting debate regarding test bias. Many tests, such as the SAT tests for college admissions, have been revised to be more gender neutral (Segal 2013).

Explanations surrounding the gender gap in educational achievements are highly contentious. Some argue that schooling is a "feminine" pursuit and boys rebel against studying since they don't want to be treated as "sissies." Some experts speculate that the school environment is more supportive of girls and that teachers are biased against boys because they present more behavioral problems in the classroom. It also has been suggested that book learning, and school structure suppress the higher physical activity drive associated with boys. It has been suggested that peer group pressures contribute to boys' underachieving.

Figure 7.8 Women earn more degrees than men, at all levels of higher education
Source: Monkey Business Images / Shutterstock.com

To address these purported biases, one proposal strongly supports separate classrooms for each sex. On the positive side, sex segregation might lead to less distraction, especially from competition to gain the attention of the other sex. Each sex behaves differently when in segregated settings, and it is believed that segregation will promote productive behaviors and better schoolwork. Critics suggest that sex separation can be a disadvantage, illuminating differences and making them seem more "real" than they are. They would also be anathema for those who support elimination of the gender binary. Another fear is that sex segregation will diminish relational skills and lead to increased occupational disparities. With respect to teaching, if classrooms had just one sex, pedagogy could become less responsive to individual styles of learning, due to the belief that a single-sex classroom represents more uniformity.

How Does Gender Impact the Work Environment?

Every aspect of work, from occupational segregation, career path, and pay, is affected by gender. More women are in the paid labor force than in previous eras, but predictions that women's participation would outrank men's have not materialized. Women's employment rate is 57 percent, while men's is 69.2 percent (Women in the Labor Force 2015). Over 70 percent of mothers with children under the age of 18 work, as do 61 percent of mothers with children under the age of three. The unemployment rate is slightly higher among men; 6.3 percent compared to 6.1 percent for women (Women's Bureau n.d.).

The gender pay gap persists; women make 79 cents to the male dollar, a figure unchanged in the last ten years. Women's wages are significantly depressed by race, ethnicity, and parental status, which is partially responsible for higher average

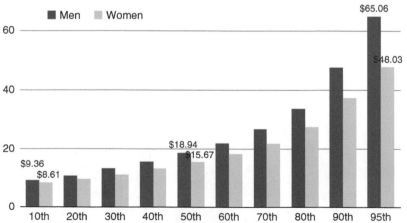

Women Earn Less than Men at Every Wage Level

Hourly wages by gender and wage percentile, 2015

■ Men   ■ Women

$65.06
$48.03
$18.94
$15.67
$9.36
$8.61

10th 20th 30th 40th 50th 60th 70th 80th 90th 95th

Source: EPI analysis of Current Population Survey Outgoing Rotation Group microdata.
For more information on the data sample see EPI's State of Working America Data Library.

Figure 7.9 Women's earnings are lower than men's at all salary levels with increased disparity among higher wage groups Source: Economic Policy Institute

incomes among White women. Asian American women are the exception, making an average of 1 percent more than White women. Gender gaps are present in virtually all occupations and at all education levels. For some highly educated women the pay gap is less dramatic, while in other occupations it is wider (AAUW 2016). For example, women comprise 40 percent of all full-time managers but earn only 73 cents to the male dollar in these positions (Coontz 2012).

Recent media attention has been focused on the depressed wages and increased unemployment of White working-class men. While it is true that males' wages have stagnated, and men without college degrees are particularly struggling, men are not disadvantaged when compared with equally qualified women. Although women's wages have risen while males' have stagnated or decreased, men still generally out-earn women (Coontz 2012). Coontz further points out that men have been entitled to a "patriarchal dividend," receiving inflated wages just for being men, though this advantage varies by race and class.

Most women work because the household relies on their contributions to survive (Reich 2013). Without the support of women, many more households would have collapsed in the "great recession." Although women's financial contributions are crucial, in 80 percent of married households they comprise a smaller portion of income than the man's. Slightly more than one third of married women contribute less than 10 percent of the family income. Women who are mothers suffer discrimination in obtaining employment and in pay. Studies where identical resumes were disseminated, with some presented as mothers, revealed that mothers were one half as likely as non-mothers to be called back (Coontz 2012).

Occupational segregation is still very high and, after a period of female gains in traditionally male occupations, is experiencing a reversal (Coontz 2012; Reeves and Sawhill 2015). Significant declines in job segregation occurred throughout the 1970s and 80s but leveled and then disappeared. Nevertheless, more women have moved into male occupations than men have into female occupational roles (Reeves and Sawhill 2015). Some fields became *more segregated*, as seen in data regarding primary school teachers, social workers, kindergarten and preschool teachers, and registered nurses. Women are a lot less likely to go into science, technology, engineering, and math (STEM) professions, even when they obtain related degrees. Women also are not "catching up" in leadership roles. Women comprise only 4 percent of Fortune 1000 CEOs (Coontz 2012) and 20 percent of Congress. Women's representation in the national legislature is relatively low, ranking 33 of 49 *high-income* countries and 75 of 137 countries studied in 2015 (McGregor 2015).

Women are evaluated with different standards at all levels of employment. **Sex discrimination** refers to unfair treatment in pay, promotion, evaluation, and other more amorphous issues such as failing to include a person in informal discussions affecting work decisions, language utilized, body language, and office space. Men, in traditionally female occupations, are usually not subjected to discrimination similar to what women face in "men's" jobs; their discrimination is more likely seen in preferential treatment.

Men in Female-Dominated Occupations

Perhaps the grimmest irony among many sex related disparities is that even in female-dominated fields, often the fastest way to advance is to be a man. A recent study found that male nurses make an average of about $5,100 more than female nurses annually, and men make more than women in other female-dominated fields such as education and social services too. In a series of interviews with male nurses and librarians, men reported feeling like they had been "fast-tracked" into leadership roles. Men also reported feeling that they were perceived as more competent, that people were more forgiving of their mistakes, and that older women in the field took on motherly roles toward them.

It's not just nursing: Men often ascend the ladder faster in other female-dominated fields. For example, in the 2011–2012 school year, 87 percent of public school teachers were women, but they made up only half of public school principals; women made up 83 percent of librarians but only 40 percent of library directors.

Even worse, the men making more than their female counterparts in these fields are likely doing less emotional labor. One study found that people make fewer emotional demands on men and that men are less likely to experience "social assaults" or "abusive treatment"—in other words, customers are less likely to subject men to childish temper tantrums. Another study found that college students expect female instructors to smile and engage in more interpersonal contact with students and rated them more poorly if they didn't. Meanwhile, smiling didn't improve the men's scores, and regardless of how friendly they were, they were still consistently rated as more effective teachers than the women. These findings are all consistent with the theory of the "status shield": men's status as stereotypically dominant and competent protects them from serving others' emotional demands and having to perform accordingly.

(Hu 2015)

The most discrete form of discrimination concerns wages. *The Equal Pay Act* (1963) mandated equal pay for workers performing the same tasks, regardless of actual job title. So, for example, a cook and a chef have to be paid equally if they are performing the same functions. Similarly, a housekeeper and a janitor require parity if their responsibilities are identical. One segment cannot be paid more simply because their position generally belongs to men while the other one has women incumbents. The concept of parity expanded in the 1980s to establish equal pay for "equivalent" work, as measured in skills, experience, and supervisory roles. So, for example, a "man's" job such as sign painter could not pay more than a "woman's" job like nursing. The supervisor of maintenance, with five employees, cannot be paid more than the supervisor of the secretarial pool, with a dozen. The concept, assigned the label "comparable worth," gained momentum through the 1980s. As a result of studies in comparable worth, 20 states adjusted pay in their workforces, effectively reducing the gender gap by 20 percent (Covert 2015). However, government agencies, and businesses, save multiple millions of dollars by not complying with comparable worth guidelines.

Box 7.8 – Equal Pay

The Equal Pay Act of 1963 established that women doing the same work as men, in the same site, should be paid the same wages as men regardless of job title. For example, a janitor and custodian, or cook and chef should be paid equally if their responsibilities are identical.

Comparable worth maintains that people who produce work of equivalent value should be paid equally. This concept addresses paying men a "family wage" since they were presumed to be supporting a family. Today, 40 percent of women are the sole, or primary, supporters of the family. Comparable worth seeks to set wages on specific elements of the job such as certifications, degrees, experience, supervisory responsibilities, specialized skills, and hazards. Job elements are awarded points and the point value would determine the pay rate. Such a process would be gender and race neutral. Organizations save millions of dollars by not adjusting for "comparable worth."

The Lily Ledbetter Fair Pay Act (2009), addressing issues of pay equity, was the first bill President Obama signed into law. The Act established the right of a person to sue for wage discrimination up to 180 days from their *last* paycheck. Previously, a person had to contest pay within 180 days of the initiation of employment.

States continue to pass legislation to address equity issues. In 2015, California passed a state bill establishing equal pay for women and men performing "substantially similar" work (Bollag 2016). This law affects everyone in the state from janitorial staffs, who have sued for equal pay, to a woman math consultant who had been hired by a California county and filed a suit (McGreevy and Megerian 2015). Massachusetts went a step further in 2016 by passing a more comprehensive "Pay Equity Act." Its mandate, among other features, clearly defines the parameters of "comparable work," and prohibits the employer from requiring any information regarding past salary history since that information leads to lifelong pay inequities (Keselenko et al. 2016).

Even with decades of legislative initiatives, pay equity remains intransigent. The investment and tech firms of Silicon Valley demonstrate deeply entrenched male power structures. Bachelor-level male employees make an average of 40 percent more than comparable women workers, while men with graduate and professional degrees make an average of 73 percent more (McGeevy and Megerian 2015). In a high-profile case charging *sex discrimination* at Kleiner Perkins, the "quintessential venture capital firm," Ellen Pao filed suit claiming she had been subjected to sex discrimination and subsequently fired in retaliation for making that complaint. Her attorney argued the case, in part, by establishing that women and men were subjected to different job evaluation criteria. They proffered evidence that she was spoken of in terms that were sexist. For example, she was given a performance evaluation in which she was "criticized for being too quiet, at least when she wasn't being too forceful." Pao lost the case, despite supporting evidence that she was judged by different criteria than her male counterparts (Streitfeld 2015, 2015a). A court order requiring Pao to pay over a quarter of a million dollars in court fees will likely discourage other potential plaintiffs from filing suit (Carson 2015).

For individual women, pay inequities not only amount to short-term financial struggles but can amount to losses of a million dollars over a lifetime. To address this problem, the first bill President Obama signed was the *Lily Ledbetter Fair Pay Act* (2009) which established the rights of a person to file charges of pay discrimination for up to 180 days after receiving the FINAL pay check. Previous laws allowed for such a charge only within 180 days of being hired. The case was inspired by the legal battles of Lily Ledbetter. Ledbetter had a 19-year tenure as a factory worker at the Goodyear Tire and Rubber Plant in Alabama. She claimed she was paid substantially less than her male colleagues but was unaware of this disparity until her retirement. At that point, she filed suit but the courts ruled against her, claiming that she should have filed a complaint within 180 days of her original employment (*Ledbetter v Goodyear Tire and Rubber Co.*). Her persistence led to the new bill, though Ledbetter never retrieved any wages.

Figure 7.10 Obama signing the Lily Ledbetter bill, with Ledbetter in attendance (to his left viewing the photo)
Source: Mark Wilson / Getty Images

Women in the workplace also suffer *sexual harassment*. *Sexual harassment* is not exclusive to women though they are commonly subjected to it. It is defined as follows:

> It is unlawful to harass a person (an applicant or employee) because of that person's sex. Harassment can include "sexual harassment" or unwelcome sexual advances, requests for sexual favors, and other verbal or physical harassment of a sexual nature.
>
> Harassment does not have to be of a sexual nature, however, and can include offensive remarks about a person's sex. For example, it is illegal to harass a woman by making offensive comments about women in general.
>
> Both victim and the harasser can be either a woman or a man, and the victim and harasser can be the same sex.
>
> Although the law doesn't prohibit simple teasing, offhand comments, or isolated incidents that are not very serious, harassment is illegal when it is so frequent or severe that it creates a hostile or offensive work environment or when it results in an adverse employment decision (such as the victim being fired or demoted).
>
> The harasser can be the victim's supervisor, a supervisor in another area, a co-worker, or someone who is not an employee of the employer, such as a client or customer.
>
> (Sexual Harassment n.d.)

Figure 7.11 Sexual harassment can be any gender-specific behavior that makes someone uncomfortable, including physically dominating body language
Source: Rommel Canlas / Shutterstock.com

> **Box 7.9 – Sexual Discrimination and Sexual Harassment**
>
> *Sexual discrimination* is differential treatment based on sex. Women are usually the group who suffer from sex discrimination in the workplace, with respect to job status, promotions, and pay. Women frequently are hired for lesser positions than men with equivalent skills, and this affects starting pay and subsequent salary scales. Women are also subjected to different standards of evaluation. Men can also be subjects of sex discrimination, though in traditionally female dominated occupations it more often leads to better pay and faster promotions.
>
> *Sexual harassment* refers to unwelcome sexual advances or hostile and intimidating behaviors. These can be in the forms of teasing, offensive comments or posturing, and any element of the environment which makes the employee feel uncomfortable. Harassment often is associated with the workplace but it can occur in any setting, on the streets, in social interactions, and in all social institutions.

Sexual Harassment

The issue of sexual harassment was brought to national attention with the televised judicial committee hearings, in the US Senate, regarding the 1991 nomination of Clarence Thomas, an African American, to the US Supreme Court. Anita Hill, then a 31-year-old African American law professor, had worked as an employee in several government agencies where Thomas had been her supervisor, and she alleged that he had harassed her while she was his employee. The hearings, the first of the kind to be televised live, attracted an audience of tens of millions. Despite multiple accusations regarding her motives, Hill actually was a reluctant witness who was approached by the FBI and asked whether she was aware of allegations of any misconduct by Thomas. Hill's testimony was rife with lurid details of conversations she recalled as offensive. Hill was variously accused of having been manipulated by the Democrats to discredit Thomas, to help their presidential candidate Bill Clinton, and was subjected to the accusation that she was a woman whose romantic interests were rebuffed by Thomas. Other commentators suggested that Hill should not have aired "dirty laundry" against an African American with a chance at the Supreme Court. It almost seemed as if anything was possible in the presentation of the case other than the actuality of the harassment.

Thomas turned the hearings into a referendum on race, famously calling the proceedings a "high-tech lynching for uppity blacks who in any way deign to think for themselves, to do for themselves, to have different ideas" (Thomas 2017). The all-White, male Senate Judiciary Committee ultimately sent Thomas' nomination to the full Senate which confirmed him by the narrowest margin of any Supreme Court nominee (52:48).

There seems ample evidence that Hill was harassed. After the confirmation, subsequent information revealed that other women were ready to testify regarding harassment by Judge Thomas. There also was a credible witness who could have attested to conversations with Hill at the time of the events cited and to their impact on Hill. She did not testify and no one obtained an affidavit from her regarding her potential testimony. The hearings were rushed and abbreviated, failing to allow for the testimony of other women subpoenaed. Multiple films have been made about the hearings, depicting Hill's ordeal as well as the politics behind the committee's actions, or inactions (Mock 2013; Famuyiwa 2016). The televised hearings were riveting to some and did result in more women making charges of sexual harassment in the workplace (Fabio 2009). HBO's presentation, *Confirmation* (Famuyiwa 2016), highlights the hypocrisy of the all-White male Senate committee whose personal behaviors, if scrutinized, likely would have revealed similar transgressions. On the occasion of HBO's 2016 *Confirmation*, and the 25th anniversary of the hearings, one commentator noted: "It brings up the uncomfortable reality of how powerful men often treat the women around them, and the problematic lack of gender and racial diversity in government" (Gray 2016).

Since that time, there have been multiple high-profile cases of sexual harassment such as those against Arnold Schwarzenegger, Bill Clinton, Donald Trump, all of whom were elected despite credible, multiple accusations. Multiple accusations that Bill Cosby had drugged and assaulted women shocked some fans, as more than one complaint emerged. He ultimately was charged with sexual assault (Ember and Bowley 2015). Then, in 2017, there seemed to be a tipping point when Harvey Weinstein, a powerful figure in entertainment, was accused by 80 women of sexual harassment and assault (Moniuszko and Kelly 2017). In the following weeks, high-profile cases emerged daily, revealing not only harassment but sexual assault by figures in politics, journalism, and entertainment. A partial list includes Senator Franken, Senate candidate Roy Moore, San Diego Mayor Bob Filner, Representative John Conyers, President George H.W. Bush, Roger Ailes, Charlie Rose, Mark Halperin, Bill O'Reilly, Michael Orestes. This is just a list of the names that emerged in the weeks immediately following the revelations with regard to Harvey Weinstein. It led to a campaign, *#metoo* movement, where women were encouraged to tell their episodes of harassment. In the first 24 hours, 12 million women responded, ranging from "everyday" workers to celebrities and movie stars (Park 2017). Several perpetrators have been revealed to have made non-disclosure settlements to their accusers and Weinstein has been shown to have hired several firms to intimidate his accusers (Farrow 2017). It seems impossible to predict how many well-known men will be identified as harassers, and worse.

What Constitutes Violence Against Women?

In his video *Tough Guise 2* (2013), Jackson Katz highlights the fact that violence and aggression are "normative" aspects of male socialization. Most violence is perpetrated by men, and this is especially pronounced in mass shootings which are almost exclusively enacted by young, White males. Violence against women is not restricted to physical assaults but is also manifested in verbal abuse and sexual exploitation. Notwithstanding some progress regarding these activities, laxity in the legal and criminal justice systems has exacerbated the silence and inaction surrounding these abuses.

With respect to language, excluding overtly sexualized words, women are prone to special vocabularies which sexualize, infantilize, or demean them. Even when referencing the same behaviors, women are described differently than men. During the 2016 presidential campaign, Hillary Clinton was described as "shrill" though she likely would have been deemed "forceful" if she had been a man.

Figure 7.12 Anita Hill testifies regarding sexual harassment during the 1991 Senate Judiciary Committee hearings for the nomination of Clarence Thomas to the US Supreme Court
Source: Rob Crandall / Shutterstock.com

Microaggression is a term recently applied to language and behaviors which carry negative, offensive, stereotypic, or derogatory evaluations based on membership in a marginalized group (Microaggression n.d.). Microaggressions typically demean the experiences of women, racial and ethnic minorities, people with nontraditional sexualities, and/or poorer people. They may be unintentional but they nevertheless indicate the automatic associations which can either credit, or discredit, a person's experiences. With respect to women, a comparison of slang words reveals that there are many more words associated with women than men.

Box 7.10 – Microaggression

The term *microaggression* refers to comments which can be construed as categorically derogatory, stereotypic, or insensitive with respect to race, ethnicity, religion, sex, sexual orientation, gender, body type, or ability. The offensiveness can be unintended but it highlights underlying assumptions regarding marginalized groups which lead to discrimination and remain unacknowledged.

Slang Words Associated with Women and Men

Slang words for women

Amazon – arm candy – astronaut's wife – Aunt Jemima – aviation blonde – b – babe – bad kitty – bag – bag bitch – BBW – beast – beav – beaver – Becky – Benjamin – Betty – biddie – biddy – Big Booty Judy – bimbo – bimho – bint – bird – bisnotch – bitch – blonde – bob – booth babe – box – breezie – breezy – bridezilla – broad – Buffy – bunny boiler – burger – bushpig – butch – butterface – butter face – butterhead – cat – chank – chica – chicadee –chick – chickabee – chickadee – chicken head – chicken hoe – chiquita – chiquita banana – classy hoochie – cougar – cow – crank whore – crockadillapig – cronk – cunt – 'c' word – dame – decent Rita – dime – dish – ditz – diva – doll – double R – dudette – f4f – fag hag – feedbag material – femme-fatale – filly – flange – flipper – floozie – floozy – foxy – gal – ghetto bird – ghetto ho – GILF – girl – girlfriend – girlie – girly – girly-girl – gold digger – good sort – Grimace – grizzly chicken – gurl – gyal – gyal dem – heina – ho bagel – hockey whore – hoe – hogbeast – homegirl – ho-nasty – hooch – hoochie – hose beast – hoss – hot ma' – hunny – hussy – huzzie – ice queen – jackpine savage – Jane Doe – Jenny McCarthy – jumper – jumpoff – karena – lass – Lolita – lumberjack – ma – ma'am – mack mamma – mami – manizer – manster – MIF – MILF – millihelen – minger – MIWLF – mole – moll – Mona Bushpig – mudpout – MWF – old bag – Omega Mu – pass around pussy – Pebbles – pigeon – poon – poontang – popcorn hoe – prostitot – puck bunny – pussy – PYT – queen bee – ragamuffin – rasp – rat – RUB – runner – sauerkraut – sausage jockey – scud – sea donkey – sea hag – sex kitten – sexy mama – shawty – Sheila – shiksa – shorty – sista – sister – skank – skeezy ho – sketel – sko – sleaze – sorostitute – space queen – split-tail – Susan Glenn – suspy – swamp donkey – sweet sister of mine – SWF – SWM – tail –tart – toots – tramp – trick – trim – troglodyte – troll – twinkie – twist – two o'clock beauty queen – vamp – village bicycle – what's-her-face – whatshername – whooty – whore – wild – woofer – Xbox – yak – younger model – yummy mummy

(Slang words for women, n.d.)

Slang words applied to men

b – babe magnet – back door man – Baldwin – Barney – bastard – big daddy long dick – bluey – boi – boy toy – bra – bro – brohan – brohanski – brother – bruv – champ – chap – chaser – cheese – chicken – chief – codger – daddio – daddy – DILF – drag queen – dreamboat – dude – fanboi – fanboy – feen – fella – FILF – girl – GQ – guy – Harrison – himbo – home boy – jack – Joe Six-pack – ladies' man – mac – mack daddy – man-slut – mate – McDreamy – Melvin – mimbo – Mr – MWM – my man – nigga – ninja – pal – pig – pimp – player – pop – prick – rhino – sausage – scrub – slick – snack – spider – sport – sugar daddy – thoroughbred – trap – vato – what's-his-face

(Slang words for men, n.d.)

Women are disrespected in myriad ways, not only in language but just by their presence, as women, in public places. Some men act as if they have the prerogative to comment on a woman's looks; apparently being out in public is enough to give them license. This presents a form of harassment, often depersonalized. Actress Shoshana Roberts walked the streets of NYC wearing jeans and a t-shirt, and reported 108 incidents of harassment, including being followed and being told to "smile." Her walk was recorded and turned into a two-minute Public Service Announcement sponsored by an anti-street harassment advocacy group (Butler 2014). The US Centers for Disease Control and Prevention report that one in three women has endured "noncontact unwanted sexual experiences" (Sullivan 2014). Another poll found two thirds of respondents reported being subjected to street harassment, with 20 percent of these incidents leading to being followed and 23 percent to physical touch. Some observers believe the figures to be low estimates (Sullivan 2014).

In a recent YouTube video, two women sportscasters discussed receiving daily tweets constituting hate crimes. These tweets assailed the appearance, sexuality, and journalistic quality of the women. Sexually graphic language and sexually profane words were used to describe the women. Some comments even promoted violence, threatening them even to the point of advocating their death. To show how harmful and hateful these tweets were, the women arranged for different men to say these things to their faces, reading from the actual tweets. In the resulting video, the men appear uncomfortable reading these aloud and are seen faltering or falling silent (Just Not Sports 2016).

Women who are overweight are viewed as fertile territory for commentary, regarding their clothing or overall appearance. A classic treatise (Orbach 1997) suggesting that "fat is a feminist issue" seems just as relevant today. Fat women are treated as "deviant" with many stereotypic characterizations attributed to them

Figure 7.13 Women feel vulnerable to street harassment and rape, just in exercising the right to walk alone in public
Source: a katz / Shutterstock.com

because of their size. The overweight female is seen as less than a woman, assumed to be non-sexual, and subjected to special derision. Heavier women have a difficult time buying clothes, especially if they want something more stylish; their shopping options, with respect to style and stores, are limited. In opposition to minimizing women's clothing sizes, which now frequently start at size 0, Melissa McCarthy has come out with a line of clothing in "straight sizing," representing styles and pricing for all shapes and budgets (Melissa McCarthy Seven7).

Notions of ideal beauty pervade the culture with images of slender, ethereal, and aloof White women. These standards are not universally applied to all groups. Leslie Marmon Silko shares some of her Laguna Pueblo upbringing on the subject:

> My great-grandmother was dark and handsome. Her expression in photographs is one of confidence and strength. I do not know if white people then or now would consider her beautiful. I do not know if the old-time Laguna Pueblo people considered her beautiful or if the old-time people even thought in those terms. To the Pueblo way of thinking, the act of comparing one living being with another was silly, because each being or thing is unique and therefore incomparably valuable because it is the only one of its kind. The old-time people thought it was crazy to attach such importance to a person's appearance. I understood very early that here were two distinct ways of interpreting the world. There was the white people's way, and there was the Laguna way, in the Laguna way, it was bad manners to make comparisons that might hurt another person's feelings.
>
> (Silko 2007)

Research shows that although the average Black woman weighs more than the average White woman, African American women display a higher self-esteem and body image. African American women are not seduced by dominant group media images which implicitly exclude them; they claim a wider variety of looks and factors as beautiful other than size:

> Princeton professor Imani Perry teaches interdisciplinary classes in African American studies and notes black women have conceptions of beauty that are "not just tied to the accident of how you look as a consequence of your genes." They include style, grooming, how you present and carry yourself, and "how you put yourself together, which I think generally speaks to the fact that we have a much broader and deeper conception of beauty."
>
> (Parker 2012)

Reproductive rights is another avenue exhibiting violence against women. Reproductive rights are greater than issues of access to birth control and legal abortion. The ability to control one's body and to make reproductive decisions without regard to external constraints is crucial in women's lives. The concept incorporates access to safe abortion and to accessing the means to securely raise a child. Another essential aspect incorporated in reproductive rights entails ending discrimination against pregnant women. This is especially significant in the workplace where it can lead to unemployment, pay inequities, and other forms of derailment in practice, law, and policy. In 1970, three years before abortion gained federal legal status (*Roe v Wade* 1973), a military captain who became pregnant was given the choice to either have an abortion or resign. The military had an exemption from the outlawing of abortion, suggesting its interest in controlling fertility. The captain in the case, Susan Struck, fought for her right to have the child while maintaining her career; she refused to be forced to relinquish either. She fought for the right to choose to give the baby up for adoption. The case never went to the Supreme Court, since the air force voluntarily changed its mandated discharge policy in 1972. A similar case, trying to force a school teacher out of work halfway through her pregnancy, was successfully argued in the Supreme Court in 1974 (Carmon and Knizhnik 2015). The underlying "right" in the area of reproduction is *choice*; a woman should have the resources to decide whether or not to have children and to feel social and legally supported in any path chosen.

Box 7.11 – Reproductive Rights

Reproductive rights assure women control over their bodies. Often associated with access to birth control and legal abortion, reproductive rights also include the provision of programs to secure a healthy pregnancy and environment for the child. The underlying "right" in reproduction is *choice*; a woman should have the resources to decide whether or not to have a child and to feel supported by social institutions and laws, whatever path she chooses.

Recent years have been especially indicative of movements to restrict abortion rights, federally guaranteed since 1973. In 2011, 92 state laws were passed restricting access to abortion. Research shows a concomitant increase in internet searches for how to obtain a self-induced abortion (Stephens-Davidowitz 2016). The most egregious law was passed in Texas where it was mandated that abortion clinic doctors must have privileges at nearby hospitals and that the clinics had to be certified as ambulatory care surgical centers. Most clinics, safely performing abortions across the country, do not qualify under these conditions (Liptak 2015). A US Supreme Court decision (2016) overturned the Texas law, ruling 5:3 that these restrictions would place an "undue burden" on women's access to safe first trimester abortions (Liptak 2016).

Abortion remains an exceptionally contentious political, religious, and emotional issue. Even the language of "pro-life" suggests that those who are "pro-choice" are somehow antithetical to supporting life. Yet "pro-life" supporters ironically do NOT support welfare and safety net programs providing for basic life needs of children (Is it Hypocritical...? n.d.). Protests have threatened the funding for *Planned Parenthood*, though performing abortions is a small part of the agency's services. *Planned Parenthood* offers a range of services, providing access to mammograms, birth control, education and preventive services, and other essential health initiatives

(Planned Parenthood 2014). In 2015 multiple accusations were made, in the press and the courts, alleging that *Planned Parenthood* sold fetal tissue. Investigations have failed to corroborate any of these (Planned Parenthood; Kurtzleben 2016; Editorial Board 2016). A national effort was initiated to prevent the Trump administration from defunding Planned Parenthood even before he took office (Hellmann 2017).

More overt forms of violence include sexual assault, rape, molestation, and sex trafficking. The CDC estimates that 19.3 percent of US women are subjected to rape or attempted rape (Jacobson 2015). The prevalence of assaults on college campuses is high and often they are uninvestigated or unpunished. In research studying 150,000 college students, 23 percent report unwanted sexual contact of some type, including sexual intercourse, and other studies support the finding (Wallace 2015; 2015a). A culture of denial leads to reluctance to file charges since women who have alleged sexual assault often must attend school with, and even live in the same dormitory, as their alleged perpetrators (Sexual Assault on College Campuses n.d.). Many women feel betrayed by the institutions which fail to protect them or to even seriously investigate the allegations (McHugh and Farrow 2016; Perez-Pena 2015).

Sexual assault in the military has also been the subject of media attention, especially with respect to the failure to investigate reported abuse and the persistent exposure of women to their alleged perpetrators. One in three women in the services will be the target of an assault. Reluctance to report the crimes pervades because it often derails careers. Frequently, the women must work with their accused assailants

Figure 7.14 Demonstrators outside the Supreme Court await the Court's decision in the case of the restrictive Texas abortion law

Source: Rena Schild / Shutterstock.com

if they do make a report. Women who report an attack are 12 times more likely to experience retaliation than to see their assailant convicted (Brook 2015). The military investigates complaints through its own ranks (Evans 2015), a situation which also discourages reporting. Women who make charges of sexual assault have been subjected to ridicule, demotion, and involuntary discharge (Speier 2012). Unreported rapes lead to persistent offenses by the perpetrator (Lisak and Miller 2002). It is estimated that only one in 20 reported rapes results in any jail time. Congressional hearings have been held to address military sexual assault, evasion of its recognition by authorities, and the complexities surrounding indictment and conviction (Speier 2017).

Human trafficking represents another threat to women. The prevalence of domestic trafficking is denied or underestimated. Predatory practices are used against desperate immigrants to enslave workers in US households, farms, factories, and service industries such as hospitality and nail salons (Vega and Woworuntu 2015). There were 3000 reported cases of trafficking in 2016, most involving sex trafficking. Human trafficking is not limited to immigrant populations; between 2008 and 2010, 82 percent of reported FBI trafficking cases involved US citizens (Tan 2016). The US government recovers only about 1 percent of these tragic cases, frequently housing youths in juvenile justice facilities ill equipped to provide necessary care or appropriate counseling (Vega and Woworuntu 2015). Nonprofit agencies committed to serving the enslaved struggle to change lives (Girls on a Journey Program 2009; Human Trafficking n.d.).

How Do Sociologists View Gender Issues?

Conflict theorists view the gender binary as an integral support of patriarchal institutional domination. This view suggests that women are unlikely to make real or lasting progress as long as traditional gender schema persist. Some progress for women is acknowledged, though the embedded nature of male dominance in major institutions limits fundamental social change. Some theorists suggest that maintaining women's subjugation is conscious or deliberate, that "power begets power." Others see it as engrained in the institutional structures and therefore unlikely to be dismantled. Conflict theorists would acknowledge that men benefit from women's oppression and have no vested interest in changing that. Men still hold the vast majority of positions of power in the economy and government. They are paid more, promoted more quickly, do less housework, and leave much of the childcare arrangement (if not the childcare) to their partners. Of course, this is not true across the board. Many men desire to free themselves from elements of traditional masculinity but retain institutionalized advantages which can only be dismantled by the will of the privileged to do so. Change necessarily depends on the recognition, by the privileged, that they are benefitting from the status quo and they must commit to changing their practices. Without that determination, if women gain significant access to sources of power, the base of the patriarchy will be threatened and individual men, as well as institutions, will suffer losses in male control. Arguably, this is part of the reason why Hillary Clinton inspires such loathing. Regardless of her political positions, she suffered attacks and censure in a way that is *gendered*. In other words, if Hillary had been Bill (or John or George), her "likeability" factor would not have been so low.

Functionalist theorists are more likely to see gender roles as useful, not just for men but for the overall social "good." In the post-World War II era, American functionalists focused on the expediency of gender roles in supporting institutional and individual well-being. They suggested that everyone benefitted when men took care of business, both at work and at home, and women took care of the household and the emotional needs of the spouse and the children. They believed that traditional family gender roles allowed for supported personal life and the economy. The man was "free" to commit to his work life, and his productivity permitted domestic consumption, which further enhanced the economy. The heterosexual, married family was seen as the "backbone" of society, supporting the education system, religious institutions, childrearing, and "community."

Although the functionalist view has been modified in deference to the reality of the dual earner family, gender is still viewed in terms of functionality. An economy requiring two incomes is also seen as "functional" since it promotes interdependency as the "necessity" of marriage. Functionalists support the idea that a two-parent family underlies the ability to produce conforming, productive members of the society. Although cultural attitudes are more inclusive of gay families, the discussion reaffirms the ideal of a two-parent heterosexual household. Although some millennials are questioning the validity of gender categorization, many continue to view change in terms of fairness regarding issues of pay, housework, and child responsibilities (see Chapters 10 and 12).

The symbolic interactionists focus on the symbolic aspects of gender in maintaining social roles and institutions. In this view, the traditional value of the nuclear family is sustained. It just may be headed by two people of the same sex or by single parents, usually as a temporary condition. Women remain the driving force of domestic life, protecting emotional well-being and accounting for 70–80 percent of all consumer purchases (Brennan 2015). Marriage remains a valued relationship, even if financial constraints have decreased its universality and delayed its occurrences. Symbolic interactionists would also be interested in the movement regarding gender fluidity. The loss of gender identities, as traditionally instituted in society, exercises enormous ramifications for the "rules" guiding social interaction. This is perhaps why so many people appear threatened by any serious challenge to the gender schema. The symbolic interactionists are less likely to judge these changes than to analyze how the population adjusts to them. These theorists are most likely to look at the consequences of change and how new "norms" of behavior become legitimated and disseminated in the population. They are more likely to address issues of gender change in the political, legal, and cultural realms for how they impact self-definition and collective life.

Key Terms

Two Spirit   Tiger Mom   Sex   Intersex   Gender   Cisgender   Transgender   Genderqueer
Sexism   Patriarchy   Misogyny   Intersectionality   Hippocampus   Lookism   Metrosexual
Title IX   Sex Discrimination   Sexual Harassment   Microaggression   Reproductive Rights

Concept Review

What Is Gender?

Gender refers to the social identity of a person as male or female. Experiences of gender are not uniform but are influenced by race, ethnicity, social class, and sexual orientation. This is reflective of **intersectionality**, referring to the differential response of the power structures to marginalized groups. A person with multiple nondominant identifications has institutional experiences in response to all of their statuses and so is differentiated from others who do not share all of them. A working-class, African American lesbian, for example, experiences society through her race, sexual orientation, and social class simultaneously.

Cisgender refers to individuals whose gender identity and biological sex are aligned in the traditional roles. **Transgender** refers to persons whose personal identity does not conform to traditional conceptualizations, establishing their gender in opposition to their apparent biology. Transgendered individuals support traditional gender roles. **Genderqueer** persons advocate the elimination of gender categories, believing them to be obsolete and restrictive. They suggest that gender should either play no role in identity or be conceived of as fluid.

What Is Sexism?

Sexism is privileging one sex over the other, resulting in the dominance of one group with respect to power, opportunities, and resources. **Sexism** is enacted through *power plus prejudice* and describes the patriarchal structure of American society. Consequently, the qualities and social roles associated with women are devalued. Women's cultural contributions are either invisible or minimized. **Misogyny** refers to this inherent degradation of women under patriarchy. Women can hold sex typed ideas regarding men but are not sexist in the same manner as men, since they do not hold the power in the society.

Are there Biological Differences in Women and Men That Contribute to Gender Differentiation?

There are biological differences between women and men but the disparities are not sufficient to explain the polarities characteristic of gender roles. Many scientists believe the similarities between the sexes to be much more significant than the differences. Some gender differences presumed to be "natural" are actually learned through culture. There is a small portion of biologically ambiguous **intersex** individuals. Advocates suggest that these people should be allowed to choose how they want to address their situation, without being forced physically or psychologically into one gender or another.

How Are Gender Differences Learned?

Gender is learned through social institutions including the family, education, media, sports, peers, and recreation. Gender inequalities pervade all social and institutional experiences. The status of women has been characterized by periods of improvement and backlash. Women's increased incorporation into traditionally male occupations has stagnated, or fallen, as have gains in wages. Women's presence in political life is increasing but minimally, especially at the federal level. Women are still vastly underrepresented in journalism, entertainment, and sports. Women have outpaced men in the educational arena but have seen no such commensurate gain in higher level positions and in pay.

What Constitutes Violence Against Women?

Women are subjected to sexual harassment, sex discrimination, sexual assault, sex trafficking, and domestic violence. Attacks on reproductive rights are another form of violence against women. Elements in the language, especially in slang expressions, also serve to demean women.

Review Questions

1. Explain the concept of the *gender binary*. What are the alternative concepts? Be sure to address issues relating to *cisgender*, *transgender*, and *genderqueer*.
2. Are you uncomfortable when you cannot say, for certain, whether the person you are talking to is a woman or man? Why does this feel uncomfortable?
3. How is sexism defined? What is the meaning of the terms *patriarchy* and *misogyny* and how do they relate to sexism? Can women be sexist?
4. How have social media affected gender experiences and have they had an equitable impact on females and males? Do you think there should be some control over representations of the genders in the media? If so, how would it be accomplished? If not, why not?
5. Do you think that *lookism* is damaging to women? Do you think that the cultural emphasis on appearance can, or should, be changed? Is lookism experienced differently with regard to race, ethnicity, and social class?
6. What is Title IX and why is it significant? What does sports involvement affect beyond sports?
7. Are occupations becoming gender neutral? Have the proportions remained steady over the past 50 years? Do you think women and men are better suited to different and specific occupations?
8. What is sexual harassment and is it the same thing as sexual discrimination? Provide an example of each and discuss its consequences.
9. What are reproductive rights and what is the status of these rights today? What do you think regarding the right to control fertility?
10. Do you think the concept of gender is necessary? Would you support a nongendered society? How do you think intimate relationships would change if there were no genders?

References

AAUW. American Association of University Women. (October 25, 2016) *What Is the Gender Gap?* Retrieved from https://www.aauw-ca.org/gender-wage-gap/

Adewumni, B. (April 2, 2014) Kimberle Crenshaw on Intersectionality: I Wanted to Come Up with an Everyday Metaphor that Anyone Could Use. *The New Statesman.* Retrieved from http://www.newstatesman.com/lifestyle/2014/04/kimberl-crenshaw-intersectionality-i-wanted-come-everyday-metaphor-anyone-could

Adiche, C.N. (2012, 2014). *We Should All Be Feminists.* NY: Anchor Books.

Alexander, M. (2010) *The New Jim Crow: Mass Incarceration in the Age of Color Blindness.* NY: The New Press

Aliferis, L. (March 7, 2016) Big Drop in Chemical Levels in Girls Who Switched Cosmetics. *KQED News.* Retrieved from https://ww2.kqed.org/stateofhealth/2016/03/07/big-drop-in-chemical-levels-in-girls-who-switched-cosmetics/

APA. American Psychological Association. (n.d.) *Definitions Related to Sexual Orientation and Gender Diversity in APA.* Retrieved from https://www.apa.org/pi/lgbt/resources/sexuality-definitions.pdf

ANAD. (n.d.) Eating Disorder statistics. *National Association of Anorexia Nervosa and Associated Disorders.* Retrieved from http://www.anad.org/get-information/about-eating-disorders/eating-disorders-statistics/

Augustin, S. (April 11, 2015) The Surprising Effect of Color on your Mind and Mood. *Psychology Today.* Retrieved from https://www.psychologytoday.com/blog/people-places-and-things/201504/the-surprising-effect-color-your-mind-and-mood

Bollag, S. (September 30, 2016) Stronger Equal-pay Protections for Women and People of Color Coming Soon in California. *Los Angeles Times.* Retrieved from http://www.latimes.com/politics/essential/la-pol-sac-essential-politics-updates-governor-signs-bills-to-expand-equal-1475261036-htmlstory.html

Brennan, B. (January 21, 2015) Top 10 Things Everyone Should Know About Women Consumers. *Forbes.* Retrieved from http://www.forbes.com/sites/bridgetbrennan/2015/01/21/top-10-things-everyone-should-know-about-women-consumers/#7258 42aa2897

Brook, T.V. (May 28, 2015) Insults to Injury: Military Sexual-assault Victims Endure Retaliation. *USA TODAY.* Retrieved from http://www.usatoday.com/story/news/nation/2015/05/18/military-sexual-assault-retaliation/27395845/

Brydum, S. (July 31, 2015) The True Meaning of the Word 'Cisgender.' *Advocate.* Retrieved from https://www.advocate.com/transgender/2015/07/31/true-meaning-word-cisgender

Butler, B. (October 29, 2014) The Story Behind that '10 Hours of Walking in NYC' Viral Street Harassment Video. *The Washington Post.* Retrieved from https://www.washingtonpost.com/blogs/she-the-people/wp/2014/10/29/the-story-behind-that-10-hours-of-walking-in-nyc-viral-street-harassment-video/?utm_term=.79c343fc2ffc

Caitlin, E. (December 21, 2016) North Carolina Bathroom Bill. *C-Span.* Retrieved from https://www.c-span.org/video/?420574-1/caitlin-emma-discusses-north-carolinas-bathroom-law

Carmon, I., Knizhnik, S. (2015) *Notorious RBG: The Life and Times of Ruth Bader Ginsberg*. New York: HarperCollins.

Carson, B. (July 17, 2015) Judge Tentatively Sets Ellen Pao's Court Costs at $275,000 – Less than One-third what Kleiner Perkins Wanted. *Business Insider*. Retrieved from http://www.businessinsider.com/ellen-pao-ordered-to-pay-275000-in-court-costs-to-kleiner-perkins-2015-6

CBS News. (October 17, 2017) More than 12 Million Facebook "Me Too" Posts, Comments, Reactions in 24 Hours. *CBS News*. Retrieved from https://www.cbsnews.com/news/metoo-more-than-12-million-facebook-posts-comments-reactions-24-hours/

Christakis, E. (2013) *Do Teachers Really Discriminate Against Boys? TIME*. Retrieved from http://ideas.time.com/2013/02/06/do-teachers-really-discriminate-against-boys/

Coontz, S. (August 29, 2012) The Myth of Male Decline. *New York Times*. Retrieved from http://www.nytimes.com/2012/09/30/opinion/sunday/the-myth-of-male-decline.html

Covert, B. (September 1, 2015) New California Law Is a Big Step Forward for Working Women. *ThinkProgress*. Retrieved from http://thinkprogress.org/economy/2015/09/01/3697387/california-equal-pay-law

Crenshaw, K. (September 24, 2015) Why Intersectionality Can't Wait. *The Washington Post*. Retrieved from https://www.washingtonpost.com/news/in-theory/wp/2015/09/24/why-intersectionality-cant-wait/?utm_term=.b9fd68040250

Davis, A.P. (December 23, 2015) Waiting to Exhale Has Aged as Well as Angela Bassett. *TheCut*. Retrieved from http://nymag.com/thecut/2015/12/20-years-later-waiting-to-exhale-still-rules.html

Editorial Board. (March 28, 2016) The State Assault on Planned Parenthood. *The New York Times*.

Ember, S., Bowley, G. (December 30, 2015) Bill Cosby Charged in Sexual Assault Case. *The New York Times*. Retrieved from https://www.nytimes.com/2015/12/31/business/media/bill-cosby-charged-in-sexual-assault-case.html

Evans, R. (October 13, 2015) Most Victims Are Men: 5 Realities of Rape in the Military. *Cracked*. Retrieved from http://www.cracked.com/personal-experiences-1966-most-victims-are-men-5-realities-rape-in-military.html

EWG (Environmental Working Group). (September 24, 2008) *Teen Girls' Body Burden of Hormone-altering Cosmetics Chemicals: Detailed Findings*. Retrieved from https://www.ewg.org/research/teen-girls-body-burden-hormone-altering-cosmetics-chemicals/detailed-findings

Fabio, M. (June, 2009) Five Biggest Sexual Harassment Cases. *LegalZoom*. Retrieved from https://www.legalzoom.com/articles/five-biggest-sexual-harassment-cases

Famuyiwa, R. (dir.) (2016) Confirmation. *Home Box Office, Inc*. Retrieved from http://www.hbo.com/movies/confirmation

Farrow, R. (November 6, 2017) Harvey Weinstein's Army of Spies. *The New Yorker*. Retrieved from https://www.newyorker.com/news/news-desk/harvey-weinsteins-army-of-spies

Frey, J. (n.d.) When Grandsons Are Out of Control. *American Grandparents Association*. Retrieved from https://www.grandparents.com/grandkids/discipline-and-behavior/when-grandsons-are-out-of-control

Frost, A. (April 17, 2015) How These 6 Countries Are Making Fashion Industry Safer. *Groundswell.org*. Retrieved from https://groundswell.org/ethical-modeling/.

Galanti, G. (July 1, 2003) The Hispanic Family and Male–female Relationships: An Overview. *Journal of Transcultural Nursing*. Retrieved from http://journals.sagepub.com/doi/10.1177/1043659603014003004

Garcia-Navarro, L. (March 5, 2016) On Verge of 70, Sally Field Navigates Aging in the Spotlight. *NPR*. Retrieved from https://www.npr.org/templates/transcript/transcript.php?storyId=469299174

Gardner, A. (June 14, 2012) Does Obesity Affect School Performance? *CNN*. Retrieved from https://www.cnn.com/2012/06/14/health/obesity-affect-school-performance/index.html

Girls on A Journey Program (November, 2009) *Youth for Tomorrow*. Retrieved from http://www.youthfortomorrow.org/Girls-On-A-Journey-Program

Gittleson, K. (June 13, 2014) Why Does Sexism Persist in the Video Games Industry? *BBC News*. Retrieved from http://www.bbc.com/news/technology-27824701

Gray, E. (April 15, 2016) Why Anita Hill's 1991 Testimony Is So Haunting Today. *The Huffington Post*. Retrieved from http://www.huffingtonpost.com/entry/anita-hill-matters-hbo-confirmation_us_570fb8f9e4b0ffa5937e5e72

Groden, C. (August 6, 2015) Study Shows How Teens Are Using Social Media. *Fortune.com*. Retrieved from http://fortune.com/2015/08/06/teens-social-media/

Hammond, C. (November 18, 2014) The 'Pink vs Blue' Gender Myth. *BBC*. Retrieved from http://www.bbc.com/future/story/20141117-the-pink-vs-blue-gender-myth

Harper, J. (March 21, 2015) 'Dramatic' Increase: Plastic Surgery for Men Up by 43 Percent as they Compete in the Job Market. *Washington Times*. Retrieved from http://www.washingtontimes.com/news/2015/mar/12/plastic-surgery-43-percent-among-men-report/

Hellmann, J. (January 5, 2017) Planned Parenthood Launches National Campaign to Take on Trump, GOP. *The Hill*. Retrieved from http://thehill.com/policy/healthcare/312886-planned-parenthood-launches-national-campaign-to-take-on-trump-gop

Hu, J. (June 15, 2015) What's the Best Way to Get Ahead in a Female-Dominated Profession? *Slate*. Retrieved from http://www.slate.com/articles/double_x/doublex/2015/06/men_in_female_dominated_fields_they_still_make_more_than_women.html

Human Trafficking (n.d.) *Freedom Network*. Retrieved from https://freedomnetworkusa.org/human-trafficking/.

IMDb. (n.d.) *Grace and Frankie*. Retrieved from http://www.imdb.com/title/tt3609352/

IMDb. (2015) *Grandma*. Retrieved from http://www.imdb.com/title/tt4270516/

Intersex. (n.d.) *Intersex Society of North America*. Retrieved from http://www.isna.org/faq/what_is_intersex

Is it Hypocritical for Pro-life Supporters to be Against Pro-life Programs Like Welfare, Food Stamps, WIC, etc? (n.d.). *Debate*. Retrieved from http://www.debate.org/opinions/is-it-hypocritical-for-pro-life-supporters-to-be-against-pro-life-programs-like-welfare-food-stamps-wic-etc

Jacobson, L. (February 16, 2015) Barack Obama Says Nearly 20 Percent of Women in the U.S. Have Been Raped or Faced Rape Attempt. *Politifact*. Retrieved from http://www.politifact.com/truth-o-meter/statements/2015/feb/16/barack-obama/barack-obama-says-nearly-1-5-women-us-has-been-rap/

Jardine, S.A., Dallalfar, A. (Spring, 2012) Sex and Gender Roles: Examining Gender Dynamics in the Context of African American Families. *Journal of Pedagogy, Pluralism, and Practice*. Retrieved from https://digitalcommons.lesley.edu/jppp/vol4/iss4/4/

Jarrett, C. (August 26, 2015) Yes, Men's and Women's Brains Do Function Differently — But It's a Tiny Difference. *thecut*. Retrieved from https://www.thecut.com/2015/08/male-female-brains-are-just-a-little-different.html

Just Not Sports (April 25, 2016) #MoreThanMean – Women in Sports 'Face' Harassment. [Video file]. Retrieved from https://www.youtube.com/watch?v=9tU-D-m2JY8

Katz, J. (2013) Tough Guise 2: Violence, Manhood, and American Culture. *Media Education Foundation*. Retrieved from https://shop.mediaed.org/tough-guise-2-p45.aspx

Keselenko, J., Anderson, A., Feudo, C. (August 3, 2016) Massachusetts Enacts New Pay Equity Law. *Massachusetts Labor & Employment Law*. Retrieved from http://www.masslaborandemploymentlaw.com/2016/08/03/massachusetts-enacts-new-pay-equity-law/

Kohn, D. (October 31, 2002) The Gender Gap: Boys Lagging. *CBSnews.com*. Retrieved from http://www.cbsnews.com/news/the-gender-gap-boys-lagging/

Kurtzleben, D. (2016) Planned Parenthood Investigations Find No Fetal Tissue Sales. *NPR*. Retrieved from http://www.npr.org/2016/01/28/464594826/in-wake-of-videos-planned-parenthood-investigations-find-no-fetal-tissue-sales

Lawrence, J. (October 14, 2015) "Why Do I Make Less than My Male Co-stars?" Retrieved from http://ew.com/article/2015/12/16/hollywood-calling-out-sexism-2015/

Ledbetter vs Goodyear Tire & Rubber Co. (n.d.) *Cornell University Law School*. Retrieved from https://www.law.cornell.edu/supct/html/05-1074.ZS.html

Lee, M.D. (dir.) (2017). Girls' Trip. *Universal Pictures*.

Lindsey, K. (2011) *Gender Roles: A Sociological Perspective* (5th edn). Boston: Pearson Publishing as Prentice Hall.

Liptak, A. (November 13, 2015) Supreme Court to Hear Texas Abortion Law Case. *The New York Times*. Retrieved from https://www.nytimes.com/2015/11/14/us/politics/supreme-court-accepts-texas-abortion-law-case.html

Liptak, A. (June 28, 2016) Supreme Court Strikes Down Texas Abortion Restrictions. *The New York Times*. Retrieved from http://www.nytimes.com/2016/06/28/us/supreme-court-texas-abortion.html

Lisak, D., Miller, P.M. (2002) Repeat Rape and Multiple Offending Among Undetected Rapists. *Violence and Victims*, 17(1): 73–84. Retrieved from http://www.davidlisak.com/wp-content/uploads/pdf/RepeatRapeinUndetectedRapists.pdf

Lobue, V., Deloache, J.S. (September 29, 2011) Pretty in Pink: The Early Development of Gender-stereotyped Colour Preferences. *British Journal of Developmental Psychology*. Retrieved from https://www.ncbi.nlm.nih.gov/pubmed/21848751

Lohmann, R.C. (June 10, 2014) Education's Great Divide: Girls Outperforming Boys. *Psychology Today*. Retrieved from https://www.psychologytoday.com/us/blog/teen-angst/201406/educations-great-divide-girls-outperforming-boys

Lopez, M., Gonzalez-Barrera, A. (March 31, 2014) Women's College Enrollment Gains Leave Men Behind. *Pew Research Center*. Retrieved from http://www.pewresearch.org/fact-tank/2014/03/06/womens-college-enrollment-gains-leave-men-behind/

Maglaty, J. (April 7, 2011) When Did Girls Start Wearing Pink? *Smithsonian.com*. Retrieved from http://www.smithsonianmag.com/arts-culture/when-did-girls-start-wearing-pink-1370097/

Marquis, M. (January 8, 2015) 2015 Word of the Year is Singular They. *American Dialectic Society*. Retrieved from https://www.americandialect.org/2015-word-of-the-year-is-singular-they

McGregor, J. (January 27, 2015) A Reality Check About U.S. Women in Power. *The Washington Post*. Retrieved from www.washingtonpost.com/news/on-leadership/wp/2015/01/27/a-reality-check-about-u-s-women-in-power/?utm_term=.d279206efd41

McHugh, R., Farrow, R. (October 16, 2016) A Hostile System? How Colleges Are Responding to Campus Sexual Assaults. *Today*. Retrieved from http://www.today.com/health/how-colleges-are-responding-sexual-assault-campus-t103823

McGreevy, P., Megerian, C. (October 6, 2015) California Now Has One of the Toughest Equal Pay Laws in the Country. *Los Angeles Times*. Retrieved from http://www.latimes.com/local/political/la-me-pc-gov-brown-equal-pay-bill-20151006-story.html

McMillan, T. (1992) *Waiting to Exhale*. NY: The Berkley Publishing Group.

Mehta, S. (December 19, 2016) Is Social Media Contributing to the Rise of Teen Suicides? *Healthify*. Retrieved from https://www.healthify.us/healthify-insights/is-social-media-contributing-to-the-rise-of-teen-suicides

Melissa McCarthy Seven7. (2017) *Melissa McCarthy*. Retrieved 13 April 2017, from https://melissamccarthy.com/

Meyer, A. (March 31, 2014) Women Now 33% More Likely than Men to Earn College Degrees. *CNS News*. Retrieved from http://cnsnews.com/news/article/ali-meyer/women-now-33-more-likely-men-earn-college-degrees

Microaggression. (n.d.) *Dictionary*. Retrieved from http://www.dictionary.com/browse/microaggression

Mock, F.L. (dir.) (2013) *Anita: Speaking Truth to Power*. Retrieved from http://www.imdb.com/title/tt2481202/

Moniuszko, S.M., Kelly, C. (October 27, 2017) Harvey Weinstein Scandal: A Complete List of the 80 Accusers. *USA Today*. Retrieved from https://www.usatoday.com/story/life/people/2017/10/27/weinstein-scandal-complete-list-accusers/804663001/

Morris, M.W. (2016) *Pushout: The Criminalization of Black Girls in Schools*. NY: The New Press.

Nelson, M.A. (2009) African-American Women: Body Image, Weight, and Depression. *Doctoral Dissertation, Emory University*. Retrieved from https://legacy-etd.library. emory.edu/view/record/pid/emory:1b1dg

News.com.au. (January 23, 2014) Parents More Likely to Google 'Is My Daughter Pretty?' and 'Is My Son Smart?' Research Shows. Retrieved from https://www. news.com.au/lifestyle/parenting/parents-more-likely-to-google-is-my-daughter-pretty-and-is-my-son-smart-research-shows/news-story/6c11f16881e9c243346f27 243ad8d330

Nunberg, G. (January 13, 2016) Everyone Uses Singular 'They,' Whether They Realize it or Not *NPR*. Retrieved from https://www.npr.org/2016/01/13/462906419/ everyone-uses-singular-they-whether-they-realize-it-or-not

Nutt, A. (2015) *Becoming Nicole: The Transformation of an American Family.* NY: Random House, LLC.

Orbach, S. (March, 1997) *Fat Is a Feminist Issue*. Bbs Pub Corp.

Park, A. (October 24, 2017) #MeToo Reaches 85 Countries, with 1.7M Tweets. *CBS News*. Retrieved from https://www.cbsnews.com/news/metoo-reaches-85-countries-with-1-7-million-tweets/

Parker, O.L. (February 12, 2012) Black Women Heavier and Happier with their Bodies than White Women, Poll Finds. *The Washington Post*. Retrieved from https://www. washingtonpost.com/lifestyle/style/black-women-heavier-and-happier-with-their-bodies-than-white-women-poll-finds/2012/02/22/gIQAPmcHeR_story.html

Pearson, Ellen Holmes (n.d.) American Indian Women. Teachinghistory.org. Retrieved from http://teachinghistory.org/history-content/ask-a-historian/23931

Pérez-Peña, R. (September 21, 2015) 1 in 4 Women Experience Sex Assault on Campus. *The New York Times*. Retrieved from https://www.nytimes.com/2015/09/22/us/a-third-of-college-women-experience-unwanted-sexual-contact-study-finds.html

Perry, M. (April 11, 2014) The College Degree Gap: Women Earned a Majority of Degrees at All Levels in 2012, and the Degree Gap for Blacks Is Stunning. *AEI*. Retrieved from https://www.aei.org/publication/the-college-degree-gap-women-earned-a-majority-of-degrees-at-all-levels-in-2012-and-the-degree-gap-for-blacks-is-stunning/

Persad, M. (April 3, 2015) France Votes to Ban Models Under a Certain Body Mass Index. *The Huffington Post*. Retrieved from https://www.huffingtonpost. com/2015/04/03/france-models-body-mass-index_n_6999244.html.

Peters, J.W., Becker, J., Davis, J.H. (February 22, 2017) Trump Rescinds Rules on Bathrooms for Transgender Students. *The New York Times*. Retrieved from https:// www.nytimes.com/2017/02/22/us/politics/devos-sessions-transgender-students-rights.html

Planned Parenthood. (January, 2014) [PDF File]. Retrieved from https://www. plannedparenthood.org/files/4013/9611/7243/Planned_Parenthood_Services.pdf

Pomerantz, D. (August 5, 2015) Women Still Ridiculously Underrepresented in Movies. *Forbes.com*. Retrieved from https://www.forbes.com/sites/ dorothypomerantz/2015/08/05/women-still-ridiculously-underrepresented-in-movies/#4f47200330ea

Quinceanera. (n.d.) Retrieved from http://www.learnnc.org/lp/editions/ chngmexico/218

Rawes, E. (November 4, 2014) How Much Do We Spend on Beauty? *Cheatsheet*. Retrieved from https://www.cheatsheet.com/money-career/how-much-do-we-spend-on-beauty.html/?a=viewall

Reeves, V.R., Sawhill, V.I. (November 14, 2015) Men's Lib. *The New York Times*. Retrieved from http://www.nytimes.com/2015/11/15/opinion/sunday/mens-lib.html

Reich, R. (2013) *Inequality For All*. Documentary, Kornbluth, J., Director.

Rob Bliss Creative. (October 28, 2014) *10 Hours of Walking in NYC as a Woman*. [Video file]. Retrieved from https://www.youtube.com/watch?v=b1XGPvbWn0A

RT News. (February 27, 2015) 58 Gender Options Not Enough? Facebook Now Allows Unlimited Custom Identities. *RT News*. Retrieved from https://www.rt.com/usa/236283-facebook-gender-custom-choice/

Sales, M.J. (2016) *American Girls: Social Media and the Secret Life of Teenagers*. NY: Penguin Random House LLC.

Schulte, B. (June 27, 2013) Does Title IX Equality for Females Come at Males' Expense? *The Washington Post*. Retrieved from https://www.washingtonpost.com/local/does-title-ix-equality-for-females-come-at-males-expense/2013/06/27/7c8beee0-df55-11e2-b2d4-ea6d8f477a01_story.html

Segal, T. (July 19, 2013) Better to Be Lucky Than Good: The Persistent Gender Gap in Standardized Testing. *Education Week*. Retrieved from http://blogs.edweek.org/edweek/reimagining/2013/07/The_SATs_Gender_Gap.html

SexInfo Online. (n.d.) *Overview of Sexual Orientations*. Retrieved from http://www.soc.ucsb.edu/sexinfo/article/overview-sexual-orientations

Sexual Assault on College Campuses: A Culture of Indifference. (n.d.) *InvestigateWest*. Retrieved from http://invw.org/sexual-assault/

Sexual Harassment. (n.d.) *U.S. Equal Employment Opportunity Commission*. Retrieved from https://www.eeoc.gov/laws/types/sexual_harassment.cfm

Silko, L.M. (2007) Yellow Woman and a Beauty of the Spirit. In Segal, M.T. and Martinez, T. *Intersections of gender, race and class*. Los Angeles, CA: Roxbury Publishing Company.

Slang Words for Men. (n.d.) *The Online Slang Dictionary*. Retrieved from http://onlineslangdictionary.com/thesaurus/words+meaning+man,+men,+male.html

Slang Words for Women. (n.d.) *The Online Slang Dictionary*. Retrieved from http://onlineslangdictionary.com/thesaurus/words+meaning+woman,+women,+female.html

Smith, L.S. (n.d.) Gender Stereotypes. [PDF File] *Annenberg.usc.edu*. Retrieved from http://annenberg.usc.edu/pages/~/media/MDSCI/Gender%20Stereotypes.ashx

Social Media and Teenage Girls: Not Your Mother's Adolescence. (February 25, 2016). *NPR*. Retrieved from http://www.npr.org/2016/02/25/468070389/social-media-and-teenage-girls-it-s-not-your-mother-s-adolescence

Sollosi, M. (December 16, 2015) *How the Women of Hollywood Call Out Gender Inequality*. Retrieved from http://ew.com/article/2015/12/16/hollywood-calling-out-sexism-2015/.

Speier, J. (June 21, 2012) Why Rapists in Military Get Away with It. *CNN*. Retrieved from http://www.cnn.com/2012/06/21/opinion/speier-military-rape/

Speier, J. (2017) *Jackie Speier*. Retrieved from http://speier.house.gov/index.php

Stahl, L. (2002) The Gender Gap: Boys Lagging. *CBS News*. Retrieved from https://www.cbsnews.com/news/the-gender-gap-boys-lagging/

Steinem, G. (1978) If Men Could Menstruate. *Ms. Magazine*. Retrieved from http://www.mylittleredbook.net/imcm_orig.pdf.

Steinem, G. (2015) *My Life on the Road*. NY: Random House.

Stephens-Davidowitz, S. (March 5, 2016) The Return of the D.I.Y. Abortion. *The New York Times*. Retrieved from http://www.nytimes.com/2016/03/06/opinion/sunday/the-return-of-the-diy-abortion.html?emc=edit_ty_20160307&nl=opinion&nlid=56728292&_r=0

Streitfeld, D. (March 24, 2015) At Kleiner Discrimination Trial, a Battle Between Legal Powerhouses. *The New York Times*. Retrieved from https://www.nytimes.com/2015/03/25/technology/at-kleiner-discrimination-trial-a-battle-between-legal-powerhouses.html

Streitfeld, D. (March 27, 2015a) Ellen Pao Loses Silicon Valley Bias Case Against Kleiner Perkins. *The New York Times*. Retrieved from https://www.nytimes.com/2015/03/28/technology/ellen-pao-kleiner-perkins-case-decision.html

Sullivan, G. (October 29, 2014) Video: Woman Harassed 108 Times as She Walks around New York. *The Washington Post*. Retrieved from https://www.washingtonpost.com/news/morning-mix/wp/2014/10/29/video-woman-harassed-108-times-as-she-walks-around-new-york/?utm_term=.d22783b056be

Tan, Y.Z. (October 18, 2016). FBI Sting Shows Child Sex Trafficking Still Thriving in United States. *The Christian Science Monitor*. Retrieved from http://www.csmonitor.com/USA/2016/1018/FBI-sting-shows-child-sex-trafficking-still-thriving-in-United-States

Thomas, Clarence. (March 21, 2017) *Wikiquote*. Retrieved from https://en.wikiquote.org/wiki/Clarence_Thomas

Title IX Anniversary. (n.d.) *Justice*. Retrieved from https://www.justice.gov/crt/title-ix-anniversary

Transgender Law Center (n.d.) *Transgender Health Benefits*. Retrieved from transgenderlawcenter.org/wp.../2014/.../Health-Insurance-Exclusions-Guide-2-WEB.p...

TrentAndLuke. (February 28, 2015) 16 Types of Sexual Orientations. *YouTube*. Retrieved from https://www.youtube.com/watch?v=7Dv25Oa0iB0

Udorie, J.E. (September 16, 2015) Social Media is Harming the Mental Health of Teenagers. The State Has to Act. *The Guardian*. Retrieved from https://www.theguardian.com/commentisfree/2015/sep/16/social-media-mental-health-teenagers-government-pshe-lessons

Underwood, M.K., Faris, R.W. (October 6, 2015) Being 13: Perils of Lurking on Social Media. *CNN*. Retrieved from https://www.cnn.com/2015/10/05/opinions/underwood-faris-being-thirteen-lurking-social-media/index.html

Urban Dictionary. (multiple dates) *Genderqueer*. Retrieved from http://www.urbandictionary.com/define.php?term=genderqueer

Uwujaren, J. (October 27, 2014) 3 Common Complaints About Political Correctness (that Completely Miss the Point). *Everydayfeminsim*. Retrieved from https://everydayfeminism.com/2014/10/complaints-about-political-correctness/

Uwujaren, J., Utt, J. (January 11, 2015) Why Our Feminism Must be Intersectional (and 3 Ways to Practice It). *Everydayfeminism*. Retrieved from https:// everydayfeminism.com/2015/01/why-our-feminism-must-be-intersectional/

Vagianos, A. (April 2, 2014) Films that Pass the Bechdel Test Actually Make More Money. *The Huffington Post*. Retrieved from http://www.huffingtonpost. com/2014/04/02/bechdel-test-women-in-film_n_5076636.html.

Van Edwards, V. (January 19, 2013) 10 Ways Color Affects Your Mood. *The Huffington Post*. Retrieved from https://www.huffingtonpost.com/vanessa-van-edwards/color-and-mood_b_2088728.html

Vedantam, S. (August 2, 2016) How a Child's Gender May Affect Parents' Willingness to Bend the Truth. *NPR*. Retrieved from https://www.npr. org/2016/08/02/488336909/how-a-childs-gender-may-affect-parents-willingness-to-bend-the-truth

Vega, G., Woworuntu, S. (July 22, 2015) How Workers Are Trafficked into the U.S.— the Ugly Truth. *CNN*. Retrieved from http://www.cnn.com/2015/07/22/opinions/ human-trafficking-laws-u-s-/

Wallace, K. (May 20, 2015) Study Has More Disturbing Findings About Campus Rape of Freshmen Women. *CNN*. Retrieved from http://edition.cnn. com/2015/05/20/living/feat-rape-freshmen-women-new-study/

Wallace, K. (September 16, 2015a) 23% of Women Report Sexual Assault in College, Study Finds. *CNN*. Retrieved from http://www.cnn.com/2015/09/22/health/ campus-sexual-assault-new-large-survey/

Waxman, O.B. (September 29, 2015) This New Dove Ad Shows How We All Have the Same Insecurities. *Time.com*. Retrieved from http://time.com/4054795/new-dove-ad-change-one-thing/

Women's Sports Foundation. (August 30, 2016) *Why Sports Participation for Girls and Women*. Retrieved from https://www.womenssportsfoundation.org/home/ advocate/foundation-positions/mental-and-physical health/benefits_why_sports_ participation_for_girls_and_women

Women in the Labor Force: A Databook. (2015) *Report 1059*. Retrieved from https:// www.bls.gov/opub/reports/womens-databook/archive/women-in-the-labor-force-a-databook-2015.pdf

Women's Bureau. (n.d.) *Women in the Labor Force*. Retrieved from https://www.dol. gov/wb/stats/stats_data.htm

Wong, A. (June 26, 2015) Thousands of America's High Schools Have Far Fewer Sports Opportunities for Girls Than for Boys. *The Atlantic*. Retrieved from http://www.theatlantic.com/education/archive/2015/06/girls-high-school-sports-inequality/396782/

Woodruff, B. (February 23, 2015) The Gender Wage Gap Is Especially Terrible in Hollywood. *Slate*. Retrieved from http://www.slate.com/blogs/ xx_factor/2015/02/23/gender_wage_gap_in_hollywood_it_s_very_very_wide.html

Zorrilla, M. (n.d.) Video Games and Gender: Game Representation. *Radford*. Retrieved from http://radford.edu/~mzorrilla2/thesis/gamerepresentation.html

CHAPTER 8

Races and Ethnicities in Society

WHAT YOU WILL READ ABOUT IN THIS CHAPTER:

- American racism persists, though it may take more subtle forms than in past eras. The concept of **race** will be presented as a socially constructed category reflecting significant life consequences. The category of **ethnicity**, which refers to the cultural background of a person and may include ancestry, country of origin, food, language, customs, and other practices specific to particular groups, also signals social divisions.

- **Racism** is a system of privilege based on power and the ability to shape social institutions and cultural standards. Racism depends upon the elevation of whiteness and its denigration of all other groups. The outcome of race privilege is the dominant group's ability to deny superordinate position. Real social equality requires that the empowered acknowledge their advantages.

- **Discrimination** and **prejudice** influence all aspects of the society but the most insidious type remains **institutional discrimination** which resides in the structure of our institutions, independently of the persons inhabiting the power positions.

- **Hegemonic** race privilege supports the coercive universality of the dominant group's standards into the social institutions. Their experiences result in the devaluation of values and standards. Discrimination pervades all social transactions. Policies such as Affirmative Action address structural discrimination and are still warranted, given the *underrepresentation* of nondominant groups in positions of power. Substantive changes in residential segregation, educational institutions, the workforce, and cultural representations will need to occur for permanent changes to be achieved.

- Although much of the history of the US has depended on the arrival of **immigrant** groups, the countries typical of newly arrived groups have changed. A century ago the immigrants were from European nations; the bulk of today's immigrants are from Latin American and Asian countries. Exploitation of immigrant labor, as well as other forms of discrimination, are a consistent feature of immigrant life. The desirability and extent of cultural **assimilation** varies by group and residence.

- The diverse backgrounds characteristic of specific nondominant groups are frequently unacknowledged and no consensus exists with regard to the terminology of address for any group.

- The economic and social status of racial and ethnic nondominant groups suffers in comparison to Whites. Issues of restitution for lost property and other forms of economic and social exploitation have been addressed for some groups and not others. Government settlements have been more symbolic than fair.

Introduction

The concepts of *race* and *ethnicity* are vague and sometimes used interchangeably. There are no biological distinctions in determining *race*; you won't find race in genes or in physical characteristics. The idea of races, as distinct categories based in biology, dates to the second half of the nineteenth century. Hierarchies were established, with no basis, where "White" was defined as superior and all other races were designated as "nonWhite," and therefore inferior. Race actually is a *social construct* which has changed over time. Racial census categories change in every decade (US Census Bureau n.d.). Not until the 2000 Census could respondents select more than one racial category. Previously, if a person did not identify with one race, the only alternative was to check the residual category of "other." The idea of separate races, with biologically distinct genetics, has been discredited. Alleged racial differences explaining diseases remain unsubstantiated (Cooper 1984).

An *ethnicity* refers to **cultural** background and includes characteristics such as food, clothing, customs, language, ancestry, national origin, and religion. One "race" can contain many cultures; for example, Asians can refer to people from Japan, China, Indonesia, Vietnam, Korea, India, the Philippines or any other country of origin associated with Asia or an ethnicity not associated with any particular country, such as Hmong. Some categories of ethnicity have no common content.

How Are Race and Ethnicity Viewed?

Preferences regarding racial and ethnic designations are disputed. "Hispanic, Latino, or Spanish Origin," actually refer to *ethnicity*, and reflect different meanings. Some Americans will assert that they "have no ethnicity." Frequently, these are White people who are from the dominant Anglican Protestant groups. Typically, dominant groups define themselves without reference to categorical labels, as simply "American." The same is true with regard to sex and sexual orientation where the dominant group does not feel it necessary to qualify their personal identity. For example, most people do not articulate their status as heterosexual, it being assumed unless otherwise specified; "White" or male are similarly considered the "default."

Box 8.1 – Race and Ethnicity

Race is a socially constructed concept associated with physical characteristics but actually having no biological basis. Categories of race have changed to reflect the political interests of the period. Currently, "Hispanic, Latino, or Spanish Origin," are listed as a race option though they are more accurately associated with ethnicity, and have different associations.

Ethnicity refers to cultural background and typically includes characteristics associated with national origin, language, food, religion, ancestry, clothing, or other practices specific to a group. One "race" can contain many cultures; for example, Asians can refer to people from Japan, China, Indonesia, Vietnam, Korea, India, the Philippines or any other country of origin associated with Asia or an ethnicity not associated with any particular country, such as Hmong. Some categories of ethnicity have no common content.

White ethnic generally refers to people of European ancestry who are not from White Anglo-Saxon Protestant (WASP) backgrounds characteristic of the early colonists. WASPs represent the dominant culture while White ethnics have largely been treated as nonWhites. *White ethnic* can include Italians, Irish, Greeks, Polish, Jews, Dutch, Swiss, or any other group generally categorized as White and having European origins outside the UK.

White people in the US who have histories of *ethnic minority status*, often referred to as **White Ethnics**, generally identify as having Irish, Jewish, Greek, Russian, or other ethnic heritages outside of the early White English Puritan colonists. Often the groups "without ethnicity" have lost the ties to their ancestry. In this concept, the *White* group tends to be understood as synonymous with *American*, making any other group essentially a subgroup, not quite deserving of the label of *American*. This status is linguistically reflected in the tendency to hyphenate the classification of marginalized groups, as in Mexican American, Native American, Asian American, or African American. Many writers attest to such delegitimation:

> for we would always have an accent, however perfect our pronunciation, however excellent our enunciation, however divine our diction. That accent would be heard in our pigmentation, our physiognomy, our names. We were, in short, *the other*.
>
> Being *the other* means feeling different; is awareness of being distinct; is consciousness of being dissimilar. It means being outside the game, outside the circle, outside the set. It means being on the edges, on the margins, on the periphery. Otherness means feeling excluded, closed out, precluded, even disdained and scorned. It produces a sense of isolation, of apartness, of disconnectedness, of alienation.
>
> Being *the other* involves a contradictory phenomenon. On the one hand being *the other* frequently means being invisible... On the other hand, being *the other* sometimes involves sticking out like a sore thumb.
>
> (Madrid 2007)

In a similar vein, Ronald Takaki highlights the tendency for people in the US to ask him where he is from because he is Asian. He relates a conversation with a taxi driver who was bringing him to a conference. The driver commented on Takaki's excellent English and then asked what country Takaki was from: "I was born in the United States ... My grandfather came here from Japan in the 1880s. My family has been here, in America, for over a hundred years" (Takaki 2007). Takaki then explains:

Questions like the one my taxi driver asked me are always jarring, but I can understand why he could not see me as American. He had a narrow but widely shared sense of the past—a history that has viewed Americans as Europeans in ancestry. Race, Toni Morrison explained, has functioned as a "metaphor" necessary to the "construction of Americanness": in the creation of our national identity, "American" has been defined as "white."

(Takaki 2007)

The experiences of nondominant groups are vulnerable to distortion, leading to feelings of exclusion. Hawaiian historian Haumami-Kay Trask writes of the confusion she felt as a youth when her family's story of her culture was completely at odds with the history of her people taught in the schools:

I understood the world as a place and a feeling divided into two: one haole (white), and the other Kanaka (Native) ... There was the world that we lived in—my ancestors, my family, and my people—and then there was the world historians described. This world, they had written, was the truth.

(Trask 2007)

Her parents raised her with a rich sense of her heritage celebrating the cultural activities surrounding fishing, planting, collectivism, dancing, and interconnectedness. The curriculum in her school described the Kanaka as "pagan," illiterate, lustful cannibals, who traded in slaves and were unmusical (Trask 2007). Her life was a

Figure 8.1 Discrimination commonly plagued nonWhite groups, and ethnic groups such as the Irish, Italians, Jews, and others who were not considered White
Source: Courtesy of National Japanese American Historical Society

contradiction resembling the "double consciousness," first described by W.E.B. Du Bois, as characteristic of the Black experience in White America.

Who is Arab?

Some categories of ethnicity are commonly perceived as vague. The term "Arab" is one such example. Some people see it primarily as an ethnic designation while others suggest Arabs do not share a common culture. In defining the group, some refer to people whose first language is Arabic. Others utilize the designation of the League of Arab Nations, incorporating 22 countries, as a reference point, though groups claiming Arabic identifications do not live only in those Middle Eastern and Northern African countries but in neighboring countries excluded from the League (ADC 2009).

A recent report on National Public Radio featured a story about modern-day Lebanon. Archaeologic research, stemming from the study of DNA in recently discovered 4000-year-old bones, has determined that the modern-day Lebanese descended from the Biblical Canaanites. This "news" apparently was met with some resistance among the Lebanese who do not identify as a unified group. There are people who are Christians and others who identify as Sunni and Shia Muslims and "they insist they are even different ethnicities" (Sherlock 2017). One young couple, she Christian and he Muslim, broke up over divisions of cultural reference. He considered them ethnic Arabs but she defined herself as Phoenician, descended from Canaanites (Sherlock 2017). Today's Lebanese are developing religiously segregated areas and, as a consequence, are developing differentiated DNA in a process one scholar has called "genetic drift."

What Is Racism and Privilege?

A person who is considered as less than a full societal member is often relegated to the category of *other.* In order to understand the full impact of being defined as *other,* we will need to understand the concept of *privilege,* especially in terms of the distortion of nondominant groups. Since the notion of race often is taken as reflecting a "natural" or biological reality, it is imagined to be immutable. Conceptualization of the *White race* as superior is essential to the system of privilege, permitting the dehumanization and subordination of other groups. The elevation of the White group to a superior status *depends* on its contrast to "lesser" groups. In his 2015 book, written as an extended letter to his son, author Ta-Nehisi Coates articulates the state of being African American in the White landscape of contemporary America. He demonstrates how the Black experience is contingent upon the *unrecognized White privilege* woven into the fiber of society, dependent on the social conceptualization of being "White." "There is no them without you, and without the right to break you they must necessarily fall from the mountain, lose their divinity, and tumble out of the Dream (Coates 2015)". This differentiation results in feelings of cultural exclusion:

> Fear ruled everything around me, and I knew, as all black people do, that this fear was connected to the Dream out there, to the unworried boys, to pie and pot roast, to the white fences and green lawns nightly beamed into our television sets.
>
> (Coates 2015)

The entitlement accompanying privilege translates into a wholly different relationship to the world and the ease of belonging and "owning" it:

> I did not understand it until I looked out on the street. That is where I saw white parents pushing double-wide strollers down gentrifying Harlem boulevards in T-shirts and jogging shorts. Or I saw them lost in conversation with each other, mother and father, while their sons commanded entire sidewalks with their tricycles. The galaxy belonged to them, and as terror was communicated to our children, I saw mastery communicated to theirs.
>
> (Coates 2015)

Racism is defined as *race power + prejudice*. If racism is both of these qualities, then it belongs specifically to the White group. Other races may hold prejudiced attitudes but lack the power to express these systemically. The "problem of racism" generally focuses on "minorities," as if they are responsible for its existence. The role of the privileged group in creating the systemic racism is denied. White people must admit, and address, the issues of *White privilege*, otherwise racism will remain entrenched. Institutional dimensions of privilege require transformation,

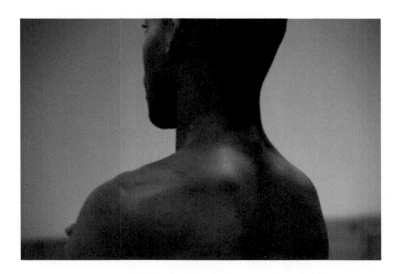

Figure 8.2 The African American body is vulnerable to stressors of discrimination and violence. This a studio portrait of a dance student Source: Photography by Rosalind Gottfried

in history, law, politics, and arts. To falsely view American history as initiated with Columbus' arrival on the shores of the "New World" annihilates the Indigenous cultures' histories. This Euro-centric version of history persists. Individual attitudes of prejudice must also be challenged and reformed.

> ## Box 8.2 – Racism
>
> **Racism** is a system where one racially designated group maintains the power and privilege in society and relegates other groups to subordinated positions of reduced resources, discrimination, and prejudice. **Racism = race power + prejudice.** In the US, racism is based upon the elevation and privilege of the White groups.
>
> **White privilege** can be described as unearned advantages associated with anyone who appears White. White privilege extends beyond institutional practices to "normative" or "correct" assessments of behaviors or attitudes. Anything associated with "White" typically is more highly valued. The term *American* is associated with White, while people from other groups are viewed as not fully *American*. The second-class status is often denoted by a hyphenated label such as Native, African, or Asian American. These groups have the status of the "**other**," since they are viewed as interlopers.

Discrimination

Discrimination refers to unfair treatment of people, based on perceived group affiliation. Discrimination takes the form of *institutional discrimination* when the very rules of the institutions, as well as informal interactions, reflect and perpetuate unfairness. The most blatant form of institutional discrimination is *legal exclusion*, also called *de jure*, as when no Blacks or women are allowed. Institutional discrimination persists *de facto*, in practice, even where it has been outlawed. Differential treatment is documented in employment, education, housing, wages, law enforcement, and the criminal justice system. Laws have been formulated to support the dominance of the empowered group, while not overtly seeming to do so. They persist, even when incumbents personally resist them. This is what is meant by *institutional discrimination*; it occurs regardless of who is currently sitting in the power positions because it is **built into the structure** of the institution. Such biases can lead to evaluating a person's resume or work performance differently, based on a person's demographics (Krugman et al. 1982). Automatic biases overtake conscious thoughts, unintentionally. This is the essence of privilege, unacknowledged and invisible, especially to those who possess it.

Because racism and stereotyping are so common, they are frequently difficult to address. The question of whether computers can be racist has been studied. Intuitively, a first response would be that they are not, since they are not sentient beings, but it must be remembered that computers are programmed by humans and bias can seep into programming despite a desire to be neutral. One person, using a *Google Photos* program to organize and label pictures of friends, found that an African American friend was given the label of an animal.

Another example of racism in technology found that people who searched for names sounding African American were more likely to be automatically contacted by search engines offering criminal record checks. The report made the suggestion that if software teams included people of color there might be a better chance of guarding against these racist associations (Siegel 2016). For example, an African American woman started a company to use computer programs to screen job applicants, without regard to their personal demographics. Her inspiration for this endeavor was the lack of diversity in Silicon Valley and the statements she frequently heard there asserting that there "just were not enough women and people of color who were qualified," something she just could not believe. As a former Microsoft employee, she was surprised to find that she felt more discrimination there as a woman than as a person of color. She was inspired to tackle the problem of personnel biases as a result of an earlier report showing that when professional symphonies ran auditions behind curtains, requiring the musicians to wear soft shoes (so as not to be influenced by hearing their heels), the result was a 500 **percent** increase in female hires (Siegel 2016). Her program hides age, names, pictures, and shows only skills, experience, and education and has successfully obtained jobs for her clients.

Behavior can be based on more personal viewpoints, as seen in *individual discrimination*, where a person's acts are a result of the demographic categories attributed to the individual. It is true that everyone discriminates; when you choose to date one person over another, you are exercising discrimination but when you make this choice based on some alleged characteristic of the person's categorical membership, then you are embodying the type of individual discrimination of concern to sociologists. *Prejudice* describes the assigning of specific attributes to an entire categorical group, frequently without any real-life interaction with any group members. These generalizations are commonly false, though prejudice can also be positive, as when, for example, an employer believes that White people are better workers. These develop into categorical *stereotypes* of a group, such as, for example, the belief that "White people can't dance." Simply integrating an environment, a school, or a workplace will not reduce prejudice by itself. In order to achieve a reduction in prejudice and stereotyping, people must be required to interact in a meaningful way, such as being given a work project to cooperate on (APS n.d.).

Box 8.3 – Prejudice/Discrimination

Institutional discrimination refers to patterns of differential treatment which are built into the structures and culture of institutions. The most blatant form of institutional discrimination occurs when one group is automatically disqualified. When colleges accept only White people, or only men, overt institutional discrimination is occurring though it often is less blatant. An example of more subtle discrimination would be when a woman and a man are held to different standards on job evaluations or when a White person and an African American are rated differently for the same level of performance at work. This type of discrimination must be addressed systemically since it operates independently of specific individuals.

Individual discrimination is when a person treats others differently based on the perception of group membership, usually indicating prejudiced beliefs. Change in this area requires personal changes, though these are best reflected in institutional and legal changes, as well.

Prejudice is when a person holds *preconceived* ideas about someone based on categorical perceptions attributed to them. Often, actual exposure to people from other groups will reduce prejudice if there is meaningful interaction. Prejudice can be either positive or negative.

Stereotypes are generalizations associated with categorical membership. An example would be to assume that all Asians are good at math, or all African Americans are athletic, or all White people have straight hair.

Is Race a Choice?

In 2015 a breaking news story revealed that Rachel Dolezal, a White woman from a privileged middle-class background, had been living as an African American. Identifying as Black, Dolezal gained a scholarship to attend the predominantly Black Howard University, utilizing resources intended to help disadvantaged people of color. She became an activist in the African American community, taught university classes as an allegedly African American person, and became president of the Spokane WA *National Association for the Advancement of Colored People* (NAACP). She claimed a deep affinity and identification with the African American cultural experience and dedicated much of her life to addressing race issues.

Her story incited much debate regarding the consequences of her actions. The conceptualization of race may be social but appropriating the experiences of another's group is offensive to some, even if the intentions were honest. As one commentator suggested (Oluo 2015), if Dolezal really wanted to address the effects of racism, it would have been more honest and effective to have done so as a White woman.

Is "passing" as a nondominant group member the same as passing as a dominant group member, as when fair-skinned Blacks "passed" as Whites? What do you think was the motivation for Rachel Dolezal and how do you feel about it?

Race and Culture

Consider public spaces and who "rules" the space. Figures displayed in public frequently represent the dominant group's "heroes." These images are monolithic, almost exclusively depicting White males. The history reflected by these men frequently speaks to events or cultural dynamics which are painful or shameful to some. Recently, there have been organized efforts to remove, or at least contextualize, some of these public depictions. In 2016, the city of New Orleans decided to remove four offensive public monuments with Confederate themes, including removing a 130-year-old statue of Robert E. Lee, as did Charlottesville VA in 2017. Another racially controversial situation emerged at Yale University regarding the possible renaming of a residence hall commemorating John C. Calhoun, a United States Senator and White supremacist (Remnick 2016). After resisting requests to change the name (Remnick 2016), the university ultimately changed its position (Wang and Svrluga 2017). Similarly, because of allegations of sexual assault brought against Bill Cosby, an artist defaced an image of Cosby in a mural on a popular D.C. restaurant's building (Rainey 2015).

Which people, or events, are selected for public celebration becomes part of collective consciousness and shapes the cultural landscape. Many of our national "heroes" reflect forces of racial and sexual oppression. These models perpetuate cultural values which are antithetical to American ideals. Renee Romano, a professor of comparative American studies and Africana studies, recommends weighing a public person's accomplishments against any negative repercussions inspired by the person. Romano uses the example of Thomas Jefferson, who owned slaves and fathered children with his slaves. She suggests that he can represent a person who did not actively take up reprehensible positions of hate though he did, of course, participate in the economy and culture that enslaved an entire group. Both of these aspects of his life can be considered in deciding whether to allow memorials with Jefferson to remain. If a person's positive contributions outweigh the negative, then commemoration may still be warranted.

An alternative tactic is to create companion memorials, alongside existing monuments, to counter the dominant content. Professor Romano suggests that this option fails to critique assumptions associated with the established heroes, simply providing additional figures. Others suggest that companion memorials could be an asset if they provoke critical thinking and discussion (The Takeaway).

The absence of nondominant heroes has the effect of confirming a "one story" version of history and contributes to the invisibility of nondominant groups. If we had more images of people reflecting diverse experiences, our automatic cultural assumptions would be modified. As it is, if any nondominant people are celebrated it is generally as a "sidebar" to the "main" history. Think about textbooks in American history. What were the Indigenous people doing before the colonial era? What were women doing during the revolutionary war? How was the Mexican population treated when their lands were taken over? What woman has ever been on our currency? What African American? Asian American? Indigenous person? What monuments are there of people from these groups to memorialize their experiences?

Figure 8.3 Images of nondominant groups, when they did exist, tended to be generic rather than memorializing a specific person, consequently supporting the view that group members were interchangeable
Source: Kaspars Grinvalds / Shutterstock.com

References to nondominant groups, when they exist at all, tend to be "generic" rather than memorializing specific people, such as in the case of the Statue of Liberty or when a woman is depicted holding the scales of justice.

Some exceptions where specific women, for example, are portrayed can be seen in the coins featuring Susan B. Anthony and Sacajewea on the silver and gold dollars respectively; interestingly neither of these was widely circulated for more than a few years. No person of color, aside from Sacajewea, has yet appeared on coins or bills. In 2016, the US Treasury Department announced major currency changes; Harriet Tubman, abolitionist and former slave, would replace Andrew Jackson on the back of the $20 bill; the ten-dollar bill will retain Alexander Hamilton's face but the back will feature an image of the 1913 march for women's suffrage and include pictures of five suffrage leaders, Lucretia Mott, Sojourner Truth, Elizabeth Cady Stanton, Alice Paul, and Susan B. Anthony; the five-dollar bill will continue to have the image of Abraham Lincoln on the front but the back of the bill will display the Lincoln Memorial as a backdrop to a concert image of African American musician Marian Anderson. Eleanor Roosevelt, who arranged the concert will also be on the back of the bill, as will Martin Luther King, Jr., who delivered his "I Had a Dream" speech from the steps of the monument. The designs will be presented in 2020, as part of the one hundredth anniversary of the 19th amendment to the Constitution granting women suffrage. The actual currency will not be disseminated until later in the decade (Calmes 2016). Interestingly, note that the images on the five and ten dollar bills will be contextualized rather than appear as stand-alone images, as in the pictures of the men on the front of the bills.

A review of national monuments reveals that among the top ten monuments to African Americans, only one features a woman, Harriet Tubman (Cganemccalla 2011). Asian American monuments are also scarce. Some have been established in commemoration of Japanese American efforts in World War II (Japanese American Memorial n.d.), though they also are generic in their portrayals. California's Angel Island, commemorating Asian immigration to the west coast, does not include images of any particular person. Cultural depictions of Indigenous persons are almost completely absent from the culture, except as stereotypes. One exception is a large

Figures 8.4a and 8.4b Susan B. Anthony and Sacajawea dollar coins; neither were produced for very long
Source: a. Daniel D Malone / Shutterstock.com; b. Vladimir Wrangel / Shutterstock.com

monument depicting the Lakota Sioux leader *Crazy Horse*, and commemorating the Native Americans buried in the vicinity of Mt Rushmore. It has been in process since the 1940s, but remains unfinished partially due to lack of funding (Crazy Horse Memorial n.d.).

National recognition of nondominant cultures generally is confined to particular dates, such as Black History, Women's History, and Asian History months (February, March, and May respectively), and Indigenous People's day (celebrated in October, sometimes as an alternative to Columbus Day). These special events recognize groups frequently overlooked but they also contribute to the exclusion of these groups from mainstream events.

Another source of cultural controversy surrounds the cooptation and perversion of Native American life by sports teams. These can be seen in the use of names and images, such as "the redskins," "the chiefs," and "the braves." These names occur in professional sports as well as in educational institutions. Agitation for change has prompted heated debates. Proponents of maintaining the practices argue the

Figure 8.5 Crazy Horse monument, South Dakota Source: Idawriter / Panoramio

importance of continuity of team identity, asserting that it does not represent a harmful practice. Those opposed demand discontinuation of the offensive imagery and names as denigrating (Martinez 2013; Native American Mascots n.d.; Qureshi 2016). Supporters of discontinuing the Native elements have been attacked as over-reacting or as hypersensitive. Such attacks on the voices of opposition invalidate genuine feelings reflecting historical abuses and derail real consideration of the identified injury to the groups.

Hegemony, defined as the imposition of the dominant group's cultural standards as universal, is pervasive. The many forms it takes are largely unrecognized. One recent study showed that adopting formal corporate power clothing, associated with White men, contributes to better outcomes in business deals. The "correct" clothes have been shown to increase the profitability of a business deal by 10 percent (Noguchi 2016).

Stereotypes can wield powerful influence. When stereotypic attitudes are articulated they can even be embraced by the people described (Noguchi 2016). A study of discrimination in the workplace found that reminding people of a stereotype perpetuates it, but simply by adding a short comment regarding the need to correct the biased viewpoint the stereotypic behaviors can be effectively reduced (Grant and Sandberg 2014). Disseminating positive images of typically stereotyped groups interrupts stereotypes. The media is the main source of stereotypic images. The absence of positive and inclusive cultural images can lead to lifelong self-doubts. Many nondominant individuals suffer from the "imposter" syndrome, indicating feelings of illegitimacy in a position. This feeling has been noted in memoirs by members of various marginalized groups, including those based on race, social class, ethnicity, and sex (Bragg 1997; Lubrano 2004; Moraga 2007; Dowd-Higgins 2012). Feelings resulting from racism deplete a person's energy which could be utilized for more positive ends:

> This need to be always on guard was an unmeasured expenditure of energy,
> the slow siphoning of the essence. It contributed to the fast breakdown of our

bodies. So I feared not just the violence of this world but the rules designed
to protect you from it, the rules that would have you contort your body to
address the block, and contort again to be taken seriously by colleagues, and
contort again so as not to give the police a reason. All my life I'd heard people
tell their black boys and black girls to "be twice as good," which is to say
"accept half as much."

(Coates 2015)

Analysis of popular media is rampant with examples of insufficient representation
of nondominant groups. A recent study survey of 400 television shows and movies
found that 28 percent of speaking parts occurred in people of color, though that
population comprises 40 percent of the population. One half of television shows had
no Asian American speakers and one fifth had no African American speakers. Movies
exhibited even smaller nondominant proportions than television, with 7 percent
approximating the actual societal demographics, compared to 17 percent of television
shows. None of the six major US movie companies passed an analysis of diversity
(Park et al. 2016; Deggans 2016).

Not only is there a marginal presence of nondominant people in media but when
they are depicted they rarely express experiences in their own "voice." The ubiquitous
and unexamined consequences of
White privilege constrain what is
shown. One example can be seen in
the pressures exerted on Margaret
Cho, star of a 1994–1995 ABC series
All American Girl (Jacobs 1994), to
portray stereotypic "Asian" femininity.
Cho was told to lose weight and
actually collapsed on the set from
exhaustion. The show was canceled
after one season and Cho writes of
feeling constantly besieged by the
producers to change her persona (Cho
2001). The show garnered criticisms
from all sides, including being unfunny,
promoting stereotypes, and featuring
a story of an Americanized daughter
of a traditional Korean mother but
with only one Korean cast member.
A later show, regarding Chinese
immigrants, did not fare much better.
In 2015, ABC produced *Fresh Off the
Boat* (Nahnatchka 2015), depicting
the experiences of Taiwanese-Chinese
American comedian Eddie Huang.
Huang, too, was offended by the

Figure 8.6 Margaret Cho at the "Rock Of Ages" opening
night, Pantages Theater, Hollywood, CA. 02-15-11. Cho was
constantly being told to lose weight, and ultimately collapsed,
on the set of her program, from dieting and exhaustion
Source: s_bukley / Shutterstock.com

Figure 8.7 Toni Morrison, a Nobel Prize-winning American author, editor, and professor during the autograph session in the L'arbre a Lettres bookstore in Paris, France
Source: Olga Besnard / Shutterstock.com

television portrayal of his written memoir and has not participated in its second season (Fernandez and Adalian 2015; De Moraes 2015). Although 20 years separate the series, it seems that not much has changed.

If images of nondominant group members are rare, their absence from leadership roles is even more pronounced. A *New York Times* review of power showed that of the 503 people studied as leaders in government, business, education, and culture, only 44 were "minorities" and 24 of these were in appointed or elected political positions (Park et al. 2016). The status of White men is rarely, if ever, scrutinized and often unreported. An August 2017 search for the category of White males in the 2016 Congress was unsuccessful. Itemized lists of women could be found but no count for White men could be located. Usually it requires extrapolation of "minority data." An earlier report, in 2015, listed Congress as 80 percent White, 80 percent male, and 92 percent Christian (Bump 2015).

Hegemony is so ubiquitous even nondominant groups reflect the dominant view. *Internalized racism* is defined as the incorporation, by nondominant group members, of cultural stereotypes disseminated by the dominant culture. One entertaining example of this phenomenon can be seen in Chris Rock's movie *Good Hair*, where he examines the ways nonWhite people desire stereotypically styled "White hair" (Good Hair 2013). *Colorism* refers to the hegemonic notion that light skin is preferable to darker skin, even within communities of color. This can be seen in "The Brown Paper Bag Rule," prevalent in the early 1900s, which held that African Americans with skin darker than a brown paper bag would be excluded from organizations representing elite African Americans (Peters 2016).

> **Box 8.4 – Hegemony**
>
> *Hegemony* refers to cultural domination in which one group's values and standards are integrated into the culture as the universal standard. Chris Rock, for example, made a video about hair and the *hegemonic* concept of "good" hair as straight and "manageable."
>
> *Internalized racism* occurs when a person from a nondominant group takes on the dominant group's image of the group or its members. One example concerns the higher valuation of lighter skin, even in communities of color. *Colorism* refers to the pervasive cultural mandate that light skin is preferable to darker skin, even within nonWhite groups.

The problem of colorism extends to other all nonWhite groups. Although this color hierarchy has been challenged, its influence can still be seen in contemporary critiques such as Spike Lee's film *School Daze* (1988) and Toni Morrison's 2015 novel *God Help the Child*. Recently, a controversy exploded regarding the choice of Zoe Saldana for a film biography of African American Nina Simone. Saldana, a light-skinned woman with Puerto Rican and Dominican roots, is a contrast to the artist/activist Simone who made a point of being dark-skinned and beautiful (Garcia-Navarro 2016). Colorism can also be seen in the Latino community, as expressed by Cherrie Moraga in *La Güera* (1983). Born to an Anglo father and Latina mother, Moraga physically favored her father and she writes about how she was encouraged to embrace her light skin: "White was right. Period. I could pass. If I got educated enough, there would never be any telling" (Moraga 2007).

Figure 8.8 In this composite image, a comparison has been made between Nina Simone and actress Zoe Saldana
Source: David Redfern / Getty Images

Figure 8.9 Spike Lee at the 46th NAACP Image Awards Press Room at a Pasadena Convention Center in Pasadena, CA
Source: Kathy Hutchins / Shutterstock.com

Affirmative Action was advanced as an initiative to combat institutional discrimination by drawing attention to automatic, often unintentional biases. Initial laws were passed by Franklin D. Roosevelt during World War II, to increase the hiring and employment of "Negroes, Mexican Americans, and Jewish" workers by contractors receiving federal monies. After initial gains, increasing the percentages of under-represented groups from 3 to 8 percent (Affirmative Action n.d.), the patterns reverted to their earlier portions by the war's end. The issue was not addressed again until the John F. Kennedy and Lyndon B. Johnson executive orders of the 1960s.

President Kennedy took up the issue of racial bias in employment with executive Order 10925, which targeted projects with federal funding. The order also established the *Equal Economic Opportunity Commission* (EEOC). In 1965 President Johnson issued Executive Order 11246, prohibiting discrimination in employment on the basis of race, color, religion, or national origin. In 1967, he extended protection to include sex. The guiding principle of Affirmative Action is to interrupt the automatic biases favoring White males since employers typically rank White males higher than others, even if their experiences are identical to other candidates' qualifications. The program goal was to attain a more diverse workforce by eliminating bias. It was never intended to replace workers with "less qualified minorities" but to protect qualified nondominant persons from being passed over. Affirmative Action developed to highlight merit over sex, race, or ethnicity.

Box 8.5 – Affirmative Action

Affirmative Action is most frequently associated with President Lyndon Johnson, though the first Affirmative Action mandates were passed during World War II to enhance the employment of "Negroes, Mexican Americans, and Jews." The 1965 Executive Order 11246, prohibiting discrimination in employment based on race, color, religion, or national origin was modified in 1967 to include the category of sex. Over the ensuing decades Affirmative Action has been challenged in the courts, and largely upheld, as long as it was not implemented with specific quotas. Court rulings have stated that diversity in education and business is considered a desirable societal goal.

The first major challenge to the use of Affirmative Action was decided in the 1978 US Supreme Court case, *The Regents of the University of CA v Bakke*. Allan Bakke was twice denied entrance to the University of CA Medical School in Davis CA (UCD). He charged that he was "unfairly" bypassed in favor of selected minority candidates with lower GPAs and Board scores. In a split decision, four of the judges ruled that using race was a violation of the Civil Rights Act while four wrote that race was a factor to be appropriately included. A fifth judge, Judge Lewis Powell Jr., sided with the first group but said that it was only wrong in the Bakke case because UCD reserved 16 of 100 admission slots specifically for minority students. He believed that the consideration of race as a factor affecting admission was legitimate but allotting a quota was not. Consequently, the resulting five to four decision resulted in Bakke's admission but left the principles of Affirmative Action intact. The influence of the Bakke decision was contained largely to abolition of the use of quotas.

Twenty-five years later, in 2013, two other cases addressing admissions in higher education reached the US Supreme Court. They were in regard to the University of Michigan undergraduate college and law school. Each case was resolved separately. In a 6:3 decision the Court voted against the current University of Michigan undergraduate admissions protocol which automatically awarded one fifth of the required admissions points to every applicant who was a member of an under-represented racial group. The Court ruled that the specific university policy could be refined by still allowing for race to be factored into the admission process but by a different policy. In the case of the law school, a 5:4 decision favored keeping race as a crucial element in attaining a diverse student body, which was deemed beneficial to the goals of the law school. Sandra Day O'Connor, widely considered a moderate judge, cast the deciding vote, asserting that perhaps in another 25 years the consideration of race would be unnecessary but that currently the law school would not achieve diversity with a *color-blind* policy. These decisions were considered a win for Affirmative Action since the conflict was not over whether race protection should exist but rather in what form (University of Michigan... 2003).

A third significant case regarding Affirmative Action in higher education was filed as *Fisher vs. The University of Texas, Austin*. Abigail Fisher, denied undergraduate admission for the fall of 2008, charged that she was the object of racial discrimination because she was White. In 1997, the University of Texas had adopted a 10 percent plan in which the top 10 percent of high school seniors from each high school in the state would be admitted to the University's Austin campus. This would account for 75 percent of the entering freshman class. The remaining 25 percent of the class would be selected by a holistic index, including multiple factors, race being one of many. The resulting score would determine who would fill the remaining spaces in the freshman class. Ms Fisher missed the cutoff for each group. In 2013, the US Supreme Court sent the case back to the US Court of Appeals Fifth Circuit saying that they had to scrutinize the 25 percent admissions criteria to advance "compelling" evidence that it was "necessary" to racially balance the school. In 2014, the Fifth Circuit Court upheld their decision (Epps 2015). The case was filed again, in the Supreme Court, in December 2015. In a June 2016 ruling, the Court upheld the right of a university to include race as one of many measures utilized to provide for a diverse student population (Liptak 2016).

Some commentators have suggested that Affirmative Action policies have resulted in *reverse discrimination*, a phrase popularized by the Bakke case. This situation would occur only if it can be demonstrated that White people have become disproportionately *under-represented* in desirable positions in education and employment. There is no evidence to support this claim. When a privileged group is treated equally to other groups, they can experience a diminished privilege they can identify as discrimination but that does not constitute reverse discrimination. In the practice of Affirmative Action, there certainly may be cases where White men have "lost" out on jobs, education opportunities, and/or contracts but that can reflect increased equity in the processes, suggesting Affirmative Action successes. Typically there will be more qualified applicants than available positions; "fairness" interrupts a process of automatic bias.

Discrimination in employment persists. There is compelling research showing that job candidates given a typically White-sounding name are significantly more likely to get a callback, across a variety of categories, than a candidate with an African American-sounding name. The White group's success rate is 150 percent of the African Americans'. If a candidate's address indicates a wealthier, more educated, predominantly White neighborhood, callback rates go up for both groups (Francis 2017). Another study shows that candidates are "whitening" their resumes by omitting any reference which alludes to their race, resulting in two times the number of callbacks from resumes which were not modified. These findings apply to a wide range of companies, including those which claim to value diversity (Gerdeman 2017).

How Do Sociologists View Race and Society?

Senator Elizabeth Warren articulates a sociological perspective in her address to the 2016 Democratic National Convention by highlighting that dividing the electorate by race dilutes the power of the working class to influence the government and big business:

> "Divide and Conquer" is an old story in America. Dr. Martin Luther King knew it. After his march from Selma to Montgomery, he spoke of how segregation was created to keep people divided. Instead of higher wages for workers, Dr. King described how poor Whites in the South were fed Jim Crow, which told a poor White worker that, "no matter how bad off he was, at least he was a White man, better than the black man." Racial hatred was part of keeping the powerful on top.
>
> When we turn on each other, bankers can run our economy for Wall Street, oil companies can fight off clean energy, and giant corporations can ship the last good jobs overseas. When we turn on each other, rich guys like Trump can push through more tax breaks for themselves and then we'll never have enough

money to support our schools, or rebuild our highways, or invest in our kids' future. When we turn on each other, we can't unite to fight back against a rigged system.

(Drabold 2016)

In the 2016 presidential race, there was much attention paid to garnering the support of specific demographic groups. Segments of the population representing common economic concerns were courted by the major parties. With respect to the increasingly elusive American Dream, Warren gave voice to the views embodied by *conflict theorists*. Conflict theorists believe that those in positions of power and privilege will promote separation of disadvantaged groups so that they will not present a threat to the establishment. The real hope for social change lies in the marginalized groups' recognition of common interests and subsequent activism.

In contrast to the conflict perspective, functionalist theorists suggest a positive aspect in specific group identity. Groups can provide elements leading to self-esteem and a sense of belonging. The functionalists also focus on the assimilation, or adaptation, of nondominant groups to the dominant culture as contributing to stability in society. These theorists underplay the development of *"hate" crimes*, perpetrated against an individual due to their affiliation with a particular group. Establishment of a special category for such crimes dates only to the 2009 *Matthew Shepard and James Byrd, Jr. Hate Crimes Prevention Act* bill (DOJ 2009). The functionalists suggest that inequality, which keeps people in low-wage jobs and insecure regarding the future, can lead to cooperation sustaining the status quo. They tend to bypass all the negative ramifications of inequality, often implying that it exists more from personal choices than social exploitation.

Figure 8.10 Protesters demonstrate against hate-speech outside the Donald Trump rally at the University of Illinois at Chicago Pavilion
Source: Marie Kanger Born / Shutterstock.com

Symbolic interactionists focus on the incorporation of symbols specific to particular groups in promoting positive self-concepts and social affiliations benefitting the groups' members. These can be expressed in clothing, ornamentation, ritual, language, and group activities. Use of these elements permits members to readily identify other members and provides a sense of familiarity and affiliation. Symbolic interactionists presume that categorical knowledge eases social interaction by providing guidelines for how to approach and respond to others. These reactions are usually automatic and can be positive or negative. A gang member, for example, utilizes symbolic colors to identify their allegiance to a group and this sends messages regarding how to behave towards them, as well as who is on board. Race, ethnic identity, and even political affiliation also are symbolically communicated leading to group solidarity.

How Is Discrimination Reflected in Issues of Immigration and Religion?

Discrimination affects all nondominant groups, including White immigrant groups lacking Anglo-Saxon origin. All nondominant groups share histories of discrimination and all have been subjected to stereotyping. The exploitation of immigrant groups is an integral part of the American story. Film writer and director Woody Allen conveys the irony of the welcoming image associated with the Statue of Liberty:

> But the huddled masses were never welcomed with open arms. Soon as they came over, each ethnic group was met with hostility. Each one had to claw and fight its way in. People always hated foreigners. It's the American way.
> (Spoken by Larry David, playing retired professor Boris Yelnikoff in Woody Allen's 2009 film *Whatever Works*)

Many immigrant groups struggle to find ways to become part of society while maintaining some group identity. Every group has had some members who have responded to exploitation, especially as new arrivals, by participating in an illicit economy or activity; such activities have not been exclusive to any particular or current group. White ethnic minorities, characteristic of turn of the twentieth century immigrants, were defined as "inferior races" and not considered "White." The development of a "White identity" took several generations and has been written about extensively, especially with respect to Jews, the Irish, Italians, and Asians (Brodkin 1998; Ignatiev 1995; Volokh 2014; Guglielmo and Salerno 2003).

Newly arrived immigrants, from the White ethnic groups of the nineteenth century to the Latino and Asian immigrants of the twenty-first century, have been "blamed" for a range of social ills including disease, poor working habits, labor unrest, low wages, unemployment, and communism. All the major White immigrant groups of the turn of the twentieth century experienced gang affiliations and Irish, Italian, and Jewish gangs vied for power in eastern cities with large immigrant populations. The immigrants also responded to the discrimination by engaging in social activism. In the early twentieth century, many members of immigrant groups contributed to the creation and membership of labor unions in order to resist the poor conditions of the

Figure 8.11 Segregation
Source: kickstand /
istockphoto.com

workplace. This history is frequently absent from standard American history classes and textbooks. The movement to win rights for workers against harsh and dangerous conditions was often violent and frequently endangered the lives and livelihoods of the activists. The workers, employed in difficult occupations of mining, farm work, and factory work, were disproportionately immigrant laborers. Issues ranged from protests of the 70-hour work week and lack of sufficient breaks and facilities, to the lack of worker protection against hazardous conditions.

Many memoirs documenting the White immigrant experience reflect the same concerns voiced by today's immigrant groups regarding wages, education, poverty, employment, and housing. Even more poignant is the documentation of family strife regarding the "Americanization" of the younger generation, and the loss of respect for the traditions of the immigrant generation. The same conditions pervade the accounts of today's nonWhite immigrants, typically from Asia, Latin America, or Africa. (Issues relating to undocumented immigrants are addressed in Chapter 14.)

The question of *cultural assimilation*, or how far to adopt the dominant American culture, is universal. This common concern of immigrant groups is highlighted by Professor Lillian Faderman, as she compares her life, born in 1940 to a mother who fled the religious persecution in the *shtetl* (a small Jewish town of eastern Europe) with the experiences of the southeast Asian Hmong immigrant community of Fresno CA:

> But much more significant ... were the many experiences as immigrants or children of immigrants in America that both groups undeniably shared. The stories of the younger Hmong people I met, first in my classes and then in the larger Hmong community, reflected back to me in so many ways my own story: my struggle, as a child of a Jewish immigrant, to become an American—the conflicting beliefs and language and outlook I had to make sense of; the

sorrows of separation from my mother's culture that I endured, as well as the guilt occasioned by that necessary separation; the realization that there was no way I could "go home again" because "home," the roots that I had inherited from her, no longer existed.

(Faderman 1998)

Many dominant group members believe that the immigrants should, through hard work and sheer will, "pull themselves up by their bootstraps." The implied desirability of assimilation is not questioned. The belief is that if people only work hard they will succeed simply by embracing American values and traditions; a failure to do so is seen as a personal flaw and not as a conscious choice. Poverty is also considered a problem of individual flaws, because in America "anyone can grow up to be president" or live out the "rags to riches" story. This perspective represents an *ideology*, defined as a set of beliefs which support the existing social order. The failure of immigrants to be "successful," as defined by the dominant culture, is attributed to bad habits and lack of character rather than to the poor working conditions and low wages associated with poverty. This attitude also permits the more advantaged groups to attribute their own successes to a "higher" character. The elevation of the dominant group can justify the dehumanization and exploitation of others. These unexamined ideologies allowed for slavery and immigrant exploitation, extending to the present day.

Box 8.6 – Cultural Assimilation

Cultural assimilation refers to the extent to which a nondominant group takes on the attributes of the dominant group. Typically, in the US, this amounts to adopting elements of the White culture.

Ideology refers to a concept which suggests that beliefs in the society persist because they justify maintaining the status quo. Ideological beliefs allow for societal practices to be sustained as desirable.

The melting pot is the belief that all nondominant groups contribute to American culture to create a new entity, characteristic of "America." It can be seen as representative of an *ideology* in that such a belief denies elements of power and negates the idea that one culture dominates the others. This theory can be represented by: $A + B + C + D... = X$.

Anglo conformity suggests that any person, or group, desiring to attain legitimacy, or success, must adopt "Anglo" elements. This can be depicted as: $A + B + C + D... = A$. This theory describes most of American history.

Cultural pluralism is a more recent conceptualization which suggests that cultures can maintain some original elements as long as they don't conflict with essential aspects of the dominant American culture. A representation of this view would be: $A + B + C + D... = A + B + C + D$, reflective of increased cultural inclusion.

Theories of assimilation operate as ideologies to support the dominant group. One theory, which often is presented as "fact," is the *melting pot*. This view incorporates the idea that all the immigrant groups arrive in the US and throw some of their "home" cultures into the pot comprising "American" culture: $A + B + C + D... = X$. American culture is constructed as the best of all worlds blended into one new culture. This position does not recognize any inequalities in the "mix" but suggests a balanced blend. There is no recognition of dominance or oppression.

Anglo conformity theory suggests that all groups must live, breathe, act, dress, speak "Anglo" in order to achieve success: $A + B + C + D = A$. Historically, the US has demonstrated Anglo conformity. Violating norms of speech by exhibiting an accent, or wearing unconventional business attire could derail a person's career. *"American"* behaviors, goals, and attitudes are desirable and individualism, the dominance of individual interest over family or group, is the guiding principle.

A third approach incorporates the idea of *cultural pluralism* (also referred to as multi-culturalism) suggesting what some believe to be the current status of diversity in the US. In this scenario, $A + B + C + D = A + B + C + D$, all the different cultures can coexist and be part of the American culture while maintaining some specific elements. Although greater inclusion of different cultures may exist today, there is still a dominant culture which devalues the others, designating them as "sub" cultural. The behaviors and standards of all groups are implicitly, if not always explicitly, measured against the dominant culture. This belief in cultural equity is harmful because it implies that equality has been attained and therefore no attention to discrimination or prejudice is required. If pluralism becomes more integrated into the culture, it can be imagined that pressures to assimilate will become less severe.

There have been some changes in the culture in recent decades, but the resurgence of Neo-Nazis, White Supremacists, racists, anti-Semitists, anti-Muslim, anti-gay, and anti-transgendered groups indicates the underlying resistance to change. Some movement towards greater inclusion of nondominant groups can be attributed to financial or political motivation. For example, if a company does not employ some workers who speak the Native language of area residents, it will lose business. If the political parties ignore the large groups of nondominant people, that can make the difference in winning or losing an election. The gay marriage market is lucrative to a market facing decreasing revenues. Origins of inclusion, stemming from economic interests are not necessarily "bad"; they are part of democratic capitalism's operating principles. Even if the original impetus for cooperation is motivated by personal or business interests, familiarity can lead to decreased tensions and stereotyping.

Immigration: Love Between the Generations

The concept assuming the desirability of *Americanization* actually represents a Euro-centric bias. Resistance to adopting Americanization, with its Anglo-Saxon roots, may be stronger in today's non-European immigrant groups. Viewing the maintenance of an immigrant's home culture as antithetical to becoming American may be shortsighted. Nevertheless, how a young person bridges the divide between the parental culture and the American culture is never easy to understand, let alone to accomplish. The comedian/actor/writer, Kumail Nanjiani, illustrates just how delicately the family feelings must be measured against personal desire.

Nanjiani immigrated as a youth and his parents made significant sacrifices, both personally and professionally, to move the family to the US. The situation is portrayed, fictionally, in the movie *The Big Sick* (Showalter 2017) which focuses on the development of Nanjiani's relationship with the Anglo-American woman, Emily Gordon, who eventually becomes his wife. His family presses him to meet Pakistani women, inviting women to "drop by" to the weekly family dinner. Nanjiani loves and respects them but is not interested in the women or in the choice of profession preferred by his parents. His deep love for them is clear as are his fears of being cast out of the family. In a heated moment, as his parents are elaborating their sacrifices, he counters by asking them why they would choose to come to America if they want him to live as a Pakistani; the question is unanswered and is met with an awkward silence. He fears that his parents will make good on the threat to disown him and so breaks things off with Emily. Ultimately, he chooses the American ideal of selecting his own spouse, whatever her background. When Emily develops a life-threatening illness he not only chooses her but decides that he can approach his parents, who have largely made good on their threat, and defies them by asserting that they can behave however they choose but he is considering himself part of the family and will continue to do so, no matter how they act or what he does. The audience is left to imagine that the older generation will come around.

What Is the Current Status of Nondominant Groups in the US?

The language referring to various groups is a major source of contention, both in the dominant culture and within communities. Controversies address what words to use in reference to a particular group: African American or Black? Latino or Hispanic? Native American or American Indian? Asian? Southeast Asian? Near Asian? White? Anglo American? Following the activism of the 1960s, "Negro" was replaced by Black and later by African American. Some Black groups resisted this modification as they are not African Americans. In this book, the words are often used interchangeably, in accordance with the usage in the studies or articles being cited. Similarly, Hispanic has given way to Latino which some people prefer because of its inclusion of cultural elements, while Hispanic focuses on language. Still, some prefer specific ethnic references, such as Mexican American, Puerto Rican, or Dominican. There is also contention in the Indigenous community surrounding the use of the term "Native American" versus "American Indian" and again, this text will reflect whatever material is being cited. When no specific reference is being utilized, the text will generally use "Indigenous" as a more neutral descriptive title. Asian will be utilized as a *Pan Asian* inclusive designation for people from the Asian continent unless we are specifically addressing a particular group. In some places, the designation will change because of the terminology, or subjects, utilized by the research being reviewed.

Asian Americans

During the half century from 1882 to 1935, three waves of Asian immigrants arrived to participate in labor-intensive, physical work. Subsequent immigration laws were passed to prohibit new group members' entry and established residents were not granted naturalization rights until 1952. Marriages between Asians and Whites were prohibited through ***anti-miscegenation*** laws, prohibiting inter-racial marriages. In 1965, through a combination of civil rights legislation and immigration reform, immigration quotas from Asian countries were set at 20,000, effectively removing *extraordinary* limitations on the group's participation. Nevertheless, legacies from historical precedents and contemporary discrimination remain. These laws varied by state (Browning n.d.) and were not made uniformly illegal until the 1967 Supreme Court decision in *Loving v Virginia* (ACLU n.d.). Though coming from different countries and cultures, the pioneering Chinese, Japanese, Koreans, Indians, and

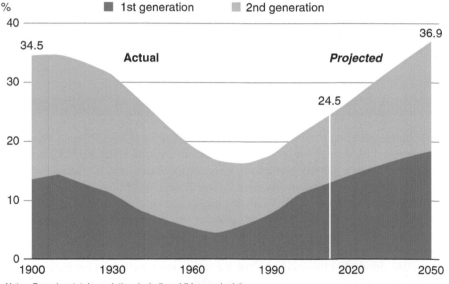

Figure 8.12a Profile of Asian American demographics
Source: "Modern Immigration Wave Brings 59 Million to U.S., Driving Population Growth and Change Through 2065," Pew Research Center, Washington DC (September 28, 2015), http://www.pewhispanic.org/2015/09/28/modern-immigration-wave-brings-59-million-to-u-s-driving-population-growth-and-change-through-2065/

First- and Second-Generation Share of the Population, Actual and Projected, 1900–2050

Notes: Based on total population, including children and adults.

Source: 2000-2012 data and all second-generation data from Pew Research Center analysis of Current Population surveys, Integrated Microdata Sample (IPUMS) files; Pew Hispanic Center projections for 2020 to 2050 from Passel and Cohn (2008); historical trend from Passel and Cohn (2008) and Edmonston and Passel (1994)

Asians Projected to Become the Largest Immigrant Group, Surpassing Hispanics

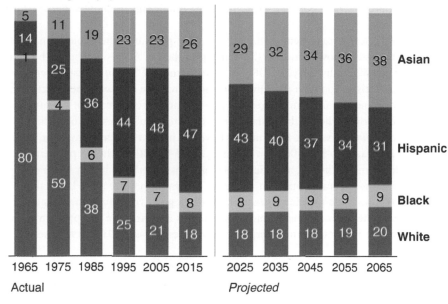

% of immigrant population

1965 1975 1985 1995 2005 2015 — Actual

2025 2035 2045 2055 2065 — *Projected*

Asian · Hispanic · Black · White

Figure 8.12b Second-generation Americans
Source: "Second-Generation Americans, by the Numbers," Pew Research Center, Washington, DC (February 7, 2013) http://www.pewsocialtrends.org/2013/02/07/second-generation-americans-by-the-numbers/

Note: Whites, Blacks and Asians include only single-race non-Hispanics. Asians include Pacific Islanders. Hispanics are of any race. Other races shown but not labeled.

Source: Pew Research Center estimates for 1965–2015 based on adjusted Census data; Pew Research Center projections for 2025–2065

Filipinos each faced similar conditions of exclusion which forged the beginnings of a common, shared Asian experience in America (Asian Americans then and now n.d.). Groups identifying as Asian American or Pacific Islanders (AAPI) are as diverse in history, culture, language, and customs as to make a broader designation virtually meaningless. The group designated as AAPI is made up of 30 countries and ethnicities speaking 100 different languages. What they share is a continent and a label. Asian Americans are 5.4 percent of the US population and will account for 9.7 percent by 2050.

The poor treatment of the Asian immigrant populations has been documented but frequently receives little attention in secondary school history courses. Many Chinese immigrants, for example, endured horrible interrogations and detentions at San Francisco Bay's Angel Island, the port of entry for many Asian immigrants. The Japanese were interned during WWII, beginning in 1942 and continuing for three and a half years. The damages in properties confiscated, educations interrupted, and families dispersed are impossible to calculate. In 1987 restitution was finally settled on the 66,000 remaining survivors, each of whom received a payment of $20,000, a figure more symbolic than realistic.

Another Asian immigration influx occurred in the mid-1970s, with the end of the Vietnam War. Refugees, some of whom aided the American military, arrived in the US, including children born to US military personnel. Subsequently, reports of the US government's failure to follow through on aid promised to Southeast Asian nationals who had supported the US effort, left some of the immigrants without support or benefits.

Asian Americans are currently 18.2 million, or 6 percent of the population, and are now the fastest growing racial/ethnic group in the US. Asians will be the biggest groups of nonWhites by the year 2065. In a large study of "Asians," respondents report more satisfaction with their lives, personal finances, and with the direction the country is moving in, than the general population. Forty percent, in the same survey cited above, believed that Asian parents put too much pressure on their children to do well in school. East Indians have the highest median income at $88,000, compared to $66,000 for all Asians, and $49,800 for the US population as a whole. Korean, Chinese, and Vietnamese groups experience higher levels of poverty than the general population. Research indicates they are more likely than the general population to value work and to hold a positive attitude towards the government. The Japanese and Filipino respondents appear more accepting than the other groups of inter-racial and intergroup marriages (Nasser 2012; Pew Research Center 2013).

The Asian immigrants are sometimes viewed as *the model minority*, as the American nondominant group possessing the highest educational level and income. While this is narrowly true today, groups within the Asian community, established over multiple generations, inflate the data and make the larger group seem more accomplished. The stereotype of the degreed, high-income Asian masks the reality that Asian immigrant groups are also among the poorest sectors of society (Garcia-Navarro 2015; Pew Research Center 2013). Poverty and high school dropout rates are staggering, especially for Hmong, Cambodian, and Laotian populations. There are many students who have "Limited Language Proficiency," or their parents do, and a Gallup poll shows more incidents of employment discrimination reported among Asian Americans than any other group, though very few file complaints with the Equal Economic Opportunity Commission (Critical Issues Facing AAPI n.d.).

The media reflect a limited portrayal of Asian Americans. American sitcoms are generally culturally monolithic, reflecting White family life. Some recent programs address nondominant groups. One acclaimed innovator is the Netflix-produced series *Master of None* which stars Aziz Ansari as an East Indian American actor trying to "make it" in New York. In the popular,

Figure 8.13 A contemporary Chinese celebration in San Francisco, CA
Source: Photography by Rosalind Gottfried

Figure 8.14 Aziz Ansari, Indian American writer, actor, comedian

Source: Jstone / Shutterstock.com

critically acclaimed series, Ansari confronts cultural issues head on. He is critical of the stereotypes conferred on the Indian population. In Season 1, Episode 4, Ansari takes on language issues when he auditions for a role and argues with the director, refusing to play the role of taxi driver with a pronounced Indian accent. Consequently, he is told he will not be receiving a "callback" (Mehta 2015). In another segment, Ansari addresses the cultural gap between the immigrant generation and their American-born offspring (Ansari and Yang 2015: Season 1, Episode 2). Ansari portrays a dinner scene with his parents, who appear in the episode as themselves. In addressing the cultural gap between the immigrant generation and the American-born, his father says: "You realize fun is a new thing, right? Fun is a luxury only your generation has." Ansari's experiences in developing this episode caused him to approach his family with new insight and he admits to feeling regret for the way he had previously disengaged from his family. He feels he is now more sensitive to his parents and he is a "better" son.

Portrayals of the Asian population as not really "American," even when born here, persist. Asians are automatically viewed as "foreign," no matter what their origins, and relegated to a "subcategory." Since cultural validity frequently is based upon visual cues, Sri Lankan performance artist Piepzna-Samarasinha writes of the "value" of keeping a "White" passport and name (2015), and of the complicated path she took to gaining a brown identity in the hegemonic White culture:

> Learning to be brown is a process some of us go through. Most of us don't talk about it. We shut the fuck up, study up, and pass into brownness as fast as we can. We don't want to admit our dorky inauthentic, mixed-race roots. We are fragile. We are making up for lost time. People already laugh at us mixed-race kids because we look weird; they're going to laugh harder if we admit what we don't know, what we were never taught by parents who were trying to survive by assimilating into whiteness, or at least not being noticed, as fast as possible. We have to get it back, get it all back.
>
> (Piepzna-Samarasinha 2015)

Indigenous Peoples

There are hundreds of Indigenous cultures residing within the US borders and how to address them remains contentious. Many Indigenous people prefer referencing their specific culture but if all Indigenous peoples are to be included, the naming preference varies. One perspective associates American Indian with European designations and consequently, their preference is "Indigenous" or "Native" (Blackhorse 2015), or "First Nations," which is the term used in Canada. The term *tribe* is viewed negatively due to its association with the European view of Indigenous cultures as "primitive," and its members as "savages" (The Trouble with Tribe 2001). With very few exceptions, the television and film industries exclude any representations of this group. When the Indigenous groups are depicted, it is generally with severe stereotyping in limited roles (Nittle 2017). In classic Anglo-American novels, Native American existence is virtually wiped out and, in the rare instances when it does occur, stereotypically portrayed. In the novel *East of Eden*, for example, Steinbeck (1952) provides a history of California's Salinas Valley, dispensing with "Native" culture in a few sentences, describing them as "barbaric" and without culture. In the past 50 years, dozens of Indigenous authors have given authentic voice to their cultural experiences (OEDB n.d.; Lee 2014). The critically acclaimed movie *Smoke Signals* (Eyre 1998) was the first feature film written, directed, acted, and co-produced by Native Americans. The movie was written by Sherman Alexie, based on a short story that appeared in his first published collection in 1993 (Alexie 2005).

It would be misleading to provide a general summary of the history of the Indigenous experience since the cultures are so diverse. The common element unifying the Indigenous population is in the **genocidal** practices of European Americans and the US government. From exposure to infectious diseases; forced removal from their lands; forced entry into White culture; broken treaties; and stolen properties, the Indigenous peoples' histories are unique when compared to other nondominant groups.

Government efforts to force Indigenous assimilation extend over centuries. Young people were forced into BIA schools, initially in 1887, and many other coercive measures were perpetrated against the groups. Youths were subjected to forced haircuts; English-only communication; forced adoption of western clothing; separation from families on reservations; and forced adoptions outside of the community. In 1978 *The Indian Child Welfare Act* provided for new regulations concerning the foster care or adoption of children with Indigenous membership or suspected Indigenous bloodlines. Under the mandate, these children were to be placed in an environment which fostered continued connection to the Indigenous community (Native American/American Indian Community n.d.).

The decimation of the Indigenous cultures has been so extreme it is difficult to accurately count the population. Ward Churchill, a historian of ethnic studies, establishes the population at 12 million in 1500, reduced to about 237,000 by 1900. The largest contributing factor to the near extinction of the Indigenous peoples was the spread of infectious diseases and unhealthy living conditions, exacerbated by multiple forced relocations (Lewy 2004). Today the Indigenous population is estimated at 5.4 million, including Native Americans, Alaskan Natives, and people of mixed race (US Census Bureau 2015). Every Indigenous group sets its own laws regarding who can qualify as a registered member, though the federal government regulates which cultures are legally recognized and therefore eligible for funded

Figure 8.15 Taos Pueblo Village, a UNESCO World Heritage Site and a National Historic Landmark is the longest, continuously inhabited community in North America. The Pueblo invites visitors to ceremonies, many of which combine Catholic and Native rituals but the Pueblo is closed to the public for about ten weeks a year during which time other festivities are celebrated
Source: Anna Morgan / Shutterstock.com

programs. Currently, there are 566 "official" groups (BIA n.d.). To be recognized as a culture, the group must prove *continuous existence* as a culture, and that has been difficult for dispersed groups. Hundreds of groups are still in the process of gaining official recognition (GAO 2002).

Multiple, long-term pending lawsuits protecting Indigenous property and financial rights were finally settled by the Obama administration. In November of 2012 a dispute over mismanagement of tribal lands, and accounts managed by the Department of the Interior, was settled for a total of 3.4 billion dollars. The case was first filed in 1996 (CNN Wire Staff 2012). In 2014, there was a 554 million dollar settlement with the Navajo nations. In 2015, there was a settlement of almost one billion dollars, in a case first filed against the Department of Justice in 1990 by the Oglala Sioux, Zuni Pueblo, and the Ramah chapter of the Navajo nation, under the *Indian Self Determination and Education Assistance Act of 1975* (Lewis 2015). Debates regarding restitution to the Indigenous populations are ongoing and likely will continue to be contested (Boxer 2009). Many Indigenous languages, due in part to forced assimilations, are at risk of extinction. Many communities have established some means of recording languages which previously had no written form (Braun 2015). Language preservation is vital to cultural sustenance.

Latinos

The linguistic preferences for labeling "Latinos" are also contentious. Many identify with two cultures, regardless of immigration status. The term *Hispanic* was first utilized in the 1970s, when the government became interested in counting people whose origins were in Mexico, Cuba and Central or South America. In the 2000 US Census, the term *Latino* was substituted and was inclusive of people from Central and South America who identified as *mestizo or mulatto*, referring to mixed race. It has been suggested that *Hispanic* highlights the importance of language while *Latino* focuses on geography. Many persons prefer referencing the country of origin rather than a generic designation (Rodriguez 2014).

The Latino population now comprises the largest minority ethnic group. Births to US nonWhites outnumber White births (Passel et al. 2012). In California, *Hispanic* births reached 15 million compared to 14.9 million non-Hispanic births (Reese and Magagnini 2015). The trend is expected to spread beyond California (Bartlett 2001). Latino demographic trends are not uniform among subgroups. Political affiliations vary with regard to country of origin, immigration status, social class, and regional residency.

Cultural assimilation of the Latino population seems to be following patterns of earlier immigrant groups in that the second generation is rapidly losing its original language. The education level of the group is increasing steadily, showing greater rates of increase than among Asians or Europeans (Gjelten 2015). The average age of the Latino population is lower than the average age of the general population; half of the Latino electorate in 2016 were millennials (Krogstad et al. 2016). Though the Latino electorate is diverse the group generally shows some favor towards the Democrats (Metla 2015).

The media continues to under-represent Latinos. While Latinos represent 17.4 percent of the population they comprise only 5.8 percent of speaking roles in film and television. Latinos comprise fewer than 2 percent of characters in top television and movie titles (Main 2014). This is reflective of the lack of diversity among

Number of Latino Eligible Voters Is Increasing Faster Than the Number of Latino Voters in Presidential Election Years

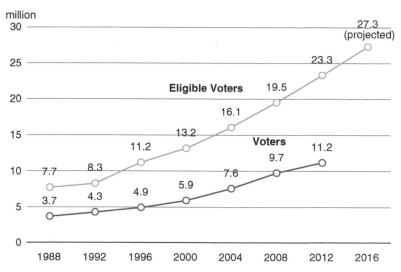

Figure 8.16 Data regarding voting demographics of the Latino population Source: "Key facts about the Latino vote in 2016," Pew Research Center, Washington DC (October 14, 2016), http://www.pewresearch.org/fact-tank/2016/10/14/key-facts-about-the-latino-vote-in-2016/

Note: Latinos are of any race. Eligible voters are US citizens ages 18 and older. Voters are persons who say they voted.

Source: Pew Research Center tabulations of the Current Population Survey, November Supplements for 1988–2012.

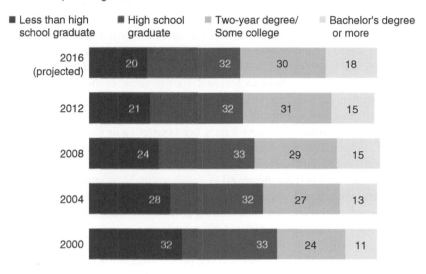

Educational Attainment of Eligible Hispanic Voters

% of Hispanic eligible voters

■ Less than high   ■ High school   ■ Two-year degree/   ■ Bachelor's degree
school graduate   graduate   Some college   or more

Year	Less than high school graduate	High school graduate	Two-year degree/Some college	Bachelor's degree or more
2016 (projected)	20	32	30	18
2012	21	32	31	15
2008	24	33	29	15
2004	28	32	27	13
2000	32	33	24	11

Figure 8.17 Hispanic voters' education attainment
Source: "Millennials Make Up Almost Half of Latino Eligible Voters in 2016," Pew Research Center, Washington, DC (January 19, 2016), http://www.pewhispanic.org/2016/01/19/millennials-make-up-almost-half-of-latino-eligible-voters-in-2016/

Note: High school graduate includes persons who have attained a high school diploma or its equivalent, such as a General Education Development (GED) certificate. Hispanics are of any race. Eligible voters are US citizens ages 18 and older. Figures may not add to 100% due to rounding.

Source: Pew Research Center tabulations of the Current Population Survey, November Supplements for 2000–2012.

entertainment writers. When characters are portrayed as Latino or Hispanic, the women are generally oversexualized while the men are shown as dominant or macho (Latimer 2016; Main 2014). A recent article highlighting the absence of diversity in the Academy Awards pointed out that Latinos are not merely misrepresented; they are virtually absent in movies. Nevertheless, this group wields some financial power since, while Latinos are 17 percent of the population, they are 25 percent of movie ticket purchases (Federa 2016). Calls for Hollywood boycotts can utilize this disparity to put demands on the industry for roles with multi-dimensional content.

Latino youths are showing increasing rates of psychological difficulties, whether as a feature of incidence or reporting is not clear. Immigrant policies and discrimination may be contributing factors to the poor mental health status of Latino youths. The rate of increase for Latino youths' mental health hospitalizations has risen 86 percent, from 2007–2014, though Latinos are less likely to seek help than White or African American families (Wiener 2016). The cause of these increased hospitalizations is unclear but explanations include a lack of appropriate help in outpatient or community centers; cuts in education, mental health services and group placements; recessionary stress; increased willingness to seek help; and the development of serious conditions due to prolonged periods lacking in available help (Wiener 2016).

African Americans

The legacy of slavery is a history that never has been sufficiently addressed by the US government or the American culture. By almost any measure, American capitalism developed, literally and metaphorically, off the backs of slaves (Baptist 2014). Slaves comprised most of an individual's wealth at the start of the Civil War. A young male might be purchased for up to 2000 dollars, while land cost less than one dollar an acre and unskilled laborers made less than a dollar a day. In 1860 there were six million slaves, representing about six billion dollars in value, or the equivalent of 300 billion dollars in today's dollars. Slaves grew their own food, made their own clothes and produced more slaves, generally paying for themselves within eight years (Baptist 2014). Demands for reparations have largely been contested or ignored. Many White people don't believe there is justification for making restitution, arguing that today's White population did not engage in slave practices. The countering argument asserts that the economy thrives from the period of enslavement. How much would 175 years of lawful slavery, and 100 additional years of legislative and legal exploitation, be worth? Residential segregation and lending practices abusing the African American population persist. As author Ta-Nehisi Coates explains:

> Having been enslaved for 250 years, black people were not left to their own devices. They were terrorized. In the Deep South, a second slavery ruled. In the North, legislatures, mayors, civic associations, banks, and citizens all colluded to pin black people into ghettos, where they were overcrowded, overcharged, and undereducated. Businesses discriminated against them, awarding them the worst jobs and the worst wages. Police brutalized them in the streets. And the notion that black lives, black bodies, and black wealth were rightful targets remained deeply rooted in the broader society. Now we have half-stepped away from our long centuries of despoilment, promising, "Never again." But still we are haunted. It is as though we have run up a credit-card bill and, having pledged to charge no more, remain befuddled that the balance does not disappear. The effects of that balance, interest accruing daily, are all around us.
>
> (Coates 2014)

Coates considers the incalculable economic contributions of slavery, and exploitation, in every realm from labor; farming; property seizures; housing and lending discrimination; denial of public education; and disenfranchisement. He supports the idea of reparation by citing the Biblical mandate to set Hebrew slaves free in their seventh year of slavery and to send them away with substantial compensation. He also refers to John Locke, the seventeenth-century English philosopher associated with the concept of the social contract. Locke maintained that a person who is injured by another, even if not defined by a criminal code, should have the right to seek reparations for the damages (Coates 2014).

Most proposals for reparations take the form of special funding for programs that would benefit the group, rather than being awarded to individuals. These would include increased school funding; mortgage subsidies; special programs

Figure 8.18 Slave quarters in Fort George Island Cultural State Park, Florida
Source: Photography by Rosalind Gottfried

for healthcare and community development, jobs, housing and businesses; and additional safety net provisions for lower income, high-density African American areas. A recent UN Working Group of Experts on People of African American Descent took this route with recommendations for reparations through special programs in education, socio-economic rights, and environmental rights. Additionally, the committee drew parallels between contemporary police killings and the trauma resulting from lynchings. The UN report also notes that the US House of Representatives, in 2008, and the US Senate, in 2009, passed bills apologizing for slavery but never signed them into law because no language was ever agreed upon. The legislators wanted to apologize for slavery in a way which would preclude the government from being held liable for reparations. They recommend the establishment of a national database to track reports of excessive force and an end to racial profiling (Pasha 2016). For wealthier African Americans, compensation proposals have been in the form of tax abatements (Quora 2014).

Discrimination in the daily life of African Americans persists. The experiences of African Americans are diverse but there is an aspect which is universal. Remarks made by President Barack Obama, who was sometimes accused of not being "Black" enough, highlight the ubiquitous nature of prejudice:

> There are very few African American men in this country who haven't had the experience of being followed when they were shopping in a department store. That includes me. There are very few African American men who haven't had the experience of walking across the street and hearing the locks click on the doors of cars. That happens to me—at least before I was a senator. There are very few African Americans who haven't had the experience of getting on an elevator and a woman clutching her purse nervously and holding her breath until she had a chance to get off. That happens often.
>
> (Obama 2013)

Discrimination of African Americans, in employment and housing, remains prevalent. In 2013, for example, the government settled a case with African American farmers who claimed that federal agricultural officials gave loans to White farmers and let the African Americans lose their farms (Brown 2013). Disparities in lending practices are common; an internet search will turn up an extensive number of lawsuits and policies exhibiting discriminatory practices against African Americans and Latinos (Rothstein 2012; Swarns 2015; Vasel 2015; Love 2016; Lee 2015; Chen

Figure 8.19 President
Barack Obama
Source: Evan El-Amin /
Shutterstock.com

2012). Redlining, the practice of delineating some neighborhoods as unstable, and therefore ineligible for insured mortgages, remains a widespread practice with origins in the Federal Housing Authority of 1934 (Coates 2014).

African Americans experience harassment in law enforcement and the criminal justice systems. They are disproportionately stopped for *driving while Black* and arrested, convicted, and incarcerated at far greater rates than Whites (see Chapter 6). Their talents in the arts and culture have been appropriated by the White culture, without purchase or credit (Berlatsky 2014; Whites, Blacks, and the Blues n.d.). The film industry's portrayal of African Americans is stereotypic and caricatured. Thorp (2016) reviewed every film featuring an African American actor nominated for a best actor/actress academy award and found that none featured "normal" people leading "regular" lives. There were 28 films in all. Most were written and directed by White men. Almost all of the ten women characters were poor, uneducated, homeless, or at risk of becoming so, and suffered absent or violent husbands, fathers, or boyfriends. Of the 20 male portrayals, 11 nominations went to four actors. Thirteen of the 20 performances featured characters arrested or incarcerated; ten were featured with a White "buddy or counterpart"; seven had no Black women characters; and seven abused or mistreated women. African American writers have pointed out that films with African American casts are held to different measures to qualify as successful. Real-life depictions of African American daily life are considered unprofitable by the industry (Clutch 2014; Gay 2014).

Muslims

The 2016 presidential election illuminated the bigotry and discrimination against Muslims, whether citizens or immigrants. The Muslim population is roughly

1 percent of the US and it is estimated to grow to about 2 percent by 2050 (Mohamed 2016). Every major news outlet has reported on the increasing rate of fear and intimidation women feel from wearing the *hijab* in public (The California Report 2016). In 2016 Obama made a public visit to a mosque to bring national attention to the issue of protecting religious freedom in the US (Ingraham 2016). The intolerance towards Muslims has led to demands for restrictive immigration policies and calls for total exclusion. In fact, the Muslim population behaves much like the rest of the population, has a long tenure in the US, and has been plagued by conversion pressures. Data reveal that Muslims are among the most highly educated groups; reside across the country, not just in large cities; have levels of religious practice similar to Christians; and have aided law enforcement in identifying terrorists and potential terrorists. Virtually all the Muslims surveyed believed that women should be able to work outside the home and Muslim women are more likely than Muslim men to have achieved college and graduate degrees (Yan 2015).

To counter these views and common misconceptions regarding the Islamic faith, Mohamed Ahmed, a Minneapolis gas station manager, has published a comic strip about the "true" and nonviolent beliefs of Islam, emphasizing aspects of the faith common among Americans. He has been doing this strip for years and takes his message to schools and churches where he can reach out to youth with accurate information and countervailing ideals (Weekend Edition Sunday 2016).

What Trends Are Appearing in the "Post-recession" Period?

All sectors of the country were hit hard by the recent recession, but Latino and African American households suffered the severest setbacks in wealth, employment, and housing. Between 2005–2009 White households lost about 16 percent of their wealth while Blacks lost 52 percent and Latinos 66 percent. In part, this was due to the portion of wealth constituted by home ownership. Whites' wealth generally extends beyond home ownership. Since 2013, the net worth of White households has increased while it continues to decrease for nonWhite households (Dickerson 2014). One third of African Americans have zero, or negative, wealth, making any unforeseen expense devastating (Coates 2014).

The unemployment rates for Whites recovered more quickly than for other groups and are now about equal to pre-recession rates. Although Black and Latino unemployment was never as low as among the White population, their recovery has been much slower, with no improvement until 2015. Generally, African Americans are twice as likely to be unemployed as Whites, while the Latino rate is one and half times the White rate. Racial disparities in employment are consistent, even with improved rates of nondominant college graduation (White 2015).

For young men in large cities, the unemployment rate is as high as 30 percent for African Americans, 20 percent for Latinos, and 10 percent for Whites. It has been suggested that the Recovery Act of 2009, which subsidized temporary employment, should have been extended by Congress. The program helped to reduce labor costs, kept employers in business and, in 37 percent of the cases, led to permanent employment (The Editorial Board 2016).

Figure 8.20 Racial wealth gaps
Source: "Wealth inequality has widened along racial, ethnic lines since end of Great Recession," Pew Research Center, Washington DC (December 12, 2014), http://www.pewresearch.org/fact-tank/2014/12/12/racial-wealth-gaps-great-recession/

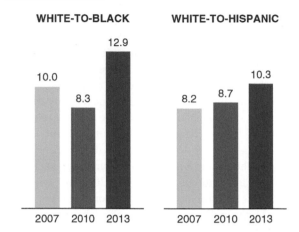

Wealth Inequality by Race and Ethnicity Has Grown Since 2007

Median wealth ratios

Note: Blacks and Whites include only non-Hispanics. Hispanics are of any race.

Source: Pew Research Center tabulations of Survey of Consumer Finances public-use data

Real Median Household Income, by Race and Ethnicity, 2000–2014

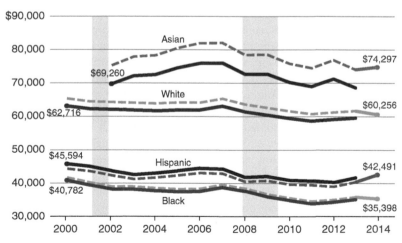

Note: CPS ASEC changed its methodology for data years 2013 and 2014, hence the break in the series in 2013. Solid lines are actual CPS ASEC data; dashed lines denote historical values imputed by applying the new methodology to past income trends. White refers to non-Hispanic Whites, Black refers to Blacks alone, Asian refers to Asians alone, and Hispanic refers to Hispanics of any race. Comparable data are not available prior to 2002 for Asians. Shaded areas denote recessions.

Source: EPI analysis of Current Population Survey Annual Social and Economic Supplement Historical Poverty Tables (Table H-5 and H-9)

Figure 8.21 Household income by race
Source: Economic Policy Institute

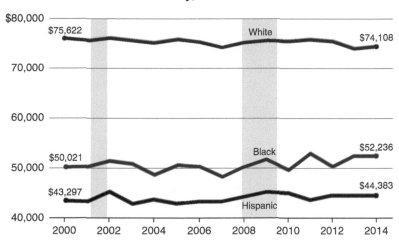

Real Earnings of Full-time, Full-year Male Workers, by Race and Ethnicity, 2000–2014

Figure 8.22 Real earnings by race
Source: Economic Policy Institute

Note: Earnings are wage and salary income. White refers to non-Hispanic Whites, Black refers to Blacks alone, and Hispanic refers to Hispanics of any race. Asians are excluded from this figure due to the volatility of the series. Shaded areas denote recessions.

Source: EPI analysis of Annual Social and Economic Supplement Historical Income Tables (Table PINC-07)

Another area of disadvantage for nondominant groups concerns the decimation of the *Voting Rights Act of 1965*. In that legislation, it was decreed that nine states, and multiple municipalities in other areas with histories of impediments to voting, would be required to obtain federal approval before changing voting laws. The Supreme Court decision (2013) revised the *Voting Rights Act* to flip the burden. With the Act, the delineated jurisdictions gained the right to change their practices while the federal government would have to show that specific groups were affected. The possibility of racial gerrymandering and picture identification requirements are potential consequences (Liptak 2013; Fausset 2016). Challenges to the revised Act persist. In July 2016, the typically conservative US Fifth Circuit Court of Appeals mandated that Texas needed to make changes to its voter photo ID laws before the November election to limit their "discriminatory effect" (Dart 2016).

Key Terms

Race   Ethnicity   White Anglo-Saxon Protestant (WASP)   White Ethnics   The "Other"   Racism
White Privilege   Prejudice   Individual/Institutional Discrimination   Stereotype   Hegemony
Internalized Racism   Affirmative Action   Reverse Discrimination   Hate Crimes
Cultural Assimilation   Ideology   Melting pot   Anglo Conformity   Cultural Pluralism
Model Minority   Voting Rights Act 1965

Concept Review

What Are Race and Ethnicity?

Essentially, these are both arbitrary designations based on cultural interests which have changed over time. **Races** have been defined by variable labels ever since the US Census Bureau began. There is nothing biologically distinctive in the categorizations. Ethnicity refers to ancestry, culture, nationality, language, and/or religion. There is sometimes little agreement on what constitutes a specific ethnicity. The language of **race** and **ethnicity** is fluid and the words utilized to identify them are contentious.

What Is Racism and Privilege?

Racism is a system which is determined by *race power + prejudice*, with one group defined as superior to others, accruing advantages over other groups. These privileges extend to economic resources, power, and status. The dominant group maintains the ability to define the elements of culture and impose them upon others in a process referred to as **hegemony**. In the US, racism is contingent upon the elevation of the White race and all things associated with it. Nondominant groups, and their members, frequently are measured against an unarticulated norm resulting in their being viewed as inherently deficient.

What Is the Immigrant History of the US?

The nation's immigrant history is one of struggle in that all groups faced **prejudice** and **discrimination**, though some groups had an easier transition to assimilation. **Cultural assimilation** refers to how the nondominant groups accommodate the dominant culture. Today, some believe there is a move towards **cultural pluralism**, where groups can maintain elements of their home culture, as long as they do not conflict with the dominant culture. The experience of immigration is largely universal, whatever group is involved, but the countries of origin shift with history. The transition to American culture is generally one which is characterized by friction between the first generation and the subsequent ones who were born in the US or arrived as minors. In the twentieth century, the majority of immigrants were White European ethnics while today the groups are more likely to be Asian, Latino, and African.

What Is the Context for the Nondominant Group Histories?

It is almost impossible to speak of the situation of any one racial or ethnic group since each group is comprised of members with disparate conditions of arrival and history. All of these groups have been subjected to economic discrimination and cultural oppression. The desirability of assimilation varies between, and within, immigrant groups. If the society is becoming more pluralistic, the nature of assimilation will likely be less pronounced.

How Are the Nondominant Groups Today?

Post-recession America has not seen parity between the dominant and the non-dominant groups in terms of foreclosures, income, wealth, home ownership status, or employment. The "recovery" has been one much more characteristic of the White group, which has regained much of what it lost in the recession. Other groups have not made significant progress, particularly in measures of wealth and employment.

Review Questions

1. Explain the concept of **White privilege** and provide at least two examples to illustrate the definition.
2. How would you define **racism**? Is racism the same for different races? Are nonWhite people racist? What is your race?
3. Explain **internalized racism** and provide at least two examples stating how they illustrate the definition. Use an example from the chapter and one from your own experiences.
4. What is **ethnicity**? What is your ethnicity? How did you determine it? Is it a significant element of your identity?
5. Is passing as a member of a nondominant group equivalent to passing as a member of the dominant group?
6. What is **institutional discrimination**? Provide two examples.
7. What do you think about **reparations** for the African American population?
8. What is **Affirmative Action**? What is the concept and how have recent legal challenges been settled?
9. How has the US treated immigrants in the past 100 years?
10. What is **cultural assimilation** and do you think it is desirable?
11. How are minorities treated in television today? Provide two examples from class material.

References

ACLU. (n.d.) *Loving*. Retrieved from https://www.aclu.org/feature/loving

ADC. American-Arab Anti-Discrimination Committee. (November 29, 2009) *Facts about Arabs and the Arab World*. Retrieved from http://www.adc.org/2009/11/facts-about-arabs-and-the-arab-world/

Affirmative Action. (n.d.) *The Leadership Conference on Civil and Human Rights*. Retrieved from http://www.civilrights.org/resources/civilrights101/affirmaction.html?referrer=https://www.google.com/

Alexie, S. (2005) *The Lone Ranger and Tonto Fistfight in Heaven*. NY: Grove Press.

Allen, W. (2009) *Whatever Works*. Sony Pictures Classics.

America's Complicated Past Stirs Battle Over Monuments, Memorials. (February 22, 2016) *WNYC*. Retrieved from http://www.wnyc.org/story/who-should-memorials-represent/

Ansari, A., Yang, A. (2015, 2017) *Master of None*. 3 Arts Entertainment.

APS. (n.d.) Engaging in a Brief Cultural Activity Can Reduce Implicit Prejudice. *Association for Psychological Science*. Retrieved from http://www.psychologicalscience.org/news/releases/engaging-in-a-brief-cultural-activity-can-reduce-implicit-prejudice.html#.WC9ls-YrKUk

Asian Americans. (2012) *Pew Research Center*. Retrieved from http://www.pewsocialtrends.org/asianamericans-graphics/

Asian Americans Then and Now. (n.d.) *Asia Society*. Retrieved from http://asiasociety. org/education/asian-americans-then-and-now

Baptist, E.E. (November 19, 2014) Without Slavery, Would the U.S. Be the Leading Economic Power? *Here & Now*. Retrieved from http://hereandnow.wbur. org/2014/11/19/slavery-economy-baptist

Bartlett, L. (December 19, 2001) Majority of Babies Born in California are Latino, UCLA Study Finds; Latino Births Reviewed County-by-County for the First Time. *UCLA Newsroom*. Retrieved from http://newsroom.ucla.edu/releases/Majority-of-Babies-Born-in-California-2893

Berlatsky, N. (May 18, 2014) Elvis Wasn't the First to Steal Black Music: 10 White Artists Who "Borrowed" from R&B Before the King. *Salon*. Retrieved from http://www.salon.com/2014/05/17/elvis_wasnt_the_first/

BIA. (n.d.) Bureau of Indian Affairs. Retrieved from https://www.bia.gov/

Blackhorse, A. (May 22, 2015) Blackhorse: Do You Prefer 'Native American' or 'American Indian'? 6 Prominent Voices Respond. Indian Country Media Network. Retrieved from http://indiancountrytodaymedianetwork.com/2015/05/21/blackhorse-do-you-prefer-native-american-or-american-indian-6-prominent-voices-respond

Blendoor App Breaks Down Computer Bias in Hiring. (March 14, 2016) *NPR*. Retrieved from http://www.npr.org/2016/03/14/470427617/blendoor-app-breaks-down-computer-bias-in-hiring

Boxer, A. (September, 2009) Native Americans and the Federal Government. *History Today*. Retrieved from http://www.historytoday.com/andrew-boxer/native-americans-and-federal-government

Bragg, R. (1997) *All Over but the Shoutin.'* NY: Random House, Inc.

Braun, M.D. (November 15, 2015) Preserving Native America's Vanishing Languages. *National Geographic*. Retrieved from http://voices.nationalgeographic. com/2009/11/15/0005_native_american_vanishing_languages/

Brodkin, K. (1998) *How Jews Became White Folks and What That Says About Race in America*. Piscataway, NJ: Rutgers University Press.

Brown, C.M. (October 2, 2013) Black Farmers to Receive Payouts in $1.2 Billion from Federal Lawsuit. *Black Enterprise*. Retrieved from http://www. blackenterprise.com/news/black-farmers-to-receive-payouts-in-1-2-billion-from-federal-lawsuit-settlement/

Browning, J.R. (n.d.) *Anti-miscegenation Laws in the U.S.* Retrieved from http:// scholarship.law.duke.edu/cgi/viewcontent.cgi?article=1544&context=dlj

Bump, P. (January 5, 2015) The New Congress is 80% White, 80% Male and 92% Christian. *The Washington Post*. Retrieved from https://www.washingtonpost.com/news/the-fix/wp/2015/01/05/the-new-congress-is-80-percent-white-80-percent-male-and-92-percent-christian/?utm_term=.b9b2909e7a64

Calmes, J. (April 20, 2016) Harriet Tubman Ousts Andrew Jackson in Change for a $20. *The New York Times*. Retrieved from http://www.nytimes.com/2016/04/21/us/women-currency-treasury-harriet-tubman.html?_r=0

Cganemccalla. (2011) Top 10 Monuments to Black Americans. *News One*. Retrieved from http://newsone.com/1458145/top-10-monuments-to-black-americans/

Chen, S. (February 26, 2012) Lending Discrimination: Black Borrowers Face Higher Hurdles, Study Shows. *The Huffington Post*. Retrieved from http://www. huffingtonpost.com/2012/02/24/lending-discrimination-black-borrowers-face-higher-hurdles-in-lending-study_n_1300509.html

Cho, M. (2001) *I'm the One that I Want*. NY: Ballantine Books.

Clutch. (June, 2014) Taye Diggs Says Studios Set Double Standard for Black Films. *Clutch*. Retrieved from http://www.clutchmagonline.com/2014/06/taye-diggs-says-studios-set-double-standard-black-films/

CNN Wire Staff. (November 27, 2012) U.S. Finalizes $3.4 Billion Settlement with American Indians. *CNN*. Retrieved from http://www.cnn.com/2012/11/26/politics/american-indian-settlment/

Coates, T. (June, 2014) The Case for Reparations. *The Atlantic*. Retrieved from https://www.theatlantic.com/magazine/archive/2014/06/the-case-for-reparations/361631/

Coates, T. (2015) *Between the World and Me*. NY: Spiegel and Grau.

Cohen, N.P. (June 25, 2012) *Do Asians in the U.S. Have High Incomes? Family Inequality*. Retrieved from https://familyinequality.wordpress.com/2012/06/25/do-asians-in-the-u-s-have-high-incomes/

Cooper, R. (1984) A Note on the Biologic Concept of Race and its Application in Epidemiologic Research. *American Heart Journal*, 108(3): 715–723. Retrieved from https://doi.org/10.1016/0002-8703(84)90662-8

Crazy Horse Memorial. (n.d.) *Google*. Retrieved from http://www.southdakota.com/crazy-horse-memorial/

Critical Issues Facing Asian Americans and Pacific Islanders. (n.d.) *The White House*. Retrieved from https://obamawhitehouse.archives.gov/administration/eop/aapi/data/critical-issues

Dart, T. (July 20, 2016) Texas Voter ID Law is 'Discriminatory' and Must Change, Court Rules. *The Guardian*. Retrieved from https://www.theguardian.com/us-news/2016/jul/20/texas-voter-id-law-voting-rights-act-federal-court-decision

De Moraes, L. (April 8, 2015) 'Fresh off the Boat' Creator Eddie Huang Continues to Trash his ABC Comedy. *Deadline*. Retrieved from http://deadline.com/2015/04/eddie-huang-fresh-off-the-boat-tweets-1201406604/

Deggans, E. (February 22, 2016) Researchers Examine Hollywood's Lack of Diversity. *NPR*. Retrieved from http://www.npr.org/2016/02/22/467621632/researchers-examine-hollywoods-lack-of-diversity

Dickerson, M. (November 18, 2014) The Economic Recovery in Black, White, and Brown. *The Huffington Post*. Retrieved from http://www.huffingtonpost.com/mechele-dickerson/the-economic-recovery-in-_b_5837664.html

DOJ. U.S. Department of Justice (2009) *The Matthew Shephard and James Byrd, Jr., Hate Crimes Prevention Act of 2009*.

Dowd-Higgins, C. (July 5, 2012) Don't Let Impostor Syndrome Sabotage your Career. *The Blog*. Retrieved from http://www.huffingtonpost.com/caroline-dowdhiggins/impostor-syndrome_b_1651762.html

Drabold, W. (July 25, 2016) Read Elizabeth Warren's Anti-Trump Speech at the Democratic Convention. *Time*. Retrieved from http://time.com/4421731/democratic-convention-elizabeth-warren-transcript-speech/

Ellen, G.I., Dastrup, S. (October, 2012) *Housing and the Great Recession*. [PDF File]. Retrieved from http://furmancenter.org/files/publications/HousingandtheGreatRecession.pdf

Epps, G. (December 10, 2015) Is Affirmative Action Finished? *The Atlantic*. Retrieved from http://www.theatlantic.com/politics/archive/2015/12/when-can-race-be-a-college-admissions-factor/419808/

Eyre, C. (dir.) (1998) *Smoke Signals*. Shadow Catcher Entertainment, Welb Film Pursuits Ltd.

Faderman, L. (1998) *I Begin My Life All Over*. Boston, MA: Beacon Press Books.

FAQs. (n.d.) *Indian Affairs*. Retrieved from http://www.bia.gov/FAQs/

Fausset, R. (March 10, 2016) North Carolina Exemplifies National Battles over Voting Laws. *The New York Times*. Retrieved from http://www.nytimes.com/2016/03/11/us/north-carolina-voting-rights-redistictricting-battles.html?&hp&action=click&pgtype=Homepage&clickSource=story-heading&module=a-lede-package-region&region=top-news&WT.nav=top-news&_r=0

Federa, A. (January 25, 2016) Why #OscarsSoWhite Isn't Very Latino. *PRI*. Retrieved from https://www.pri.org/stories/2016-01-25/why-oscarssowhite-isnt-very-latino

Fernandez, E.M., Adalian, J. (September 22, 2015) Eddie Huang Isn't Narrating 'Fresh off the Boat' Anymore. *Business Insider*. Retrieved from http://www.businessinsider.com/abc-fresh-off-the-boat-eddie-huang-narrator-2015-9

Francis, D.P. (August 15, 2017) Employers' Replies to Racial Names. *The National Bureau of Economic Research*. Retrieved from http://www.nber.org/digest/sep03/w9873.html

GAO. U.S. Government Accountability Office. (September 17, 2002) *Indian Issues: Basis for BIA's Tribal Recognition Decisions Is Not Always Clear*. Retrieved from http://www.gao.gov/products/GAO-02-936T

Garcia-Navarro, L. (October 11, 2015) America's Immigration Rhetoric out of Touch with the Numbers. *Weekend Edition Sunday*. Retrieved from http://www.npr.org/2015/10/11/447688060/america-s-immigration-rhetoric-out-of-touch-with-the-numbers

Garcia-Navarro, L. (March 5, 2016) Saldana as Simone Resurfaces a Debate Beyond Black and White. *Weekend Edition Sunday*. Retrieved from www.npr.org/2016/03/05/469298260/saldana-as-simone-resurfaces-a-debate-beyond-black-and-white).

Gay, Roxanne. (2014) *Bad Feminist: Essays*. NY: HarperCollins Publishers.

Gerdeman, D. (May 17, 2017) Minorities Who Whiten Resumes Get More Job Interviews. *Forbes.com*. Retrieved from https://www.forbes.com/sites/hbsworkingknowledge/2017/05/17/minorities-who-whiten-resumes-get-more-job-interviews/#44719a5b7b74

Gjelten, T. (October 3, 2015) Should Immigration Require Assimilation? *The Atlantic*. Retrieved from https://www.theatlantic.com/politics/archive/2015/10/should-immigration-require-assimilation/406759/

Good Hair. (October 20, 2013) [Video File]. Retrieved from https://www.youtube.com/watch?v=Hz4lfFS_7fk

Grant, A., Sandberg, S. (December 6, 2014) Adam Grant and Sheryl Sandberg on Discrimination at Work. *The New York Times*. Retrieved from http://www.

nytimes.com/2014/12/07/opinion/sunday/adam-grant-and-sheryl-sandberg-on-discrimination-at-work.html

Guglielmo, J., Salerno, S. (2003) *Are Italians White?. How Race Is Made in America.* London UK: Psychology Press.

Ignatiev, N. (1995; 2009) *How the Irish Became White.* NY: Routledge.

Ingraham, C. (February 3, 2016) The Importance of Obama's Mosque Visit in an Era of Hate Crimes Against Muslims. *The Washington Post.* Retrieved from https://www.washingtonpost.com/news/wonk/wp/2016/02/03/the-importance-of-obamas-mosque-visit-in-an-era-of-hate-crimes-against-muslims/

Jacobs, G., (creator.) (1994–1995) *All American Girl.* Produced by Sandollar Television, Heartfelt Productions, and Touchstone Television.

Japanese American Memorial to Patriotism During World War II. (n.d.) *Wikipedia.* Retrieved from https://en.wikipedia.org/wiki/Memorial_to_Japanese-American_Patriotism_in_World_War_II

Kochhar, R., Fry, R. (December 12, 2014) Wealth Inequality Has Widened Along Racial, Ethnic Lines Since End of Great Recession. *Pew Research Center.* Retrieved from http://www.pewresearch.org/fact-tank/2014/12/12/racial-wealth-gaps-great-recession/

Krogstad, M.J., Lopez, H.M., López, G., Passel, S.J., Patten, E. (January 19, 2016) Millennials Make up Almost Half of Latino Eligible Voters in 2016. *Pew Research Center.* Retrieved from http://www.pewhispanic.org/2016/01/19/millennials-make-up-almost-half-of-latino-eligible-voters-in-2016/

Krugman, P., Persson, T., Svenson, L.E.O. (September, 1982) Inflation, Monetary Velocity, and Welfare. *National Bureau of Economic Research.* Retrieved from http://www.nber.org/papers/w987

Latimer, B. (February 22, 2016) Latinos in Hollywood: Few Roles, Frequent Stereotypes, New Study Finds. *NBC News.* Retrieved from http://www.nbcnews.com/news/latino/latinos-hollywood-few-roles-frequent-stereotypes-new-study-finds-n523511

Lee, H.T. (January 15, 2014) Fine Print: 7 American Indian Women Novelists You Have to Read. *Indian Country Media Network.* Retrieved from https://indiancountrymedianetwork.com/culture/arts-entertainment/fine-print-7-american-indian-women-novelists-you-have-to-read/

Lee, J. (July 28, 2015) Getting a Home Loan Is Expensive—Especially for Black Women. *Mother Jones.* Retrieved from http://www.motherjones.com/mojo/2015/07/race-gender-interest-rates-mortgages

Lee, S. (1988) *School Daze.* Columbia Pictures Corporation.

Lewis, R. (September 18, 2015) Feds to Pay $940M to Settle Claims Over Tribal Contracts. *Aljazeera America.* Retrieved from http://america.aljazeera.com/articles/2015/9/17/feds-to-pay-940m-to-settle-tribal-contract-claims.html

Lewy, G. (September, 2004) Were American Indians the Victims of Genocide? *History News Network.* Retrieved from http://historynewsnetwork.org/article/7302

Liptak, A. (June 25, 2013) Supreme Court Invalidates Key Part of Voting Rights Act. *The New York Times.* Retrieved from http://www.nytimes.com/2013/06/26/us/supreme-court-ruling.html

Liptak, A. (June 23, 2016) Supreme Court Upholds Affirmative Action Program at University of Texas. *The New York Times*. Retrieved from http://www.nytimes.com/2016/06/24/us/politics/supreme-court-affirmative-action-university-of-texas.html

Love, D. (January 31, 2016) Study: Racial Discrimination in Mortgage Lending Continues to Impact African Americans, with a 'Black' Name Lowering One's Credit Score by 71 Points. *Atlanta Black Star*. Retrieved from http://atlantablackstar.com/2016/01/31/study-racial-discrimination-in-mortgage-lending-continues-to-impact-african-americans-with-a-black-name-lowering-ones-credit-score-by-71-points/

Lubrano, A. (2004) *Limbo: Blue-Collar Roots, White-Collar Dreams*. NJ: John Wiley & Sons.

Madrid, A. (2007) Missing People and Others: Joining Together to Expand the Circle. In Andersen, M.L. and Collins, P.H. (2007) *Race, Class, and Gender*, 6th edn. Belmont, CA: Thomson Higher Education.

Main, J.S. (September 20, 2014) Latinos in Mainstream Media Are a Disappearing Act: The Latino Media Gap Crisis. *The Huffington Post*. Retrieved from http://www.huffingtonpost.com/sj-main/the-latino-media-gap-crisis_b_5604714.html

Martinez, M. (October 12, 2013) A Slur or Term of 'Honor'? Controversy Heightens Over Redskins. *CNN*. Retrieved from http://www.cnn.com/2013/10/12/us/redskins-controversy/

Mehta, M. (November 18, 2015) Aziz Ansari's 'Master of None' Episode 'Indians on TV' Gets Representation Painfully Right. *Bustle.com*. Retrieved from http://www.bustle.com/articles/122532-aziz-ansaris-master-of-none-episode-indians-on-tv-gets-representation-painfully-right

Metla, V. (May 2, 2015) What Part Will Hispanic Voters Play in the 2016 Elections? *Law Street*. Retrieved from https://lawstreetmedia.com/issues/politics/part-will-hispanic-voters-play-2016-elections/

Mohamed, B. (January 6, 2016) A New Estimate of the U.S. Muslim Population. *Pew Research Center*. Retrieved from http://www.pewresearch.org/fact-tank/2016/01/06/a-new-estimate-of-the-u-s-muslim-population/

Moraga, C. La Guera. (2007) In Andersen, M.L. and Collins, P.H. (2007) *Race, Class, and Gender*, 6th edn. Belmont, CA: Thomson Higher Education

Morrison, T. (2015) *God Help the Child: A Novel*. NY: Alfred A. Knopf.

Nahnatchka, K. (creator) (2015–2018). *Fresh off the Boat*. Fierce Baby Productions, Detective Agency, 20th Century Fox Television.

Nasser, El.H. (June 19, 2012) Study: Asian Americans Value Hard Work, Family. *USA TODAY*. Retrieved from http://usatoday30.usatoday.com/news/nation/story/2012-06-18/asian-american-study/55677050/1

Native American/ American Indian Community. (n.d.) A Family for Every Child. Retrieved from http://www.afamilyforeverychild.org/Adoption/AdoptionAgency/Diversity/Native_American_Community.php

Native American Mascots. (n.d.) *The Huffington Post*. Retrieved from http://www.huffingtonpost.com/news/native-american-mascots/

Nittle, K.N. (March 2, 2017) 5 Common Native American Stereotypes in Film and Television. *ThoughtCo*. Retrieved from http://racerelations.about.com/od/hollywood/a/Five-Common-Native-American-Stereotypes-In-Film-And-Television.htm

Noguchi, Y. (March 18, 2016) Power Suits: How Dressing for Success at Work Can Pay Off. *Morning Edition*. Retrieved from http://www.npr.org/2016/03/18/469669877/power-suits-how-dressing-for-success-at-work-can-pay-off

Nonwhite U.S. Births Become the Majority for First Time. (May 17, 2012) *Bloomberg*. Retrieved from http://www.bloomberg.com/news/articles/2012-05-17/non-white-u-s-births-become-the-majority-for-first-time

Obama, B. (July 19, 2013) *Remarks by the President on Trayvon Martin*. Retrieved from https://obamawhitehouse.archives.gov/the-press-office/2013/07/19/remarks-president-trayvon-martin

OEDB. Open Education Database. (n.d.) *20 Native American Authors You Need to Read*. Retrieved from http://oedb.org/ilibrarian/20-native-american-authors-you-need-to-read/

Oluo, I. (June 15, 2015) How Rachel Dolezal's Lies Hurt Black People. *The Seattle Globalist*. Retrieved from http://www.seattleglobalist.com/2015/06/15/rachel-dolezal-lies-hurt-black-people-spokane-ijeoma-oluo/38338

Park, H., Keller, J., Williams, J. (February 24, 2016) The Faces of American Power, Nearly as White as the Oscar Nominees. *New York Times*. Retrieved from https://www.nytimes.com/interactive/2016/02/26/us/race-of-american-power.html?hp&action=click&pgtype=Homepage&clickSource=story-heading&module=photo-spot-region&region=top-news&WT.nav=top-news&_r=1

Pasha, H. (October 18, 2016) The UN Working Group of Experts on People of African Descent's Report on the United States – An International Perspective on Race in America. *Human Rights Brief*. Retrieved from http://hrbrief.org/2016/10/un-working-group-experts-people-african-descents-report/

Passel, J.S., Livingston, G., Cohn, D. (May 17, 2012) *Explaining Why Minority Births Now Outnumber White Births*. Retrieved from http://www.pewsocialtrends.org/2012/05/17/explaining-why-minority-births-now-outnumber-white-births/

Peters, B. (August 19, 2016) Urban Dictionary: Brown Paper Bag Test. *Urban Dictionary*. Retrieved from http://www.urbandictionary.com/define.php?term=brown+paper+bag+test

Pew Research Center (2013, February 7) Second Generation Americans: A Portrait of the Adult Children of Immigrants.

Pew Research Center (April 4, 2013) The Rise of Asian Americans. Retrieved from http://www.pewsocialtrends.org/2012/06/19/the-rise-of-asian-americans/

Piepzna-Samarasinha, L.L. (2015) *Dirty River: A Queer Femme of Color Dreaming her Way Home*. Vancouver, Canada: Arsenal Pulp Press.

Pratt, M.B., Hixson, L., Jones, A.N. (n.d.) Measuring Race and Ethnicity Across the Decades: 1790–2010. *U.S. Census Bureau*. Retrieved from http://www.census.gov/population/race/data/MREAD_1790_2010.html

Quora. (2014) How Much Did Slavery Contribute to American Wealth? *Quora*. Retrieved from https://www.quora.com/How-much-did-slavery-contribute-to-American-wealth

Qureshi, F. (February 10, 2016) Native Americans: Negative Impacts of Media Portrayals, Stereotypes. *Journalist's Resource*. Retrieved from https://journalistsresource.org/studies/society/race-society/native-americans-media-stereotype-redskins

Rainey, C. (October 20, 2015) The Ben's Chili Bowl Bill Cosby Mural Was Finally Defaced. *Grub Street*. Retrieved from http://www.grubstreet.com/2015/10/bens-chili-bowl-cosby-mural-defaced.html

Reese, P., Magagnini, S. (June 30, 2015) Census: Hispanics Overtake Whites to Become California's Largest Ethnic Group. *The Sacramento Bee*. Retrieved from http://www.sacbee.com/news/local/article25940218.html

Remnick, N. (April 27, 2016) Yale Defies Calls to Rename Calhoun College. *New York Times*. Retrieved from https://www.nytimes.com/2016/04/28/nyregion/yale-defies-calls-to-rename-calhoun-college.html

Rodriguez, Y.C. (May 3, 2014) Which Is It, Hispanic or Latino? *CNN*. Retrieved from http://www.cnn.com/2014/05/03/living/hispanic-latino-identity/

Rothstein, R. (January 23, 2012) A Comment on Bank of America/Countrywide's Discriminatory Mortgage Lending and its Implications for Racial Segregation. *Economic Policy Institute*. Retrieved from http://www.epi.org/publication/bp335-boa-countrywide-discriminatory-lending/

Sherlock, R. (August 12, 2017) Unearthed Canaanite Graves Shed Light on Descendants in Lebanon. *Weekend Edition Saturday*. Retrieved from http://www.npr.org/2017/08/12/542998587/unearthed-canaanite-graves-shed-light-on-descendants-in-lebanon

Siegel, R. (March 14, 2016) Blendoor App Breaks Down Computer Bias in Hiring. *KQED Radio*. Retrieved from http://www.kqed.org/news/story/2016/03/14/192044/blendoor_app_breaks_down_computer_bias_in_hiring

Staff Writers. (November 15, 2012) 20 Native American Authors You Need to Read. *OEDB*. Retrieved from http://oedb.org/ilibrarian/20-native-american-authors-you-need-to-read/

Steinbeck, J. (1952) *East of Eden*. NY: Penguin Random House LLC.

Swarns, L.R. (October 30, 2015) Biased Lending Evolves, and Blacks Face Trouble Getting Mortgages. *The New York Times*. Retrieved from http://www.nytimes.com/2015/10/31/nyregion/hudson-city-bank-settlement.html

Takaki, R. (2007) A Different Mirror. In Andersen, M.L. and Collins, P.H. (2007) *Race, Class, and Gender,* 6th edn. Belmont, CA: Thomson Higher Education.

The California Report. (January 8–10, 2016) California Muslim Women Reconsider Wearing Hijab over Safety Concerns. *KQED*. Retrieved from http://audio.californiareport.org/archive/R201601081630/b

The Editorial Board. (February 20, 2016) The Crisis of Minority Unemployment. *The New York Times*. Retrieved from https://www.nytimes.com/2016/02/21/opinion/sunday/the-crisis-of-minority-unemployment.html?action=click&pgtype=Homepage&clickSource=story-heading&module=span-abc-region&region=span-abc-region&WT.nav=span-abc-region&_r=0

The Takeaway. (February 22, 2016) America's Complicated Past Stirs Battle over Monuments, Memorials. *PRI and WNYC*. Retrieved from http://www.wnyc.org/story/who-should-memorials-represent/

The Trouble with Tribe. (November 19, 2001) *Teaching Tolerance*. Retrieved from http://www.tolerance.org/magazine/number-19-spring-2001/feature/trouble-tribe

Thorp, B.K. (February 21, 2016) What Does the Academy Value in a Black Performance? *The New York Times*. Retrieved from https://www.nytimes.com/2016/02/21/movies/what-does-the-academy-value-in-a-black-performance.html

Trask, H-K. (2007) From a Native Daughter. In Andersen, M.L. and Collins, P.H. (2007) *Race, Class, and Gender,* 6th edn. Belmont, CA: Thomson Higher Education.

University of Michigan Supreme Court Ruling. (June 23, 2003) Retrieved from http://ns.umich.edu/new/releases/20237-us-supreme-court-rules-on-university-of-michigan-cases?tmpl=component

US Census Bureau. (November, 2015) *Facts for Features: American Indian and Alaska Native Heritage Month*: Retrieved from https://www.census.gov/newsroom/facts-for-features/2015/cb15-ff22.html

US Census Bureau. (n.d.) *Race*. Retrieved from https://www.census.gov/topics/population/race.html.

Vasel, K. (September 24, 2015) Bank to Pay $33 Million for Discriminatory Mortgage Lending. *CNNMoney*. Retrieved from http://money.cnn.com/2015/09/24/real_estate/cfpb-hudson-city-savings-bank-order/

Volokh, E. (May 29, 2014) How the Asians Became White. *The Washington Post*. Retrieved from https://www.washingtonpost.com/news/volokh-conspiracy/wp/2014/05/29/how-the-asians-became-white/?utm_term=.4c8d5fbfa03f

Wang, M., Svrluga, S. (February 12, 2017) Yale Renames Calhoun College Because of Historic Ties to White Supremacy and Slavery. *The Washington Post*. Retrieved from https://www.washingtonpost.com/news/grade-point/wp/2017/02/11/yale-renames-calhoun-college-because-of-historic-ties-to-white-supremacy-and-slavery/?utm_term=.20faf72795a4Yale renames Calhoun College because of historical ties to white supremacy and slavery

Weekend Edition Sunday. (February 21, 2016) Taking on the Appeal of ISIS, with Cartoons. *NPR*. Retrieved from http://www.npr.org/2016/02/21/467501423/taking-on-the-appeal-of-isis-with-cartoons

White, B.G. (August 7, 2015) The Racial Gaps in America's Recovery. *The Atlantic*. Retrieved from http://www.theatlantic.com/business/archive/2015/08/jobs-numbers-racial-gap-recovery/400685/

Whites, Blacks, and the Blues. (n.d.) *PBS*. Retrieved from http://www.pbs.org/theblues/classroom/intwhitesblacks.html

Wiener, J. (March 1, 2016) Big Rise in Psychiatric Hospitalizations for California's Latino Youth. California Healthline. *KQED*. Retrieved from http://ww2.kqed.org/stateofhealth/2016/03/01/big-rise-in-psychiatric-hospitalizations-for-californias-latino-youth/

Yan, H. (December 9, 2015) The Truth About Muslims in America. *CNN*. Retrieved from http://www.cnn.com/2015/12/08/us/muslims-in-america-shattering-misperception/index.html

CHAPTER 9

Health and Healthcare

WHAT YOU WILL READ ABOUT IN THIS CHAPTER:

- **Health** is defined as a sense of well-being physically, mentally, and emotionally. The absence of "disease" does not assure health. Good health is enhanced by both personal behaviors and social policies. On the personal level, health maintenance requires a good healthy diet; adequate sleep and exercise; access to regular healthcare; and refraining from poor practices relating to these. On a social level, good healthcare requires universal access to health services; protection from toxins with environmental policies; clean water and fresh foods, and other public policies to support health maintenance.

- The **health status** of the US population is generally poor. The US lags far behind other countries on multiple measure of health including accessibility; longevity; mental health; management of chronic conditions; and preventable death. The US has high rates of death from smoking, obesity, and alcohol use. Conversely, we do have the most costly system, with expenditures close to double that of the next most expensive country.

- The healthcare system in the US is fragmented, with **insurances** and **services** coming from a variety of sources. A large portion of the population has private insurance, generally through employers. The rest of the population received insurance through government programs such as **The Affordable Care Act**, passed in 2010, or through **Medicaid** or **Medicare**. Historically, healthcare has been delivered by a fee-for-service system where a person is billed for service as received. Today, a significant portion of the population are enrolled in a Health Maintenance Organization (HMO), where the services and the provider are the same entity and payments are made on a regular monthly basis.

- The **pharmaceutical industry** is vast and highly profitable. There are many controversies surrounding the industry especially with respect to drug testing; drug costs; branding; shortages; and efficacy. It has been suggested that American medicine "overmedicates," utilizing ineffective medicines which can sometimes be dangerous or have no effect on the condition they are prescribed for.

- **Epidemiology** is a science which investigates the frequency, prevalence, and distribution of disease and health conditions. Epidemiologists have established that nondominant groups are treated differentially with respect to access; diagnosis; treatment; and medications. This is true of nondominant groups in race, ethnicity, sex, gender, ability, and sexual orientation.

- The **functionalists** tend to focus on the ways that the healthcare system "works," including treatment of disease, economic interests, and social stability. The **conflict** theorists suggest that inequality persists because it is highly profitable with regard to hospitals, pharmaceuticals, and insurance corporations.

- Sociologists have also described a condition of **medicalization**, where a disease is "treated" but no medical problem actually exists, such as in some forms of hyperactivity, pregnancy, childbirth, and death.

Introduction

In this chapter, we will explore the definition of health, the status of the American population's health, the history and cost of the healthcare system, the *Affordable Care Act*, the pharmaceutical industry, and the Trump administration's plans regarding healthcare.

What Is Health?

The World Health Organization defines *health* as "a state of complete physical, mental, and social well-being, and not merely the absence of disease or infirmity." To assure attainment of well-being, a person needs access to affordable housing, adequate nutrition, a safe environment, and social support systems. The National Wellness Institute identifies six areas of significance: physical, spiritual, intellectual, social, occupational, and emotional (NWI n.d.). Achieving a minimal level of health has far-reaching consequences. Ill health impacts many spheres of life, including a child's physical and cognitive development; a person's likelihood of developing diseases; and the ability to perform social roles. Poverty and racism constitute stressors only now being acknowledged as contributing to low achievement, disease, and early death.

> ### Box 9.1 – Health
>
> The *World Health Organization* defines **health** as achieving well-being in physical, mental, and emotional dimensions. Basic life needs in diet, exercise, shelter, and access to services contribute to enhanced health. Diminishment of life stressors, including poverty and discrimination, also support good health. Personal behaviors, accompanied by social programs, promote the accomplishment of these goals.

Good health starts with a healthy lifestyle, including physical exercise and a balanced diet. Many Americans fall short in these areas. We are increasingly a sedentary (nonmoving) society. Recent research indicates that sitting for more than an hour at a time will shorten your life span. This lack of mobility, judged to affect 60–85 percent of the world population, is likely increasing (WHO 2017; Neighmond 2011). Consequences of immobility include: increases in colon and breast cancer; insulin resistance leading to increased Type 2 diabetes; cognitive decline; increased risk of heart attack and stroke; increased bone loss; increased weight gain; loss of lean muscle tissue; and a less effective immune system (NCHPAD n.d.). Physical activity also increases a person's mental health since it can bolster mood, boost energy, promote sleep, enhance sex life, and increase sociability (Mayo Clinic Staff 2017). Exercise has been shown to be effective therapy for mild to moderate depression (Taylor et al. 1985). Recommendations regarding dietary guides have been controversial and continue to fall short of agreement.

Figure 9.1 Americans are sedentary at work and fail to get even a minimal level of exercise, essential for maintaining health
Source: Cecilie_Arcurs / istockphoto.com

Dietary Issues

A good diet is vital to health, though experts rarely agree as to what constitutes an optimally healthy diet. The US Department of Health and Human Services, in conjunction with the Department of Agriculture, publishes dietary guidelines every five years. These recommendations impact the health of the population, particularly lower income groups whose supplements are based upon these recommendations. These mandates are incorporated into the Women Infants and Children (WIC) Program, Supplemental Nutrition Assistance Program (SNAP), and school lunch menus. Much of the research upon which dietary recommendations are based, is observational, lacking scientific validation. Such research demonstrates associated trends but lacks controlled clinical trials (Teicholz 2015). In 1961, the government's dietary guidelines promoted low fat, low cholesterol diets, especially for cardio-vascular health, and consequently changed the eating habits of the American public. Recent research strongly suggests that there is no significant relationship between dietary cholesterol and blood cholesterol, and that the restriction on fat intake be dropped (O'Connor 2015). The 25 percent decrease in fats seen in the last 50 years was matched by an increase of 30 percent in carbohydrate consumption. Increased consumption of carbohydrates has been linked to greater risks of obesity, heart attack, and diabetes while the purported relationship of saturated fat to heart disease remains unsubstantiated (Teicholz 2015). Carbohydrates are also suspected of causing inflammation, which is thought to be a leading cause of immune system breakdown (Robert 2017; Morgan 2015). Current recommendations to limit the consumption of lean meat are cautioned against as another factor leading to increased carbohydrate intake. Advice to reduce salt, still currently in the guidelines, is not supported by research from the Institute of Medicine (Teicholz 2015). It is recommended that people get no more than 10 percent of daily calories from sugar, yet the typical American's diet has more than two times that amount (O'Connor 2015). Sodas, juices, and other sugary drinks account for the greatest part in sugar consumption yet are empty calories, with no nutritional value. Sugared drinks, whether made with "natural sugar" or artificial sweeteners, do not alleviate thirst.

> ## Box 9.2 – Dietary Guidelines
>
> *The Dietary Guidelines* are published every five years. These guidelines establish the parameters of a healthy diet believed to promote optimal nutrition. The 1960s was a time where reductions in fat were promoted by a low cholesterol diet. These calories were often replaced with carbohydrates, which many experts feel are contributing to increases in obesity and Type 2 diabetes. A diet high in carbohydrates is now widely considered unhealthy. The Mediterranean diet, rich in fruits, vegetables, whole grains, beans, nuts, legumes, olive oil, and fish is often recommended as supporting good nutrition, health, and weight control. Dairy products are also controversial since a significant portion of the population, especially among African Americans, is lactose intolerant.

Figure 9.2 The Mediterranean diet, rich in vegetables, fruit, and "good" fat, is shown in some research to be the best option
Source: Photography by Rosalind Gottfried

There is some agreement that the Mediterranean diet, rich in fruits, vegetables, whole grains, beans, nuts, legumes, olive oil, and fish is one of the best for overall nutrition and avoidance of diseases (Mediterranean Diet n.d.; O'Connor 2015). Recent modifications in guides for American diets incorporate these elements by suggesting a diet with a variety of vegetable types; whole fruits; grains, especially whole grains; no fat or low-fat dairy products; oils; and protein derived from various sources of meat, seafood, nuts, legumes; seeds; eggs; and soy products. The hierarchical structure of the "food pyramid" has been replaced by a stratified image permitting more flexibility in the balance of foods selected from each group (Dietary Guidelines 2015). The current recommendations may still be less than optimal, and even damaging, to some groups. Guidelines recommend two to three servings of dairy a day but dairy is not well tolerated by a significant portion of the population. African Americans, with rates of 70 percent lactose intolerance, are at greater risk for negative effects than the corresponding 25 percent of the White population (PCRM n.d.; Harkinson 2015). This type of divergence suggests the fallacy in creating a 'one size fits all' dietary guideline. Calcium, a mineral basic to good health, is associated with dairy products but it can be found in other foods. Collard greens, kale, broccoli, and beans are rich calcium sources and additionally provide high fiber and vitamins and contain no cholesterol (Almendrala 2016).

Evidence suggests that diet may be more significant in health outcomes than genetics. Research comparing the diets of Pima Indians in Arizona to a Pima group located in Mexico demonstrates significant differences in health status. The Mexican Pima, who maintain a more traditional lifestyle and diet, are assessed as much healthier than their Arizona cohort; they fare better in measures of weight, height, body fat, blood pressure, cholesterol, glucose, and diabetes (Melillo 1993).

Environmental Issues

Health threats from environmental factors are proliferating. These concern both toxins and behavioral factors. The fiasco of the lead-contaminated water of Flint MI (see Chapter 14) is not an isolated event. Many people have been exposed to lead in the water supply, and other environmental sources, though its destructive effects are well documented (WHO 2016).

Another health concern, linked to environmental factors, concerns the age at which young girls are entering into puberty. Many theories have been advanced to explain a trend towards early onset of menstruation, seen in girls as young as seven and eight. Chemical additives and hormones in foods have been chief suspects but the most convincing argument suggests the culprits are obesity and persistent family stress (Greenspan and Deardorff 2015). Body fat secretes estrogen which stimulates breast development. Twenty-three percent of Black girls, 25 percent of Hispanic girls, and 10 percent of White girls show breast development at the age of seven (Greenspan and Deardorff 2015). Consuming sugary drinks enhances the likelihood of early breast development even without being overweight. Emotional stress also ignites early menstruation. High family conflict, instability, and sexual abuse all enhance the likelihood of early onset of menstruation, as do stressors linked to living in a fatherless household (Greenspan and Deardorff 2015).

Early onset of menstruation disrupts physical health in a number of ways. Early puberty is linked to eating disorders, substance abuse, early sexual activity, and breast cancer later in life. Chemical exposure effects the endocrine system, influencing puberty and potentially disrupting reproductive development. Studies suggest that breast feeding, healthy weight of the mother before and during pregnancy, and consuming soy foods can potentially inhibit early menstruation (Greenspan and Deardorff 2015). A warm emotional environment also is a deterrent to early onset and can mitigate its consequences (Greenspan and Deardorff 2015). Hormone-disrupting elements in cosmetics also pose a danger to girls, who are heavier users of these products than adult women (EWG 2008).

Americans' lack of sleep also is implicated in negative health outcomes. A recent Centers for Disease Control and Prevention (CDC) study found that one third of Americans consistently fail to get the seven hours of sleep recommended by experts (CDC 2016). Another poll shows the figure at 40 percent (Jones 2013). Sleep shortage can result in increased risk of diabetes, hypertension and heart disease, stroke, and mental distress (CDC 2016). Increases in the use of smart phones, from even younger ages than among the millennials, are related to more sleep deprivation in adolescents, who require about nine hours of sleep. Between 2012 and 2015 there was an increase of 22 percent in teens getting less than seven hours (Twenge 2017).

Mental Health Issues

There are persistent discriminatory practices against women in the assessment, diagnosis, and treatment of mental illness. Women are more likely to receive a psychiatric diagnosis and to be prescribed mood stabilizers and other psychiatric drugs. Clinical assessments of women describe them as weak and in need of paternalistic social control. These trends were first publicized 50 years ago and persist virtually unchanged. Investigation of gender and mental disorders, initiated in the early 1970s identified the possession of stereotypic femininity as psychologically "normal," while deviations from prescribed gender characteristics were deemed to be mental instability or illness (Chesler 1972; Miller 1976). Overall, women are more likely to be considered as psychologically impaired; one in four women, compared to one in seven men, takes a psychiatric drug. The prevalence of psychiatric drug prescriptions is high; *abilify*, an antipsychotic drug, outsells every other drug for any mental or physical condition (Joiner 2014). Mood-stabilizing drugs, more prevalent in women, work to level moods, eliminating "lows" or depressive symptoms, and also resulting in the loss of any emotional reaction. Holland (2015) suggests that these drugs make women behave more like men, and therefore appear more "acceptable." She contends that medicating women out of their feelings is not only "unnatural" but dangerous to the culture which benefits from women's compassion.

The institutionalization of personal behavioral changes is insufficient to improve the general societal health; social policies affecting behaviors and environment must also support good health. The safety of our food sources is one avenue for change (Bollinger n.d.). Pesticides banned elsewhere are still allowed in the US (Kim 2013). The real dangers these substances pose is debated but some feel that the Food and Drug Administration is not cautious enough in its regulation of the food supply. The ramifications of genetically modified foods for the environment and the food chain (see Chapter 14) remain controversial. Comprehensive affordable healthcare; parental leaves; early childhood support programs; free preschool; food aid; strict environmental regulations affecting pollution, chemical dumping, and toxic exposure; access to recreational areas and good public transportation are all standard policy provisions in comparable countries to enhance the population's wellness.

What Is the Status of the US Population's Health?

By just about any measure, the health status of the US population trails behind comparable nations. Our most distinctive feature is the exceptionally high cost of the system, where we exceed any other nation by nearly 200 percent. We also stand out in rates of obesity, where we rank number one among the Organization for Economic Cooperation and Development (OECD) nations, with 36.5 percent qualifying as obese compared to an average of 22.8 percent (US Life Expectancy... 2013). In the same study, the US ranked 26 out of 36 in longevity. Average longevity is 78.8, 81.2 for women and 76.4 for men (Copeland 2014). US longevity gains of nine years, between 1960–2011, are smaller than in other countries where increases were greater—15 years in Japan and an average of 11 years across the study. International comparisons of the aging population also rank the US lower than most comparable countries. We rank 43 out of 96 nations in life expectancy at 60, a measure often utilized to assess overall health and healthcare (Global Age Index Inventory 2015). Obesity now surpasses smoking as the leading cause of preventable death (Cleveland Clinic 2017). We ranked 19 out of 19 developed nations in "avoidable mortality" (Nolte and Martin McKee 2008).

In the US, social class is strongly implicated in health and longevity. Individuals from lower socio-economic statuses are three times more likely to experience a premature death than affluent people. Research shows that the earlier death of lower income people is also affected by geography since it varies by city of residence. Wealthy Americans have made significant gains in longevity regardless of location. Poorer families generally show little increase in longevity though there are some gains specific to certain localities. Researchers suggest that contributing factors to increased longevity are behavioral, such as more exercise, less smoking, and better access to healthcare which reduces stress (Zarroli 2016; Irwin and Bui 2016).

People in lower income groups also are more likely to suffer from chronic conditions such as depression, heart disease, high blood pressure, arthritis, and diabetes. Childhood stress, related to poverty, produces consequences sustained into adulthood. Poverty affects the nervous system and may even accelerate the aging process (Velasquez-Manoff 2013). People born into low-income households who attain affluence are more prone to illness than people who never were poor. Lower income youths who graduate college experience more health issues than their less educated counterparts. These "successful" students have higher rates of obesity, high blood pressure, and stress hormones. These are attributed to the drive to perform well, particularly in view of parental sacrifice. Other potential culprits are feelings of social isolation from their current peer group, as well as racism and discrimination. It is also suggested that competitive lifestyles might contribute to poor habits in sleep, diet, and exercise (Miller et al. 2014). A British epidemiologist has labeled this tendency *the status syndrome*, indicating the higher your social status as a child, the better your health (Velasquez-Manoff 2013).

The US ranks 26 of 29 countries assessed for childhood well-being (Velasquez-Manoff 2013). Recent upsurges in child poverty have raised concern regarding

Exhibit 9. Select Population Health Outcomes and Risk Factors

	Life exp. at birth, 2013[a]	Infant mortality, per 1,000 live births, 2013[a]	Percent of pop. age 65+ with two or more chronic conditions, 2014[b]	Obesity rate (BMI>30), 2013[a,c]	Percent of pop. (age 15+) who are daily smokers, 2013[a]	Percent of pop. age 65+
Australia	82.2	3.6	54	28.3[e]	12.8	14.4
Canada	81.5[e]	4.8[e]	56	25.8	14.9	15.2
Denmark	80.4	3.5	–	14.2	17.0	17.8
France	82.3	3.6	43	14.5[d]	24.1[d]	17.7
Germany	80.9	3.3	49	23.6	20.9	21.1
Japan	83.4	2.1	–	3.7	19.3	25.1
Netherlands	81.4	3.8	46	11.8	18.5	16.8
New Zealand	81.4	5.2[e]	37	30.6	15.5	14.2
Norway	81.8	2.4	43	10.0[d]	15.0	15.6
Sweden	82.0	2.7	42	11.7	10.7	19.0
Switzerland	82.9	3.9	44	10.3[d]	20.4[d]	17.3
United Kingdom	81.1	3.8	33	24.9	20.0[d]	17.1
United States	78.8	6.1[e]	68	35.3[d]	13.7	14.1
OECD median	81.2	3.5	–	28.3	18.9	17.0

[a] Source: OECD Health Data 2015.

[b] Includes hypertension or high blood pressure, heart disease, diabetes, lung problems, mental health problems, cancer, and joint pain/arthritis. Source: Commonwealth Fund International Health Policy Survey of Order Adults, 2014.

[c] DEN, FR, NETH, NOR, SWE, and SWIZ based on self-reported data; all other countries based on measured data.

[d] 2012. [e] 2011.

the long-term health and well-being of these youths, both now and in adulthood. Help for poor children needs to begin early in life, even pre-natally. More support for pregnant women who use alcohol, drugs, tobacco, and suffer exposure to toxins can reduce long-term effects on their children. Increased expenditures can significantly reduce the cost of subsequent outcomes in ill health, joblessness, and incarceration.

Early life stress can lead to inflammation later in life, which can increase the risk of degenerative diseases such as heart disease and diabetes. African American men live, on the average, five years less than White men and are at greater risk of cardiovascular disease and hypertension; most of this difference comes from income, not genetics (Velasquez-Manoff 2013). Racism plays a part in stress and in women it manifests in visceral fat accumulation which increases the risk of *metabolic syndrome* leading to heart disease and diabetes. There is evidence that vulnerability to infection later in life also is linked to childhood stress (Velasquez-Manoff 2013).

Reducing the stress of parents, especially single parents, will significantly impact the well-being of their children. Nurturing has been shown, in multiple studies, to

Figure 9.3 Of OECD nations, the US ranked highest in rates of obesity, infant mortality, and chronic condition of the aging population, and lowest in longevity Source: OECD Health Data 2015

protect a child against environmental stressors. Rat research shows that adult licking and cuddling of the young creates more confident, curious, intelligent, healthier rats with increased longevity (Kristof and WuDunn 2014). This phenomenon holds true even if the grooming adult is not biologically related to the baby. Cortisol is the hormone that is released when an organism feels stress and it has been shown to dissipate when rats are tended to by adults. Similar studies exist for humans. When a baby is in a stress response, the level of cortisol can be reduced by attentive parents. Cortisol levels are implicated in aggressive behaviors and are especially influential when high levels are sustained by persistent tension (Kristof and WuDunn 2014).

Chronic stress is a factor in the lives of many people, particularly those in nondominant groups. With regard to the attacks of 9/11, middle-class Americans were catapulted into awareness of vulnerability and insecurity more typically characteristic of lower class Americans. These less fortunate groups suffer daily fear and anxiety. Consequently, large portions of the American population sustain negative health affects which can be reduced, if not eliminated by better social policies. The society benefits when access to adequate health services is assured, along with the ability to purchase treatment and medications. Good healthcare contributes to healthy brain development and the ability to accomplish the necessary skills of adulthood (Velasquez-Manoff 2013; Kristof and WuDunn 2014). Numerous studies document achievement deficits in bright lower income children.

Stress initiated later in life is also being recognized as a vital element of disease. In recent years, many media reports have highlighted the widening epidemic of premature death among middle-aged White men. This has been attributed to the changing economy, and the scarcity of jobs with adequate wages, especially among men without college degrees. These men are dying from heart disease, suicide, and substance abuse.

More revelatory aspects of American healthcare occur with regard to systemic flaws, which can be alleviated by better practices. Four hundred thousand Americans die from medical mishap, the third leading cause of death in the US. These "mishaps" refer to misdiagnosis, accidents in the treatment process, and misuse of prescriptions (McCann 2014). On many measures the US ranks poorly in comparison with other advanced nations. The US ranked 15 of 19 nations in number of deaths resulting from normally non-fatal conditions; ranked lowest in survival rates from kidney transplants; and exhibited comparatively high levels of death from circulatory diseases, respiratory diseases, and diabetes. Levels of patient dissatisfaction surpassed most other developed nations with 40 percent reporting negatively to a question regarding patient satisfaction (Editorial Board 2007).

Box 9.3 – Health Status

Health status refers to the overall health of the citizens of a country. Common measures in assessing health status include rates of infant mortality; longevity; longevity at age 60; prevalence of chronic diseases such as diabetes and cardio-vascular disease; obesity; and accessibility. By virtually all the measures commonly used, the US falls far behind countries with comparable levels of development. Americans' lack of universal access to healthcare remains unique in the developed world.

The US spends $10,348 on healthcare per capita in contrast with an average of $4908 for nations of the OECD. The nearest nation, Switzerland, spends $7919, making the US the most expensive current system, and yet it fails to provide universal coverage as is the norm in comparable countries (Sawyer and Cox 2018). In spite of our greater spending, healthcare services are deficient. For example, 37 percent of adults went without recommended care, didn't see a doctor, or didn't fill a prescription because of the cost. Twenty-six percent of patients with chronic diseases obtained a same day appointment to see a provider, compared to 40–60 percent in other countries. We rank well in access to specialists, but this carries its own set of problems, particularly since the cost of seeing a specialist is significantly higher than seeing a general doctor and there is a shortage of general practitioners who often can more cheaply supervise treatment once a plan is constructed (Commonwealth Fund 2015).

How Is our Health System Structured?

Historically, the United States has had a "fee-for-service" system where a person is billed for each service provided at the time of the service. The patient is responsible for the payment unless she or he has health insurance. Most commonly, insurance is obtained through employers. The insurance premium may be completely paid by the employer or the employee may contribute a portion of it. An additional co-payment may be required per service, depending on the plan. Fee-for-service was universal until gradual changes were introduced, mostly in the past 50 years.

In the years since World War I, alternative forms of insurance, and healthcare delivery were available on a very limited basis, affecting about 3 percent of the population. The alternative system is known as a *Health Maintenance Organization* (HMO). In an HMO, the insurer and the system of delivery are the same entity. Monthly payments cover both the insurance premiums and the services provided. The patient sustains minimal out of pocket costs. The guiding principle of the HMO is that reducing out of pocket expenses ultimately will increase the health of the patient by encouraging preventive measures and early intervention. The HMO charter mandates free or low-cost educational opportunities to promote health and control costs. These would include programs for smoking cessation, childbirth classes, nutrition education, exercise, and stress reduction techniques. The Nixon administration passed a federal act, in 1973, promoting HMOs. Today HMO enrollment is over 87 million people. Assessment shows that decades after its expansion, HMOs have failed to reduce the overall cost of healthcare. Although some HMO plans cost slightly less than traditional insurance plans, they are basically comparable. In addition to premiums, charges for co-payments, deductibles, and prescriptions have increased. The level of these out of pocket expenses will vary depending on the plan purchased. The same is true for *Preferred Providers*

Organizations (PPOs) plans, which operate in a fee for service structure and include deductibles and out of pocket expenses contingent on the level of the plan; the higher the cost of the plan, the lower the out of pocket costs. Recent years have seen significant increases in both premiums and co-payments and deductibles.

Box 9.4 – Healthcare System

The healthcare system refers to the organization and dissemination of healthcare. The American system is the most expensive system in the developed world, accounting for about 18 percent of GDP, even with a large portion of the society lacking health insurance (CMS.gov 2018).

In a *fee for service* structure, a person receives a bill for services rendered, at the point of service. Payment for the services may be the responsibility of the individual or their insurance company. Insurance generally has been obtained through an employer, or government programs such as the Veterans Administration, Indian Health Services, *Medicaid*, or *Medicare*. Expanded access to purchasing insurance was made possible with the passage of the *Affordable Care Act* (ACA) in 2010. Although estimates vary, approximately 30 million people remain uninsured in 2016.

Health Maintenance Organizations are systems of healthcare in which the provider and the insurer are the same entity. An HMO client makes a monthly payment, either out of pocket or through an employer, which provides for most healthcare services, minus any deductible or co-payment in the selected plan. HMOs include a mandate to provide low-cost, or no cost, education and preventive programs. Until President Nixon's administration signed a bill of support for HMOs (1973), only 3 percent of people participated in these programs. Today the figure for HMO membership is more than 87 million.

For people who do not have health insurance, the costs of services are prohibitive. People without any type of insurance are typically billed more than those with insurance because the large volume of consumers represented by insurance plans allows for fee negotiations. A diagnostic center will lower fees to increase the volume of clients. In a PPO, physicians accept a small fee discount to become part of the "preferred network." Choosing a doctor, or service, outside of the preferred providers will generally result in the consumer making a payment compensating for the discount.

A limited portion of the population is eligible for government programs which include **Medicaid** and **Medicare**. Medicaid is generally for the indigent and Medicare is for seniors, available to everyone at the age of 65. These programs were initiated in 1965, by Congressional vote, as amendments to the *Social Security Act* (1935). There are additional specialized programs such as the Veterans' Administration (VA) and the Indian Health Services (IHS), for which a person must meet eligibility requirements. In 2010, the Obama administration passed an Act to insure more of the population.

The structure of the systems in other countries varies but they all include universal coverage. The US is the sole developed country failing to provide access to care for the entire population. Some countries feature a single payer plan, where a government entity collects and distributes the monies for healthcare. In other countries, private insurance companies provide for payments but these agencies are not for profit. The funding for the coverage usually comes from employers but it is covered by the government, should a person not have access to coverage from a job. These programs are not socialized medicine because the services are provided by private, nonprofit agencies. Most of these countries provide comprehensive services. Some countries engage in what is considered socialized medicine in that the government collects and disseminates funding and provides the services (Reid 2009).

Current Costs in the US Health System Under the Affordable Care Act

The Patient Protection and Affordable Care Act (ACA), signed into law by President Obama in 2010, assists individuals to buy health insurance if they are unable to do so through an employer.

> Like many people, I've been out of a job for a little while but looking, and things are looking better, but the timeline is always unfortunately indefinite. Debt and expense have been racking up while I burn through back up savings, and things have not been ideal, and frankly have been tough. I did not have health insurance for a couple months, and finally got around to applying on the exchange. It was simple, fast, easy and got things done well for me. My mind is now at ease. I qualified for a subsidy thankfully which allows me to be on a great plan with everything I need at a very manageable monthly cost. I need health insurance and simply would not be able to have such good coverage at such a low price without Obamacare/Affordable Care Act.
> Thank you for everything President Obama.
>
> (Real Life Stories n.d.)

The ACA has remained fundamentally intact despite several successful legal challenges altering some programs made during Obama's administration. The impact, and intent, of the ACA has been widely misunderstood. One half of people surveyed in a recent 2017 poll believe that the number of the uninsured increased, or stayed the same, after inception of the ACA. Prior to the passage of the Act, estimates of the uninsured were at about 50 million people (Kodjak 2017). With passage of the Act, 20 million people gained coverage, making the uninsured rate the lowest in American history. Attempts to "repeal and replace," initiated with a Republican president and Congress in 2016, so far have been unsuccessful (Newkirk 2017). The programs promoted by Trump would have resulted in over 24 million Americans losing their health plans, according to the Congressional Budget Office (Maddow 2017). The Republicans have turned some attention to making the system more efficient and also have waged attempts to chip away at it through other means, rather than full repeal.

Various aspects of the ACA were phased in between 2010 and 2016. Citizens were mandated to buy insurance or pay a tax penalty, an element of the ACA overturned in the tax reform of 2018. The expansion of insurance to all would result in a larger pool of premiums, paid by healthier insured persons, who could support costs for the less healthy. Consumers could "shop" for plans on exchanges comparing a variety of plans. These followed the idea that competition between insurance plans would serve to regulate the cost of the plans. People are compelled to purchase insurance either through the federal government's exchange, or a state one, if the state opted to have one. Contrary to some of the attacks against the ACA, the program is in no dimension "socialized" medicine. It actually relies on basic capitalist principles in which competition results in a self-regulating market. The government is not regulating the price of insurances or services. Medical practices, health insurance, clinics, hospitals, and pharmaceuticals remain private and profit making. The ACA mandate that all people be covered was established to protect those with pre-existing conditions who formerly were virtually unable to obtain insurance; surcharges for pre-existing conditions are prohibited. Older persons can be charged more but the government imposed limitations on the rates (Kodjak 2017).

Box 9.5 – Patient Protection and Affordable Care Act 2010

The *Patient Protection and Affordable Care Act 2010 (ACA)* mandates that all persons should have health insurance or pay a penalty though this element was eliminated by the tax reform of 2018. The ACA contains many elements but the provision that all must be eligible for insurance, regardless of previous or current health, is a major shift in the insurance industry. Other elements include free preventive services for basic health maintenance such as contraception, vaccinations and certain diagnostic tests; federal government subsidies to the states, including the voluntary expansion of Medicaid; and the requirement that employers with more than 50 workers must offer insurance or suffer a tax penalty. Many Americans have obtained insurance under the ACA, and as many as 32 million are estimated at risk of losing it if Congress passes a repeal.

Predictions that the cost of healthcare under the ACA would balloon have not come to pass. In fact, the rate of increase in the cost of healthcare actually has slowed since the inception of the act (Krugman 2016). Systemic changes, phased in over several years, have occurred as a result of the mandate. Under the ACA, persons earning between 130–400 percent of the poverty level, pro-rated for family size, are eligible for some amount of subsidy from the federal government. Employers have to offer insurance to their employees or incur a tax penalty. In 2015, this provision was enacted for companies with over 100 employees and in 2016 it was extended to those with over 50. Consequently, many companies are cutting back on hours for their workers, so they will not achieve the 30 hours of "full time" employment necessary to require insurance. One example is represented by fast food workers in the Central Valley of California, where workers' hours were cut from 40 to under 30. One Burger King franchise permitted only managers to work full time. The Chamber of Commerce estimates that 60 percent of small businesses or franchises will cut hours to avoid insurance (Dembosky 2016).

Another common employer response is simply to cut back on the number of employees. To avoid tax penalties, a company has to show that employees were offered insurance and declined it. National Public Radio (NPR) reports show how California companies are sidestepping this requirement. For example, many farm workers are hired by contractors as a casual labor force; workers make about ten dollars an hour, when they are working. One contractor, with 100 workers on her payroll, said that insurance would cost the company $30,000 a month, a cost she cannot cover. The workers cannot afford premium payments from their wages. The contractor protects herself against litigation by including a form establishing that the worker declined insurance in the pile of papers the worker must sign to be officially employed. Many of the workers are undocumented and are ineligible for any government assistance, so they remain uninsured. The labor contractors feel the provision of healthcare is an integral aspect of the immigration issue, which they urge Congress to address (Dembosky 2016).

The ACA also provides for the federal government to fund an expansion of the Medicaid program, allowing for persons earning up to 138 percent of the poverty level to qualify, whereas previously income had to be less than the poverty level. The federal government covers all of the increased costs through 2016, and will gradually reduce its portion to 97 percent in 2017, and 90 percent by 2020. Thirty-one states, and the District of Columbia, adopted the Medicaid expansion as of 2016 (Garfield and Damico 2016). Most of the states choosing to opt out of the expansion are Republican governed states and some are reconsidering since, without the Medicaid expansion, they have to assume the burden of the healthcare costs of their poor population. The future of this program is unstable with the Republican administration.

There are elements in the ACA guidelines which remain problematic and have caused criticism of the Act. People who obtain insurance through the exchanges

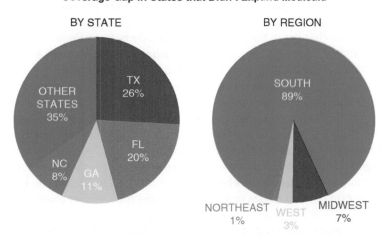

Coverage Gap in States that Didn't Expand Medicaid

BY STATE

BY REGION

Distribution of adults with incomes above Medicaid eligibility limits but below lower limit for tax credits

Figure 9.4 Percentage of population ineligible for either Medicaid or tax subsidies for health insurance
Source: The Kaiser Family Foundation, 2016

still pay a significant amount of their income for coverage and, to stretch their budgets, remain without needed services. Nevertheless, insured persons have access to some tests and treatments previously excluded. These include coverage for tests like mammograms and colonoscopies, with no out of pocket cost. Free preventive measures, such as vaccinations, are a part of the ACA mandate, as are services such as routine gynecologic services for women. Mental health is to be treated with the same coverage as other conditions. Premiums can cost up to 10 percent of a person's income and, when deductibles, co-payments and costs of other services are factored in, the figure can go higher (Rosenthal 2015). Twenty percent of people with insurance report having trouble paying medical bills while 53 percent of people without insurance suffer the same fate (Sanger-Katz 2016). For some medical needs, due to high deductibles, many people have had to dip into savings, work extra hours or jobs, use credit cards, borrow money, or reduce other expenses such as food, heat, and housing to obtain care; some people even have moved their household, or accepted charity, to meet healthcare needs (Sanger-Katz 2016). Some elect to avoid the insurance expense and pay the tax penalty, as a more cost-effective option. In 2015 the penalty was $695, or 2.5 percent of a household's income, whichever is greater (Pear 2015). Although politically tumultuous, the ACA has helped many people and it has been shown that efforts to repeal it will result in as many as 32 million people rejoining the ranks of the uninsured (Luhby 2017). Enrollment for 2018, amid the uncertainty of the ACA's future, outpaced the previous year. This is in spite of increased costs of premiums, 90 percent less advertising funding, and less money for "navigators" who help consumers select plans (Fite 2017).

My Experience with the Affordable Care Act (Obamacare)

I am one of the 5–6 percent of Americans who buy their insurance in the individual marketplace. I currently have a high deductible plan, which is one of the plans that will not meet the minimum requirements of the new law so my old plan is being phased out.

With the changes in the law that have already been implemented, I have already benefited from Obamacare. Before the law changed and health insurance policies were required to cover preventative screenings, I had put off getting a colonoscopy because I would have had to pay for the entire amount myself (the $3000 cost being less than my deductible).

My family history for colon cancer is downright scary. My father and both of his parents had colon cancer. My father was diagnosed at age 45 and died 4 years later from the disease after "living" with several surgeries, radiation treatment and chemotherapy during his last years. His mother lived into her 80s before succumbing to the disease and his father died of other causes in his 50s before the colon cancer could get him.

In the years leading up to and past the age that my father was diagnosed and then died of colon cancer, I had a nagging fear that the disease would visit me also.

Finally, in my later 50s, the ACA changed what my policy was required to cover and I scheduled my test since my insurance company was now required to pick up the tab.

Years of stress melted in relief when I saw the photos of my healthy, pink colon after my test. Another test isn't needed for 10 years. The peace of mind I was able to experience because of the new law is more valuable even than the money I was able to save.

I recently found out through coveroregon.com that I qualify for a substantial subsidy toward my health insurance premiums under the new law. So although my current plan is being phased out, I have the choice of upgrading my plan and keeping my premiums about the same or paying even less, or signing up for a similar (but better) plan to the one I currently have and paying much less than I have been.

I am sure there are hundreds of thousands, and probably eventually millions of stories similar to mine. I understand that there are a small percentage of people who will end up paying more for health insurance, but almost all of them are so well off that they do not qualify for government subsidies. Most of these people can afford to pay a bit more.

There is a lot of noise from the people who want to kill, stop, impede and otherwise throw a monkey wrench into what is being called Obamacare. The true source of this noise is not anyone who actually cares about helping people – it is about protecting power and money. Too bad the press has been giving this B.S. so much airtime.

If I had my way, there would be universal healthcare for everyone – but the political climate makes that impossible right now. I think the Affordable Care Act is probably about as much improvement to our broken healthcare system as we could have hoped for right now.

(John G., Ashland Oregon, http://obamacarefacts.com/obamacare-stories)

Systemic Challenges in Healthcare

Although the ACA has widened the accessibility of insurance, the Act failed to accomplish any restructuring of the system or any cost containment measures for services, tests, or pharmaceuticals. Length of average hospital stays have decreased. Though a shorter stay is not always bad for the well-being of the patient, it has been linked to increases in ER visits and "observational status" visits. Frakt (2016) suggests the shortened hospital stays are in direct response to a Medicare program which links the length of a stay to specific diagnoses. If the hospital releases the patient before the allotted days, it can earn the hospital some savings. It is a gamble because readmission within 30 days can cause the hospital to lose money. Consequently, financing decisions, rather than medical ones, determine admission and discharge schedules (Frakt 2016).

Hidden costs also contribute to the price of surgeries. An increasingly common practice allows for calling in "contract workers," including "assistant surgeons," during a surgery. The patient will sign a packet of consent forms not realizing the potential for huge out of network expenses. Patients can be billed separately for any "contractual worker" attending to them, when a nurse or other staff person could have provided the service. These practices are expensive, stressful for the patient, and contribute to the exorbitant 2.7 trillion-dollar annual healthcare bill. Disputes regarding out of network charges are now the leading complaint at the New York state agency which regulates insurance companies (Rosenthal 2014).

Cost containment measures remain unaddressed by the ACA. Only mandated federal programs, such as Medicaid or Medicare, put a cap on charges. For example, Medicare sets a price for knee replacement of about $12,000, slightly adjusted for location, with private insurance bills anywhere from $3400–$55,800, varying even within a city (Quealy and Sanger-Katz 2015). In the open market, prices for procedures cover a wide range and the final cost to the patient frequently is undiscoverable until after the fact. Colonoscopies, for example, used to be done in doctors' offices for under a thousand dollars (Rosenthal 2013). In 2000, the American College of Gastroenterologists recommended colonoscopies as the preferred method for screening for colon cancer even though there are cheaper, equally effective procedures. The prevalence of the procedures ballooned even though "studies have not clearly shown that a colonoscopy prevents colon cancer or death better than other procedures" (Rosenthal 2013). The average cost of the procedure ranges from 2000 to 9000 dollars, depending on where the procedure is performed and by whom. Clinics establish a "facility" use fee and payments for the specialist performing the procedure, the anesthesiologist, and other clinic expenses. One colonoscopy in Durham NC was billed at $19,438, including removal of one polyp (Rosenthal 2013).

Costs of diagnostic tests also vary and are largely unrelated to actual costs of the procedure. Diagnostic testing has become "a profit center with large and arbitrary markups" (Rosenthal 2014). Some of the testing could be done with less expensive machines though the medical professionals maintain the more expensive models. Echo-cardiograms, for example, exhibit a huge range of pricing, and often are ordered when they are not indicated. New technology has created pocket-sized echocardiogram machines that provide snapshots of the heart which are billed for as little as $700 or as much as $12,000. New pocket-sized echocardiogram machines can be purchased for $10,000 and easily carried and utilized by primary physicians (Rosenthal 2014a). Low-cost medical procedures frequently are billed at highly inflated prices. For example, Americans are billed at four times the rate for hip replacements and three times the cost for C-sections than in other countries (Rosenthal 2013).

Another inflationary element of the healthcare system concerns the coding and billing of services, obtaining pre-approval, and other administrative support tasks, estimated to cost 25–32 percent of the total healthcare budget. Administration costs alone are estimated to be 20–30 percent of the $2.7 trillion healthcare bill (Rosenthal 2014). Hospital and insurance executives are the best paid personnel in the health field. An insurance chief executive makes an average of $584,000 and a hospital administrator about $237,000. Insurance executives often get a compensation package worth much more when stocks and other options are figured in. By comparison, the average general doctor makes about $185,000 and a surgeon about $306,000. Average nursing salaries are $61,000 a year while the corresponding figure for emergency medical technicians is $27,000 (Rosenthal 2014). The US physician pool relies disproportionately on the employment of specialists, with only one third *generalists* (which include pediatricians), a decrease from almost one half in 1961 (Frances 2017). In other countries' systems, the generalist/specialist ratio is reversed. Generalists make considerably less than specialists and often supervise treatments for many problems once the specialist has devised a treatment plan. The US is experiencing a shortage of generalists, particularly in less desirable rural areas and inner cities lacking a major research university. Though these shortages pre-date the ACA, they are becoming more dramatic with the increased enrollments of the ACA.

Pharmaceutical Issues

Common pharmaceutical company practices make the industry one of the most profitable. The last several years have witnessed price upsurges, even in generic drugs, making many prescriptions prohibitively expensive (Gutt 2016). Some patients are being charged as much as $100,000 for a drug, though the actual cost is a small fraction of that amount. The industry attributes the high cost of drugs to the expenses involved with research, though expenditures on advertising are more accurately the culprits (Goodman 2007). In one year, GlaxoSmithKline spent 99 million dollars to advertise Advair while Merck spent 46.3 million dollars to push Nasonex in the market (Rosenthal 2013). Profit margins for the five largest companies were 20 percent or more in 2013 (Anderson 2014). The cost of drugs is 10 percent of the total annual $2.7 trillion healthcare bill. Pharmaceutical lobbying expenditures are $250 million annually. The pharmaceutical industry spent $272,000 in campaign donations **per member of Congress** and has more lobbyists than Congress has members. The lobby focuses on preventing the government from bargaining for the cost of drugs on Medicare. The lack of price control in pharmaceuticals amounts to a 50 billion dollar annual gift to the companies (Kristof 2016).

Box 9.6 – Issues Affecting Costs in the System

Cost containment refers to measures which limit the costs of services. Private insurance plans have no limits on the pricing of diagnostic tests, clinical services, surgeries, or medications. As a result, fees for the same procedures can vary widely. Most of the time the consumer is not informed of the costs until after services are rendered. The only caps on costs are in the publicly funded programs such as Medicaid and Medicare, causing some physicians and facilities to deny coverage to these patients. A large portion of the costs of healthcare are attributable to administrative costs associated with billing, pre-approval, and coding.

Pharma refers to the whole industry involved with the development and sale of pharmaceuticals. The purchasing of drugs accounts for 10 percent of the cost of the healthcare system. Theoretically regulated by the Food and Drug Administration (FDA), there are few, if any, limitations on consumers' medication costs. The FDA regulates the patenting, development, and approval of new drugs and treatments. The efficacy of drugs often is not established by research. Patenting is frequently controlled by a company which either produces a slightly changed version of a drug, extending the patent, or pays other companies to refrain from issuing a comparable drug. Congress is heavily lobbied, by the pharmaceutical industry, which has been successful in controlling limiting government regulations.

Controlling the availability of generic drugs is one way drug companies obtain exorbitant prices while retaining a monopolistic advantage. Because of changes in regulations and pricing, drugs were more likely to become generic 20 years ago than now (Rosenthal 2013). When a drug company's patent is running out, it will either pay other companies not to make a competing product or it will create a new product, slightly different in formula, to re-patent. Companies buy up rights to drugs and lock out competitors. They also refuse to allow drugs sold over the counter elsewhere to become non-prescription since people generally will not pay more than about 20 dollars for over the counter products. Evidence suggests that just a simple threat to control US prescription drug prices will lead to companies reducing prices in order to avoid government regulation (Frakt 2016).

In the US, regulations mandate that drugs must be available to everyone, regardless of cost or effectiveness, while other countries make do with similar drugs. In Europe, commonly used drugs, like those used in cancer treatments or for treatment of parasitic infections, cost about half of what people pay in the US (Bach 2015). In Europe, where providers can limit the drugs available to patients, the reduction in available drugs is not dramatic. Germany maintains the availability of 97 percent of the drugs found in the US and France provides for 86 percent availability (Bach 2015). In 2015, the executive of Turing Pharmaceuticals ignited a scandal when he purchased the rights to a drug for parasitic infections, previously sold in the US for $13.50 a dose, and raised the cost to $750.00. A similar product, benzidazole, available for treating a parasitic infection affecting 300,000 Latin American immigrants in the US, was available free of cost, but only from the CDC. The onerous paperwork dissuaded its use. If the FDA sells the rights to bring the drug to market it is feared that it would cost about 60–100 thousand dollars for a round of treatment (Pollack 2015). The same drug is available in Latin America for between 50 and 100 dollars for a month's supply (Pollack 2015).

Many drug companies' practices violate the public trust. The documentary *Big Bucks, Big Pharma* (Goodman 2007) reveals a host of these activities. A particularly egregious practice concerns making relatively rare conditions sound "normal" and in need of medication. One example concerns the alleged "restless legs syndrome," which is not typically medically dangerous. Another case concerns "social anxiety," which is frequently just a person who is shy or reserved, and not in need of medical treatment. Some behavioral supports might be beneficial in creating a more satisfying life but medication is likely unnecessary and potentially comes with side effects. Sometimes prescribed drugs actually show no efficacy in treating symptoms. The documentary also highlights how the guidelines for prescribing a medication can change by increasing the parameters of "pathology," extending the range of people who require them and garnering more revenue.

Another strategy promotes the use of an established drug for new purposes, as in the case of Selective Serotonin Reuptake Inhibitors (SSRIs) like Prozac, now used for anxiety and a range of mood disorders, though its original use was specifically for major depression. When a drug is approved for new conditions, the patent is extended, potentially expanding profits by tens of millions of dollars. Amy Goodman (2007) illustrates this point by quoting a Paxil (an SSRI drug) product manager as stating, "Every marketer's dream is to find an unidentified or unknown market and develop it. That's what we were able to do with social anxiety disorder" (Goodman 2007). The company's public relations department waged a wide campaign for the condition warranting the drug, even getting the media to highlight the condition in feature stories.

Much controversy surrounds the use of statins, a drug for reducing cholesterol levels. Changing the parameters for the diagnosis of problematic levels of cholesterol ballooned the prescriptions for the drugs. New guidelines issued by cardiologists in November 2013 would increase the users of statins from 43.2 million Americans to 56 million, or one half of adults 40–75 (Pollack 2015). The extended criteria designate a population that actually has not been shown to benefit from the drug and the use of the drugs has been emphatically contested (Goodman 2007; Pollack 2015; Moyer 2012). The effectiveness of primary statin use, defined as occurring *before* any cardio-vascular disease is present, has not been supported by research since most studies of the drug relied on a population already diagnosed as suffering from heart disease. The initial use of statins was for secondary care of people who already had a cardio-vascular event or diagnosis (Moyer 2012). The ill effects of statins, according to some experts, make them undesirable, especially if their efficacy is uncertain.

Another drug issue, rarely addressed in the media, concerns the prevalence of shortages. Consistent shortages occur in anesthetics, painkillers, and certain cancer drugs. Sometimes alternative treatments are substituted, even though they present a greater risk of side effects, medication errors, and disease progression or death (Fink 2016). Many patients are unaware of the fact that treatment delays, or the provision of alternative treatments, stem from drug shortages. These problems have no universal solution. Some organizations prioritize young people, or people who could benefit the most from the treatment, while others just resort to a "first come, first served" approach. The Cleveland Clinic compensates by mixing its own compound to compensate for shortages (Fink 2016). The causes of the shortages vary; sometimes the companies deliberately under-produce medications, while other times components are hard to obtain. Current drug shortages impact over 150 drugs (Eban n.d.).

Sex and Race Issues

Epidemiology is the branch of science dealing with the frequency, prevalence, and distribution of diseases, and other health factors, in a population (Epidemiology n.d.). Research concerning the efficacy of treatments is often done with a restricted subject pool. Drug effects frequently are disparate by sex, age, race, and ethnicity but the research does not address these differences. For example, women who take statins appear to show a higher likelihood of developing diabetes than men. Adolescent use of anti-depressants shows elevations of suicidal ideation and proclivities. These outcomes were not seen in early research because they were tested only on limited subjects.

Group differences also are seen in the presentation of symptoms of disease. Heart disease is the number one killer of American women; more women than men die annually from heart disease. Until the last several decades there was no recognition that women's symptoms deviated from those of men. Women typically present with milder chest pain or discomfort, or even no chest pain, but express the disease by nausea, sweating, dizziness, and fatigue (Mayo Clinic 2017). Shortness of breath and flu like symptoms are also more commonly associated with heart symptoms in women (AHA 2017).

Longevity and prevalence of particular diseases also differ by sex (Castillo 2015). The cause of these differences has not been identified but chief contenders are chromosomes and hormones. Some evidence suggests that women's double X chromosome is protective. Women's immune system cells stay active to older ages. Women have twice the inflammation proteins in their immune cells, leading to higher incidences of auto-immune diseases such as lupus, multiple sclerosis, rheumatoid arthritis, and Type 1 diabetes. Auto-immune diseases are notoriously difficult to diagnose and treat and are not well understood. Three quarters of auto-immune diagnoses are in women (O'Rourke 2013). Women's greater susceptibility to auto-immune diseases also has been linked to sex differences in intestinal bacteria which can affect immunological responses (Burne 2013). Men's immune systems are not as responsive as women's and there seems to be some evidence that testosterone "dampens down" the immune system, perhaps increasing vulnerability to certain cancer cells. One proposal suggests that lowering testosterone levels will boost the male immune response and research is being conducted to test this thesis (Burne 2013).

Racial disparities in US cardio-vascular disease (CVD) are alarming. The rate of hypertension (high blood pressure) is higher among African Americans, and the age of onset lower, than for people of African descent living elsewhere (AHA n.d.; Collins 2015). A partial explanation lies in the greater rates of obesity and diabetes in the population but stressors relating to racial discrimination also are implicated. Death from CVD, adjusted for age, is 33 percent higher in Blacks than Whites. African Americans are also twice as likely to experience a stroke and more likely to die from it. American Indians and Alaska Natives also have a higher death rate from CVD with 36 percent dying before the age of 65 compared to 17 percent of the general population (AHA n.d.). According to the Black Women's Health Imperative (2017), 49 percent of Black women over 20 have heart disease, and most Black women are unaware of the risk.

Access to healthcare is still skewed by race and class. Even with the ACA, thirty-three million Americans remain uninsured and one half of these are minorities (Castillo 2016). Variations in treatment plans also persist:

Implicit stereotypes about how different groups deserve to be treated may also affect the health care that minorities and women receive. Studies, for example,

Figure 9.5 Stress relief is thought to help in reducing cardio-vascular diseases. Meditation has been shown to be significant in reducing blood pressure and other stress-related measures
Source: kali9 / istockphoto.com

have shown that African-American patients are prescribed less pain medication than white patients with similar complaints. During childbirth, women often experience "poor treatment ... including abusive, neglectful, or disrespectful care," a report published in the Public Library of Science revealed. A 2014 survey of 2,000 women highlighted how out of tune doctors can be with their female patients when they experience pain. Forty-five percent of respondents, for example, said their doctor told them "the pain is all in your head."

(Collins 2015)

The rate of medical school admissions for individuals in minority groups is low. Some suggest that diversification of healthcare professionals can be effective in reducing some of the disparities in the system (Collins 2015).

The *lesbian, gay, bisexual, transgendered, and queer* (LGBTQ) communities are all subjected to discrimination in healthcare. Many practitioners are unfamiliar with the health needs of these groups and some are uncomfortable treating them. Additionally, many people in these groups are reluctant to seek healthcare since they fear being mistreated and/or misunderstood. Gay and lesbian individuals report discrimination in healthcare settings and this is compounded for persons of color. Thirty-one percent of transgendered persons report lack of access to healthcare (Ulaby 2017; Neel 2017; Prichep 2017).

How Are Sociological Perspectives Applied to Healthcare Systems?

Structural functionalists feel that the healthcare system is generally working well. These theorists would suggest that even what some consider flaws in the system actually are functional for the sustenance of the system. The system creates jobs in healthcare delivery, insurance, pharmaceuticals, and government agencies. Employment opportunities extend to multiple healthcare roles. Support staff, administrators, clinicians, lab techs, insurance personnel, and research scientists are integral to the system. At costs nearing 18 percent of the GDP, healthcare contributes significantly to the economy. The government protects the safety of the population through the licensing and regulation of healthcare professionals and facilities. Functionalists would suggest that any inequities inherent in a capitalist system are inevitable because they promote competition for clients and for innovative procedures and patents. The better care some receive is seen as motivation for social mobility. These theorists would point to government programs which help the needy as sufficient to sustain basic needs. Functionalists might support "tweaking" the system but they would not advocate major changes.

Functionalist also believe that medicine contributes to the overall stasis of society by permitting some variation in social roles. The institutional roles of illness and healthcare are viewed as playing a social function. Clinicians can not only supervise treatment but they also support the "patient" and intervene in work by regulating the medical leaves and financial compensation. The *sick role* allows for special treatment of a person, up to a certain extent, to tend to health concerns. Generally, there are limits to the tolerance of the sick role; a person who is seen to malinger is violating the sick role by not getting better and resuming "normal" roles. Ill people gain social sympathy which can dissipate if they don't comply with the other demands of the sick role to get better. Health, and illness, are conditions which support cultural values of work, discipline, and responsibility. A temporary "leave" from these, in a Durkheimian perspective, serves to remind us of the general expectations to return to productive social roles or suffer informal, and formal, consequences. Accordingly, American culture is not sympathetic to the needs of people with chronic conditions or disabilities, who are largely unsupported by social institutions.

Conflict theorists do not share the benevolent views of the functionalists. The conflict theorists highlight the ways in which the healthcare system perpetuates inequality by providing for disparate care based on race, sex, social class, and employment status. Not only would they view the differential access to care as a consequence of privilege but they would point out that the ill health of the poor reproduces these inequalities. They would maintain that the privileged class has little incentive to make affordable care universal when it can get away with not providing it. They might suggest that some people should have better access because they "earned" it by working. Conflict theorists would also highlight the lack of regulations in the system which contribute to substantial corporate profits for services and drugs. Medicaid and Medicare also support the system by contributing revenues for people who otherwise would not generate income for the system. Additionally, counting health insurance premiums as part of a person' wages allows for the depression of salaries and serves to keep people tethered to their jobs. These theorists suggest that with so much to gain, and lobbyists to help secure it, there is little likelihood of fundamental systemic change, though, unlike the functionalists, they would support major changes such as universal coverage.

Symbolic interactionism focuses on symbolic issues relating to the healthcare system. These theorists look at "normal" life processes and analyze how they are defined and controlled by the healthcare system. They also look at the sick role in "micro" level analysis and analyze how it can be utilized in social interaction to get the "patient" sympathy or support from family, friends, and co-workers and other special treatment. A time-limited "vacation" from the usual roles can be beneficial, to the person and to the social system, as long as it isn't sustained. Symbolic interactionists will view labels associated with health and illness and analyze their integration into society. For example, certain disability labels will earn the individual social support, including disability payments, while others will not. Some will earn a person sympathy while others, such as "addict," are more likely to be met with intolerance. They will look at how these factors impact the "career" of the person in the sick role, legitimizing some while stigmatizing others. Certain illnesses tend to be seen as malingering, by definition, and the person suffering from them may have to fight for disability supports. Chronic fatigue syndrome and fibromyalgia are sometimes treated as psychological rather than originating in an organic cause, and so the burden of cure can be leveled at the individual rather than the medical establishment. These theorists would advocate activism to publicize the consequences of labels and to promote social roles devoid of stigma.

Have Medical Conditions Proliferated?

The term *medicalization* has been used to describe natural life events or conditions which are increasingly treated as "*diseases*" requiring medical intervention. Physical differences, mental conditions, and the processes surrounding childbirth and dying represent a few examples. Some people who fall into these categories, and their supporters, view the designation of "disease" or "illness" as a means of social control.

Disability Issues

The *Disability Rights Movement*, inspired by the civil rights movement of the 1960s, promoted the rights of 50 million "disabled" Americans to be independent. Advocates promoted the disabled to be seen as whole human beings entitled to the rights and living standards of the rest of the population (ADL n.d.). The rights of the disabled to access public spaces and health services and to achieve full inclusion are central to the activists. Shedding the devaluation of the label *disabled* also was a central theme. More recently a *Disability Justice Movement* has emerged which articulates demands moving beyond issues of accessibility, language, and logistics. They critique the cultural notions of what constitutes a "body," rejecting the standard of a universal "norm." They assert that just as White and male are not inherently the mandate for legitimacy in sex and race, ability should not be defined as setting a physical or biological standard: "There is no neutral body from which our bodies deviate" (Morales n.d.).

Disability *Justice* Activists promote a more politicized message than advocates supporting *Rights*. Disability Justice demands include seeking community reform and contesting the oppressions of the capitalistic, heterosexist, misogynistic,

White-dominant power structure. They maintain (n.d.) that these structures also create the invisibility of other oppressed groups, such as the transgendered, queer, or indigent in addition to the more standardly recognized categories of nondominant groups in sex, race, ethnicity, religion, and ability. They do not seek *inclusion* but *transformation*. To define the "disabled" permits the "abled" to feel better and to claim an entitled privilege without awareness of this benefit, much as Ta'Nehisi Coates (2015) argues that White privilege depends on the subordination and dehumanization of all other groups (see Chapter 8). Disability Justice activists proclaim the normative state of physical independence as a bias of the privileged. They raise the issue as to why independence is more essential or "better" than inter-dependence. They contend that inter-dependence of humans is the actual state of the human condition and promote this as the desired state for all people.

Mental illness is another component of the disability movement, comprising the largest grouping under the designation of *disability*. Neuropsychiatric illnesses are the leading cause of disability, according to the *National Institute for Mental Health* (including both neurological disorders and behavioral and mental ones) (NIMH n.d.). It includes everything from diagnoses of depression, autism, dementia, and learning disabilities, to eating disorders. Assessments garnered from government disability claims disagree with this ranking (CDA n.d.), suggesting that separating behavioral and mental disorders from neurological illnesses drops their prevalence.

One element in the ACA mandates that mental health benefits be equivalent to those provided for physical health, though this has failed to reach many of the affected population. Some people suffering from mental ailments feel they are blamed for their conditions while others believe that their "conditions" are just different ways of being in the world and should not be defined as illness. Mental health activists discourage the view that these are medical conditions requiring "management" by experts. The medical model of health assumes a particular desired norm and defines any deviation as "sick" or "abnormal," requiring expert intervention. This creates a narrow view of health and relegates a portion of the population to a lesser social status.

The Council for Disability (CDA) lists muscular/connective tissue disorders as the leading cause of federal disability claims, according to government agencies. The corresponding placement for mental disorders is fifth, for established claims, and fourth for long-term claims. Mental illness is pervasive, though it may not be diagnosed and/or treated. Twenty percent of the population expresses at least one symptom of depression in a given month (MHA n.d.). Mental health activists promote defining the mentally ill as "different" rather than needing to be "fixed."

Eating disorders include five categories and are the leading cause of deaths associated with mental conditions (NEDA n.d.). The sex and racial/ethnic ratios with respect to eating disorders have reached parity, with the exception of *Anorexia Nervosa*, which is more prevalent in non-Hispanic Whites (NEDA n.d.). People exhibiting eating disorders are very likely to have seen a healthcare practitioner, including a counselor, a general practitioner, and/or a social services provider but only in a small portion of these visits are they identified as exhibiting issues related to eating, weight, or health and so the sufferer is not appropriately diagnosed or

Figure 9.6 Eating disorders are the leading cause of death from mental illness
Source: Photographee.eu / Shutterstock.com

offered services. This suggests that practitioners still possess insufficient knowledge regarding the identification and intervention of eating disorders. Eating disorders are exceptionally underfunded when compared to other conditions. Per patient expenditures are 93 cents compared to 88 dollars per autistic patient and 81 dollars for schizophrenia.

Box 9.7 – Medicalization and Personal Rights

The term **medicalization** refers to identifying a medical condition where none actually exists. This has resulted in the loss of personal control over certain life experiences and in marginalizing a portion of the population. This trend has resulted in stigmatizing portions of the population, over-medicating, and imposing universal standards on diverse populations.

The **Disability Rights Movement**, originating in the 1960s, promotes the disabled to be seen as whole human beings entitled to the rights and living standards of the rest of the population. The rights of the disabled to access public spaces and health services, and to shed the label *of disabled* with its connotation of subordination, are core objectives of the movement. The goal sought is full inclusion.

The **Disability Justice Movement** goes beyond fighting for the "rights" of the disabled. The movement promotes the concept that there is no fixed standard of the "correct" body and that differences should not be interpreted as being in need of "fixing." The *Disability Justice Movement* challenges ideas of what it means to be a "productive" member of society, promoting the inherent worth and contributions of all human beings. They suggest that independence is not the inherent goal but rather inter-dependence, which is understood as the "natural" state of humanity.

Mental illnesses include difficulties in *mood, thought, or behavior*. These can range from extreme conditions in which a person cannot function adequately for a period of time, such as clinical depression or schizophrenia, to less severe mood and personality difficulties. Learning disabilities, eating disorders, and brain disorders such as autism are also considered as part of the mental health category. Mental health activists are bringing attention to the difficulties faced by people diagnosed with mental illness and promoting the idea that such people, like those with other disabilities, do not need to be "fixed" but fully accepted just as they are. One element uniting all mental illness designations is the *stigma*, or negative associations they carry.

The proliferation in the diagnosis of learning disabilities has raised questions regarding the etiology of these conditions. Some feel that the significance of these categorizations is most essential for producing chronic drug prescriptions. Specifically, the excessive reliance on prescriptive drugs for treating Attention Deficit Disorders, which reached the level of 9 billion dollars in 2012, has been challenged. Costs of treatment escalate when counseling, doctor visits, and academic interventions are included. As many as one in five high school boys receive the diagnosis (Briody 2013). Boys outnumber girls in the diagnostics category by a factor greater than 2:1 (CDCa n.d.). As many as 11 percent of the population aged 4–17 have been diagnosed as having Attention Deficit Disorder with Hyperactivity (ADHD). Whether the increase in the diagnosis is a result of expanding criteria, or to more attention to looking for "symptoms," the increased use of prescriptive drugs is considered suspect (Herman 2015). Some experts suggest that youths diagnosed with alleged attention deficit conditions do not fit the official diagnostic criteria. They suggest that some labeled as having ADHD would be better served by innovations in the classroom, rather than in the pharmacy. They point to the deficiencies in classroom management and resources as the source of the "bad" behaviors. Moving children into special education classrooms has been suggested as exacerbating the problems by stigmatizing students and affixing them with a harmful label. Additionally, assigning children to special ed classrooms siphons money from mainstream classrooms. Such segregation is considered detrimental to both groups of students (see Chapter 11).

Childbirth Issues

Medicalization issues can also be seen in the history of childbirth. In the mid-twentieth century, birthing moved from the domain of women, in the person of lay and nurse midwives, to that of men in the specialty of obstetrics and gynecology. Today 64 percent of ob/gyns are male, though when birth first became the purview of medical doctors they were almost exclusively men. Hospital births became prevalent in the 1950s and 1960s although they were seen earlier among privileged urban residents. As medicine took over childbirth, it also mandated certain protocols for the course of labor and delivery, compromising the natural process of the woman, and resulting in undesired and unnecessary interventions.

Today's advanced diagnostic testing and technological interventions can save the lives and promote the well-being of both babies and mothers. At the same time, interventions also can create concern where there is no indication of a problem. Such designations lead to further intervention and poor outcomes for the mother, the baby, or both. In the 1970s, a movement to "take back" control of childbirth was initiated. Natural childbirth, with relaxation and breathing approaches, gained adherents. Other innovations, such as water immersion childbirths, also were introduced (Lothian and DeVries 2005; McCutcheon 1996; Bradley 1981; ACNM 2016). Women articulated preferences for midwife deliveries, viewing them as more "woman centered." Lay midwives, trained outside the medical establishment, are sometimes seen as more responsive to the mother than traditionally trained nurses and nurse midwives, who are trained in medical fields and licensed by government agencies. *Certified nurse practitioners* are both nurses and midwives (MANA n.d.).

Many hospitals and medical practices now offer a *nurse midwife* delivery option. Not only do women prefer the midwife delivery but it is less expensive than a doctor assisted birth. For "low risk' births, those having no indication of any potential complication, midwife deliveries are, at the very least, as safe as doctor-assisted deliveries (MANA n.d.). A recent study of 17,000 births of planned home deliveries with low-risk mothers showed no increase in adverse outcomes for mother or babies and the rate of cesarean section was 5.2 percent compared to 31 percent nationally (MANA n.d.).

In addition to a birthing professional, many women choose to have a *doula*, or birthing attendant. These "lay" women are trained to assist the mother in the pregnancy, birthing, and early parenting of a newborn. *Doulas* are associated with

Figure 9.7 Natural childbirth has proliferated in recent decades; one approach is to have a water birth
Source: myrrha / istockphoto.com

greater comfort and better outcomes in childbirth, nursing, and early adjustment to mothering. It is ironic that in the 1950s, when becoming a mother was considered the ultimate goal of the feminine role (Friedan 1963), the process of becoming one was the most impersonal and medicalized in modern times. At that time, partners were remanded to waiting rooms and the pregnant woman typically received drugs rendering her unconscious.

Illness and Death Issues

Life expectancy has increased by an average of about 25 years since 1900. The aging population is expanding and so are their medical needs, though on the whole they are healthier than earlier generations. Today, four out of five adults, 50 and over, have a chronic condition, such as diabetes, hypertension, cardio-vascular disease, or depression. One half of this population has more than one condition (AARP n.d.). Many of these can be managed with medications or lifestyle changes. As the boomers reach Medicare eligibility, the pressures on the system will be extensive.

With all the medical interventions, *end of life* costs are exorbitant. Reports assert that "30 percent of all Medicare expenditures are attributed to the 5 percent of beneficiaries that die each year, with 1/3 of that cost occurring in the last month of life" (Bell 2013). Some suggest that rather than sustain these costs, people should be able to elect discontinuance of treatment (Gawande 2014), with informed consent, and supported to die at home. Almost nine out of ten Americans, in a Gallup survey, say they would like to die at home, surrounded by family and friends (NHPCO n.d.). The hospice movement has emerged to help people to orchestrate more of the process of dying. Hospice care can be elected when death is imminent, defined as likely to occur in less than six months. Hospice provides visiting nurses and aides to help people remain at home, access pain control measures, and be made as comfortable as possible until the end of life (care is not terminated if a person is still alive after six months). This palliative care, offering comfort and ceasing medical intervention, is the essence of the US hospice movement which began in 1974. It is estimated that well over one and a half million deaths are supervised by hospice services today.

Box 9.8 – Medicalization of Life and Death

Childbirth became the exclusive domain of the medical establishment by the mid-twentieth century. Up until that time it was attended by midwives, most of them trained outside of the medical field. The process of childbirth became controlled by medical protocol, attended by physicians or medically trained midwives. Child birthing became "managed" by the medical field to the detriment of the experience of the mothers and children. A movement was formed to promote the enhancement of the experience for mothers and newborns and to promote more healthy outcomes and minimal medical intervention. Many systems now employ medically trained midwives to achieve this goal, which also frequently costs less than doctor-assisted births. Doulas, or lay birth attendants, support women in childbirth and the care of newborns and also have been documented as contributing to superior outcomes.

The **hospice** movement is a program supporting the terminal patient by alleviating pain and offering support services, usually at home, but sometimes in a facility. Hospice care is initiated when medical intervention is considered ineffective, or undesirable, and a person is judged to have fewer than six months to live.

The **right to die**, sometimes referred to as **"death with dignity,"** concerns the right of a terminal person to request a doctor-assisted suicide. Currently, five states have *right to die* laws which clearly elaborate conditions to be met to qualify for such aid. The right to die is very controversial; it goes against many people's religious or ethical beliefs and some doctors feel it violates the Hippocratic oath.

Some people advocate more decisive action with regard to dying. The right to take one's own life, when life is judged to be "not worth living," is controversial and the subject of recent legislation. Suicide "rights" are strongly contested by some, regardless of the severity of a person's illness or outside of any personal desires. For some, suicide violates religious beliefs, while for others it crosses ethical values. Some doctors perceive doctor-assisted suicide as a violation of the Hippocratic oath. Nevertheless, there are some people who feel the right to die with dignity should be a basic human right and there are some clinicians who support it. Five states have

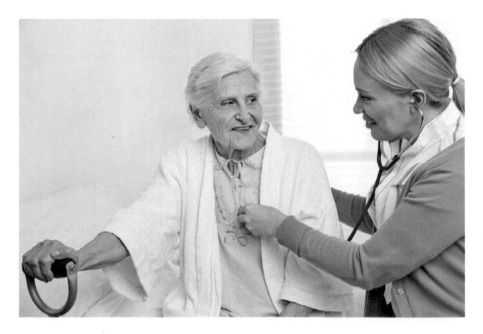

Figure 9.8 Most ill or dying people prefer to stay at home, with home visits for treatment and monitoring
Source: Robert Kneschke / Shutterstock.com

"right to doctor-assisted suicide laws." The breadth of these laws is clearly limited. To invoke the laws, two physicians must agree that the prognosis establishes that the person has less than six months to live; has the mental competency to make the decision; and is not under any pressure to choose assisted suicide. Oregon was the first to pass such a law, in 1998, and so it offers the most comprehensive data available. The state recorded 218 people as receiving prescriptions in 2015 and 132 as having died from these drugs by January 1, 2016 (OHA 2016). In California, where the state legislature approved a 2015 bill regarding the "right to die," there was no assurance that Governor Jerry Brown would sign the bill. Since Governor Brown was educated in Jesuit institutions, no one had been willing to predict his action. In October of 2015, he signed the bill with the following explanation:

"In the end, I was left to reflect on what I would want in the face of my own death," Brown wrote in a signing message. "I do not know what I would do if I were dying in prolonged and excruciating pain. I am certain, however, that it would be a comfort to be able to consider the options afforded by this bill. And I wouldn't deny that right to others."

(McGreevy 2015)

Many people who theoretically support the right to die might not be able to predict the choices they would make once in the actual circumstances where a decision is needed. The issue has received wider press in recent years with the book and movie *Still Alice* (Genova 2007, 2009; Glatzer and Westmoreland 2014), centering around the question of the suicide of a woman suffering from early onset Alzheimer's disease. The character, Alice, sets up a system of reminders to kill herself

Figure 9.9 The much-publicized activism of Brittany Maynard to end her own life, as she suffered from terminal brain cancer, was part of the campaign to pass the CA legislation ensuring the "right to die"
Source: Carl Costas / AP Images

when she arrives at a time when she will not want to live. As her disease progresses, she ultimately changes her mind. By contrast, an actual Alzheimer's sufferer, whose story was featured in the *New York Times* magazine, chooses suicide. Sandra Bem, a retired Cornell University psychology professor, obtained a lethal prescription through a mail order service. She expressed a strong determination of the point at which she would invoke her choice and was supported by her family and close friends. By all accounts, she had no ambivalence regarding her decision to choose her time to die (Henig 2015).

The *right to die*, sometimes referred to as *"death with dignity,"* evokes intensive emotional responses. The social climate is moving towards promoting compassion for the terminally ill (Gawande 2014). Beyond the humane aspects, there are concerns regarding the high costs of medical interventions and the need for limiting medical expenditures. In 2015, the Republicans repealed a part of the ACA which would have established an Independent Payment Advisory Board tasked with making recommendations of how to contain Medicare expenditures. This panel had been constructed to look for ways to cut costs while maintaining coverage and treatment but fears of denial of treatments ultimately led to its demise (Stromberg 2015). The issue is likely to become increasingly urgent, as the baby boomers fill the ranks of the elderly.

Key Terms

Health   Mediterranean Diet   Health Status   Longevity   Fee for Service   Health Maintenance Organization (HMO)   Preferred Providers Organization   Patient Protection and Affordable Care Act (ACA)   Epidemiology   Sick Role   Medicalization   Disability Rights Movement   Disability Justice Movement   Eating Disorders   Midwives   Hospice   Right to Die

---

Concept Review

What Is Health?
Health is defined as "a state of complete physical, mental, and social well-being, and not merely the absence of disease or infirmity" (WHO). Health maintenance is supported by a good diet; sufficient exercise; secure and safe housing; reproductive freedom; and environmental and public health protections through established social policies. Access to comprehensive healthcare is also fundamental in maintaining health. Poverty and discrimination have been recognized as persistent stressors affecting health and implicated in the poor health of the impoverished and nondominant group members.

What Is the Status of the Health of the Population in the United States?
Overall, the status of Americans' health compares unfavorably to comparable countries. Our **obesity** rate is the highest in the developed world and our **longevity** among the lowest. The well-being of our aged population compares negatively to measures in other developed countries. The US is the only developed country which fails to provide universal, comprehensive healthcare to its citizens. We also rank poorly with respect to "avoidable mortality." Leading causes of preventable death in the US are smoking,

obesity, and alcohol. Our infant mortality rate also is higher than in comparable countries.

How Is the US Healthcare System Structured?

A *fee-for-service* system characterized healthcare for most of the history of US healthcare. In such a system, a person is billed per service and is responsible for payment. If they are insured, then the insurance covers part, or in some cases, all of the cost. Most plans contain a co-payment and an annual deductible. The Nixon administration passed a bill in the 1970s promoting Health Maintenance Organizations (HMOs), where the insurance and service provider are the same entity. In this system, payments are made to the institution all year though the person may be responsible for co-payments and/or deductibles. The insured person does not receive a bill for each service. A significant portion of the American population is subscribed to HMO plans.

Until the **Affordable Care Act (ACA)** was passed in 2010, close to one sixth of the population had no insurance from work, private plans, **Medicare**, or **Medicaid**. Expanded access to purchasing health insurance, and federal extension of the Medicaid program, has led to 20 million more Americans gaining access to services. Many agree that there are problems with the ACA bill, which does not restructure the health insurance system, but they applaud the program for expanding access. Issues of increasing expenses relating to the cost of premiums, co-payments, deductibles, drug costs, and uncovered expenses continue to plague consumers. Efforts of the Republican party to "repeal and replace" the ACA have not been successful.

Why Do Drugs Cost So Much in the US?

The cost of drugs accounts for one tenth of total healthcare expenditures. Many pharmaceutical practices affect the current cost of drugs. Though the industry would suggest that high costs are due to research and development, practices relating to patents, production, and marketing are more crucial determinants of pricing. Drugs sold overseas, even in European and developed countries, are sold at costs of less than half of the domestic prices. Shortages of drugs have affected the treatment and course of illnesses, though many Americans are unaware of this problem. The pharmaceutical lobby is extensive in numbers, expenditures, and influence.

How Do Science and Social Sciences Study Healthcare Issues?

Epidemiology is the field of science which studies the frequency, prevalence, and distribution of disease in a population. A person's sex, race, social class, gender, and sexual orientation are strongly associated with health status.

Sociological theories assess the health system very differently. Functionalists tend to see the positive aspects in the highly specialized system which promotes good care for some and contributes enormously to the GDP. Conflict theorists are more likely to focus on group disparities in the system and its contribution to perpetuating inequalities.

What Issues Are Prevalent in Considering Healthcare in America?

The *medicalization of life* has impacted multiple areas of life which actually are not in need of medical supervision. Issues of *disability justice*, addressing individuals with physical and mental differences, have moved beyond demanding individual rights and logistical access to asserting that *difference* does not mean "flawed" or in need of being "fixed." Advocacy highlights the concept of *equal* and *different*. Demands to make personal choices, especially with regard to childbirth and death, have contributed new approaches and laws. "Natural" childbirth and midwife-assisted births are gaining greater adherents. The hospice movement is proliferating and several states have instituted "right to die" or "death with dignity" legislation. People are resisting medical management in all of these areas.

Review Questions

1. What are the current **dietary** recommendations and how have they changed in the past 50 years? List at least three dietary issues and explain them.
2. How does the **status of health** in the US compare to other countries? List at least three issues such as longevity, chronic disease, and exercise and explain how they affect people.
3. How effective is the **ACA**? How many people have coverage? Discuss three distinct problems with the program. What can you imagine as a viable alternative?
4. What is the current status of the ACA? What is the future of the ACA?
5. How do you think health insurance, and healthcare, should be structured in the US? Address issues of payment, cost containment, access, and pharmaceuticals.
6. What are the problems with **Medicaid** and how has it been impacted by the ACA?
7. Do you think **Medicare** is viable for the future? Why or why not?
8. What is a **single payer** plan and is there any such plan in the US?
9. What is an **HMO** and what is distinctive about it?
10. What is the **"sick role"** and how does it affect social interaction?
11. Compare and contrast the functionalist and conflict views of the healthcare system.
12. Explain the concept of **medicalization** and provide two examples.

References

AARP. (n.d.) Chronic Conditions Among Older Americans. *American Association of Retired Persons*. Retrieved from https://assets.aarp.org/rgcenter/health/beyond_50_hcr_conditions.pdf

ACNM. (October 26, 2016) *American College of Nurse-Midwives' Statement Regarding the New ACOG/AAP Committee Opinion, "Immersion in Water During Labor and Delivery"* Retrieved from http://www.midwife.org/ACNM-Water-Birth-Statement

ADL. (n.d.) A Brief History of the Disability Rights Movement. *Anti-defamation League.* Retrieved from https://www.adl.org/education/resources/backgrounders/disability-rights-movement

AHA. (n.d.) *Bridging the Gap: CVD and Health Equity*. American Heart Association. Retrieved from https://www.heart.org/idc/groups/heart-public/@wcm/@adv/documents/downloadable/ucm_301731.pdf

AHA. (2017) Go Red For Women®. *The American Heart Association*. Retrieved from https://www.goredforwomen.org/

Almendrala, A. (April 9, 2016) What the World's Healthiest Diets Have in Common. *The Huffington Post*. Retrieved from http://www.huffingtonpost.com/2015/01/16/healthy-diets-around-the-world_n_6446140.html

Anderson, R. (November 6, 2014) Pharmaceutical Industry Gets High on Fat Profits. *BBC News*. Retrieved from http://www.bbc.com/news/business-28212223

Bach, P.B. (January 15, 2015) Why Drugs Cost So Much. *The New York Times*. Retrieved from https://www.nytimes.com/2015/01/15/opinion/why-drugs-cost-so-much.html

Bell, M. (January 10, 2013) Why 5% of Patients Create 50% of Health Care Costs. *Forbes*. Retrieved from https://www.forbes.com/sites/michaelbell/2013/01/10/why-5-of-patients-create-50-of-health-care-costs/#7d41499128d7

Bever, L. (November 2, 2014) Brittany Maynard, as Promised, Ends her Life at 29. *The Washington Post*. Retrieved from https://www.washingtonpost.com/news/morning-mix/wp/2014/11/02/brittany-maynard-as-promised-ends-her-life-at-29/?utm_term=.55d747396110#comments

Black Women's Health Imperative. (July, 2017) *Heart Disease in Black Women: The Big Issue You Might Not Know About*. Retrieved from https://www.bwhi.org/2018/02/12/heart-disease-black-women-big-issue-might-not-know/

Bollinger, T. (n.d.) Does America Have the Worst Food Quality & Safety? *The Truth About Cancer*. Retrieved from https://thetruthaboutcancer.com/america-worst-food-quality-safety/

Bradley, R.A. (1981) *Husband-Coached Childbirth: The Bradley Method of Childbirth*. 4th edn. New York: Harper and Row.

Briody, B. (April 1, 2013) The Shocking Cost of Your Child's ADHD. *The Fiscal Times*. Retrieved from http://www.thefiscaltimes.com/Articles/2013/04/01/The-Shocking-Cost-of-Your-Childs-ADHD

Burne, J. (August 27, 2013) Why Women Really Are the Stronger Sex: Research Suggests Testosterone Weakens the Immune System (Which Means Man Flu Could Actually Be Real). *Mail Online*. Retrieved from http://www.dailymail.co.uk/health/article-2402553/Why-women-really-stronger-sex-Research-suggests-testosterone-weakens-immune-means-man-flu-actually-real.html

Castillo, S. (March 9, 2015) Science Says that Women are Physically Stronger than Men—Duh! *Your Tango*. Retrieved from http://www.yourtango.com/2011104494/study-women-are-stronger-sex

Castillo, S. (February 11, 2016) Why Women of Color Need Targeted Treatment for Heart Health. *Medical Daily*. Retrieved from http://www.medicaldaily.com/heart-disease-risk-women-color-373138

CDA. (n.d.) Chances of Disability: Me, Disabled? *Council for Disability Awareness*. Retrieved from http://www.disabilitycanhappen.org/chances_disability/causes.asp

CDC. (February 16, 2016) 1 in 3 Adults Don't Get Enough Sleep. *Centers for Disease Control and Prevention*. Retrieved from http://www.cdc.gov/media/releases/2016/p0215-enough-sleep.html

CDCa. (n.d.) Attention-Deficit/Hyperactivity Disorder. Data and Statistics. *Centers for Disease Control and Prevention*. https://www.cdc.gov/ncbddd/adhd/data.html

Chesler, P. (1972, 1989, 1997) *Women and Madness: Revised and Updated*. New York: Four Walls Eight Windows.

Cleveland Clinic (April 22, 2017) Obesity is Top Cause of Preventable Life-years Lost, Study Shows. *ScienceDaily*. Retrieved from https://www.sciencedaily.com/releases/2017/04/170422101614.htm

CMS.gov. (April 17, 2018) *NHE Fact Sheet*. Retrieved from https://www.cms.gov/Research-Statistics-Data-and-Systems/Statistics-Trends-and-Reports/NationalHealthExpendData/NHE-Fact-Sheet.html

Coates, T. (2015) *Between the World and Me*. New York: Spiegel & Grau.

Collins, P.K.S. (August 25, 2015) Diversity Is Sorely Needed in Medicine. Why Is it Lacking in Certain Specialties? *ThinkProgress*. Retrieved from http://thinkprogress.org/health/2015/08/25/3694946/women-and-minorities-underrepresented-medicine

Commonwealth Fund (October, 2015) *U.S. Health Care from a Global Perspective*. Retrieved from http://www.commonwealthfund.org/publications/issue-briefs/2015/oct/us-health-care-from-a-global-perspective

Copeland, L. (October 8, 2014) U.S. Life Expectancy Hits Record High. *USA Today*. Retrieved from https://www.usatoday.com/story/news/nation/2014/10/08/us-life-expectancy-hits-record-high/16874039/

Dembosky, A. (January 25, 2016) To Avoid Obamacare, Some Fast Food Restaurants Cut Staff. Did it Work? *KQED*. Retrieved from http://ww2.kqed.org/stateofhealth/2016/01/25/to-avoid-obamacare-some-fast-food-restaurants-cut-staff-did-it-work/

Dietary Guidelines (2015) Key Recommendations: Components of Healthy Eating Patterns. *Health.gov*. Retrieved from https://health.gov/dietaryguidelines/2015/guidelines/chapter-1/key-recommendations/

Eban, K. (n.d.) Drug Shortages: The Scary Reality of a World Without Meds. *Reader's Digest*. Retrieved from http://www.rd.com/health/conditions/drug-shortages/

Editorial Board. (August 12, 2007) World's Best Medical Care? *The New York Times*. Retrieved from https://www.nytimes.com/2007/08/12/opinion/12sun1.html

Epidemiology. (n.d.) Definition. *Medical-Dictionary*. Retrieved from http://medical-dictionary.thefreedictionary.com/epidemiology

EWG. (September 24, 2008) Teen Girls' Body Burden of Hormone-Altering Cosmetics Chemicals. *Environmental Working Group*. Retrieved from http://www.ewg.org/research/teen-girls-body-burden-hormone-altering-cosmetics-chemicals

Fink, S. (January 29, 2016) US Drug Shortages Forcing Hard Decisions on Rationing Treatments. *The New York Times*. Retrieved from https://www.nytimes.com/2016/01/29/us/drug-shortages-forcing-hard-decisions-on-rationing-treatments.html

Fite, E. (November 30, 2017) Affordable Care Act Enrollment Outpacing Last Year's Sign Ups. *Times Free Press*. Retrieved from http://www.timesfreepress.com/news/local/story/2017/nov/30/affordable-care-act-enrollment-outpacing-last/458157/

Frakt, A. (January 19, 2016) Even Talking About Reducing Drug Prices Can Reduce Drug Prices. *The New York Times*. Retrieved from https://www.nytimes.com/2016/01/19/upshot/even-talking-about-reducing-drug-prices-can-reduce-drug-prices.html

Frances, A. (January 21, 2017) We Have Too Many Specialists and Too Few General Practitioners. *HuffPost*. Retrieved from http://www.huffingtonpost.com/allen-frances/we-have-too-many-speciali_b_9040898.html

Friedan, B. (1963) *The Feminine Mystique*. New York: W.W. Norton and Company.

Garfield, R., Damico, A. (October 19, 2016) The Coverage Gap: Uninsured Adults in States that do not Expand Medicaid. *Kaiser Family Foundation*. Retrieved from http://www.kff.org/uninsured/issue-brief/the-coverage-gap-uninsured-poor-adults-in-states-that-do-not-expand-medicaid/

Gawande, A. (2014) *Being Mortal: Medicine and What Matters in the End*. New York: Metropolitan Books.

Genova, L. (2007, 2009) *Still Alice*. New York: Gallery Books.

Glatzer, R., Westmoreland, W. (2014) *Still Alice*. Litzus-Brown, Killer films. BSM Studio.

Global Age Index Inventory (2015) *Life Expectancy at 60*. Retrieved from http://www.helpage.org/global-agewatch/population-ageing-data/life-expectancy-at-60/

Goodman, A. (January 19, 2007) Big Bucks, Big Pharma: Marketing Disease & Pushing Drugs. *Democracy Now!* Retrieved from http://www.democracynow.org/2007/1/19/big_bucks_big_pharma_marketing_disease

Greenspan, L., Deardorff, J. (February 5, 2015) What Causes Girls to Enter Puberty Early. *The New York Times*. Retrieved from https://www.nytimes.com/2015/02/05/opinion/what-causes-girls-to-enter-puberty-early.html

Gutt, D. (November 15, 2016) Our Broken System: Modifying the U.S. Pharmaceutical Regulatory Scheme to Decrease Surging Prescription Drug Prices. *University of Illinois Board of Trustees*. Retrieved from https://publish.illinois.edu/illinoisblj/2016/11/15/our-broken-system-modifying-the-u-s-pharmaceutical-regulatory-scheme-to-decrease-surging-prescription-drug-prices/

Harkinson, J. (November/December, 2015) The Scary New Science that Shows Milk Is Bad for You. *Mother Jones*. Retrieved from http://www.motherjones.com/environment/2015/11/dairy-industry-milk-federal-dietary-guidelines/

Henig, M.R. (May 14, 2015) The Last Day of Her Life. *The New York Times*. Retrieved from https://www.nytimes.com/2015/05/17/magazine/the-last-day-of-her-life.html

Herman, E.D. (April 21, 2015) Using Adderall to Get Ahead, Not to Fight A.D.H.D. *The New York Times*. Retrieved from https://www.nytimes.com/roomfordebate/2015/04/21/using-adderall-to-get-ahead-not-to-fight-adhd

Holland, J. (February 28, 2015) Medicating Women's Feelings. *The New York Times*. Retrieved from https://www.nytimes.com/2015/03/01/opinion/sunday/medicating-womens-feelings.html

Irwin, N., Bui, Q. (April 11, 2016) For the Poor Geography Is Life and Death. *The New York Times*. Retrieved from https://www.nytimes.com/interactive/2016/04/11/upshot/for-the-poor-geography-is-life-and-death.html

Joiner, J. (November 10, 2014) America's Highest Selling Drug is an Anti-psychotic. *Esquire*. Retrieved from http://www.esquire.com/news-politics/news/a31912/turns-out-everyone-is-psychotic/

Jones, J.M. (December 19, 2013) In U.S., 40% Get Less Than Recommended Amount of Sleep. *Gallup*. Retrieved from http://www.gallup.com/poll/166553/less-recommended-amount-sleep.aspx

Kim, S. (June 26, 2013) Foods Ingredients Banned Outside the US. *ABC News*. Retrieved from http://abcnews.go.com/Lifestyle/Food/11-foods-banned-us/story?id=19457237#1

Kodjak, A. (January 12, 2017) We Asked People What They Know About Obamacare. See if You Know the Answers. *NPR*. Retrieved from http://www.npr.org/2017/01/12/509314717/we-asked-people-what-they-know-about-obamacare-see-if-you-know-the-answers

Kristof, N. (February 18, 2016) America's Stacked Deck. *The New York Times*. Retrieved from https://www.nytimes.com/2016/02/18/opinion/americas-stacked-deck.html

Kristof, N., WuDunn, S. (September 12, 2014) The Way to Beat Poverty. *The New York Times*. Retrieved from https://www.nytimes.com/2014/09/14/opinion/sunday/nicholas-kristof-the-way-to-beat-poverty.html

Krugman, P. (February 5, 2016) Who Hates Obamacare? *The New York Times*. Retrieved from https://www.nytimes.com/2016/02/05/opinion/who-hates-obamacare.html?_r=0

Lothian, J., DeVries, C. (2005, 2010) *The Official Lamaze Guide*. New York: Meadowbrook Press.

Luhby, T. (June 30, 2017) 32 Million People Would Lose Coverage if Obamacare Was Repealed. *CNN Money*. Retrieved from http://money.cnn.com/2017/06/30/news/economy/obamacare-repeal-trump/index.html

Maddow, R. (March 13, 2017) 24 Million Would Lose Insurance Under GOP Plan: CBO. *MSNBC*. Retrieved from http://www.msnbc.com/rachel-maddow/watch/24-million-would-lose-insurance-under-gop-health-plan-cbo-897235011622

MANA. (n.d.) *Midwives Alliance of North America*. Retrieved from https://mana.org/

Mayo Clinic. (2017) Retrieved from http://www.mayoclinic.org/

Mayo Clinic Staff. (2017) *Exercise: 7 Benefits of Regular Physical Activity*. Retrieved from http://www.mayoclinic.org/healthy-lifestyle/fitness/in-depth/exercise/art-20048389/

McCann, E. (July 18, 2014) Deaths by Medical Mistakes Hit Records. *Healthcareitnews*. Retrieved from http://www.healthcareitnews.com/news/deaths-by-medical-mistakes-hit-records

McCutcheon, S. (1996) *Natural Childbirth the Bradley Way*. Revised edition. New York: Penguin Books.

McGreevy, P. (October 5, 2015) After Struggling, Jerry Brown Makes Assisted Suicide Legal in California. *Los Angeles Times*. Retrieved from http://www.latimes.com/local/political/la-me-pc-gov-brown-end-of-life-bill-20151005-story.html

Mediterranean Diet. (n.d.) *U.S. News*. Retrieved from http://health.usnews.com/best-diet/mediterranean-diet

Melillo, W. (March 30, 1993) Why Are the Pima Indians Sick? Studies on Arizona Tribe Show Excessive Rates of Diabetes, Obesity, and Kidney Disease. *The Washington Post*. Retrieved from https://www.washingtonpost.com/archive/lifestyle/wellness/1993/03/30/why-are-the-pima-indians-sick-studies-on-arizona-tribe-show-excessive-rates-of-diabetes-obesity-and-kidney-disease/1f978958-e73b-483a-9af9-47d9efdad534/

MHA. (n.d.) Mood Disorders. *Mental Health America*. Retrieved from http://www.mentalhealthamerica.net/conditions/mood-disorders

Miller, G.E., Chen, E., Brody, G.H. (January 4, 2014) Can Upward Mobility Cost You Your Health? *The New York Times*. Retrieved from https://opinionator.blogs.nytimes.com/2014/01/04/can-upward-mobility-cost-you-your-health/

Miller, J.B. (1976, 1986) *Toward a New Psychology of Women*. Boston: Beacon Press.

Morales, A.L. (n.d.) *Sins Invalid: An Unashamed Claim to Beauty in the Face of Invisibility*. Retrieved from http://sinsinvalid.org/

Morgan, C. (January 15, 2015) The Inflammation Epidemic: Your Number One Health Concern 2015 (and What Sugar's Got to Do With It). *High50*. Retrieved from http://www.high50.com/health/the-inflammation-epidemic-your-number-one-health-concern-2015

Moyer, M.W. (May 21, 2012) The Stats on Statins: Should Healthy Adults Over 50 Take Them? *Scientific American*. Retrieved from https://www.scientificamerican.com/article/statins-should-healthy-adults-over-50-take-them/

NCHPAD. (n.d.) *Building Healthy Communities*. Retrieved from http://www.nchpad.org/

NEDA. (n.d.) FAQs. *National Eating Disorders Association*. Retrieved from https://www.nationaleatingdisorders.org/learn/general-information/faqs

Neel, J. (November 21, 2017) Poll: Majority of LGBTQ Americans Report Harassment, Violence Based on Identity. *Capital Public Radio*. Retrieved from https://www.npr.org/2017/11/21/565327959/poll-majority-of-lgbtq-americans-report-harassment-violence-based-on-identity

Neighmond, P. (April 25, 2011) *Sitting All Day: Worse for You than You Might Think*. Retrieved from http://www.npr.org/2011/04/25/135575490/sitting-all-day-worse-for-you-than-you-might-think

Newkirk II, V.R. (January 24, 2017) The Trump Administration's First Blow to Obamacare. *The Atlantic*. Retrieved from https://www.theatlantic.com/politics/archive/2017/01/the-trump-administrations-first-blow-to-obamacare/514103/

NHPCO. (n.d.) Key Hospice Messages: It Is about How You LIVE. *National Hospice and Palliative Care Organization*. Retrieved from https://www.nhpco.org/press-room/key-hospice-messages

NIMH. (n.d.) U.S. Leading Categories of Diseases/Disorders. *The National Institute of Mental Health*. Retrieved from http://www.nimh.nih.gov/health/statistics/disability/us-leading-categories-of-diseases-disorders.shtml

Nolte, E., Martin McKee, C. (January 8, 2008) U.S. Has Most Preventable Deaths Among 19 Nations. *PNHP*. Retrieved from http://www.pnhp.org/news/2008/january/us-has-most-preventable-deaths-among-19-nations

NWI. (n.d.) The Six Dimensions of Wellness. *National Wellness Institute*. Retrieved from http://www.nationalwellness.org/?page=Six_Dimensions

O'Connor, A. (February 19, 2015) Nutrition Panel Calls for Less Sugar and Eases Cholesterol and Fat Restrictions. *Well blogs*. *New York Times*. Retrieved from https://well.blogs.nytimes.com/2015/02/19/nutrition-panel-calls-for-less-sugar-and-eases-cholesterol-and-fat-restrictions/?_r=0

OHA. (February 4, 2016) Oregon Death with Dignity Act: 2015 Data Summary. [PDF File]. *Oregon Health Authority*. Retrieved from https://public.health. oregon.gov/ProviderPartnerResources/EvaluationResearch/DeathwithDignityAct/ Documents/year18.pdf

O'Rourke, M. (August 26, 2013) What's Wrong with Me? *The New Yorker*. Retrieved from http://www.newyorker.com/magazine/2013/08/26/whats-wrong-with-me

PCRM (n.d.) *Health Concerns about Dairy Products*. Physicians Committee for Responsible Medicine. Retrieved from http://www.pcrm.org/health/diets/vegdiets/ health-concerns-about-dairy-products

Pear, R. (November 15, 2015) Many Say High Deductibles Make their Health Law Insurance All but Useless. *The New York Times*. Retrieved from https://www. nytimes.com/2015/11/15/us/politics/many-say-high-deductibles-make-their-health-law-insurance-all-but-useless.html

Pollack, A. (December 11, 2015) *Martin Shkreli's Latest Plan to Sharply Raise Drug Prices Causes Outcry*. Retrieved from https://www.nytimes.com/2015/12/12/ business/martin-shkrelis-latest-plan-to-sharply-raise-drug-price-prompts-outcry.html?hp&action=click&pgtype=Homepage&clickSource=story-heading&module=second-column-region&region=top-news&WT.nav=top-news

Prichep, D. (November 25, 2017) For LGBTQ People of Color Discrimination Compounds. *Weekend Edition Saturday*. Retrieved from https://www.npr. org/2017/11/25/564887796/for-lgbtq-people-of-color-discrimination-compounds

Quealy, K., Sanger-Katz, M. (December 15, 2015) The Experts Were Wrong About the Best Places for Better and Cheaper Health Care. *The New York Times*. Retrieved from https://www.nytimes.com/interactive/2015/12/15/upshot/the-best-places-for-better-cheaper-health-care-arent-what-experts-thought.html

Real Life Stories on Obama Care. (n.d.) *Obama Care Facts*. Retrieved from http:// obamacarefacts.com/obamacare-stories/

Reid, T.R. (2009) *The Healing of America: A Global Quest for Better, Cheaper, and Fairer Health Care*. USA: The Penguin Group.

Robert, C. (January 20, 2017) The Inflammation Epidemic: Your Number 1 Health Concern (and Sugar's Role in it). *High 50 Health*. http://www.high50.com/health/ the-inflammation-epidemic-your-number-one-health-concern-2015-and-what-sugars-got-to-do-with-it

Rosenthal, E. (June 1, 2013) Colonoscopies Explain Why U.S. Leads the World in Health Expenditures. *The New York Times*. Retrieved from http://www.nytimes. com/2013/06/02/health/colonoscopies-explain-why-us-leads-the-world-in-health-expenditures.html?pagewanted=all

Rosenthal, E. (May 18, 2014) Medicine's Top Earners Are Not the MDs. *The New York Times*. Retrieved from https://www.nytimes.com/2014/05/18/sunday-review/ doctors-salaries-are-not-the-big-cost.html

Rosenthal, E. (December 15, 2014a) The Odd Math of Medical Tests: One Scan, Two Prices, Both High. *The New York Times*. Retrieved from https://www.nytimes. com/2014/12/16/health/the-odd-math-of-medical-tests-one-echocardiogram-two-prices-both-high.html

Rosenthal, E. (February 7, 2015) Insured, but Not Covered. *The New York Times*. Retrieved from https://www.nytimes.com/2015/02/08/sunday-review/insured-but-not-covered.html

Sanger-Katz, M. (January 6, 2016) Even Insured Can Face Crushing Medical Debt, Study Finds. *The New York Times*. Retrieved from https://www.nytimes.com/2016/01/06/upshot/lost-jobs-houses-savings-even-insured-often-face-crushing-medical-debt.html

Sawyer, B., Cox, C. (February 13, 2018) How Does Health Spending in the U.S. Compare to Other Countries? *HealthSystemTracker*. Retrieved from https://www.healthsystemtracker.org/chart-collection/health-spending-u-s-compare-countries/#item-start

Squires, D., Anderson, C. (2015) US Health Care from a Global Perspective: Spending, Use of Services, Prices, and Health in 13 Countries. Issue Brief *(Commonwealth Fund)*, 15: 1–15. Retrieved from http://www.commonwealthfund.org/publications/issue-briefs/2015/oct/us-health-care-from-a-global-perspective

Stromberg, S. (March 22, 2015) The GOP's Obamacare 'Death Panel' Nonsense Won't Die. *The Washington Post*. Retrieved from https://www.washingtonpost.com/blogs/post-partisan/wp/2015/03/22/the-gops-obamacare-death-panel-nonsense-wont-die/

Taylor, C.B., Sallis, J.F., Needle, R. (March/April, 1985) The Relations of Physical Activity and Exercise to Mental Health. *Public Health Reports*. 1985, March/April 100(2). Retrieved from https://www.ncbi.nlm.nih.gov/pmc/articles/PMC1424736/

Teicholz, N. (February 20, 2015) The Government's Bad Diet Advice. *The New York Times*. Retrieved from https://www.nytimes.com/2015/02/21/opinion/when-the-government-tells-you-what-to-eat.html

Twenge, J.M. (September, 2017) Has the Smartphone Destroyed a Generation? *The Atlantic* 320 (2): 58–65.

Ulaby, N. (November 21, 2017) Healthcare System Fails Many Transgendered Americans. *All Things Considered*. Retrieved from https://www.npr.org/sections/health-shots/2017/11/21/564817975/health-care-system-fails-many-transgender-americans.

US Life Expectancy Ranks 26th in the World, OECD Report Shows. (November 21, 2013) *Huffington Post*. http://www.huffingtonpost.com/2013/11/21/us-life-expectancy-oecd_n_4317367.htmlU.S.

Velasquez-Manoff, M. (July 27, 2013) Status and Stress. *The New York Times*. Retrieved from https://opinionator.blogs.nytimes.com/2013/07/27/status-and-stress/

WHO. (September, 2016) Lead Poisoning and Health. *World Health Organization*. Retrieved from http://www.who.int/mediacentre/factsheets/fs379/en/

WHO. (February, 2017) Physical Activity. *World Health Organization*. Retrieved from http://www.who.int/mediacentre/factsheets/fs385/en/

Zarroli, J. (April 11, 2016) Life Expectancy Study: It's Not Just What You Make, It's Where You Live. *NPR*. Retrieved from http://www.npr.org/sections/thetwo-way/2016/04/11/473749157/its-not-just-what-you-make-its-where-you-live-says-study-on-life-expectancy

CHAPTER 10

Families

WHAT YOU WILL READ ABOUT IN THIS CHAPTER:

- **Family** is the most crucial social institution, tasked with primary socialization and emotional support of its members. The state of family life has been in flux, especially in terms of gender roles, longevity, and composition. Definitions of family extend beyond blood or legal relationships. Close friendships can define "family," especially for single people. The varieties constituting family life make it very difficult to come up with a meaningful definition of family, though it remains an essential aspect of identity.

- Less than half of American children live with their original, heterosexual parents and more than *40 percent of children are born to women who are unmarried.* The majority of births to single women are to women in their 20s. Increasingly, marriage has become a characteristic of educated, middle-class people. Less educated and lower income people are especially unlikely to marry, in part because of the fear of financial responsibilities. **Gay marriage** became nationally legal in 2015, as a result of a Supreme Court case.

- Family life has changed over time and with the **life cycle of the family**. More people today meet online and issues relating to housework, parental responsibilities, and wage earning are in flux. Mothers are still evaluated differently than fathers but more fathers than in previous generations are taking an active or primary role in childrearing. The division of **housework** remains a challenging aspect of married life.

- **Divorce** has decreased in recent decades, having peaked around 1980. Current statistics indicate that millennials who marry are less likely to experience divorce than the Gen Xers or boomers. Divorce is traumatic for all family members, and particularly for children, though research regarding the impact of divorce on the children, as adults, is mixed.

- Women are still the primary persons struggling with the balance of work and **childrearing**. Women also are likely to suffer financial losses at work due to parenting responsibilities. The primacy of women's childrearing role stems from a mixture of personal choice and societal mandate.

- More older adults are taking significant roles in the lives and care of grandchildren than in previous generations. The relationship is beneficial to both the children and the **grandparents**.

- Domestic violence is pervasive. Abuse occurs between spouses/partners; parents and children; adult children and the elderly; and siblings. These represent various forms of domestic violence. Runaway and homeless youths often are fleeing violence at home.

Introduction

Imagine a young woman who decided to propose marriage to her boyfriend. She orders a ring, sets up a special date, has a special kaleidoscope made to put the ring in, and picks the night prior to graduation from the State Police Academy to pop the question. When asked about her attitudes towards marriage, the young woman said that she and her boyfriend already had agreed they would marry and that she did not care if there was a big wedding celebration, she would feel fine if they decided to marry while his family was in town for graduation. The young woman is the friend of the author's daughter. I was struck by the young woman's unromanticized view of the engagement process and her role reversal in taking the initiative to propose. The proposal was successful, the couple married ten months later, with a traditional marriage ceremony, complete with white gown, two bridesmaids, a best man, and a groom's man.

Do you believe this scenario to be unusual? The lack of sentimentality with which the young woman above approached her engagement was strikingly deviant from the cultural norm. Many women are following non-traditional paths with regard to marriage and family gender roles. Many couples cohabitate prior to marriage, discussing marriage extensively before becoming "officially" engaged. It seems incongruous to have a formal wedding after cohabitation and even, in some cases, after having children, though this occurs. The tremendous attention to dating "rules," engagement rings, and weddings in books, magazines, and the internet, would indicate this young woman was not typical but it is hard to know for sure. Many traditions surrounding marriage actually reflect corporate interests. Several years ago, there was a concerted diamond industry campaign promoting the "proper" amount a man should spend on an engagement ring. The "mandate" originated with the diamond lobby to increase profits. It was recommended to be three months, or 25 percent, of the male's salary (Saad 2009). The article stated that many spend less, about 8 percent of their annual salary, on the ring, and some marry without a diamond. The idea that the diamond represents love and commitment pervades the culture, particularly among the young. The diamond has become a "requirement" of the engagement process and even has been integrated into anniversary celebrations, with a three diamond version. The diamond industry consciously made this effort to enhance product sales (Jhally 1997). The expectation becomes part of romance, at least theoretically, and is symbolized in the industry's campaign slogan, "Diamonds are forever," though for some they may very well outlive the marriage. Some millennials are rejecting diamonds in favor of less expensive alternate stones, and others are rejecting marriage, possibly in the largest numbers of any generation. While the diamond industry sold 26 billion dollars in diamonds in 2015, it has started a campaign to press the purchase of a diamond to celebrate any "real" relationship, even if not a legal marriage (Martin 2017). Today, the divorce rate is decreasing, but so is the marriage rate, especially for the population without college degrees.

Figure 10.1 More non-traditional roles characterize the family. Here, a young woman proposes to her boyfriend
Source: Antonio Guillem / Shutterstock.com

Are Attitudes Towards Marriage Changing?

Cultural and personal ideals relating to family pervade the media and largely represent the practices of the dominant group. Recent trends indicate that they are the most likely to marry. Most people hold strong beliefs regarding romance and childrearing, though they are frequently unexamined. Often childrearing standards are culled from personal experiences and absorbed from the culture, especially mass media. Cultural norms surrounding childrearing can become as much a source of anxiety as of guidance. Family can be a source of support and nurturance but it can also descend into pain, disappointment, anger, and violence. Is the family undergoing a metamorphosis or are its problems just becoming more exposed? The millennial generation seems to be showing increased rates of remaining single, cohabitating outside of marriage, parenting outside of marriage, and gay marriage. In this chapter, we will evaluate the sources and extent of these changes.

How Is Family Defined?

If you were asked to describe your family, who would you include? Who would you exclude? Is there a distinction between your *given* family, of blood and legal relatives, and your *chosen* family, of psychological and emotional supports? Family definitions have typically specified that members have a legal or blood relationship and that they live together. We can see, however, that such a definition excludes many situations. If a divorced parent doesn't live with a child, does she or he still have a *family*? If you live with a partner whose child(ren) are not "yours," are they your family? Is a couple household, with no children, a "family"?

A meaningful practical definition of family is challenging, if not impossible. We can say that family is "whoever is designated as family," but that argument is circular and would fail to communicate the nature of the term. The vast majority of Americans will eventually marry, and many still regard the institution as meaningful, but as family historian Stephanie Coontz remarks, "Marriage is no longer the only place where people make major life transitions and decisions, enter into commitments or incur obligations" (Coontz 2013). To broaden the concept, a statement regarding emotional and financial interdependence might be pertinent but some families are not emotionally supportive and some partners choose to keep their finances separate. There seems to be a growing importance of "nonfamily" family, or the friendships and voluntary relationships people depend upon for intimacy. Think of the characters in the television shows *Grey's Anatomy*, *The Mindy Project*, *Master of None*, *Friends*, *Seinfeld*, *Being Mary Jane*, and *Girls*, to name just a few.

We will define *family* as the most significant people with whom an individual has a **primary group relationship**, including some combination of emotional identification, social support, and financial obligation and who may reside in the same household. This definition is clumsy, and somewhat vague, but it allows for those whose "family" is not the traditional nuclear family. Do you think this covers it? Try composing your own definition.

> ## Box 10.1 – Family Definition
>
> The nature of the American *family* is in flux. In earlier decades, it was defined as people sharing either a legal or blood relationship but this fails to include many of the variations people now include as "family."
>
> *Family* is best described as anyone who is designated as such, though admittedly that is a circular definition. A working definition of family suggests it be defined as the most significant people with whom an individual has a *primary group* relationship, including some combination of emotional identification, social support, financial obligation, and co-residence.

Theorists distinguish a variety of family types. A *nuclear family* is a two-generational household with parents and children. This could contain both legal and non-legal partnerships, biological and adopted children, as well as step children, though the term "nuclear" is most often associated with a married couple and their original children. The term *extended family* would include people outside of these dimensions. Extended family households can include the couple's parents, siblings, nieces or nephews, or cousins.[1]

> ## Box 10.2 – Family Composition
>
> A *nuclear family* refers to a two-generational household with parent(s) and child(ren). This can include legal and non-legal adult partnerships. Children

in a household can be biological, adopted, fostered, or "step." A single parent household can also be designated as "nuclear." The arrangement most typically associated with the term "nuclear," is when children under the age of 18 are living with two original parents, in a heterosexual marriage.

An **extended family** would include people of other generations, such as the couple's parents, or people who have another relation to the family such as the children's cousins or the adults' siblings.

Polyamory is the practice of maintaining more than one primary relationship, which may, or may not, incorporate a sexual aspect.

Family structures have been fluid since the post-World War II era, especially influenced by the Women's Movement of the 1960s. It is misleading to speak of a "norm," since there are so many variations. Family norms differ with social class, race, ethnicity, and immigration status. Many issues associated with the family actually stem from changes due to the industrial era, and the consequent separation of work and domestic life. Divorce rates, which began to rise after World War II, peaked around 1980 and have since been demonstrating a gradual decline. With today's large segment of single-parent households and those with two working parents, much attention has been focused on the pressures of balancing work and family life. US domestic policies provide few tangible family supports.

The same family is experienced differently by its participants. The couple, children, grandparents live in 'different' families even while residing in the same household. It is not unusual for one sibling to remember some childhood event vividly while

Growing Complexity

Almost half of adults today do not live with a spouse

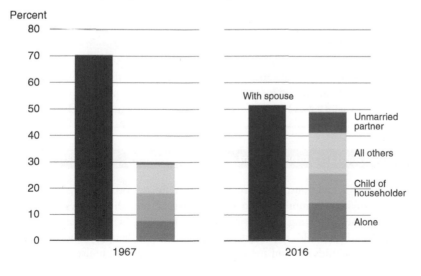

Figure 10.2 Slightly more than one half of adults live with a legal spouse while a significant portion (slightly less than 10 percent) live with an unmarried partner
Source: US Census Bureau, Current Population Survey, Annual Social and Economic Supplement, 1967–2016

another does not even recall the episode. Personal situations (micro level) also are subject to historical changes such as legalization of gay marriage, war, or economic shifts (macro level). The experiences of a family generally undergo "lifecycle" changes resulting from phases associated with being a new couple, often referred to as the honeymoon era (with or without a legal marriage or honeymoon), a period of childrearing, an empty nest period, a grandparent phase, and, usually for one partner, the loss of the partner.

Polyamory

Polyamory refers to people who believe that a person can have significant, loving relationships concurrently with more than one adult person, either for life or for some other defined period of time. Polyamorists do not believe in the principles of monogamy, seeing it as possessive and potentially destructive of authentic loving relationships. Polyamory tenets assert that loving one person does not detract from feelings towards another nor does it minimize the essence of any established relationship. Polyamorists focus on navigating routes to fulfilling relationships.

There are a variety of relational forms adopted in the polyamory community. Polyamorists may define their families by a permanent or semi-permanent relationship, with more than one "spouse," living together or not. They also may identify one primary partner while maintaining relationships with one, or several, others. Sometimes participants construct a "group marriage," where several adults live together with reciprocal involvement, though this may or may not include sexual relationships in all possible configurations. Polyamorists can be heterosexuals, bisexuals, homosexuals, "queer," or asexual but are in emotionally committed relationships. Polyamorist principles guiding relationships incorporate honesty, respectful ethics, and good communication skills to assure the processing, and troubleshooting, in relationships.

There is a nonprofit organization which provides information to the community, such as guidelines to establish contractual agreements between parties and to protect any juveniles involved. Polyamorists believe in establishing social institutions which would be welcoming to alternative forms of family and to aid in the institutional support of these alternatives. The Polyamory Society was formed in 1996 (History of Polyamory Society n.d.).

What Is the Actual Composition of Families Today?

"Traditional" nuclear households are not in the majority today. Currently, 41 percent of children are born to mothers who are not married, though this does not necessarily indicate that they are living alone at the time of the birth. Eighty-three percent of single heads of households are female, and 49 percent of them were never married. Single-dad households account for 17 percent of single-parent households. Single parents are at greater risk for poverty; 36.5 percent of single-mom households; 22 percent of single-dad households, while 7.5 percent of two-parent households are impoverished (Lee 2017). Twenty-three percent of children live only with their mothers while 69 percent live with two parents (not necessarily the original two), 4 percent live only with their fathers, and 4 percent live with no parent in the household. Sixteen percent of children live in a blended family, with step-parents, step-siblings, or half siblings (Pew Research Center 2015). In married households, with children under 15, 24 percent live with stay at home mothers and 1 percent with stay at home fathers (US Census Bureau 2015). In 2013, 536,000 grandparents, 65 and older, had primary responsibility for their grandchildren (Profile of Older Americans 2017). Households are volatile. One study showed that 31 percent of children less than six years old underwent a major change in the family structure over a period of three years (Pew Research Center 2015).

Twenty-seven percent of the population lives alone. Women are slightly more likely to live alone, with 15 percent of single-person households belonging to women and 12 percent to men. This relatively new household form, up from 5 percent in the 1920s, reflects several demographic trends. The average ages of marriage, currently around 29 years for men and 27 years for women, are among the highest averages recorded. Divorce, death of a partner, and increased life expectancy also create more single households. These trends of delayed marriage, divorce, and widowhood explain the increased likelihood of living alone. Living alone has less stigma than in the past, even being chosen by some (Henderson 2014).

Family and household trends are transitioning yet the institution of marriage and the family remains a cultural ideal. Ninety percent of Americans will marry and the desirability of marriage is still high, as can be seen in the fight to legalize gay

Figure 10.3 Good jobs increase the likelihood of marriage
Source: Ann Little / Alamy Stock Photo

marriage, nationally obtained in 2015. The majority of unmarried households are from lower socioeconomic groups, since economic stability is a contributing factor to legal marriage. Disparities in the rate of marriages for different social classes is greatest when disparities of income between social classes is the highest, as it was in the 1890s and in the recent "great recession" (Cherlin 2014).

What Are the Cycles of Family Life?

Finding a Partner

Who do you define as a potential life "partner" or "significant other"? Does your conception match your family's ideal? Most people gravitate to *homogamy*, referring to the likelihood that a person will choose a partner similar in race, ethnicity, religion, education, social class, and personal values. These are contributing factors to a successful outcome, as is family approval. We like to think we are "free" to marry whomever but there frequently are constraints relating to money, race, religion, ethnicity, and family background. The belief in *romantic love*, where music erupts, the earth moves, and a person believes they have found "the one" is a development of the industrial era. The separation of the work and domestic spheres weakened the family's control of the individual. Personal fulfillment, and the creation of emotional bonds based upon shared interests, activities, and values began to replace familial obligation (Oatman-Stanford 2013). Prior to this time, marriages often were arranged by the older generation to solidify family connections and assure complementary statuses in social class, race, ethnicity, and religion. Even with the advent of personal choice as a major element of mate selection, proximity frequently was a determining factor in the pool of available prospects. Today's lifestyles make locale much less limiting in finding a partner.

Box 10.3 – Romantic Love

The notion of *romantic love*, based on personal choice and the ideal of passionate attachment, dates back to the Industrial Revolution. Prior to that time, marriages were engineered by parents to ensure continuity in their offspring's social status or limited by geographic proximity.

Homogamy refers to marriage between persons who have similar demographic characteristics with respect to social class, education, race, ethnicity, religion, and age. In arranged marriages the older generation made sure these criteria were compatible in the couple. Today, more people are moving away from homogamy, though the vast majority of marriages still are between partners who are demographically similar.

Dating has undergone cultural changes among the millennial generation as it has in previous generations. Young people refer to "talking to someone" as a first step in getting to know someone and seem less likely to refer to this as "dating," though it frequently includes spending time alone with the person (Twenge 2017). "Dating" seems reserved for a relationship which is established and implies monogamy. A 2014 online survey, regarding dating in the US (7 Things … 2014), shows that respondents felt a lack of clarity regarding what actually constitutes a "date." Williams (2013) suggests a redefinition to a much more casual encounter, maybe even in a group setting, as a "date." The "hook up" refers to casual encounters for sex, minus the date or emotional entanglement. Today's women are interested in "hooking up," and not just led there by male pressure (Taylor 2013). This seems to be particularly true of women who are seeking competitive professional goals. Although young adults show a tendency towards hook-ups, research indicates that many young people desire a relationship (Fellizar 2017).

Surveys of dating behaviors reveal what a person looks for in a prospective mate. A survey of 2647 people through an online dating site identifies the highest ranking "deal breaker" as poor hygiene. For women, unemployment, excessive use of alcohol, and smoking were also deterrents. Men were most likely to list smoking or being overweight as "turn offs." "Rules" emerging as significant included a good sense of humor, good appearance, and confidence. Asking a person for a date by texting is viewed negatively. Young people hope to marry between 26 and 30 and most respondents stated they would want to move in together between six months and two years of dating.

Box 10.4 – Online Dating

Online dating refers to meeting a potential partner on the internet, frequently from sites set up for this purpose. Research shows that 22 percent of heterosexual couples, and 61 percent of homosexual couples, make initial contact through online sites. Sites such as Match.com get as many as 25,000 people registering daily. Thirty-eight percent of people identifying as "single and looking" use online or mobile dating sites.

An increasing number of people are relying on online dating to identify potential partners. In 1992 only 1 percent of people found partners through ads or matchmaking. In 2009, 22 percent of heterosexual couples and 61 percent of gay couples met online. One third of couples recently married met online (Jayson 2013; Fottrell 2013). The popularity of online dating is growing. Usage of online dating sites increased 300 percent, for 18–24-year-olds between 2013 and 2016. Significant increases were also seen in the 55–64 age group (Smith and Anderson 2016). Thirty-eight percent of people in 2013 who identified as "single and looking" used online or mobile dating apps (Smith and Duggan 2013). The success rate of dating relationships originating online appears mixed. On the negative side, online dating can create unrealistic expectations and encourage a "shopping" mentality where if one "product" is not suitable there are others to choose from. Additionally, the poor matching standards of sites, coupled with ambiguous or outright dishonest communications in profiles and personal communications, can be detrimental to the process or eventual outcome (Adams 2015). On the positive side, research shows that online dating relationships are slightly more likely to succeed than offline meetings (Jayson 2013; Fottrell 2013). The online services widen the available pool, and can be especially expedient for specific populations, such as gay and bisexual persons, older persons, or those seeking partners in specific religious, ethnic, or racial groups. Online daters also tend to be wealthier and more educated than the general population (Toma 2014). The manner of the meeting source is less significant than what develops. Successful long-term relationships depend on similar values, attitudes, and beliefs which develop with time spent together.

Dating behaviors, especially as influenced by technology, have been the source of speculation, research, and comedy. Actor and comedian Aziz Ansari teamed up with sociologist Eric Klineberg to study emerging norms. They were especially interested in how to approach a woman to get a first date. They ran focus groups to determine what type of text messages were successful in getting women to respond favorably to a man's overture. They concluded, after talking with multiple groups of women and men, and reviewing sample texts, that there were some general rules for success. These were: invite the woman to a specific event rather than make a general comment about "getting together" at some vague future time; say something which referenced an earlier conversation to show that the writer is paying attention; and, say something funny. Their study was published as the book *Modern Romance* (Ansari and Menjivar 2015).

Marriage

The millennial generation (born between 1980 and 2000) is more likely than any previous generation to remain unmarried by age 25. Never married younger adults rose to 25 percent in 2012, compared to 9 percent in 1960, according to Pew Research. The never married rate for those 25 and older is more than doubled for African Americans (36 percent), slightly higher for Asians (19 percent), and 26 percent for Hispanics when compared to the rates among Whites (16 percent). Younger

Figure 10.4 Online dating, increasingly utilized to meet potential partners, can carry unrealistic expectations as well as false information and a sense of unlimited choices making it difficult to move towards commitment
Source: Andy Dean Photography / Shutterstock.com

Education and Marriage: Shifting Patterns for Women and Men

% of men and women ages 25 and older who have never been married, by education

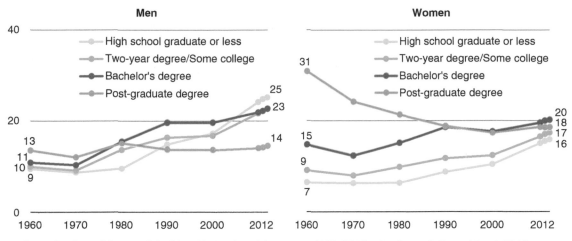

Source: Pew Research Center analysis of the 1960–2000 decennial censuses and 2010–2012 American Community Survey, Integrated Public Use Microdata Series (IPUMS)

African Americans were more likely than other groups to say it was very important for a couple to marry if they planned on spending their lives together. The three main reasons reported for remaining single are, in order: not finding the right person, not being financially stable, and not feeling ready to settle down (Wang and Parker 2014).

In previous generations, uneducated women were more likely than educated women to marry but women with higher levels of income and education are now equally likely to marry and less likely to divorce (Coontz 2013). Educated women marry at later ages; there are 77 never married 25–34-year-old men for every 100 women with *post-graduate* degrees (note: when they marry, it may not be their partner's first marriage). Among never married people with *bachelor's* degrees the comparable male to female ratio is 100:102.

Employment is a big factor in marriage rates; women persist in listing secure employment as the most important quality when evaluating a potential spouse. The rate of male employment, especially in relation to female employment, is low, with a ratio of 91:100 single employed males to single employed females. By comparison, the 1960 figure was 139:100. Employment for all males is 82 percent (2012) compared to 93 percent in 1960. Forty percent of women are the sole or primary breadwinners for families with children under 18 (Marche 2013). The median income for male workers, aged 25–34, is down 20 percent from 1980. Women's earnings, in comparison to male wages *in this age group*, have improved from 70 percent in 1980 to 93 percent in 2012. Men with just a high school diploma or less are more likely never to have married. For men, the most common response for evaluating a potential spouse is similar ideas about childbearing (62 percent). Men are a lot less likely than women to see steady employment as an essential quality (46 percent to 78 percent) (Wang and Parker 2014).

Figure 10.5 The "marriage penalty" women face for higher education appears to be significantly diminishing, while the rate of "never married" for less uneducated men is climbing
Source: "Record Share of Americans Have Never Married," Pew Research Center, Washington, DC (September 24, 2014), http://www.pewsocialtrends.org/2014/09/24/record-share-of-americans-have-never-married/

Cohabitation is becoming more common and less stigmatized. About one quarter of never-married adults aged 25–34 are cohabitating; the average length of cohabitation is 18 months. College-educated women are less likely than other women to cohabitate before marriage and more likely to marry the man if they do. Fifteen percent of cohabiters in this age group are widowed, divorced, or separated. Slightly less than half of people surveyed agreed with the statement: "Society is better off if people make marriage and having children a priority." Fifty percent said that society is just as well off if people choose other priorities (Wang and Parker 2014). Previously married women are a lot less likely than previously married men to say that they want to marry again. Research shows that marriage improves the health of men but has no significant impact on women's health. Divorce does not seem to impact the future health of either women or men, though earlier research suggested that it had a detrimental effect on men (Knapton 2015). Married women are less satisfied with marriage than men and initiate two thirds of divorces. Women in *non-marital* relationships do not report less satisfaction than married women (Shpancer 2015). Married people are generally happier than their *single* counterparts and this is especially true when the marital partners consider themselves best friends (Curtin 2018). Today's happily married couples are happier than married people of past generations. Perhaps this is due to the acceptability of remaining single and the removal of the stigma associated with divorce.

Family research has focused more on the consequences of divorce than investigating the quality of intact marriages. One exception is psychologist John Gottman, who has spent much of his career studying marriage in *The Relationship Research Institute*, commonly referred to as "the love lab." He claims that he

Figure 10.6 Investigation regarding the characteristics of happy marriages seems less of a priority than studying what goes wrong. With today's longevity, many couples can experience long marriages. What makes them successful?
Source: Shutterstock.com

can predict the likelihood of divorce with over 90 percent accuracy by watching couples interact in order to identify what he calls the "Four Horsemen of the Apocalypse." The four negative behaviors include: using critical language towards a partner; showing contempt; becoming defensive; or disengaging. He also identifies positive aspects in successful relationships, such as possessing knowledge of the details of the partner's history and world; honoring and respecting your partner; daily supporting your partner; sharing power; utilizing positive communication styles to resolve problems; avoiding getting stagnant; and creating shared meaning (Johnson 2009).

Accurately assessing the status of a marriage is a tricky business, especially since partners' descriptions can be disparate. In no arena is this more obvious than when it comes to housework. The majority of coupled households show a marked inequality in the hours each partner commits to household responsibilities. Although women comprise half of the labor force, men have not commensurately increased their domestic labor. There is some research that shows men are doing more housework than they used to, but not much more. Women are doing less than in the past, but not much less, even if they work full time. This has been referred to as the *Second Shift*, where a woman works full-time in the paid labor force and does another full- time "job" at home (Hochschild and Machung 1989).

> ### Box 10.5 – Women and Family Life
>
> *The Second Shift* refers to the trend where women work full time in the paid labor force and have another full-time "job" at home.
>
> The ideal concept of the family, proliferating in the suburban expansion of the 1950s, embodied the father/ breadwinner and mother/housewife in monogamous heterosexual marriage. This ideal is no longer feasible for most of the middle or working class. Today, 40 percent of women are either the sole or *primary breadwinner*, supporting their children.

Contrary to much of the media stereotypes, working-class men do more housework than middle-class and professional men (Ellen 2015). The greater household equality in less well-off families can be attributed to the lack of money to buy household help and to less flexible work schedules. One study showed that even unemployed men spend less time on housework than their wives. Explanations for this reluctance suggest that men feel emasculated by housework and that being unemployed is a further threat to masculinity (Marcotte 2015). One recent study found that just having a husband creates seven more hours of housework for women, while saving the husband one hour of chores (Reaney 2016; Klein et al. 2013). Research also shows that though couples express the desire to be equitable they are likely to fall into traditional roles, particularly if the man works more than 40 hours a week (Klein et al. 2013; Hillin 2014; Gottlieb 2014). To address the unequal burden of household chores, one author suggests (Marche 2013) that we can all just learn to live with more "filth."

Marriage also impacts women's wages. Married women make an average of 78
cents to the male dollar. The marital income gap is highest in couples where the man
is particularly well paid. In married households, 25 percent of couples earn within
$4999 of each other; 35 percent have households where men make $30,000 more
than the woman while the comparable figure for women is 9 percent (US Census
Bureau 2015). Contrary to the situation among the baby boomers where spousal
careers often were not equivalent, today's professional and graduate educated men
are increasingly likely to marry spouses with similar achievements and interests. These
dual professional marriages have instigated more concentrated social class segregation
(Miller and Bui 2016).

There is insufficient research, and some contradictory findings, regarding the
influence of the division of labor and financial contributions in marriages. Research
suggests that more equality at home can translate into more and better sex (Bratskeir
2015) though some research shows that the men who do more "female" chores in
the home may be getting less sex (Gottlieb 2014). One clearly emergent trend is that
marriages are happier than in the past, possibly an artifact of easy access to divorce as
well as "partnership" marriages based on similar work and education status.

Divorce

Divorce is never the anticipated outcome in marriage though it may be preferable to
staying in a dysfunctional or abusive situation. Research suggests that two parents
are better than one and, ideally, parents should stay together, but many people feel
consistent hostility between parents has a negative effect on everyone concerned.
Earlier research on marriage and family tended to compare the children of divorce

144 Years of Marriage and Divorce in the US

WWII ends

The Great Depression

WWI ends

per 1,000 people

Figure 10.8 Divorce rates peaked around 1980 and have declined. Marriage rates are at the lowest recorded rate Source: Adapted from Randy Olson / randalolson.com. CDC NCHS

to those of intact families, without controlling for other factors such as parental involvement or levels of marital hostility. More recent research includes comparisons of married couples, married couples with high conflict, and divorced couples. In these cases, the highly-conflicted marriages fare worse than the divorced cases. No one would argue that two loving adults in the household isn't optimal for the health of the adults and children but sometimes that is just not possible.

The process of divorce has undergone significant change in the past 50 years. Until the 1960s, before the dominance of "no-fault" divorce, one spouse had to sue the other on legal grounds such as cruelty, infidelity, or abandonment. Divorce was an inherently adversarial and public event and carried a severe stigma. More recent laws support the premise of "irreconcilable differences," where no fault is assigned and the marriage is consensually dissolved. In 17 states, there are only "no-fault" divorces. In the other 33 states, a couple can file for cause, although *no fault* is an option and a way to stay out of court. California passed the first *no fault* law in 1970, while New York did so only in 2010 (Vlosky and Monroe 2002; Coontz 2010). There are nine *community property* states. Community property means that both spouses co-own everything accrued during the marriage, including assets such as retirement accounts and real estate. Everything which is a joint asset is divided equally between spouses upon divorce, as is any debt accrued during the marriage. Property that is excluded would be anything that was obtained separately prior to marriage, or during the marriage with separate funds, such as inheritance. Separate money comingled with the couple's accounts is considered community property (Johnson 2010). Legal pre-marital agreements (*prenups*) can over-ride these laws. In states without community property laws, assets are not presumed to be equally owned and a couple may litigate if they cannot agree on a settlement. In property settlements, as in child custody and support, it is generally preferable to make compromises and settle disputes without the court's intervention because once a case goes to court the couple loses control and gains expenses in legal fees.

Divorce tears people's worlds apart. Even if the couple believes it is for the best, it is still a devastating blow. Parents often are suffering so much that they cannot provide the emotional support their children need at the time of the divorce, when the children are most vulnerable as well. Even if the parents appear affable, the kids suffer long-term effects and there is some evidence that it affects their future relationships (Gottlieb 2014). Children are prone to believing that they somehow are to blame for the divorce and feel guilty about not being "better" kids. For the children, visiting between households can be disruptive. Imagine yourself, even as a young adult, changing your residence multiple times in the same week, having to keep track of your things and manage the logistics of your school, work, and social life. It is not that divorce can't be managed, and even in some ways positively, but it should be acknowledged that the changes frequently are devastating, at least in the short term, and possibly in the long term.

> We all pretend, us Kids. We learn quickly to "adapt" as they say. But they're the fools. Children pick up new languages easily—hear the sounds and imitate. We become so distracted with futile attempts to act as we should, to say what they want to hear, to please, that we forget ourselves and our lives. Next thing we know, there's a plethora of parents, new houses and a formulated schedule for moving between them. We learn to show just how okay we are. For a while, we get nervous, tiptoeing parents, their guilt radiating through the air and piercing our young souls. Then they find new people and can start again, anew. That's exactly when it hits us.
>
> (Channa Joffe-Walt, in Shandler 1999)

Child custody issues are difficult to resolve and there is no formula that works for everyone. Additionally, laws and practices regarding custody vary by state. Through much of western history children were the automatic responsibility of the father, since he had legal "rights" to them under property laws, as he did to the wife. A woman who was "at fault" in a divorce case ran a high risk of losing her children unless the man agreed to relinquish physical custody. The twentieth century brought two big changes with regard to child custody. On the social level, the familial division of labor associated with industrialization made the home the "work" of the woman. Secondly, the "tender years" doctrine established that the psychological health of children, particularly young ones, depended on the integrity of the mother/child bond.

Box 10.6 – Divorce

Divorce is the dissolution of a legal marriage. Divorce rates increased steadily since World War II, peaked around 1980, and have declined gradually. There is speculation that the decline will be more pronounced in millennial marriages since millennials marry later in life and tend to be affluent and educated, all factors associated with intact marriages. Much of today's divorce is "no fault," referring to the dissolution of a marriage due to "irreconcilable differences" where neither party is assigned blame.

Whether due to divorce or lack of marriage, single parenting is particularly stressful, especially if the parent has little social support. Custody is an especially problematic feature of divorce. Children often suffer if they feel compelled to "choose" between parents. Child custody arrangements follow a legal mandate of "the best interest of the children," though there is evidence that courts' efforts to be equitable to the parents' interests can interfere with the optimal arrangement for the children. The courts draw a distinction between "legal custody" and "physical custody" or "visitation," which is sometimes also called "periods of responsibility." In joint legal custody, each parent theoretically has equal input with regard to issues of childrearing, from schooling to religion, to sports and vacations. Joint physical custody refers to sharing equivalent time with each of the parents. Joint physical custody does NOT require a 50/50 split in time with each parent.

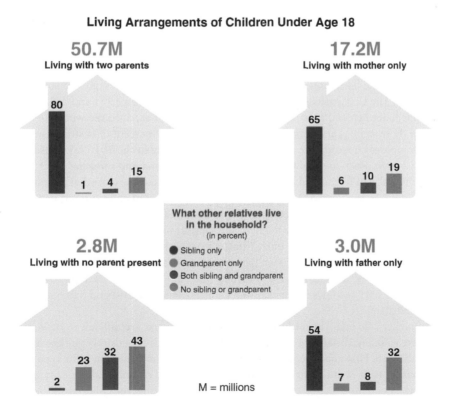

Figure 10.9 The majority of US children (about 69 percent) live with two parents while close to one quarter live only with a mother
Source: US Census Bureau, 2016 Current Population Survey Annual Social and Economic Supplement

Child support laws vary from state to state and the specific codes can be very complicated. Federal guidelines were initiated in 1974–1975 as amendments to the Social Security Act, to reduce the cost of welfare for the federal government. In 1987, in response to changes in work and custody, guidelines incorporated the resources of both parents when establishing child support payments. In 1992, laws were passed making a parent responsible for paying child support for a child living in a different state. Prior to that time, a parent could "beat" child support responsibility by moving out of state. In 1994, child support payments were exempted from personal bankruptcy, so that a parent was still responsible for payment, even if she or he declared bankruptcy (History of Child Support 2003). A parent can appeal to a court for modification of support if their circumstances have changed. Most of the time, if the parent is capable of work, the court will not excuse them from payment.

It is difficult to assess how many parents collect child support and how much they average. Child support calculations depend on multiple factors involving employment, income, and resources. In most states, child support is awarded to the *custodial* parent in whose house the child spends the most time. Some states reduce support payments, based on the amount of time a noncustodial parent spends with the child. In many states, a quarter of the year (measured in overnights) will lower payments. In many cases, the custodial parent will also get the "dependent" credit on their taxes. The current tax structure does not award a deduction for the parent paying the support, though doing so might increase compliance. Any measure enhancing the likelihood of support payments benefits the child, the family, and government budgets. (Because of variations between states, and in forms of support, child support can be tax deductible if it is labeled "family support," incorporating the financial needs of the spouse.) The maintenance of the standard of living of the child, within the limitations of the parents' incomes, is supposed to govern support guidelines. The US Census Bureau reports (2018) that between 1993 and 2015, less than one half of custodial parents awarded child support received the whole amount. During those same years, between 24.2 percent and 30.7 percent of custody awards were completely unpaid. The average payment, according to the 2010 US Census, was $430 a month. Keep in mind that some parents get nothing and some get much more, so "averages" can be misleading. For a variety of reasons, some custodial parents choose not to seek support. Modifications in the awarding of child support can occur frequently, based on shifting income of one, or both, of the partners. Changes in the child's residency can also create the need for support modifications. If a couple cannot agree on terms, they can go to court. Women have been ordered to pay support to men, usually in cases where the men have equal childcare responsibility but make little or no money. Men can also be awarded child support if they have physical custody and have incomes lower than the woman's, or if the husband had been a "househusband."

Summary statements regarding post-divorce adjustment are difficult to make since there are so many variables at play. A few basic standards for custody guides can be established. First and foremost, children benefit from maintaining some type of relationship with each parent, except in cases of physical or sexual abuse or neglect. Even when parents disagree on issues regarding childrearing, the children still need to experience each parent. Child custody in which the physical management of children is shared is best, though it does not have to be a 50/50 split. Some research actually shows that 50/50 arrangements only work when the parents live in close proximity and have similar household rules and lifestyles. An arrangement of 75/25 can be beneficial for the children, as long as the parent who has the lesser amount of time actually spends the time in parenting activities, such as attending the child's activities, taking them to appointments, supervising homework and personal cleanliness and other childrearing and household responsibilities. Only 10 percent of divorced couples have joint physical custody.

Assessment of custody arrangements is further complicated because many people fail to maintain their legal agreements and because situations change as children age and parents gain a new partner. There is some evidence that when men are involved parents and fight for the custody of the children, they are successful in gaining primary custody (DiFonzo 2014; Cancian et al. 2014; USCRossier Online 2014). A single man, when listed as the father on a birth certificate, has all the same rights to child custody and visitation as a married man, even if he never lived with the mother. Ideally, the parents cooperate but the father can go to court to get legally binding periods of responsibility for his child. Many men feel wary of the system. Edin and Nelson's (2013) research on low-income men found that fathers listed on birth certificates are highly likely to be contacted for child support and unlikely to get visitation without fighting for it. They further point out that even when visits are ordered by the court, it can be difficult to enforce them.

Simple aids to support children of divorce include: do not utilize the child to communicate between parents; do not speak badly of the other parent to the children; do not separate siblings; allow children to voice their feelings about the situation; try to maintain some type of consistent discipline between households; permit deviations from the schedule for special events; communicate effectively between households, while respecting the boundaries of each. Children's feelings should be considered, in custody arrangements, but should not be relied upon as the determining factor. Parents can learn to pick up on cues the child may be giving regarding their feelings, rather than asking the child directly, which can cause emotional turmoil. Children try to protect the parents, fearing for a parent's stability or the loss of their affections. Consultation with mental health professionals is important since judges may not be adequately trained in family psychology. Some jurisdictions routinely employ mental health professionals' input in making child custody decisions.

Parenting

A few mothers seem happy with their children all the time, as if they're sailing through motherhood, entranced. However, up close and personal, you find that these moms tend to have tiny little unresolved issues: They exercise three hours a day or check their husband's pockets every night looking for motel receipts. Because not only do moms get very mad; they also get bored. This is a closely guarded secret, as if the myth of maternal bliss is so sacrosanct that we can't even admit these feelings to ourselves. But when you mention these feelings to other mothers, they all say, "Yes, yes!" You ask, "Are you ever mean to your children?" "Yes!" "Do you ever yell so that it scares you?" "Yes, yes" "Do you ever want to throw yourself down the back stairs because you're so bored with your child that you can hardly see straight?"

(Anne Lamott, in Peri and Moses 2000)

Modern western cultures have put intensive pressures on mothers, especially when being a mother became a "career" in the post-World War II era and parenting theories regarding the impact of mothering became standard psychological fare. Prescriptions for good mothering have changed with different generations and cultures. Mothers who fail to behave appropriately are vilified. Marilyn Frye (2004) defined oppression as the absence of choices, as being "locked in." An oppressed person will be viewed in a negative manner, no matter what course is taken. In contemporary settings, a woman who commits herself to mothering is idealized if she is a middle-class stay at home mom and demonized if she is poor and does the same thing, especially if she receives welfare:

The "success stories" of welfare reform typically involve single mothers who land minimum-wage jobs requiring up to a two-hour commute each way by public transportation. While the largest national study to date found that good child care plus good parenting confers a double advantage on children, former welfare recipients must often leave their children in substandard care for ten to twelve hours a day.

(Stephanie Coontz, in Peri and Moses 1999)

In a similar vein, women who are too professionally involved are also suspect. While many women need to work outside the home, "too much ambition" can be viewed negatively, even causing the woman to lose custody of her children. Men are considered to be "good" fathers if they simply show interest in their children while women are invariably viewed as deficient, no matter how they behave (Glassner 1999). "Bad" mothers have been blamed for everything from falling standardized test scores, to juvenile delinquency, to violence.

Box 10.7 – Parenting

Parenting refers to the social role of caring for a child. The concepts of "mother" and "father" generally carry disparate expectations. These frequently result in women and men being judged differently, even for similar behaviors. Many children, perhaps as many as 50 percent, will live in a single-parent household prior to the age of 18.

Sociologist Barry Glassner (1999) analyzes the particular maligning of teenage mothers. He notes that these mothers represent few parenting differences from mothers of comparable backgrounds who have their children later in life. Glassner suggests a confusion regarding cause and effect; being a teen mother does not cause poverty but reflects poverty's inadequate opportunity structures. The best "birth control" is for a woman to feel she has life choices. There is research that shows that very bright Latino and Black women are actively recruited to join the military as an alternative to early pregnancy, while encouraging them to apply to college is bypassed (Goodman 2002). Researchers have noted the causal link between poor schooling and blocked mobility in young motherhood.

Women most at risk for early pregnancy view motherhood as a bridge to adulthood and a status they can achieve. A significant portion of teenaged mothers quickly adapt to their new responsibilities by increasing their educational goals and employment, and giving priority to childrearing. The stereotype is based on the ones who do not meet their obligations, though they are not the majority. Another misconception concerns the alleged increases in teen mothering, though the incidence actually is decreasing. Teen pregnancies have hit an all-time low for the modern era, having decreased 67 percent between 1991 and 2016 (Twenge 2017). The majority of single women giving birth today are in their 20s. Additionally, young women frequently are penalized for behaviors that have no consequence for young men, especially with regard to parenting. In 1998 two teenaged mothers sued a Kentucky school board for prohibiting them from being inducted into the *National Honor Society* because they were unwed mothers (Glassner 1999). Though the women had excellent academic records, they were denied admission to the honor society on the basis of possessing a "character flaw." Nothing happened to the fathers.

Judgements regarding parenting are not limited to teen mothers. Older women who choose not to have children often are accused of having a personality flaw, lacking in "nurturance," or being selfish. Unmarried women who deliberately choose to become mothers also are prone to accusations of selfishness, the implication being that married women never choose to have children for "selfish" reasons. Single parents, no matter what age or circumstances, are still viewed as "deviant" and scrutinized for potential deficits. Often, the lack of structural cultural support for single parents of any sex is ignored:

> Yes, there were great times (in single parenting) and truly parenting is the most enriching and joyful of times (if you have the luxury of relishing it) but it also was grueling, tedious, and exhausting … The chief culprit is that there is no relief … You are "on" all the time, and there is no pinch hitter. I notice that there are endless novels and memoirs about romance, discussing, dreaming, dissecting the experience. Close friends can spend hours probing marital relationships; the good, bad, and the ugly (all with the same partner) but they don't want to hear about the challenges of a single person.

All women who are mothers, whether step, married, single, heterosexual or homosexual, can bond over the tribulations of mothering, in general, granting a nod to the phenomenon of mother guilt because we all share the cultural experience of mother blame for everything our children are and are not. Yet, it seems no one really wants to hear what it feels like to be a *single* parent … not the reality of it from day to day … Here is the reality: you are up all night vomiting, having caught an intestinal bug from the kids, and you are feverish, sleep deprived, weak, and the children are still up at 5 AM, wanting whatever it is they want at that time—love, food, stimulation, a diaper change or, more likely, all of these … and you can't imagine how you will prop your eyes open, or ignore the pain in your head, even though you know that you can't sleep because you are needed and, even if given the chance, the moment for sleep has somehow passed.

In searching for relief from friends or family, the single parent finds that she is no one's priority when she should always be ready to provide for any need in her children, without respite, oh, and not complain.

(Notes from a single parent, personal communication)

Can a "father" be a "mother"? Cultural ideas relating to gender and parenting have a far-ranging impact on the family. Most people would admit that women and men parent differently, bringing specific elements to the task. Can men be the primary nurturers? Can men "mother"? Men, single and in pairs, are more likely to be raising children today than in the past. When men take on the "mothering" role often they are celebrated for their courage and commitment while women, especially if they are single, typically are subjected to scrutiny and criticism.

Fathers also are stereotyped as parents but more often favorably. If "bad" mothers are the problem, the mere presence of fathers has been posited as the solution, though men frequently suffer from being relegated to the role of "banker":

American society tends to assess the unwed father's moral worth with a single question; how much money does he provide? But the men that we interviewed in Philadelphia and Camden [N.J.] vehemently reject the notion that they

Figure 10.10 A son helps his father with kitchen chores; generally, men are not doing much more housework than in past generations
Source: Oliveromg / Shutterstock.com

should be treated as mere paychecks. Instead, they desire, and even demand, at least a slice of the "whole fatherhood experience" in exchange for a portion of their hard earned cash. When mom acts as gatekeeper or when a child refuses contact, even this relatively weak breadwinner norm can be eroded or nullified.

(Edin and Nelson 2013)

But many men want to be more, they want to be a full parent, in every sense:

"Just know that I love you, and that everything that I have done is because of you," his father answers. "To see you every day, to answer your questions about life just like we are doing right now, that is to me the most important thing."

(A Veteran speaks to his son, NPR Staff 2016)

Single fathers are more likely to receive social, and parenting, support from other adults while single mothers often are the subjects of disdain. The very presence of a father, even a completely uninvolved one, is thought to save "children and the nation from ruin" (Glassner 1999). One theorist, David Blankenhorn (1995) asserts that no mother can possibly raise a healthy male child because she cannot teach him to "be a man." Some men are making a point of spending more time with their children, tripling their time with kids compared to fathers of earlier generations. Still, this is seen as a choice, sometimes brought about by the special needs of the child (Polakow-Suransky 2016).

Different gender standards relating to work and family balance persist. Vice President Biden was praised for returning home to his children when he was a Senator, even if it was late at night and his kids were asleep. Obama has been noted

Figure 10.11 More attention is being given to the nurturant role of fathers and some men have voiced concern for having more flexible work time to spend with their families

Source: Olesia Bilkei / Shutterstock.com

for skipping ceremonial dinners to be at home with his children. These are good trends but women often are criticized for doing the same thing. In the summer of 2012 Anne-Marie Slaughter (2012) published an article in the *Atlantic* magazine, "Why Women Still Can't Have It All," which explained why she was leaving a high-level state department job in Washington DC to return to Princeton to be with her husband and family. Slaughter had many advantages, unavailable to many working mothers, since Princeton was close enough to DC for a weekend commuting life and money was no object. Additionally, her husband was a college professor who agreed to take on the bulk of the parenting activities while she worked at her state job. His "agreement" reflects his choice whereas most women do not perceive themselves as having a choice when it comes to childrearing responsibilities. Slaughter, after her two years with the State, would have had to resign her position at Princeton if she wanted to continue with her DC position but she admits that the decisive factor in her return was her family, since her older boy was having some difficulties with the transition to adolescence. She felt a strong compulsion to be with her family, even though she completely trusted her husband's capabilities. She wrote about the difficulty of finding a work/family balance, even considering the many advantages available to her. The *Atlantic* received more commentary on Slaughter's article than on any other in the magazine's history. Slaughter continued her reflection on the issues with the publication of her book, *Unfinished Business: Women, Men, Work, Family* (2016).

Cultural attitudes regarding working mothers remain mixed though the reality is that most work. Forty-one percent of respondents in a large study believe that it is bad for moms to work, though 75 percent of women with kids at home do so. Research shows that working moms create social, educational, and economic benefits. Daughters of working mothers achieve better paying jobs and more education. Their sons, whose work and income are not affected, are more involved in household chores and childrearing (Miller 2015).

Slaughter's story highlights the unfriendly nature of work structures in the US, even among the most privileged sectors. Unlike other countries with advanced economies, many US jobs fail to provide for sick days, parental leave, or "family days" (where parents can visit with kids' schools), and have fewer paid holidays and shorter vacations. Research definitively shows that American parents experience the least happiness with regard to parenting when compared to other English-speaking and European populations, and the difference is entirely attributable to the lack of social policies (Coontz 2017; Knox 2016). In other high-income countries, paid leave is generally guaranteed by the government, employer, or some combination of the two. Paid leaves can usually be taken by either parent, or shared by the partners, though they must be consecutive rather than simultaneous. Parental leaves can range from 20 weeks to a year, and extend to two years in some countries. The portion of income retained while on leave varies by country and by the duration of the leave time, but 80–90 percent of the regular salary is not uncommon and health benefits are not affected.

The only national policy in the US is the *Family and Medical Leave Act* of 1996 which covers a maximum of 12 weeks of unpaid leave for family emergencies in companies with 50 or more employees. Only 14 percent of private companies

(McGregor 2014) offer any paid parental leave. These employers offer anywhere from six weeks to six months of paid parental leave. Only five states, 23 cities, and one county have paid sick time laws on the books. Obama signed an order providing for six weeks of paid leave for federal employees. Lower level workers are unlikely to have paid parental leave, or even any paid sick leave, and generally have less flexible workday schedules (ABB 2016). Some companies, especially in Silicon Valley, have been instituting more liberal leave policies, with *Facebook* offering four months and *Yahoo* eight weeks (McGregor 2014). Additionally, some high-profile individuals, such as Mark Zuckerberg, Kanye West, Justin Timberlake, and Prince William are taking time to be at home with a new baby. Quebec reserves five weeks of parental leave exclusively for fathers (Covert 2015).

Research also shows interesting trends in the millennial generation. Equality of roles appears to have peaked in the mid-1990s. Research shows a recent increase in the desirability of a traditionally oriented two-parent household, with a father as the main breadwinner and a mother who takes care of the home. This trend is statistically significant and even more pronounced among young men (Coontz 2017). One study indicates this sentiment is largely the result of watching the parental generation struggle with work and family stressors (Coontz 2017). It is also clear that progressive family policies make a difference. One study showed that dads who receive paid paternity leave took it all, but many fathers surveyed said they would not take unpaid leave or leave paid at less than 70 percent of their salaries (McGregor 2014). Research also shows that, aside from enhanced family life, the short-term costs of paternity leave may be compensated for by the long-term gains in increased productivity and decreased worker turnover (Covert 2015).

> ### Box 10.8 – Parental Leave
>
> **Parental leave** is paid leave a person can take at the birth or adoption of a child. The United States has **NO** policy guaranteeing parental leave. About 12 percent of private companies offer parental leave and President Obama signed an order providing six weeks of paid leave for federal employees. *The Family and Emergency Medical Leave Act,* signed into law by President Clinton in 1993, mandates up to 12 weeks of *unpaid* leave for workers employed by a company with 50 employees or more. This can be utilized for the birth or adoption of a child or any other family medical or emergency leave issue, such as illness or a problematic pregnancy.

Families and Aging

Later in life divorces are on the rise. Previously, the longer a person was married the less likely they were to divorce but the portion of people divorcing at age 50 and older has doubled since 1990. For the age group over 65 the increase is even greater. There are a variety of reasons for this development: an individual's longevity can enhance the likelihood that a couple will grow apart, especially after the kids are grown. For some women, financial independence has provided the security to leave an unfulfilling situation. Finally, the general vulnerability of second marriages makes them harder to sustain, especially if the adults each have children and grandchildren (Ellin 2015). Many people blossom after a divorce from a marriage which had been stultifying, pursuing interests stagnant during the marriage, or newly discovered. For others, the aftermath of the divorce can be devastating with feelings of loss, loneliness, and depression, sometimes accompanied by substance abuse. For older persons, a later divorce can rekindle past trauma since 53 percent of people who divorce after 50 have had a previous divorce (Bloom and Bloom 2012).

In general, men have more difficulty after divorce, suffer more depression and loneliness, and are more prone to develop bad habits. Substance abuse, unhealthy lifestyles, and avoiding routine health maintenance are more characteristic in divorced men than women. Women are more likely to initiate divorce but regardless of who initiates a divorce, a man is more likely to remarry than a woman (McClintock 2014). For many men, sociability occurs through work or the wife's planning so divorce significantly reduces their activities. Women typically maintain an active social support network which may mitigate against the desire to remarry. They also tend to have more responsibilities in the marriage and so are less likely to see remarriage as a desirable outcome.

One in seven Americans is 65 or older. Over 72 percent of men and 46 percent of women in this group were married in 2013. Twenty-eight percent of noninstitutionalized elderly live alone (Ortman et al. 2014). Isolation and loneliness are difficult to quantify. There are dating websites especially for widowed persons. The relationship between isolation and depression is reciprocal, perpetuating a negative cycling. In a UCSF study of the elderly, 43 percent of respondents reported feeling lonely on a regular basis and two thirds of these were living with a partner (Botek n.d.). Living alone does not consistently indicate that a person is lonely, particularly among the young, but among the elderly there is a greater risk that living alone indicates a scarcity of social connection. Being an active grandparent can protect against feelings of isolation. Stahl (2016) documents the beneficial impact of grandparent/grandchild relationships for both participants. Becoming an active grandparent can also bring new dimensions to the relationship with the adult child. Increased longevity has made the grandparent role an increasingly significant relationship, even extending into the grandchild's adulthood.

Box 10.9 – Grandparents

Increased longevity has resulted in many more **grandparents**. Many of today's grandparents are relatively young and in good health, taking active roles in their grandchildren's lives. Research shows that the grandparent/grandchild relationship is beneficial to both participants, as well as supporting the working parents.

How Is Family Lived?

Living Single

More than one quarter of adults live alone, though the exact number varies with different sources. This is a significant development in human history, since in the past solo life was literally impossible. Today, with delayed age of marriage, coupled with divorce and widowhood, many people can expect to spend a significant portion of their lives living alone. There is some evidence that many nonelderly single people enjoy active social lives, spend much time in the company of others, and enjoy their independence. Friendships between women are places of deeply held intimacy, even life altering, and remain essential even if the women take on heterosexual life partners (Traister 2016; Drexler 2014).

There is some research which suggests that living alone can be literally unhealthy. A national research study (Klinenberg et al. 2016) shows that social isolation can influence mortality in equal measure to risk factors such as smoking, obesity, high blood pressure, and high cholesterol. Certain populations are more vulnerable to risks associated with single living. These include older people, men, and members of the LGBTQ communities. More research is needed to distinguish between living alone, feeling lonely, and social isolation. Single people, living alone, may not feel lonely or be isolated since they spend more time volunteering and visiting with friends. Environment makes a difference as well. It was found that poor people living in vibrant communities with social and commercial activity, designated as having "robust infrastructures," fare better than their counterparts in more run-down neighborhoods lacking in such infrastructures (Klinenberg et al. 2016).

African American Families

There are many cultural stereotypes promoting the idea that the African American family is dysfunctional, matriarchal, and characterized by absent fathers. Blow (2015) dispels these stereotypes by looking beyond statistics. Although unmarried births describe 72 percent of Black, non-Hispanic women's experiences, he suggests this is due to mass incarceration and early death, and that, due to the consequent scarcity of African American men, some men have children with more than one woman. Blow establishes that many men are living with women, just not married, while other men are active with their children and women but not living with them. He also shows that the birthrate for African American women is decreasing and the birthrate for married African American women is lower than that of married White women, causing the portion of unwed births to appear more significant than it is. The Centers for Disease Control (CDC) has found that African American men, by several measures utilized, are **more** active in the daily lives of their children than other fathers.

The entire conceptualization of the African American family is distorted by the history of slavery and the cultural bias of White European norms. The historical enslavement of Africans in the US is frequently suggested as responsible for the "disintegration" of the nuclear family. This view obscures the ways in which African

Figure 10.12 African American men, contrary to popular images, are more active with children than White men (CDC) Source: DGLimages / Shutterstock.com

American family structures have shown extraordinary resilience. African peoples enjoyed large extended families in strongly unified communities. Although there were many distinct cultures in Africa, the social organization typically evidenced whole communities operating as extended families and these have been sustained in the US. This structure, where the community members all tended to responsibilities of childrearing, was adaptive against the travails of enslavement. It reflects a healthy model with multiple adults invested in raising the children of the community. Children can never have too many "parents." Women were not identified by roles commensurate with the modern "housewife" devoted primarily to her home, spouse, and children. The "housewife" represents a Euro-centric ideal and generally signifies a somewhat isolated nuclear unit. African American women have a lifestyle based in intensive social and community participation and leadership (Hill Collins 2000).

Afrocentric feminist notions of family reflect this reconceptualization process. Black women's experiences as bloodmothers, othermothers, and community othermothers reveal that the mythical norm of a heterosexual, married couple, nuclear family with a nonworking spouse and a husband earning a 'family wage' is far from being natural, universal and preferred but instead is deeply embedded in specific race and class formations. Placing African-American women in the center of analysis not only reveals much-needed information about Black women's experiences but also questions Eurocentric masculinist perspectives on family.

(Patricia Hill Collins, Boston, 1990, http://www.hartford-hwp.com/archives/45a/252.html)

African American married couples historically have exhibited greater gender role equality, with women playing the role of independent partner. African American parents, due to concern for the racial discrimination of their children, addressed issues of power, work, brutality, and violence, especially with their sons. African American women, even before the recently publicized string of deaths of Black men by law enforcement officials, were likely to have "the talk" with their sons about how to survive in a White, racist society (Sultan 2014).

Latino Families

Children absorb spoken and unspoken messages from observing the adults in their communities way before they can articulate them. Children are aware of different behaviors their parents exhibit at home, and in their community, than in dealing with the world outside of these. Latina author Cherrie Moraga states: "I have had to confront the fact that much of what I value about being Chicana, about my family, has been subverted by Anglo culture and my own cooperation with it" (Moraga 2007). Living with a double consciousness, as a nondominant group member, is a dynamic commonly articulated among all marginalized groups. W.E.B. Du Bois revealed this dynamic in a 1903 essay "The Souls of Black Folk." Latinos also write of a sense of "otherness," or not really belonging or feeling validated in the culture (Madrid 2007). In the video, *The Color of Fear* (Wah 1994), a middle-aged Chicano speaks of being surrounded by people who do not "act like him, think like him, smell like him, or laugh and cry" like he does. Another man in the video remarks that he cannot wait to leave the corporate world, to go home and "be Black again."

Latino families generally embrace pronounced familial bonds which can over-ride individual needs. Families are closely knit and, if not actually living in extended households, commonly live close enough to relatives to visit frequently, sometimes daily. Gender roles are traditionally oriented, with a father breadwinner and mother homemaker. Older family members are respected and deferred to and, though the structure is patriarchal, women are revered as nurturers and central domestic figures. Children are expected to be loyal to their family of origin:

> Unless you're exiled from your father's house for some transgression, you really are expected to live there ... And if you don't marry, you're expected to stay there and take care of your parents. I'm an only daughter in the middle of six brothers. And I think I did things that were rather shocking if I had been a man.
> (Sandra Cisneros, NPR Staff 2015)

Latino families today represent a variety of forms. Acculturation to Anglo customs creates tensions in the family, especially with regard to the liberalization of gender roles and peer relations in the younger generation. Rates and manner of acculturation vary with immigration status, language, longevity of residence, education, family composition, and locale. Research indicates that higher acculturation is associated with greater use of public services, increased social supports, higher perceptions of health, and more agency or control. Contrarily, it also indicates a predilection to anxiety, depression, and suicide. Deeply held notions of the respect men should receive are tied to the concept of *macho or machismo*. Women are similarly held to standards relating to *Marianism*, or the image of the Virgin Mary; the woman is viewed as the moral force of the family and the family is built around her. These terms *machismo* and *Marianism* are utilized in Mexico, though it is suggested that the themes, if not the language, permeate many of the Latino cultures (Fernandez 2009). The most extreme manifestations of these roles may be decreasing but the differential gender roles persist in many Latino families, while accommodating some of the more egalitarian elements of contemporary society. Some research indicates a close identification of males with the role of father but there is little research on investigating actual interactions, with respect to time and content, between fathers and children.

Asian American Families

The Asian population is varied in ethnicity, country of origin, and immigration status, highlighting the diversity in the designation of Asian. A recent survey of 3511 Asian Americans, drawing heavily from the Chinese, Filipino, Indian, Vietnamese, Korean, and Japanese populations indicates they are doing better and feel more positively about the US than the general population, although this trend is not uniformly found across included groups. Newly arrived Asian immigrants are more educated than the general population, with 60 percent having college degrees, and they are more likely to be working in science and technology fields. They are the best educated cohort in US immigrant history. All of the Asian groups reported on were more likely than the general population to identify a successful marriage and good parenting as significant life goals (Nasser 2012). Earlier groups of Asian immigrants were brought to the US with very different intent and circumstances, ranging from indentured servitude to escaping the Southeast Asian wars of the mid-twentieth century.

Asian families are highly likely to embrace family loyalty, respect for elders, and family affiliations as central to personal identity. Emotional and verbal reticence are valued, while direct questioning of others is considered rude. Asian parenting is generally strict and parental control firm, making openly warm or demonstrative behavior rare. Youth often experience conflict between the US cultural norms and parent cultural norms (Carteret n.d.; Faderman and Xiong 1998; Frances McClelland Institute n.d.).

Chinese American law professor, Amy Chua, created an international controversy with her book, *Battle Hymn of the Tiger Mother* (2011), regarding the way she raised her two daughters. In contrast to her children's peer group, she did not allow them to watch television, have play dates or sleepovers, choose their own extra-curricular activities, or get lower grades than an A. Her focused, non-permissive parenting style drew much criticism and praise. The book, intended as a memoir regarding her personal dual cultural conflicts, incited a frenzy of attacks regarding over-involved *helicopter parenting*. Perhaps more significantly, it released a flood of sentiments revealing the angst many parents experience regarding the "right" way to raise children. This initially surprised Chua since she had set out to tackle issues of acculturation rather than to dispense parenting advice. Many chastised her for being unrelentingly domineering, rigid, and controlling, though that was not how she saw herself. Subsequent to the furor surrounding the book's publication, one of her daughters published an article defending her mother and both daughters expressed positive feelings regarding their upbringing. Nevertheless, the media frenzy reinforced many stereotypes of the Chinese American culture.

Extending Chua's personal experiences to Chinese American families, or Asian cultures, is symbolic of the tendency to address these cultures uniformly. Asian families demonstrate the same diversities seen among the general population and are influenced by immigration status, social class, country of origin, religion, and locale. Among the traditional Hmong, for example, marriage for girls is arranged and occurs early, at around age 15. Education is not seen as important to this culture's agrarian roots and is especially viewed as unimportant for girls. Acculturation has led youth to participate in American dating, mate selection, education, and career trends. This transitioning of the Americanized youths has created tension with the older generation, similar to that seen in many other groups, including the European ethnic immigrants of the last century (Faderman and Xiong 1998).

Indigenous Families

The policies and practices of the US government have compromised Indigenous families and cultures. Accurate histories and research are difficult to locate.

The following is a summary statement of a PBS series on Native American family life:

> Each tribe's historic relocation or genocide experience also damaged traditional family structures and family mores. Some Native American tribes were patriarchal, but most were matriarchal tracing lineage through the mother. In general, women held honored places in the society. For instance, among the Cherokees, women owned the homes and garden plots, which were passed from mother to daughter. It was also the Cherokee Women's Council who determined which men were worthy of performing sacred duties or holding public office. Many other tribes had similar matriarchal systems.
>
> According to many tribal elders and oral traditions, "wife-beating" was a practice learned from non-Indian society. Or at least, the stresses introduced by the Europeans may have contributed to domestic abuse.

Policies of the *Bureau of Indian Affairs*, which removed children from local reservations and communities to boarding schools, resulted in forced assimilation in language, clothing, and education. These cultural impositions did not erase the cultures' religion, ethics, and behaviors. In the second half of the twentieth century, many Indigenous families moved to urban areas and suffered losses as a result of the loss of the community cultural supports. The decimation of the culture has had incalculable consequences for the Indigenous populations' well-being. Many problems characteristic of the Indigenous peoples, such as alcohol or substance abuse, can best be understood as reactionary symptoms to the violence against their cultures. In recent decades, increased attention to preserving cultural elements has led Indigenous groups to create written forms of their languages and develop special events and programs to expose young people to cultural practices, beliefs, and histories.

White Families

Internet searches on "White families" turn up nothing regarding White family life as expressive of the values of "the White culture." Partially this reflects the dominant role of White culture but it is also a mistake to view all White cultures as uniform. White culture has assimilated White "ethnics" into the dominant European Anglo-Saxon Protestant practices and attitudes. As the dominant culture, "White" families' structures and customs are integrated as societal norms. The traditional nuclear family model, with two parents and their children, who will "launch" into individualist, independent adult identities broadly typifies this group, though some "ethnic" groups maintain closer family ties and proximity. Geographic mobility requiring separation from parents in pursuit of career advancement is considered normative.

Research on "White families" mostly is limited to comparisons with nonWhite races. Comparisons often are drawn with respect to marriage patterns, childrearing style, employment, education, income, and wealth. Descriptions articulating the practices of "White" family life are nonexistent. White identity hinges on defining other races as the "other" (Coates 2015), and so frequently is not investigated as a discrete entity. The White working-class patterns with regard to marriage rates, unwed births, and single parenting are similar to those identified in less educated African American communities, suggesting the primacy of social class in family outcomes (Sawhill 2013).

Figure 10.13 In 2015 a Supreme Court decision made gay marriage legal in all 50 states and the District of Columbia Source: cunaplus / Shutterstock.com

Gay Families

In the 2010 Census, .6 percent of households were reported as headed by a same sex couple. This represents a growth of 80.4 percent from 2000. A small fraction of the 2010 same-sex households reported being married (Youth Blog n.d.). Under-reporting makes it difficult to say anything about the actual number of same-sex households. It is safe to say that the portion of couples reporting cohabitation, as well as marriage, will show a significant increase by the 2020 Census. Gay marriage became legal in June 2015 as a result of the Supreme Court case of *Obergefell v. Hodges*. The decision affirmed the Constitutional right of due process and equal protection of marriage for same-sex couples. Cultural support for gay marriage has grown significantly, increasing to 62 percent in 2017, compared with 37 percent ten years earlier. Nonaffiliated religious persons are more likely to support gay marriage, as are the millennials (Masci et al. 2017). Millennials, even among those who generally show conservative attitudes, are likely to support gay marriage (Blake 2009).

Gay couples represent many similarities to heterosexual ones. They are as likely as other couples to list "love" as a major reason for the desire to marry (88 percent) (Masci et al. 2017). Legal marriage carries benefits over cohabitation, such as rights to inheritance and to be named as decision makers in medical directives. Registering as domestic partners can bring some legal advantages but does not provide for a fully legal relationship. Gay marriage can yield economic advantages for the couple. Culturally, it presents the opportunity for a boost to the wedding industry, which has suffered setbacks in recent years, and other enterprises supporting domestic life (Stein and Bobic 2015).

Box 10.10 – Gay Marriage

Gay marriage became legal everywhere in the US by a 2015 Supreme Court decision granting same-sex couples the same due process and equal protection awarded to heterosexuals. It is difficult to know what portion of the US population live in long-term same-sex partnerships since they are under-reported. Future data, culled from government sources of domestic partnerships or marriages, are likely to yield more reliable information by the 2020 Census.

Research regarding the effects of gay parents on children's well-being is difficult to assess because there are so many factors to control for. In addition to accounting for socio-demographic differences, there are also issues of parenting approaches and household composition. Many of the children of gay and lesbian parents were initially born into heterosexual households and demonstrate little conformity. Separating the threads of cause and effect becomes almost impossible, especially because many of the studies have a limited number of cases. In a review of the literature on gay parenting (What We Know n.d.), the authors state that 75 of 79 studies found no discernible differences in the youths studied. Two studies, with large samples, showed no differences in the school achievement of children from gay or straight

households, when controlling for family background. Four found an increased risk in outcomes for the youths but lacked clarity in assigning causality since the dissolution of a heterosexual partnership was a frequent confounding factor. Only a handful of these children were actually raised by a gay or lesbian couple. Research from a study of over 300 same-sex couples, compared with almost 200 heterosexual couples, shows that the children of same-sex couples are healthier. Analysis attributes these differences to equal parenting roles rather than to the sexual orientation of the parents (CNBC 2014).

Another factor making assessment of the research on gay couples difficult stems from the failure to consider the effects of social stigma and discrimination on the family members, a situation which seems more impactful than the sexual orientation of the parents (Blake 2009). One research project shows that children of gay couples possess more liberal attitudes than other groups, especially with regard to gender but also politically, which appears to be more attributable to the gender identities of the parents than to sexual orientation (Chamberlin n.d.). The explicit impact of sexual orientation requires more isolation of its affect than is presently available.

Youth Without Families

It is difficult to estimate the number of youth who are either on the streets or in the foster care system. The best estimates indicate that there were roughly 415,000 children in foster care in 2014 (ACF 2015) and between 1.6–2.8 million runaways. Foster care mandates vary by state and county. A foster child typically undergoes multiple placements and relocations, without notice or preparation time. Children often have little time to say goodbye or to obtain contact information for friends and foster family members. The transient nature of placements can be disorienting, at best. Some children run away due to abusive actions in the foster family.

> ### Box 10.11 – Youth Without Family
>
> Some *legal minors* live without parental or guardian supervision. Youths can be the legal responsibility of the government, as in foster care, or they can be on their own without legal guardianship, as in the case of runaways.

Some states offer extended support to foster youth after they turn 18 years old, but often the youths either don't know about it; don't know how to access it; are put off by cumbersome paperwork; or have other issues which act as impediments to extending services. As a result, many youths have difficulties in education, housing, healthcare, and finances when they become independent. Investment in less abrupt discharging of state obligations by providing "aftercare" programs seems advantageous. If government commitment to the provision of funds for extended services is not made on humane grounds, there are sound fiscal reasons for doing so: one in five foster youths is homeless after age 18, one half are unemployed at 24, fewer than 3 percent obtain a college degree, and 71 percent of the young women are pregnant by 21. Providing for social and financial support would not only help the youth to gain college educations but would likely reduce early pregnancy and further system dependency. There are programs which have helped foster youth and runaways to succeed but these frequently are either underfunded or discontinued (Soronen 2014). Homeless LGBTQ foster youth are exceptionally at risk for tragic outcomes. These youths are at elevated risk for suicide, sexual abuse, and hunger even when compared to their homeless heterosexual counterparts (National Runaway Safeline n.d.).

Domestic Violence

Domestic violence refers to any physical, psychological, emotional, sexual, or financial damage a person perpetrates in primary interpersonal relationships. Abuse occurs between parent and child; between siblings; between a family member or provider and an elderly person; and partner abuse occurs in married, cohabitating, and dating couples. Domestic violence is pervasive, cutting across all family forms and socioeconomic levels. The one common thread in all domestic violence is the perception, on the part of the abuser, of having power over the person who is abused; control is the motivating element. If the power differential shifts, the abuse may drop off, as when a child becomes physically stronger than the parent. The situation is also vulnerable to external factors. When, for example, the economy tanks, abuse increases. Loss of income or a job can exacerbate a person's self-esteem, leading to abusive behaviors. Financial fear can cause women to stay in abusive relationships. Contracted government budgets can lead to cuts in human services, also contributing to lack of alternatives to remaining in the abusive situation (Firestone 2012).

> **Box 10.12 – Domestic Violence**
>
> *Domestic violence* refers to any physical, sexual, or mental abuse occurring in a domestic setting. This includes spousal abuse; parental abuse; child abuse and neglect; elderly abuse and neglect; sibling abuse; and rape and sexual molestation. All domestic violence incorporates a dynamic of **perceived power** of the abuser over the target of the abuse. Typically, these forms of violence emerge from the customary expectations assigned to each of the social roles.

Domestic violence is so prevalent that it may be considered "normal" behavior. Twenty people per minute experience intimate partner violence and 40–45 percent of these incidents include sexual assault. One in four women will suffer severe violence in her lifetime and one in seven men will. A woman is beaten every nine seconds. Gay men are at high risk, with 40 percent estimated to have experienced domestic violence. Fifty percent of lesbians have suffered some form of abuse though not necessarily from a partner. It is estimated that eight million days of work are missed annually from abuse. Some 18,500,000 mental health visits are attributable to domestic violence. The average ER visit for a woman, stemming from domestic abuse, costs $948 while the corresponding male figure is $387. Women with physical disabilities are at greater risk, estimated as 40 percent more likely than other women to experience physical violence. More than 61 percent of murdered women are killed by an intimate partner, amounting to three women a day. Women are eight times more likely to be killed if there is a firearm in the home. The vast majority of women who are stalked also are abused by that partner. Men who experience domestic violence as children are three to four times more likely than other men to perpetrate as adults (Vagianos 2015). Only 25 percent of physical assaults on women are reported to police. A person can obtain a restraining order but people who have been subjected to severe abuse know that these are largely ineffective and may even incite the abuser to act. Nicole Brown Simpson's calls to the police regarding her restraining order against O.J. Simpson are a case in point, as she is widely believed to have been murdered by him despite his acquittal. In spite of a documented history and reports of abuse, O.J. Simpson was at her house the night she was killed, and she made 911 calls saying she feared he would kill her.

In recent years, more attention has been focused on women who commit violence against their partners. Retaliation and self-defense are more often associated with women's acts of violence than control. This is not to say that women never initiate violence but that they are less likely to do so. Research also indicates that domestic violence has a greater impact on women, even in situations of reciprocal abuse. Men are more likely to initiate "serious" abuse (more severe injuries), sexual abuse, and stalking (Swan et al. 2008; Weinberger 2016).

The emotional consequences of domestic violence are far more difficult to assess than the physical ones. Many women perceive no way out, and this attitude is part of the consequence of living in a dynamic of abuse. Ninety-eight percent of women who are abused have no access to financial resources (Vagianos 2015). Women who work may also feel defenseless since the partner may manage her paycheck, prohibiting her from accessing funds. This is one of the reasons why shelters are so important because women, and other victims of violence, need a safe place of refuge.

Women also are fearful of leaving because they are afraid of escalating their partner's reactions. There is justification for this fear. In the first few weeks after leaving her abuser, a woman's risk rate increases by 70 times. Many emotions, pressures, and fears feed into a person's likelihood of staying. Many observers ask: "Why doesn't she just leave?" This attitude reflects a lack of understanding of the dynamic of abuse and evades a bigger issue concerning why abuse is so "acceptable." Abuse contributes to feelings of dependency and shatters self-esteem, even in women who are working or otherwise functioning outside of the home, and who entered the relationship with their self-confidence intact. Persons subjected to violence exhibit response patterns typically identified in brainwashing. These represent situational dynamics which are inherently immobilizing and could promote "victim" behavior in anyone so exposed. Gender roles contribute by promoting the idea that the failure of a relationship is due to the women's inability to be a "good" wife. Additionally, many women believe that their children are better off with two parents in the home and are fearful of the consequences of leaving, though it is preferable in violent settings (Shoener 2014). Domestic violence is a complicated syndrome, and so is its emotional, social, and financial fallout. Children who *witness* domestic violence are at greater risk, even more than child victims, for future involvement in domestic violence. Perhaps this is due to viewing the behavior without experiencing its devastation firsthand. Domestic violence is the third leading cause of family homelessness and it is implicated in the rate of runaways.

Child abuse is defined as the physical harming of a child due to punching, beating or other physical attacks, such as striking a child with a belt or other implement or medical neglect which endangers the child. Contrary to popular beliefs, it is permissible by law to hit your child with an open hand between the shoulders and above the knees, though codes vary by jurisdiction. A parent can use physical discipline "mildly" and there are some experts who do not think this is a negative thing. The rate of child abuse is extensive. *Child neglect* is the failure to provide for basic human needs such as adequate nutrition, shelter, clothing, warmth (in winter), and supervision appropriate to a child's age. Sexual abuse refers to any sexualized touching or assault. Scxual abuse of a child or adolescent is by definition *coercive*; a child who is dependent on an adult or caretaker can never be considered to be consenting.

Published rates of child abuse and neglect are often inconclusive, differing by study and reflective of under-reporting. Abuse frequently is unrecognized and/ or unreported. There are 2.9 million reports of child abuse and neglect annually. Girls are more likely to be abused; 36 percent of females and 14 percent of males are estimated to have been abused as children (Do Something n.d.). This number likely excludes unsubstantiated reports as well as those never reported. "Mandated reporters" refer to anyone who comes into contact with children in a professional setting such as in a school, medical facility, or youth setting/activity. This incorporates support and paraprofessional staff, as well as professionals. Sometimes a person is reluctant to make a report, because they fear retaliation or worry about the child landing in a worse situation. The name of the reporter is anonymous, though fear of being identified by the abuser can act as a deterrent. In most jurisdictions, a report of suspected abuse will result in an automatic removal of the minor, usually for 72 hours, to make a preliminary study of the situation. States and counties delineate the process for more extended or permanent removal but the system is theoretically obligated to put the safety of the child first and foremost.

Child neglect is under-reported and, when occurring with no other form of abuse, rarely results in any removal of a child unless it is severe enough to be life threatening. Nevertheless, the consequences of neglect, both physically and psychologically, can be devastating and long term. Abuse and neglect result in a 59 percent increased likelihood of juvenile arrest and a 28 percent increase in arrest as an adult. Eighty percent of adults, 21 and over, who experienced child abuse meet the criteria for at least one psychological disorder. People who experience child abuse and neglect are also more at risk of committing a violent crime. Female subjects are 25 percent more likely to have a teen pregnancy (Do Something n.d.).

Statistics regarding the extent of sexual abuse are even harder to assess. It is estimated that one in three females and one in five males will experience an incident of sexual abuse by the age of 18. Ninety percent of these will entail people known to the child and 68 percent will be family members (Do Something n.d.). Children who have been sexually abused can have long-term consequences from the abuse ranging from depression, anger, and substance abuse to an inability to form long-term relationships or to trust people. The child who is sexually abused not only suffers feelings of betrayal, due to the acts of the abuser, but also feels angry or betrayed by the non-abusing parent, or adult, who failed to secure their safety.

Sibling Abuse

Psychologists often have insisted that sibling "sparring," both verbal and physical, is a "normal" part of sibling interaction and can even be beneficial since it can toughen kids against peer assaults (personal communications). Sibling abuse includes verbal intimidation, physical assaults, and sexual molestation or intercourse. Sibling abuse, as estimated from a recent study of 3600 youths under the age of 17, is estimated at incidences four to five times those of spousal and child abuse. One half of the children reported being kicked, punched, or bitten and 15 percent reported being assaulted repeatedly. In a study from the *National Survey of Child's Exposure to Violence,* 6 percent reported experiencing some form of sexual assault (Finkelhor et al. 2009). Sibling assaults result in increased levels of depression, anger, and anxiety. Victimization by siblings should be treated with equal concern as bullying in school or by peers; it may actually do more long-term damage since it erodes self-esteem and identity in the very place that should be supporting safety. Even with the level of incidences being reported at one third of youths in any given year, the data is likely under-estimated since most people are reluctant to accuse their children or to recognize sibling "bantering" as potentially damaging.

Elderly Abuse

Elderly abuse includes physical and sexual abuse; psychological, emotional and verbal abuse; financial exploitation regarding money and/or property; abandonment;

and failure to assist persons who cannot care for themselves. Elderly abuse is estimated to occur in 10 percent of the population with 90 percent of incidences involving family members as the perpetrators. This problem is literally growing, not only in its recognition but in the fact that the elderly population, currently 13 percent of the whole population, is predicted to reach 20 percent by 2050. The portion of older elderly, 75 years and older, represent greater risk and will likely increase at a faster rate.

Financial abuse, reported as occurring in 41 of 1000 elderly persons, is the most common form of abuse. Physical abuse and neglect occur in institutional settings, particularly those with long-term care patients. The high turnover of personnel, low pay, and heavy patient loads are all contributing factors in the increased vulnerability of long-term care patients. Since fewer of the elderly live in these settings, the prevalence is higher in private settings (Heitz 2014; APA n.d.). More social policies supporting the elderly and their caretakers likely would reduce abuse rates.

Key Terms

Nuclear Family   Extended Family   Polyamory   Homogamy   Romantic Love   Second Shift   No Fault Divorce   Community Property   Tiger Mom   Helicopter Parents   Domestic Violence   Child Abuse   Child Neglect

Concept Review

How Can We Define Family when the Institution Is Varied and In Flux?

Family can be seen as the people who are most significant in a person's life, forming a primary group and representing some combination of emotional identification, social support, or financial support. The people so defined may, or may not, be living in the same household. "Family" members may be chosen from friendships or constructed by blood or legal relationships.

What Is the Composition of Families Today?

There are various family and household arrangements and much of the research reveals contradictory data. One fact is clear—there are more children being born to unmarried women today, around 40 percent. Another change is that fewer children live with two parents, particularly the original biological two. One historical innovation is the 27 percent of single-person households. This can be attributed to delayed marriage, nonmarriage, divorce, and widowhood.

How Can We View Family Changes Over Time?

Familial and personal concerns change over time. The "life cycle" of a family begins with choosing a mate, followed by marriage or cohabitation; childrearing for some couples; divorce for some couples; the formation of step or "blended" families for some; and a period of widowhood or single aging. Sexual orientation; race and ethnicity; single-parent status; and social class all affect family life. Single life, gay marriage, and non-familial households also characterize domestic life.

What Is Domestic Violence and How Prevalent Is It?

Domestic violence refers to physical, sexual, or emotional abuse; child abuse and neglect of basic life needs; partner sexual, physical, or psychological abuse; physical, sexual, or financial abuse of the elderly; and physical, sexual, and verbal abuse between siblings. All domestic violence is predicated on the desire to control another person and the perception of having the power to do so. Domestic violence results in physical and psychological damage which can follow a person throughout life. It is difficult, if not impossible, to assess the prevalence of domestic violence. Sibling abuse, in particular, is not well researched though it is estimated to be the most common form.

Review Questions

1. How would you account for an inclusive definition of family? What characteristics would you select in differentiating it from other social groups? Is the traditional concept of family obsolete?
2. What demographic changes have impacted today's households? Do you think family is losing its importance as a major social institution?
3. Has the division of household labor changed much in recent decades? What is the cultural significance of housework?
4. Should parents remain together, for the sake of raising their children? Explain.
5. Are the standards of parenting different for women and men? Explain.
6. Are gender roles in Anglo American families and in nondominant American families similar? Explain.
7. Is gay parenting substantially differentiated from straight parenting?
8. How should children who cannot stay at home best be served? Provide details.
9. What do all types of domestic violence have in common?
10. What can be done to make the society more supportive of family life? Explain.

References

7 Things You Should Know About Dating in America. (January 25, 2014) *The Huffington Post*. Retrieved from http://www.huffingtonpost.com/2014/01/22/state-of-dating-in-america_n_4639717.html

ABB. A Better Balance. (November 15, 2016) *Paid Sick Time Legislative Successes*. Retrieved from http://www.abetterbalance.org/web/images/stories/Documents/sickdays/factsheet/PSDchart.pdf

ACF. (July, 2015) The AFCARS Report. *Administration for Children and Families*. Retrieved from https://www.acf.hhs.gov/sites/default/files/cb/afcarsreport22.pdf

Adams, R. (July 7, 2015) 7 Drawbacks of Online Dating, According to Science. *The Huffington Post*. Retrieved from http://www.huffingtonpost.com/2015/07/07/online-dating-science_n_7745108.html

APA. (n.d.) Elder Abuse and Neglect: In Search of Solutions. *The American Psychological Association*. Retrieved from http://www.apa.org/pi/aging/resources/guides/elder-abuse.aspx

Ansari, A., Menjivar, J. (June 26, 2015) 559: Captain's Log. *This American Life*. Retrieved from https://www.thisamericanlife.org/radio-archives/episode/559/captains-log?act=2

Blankenhorn, D. (1995) *Fatherless America: Confronting our Most Urgent Social Problem*. NY: Basic Books.

Blake, J. (June 29, 2009) "Gaybyboom": Children of Gay Couples Speak Out. *CNN*. Retrieved from https://cola.unh.edu/sites/cola.unh.edu/files/student-journals/ShelbyChamberlin.pdf

Bloom, L., Bloom, C. (April, 2012) The Epidemic of Gray Divorces. *Psychology Today*. Retrieved from https://www.psychologytoday.com/blog/stronger-the-broken-places/201204/the-epidemic-gray-divorces

Blow, M.C. (June 8, 2015) Black Dads Are Doing Best of All. *The New York Times*. Retrieved from https://www.nytimes.com/2015/06/08/opinion/charles-blow-black-dads-are-doing-the-best-of-all.html?_r=0

Botek, A. (n.d.) The Elder Loneliness Epidemic. *Agingcare.com*. Retrieved from https://www.agingcare.com/Articles/loneliness-in-the-elderly-151549.htm

Bratskeir, K. (November 15, 2015) Couples Who Share Chores May Have Better Sex, and Sex More Often. *The Huffington Post*. Retrieved from http://www.huffingtonpost.com/entry/share-chores-better-sex-couples_us_5638eefbe4b00a4d2e0c0594

Cancian, M., Meyer, D.R., Brown, P.R., Cook, S.T. (2014) Who Gets Custody Now? Dramatic Changes in Children's Living Arrangements After Divorce. *Demography*, 51(4): 1381–1396. http://dx.doi.org/10.1007/s13524-014-0307-8

Carteret, M. (n.d.) *Cultural Values of Asian Patients and Families. Dimensions of Culture*. Retrieved from http://www.dimensionsofculture.com/2010/10/cultural-values-of-asian-patients-and-families/

Chamberlin, S. (n.d.) *The Effects of Lesbian and Gay Parenting on Children's Development*. Retrieved from https://cola.unh.edu/sites/cola.unh.edu/files/student-journals/ShelbyChamberlin.pdf

Cherlin, J. A. (December 6, 2014) The Real Reason Richer People Marry. *The New York Times*. Retrieved from http://www.nytimes.com/2014/12/07/opinion/sunday/the-real-reason-richer-people-marry.html

Chua, A. (2011) *Battle Hymn of the Tiger Mother*. England: Bloomsbury Publishing plc.

CNBC. (July 7, 2014) Children of Same-sex Parents Are Healthier: Study. *CNBC.com*. Retrieved from https://www.nbcnews.com/https://www.nbcnews.com/health/kids-health/children-same-sex-parents-are-healthie

Coates, T. (2015) *Between the World and Me*. NY: Spiegel and Grau.

Collins, P.H. (n.d.) *Black Feminist Thought in the Matrix of Domination*. Hartford Web Publishing. Retrieved from http://www.hartford-hwp.com/archives/45a/252.html

Coontz, S. (June 16, 2010) Divorce, No-fault Style. *The New York Times*. Retrieved from https://www.nytimes.com/2010/06/17/opinion/17coontz.html

Coontz, S. (June 22, 2013) The Disestablishment of Marriage. *The New York Times*. Retrieved from http://www.nytimes.com/2013/06/23/opinion/sunday/coontz-the-disestablishment-of-marriage.html?_r=0

Coontz, S. (March 31, 2017) Do Millennial Men Want Stay at Home Wives? *The New York Times*. Retrieved from https://www.nytimes.com/2017/03/31/opinion/sunday/do-millennial-men-want-stay-at-home-wives.html?_r=0

Covert, B. (February 13, 2015) How Everyone Benefits When New Fathers Take Paid Leave. *Thinkprogress*. Retrieved from https://thinkprogress.org/how-everyone-benefits-when-new-fathers-take-paid-leave-862836d2f843/

Curtin, M. (March 21, 2018) Spouses Who View their Partners in this 1 Specific Way Are Twice as Satisfied in Life. *Inc*. Retrieved from https://www.inc.com/melanie-curtin/spouses-who-view-their-partners-in-this-1-specific-way-are-twice-as-satisfied-in-life.html

DiFonzo J.H. (November 14, 2014) There's a Great Way to Figure Out Child Custody. Most Divorce Courts Don't Use It. *The Washington Post*. Retrieved from https://www.washingtonpost.com/posteverything/wp/2014/11/14/no-children-should-not-spend-equal-time-with-their-divorced-parents/

Do Something. (n.d.) *11 Facts About Child Abuse*. Retrieved from https://www.dosomething.org/us/facts/11-facts-about-child-abuse

Drexler, P. (April 29, 2014) Friendships Between Women Have Health Benefits. *Psychology Today*. Retrieved from https://www.psychologytoday.com/blog/our-gender-ourselves/201404/friendships-between-women-have-health-benefits

Du Bois, W.E.B. (1903) *The Souls of Black Folk*. Chicago: A. C. McClerg & Co.

Edin, K., Nelson, T.J. (2013) *Doing the Best I Can: Fatherhood in the Inner City*. CA: University of California Press.

Ellen, B. (February 8, 2015) Gender and Housework: Men, You Can't Sweep This One Under the Carpet. *The Guardian*. Retrieved from http://www.theguardian.com/commentisfree/2015/feb/08/men-women-cleaning-gender-divide-middle-class-men-do-less

Ellin, A. (October 30, 2015) After Full Lives Together, More Older Couples Are Divorcing. *The New York Times*. Retrieved from http://www.nytimes.com/2015/10/31/your-money/after-full-lives-together-more-older-couples-are-divorcing.html

Faderman, L., Xiong, G. (1998) *I Begin My Life All Over: The Hmong and the American Immigrant Experience*. Boston: Beacon Press.

Fellizar, K. (June 5, 2017) Millennials Want Emotional Connections, Not Hookups, Report Finds, but Many Don't Really Know How. *Bustle*. Retrieved fromhttps://www.bustle.com/p/millennials-want-emotional-connections-not-hookups-report-finds-but-many-dont-really-know-how-59995

Fernandez, J. (2009) The Role of Machismo and Marianismo in the Construction of Sexes in Latin America. *SCRIBD*. Retrieved from https://www.scribd.com/doc/58332662/The-role-of-Machismo-and-Marianismo-in-the-construction-of-sexes-in-Latin-America

Finkelhor, D., Turner, H., Ormrod, R., Hamby, S., Kracke, K. (2009) Children's Exposure to Violence: A Comprehensive National Survey. *OJJDP*. *Juvenile Justice Bulletin*. Retrieved from https://www.ncjrs.gov/pdffiles1/ojjdp/227744.pdf

Firestone, L. (October 22, 2012) *Why Domestic Violence Occurs and How to Stop it*. Retrieved from https://www.psychologytoday.com/blog/compassion-matters/201210/why-domestic-violence-occurs-and-how-stop-it

Fottrell, Q. (June 5, 2013) Does Online Dating Lead to Happier Marriages? *MarketWatch*. Retrieved from http://www.marketwatch.com/story/does-online-dating-lead-to-happier-marriages-2013-06-05

Frances McClelland Institute (n.d.) Latino Families Research Initiative. Retrieved from https://mcclellandinstitute.arizona.edu/latino-families

Frye, Marilyn (2007) Chapter 3, in Anderson, M.L. and Collins, P.H. *Race, Class, and Gender*. Belmont, CA: Thomson Wadsworth, pp. 29–32.

Glassner, B. (1999) *The Culture of Fear: Why Americans Are Afraid of the Wrong Things: Crime, Drugs, Minorities, Teen Moms, Killer Kids, Mutant Microbes, Plane Crashes, Road Rage, & So Much More*. NY: Basic Books.

Goodman, D. (January/February 2002) Recruiting the Class of 2005. *Mother Jones*. Retrieved from https://www.motherjones.com/politics/2002/01/recruiting-class-2005/

Gottlieb, L. (February 6, 2014) Does a More Equal Marriage Mean Less Sex? *The New York Times*. Retrieved from http://www.nytimes.com/2014/02/09/magazine/does-a-more-equal-marriage-mean-less-sex.html?_r=0

Heitz, D. (January 27, 2014) U.S. Official: Elder Abuse Is 'Broad and Widespread.' *Healthline*. Retrieved from http://www.healthline.com/health-news/senior-elder-abuse-more-common-than-you-think-012714#3

Henderson, T. (September 28, 2014) More Americans Living Alone, Census Says. *The Washington Post*. Retrieved from https://www.washingtonpost.com/politics/more-americans-living-alone-census-says/2014/09/28/67e1d02e-473a-11e4-b72e-d60a9229cc10_story.html

Hill Collins, P. (2000) *Black Feminist Thought: Knowledge, Consciousness, and the Politics of Empowerment*. NY: Routledge.

Hillin, T. (May 9, 2014) The Way Couples Divide Household Chores Can Make or Break a Marriage. *The Huffington Post*. Retrieved from http://www.huffingtonpost.com/2014/05/09/marriage-happiness-study_n_5298235.html

History of Child Support in the USA. (December 18, 2003) *Child Support Analysis*. Retrieved from http://www.childsupportanalysis.co.uk/information_and_explanation/world/history_usa.htm

History of Polyamory Society. (n.d.) *Polyamory Society*. Retrieved from http://www.polyamorysociety.org/page7.html

Hochschild, A.R., Machung, A. (1989) *The Second Shift: Working Parents and the Revolution at Home*. NY: Viking/Penguin.

Jayson, S. (June 3, 2013) Study: More than a Third of New Marriages Start Online. *USA Today*. Retrieved from https://www.usatoday.com/story/news/nation/2013/06/03/online-dating-marriage/2377961/

Jhally, S. (1997) DVD Advertising and the End of the World. *Media Education Foundation*. Retrieved from https://shop.mediaed.org/advertising--the-end-of-the-world-p59.aspx

Johnson, L.C. (October, 2010) Do You Live in a Community Property State? *Legal Zoom*. Retrieved from https://www.legalzoom.com/articles/do-you-live-in-a-community-property-state

Johnson, L.L.C. (October 24, 2009) Inside the Love Lab: Seven Principles of Making Marriage Work. *Positive Psychology News*. Retrieved from http://positivepsychologynews.com/news/laura-lc-johnson/200910244255

Klein, W., Izquierdo, C., Bradbury, T.N. (March 1, 2013) The Difference Between a Happy Marriage and a Miserable One: Chores. *The Atlantic*. Retrieved from https://www.theatlantic.com/sexes/archive/2013/03/the-difference-between-a-happy-marriage-and-miserable-one-chores/273615/

Klinenberg, E., Taylor, H.O., Taylor, B., Nguyen A.W., Chatters, L.M. (October, 2016) Social Isolation, Loneliness, and Living Alone: Identifying the Risks for Public Health. *American Journal of Public Health*. Retrieved from https://www.researchgate.net/publication/300366837_Social_Isolation_Loneliness_and_Living_Alone_Identifying_the_Risks_for_Public_Health

Knapton, S. (June 11, 2015) Marriage Is More Beneficial for Men than Women, Study Shows. *The Telegraph*. Retrieved from http://www.telegraph.co.uk/science/2016/03/14/marriage-is-more-beneficial-for-men-than-women-study-shows/

Knox, A.J. (June 28, 2016) American Parents Are Some of the Unhappiest. *Mothering*. Retrieved from http://www.mothering.com/articles/american-parents-unhappiest/

Lee, D. (August 6, 2017) *Single Mother Statistics*. Retrieved from https://singlemotherguide.com/single-mother-statistics/

Madrid, A. (2007) Missing People and Others: Joining Together to Expand the Circle. In Andersen, M.L., Collins, P.H. (2007) *Race, Class, and Gender,* 6th edn. Belmont, CA: Thomson Higher Education.

Mail Online Reporter. (January 12, 2015) Married Couples are Happier than Singles Says New Study. *Mail Online*. Retrieved from http://www.dailymail.co.uk/news/article-2904986/There-really-thing-wedded-bliss-Married-couples-happier-singles-says-new-study-following-benefits-matrimony.html

Marche, S. (December 7, 2013) The Case for Filth. *The New York Times*. Retrieved from http://www.nytimes.com/2013/12/08/opinion/sunday/the-case-for-filth.html

Marcotte, A. (January 6, 2015) Even When They Don't Have Jobs, Men Do Less Housework than Women. *Slate Magazine*. Retrieved from http://www.slate.com/blogs/xx_factor/2015/01/06/gender_and_housework_even_men_who_don_t_work_do_less_than_women.html

Martin, E. (May 20, 2017) 3 Reasons Millennial Couples Are Ditching Diamonds. *CNBC*. Retrieved from https://www.cnbc.com/2017/05/20/millennial-couples-arent-buying-diamonds.html

Masci, D., Brown, A., Kiley,J. (June 26, 2017) 5 Facts About Same Sex Marriage. *Pew Research Center*. Retrieved from http://www.pewresearch.org/fact-tank/2017/06/26/same-sex-marriage/

McClintock, A.E. (December 19, 2014) Why Breakups Are Actually Tougher on Men. *Psychology Today*. Retrieved from https://www.psychologytoday.com/blog/it-s-man-s-and-woman-s-world/201412/why-breakups-are-actually-tougher-men

McGregor, J. (June 9, 2014) When Dads Take Paternity Leave. *Washington Post*. Retrieved from https://www.washingtonpost.com/news/on-leadership/wp/2014/06/09/when-dads-take-paternity-leave/?utm_term=.f9d649deaa2d

Miller, C.C. (May 15, 2015) Mounting Evidence of Advantages for Children of Working Mothers. *The New York Times*. Retrieved from http://www.nytimes.com/2016/01/13/opinion/teach-your-teachers-well.html

Miller, C.C., Bui, Q. (February 27, 2016) Equality in Marriages Grows, and So Does Class Divide. *The New York Times*. Retrieved from http://www.nytimes.com/2016/02/23/upshot/rise-in-marriages-of-equals-and-in-division-by-class.html

Moraga, C. La Guera. (2007) In Andersen, M.L., Collins, P.H. *Race, Class, and Gender*. 6th edn. Belmont, CA: Thomson Higher Education.

Nasser, El., H. (June 19, 2012) Study: Asian Americans Value Hard Work, Family. *USA Today*. Retrieved from http://usatoday30.usatoday.com/news/nation/story/2012-06-18/asian-american-study/55677050/1

National Runaway Safeline. (n.d.) *Third Party Statistics*. Retrieved from http://www.1800runaway.org/runaway-statistics/third-party-statistics/#LGBTQ

NPR Staff. (October 6, 2015) Sandra Cisneros Crosses Borders and Boundaries in 'A House of My Own'. *NPR*. Retrieved from http://www.npr.org/2015/10/06/446301433/sandra-cisneros-crosses-borders-and-boundaries-in-a-house-of-my-own

NPR Staff. (June 17, 2016) After Deployment, Marine Returns to Find his 'Most Important Thing': Fatherhood. *StoryCorps*. Retrieved from http://www.npr.org/2016/06/17/482342610/after-deployment-marine-returns-to-find-his-most-important-thing-fatherhood

Oatman-Stanford, H. (November 1, 2013) Can't Buy Me Love: How Romance Wrecked Traditional Marriage. *Collectors Weekly*. Retrieved from http://www.collectorsweekly.com/articles/how-romance-wrecked-traditional-marriage

Ortman, J.M., Velkoff, V.A., Hogan, H. (May, 2014) An Aging Nation: The Older Population in the United States. *U.S. Census*. Retrieved from https://www.census.gov/prod/2014pubs/p25-1140.pdf

Peri, C., Moses, K. (1999). *Mothers Who Think: Tales of Real-life Parenthood*. NY: Washington Square Press.

Pew Research Center. (December 17, 2015) The American Family Today. *Pew Research Center*. Retrieved from http://www.pewsocialtrends.org/2015/12/17/1-the-american-family-today/

Polakow-Suransky, S. (January 13, 2016) Teach Your Teachers Well. *The New York Times*. Retrieved from http://www.nytimes.com/2016/01/13/opinion/teach-your-teachers-well.html

Profile of Older Americans: 2014 Profile. (March 9, 2017) *Administration for Community Living*. Retrieved from https://aoa.acl.gov/aging_statistics/profile/2014/2.aspx

Reaney, P. (February 19, 2016) Husbands Create 7 Hours of Extra Housework for their Wives. *The Huffington Post*. Retrieved from http://www.huffingtonpost.com/entry/husbands-create-7-hours-of-extra-housework-for-their-wives_us_56c72146e4b0ec6725e23e2c

Saad, G. (November 15, 2009) *How Much Should One Spend on an Engagement Ring*. Retrieved from https://www.psychologytoday.com/blog/homo-consumericus/200911/how-much-should-one-spend-engagement-ring

Sawhill, I. (2013) The New White Negro. *Washington Monthly*. Retrieved from http://washingtonmonthly.com/magazine/janfeb-2013/the-new-white-negro/

Shandler, S. (1999) *Ophelia Speaks: Adolescent Girls Write About their Search for Self*. NY: Harper Perennial.

Shoener, S. (June 21, 2014) Domestic Violence and Two-Parent Households. *The New York Times*. Retrieved from http://www.nytimes.com/2014/06/22/opinion/sunday/domestic-violence-and-two-parent-households.html?_r=0

Shpancer, N. (October 1, 2015) Is Marriage Worth the Trouble for Women: The Benefits Go Mostly to Men. *Psychology Today*. Retrieved from https://www.psychologytoday.com/blog/insight-therapy/201510/is-marriage-worth-the-trouble-women

Slaughter, A.M. (July, 2012) Why Women Still Can't Have it All. *The Atlantic*. Retrieved from https://www.theatlantic.com/magazine/archive/2012/07/why-women-still-cant-have-it-all/309020/

Slaughter, A.M. (2016) *Unfinished Business: Women, Men, Work, Family*. NY: Random House.

Smith, A., Anderson, M. (February 29, 2016) 5 Facts About Online Dating. *Pew Research Center*. Retrieved from http://www.pewresearch.org/fact-tank/2016/02/29/5-facts-about-online-dating/

Smith, A., Duggan, M. (October 21, 2013) Online Dating Relationships. *Pew Research Center*. Retrieved from http://www.pewinternet.org/2013/10/21/online-dating-relationships/

Soronen, R. (April 17, 2014) Opinion: We Abandon Thousands of Foster Case Children a Year. *CNN*. Retrieved from http://www.cnn.com/2014/04/16/opinion/soronen-foster-children/

Stahl, L. (2016) *Becoming Grandma: The Joys and Science of the New Grandparenting*. NY: Blue Rider Press.

Stein, S., Bobic, I. (June 30, 2015) Wedding Vendors Gear Up for a $ame-$ex Wedding Boom. *HuffPost*. Retrieved from https://www.huffingtonpost.com/2015/06/29/same-sex-marriage_n_7691650.html

Sultan, A. (September 29, 2014) Black Moms Tell White Moms About the Race Talk: Parents Talk Back. *Uexpress*. Retrieved from http://www.uexpress.com/parents-talk-back/2014/9/29/black-moms-tell-white-

Swan, S.C., Gambone, L.J., Caldwell, J.E., Sullivan, T.P., Snow, D.L. (2008) A Review of Research on Women's Use of Violence with Male Intimate Partners. *Violence and Victims*, 23(3): 301–314. Retrieved from https://www.ncbi.nlm.nih.gov/pmc/articles/PMC2968709/

Taylor, K. (July 12, 2013) Sex on Campus: She Can Play that Game, Too. *The New York Times*. Retrieved from https://www.nytimes.com/2013/07/14/fashion/sex-on-campus-she-can-play-that-game-too.html

Toma, C. (June 17, 2014) Why Is Online Dating Successful? *Psychology Today Blog*. Retrieved from https://www.psychologytoday.com/blog/virtual-you/201406/why-is-online-dating-successful

Traister, R. (February 27, 2016) What Women Find in Friends That They May Not Get from Love. *The New York Times*. Retrieved from http://www.nytimes.com/2016/02/28/opinion/sunday/what-women-find-in-friends-that-they-may-not-get-from-love.html

Twenge, J.M. (September, 2017) Has the Smartphone Destroyed a Generation? *The Atlantic*, 320(2): 59–65.

US Census Bureau (2015) *Data Tables on Family Arrangements*. Retrieved from https://www.census.gov/data/tables/2015/demo/families/cps-2015.html

US Census Bureau (January 30, 2018) *Child Support Payments Received by Custodial Parents*. Retrieved from https://www.census.gov/library/visualizations/2018/comm/child-support.html

USCRossierOnline. (2014) What are my Chances of Gaining Full or Primary Custody of my Child as a Father? *Quora*. Retrieved from https://www.quora.com/What-are-my-chances-of-gaining-full-or-primary-custody-of-my-child-as-a-father

Vagianos, A. (February 13, 2015) 30 Shocking Domestic Violence Statistics that Remind Us it's an Epidemic. *The Huffington Post*. Retrieved from http://www.huffingtonpost.com/2014/10/23/domestic-violence-statistics_n_5959776.html

Van Campen, K.S., Russell, S.T. (2010) Cultural Differences in Parenting Practices: What Asian American Families Can Teach Us. *University of Arizona*, 2(1). Retrieved from https://mcclellandinstitute.arizona.edu/sites/mcclellandinstitute.arizona.edu/files/ResearchLink_2.1_Russell_AsianFam.pdf

Vlosky, D.A., Monroe, P.A. (October 2002) The Effective Dates of No-Fault Divorce Laws in the 50 States. *Family Relations*, 51 (4): 317–324.

Wah, L.M., (dir.) (1994) *The Color of Fear*. Stir Fry Seminars and Training. Retrieved from http://www.diversitytrainingfilms.com/

Wang, W., Parker, K. (September 24, 2014) Record Share of Americans Have Never Married. *Pew Research Center*. Retrieved from http://www.pewsocialtrends.org/2014/09/24/record-share-of-americans-have-never-married/

Weinberger, Z.B. (October 15, 2016) It's Time to Acknowledge Male Victims of Domestic Violence. *The Huffington Post*. Retrieved from http://www.huffingtonpost.com/bari-zell-weinberger-esq/its-time-to-acknowledge-m_b_8292976.html

What We Know. (n.d.) What Does the Scholarly Research Say About the Wellbeing of Children with Gay or Lesbian Parents? *Columbia Law School*. Retrieved from http://whatweknow.law.columbia.edu/topics/lgbt-equality/what-does-the-scholarly-research-say-about-the-wellbeing-of-children-with-gay-or-lesbian-parents/#Sullins_15

Williams, A. (January 11, 2013) The End of Courtship? *The New York Times*. Retrieved from https://www.nytimes.com/2013/01/13/fashion/the-end-of-courtship.html

Youth Blog. (n.d.) *Impact*. The LGBT Health and Development Program at Northwestern University. Retrieved from http://www.impactprogram.org/lgbtq-youth/youth-blog/

Note

1. A survey of family and sociology textbooks failed to show consensus in the ways these terms, as well as *family*, were defined.

CHAPTER 11

Education

WHAT YOU WILL READ ABOUT IN THIS CHAPTER:

- **Public education** has been an integral feature of American society and has played an important role in Americanizing generations of immigrant children. In addition to teaching a core curriculum, the school system promotes a **hidden curriculum** of social and cultural values and norms, leading to assimilation into the dominant culture.

- The American system, with its historical reliance on local and state funding, has sustained disparate educational experiences with regard to social class, sex, and race. Although there have been attempts to equalize funding and create more uniform curricula, these goals have not yet been reached.

- Research has been inconclusive on what would best aid the improvement of the educational experience but two emergent elements, supported by research, are superior **teacher training** and **parental involvement**. Most educators and social scientists agree that poor children are significantly disadvantaged before they enter formal education institutions. Research definitively indicates that intervention in early childhood and preschool can enhance the school and life achievements of these children.

- The **Common Core Initiative**, adopted by 44 states and the District of Columbia, was developed to standardize the education of US students, as well as to raise standards. Elements of the program, especially with regard to the administration and uses of standardized testing, have garnered intensive debate.

- In spite of various initiatives and legal challenges, the American school system remains highly **segregated by race**. These differences are persistently evident in performance on standardized testing, raising the question of what is being measured, and how the results should be interpreted.

- The importance of **teacher training**, conditions and pay for teachers, and the recruitment and retention of non-white teachers are major elements of concern in working for more effective educational outcomes, especially for children from nondominant groups.

- **Higher education** is an essential predictor of adult well-being. Women are significantly more likely than men to graduate college and to pursue post-graduate education. Students from nondominant groups, both racially and economically, frequently face significant challenges in higher education. Issues of racial and gender bias, censorship on campuses, and sexual harassment have been particularly highlighted in the past decade.

Figure 11.1 Children studying a globe
Source: Pressmaster / Shutterstock.com

Introduction

Education is frequently viewed as the major mechanism of social mobility. As such the optimal functioning of the system is especially crucial to the lower income sectors of society, yet these are the groups generally underserved in a variety of ways. Many controversies surround the efficacy of the education system at all levels, from preschool to higher education. It is difficult to evaluate systemic issues since they are compounded by inconclusive findings regarding the nature of the problems, their causes, and their solutions.

US public education is unique in that there are no national laws creating a uniform curriculum or funding mechanism. The US laws governing public education are state mandates, with state and local entities controlling the public schools. This local focus dates to the inception of public education in the colonies. The first mandate was established in the Massachusetts *colony* in 1647, and it declared that any town or village with 15 or more families had to provide a primary education, including grammar and arithmetic. Massachusetts also became the first *state* to institute a similar law in 1852, making it punishable by fine, or even state seizure of the children, if parents did not comply. Over the next 60 years all the states adopted laws making education compulsory. The final state was Mississippi in 1917. Prior to the initiation of free public education, such educational institutions which existed were run by churches and charged tuition (Race Forward 2006).

The typical rationale for promoting compulsory education generally is attributed to creating an informed, cohesive citizenship. However, probing the underlying motivations for implementing free public education reveals other agendas. One goal was to wrest education from religion, especially from the Catholic Church. The early Protestant settlers were suspicious both of "immigrant values" and of the Catholic Church, and sought to control education (Find Law n.d.). Another stated motive was to protect children from the harsh conditions of factory work but this, too, is largely fictional in that it is equally likely that adults wanted children in school to protect their own jobs. Conversely, historically the "rights" to an education were suspended when industry had a need for child labor as when, for example, Alabama temporarily repealed its law under pressure from a large textile company. Today compulsory education, depending on the state, applies to youths up to 16–18 years. Some minor exclusions are granted as, for example, in the case of the Amish or in-home schooling, but even these exceptions must comply with legal requirements.

Boston Latin: The First Public Secondary School, and Race/Ethnicity Today

The first public secondary school, Boston Latin, was created in 1635. At that time, the school charged tuition. Today the school serves grades 7–12 and is regarded as one of the best public schools, on a par with the most highly ranked private US academies. Boston Latin is the most competitive public school in Boston. The school is highly competitive; admission is by exam and grade point average, and students are admitted at only the 7th and 9th grades. The school's admissions policies have been the subject of critical review, exposing its systemic unfairness to minority students. In 1995 a court invalidated a mandate reserving a certain portion of seats for nondominant students. As a result, the school's student population failed to reflect the district's racial and ethnic distributions, suggesting inequalities in education prior to the point of application. The district's public-school student population is 42 percent Latino, 32 percent Black, and 14 percent White while the school's population is 11.6 percent Latino, 8.5 percent Black, and 47 percent White. It has been suggested that the lure of a potential admission is responsible for keeping some White families within the district. In recent years, the school has been accused of failing to provide a welcoming atmosphere to its minority students and the administration has been charged with mishandling complaints regarding its racial climate. As a result of these accusations, the headmaster and assistant headmaster resigned in June 2016 (Ebbert 2016; Editorial Board 2016).

How Is American Education Funded?

Issues of equity, funding, curricula, pedagogy, hegemony, teacher quality and certification, and relevance to the job market are common areas of contention. The manner of American public education funding is at the core of education debates. Education funding usually originates from three sources: 45 percent from state allotment to the district; 45 percent from the local property taxes; and 10 percent from the federal government. Federal money frequently is dedicated to specific programs such as remedial reading or disability programs. A US Supreme court case, filed in Texas in 1968, which sought to have the federal government guarantee equal funding between states and districts failed by a 5:4 vote. The majority opinion stated that it was not the obligation of the federal government to make the system fair or balanced and so the problem remained one for the states to grapple with. In his dissenting opinion, Thurgood Marshall, who had successfully argued *Brown v. The Board of Education* in 1954 establishing federal support for the desegregation of schools, wrote: "I cannot accept such an emasculation of the Equal Protection Clause in the context of this case" (Turner et al. 2016). As a result of state funding, it is difficult to make broad statements regarding funding, or how education is managed, since each state is different (Turner et al. 2016, 2016a). The inequalities inherent in the organization and funding of the education system have led to law suits against every state in the union over the past few decades (School Funding Fairness n.d.).

Average spending per student across the country, controlled for regional differences in costs, is $11,841. Funding ranges from a low of $7900 to a high of

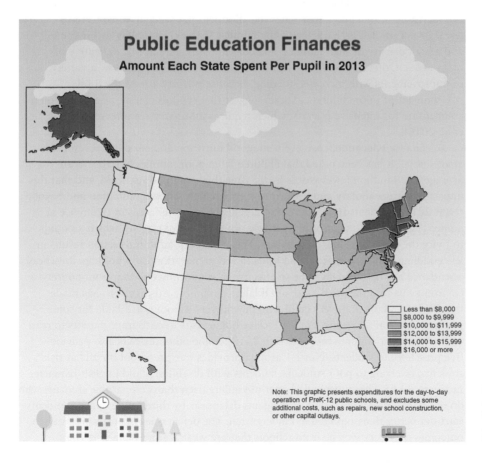

Figure 11.2 A broad look at state funding 2013 Source: US Census Bureau, 2013 Annual Survey of School System Finances

over $28,000 per annum. Budgets impact classroom size; the ability to attract and keep good teachers; curricula updates; resources such as textbooks and technology; and even the provision of decent meals for the students. If the local tax base of an area is good, the budget will reflect the community's status, often augmenting insufficient state budgets. As a consequence of the "great recession," 35 states spent less per student in 2014 than they did in 2008 and 23 states were still spending less in 2016–2017 (Brown 2016). Differences in local budgets, of as much as 300 percent more money for affluent students, exacerbate inequalities since wealthy families also provide resources outside of the schools that are unavailable to poorer students. In cities like Chicago and Philadelphia, disparities between urban and suburban districts are documented by any measure of student success utilized.

Inequality and Achievement

The efficacy of simply pumping more money into poor, and low-performing, schools is questionable. Most research suggests that money does make a difference, particularly if the way in which the money is spent is examined, although there is some evidence to the contrary. One project showed that the infusion of extra money failed to remedy the consequences of the very extensive poverty of Camden, NJ; increases of two and a half times the allotment per student failed to raise test scores. Camden is characterized by families with exceptionally low incomes and a high density of such families, and consequently may not be indicative of other areas. Other districts, with less extreme circumstances, do show a variety of improvements with increased funding. Because poverty affects the total environment of poor children, experts suggest that schools cannot be counted on to compensate for intensive poverty, which requires more areas of intervention (Turner et al. 2016).

To enhance educational achievement, good nutrition and enrichment resources are essential. It has been noted that children from poor families have heard an average of 30 million fewer words by the time they are three years old, and that this impacts their vocabulary and test scores through high school graduation and beyond (NPR 2015). Students from poorer families also have other areas of difference at home. They spend 40 percent of their free time in front of screens, which amounts to twice the time of middle-class babies. This paucity of adult interaction results in less cuddling and conversation and leads to less preparation for schooling. Preschool attendance has been shown to be so effective in supporting children from poorer environments that the "red" state of Oklahoma, in a bipartisan effort, has made it publicly available for every child. Full day nursery school is available for some younger children and some families receive home visits to encourage parents to read and talk to their children more (Kristof 2013). Some other districts also provide free preschool to students. North Carolina provides free preschool for all "at risk" students, referring to poor students, students with disabilities, and English Language Learners (ELL). The students do better in kindergarten than comparable students who do not attend preschool. Some of the gains disappear by third grade but the students start out better than expected in kindergarten. The deficiencies in post-kindergarten outcomes may very well be from schools that are weak, rather than from the weaknesses in the preschool experience (Turner et al. 2016a). Schools lacking in rigor likely are more detrimental to low-income students who are more vulnerable to being relegated to remedial classrooms:

> [Kiana Hernandez] failed the Florida reading test every year since sixth grade and had been placed in remedial classes where she was drilled on basic skills, like reading paragraphs to find the topic sentence and then filling in the right bubbles on a practice test. She didn't get to read whole books like her peers in the regular class or practice her writing, analysis, and debating—skills she would need for the political science degree she dreamed of, or for the school board candidacy that she envisioned. (Sorting students into remedial classes, educational research shows, actually depresses achievement among African American and Latino students in many cases, yet it remains common practice.)
> (Rizga 2015, parenthesis in original)

Research further shows that when a student acquires a home computer between the 5th and 8th grades, the amount of time he or she spends on homework *decreases*. The weaker students were shown to suffer more losses with the addition of the computer, perhaps due to spending more time on socially oriented sites (Pinker 2015).

Box 11.1 – Education Funding and Inequality

American school districts receive unequal *funding* since the majority of education funding relies on state and local measures. About 45 percent of the funding is generated by per pupil allotments provided by the state. Another 45 percent is drawn from local property taxes. The remaining 10 percent comes from the federal government and generally is restricted to use either in specific programs or populations. Each state maintains its own formula for funding public education, resulting in different resources between, and within, states.

Not all *inequality* of education outcomes can be attributed directly to budgetary considerations, though there is a wealth of evidence that poor students are educationally disadvantaged in multiple ways. One means to address this differential, supported by many educators and across the political spectrum, is to offer public preschool education. Other recommendations generally center on family support and the availability of enrichment experiences.

Long summer vacations further promote social class differences in education. The basis for these long breaks has its origins in the farming calendar, when children were needed to help with chores. Currently, most children are not needed for labor in the summer and suffer educational setbacks if the family cannot afford supervised or enriched summer activities. The cost of programs or care is high and lower income parents, who already are struggling to meet their basic needs, cannot stretch their budgets to pay for programs. Only one quarter of school children have a parent at home during the summer time. As a result, young kids are frequently left in the care of older siblings, who would also benefit from adult supervision. Some older children, still too young for unsupervised days, are left inside all day where they will, the parents hope, remain unnoticed by authorities. Not only is this situation unhealthy and potentially dangerous for kids, but research shows that it has a devastating effect on skills. All children lose math skills during the summer but lower income children lose reading skills they never recover; reading deficits can reach three years by fifth grade (Dell'Antonia 2016). The loss of skills during summer is thought to account for up to one half of the overall achievement gaps between lower and higher income students. If a child cannot read at a proficient level by third grade, the likelihood of failure to achieve high school graduation increases by six times (Early Warning 2013). Publicly funded subsidized programs frequently cannot accommodate all the qualifying families. Other gaps in the school calendar also contribute to deficits in the less privileged students. Equity in education necessitates a rethinking of how a society of working parents, particularly single and lower income parents, should enhance the quality of education for all youths.

Achievement gaps formerly were documented only between the poor and the wealthy. Today they are more pervasive. In a review of a dozen studies, from 1960–2010, Stanford University Professor Sean Reardon (2013) found that the rich–poor gap in test scores had increased by 40 percent in the later 30 years. The gap exists today, in equal measure, between the rich and the middle class and again between the middle class and the poor. Reardon also shows that family income surpasses race as a predictor of school success. Rich and poor gaps in extracurricular activities, school leadership, graduation rates, sports, church attendance, and volunteer work also have increased. Reardon attributes these differences to school readiness measures, rather than to the schools themselves (Reardon 2013, 2011). This is reflected in the evidence showing that performance gaps close during the school months and widen in the summer.

It is likely that the increased gap in readiness reflects the better access to out of school environments available to better off children, which persists throughout the school years. Wealthy families are spending more money on enrichment activities, and though middle-class and lower income families are also spending more on such activities, the increase among the wealthy is 150 percent, compared to 57 percent among the low income. Increasing disparities in income gains account for this data. Residential segregation often promotes economic homogeneity within a school, consolidating the advantages of kids from wealthier households. Gaps within schools, when they contain students of different economic backgrounds, can reach four years. This represents further evidence that a school is not experienced equivalently by all its students, largely because they are not beginning at the same levels. As a remedy, Reardon makes a strong argument for investing in early childhood programs and preschool, and in supporting parents to better help their children. School success snowballs in that it leads to adult economic success, benefiting society (Reardon 2013, 2011; Rich et al. 2016). The academic achievement of American students compares unfavorably to students in comparable countries. This has been attributed

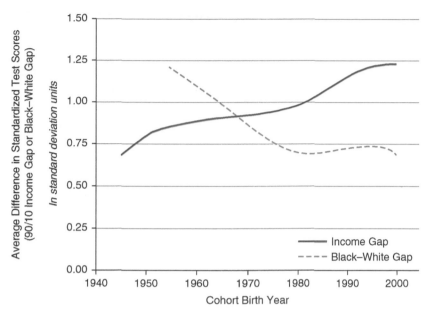

Figure 11.3 The gap in test scores has been rising for income and falling for race
Source: Adapted from "The Widening Socioeconomic Status Achievement Gap: New Evidence and Possible Explanations" (p. 98) by S.F. Reardon, in R.J. Murnane and G.J. Duncan (eds), *Whither Opportunity? Rising Inequality, Schools, and Children's Life Chances*, 2011, New York: Russell Sage Foundation

Figure 11.4 It is important for children to read at grade level by third grade or they will never compensate for the deficiency
Source: Monkey Business Images / Shutterstock.com

to the stagnation of the American system, rather than to appreciable advances in other countries (Bidwell 2013a).

How Do Sociologists View the American Education System?

Sociological theories offer different interpretations of the American school system. The functionalists maintain that there are multiple tasks, beyond imparting knowledge and skills, involved in the education system. They suggest that the smooth sustenance of the social fabric, from personal communication skills to cultural conformity, are as much a part of the school's agenda as is imparting information and competence. The general goal is to create people who conform to the expectations and needs of the community, workforce, family, and economy. For the functionalist, the schools are seen as institutions of social stability, in that that they ultimately subdue any emerging elements which challenge the system. According to this view, the system will select and sort students for different roles in society and it will successfully reproduce itself. Functionalists are likely to see personal educational attainment as a ***meritocracy***. A meritocracy is the belief a person can accomplish as much as her or his skills and motivation allow; this perspective minimizes the influences of inequalities in society, if it recognizes them at all. These sociologists do not attribute educational inequities to systemic unfairness.

In contrast, the conflict perspective suggests that the education system is structured to maintain the advantages of the more powerful groups in society. This is accomplished through unequal education funding, both in the public K-12 system and in higher education. The disparate funding and education experiences of the lower income students makes it difficult for them to compete in higher education

Figure 11.5
Functionalist theorists see schools as promoting conformity
Source: BraunS / istockphotos.com

and perpetuates the inequalities of social class. These groups often struggle to finance their higher education as well. Different levels of cultural capital, or the ability to know what to expect in a social institution and how to "work it," also influence educational outcomes. Latina author/poet Cherríe Moraga belatedly recognized that the brilliance she attributed to affluent classmates was not actually talent but privilege:

> For years I had berated myself for not being as "free" as my classmates. I
> completely bought that they simply had more guts than I did—to rebel against
> their parents and run around the country hitchhiking, reading books and studying
> "art". They had enough privilege to be atheists, for chrissake. There was no one
> around filling in the disparity for me between their parents, who were Hollywood
> filmmakers, and my parents, who wouldn't know the name of a filmmaker if their
> lives depended on it (and precisely because their lives didn't depend on it, they
> couldn't be bothered). But I knew nothing about "privilege" then. White was right.
> Period. I could pass. If I got educated enough, there would never be any telling.
>
> (Moraga 2007)

Cultural capital provides a wide range of skills leading to ease of interaction, such as in how to address authority figures; how to negotiate peer relationships; and how to access opportunities. Being able to "fit in" and feel comfortable with others promotes greater success in school, beyond the acquisition of good grades and test scores. Success in these spheres is more accessible to the more affluent, whose exposure and comfort with these elements begins much earlier. The ways in which the school perpetuates these behaviors and evaluates students with regard to them are referred to as the *hidden curriculum*. These aspects of privilege are unacknowledged and contribute to the disadvantages which adhere to lower income students. The "street smarts" of lower income students do not usually yield a similar benefit. Lower income students are not barred from high achievements, but their paths will contain more obstacles and challenges. The conflict theorists conclude that the game is stacked and not at all a meritocracy. With regard to high school students who are not college bound, the evidence shows that they perform poorly, especially in low performing schools with a preponderance of students who are not college bound.

Box 11.2 – Sociological Perspectives

Functionalist theory focuses on the role of education for the smooth sustenance of the social fabric of society. Cultural conformity is viewed as equally important to the imparting of knowledge and skills. Overall, the general needs of the community, workforce, family, and economy are the central factor in the education system. The functionalists believe in the existence of a *meritocracy*, where any person can achieve the level their talents, skills, and hard work yield. The concept of a meritocracy incorporates the false belief that all students start on an even playing field.

In contrast, *the conflict perspective* suggests that the education system is structured to maintain the advantages and position of the more powerful groups in society. The disparate funding and experiences of the lower income students make it difficult for them to compete in higher education and perpetuate the inequalities of social class. Conflict theorists elaborate a *hidden curriculum* that promotes the unequal access and assessment of students from disparate demographic groups. *Cultural capital* is the ability to excel in the unarticulated ways of the dominant group which contribute to the comfort a person feels in institutional settings, as well as the ways in which she will be assessed. The more privileged students gain familiarity in these at an earlier age.

What Are Current Issues and Trends Affecting Education?

Testing

Controversies surrounding the validity and role of standardized testing are explosive. The validity of the tests as a measure of achievement is challenged; some believe them to be more accurately a measure of social class. Testing has become a priority among some administrators, parents, and educators to hold the education system accountable for achieving specific, standardized student outcomes in the classroom. The proliferation of testing, and its uses, has raised many questions. Student populations mandated for, or excluded from, test taking are thought to skew the outcomes, lending even more ambiguity to the value and purpose of the testing. The No Child Left Behind (**NCLB**) mandate of 2002 requires children to be tested in grades 3–8 and at least once in high school. With the **NCLB** mandate, annual state dollars spent on testing rose from $423 million in 2002 to $1.1 billion in 2008. The mandate was renewed in Obama's last term in office though he warned against spending an inordinate amount of time on testing and test preparation.

States generally administer the National Assessment of Educational Progress (NAEP), which provides some measure of achievement between states. Each state also uses specific state tests, representing different testing instruments, which can result in unreliable comparisons. Even when specific test scores show increases, it is difficult to draw conclusions from them. The scores are not necessarily indicative of advances in cognitive abilities (Trafton 2013). A study of 1400 eighth grade students in a variety of schools in Boston, found that better scores on tests did not show commensurate increases on measures of cognition such as working memory, processing speed, and abstract reasoning. The type of school attended, whether public, charter, or those requiring entrance exams, showed no influence on cognitive abilities such as fluid reasoning and executive functioning associated with school performance, drug usage, criminality, and goal achievement. Students who gained admission to high-performing charter schools showed increased state standardized test scores but no commensurate gains in fluid reasoning. The researchers conclude that fluid reasoning skills are not integrated into school curricula (Trafton 2013).

Figure 11.6 The efficacy and validity of standardized testing has been questioned, along with instructional time lost to testing
Source: Bart Sadowski / Shutterstock.com

Critics suggest that tests assess aptitude on a limited set of skills. School failure often is attributed to poor test scores but some schools, showing little or no improvement on tests, exhibit increased rates of graduation and college attendance (Rizga 2012; Kamenetz 2015). This suggests that attributes not incorporated in testing may be at work in producing educational advancements. Opponents of

Higher Percentages of Students Perform at *Proficient* and *Advanced* in Reading than in 1992 and 2011

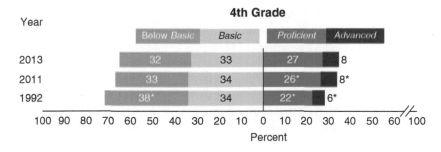

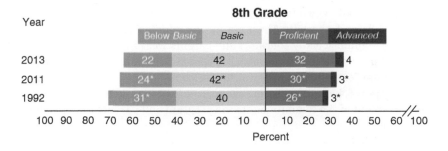

Figure 11.7 Test scores, 1992–2013
Source: Bidwell 2013a

testing suggest that there has been no notable improvement in achievement since the inception of the **NCLB**. The gap between White and minority scores has not closed, though modest gains have been seen in the test scores of racial minorities since the early 1990s. Research indicates that, on average, students of color are scoring at the level of White students a generation ago, with the exception of a decreased gap in the reading scores of 13-year-old White and Hispanic students (Bidwell 2013c). The NAEP reveals that 2013 scores were weak, with more than half of fourth graders at or below basic skills in math and 65 percent at or below basic scores in reading. In eighth grade, the comparable scores were 64 percent at or below basic in both math and reading (Bidwell 2013a).

The Common Core Initiative

In 2009 a new pedagogical approach was developed to improve the math and language arts curricula. Developed as the Common Core Initiative, 45 states and the District of Columbia adopted the program. The *Common Core* emphasizes critical thinking, application of skills to real-life problems, writing skills, and creativity. It also represents an effort to make curricular content more uniform across states. Though many teachers feel the program is solid, some states have tried to renege on their adoption of the program. A good deal of the dissension stems from the student testing of the program, widely instituted in 2015. Many teachers feel they have not been given suitable time and training to feel comfortable with the new material. They are also vehemently opposed to their performance evaluations being tied to these test results (Rizga 2012; Polakow-Suransky 2016; Kirp 2014a).

Box 11.3 – Education Initiatives

The No Child Left Behind Act (NCLB) was signed into law in 2002 by President George W. Bush. It was developed to extend the Elementary and Secondary Education Act of 1965, an element of President Lyndon B. Johnson's *Great Society* programs providing federal monies to schools. The ***NCLB*** mandates testing in reading and math for students in the 3rd–8th grades and at least once in high school. The act was renewed in 2013. Controversies surround the NCLB mandate, especially in relation to the time and costs devoted to testing, and to the use of the test scores in evaluating the quality of education and teaching in a school.

The Common Core refers to an approach to math and language arts curricula, developed in 2009, which focuses on critical thinking, problem solving, writing skills, and creativity. The program was adopted by 45 states and the District of Columbia. Many educators and parents were initially in favor of the program but some of the enthusiasm has waned. Pressures to perform on tests geared to the Common Core material, for which many teachers and students feel unprepared, have turned some against the initiative. Some states have tried to opt out of the commitment to the program and parents can opt out of the testing.

The *American Federation of Teachers* (AFT) initially supported the *Common Core* but the leadership apparently withdrew their support in 2014. Public statements emanating from the AFT leadership diverge from the more positive views of the rank and file. Members of the other large teachers' union, the National Educators Association (NEA), also appear to support the *Common Core*. The teachers' basic support of the standards is not extended to implementation of its associated testing (Russo n.d.). Teachers are frustrated with the pressures the initiative has placed on the students, the classroom, and pedagogy. Some parents have chosen to opt out of testing, though this is more prevalent among White, middle-class parents. Other parents seem to be more positive about testing because they feel that it will hold the schools accountable for the deficiencies in their kids' education (Taylor 2016).

Much of the test results where the Common Core has been implemented has shown downward trends. Educators are wary of interpreting the outcome of the tests. *Common Core* testing in Minnesota shows a significant drop in reading scores. One of the largest changes occurred in the third grade where proficiency dropped from 80 percent in 2012 to 57 percent in 2013. There were smaller changes seen in lower math scores. New York first tested for *the Common Core* in 2012 and found that fewer than one third of the students in the third to eighth grades met or exceeded the standards for math and English (Bidwell 2013b). New York City passed a resolution, to develop "multiple forms of assessments" to more comprehensively evaluate student progress, rather than require "extensive standardized testing" (Mark-Viverito 2012).

The Gates Foundation, largely responsible for the development and implementation of the *Common Core*, recently released a statement admitting that school reform was much harder to address than they had anticipated and that they made mistakes in developing the *Common Core*. Specifically, they admitted that they should have worked more closely with educators, particularly teachers, and that they were too hasty in developing tests to assess the standards. Critics also suggest that the Gates Foundation, as a philanthropic institution, should not be the organization spearheading education reform (Strauss 2016).

Teacher Training

Substantial evidence reinforces improving teacher training and support. Teacher testing has been widely instituted as a means of assuring adequate qualification, though there is no data to suggest that testing serves this purpose. Suggestions for enhancing teacher effectiveness include more on the job training for teachers, where new teachers can work with master teachers and be actively mentored in the classroom. The countries with the best education systems provide more opportunities for extensive training and long-term mentoring (Polakow-Suransky 2016; Pinker 2015). Finland's comprehensive system of training supports a system with high standards. Experts believe it to be an exemplary, comprehensive system:

- The Finnish school system uses the same curriculum for all students (which may be one reason why Finnish scores varied so little from school to school).
- Students have light homework loads.
- Finnish schools do not have classes for gifted students.

- Finland uses very little standardized testing.
- Children do not start school until age seven.
- Finland has a comprehensive preschool program that emphasizes "self-reflection" and socializing, not academics.
- Grades are not given until high school and, even then, class rankings are not compiled.
- Teachers must have Master's degrees.
- Becoming a teacher in Finland is highly competitive. Just 10 percent of Finnish college graduates are accepted into the teacher training program; as a result, teaching is a high-status profession. (Teacher salaries are similar to teacher salaries in the US, however.)
- Students are separated into academic and vocational tracks during the last three years of high school. About 50 percent go into each track.
- Diagnostic testing of students is used early and frequently. If a student is in need of extra help, intensive intervention is provided.
- Groups of teachers visit each other's classes to observe their colleagues at work. Teachers also get one afternoon per week for professional development.
- School funding is higher for the middle school years, the years when children are most in danger of dropping out.
- College is free in Finland (Wilde 2015).

A Student View

Students attest to the quality of their teachers as a priority for enhancing success. In a personal commentary, an inner-city Latino high school student wrote the following, in response to bond money being spent on buildings:

> I was fortunate to have a few amazing teachers, who, along with my brother, paved the path to college for me. After being accepted into UC Davis, I realized that a small, vulnerable kid from the projects could actually have a future and opportunities in life.
>
> The quality teachers I had should not have been so few and far between. They were my only ticket to academic success. Underserved communities in California must demand that school boards focus on what will really get students like me to college – better teachers, not better buildings.
>
> With a Perspective, I'm Eduardo Martinez.
>
> (Martinez 2015)

The dynamics of the classroom may be more central to learning but they remain largely unmeasured. Some evidence suggests that pedagogical innovation focusing on the skills for creating and completing student-oriented projects is more desirable in promoting success. Project-based, experiential learning has had only intermittent utilization in schools. This approach is "labor intensive" since the teachers must devote intensive planning to the project or risk a poor outcome. These types of projects align more closely to the targets of the *Common Core* standards than traditional classroom techniques. These projects tend to be introduced into schools that are "underperforming" as a way to more fully engage students. Because it has been associated with low performing schools, project learning often is unfairly associated with low test scores. In San Jose CA, project learning was adopted in a low-performing school and test scores relating to research skills improved, as did attendance and grades, though scores in math and English remained unchanged (Tintocalis 2015). This may be attributable to poor test construction and the difficulties surrounding accurate assessment of skill sets.

Has the United States Accomplished Racial Integration in Schools?

Commonly, the 1954 *Brown v. the Board of Education* Supreme Court decision is the legal case most closely associated with school desegregation but it was not the first significant case challenging segregation. Demands for school integration are largely associated with the African American population but such activism is common in many nondominant groups. With regard to the African American population, the first major mobilization to gain access to public education occurred in the post-Civil War period in the south. In the early 1900s, immigrant lawsuits resulted in a US Supreme Court mandate instructing California to extend public education to the children of its immigrant populations (Race Forward 2006). By 1930–1950 the *National Association for the Advancement of Colored People* (NAACP) agitated to obtain equal pay for Black teachers in the south. Significant strides towards racial integration, following the Brown decision ordering the racial desegregation of school, extended into the 1980s, but the trends have since been reversed, with segregation rates now similar to those of the 1960s. Residential segregation is a persistent phenomenon with patterns of racial segregation in the cities recreated by various groups occupying distinct suburban areas outside of major cities (Nasser 2014).

National Origin and School Integration

In 1946, **Mendez v. Westminster** in Orange County CA established the unconstitutionality of segregation based on national origin and provided precedence for the Brown decision. The case, filed by the Mendez family and other families against the county, ultimately was resolved for the plaintiffs by the US Ninth Circuit Court of Appeals. A thriving citrus fruit industry led to increases in the Mexican and Mexican American population, creating a significant demographic shift in the early part of the twentieth century. The farm worker parents sued four districts for the segregation of the immigrant population, both between schools and within schools. At the time, the justification for the separation included the lack of English proficiency in the Latino students. The California governor, Earl Warren, initiated state legislation repealing the state code which permitted the segregation. The District Court ruled in favor of Mendez and mandated integration based on the 14th amendment of the Constitution, guaranteeing equal protection. The case was settled without appeal to the US Supreme Court and had a significant impact on a large segment of the population.

In 2013, the American public-school student body was 50 percent White, 15 percent Black, and 29 percent Hispanic (NCES 2016). Currently, it still exhibits widespread segregation, significantly impacting the education and experiences of all the students: "In many respects, the schools serving White and Asian students and those serving Black and Latino students represent two different worlds" (UCLA Civil Rights Project cited in Breslow et al. 2014):

- Gains in racial integration in the southern states, made since the 1954 Supreme Court decision, have reversed to just below their 1968 level.
- Schools released from desegregation orders have multiplied in the years between 1990 and the 2000s, as districts were removed from court oversight.
- Segregation does increase when oversight is removed.
- Since 2011 the most segregated group is the Latino population. The typical Latino will go to a school which is about 57 percent Latino.
- White students have the least exposure to other races. The typical White student attends a school which is 75 percent White, one eighth Latino, and one twelfth Black.

Figure 11.8 Busing was a prevalent mechanism for accomplishing integration within school districts
Source: Monkey Business Images / Shutterstock.com

- More than half of the students, in the schools with the highest poverty are Black or Latino while they comprise only 11 percent of the students in the least impoverished schools.
- A researcher at UC Berkeley studied the effects of attending integrated schools, for children born between 1945–1970 and found a significantly increased rate of high school graduation; these schools had higher per pupil spending and lower teacher–student ratios.
- Students attending integrated schools for five years had an average increase of 15 percent in wages and an 11 percent decline in yearly incidences of poverty. Additionally, there was no ill effect to the Whites in these schools (Breslow et al. 2014).

Equitable access remains a crucial goal since education is almost universally regarded as a major mechanism of social mobility. The means of accomplishing equity is still hotly debated. The civil rights movement promoted full integration in education, housing, voting, and other civic activities. But was forced school desegregation really good for the nonWhite students and their communities? Evidence suggests that desegregation impacts educational attainment and reduces adult poverty but it appears that the gains are attributable to improved neighborhoods and school budgets rather than to inter-racial groupings (Edsall 2017). There is evidence that African Americans' school performance suffers in predominantly White schools, due to alienation, impersonal relations, and isolation.

Integrated schools do not necessarily translate into integrated classrooms. The use of standardized testing to assign students to different educational tracks began in 1932 when intelligence testing was employed for this purpose (Race Forward 2006). Tracking is the practice of using standardized test scores to sort students into different programs of study, and/or into different classrooms or groups, based on perceived "ability." Tracking is generally regarded as correlated with social class and race and is an unreliable measure of student potential. When assigning students to tracks, the bias in testing is not considered nor is the interest and motivation of the students, which is an essential element of achievement. Nondominant students are less likely to be allowed access to honors, accelerated, or advanced placement courses (Quinton 2014).

Prior to integration, African American students were more likely to have Black teachers, excel academically, attend schools with high expectations, and feel part of the community. The advent of integrated schools, some believe, is responsible for smart, high-achieving African American children being seen as "acting White" (Chiles 2014; hooks 1994; Jenkins 2016; personal communication). Many students might have been better served in their own communities, where they felt enmeshed in community and expected to excel. Increased school funding, and greater proportions of African American teachers, administrators, and personnel, are indicative of greater student achievement. Greater access to higher education and scholarships may also be more significant in producing gains for the African American population.

Educators raise the question as to whether it is essential to have teachers who reflect the culture and background of their students. In terms of measures of academic performance on testing, the effect can amount to a month of additional learning in a school year. More essentially, the effects of cultural mirroring may have a more dramatic impact but they are difficult to measure and generally not considered in school assessments. Experts have established that psychological identification with a mentor, or role model, powerfully affects self-image, confidence, and aspirations. Though minorities make up half the nation's student body, more than 80 percent of teachers are White, with some districts exhibiting larger disparities than others. In Boston, for example, there is one Hispanic teacher for every 52 Latino students and one Black teacher for every 22 African American students; for White students and teachers the ratio is less than one to three. In NYC, where the student body is 85 percent minority, 60 percent of the teachers are White.

Diversity in teachers' education programs is not extensive but the largest problem regarding nondominant teachers is teacher retention. Nonwhite teachers are more likely to resign than their White counterparts and more likely to do so as a result of frustration with management and lack of autonomy. Nonwhite teachers are also more likely to work in schools with high proportions of impoverished students, rigid curricular control, and top-down management (Rich 2015).

Box 11.4 – Integration of Schools

Brown v. The Board of Education of Topeka Kansas was the 1954 class action Supreme Court case which resulted in the desegregation of schools, asserting that racial separation in schools was *inherently* unequal. Less well known was the case of *Mendez v Westminster*, ultimately decided by the US Ninth Circuit Court of Appeals, which established the illegality of separating children in schools due to national origin. The case set the stage for the ultimate success of *Brown v the Board*. Subsequent to the Brown decision, gradual integration took place, peaking in the 1980s and followed by a period of resegregation, largely due to patterns of residential segregation.

Tracking is the practice of grouping students together by perceived abilities, generally by standardized test scores. Tracking can occur through separation into different classrooms or into different groups within a classroom. Many parents, and educators, support tracking as a means of using the classroom efficiently but the practice is controversial. Tracking is strongly correlated with social class and consequently perceived as an unreliable source of intellectual potential.

Graduation and Attrition

High school graduation rates currently are considered to be at an all-time high. However, the data is inconsistent. The means of assessing graduation rates varies by researchers' methods of assessment. The chart below includes data by income, language proficiency, and disability, as compiled by the White House.

Graduation Rates by Subgroup of Students						
	2010–2011	2011–2012	2012–2013	2013–2014	2014–2015	*Change from 2010–2011 to 2014–2015*
Total	79	80	81.4	82.3	83.2	**4.2**
American Indian/Alaska Native	65	67	69.7	69.6	71.6	**6.6**
Asian/Pacific Islander	87	88	88.7	89.4	90.2	**3.2**
Hispanic	71	73	75.2	76.3	77.8	**6.8**
Black	67	69	70.7	72.5	74.6	**7.6**
White	84	86	86.6	87.2	87.6	**3.6**
Low Income Students	70	72	73.3	74.6	76.1	**6.1**
English Learners	57	59	61.1	62.6	65.1	**8.1**
Students with Disabilities	59	61	61.9	63.1	64.6	**5.6**

Figure 11.9
Graduation rates
Source: The White House, 2016

The figure for African American youth is reported as 74.6 percent for 2014–2015. African American commentator/journalist Tavis Smiley believes the data on African American males understates the severity of the problem. He asserts that only 54 percent of African American students graduate high school as compared to three quarters of White students. He also establishes that the average African American high school senior reads at the same level as the average eighth grade White student and only 14 percent of African Americans score "proficient" on eighth grade testing (Thompson n.d.). Less information is available on African American females. There

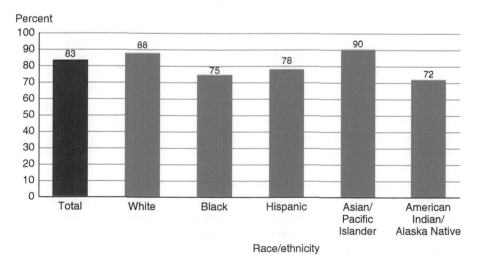

Figure 11.10
Graduation rates for Black, Hispanic and American Indian students grew at a faster pace than the rate for White students
Source: Adapted by National Center for Education Statistics from US Department of Education, Office of Elementary and Secondary Education, Consolidated State Performance Report, 2014–2015.

is no research data reported specifically on African American women. According to the Schott Foundation for Public Education, the rate of high school graduation for the year 2012–2013 was 59 percent for African American males, 65 percent for Latino males, and 80 percent for White males; the report noted that the rate was 61 percent for African American males in 2011 and that the Black–White gap is growing (Schott Foundation n.d.). According to data for 2012–2013 from the Department of Education, the rate of increase in high school graduation for African Americans, Hispanics, American Indians, English language learners, and students with disabilities outpaced the rates for White students; the only group which showed a lesser growth rate than White students was the Asian/Pacific Islander category. This data is also reported solely by race, so the report reflects rates inclusive of both sexes (Bidwell 2015).

Although the high school graduation rate for African American women is better than for men, problems confronting African American women who are "off track" receive significantly less attention than those experienced by men. The criminalization of African American girls expelled from schools shows that they are more at risk than African American boys in the school to prison pipeline. Most media attention focuses on the plight of the males and ignores the consequences for females. Black females are six times more likely than White females to be suspended and to receive excessive discipline measures. African American boys are three times more likely than their White peers to experience these sanctions. President Obama has drawn attention to addressing these issues for boys, completely ignoring the girls. Girls are especially likely to have histories of sexual victimization and to be punished for minor transgressions in clothing, language, and behaviors or just for expressing opinions, even when asked. African American girls are less likely to be invited or allowed into Advanced Placement classes and generally receive little teacher attention, even when they are excellent students (AAPF 2014; White 2015; Krasny 2016).

Box 11.5 – The School to Prison Pipeline

The school to prison pipeline refers to the high dropout rate of kids from poor neighborhoods, with deficient schools, who end up in the criminal justice system. These students are more likely to be subjected to disciplinary actions such as detention, suspension, and expulsion and have greater rates of truancy and attrition. Failure to complete high school is correlated with incarceration. Attention regarding the "school to prison pipeline" exclusively pertains to African American boys, though the problem is even more extensive among African American girls.

Monique Morris, author of the book *Pushout: The Criminalization of Black Girls in School* (2015), suggests changing the culture of schools by "co-constructing" the environment with the community, rather than imposing policy, curriculum and pedagogy. Community involvement is central to reforming the cultural climate in schools and education policies. The special needs accruing to African American

Figure 11.1 The school to prison pipeline has gained media attention but most has focused on boys, though it affects girls as much and possibly more since girls often are incarcerated for status offenses not applied to boys
Source: Skyward Kick Productions / Shutterstock.com

girls with respect to the multiple statuses of race, sex, gender, poverty, and other characteristics cannot be bypassed or isolated. The experiences of poor, young, African American lesbians are qualitatively different from poor Whites, or White lesbians, or African American heterosexual women, or any other combination. Morris especially promotes the need for more restorative measures in regard to individuals and to the institution.

Native Americans students also have a long history of indifference and abuse in the educational system. In 1864 Congress passed legislation making it illegal to teach Indigenous children in their Native language. Indigenous youths were forcibly removed for years at a time, from as young as four years old, to Bureau of Indian Affairs (BIA) schools where they were compelled to learn English, dress like "Americans," and separated from their families and culture. In 1934, some progressive measures were taken under the Indian Reorganization Act to provide more culturally specific, child-centered education. In 1979, the American Indian Movement sponsored their own schools as culturally relevant alternatives to public and BIA schools. In the 1970s local Indigenous community colleges were instituted, the first in the Navajo homeland, and by the late 1970s there were 35 natively run community colleges in 13 states. In the 1980s laws were passed ensuring that every Indian reservation had a community college to provide for local access to at least the first two years of college (Reyhner n.d.).

Native American and Alaskan Natives have the worst dropout and graduation rates of any group. The dropout rate is two times the national average, or three in ten, and it is consistent for urban and Native land populations. The graduation rate is 65–67 percent, compared to the national average of 80 percent. Native American schools exhibit major physical impediments such as poorly maintained facilities,

frequently with no heat or plumbing. Native American test scores did not improve with the passage of the NCLB initiative, though other groups' have (Reyhner n.d.). Native Americans tend to experience the curriculum as hostile to their experiences, as it lacks any connection to their culture and history. This cultural distance, often accompanied by stereotypic depictions, is more illuminating with regard to the educational impediments of the groups than any data. This marginality can be addressed by greater efforts of school officials working in conjunction with parents and communities to integrate more inclusive practices and curriculum. Training community members to teach in their schools has been shown to be beneficial and should be promoted by policy and financial aid (American Indian School Dropouts and Pushouts 2016; Camera 2015).

Influence of Family and Technology

Parental support of education is highly effective in improving outcomes. High-achieving Asian American students have been shown to come from homes across the social class spectrum, emphasizing the value of hard work in education. Kristof (2015) attributes this to the high valuation of education and learning and to strong family involvement. The presence of two parents is also helpful in that it indicates more available time for assistance (Kristof 2015). In a similar vein, Latino journalist Ruben Navarrette suggests that though Latino parents highly value education, and impress this in raising their kids, they don't take English courses or community college classes. He suggests that modeling education is just as important as promoting it with words (Navarrette 2005). Only 10 percent of American Latinos are college educated, significantly lower than other racial and ethnic groups. Research also suggests that Latino students are being overlooked when it comes to being selected, tested, or tracked into gifted programs, especially if they are English Language Learners (Sanchez 2016).

Another study adds evidence to the importance of parental commitment to involvement in their children's education. UC professor John Ogbu, hired by affluent African American professional parents in Shaker Heights Ohio to investigate why their children's achievements lagged significantly behind their White peers, concluded that the parents were not sufficiently engaged with their children's school work to promote its importance. He asserted that the busy parents failed to engage in school-related activities, relying on their belief in the excellence of the local schools to get results. He established that the parents spent no more time supervising the homework of their children than poor White parents did. He also suggested that the peer group supported the idea that excelling in school was "acting White" (Lee 2002). These varied situations all have the same underlying theme: parental support and involvement is a major element of student achievement, particularly if matched with demands to eliminate discrimination in selecting students for advanced placements and other enriching activities.

Questions have been raised regarding the impact of technology on educational achievement, especially in its effect on nondominant groups. Research shows that access to the internet and smart phones is equal between different racial and social class groups. There is some evidence, however, that internet access can actually promote disadvantages in children from lower income homes. Data from a longitudinal study, of one million fifth to eighth grade students provided with a home computer, showed a persistent decline in math and reading scores. Increased time spent on games and social media yielded a commensurate decrease in homework time. In contrast, research shows that one year with a gifted middle school teacher produces a significant impact in reductions of early pregnancy; increased college attendance; better adult incomes; access to "good" neighborhoods as adults; and gains in retirement savings (Pinker 2015). Research in countries with high-achieving students also shows that technology does not generally improve reading, science, and math test scores. For disadvantaged students, heavy use of technology is particularly detrimental. The overall quality of the schools, in terms of teacher quality and optimal connection between instruction and technology, is more significant than time spent with technology (Klein 2015).

How Can Schools Be Made Better?

Teachers

As indicated above, research shows that money spent to hire, train, and retain good teachers is especially helpful and it significantly increases the high school graduation rate. Increased funding to bolster teacher support helps achievement in several measures. In one study, it was shown that increased funding decreased the gap in scores between low income and affluent students by 20 percent. In the absence of additional funding, the gap between these groups grew. A second study investigated the future educational attainment and income of poorer students. When the funding increased steadily, over the 12 years the students were in school, the lower income

Figure 11.13 Increased budgets leading to more teacher enrichment and mentoring improves student achievement
Source: Karin Hildebrand Lau / Shutterstock.com

students were less likely to remain poor as adults and high school graduation rates improved. Although all students made slight gains, the impact was greater among poorer students (Turner et al. 2016a).

Improving teacher training and quality may be the most significant asset for supporting low-performing students. In the US, pressures to assess teachers have led to increased teacher testing and credentialing requirements, which do not actually emphasize the kind of training seen in the model systems of other countries. Most states have credential programs extending beyond the bachelor diploma, ranging from one to three semesters of additional schooling. Teacher credentialing is controlled by state boards and consequently varies from state to state. No state must accept the credential from another state, though some have implemented reciprocity. Teacher testing is accomplished by corporate entities entrusted with the task and many of these sources have been criticized for weak and culturally biased measures (Barmore 2016; Harris 2015).

Possibly due to some of the escalated pressures on teacher evaluation, evidence suggests that the desirability of a teaching career is waning. There is a shortage of teachers, which is predicted to become more severe. Veteran teachers say they would not choose the same career again. Three fourths of teachers surveyed say that they feel "profoundly undervalued." Teacher job satisfaction is at its lowest level in 25 years and between 40–50 percent of teachers leave the profession within five years of beginning teaching. The highest attrition rates are found among teachers who attended top colleges and among minority teachers. The chief reason given for leaving teaching concerns the lack of autonomy in the classroom. Excessive student testing is also a factor in discouraging new teachers. Fewer candidates are willing to subject themselves to the credentialing process, feeling their creativity and professionalism is discredited. Many minority candidates are especially discouraged and are not just resigning but also failing to enroll in teacher training programs (Weingarten 2016;

Phillips 2015; Kim 2016; Morrison 2015). Only two percent of public school teachers are Black men. Black men are particularly likely to dismiss teaching as a career option (Hanford 2017).

Teacher salaries are low, considering the education and training required for the job. The average US starting salary is $36,141, frequently an amount insufficient to cover living expenses (2012–2013 Average Starting Teacher Salaries by State 2013). The annual cost of US teacher *turnover* is 2.2 trillion dollars. Attacks on unionization have accelerated the teacher shortage and decimated the quality of education. The best example can be seen in the state of Wisconsin, where Republican Governor Scott Walker signed an Act in 2011 reducing the ability of public unions to collectively bargain. The Democratic Caucus was sufficiently alarmed to physically vacate the state in a failed effort to stop the vote. Efforts to recall Governor Walker also were unsuccessful. Consequently, public workers cannot negotiate retirement and health benefits and cannot achieve raises over the rate of inflation. Employees have lost job security measures, such as tenure for the state's teachers, and employee management can fire workers without cause. Additionally, unions must undergo a recertification vote annually where 51 percent of the total membership, including nonvoters, must support the union (Caldwell 2017).

As a consequence of this Act, Wisconsin has suffered a significant decrease in students enrolled in teacher training and many of those who are enrolled plan to seek work out of state. Veteran teachers are leaving in droves, since the governor has threatened to reduce benefits that allow for early retirement. Remaining faculty are teaching larger classes and extra classes, and have shown a marked trend in reduced participation in extracurricular assignments. In 2011, Walker also cut state funding for K-12 education by $792 million over two years, and any district that seeks a tax increase for education must pass a referendum. Public schools lost an additional $41.4 million in two years from 2015–2016, as a result of expansions in the state's school voucher program (see below), a program which generally has little national support among educators. Many observers fear that other states will follow in the wake of the Wisconsin reforms (Caldwell 2017).

In California, the state with the largest population, the teacher shortage is severe enough that it is feared to be moving towards crisis. In the years between 2011–2012 and 2013–2014, enrollment in teacher training programs fell by 21 percent and the number of district openings doubled (Mader 2016). Mandates for smaller primary grade classrooms, initiated for the fall of 2016, also are a contributing factor. Vacancy growth is partially due to the layoffs of the "great recession" as well as to prolonged teacher training programs and to teacher testing requirements, all of which discourage young people from entering the profession. The extensive teacher training programs in CA show no evidence of improving teacher quality or longevity. One assessment of the training highlights the lack of congruence between the credential process and the classroom:

> Some of California's problems stem from the state's unique, and uniquely
> dysfunctional, approach to teacher preparation. Prospective teachers in
> California must first earn a bachelor's degree in a non-education subject area

and then complete a post-graduate teacher training program. This means that teachers' preparation is fragmented and increases the costs of earning a credential. But many of the problems with teacher preparation in California also exist in other states: Students enrolled in teacher preparation programs are far less diverse than the state's K-12 students. Admissions standards are low. The training that prospective teachers receive is disconnected from the reality and needs of K-12 schools. Prospective teachers aren't adequately prepared to work with children with disabilities or English language learners. Some preparation programs do a better job than others, but the state doesn't have a way to tell the good from the bad. Although teacher preparation is highly, some would say excessively, regulated, regulations focus on program inputs, not how graduates perform in the classroom.

(Mead 2015)

And a personal reaction to having been trained in CA:

I always wanted to be a teacher, ever since I was a kid who struggled with school myself. I graduated from college, in the program for future teachers, and spent one year as an assistant teacher in AmeriCorps. I worked in a third-grade classroom in a New Orleans charter school considered one of the very toughest in the state. I worked a 60-hour week for a stipend of 1000 dollars a month. It was not a good experience but I did learn some things from my classroom teacher. I was dismayed, when I started the credential program, that it was another three semesters, over ten thousand dollars in tuition and I learned nothing in the program's classes though I did get something out of working with the teachers in my student teaching placement. I received no credit hours for my year with AmeriCorps.

In the credential program, we had to take all these tests and we had to pay a lot for them, each time we took them. When I failed one of them, for the second time, I really thought I would quit, I even went to talk to a career counselor. But then I went to my student teaching class and I loved being with the children so much, and working with them, I decided to stay and try. I eventually passed the tests but now, in my last month of the program, I have to turn in an edTPA [a portfolio initiated in CA, in 2014, and scored by Pearson Corp], even though I have to lead teach next week [solo teach without a classroom teacher there], and I am so stressed and I don't even know what grade I will get on the portfolio, or if it will be enough to pass, and I start teaching in two days.

(personal communication)

[This student ultimately received her credential, obtained a job, and had exceptional teacher and principal recommendations and her experiences are common to others this author has heard. Many supervising teachers report that their student teachers are so stressed they frequently break down and cry, and say they want to quit.]

(personal communication)

Figure 11.14 City year is a program of AmeriCorps which provides a stipend for about ten months of full-time service to underserved schools; the volunteers are hired essentially as aides, they gain classroom experience but are not the classroom teacher
Source: Photography submitted by Kara Gottfried, taken by anonymous citicorps staff

Another stressor impeding the satisfaction of teachers concerns issues of special education. Increases in resources devoted to special education affect all teachers since money for special education results in less money for general education programs. Though 1970s legislation improved the education rights of disabled students, some teachers feel overuse of disability categorizations has siphoned money to the few, at great cost to the many. Since the new legislation, however, there has been a 63 percent increase in the diagnoses of disabilities and virtually all of this has been in two of 13 categories covering dyslexia and attention deficit disorders. Critics suggest that parents abuse the disability label as an avenue to getting extra financial support and services for their children as well as benefits such as extra time for tests (Big Think Editors n.d.). Although 12 percent of US children are labeled as disabled, 22 percent of school funding is devoted to special education needs. Teachers complain of lost instructional time due to increased class size and time devoted to classroom management (personal communications). Disability legislation has been essential in providing needed aid for children previously excluded from the public system but the concern is that some of the students, whose needs are not as extreme, could be "mainstreamed" (retained in "regular" classrooms).

School Reform

There are many proposals for what can be done to improve schools. We have seen that better teacher training and conditions of employment have been established as crucial. Setting high expectations for student performance, improving the curricula, and strong parent involvement are also supported by research. Another area of concern reflects the schools themselves. In 1999, the Gates Foundation allotted significant funding to support the breakup of large urban schools, either by building small schools of no more than 500 students, or by creating Small Learning Communities (SLC) within urban high schools. An SLC would establish student groupings of no more than 500 students in the combined grades, and each would function as a discrete school, within the existing structures. The more personalized environment would facilitate better student/teacher relationships and greater peer solidarity. Additionally, the SLCs could each offer specialized programs focused on particular career goals. Examples include health professions, technology, performing arts, visual arts, or academically advanced programs. Ten years following the implementation of SLCs, the Gates Foundation admitted that the program was not working well and that it might have been more beneficial if they had allowed principals to have more control over reforms, especially in areas of direct classroom impact. Though gains in attendance and graduation rates were accomplished, there were no gains in college readiness among graduates (Strauss 2016).

Box 11.6 – School Reforms

Small Learning Communities (SLCs) are smaller groups of students in discrete programs attending the same large high school. Each SLC would retain the same students and teachers for the four years of high school, providing a more personalized and cohesive environment. They also could provide specialized programs addressed to particular student interests.

Charter schools are schools which are funded by public monies but operate like private schools. They were developed to enhance school quality by promoting competition. They are made possible by the state governments passing bills allowing for them. Charter schools must be approved by local school boards but once accepted only are subject to the elements outlined in the charter. The only mandate is that they must administer state testing.

Magnet schools refer to schools within a district which offer special programs to attract students to under-enrolled schools. These schools would enhance the desirability of underperforming, or under-enrolled, schools. One potential problem concerns the possibility for local students to be pushed out of such schools if they become too competitive.

Other school reforms, such as charter and magnet schools, have yielded mixed results. Each of these developed as a partial attempt to compensate for low-performing and/or low-enrolled schools. A **charter school** is a school which is publicly funded but operates like a private school. Charter schools are possible when states pass mandates allowing for their development. Any group can propose a charter school to a local school board and, if accepted, the charter will be enacted upon as proposed. These groups can be comprised of parents, educators, community groups, or any combination of these. Once approved the school receives state and federal money, just like the public schools, but is run entirely according to the guidelines in the charter; the school will hire its own teachers, have its own calendar and hours, its own staffing and pay scale. Usually, the only district-imposed requirement is that the school must administer state-required standardized tests (NEA n.d.). Charter schools have taken a variety of forms and curricula and have shown mixed results with regard to improved student achievement. One recent study, however, showed one type of charter school did exceptionally well in improved student achievement. These were schools devoting more time and resources to classroom teaching and providing essential teacher feedback in a meaningful process. A fear concerning the expansion of charter schools is that it will cause further deterioration of the public system by draining more students from the system, though so far this has not occurred (Leonhardt 2016).

Magnet schools are public schools which are developed to draw enrollment to a failing school. Frequently these are "underperforming," minority-enrolled, and/or under-enrolled schools. The concept of the magnet school entails attracting students to achieve a diverse student body and elevated enrollment by providing specialized, high-quality programs. Sample programs include performing arts, computer technology, health professions, business, or "basic skills." One problem resulting from successful magnet schools is that the competition for admission can result in shutting out the kids in the vicinity of the school who were supposed to be designated beneficiaries of these innovations. The emphasis on basics, particularly in elementary schools, also has been a draw in many communities among both magnet and charter schools (Chen 2017). Magnet schools differ from charter schools in that they have full district status.

School vouchers represent an effort to maximize parent choice in education. Instead of student monies being paid to a district school enrolling a student, the voucher would be given to the parent or guardian for use in whatever institution they choose. Vouchers generally have been a program of the Republican Party, strongly promoted in the George W. Bush era, but subjected to legal challenges. Fears surrounding vouchers concern a challenge of the American mandate of the separation of Church and State, since vouchers theoretically can be applied to any school, including religiously based institutions. It is also feared that by subsidizing the costs of private schools, the public schools would suffer from loss of students and the consequent reduction of financial allotments. Some areas have voluntarily adopted voucher programs. Expanded voucher programs in Wisconsin, for example, resulted in losses of $41.4 million in funding for one two-year period (Caldwell 2017). Debates regarding vouchers reappeared with President Trump's appointment of Betsy DeVos to the position of Secretary of Education. DeVos is a strong advocate of school vouchers, and her nomination was strongly opposed by many educators and politicians though ultimately she received confirmation to the office (Brown 2016a; ADL 2012; Fischer 2016; Hess 2015).

Some education critics take a more radical stand in promoting educational change, suggesting that simply modifying the current system will not suffice. One suggestion is to reduce the length of high school for students choosing a four-year degree program since often they already are enrolled in college-level classes, either in AP classes or in joint programs available at local community colleges. Another reform recommends block scheduling of classes, so that classes meet for longer periods several times a week, which allows for more focused study and is seen as more closely aligned with the college classroom. Proposals addressing students who are not college bound recommend a four-year diploma with more focused vocational training to obtain occupational skills required in the "new" economy. Community colleges can also address the needs of the local job market with programs tailored to regional employment needs (Obama 2016).

Is College "Worth It"?

As the cost of college expands much more rapidly than income, some have questioned its efficacy with regard to employment opportunities. A college education does add value in future income, job potential, and decreased unemployment. Education also has an effect on personal values. Degreed persons generally possess more liberal views, though not all research supports this claim. Education is thought to lead to increased tolerance regarding social issues of difference, such as gender equity. Newer research suggests that highly educated people are becoming more liberal, as a group, than in the past. This shift to the "left" has been attributed to growing polarization between conservatives and liberals; increased participation of women who generally show higher levels of liberal social ideas; and insularity, or the tendency of people to coalesce in areas of like-minded people, particularly in major urban areas (Kurtzleben 2016).

With regard to earnings, data from the Bureau of Labor Statistics (Josephson 2018) reveals that the median income for a person with a BA in 2015 was $59,124 while it was just $35,256 for a person with a high school diploma, amounting to a lifetime difference of 1.5 million dollars. Millennials with college degrees had a

Figure 11.15
Celebrating graduation
Source: Monkey Business
Images / Shutterstock.com

median annual income, in constant 2012 dollars, which increased by 7000 dollars between 1965–2012. During the same time period, incomes decreased by 3000 dollars for high school graduates. In 2012, the unemployment rate for a college graduate was 3.8 percent and 12.2 percent for those with only a high school diploma (Pew Research Center 2014). Income for skilled work, requiring a bachelor's degree, has increased significantly in the past 40 years. The income gap between individuals with high school diplomas and those with college degrees has doubled in this time period, the highest increase ever recorded. Baby boomers (born 1946–1964) had a college graduation rate of 24 percent while the millennial rate is 34 percent, the highest ever recorded. Yet, in international comparisons, the level of college completion for 25–29 year olds has fallen from number 1 to 16 (Gordon 2013).

Box 11.7 – Higher Education

Higher education refers to any post-secondary program for education and/ or training. These programs include vocational programs; two-and four-year colleges and universities; and graduate and professional schools.

Undermatched refers to the tendency of first-generation, and lower income, students to apply to schools which are less competitive than they can qualify for.

First generation refers to students who are the first in their families to attend college. The special needs of these students, accompanied by programs to address them, have only recently been addressed by colleges.

Prognostications for the future offer good reasons to promote the accessibility of college enrollment. The first is that, by 2020, two thirds of jobs will require some post-secondary education and training, while research projects a shortage of five million people to fill these positions (Bui 2016). This situation suggests a lack of workers with appropriate skills. Additionally, it points to the need to seriously address the high cost of college. College education has become increasingly costly, even when controlling for inflation. Students struggling with financial pressures are more at risk for failing to graduate. Not only do we need more skilled workers, but college-degreed persons contribute to the economy in multiple ways. Non-completion leads to poor wages, lower tax revenue, more government expenditure, decreased consumerism, and delinquent student loan repayment.

The dropout rate is staggeringly high. About one half of the students who start in a four-year college will graduate, while the figure is only about one third for students who begin in community colleges. Community college enrollment represents about one half of total American college enrollment. The majority of community college students are from families in the lower half of household income (Kirp 2014; Bellafante 2014). Some critics suggest that attending a four-year college from the beginning will increase graduation rates. Research shows that many high school students, falling just below the admissions standards for a four-year school, will show great future benefits if they are given a chance to attend these schools upon high school graduation. Enrollment at a four-year school is especially significant for low-income students and for men, who typically attend college at lower rates (Leonhardt 2014). Research also shows that many low-income students attending a four-year program, "undermatch"; they do not apply to the more selective schools for which they can qualify. Reasons for this omission include poor counseling, lack of confidence, and fear of the costs. The acceptance of low-income students by more selective colleges and universities can be extended by 30 percent without compromising admissions standards. In the 193 most selective colleges and universities, only 14 percent of students came from American households in the lower 50 percent of income, and only 5 percent came from the bottom 25 percent (Madden 2014; Pappano 2015). Only one in three top-performing lower income students attends an institution with a 70 percent graduation rate.

Because bright low-income students often fall through the cracks, some high schools are providing free SAT testing to their juniors and making sure that students get better advice. One pilot program hired 130 full-time counselors and 4000 college students to be part-time advisors, to help students with the application process. Some institutions of higher education are initiating programs which include the consideration of impoverished backgrounds in the admissions process (Leonhardt 2014a).

Costs of Higher Education

Students from low-income homes face many challenges in pursuing higher education, mostly for financial reasons. Many students remark how hard it is to be a full-time student, work, and get enough study time. At residentially oriented schools, these students are less likely than their more affluent peers to fully participate in campus life. Many students struggle with paying for food and maintaining shelter, and are very anxious about bills, even with financial aid.

The costs of states' public institutions of higher education have increased and they have suffered from state funding cutbacks in the "great recession," resulting in higher tuition costs (Mitchell et al. 2016). In one recent publication, *Paying the Price: College Costs, Financial Aid, and the Betrayal of the American Dream* (2016), sociologist Sara Goldrick-Rab investigates the hardships faced by lower income students attending college. She examines issues such as receiving financial aid that allegedly covers 75 percent of the cost against a reality that it provides only about 30 percent of the "real" cost. Pell grants to low-income students now cover only about 36 percent of a public university education and 62 percent of a community college program, representing a significant decrease from past decades. One study of 4312 respondents, drawn from seven community colleges across the country, found that one in five students had been food deprived in the past month and 10 percent had unstable living situations, resulting in a period of homelessness. One in five Black students reported being homeless during the previous month. Black, Asian, and Latino students are more likely to suffer food insecurity than White students (Kolowich 2015).

Goldrick-Rab criticizes federal financial aid forms for utilizing a formula which presumes that a family can make a contribution to the student when, in fact, the student frequently is still helping the family and therefore is experiencing a more dramatic deficit. She shows that data regarding the employment of students omits the large number of students who seek work but can't find jobs. Some students suffer in classroom performance due to fatigue from work, which frequently is full time, sometimes incorporating the graveyard shift which further interrupts elements leading to college success (Kamenetz 2016). The need to address public higher education funding and student financial aid assessment seems imperative (Goldrick-Rab 2016; McGuire 2016).

In private universities with large endowments the situation can actually be financially easier. In selective four-year universities, low-income students appear to receive more adequate financial aid. The portion of students officially reported as receiving financial aid is misleading since many of these students receive only partial financial aid, and so are counted in the data of supported students though they are from middle-class families. Lower income students suffer other setbacks since they are frequently unable to purchase books, tickets home, meals or shelter during breaks when dorms are closed, clothing for cold weather, and many other "incidentals" that more affluent students take for granted.

Student Issues in Higher Education

When students complete undergraduate study, it takes them longer than in the past, with fewer achieving success in the "traditional" four-year period. In public four-year universities, only 19 percent of full-time students finish in four years while the corresponding figure is 36 percent for the most selective campuses in the system. Explanations include reduced availability of required courses; credits lost to transfer; remediation classwork; failure of remediation to prepare the students; and enrollment in too few credits per term. External factors such as family, financial, and personal stressors also impact expanded enrollment time. In community colleges and public colleges, the severe budget cuts of the recession led to reductions in faculty and course sections. Only 5 percent of students attending community colleges complete an associate level degree in two years and those who receive a bachelor's level degree will also experience prolonged enrollment (Meraji 2015; Lewin 2014; Gates 2015).

When low-income, and first-generation, college students attend more selective universities, they frequently suffer from feelings of alienation and marginality. Research shows that the lecture format is inherently biased, advantaging White, affluent males (Paul 2015). Lectures typically require passive engagement with material more characteristic of the dominant group. Active learning has been shown to provide more engagement with the material, allowing for the incorporation of more personal experiences of the groups implicitly left out of lectures. Non-lecture formats significantly increase assignment completion for all students but more significantly for minority and low-income students. It has been shown that new knowledge is anchored to previous knowledge, and low-income students generally do not have the same level of preparation as the more affluent students, resulting in more difficulties with the material. Many students record lectures, or use laptops, though research shows note taking by hand promotes better retention resulting from active selectivity of what is recorded. More conceptual sophistication is utilized and may point to another disadvantage in students with inferior secondary school educations (Doubek 2016).

Low-income, minority, and first-generation students are also less likely to participate verbally in class and feel less integrated into the school setting. This alienation has been shown to be a significant contributor to academic performance and is considered a contributing factor in the poorer performance of women in math and science programs (Paul 2015). These students can also be assessed less strongly, even when their assignments are equivalent to the more verbal students' work. Research shows that having first-generation freshmen attend an orientation panel where a person of similar background simply addresses the issues of student backgrounds has an impact on performance. Freshmen attending such a session closed the small gap in grade point average typical of the group. These students also reported feeling happier, less stressed, and more willing to seek help than students who did not participate in such a presentation (Pappano 2015). To alleviate some of the exclusionary dynamics, some elite schools have established clubs for first-generation students and Brown University hosted an initial national conference in 2015.

Undocumented students face many issues in obtaining higher education. Even in states where the schools are protective, the students are fearful and distracted. Since public tax money cannot be utilized by undocumented students, even in "sanctuary" states, it can be difficult to raise money for school. Currently, 18 states provide for students to get in-state tuition while three states specifically prohibit it (NCLS 2015).

Subtle forms of discrimination and hostility persist towards students of color and students with nondominant gender identities, sexualities, nationalities, religions, social class, and abilities. In the student movement of the 1960s and 1970s, students demanded more relevant curricula and ultimately gained specialized classes addressing race, ethnicity, gender, labor history, and sexual orientation. It was suggested that these courses were necessary to compensate for the hidden bias of the standard history, social science, and literature curricula. Since then, there has been some discussion of whether these specialties are still needed or whether the material has been incorporated into the "mainstream" courses. Contemporary student activism suggests that the mainstream classes are not inclusive, with students identifying persistent overt and covert biases. Students with nondominant demographics feel that professors are, at best, insensitive or oblivious. The manifestations of these biases, particularly when covert, have been viewed as *microaggressions*. These can take the form of stereotyping, generalizations, presumptions of others' experiences, and/ or choice of language (Lukianoff and Haidt 2015). An incidence of class bias, for example, might occur with a professor asking students where they went on semester break. Such a question ignores the reality that some students have no place to live, or need to work, during the school break. Students also protest the assumption of normative gender roles and do not want to be presumed to adhere to the typical gender binary. In some settings, students now receive forms asking by what pronoun they wish to be addressed.

Student demands have extended to protection against uncomfortable conditions in class or on campus. Some students are demanding trigger warnings on material representing the potential for rekindling a person's past traumas. These would be included in course syllabi, assigned readings, lectures, or special events. Controversies regarding their inclusion have become so incendiary some faculty are saying that they threaten the academic freedom of the classroom and campus. Some faculty and students fear for a climate antithetical to any critical thought or divergent perspectives. Faculty fear that this trend will result in censorship and contract terminations and some have initiated campaigns to educate around issues of protecting free speech (Raphelson 2017).

> The current movement is largely about emotional well-being. More than the last, it presumes an extraordinary fragility of the collegiate psyche, and therefore elevates the goal of protecting students from psychological harm. The ultimate aim, it seems, is to turn campuses into "safe spaces" where young adults are shielded from words and ideas that make some uncomfortable. And more than the last, this movement seeks to punish anyone who interferes with that aim, even accidentally. You might call this impulse *vindictive protectiveness*. It is creating a culture in which everyone must think twice before speaking up, lest they face charges of insensitivity, aggression, or worse.
>
> (Lukianoff and Haidt 2015)

In one example, where a speaker coming to Brown University was believed to hold a critical view of the concept of the *rape culture* (which suggests that rape is a normative aspect of violence in the US), students protested saying that such an assertion would invalidate the experiences of women students. As a result, the campus ran a simultaneous lecture on the culture of rape and sexual assault and provided a

Figure 11.16 Some educators fear that the sensitivities of students, and the demand for trigger warnings and safe spaces, will impede critical thinking and the inclusion of controversial issues on campuses, both inside and outside of the classroom
Source: Lightspring / Shutterstock.com

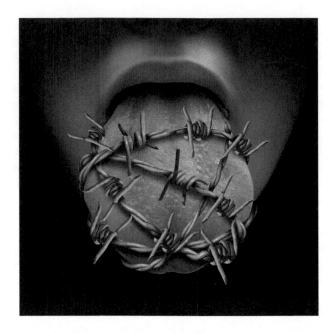

safe space in a room with arts and crafts and snacks, where a student could go if she or he felt *triggered*. Other campuses have had speakers back out of scheduled talks, or actually be uninvited, because of student protests. These speakers were discouraged as a result of their views, not because they engaged in dangerous practices (Parker 2015; Shulevitz 2015). Some educators are concerned about the well-being of students, believing that the millennial generation is so coddled that they actually are mentally fragile, exhibiting symptoms associated with depression and anxiety as well as an inability to resolve simple chores of daily life (Lukianoff and Haidt 2015).

Quality of American Higher Education

Evaluating the quality of American institutions of higher education has been a source of contention. Americans with high school diplomas fare only as well as high school dropouts from other countries. In *Organization for Economic Cooperation and Development* (OECD) studies the US came in last on tests of simple technical skills such as file naming, drop menu use, email and text messaging, and making purchases online (Emanuel 2016). The standards of student performance have been scrutinized, especially in relation to grade inflation (Weller 2017). It is frequently asserted that the US has the best universities in the world. While it is true that the US houses the majority of the 25 institutions of higher education listed as the best in the world, graduates of the more typical American colleges do not compare well to those in 69 other countries in the OECD. US students with associate and graduate degrees also fall short by comparison to international peers (Carey 2014).

Also under scrutiny is the issue of what constitutes a curriculum appropriate for higher education. Due to the technological demands of the current economy, the value of a **liberal arts** education has been debated. The push has been towards **STEM** degrees (science, technology, engineering, and math) and extra money and initiatives have moved in that direction. Proponents of STEM initiatives suggest that America is not competitive with other countries in producing these graduates (Neuhauser 2016). However, there is evidence that only a small portion of jobs require STEM degrees and that a liberal arts degree is great preparation for any work and for other areas of life (Teitelbaum 2014). The liberal arts, including anything from history and anthropology to music and dance, are increasingly devalued, particularly in terms of their alleged impracticality. Supporters of liberal arts suggest that a general liberal arts background is essential to develop creativity, imagination, and approaches to learning that are of significant value to the work environment and cannot be replaced by modern technological innovations. They suggest that technology is a tool of human endeavor, requiring other skills to be effectively utilized (Woodcock 2015). Improving American education, work, and the economy is best addressed by enhancing academic standards (Worstall 2012).

Box 11.8 – Student Issues in Higher Education

Students feel that the education environment is biased and degrades the experiences of particular groups. *Microaggressions* refer to any communication which contains potentially offensive or stereotypic depictions of nondominant groups, though frequently they are unintended or unrecognized by the person exhibiting them. Some students are agitating for control over who speaks on campus and what topics can be addressed. Some educators feel that this is compromising the critical thinking on campus and risking free speech.

Sexual assault and harassment are considered prevalent on college campuses and generally have garnered little serious attention or consequences. Several recent cases have been widely reported in the media and have resulted in more attention to these issues.

Liberal arts courses refer to a curriculum based on general studies in humanities, social sciences, languages, arts, and sciences. Some experts suggest that liberal arts have become obsolete, since they do not address the needs of the technical economy of the twenty-first century. Liberal arts critics promote the expansion of science, technology, engineering, and mathematics (*STEM*) as a curriculum more responsive to global interests. Liberal arts proponents believe critical and learning skills constituting a general education are transferable to occupational and other life sectors.

Nonacademic Issues Affecting Education

Several non-academic issues on college campuses have garnered recent attention. One such issue is sexual assault. Campus sexual assaults are pervasive in sports and academic settings and are frequently unreported, covered up, unprosecuted, or lacking in consequences for the perpetrators. The widely-publicized Penn State athletics scandal, pertaining to sexual abuse perpetrated against male athletes by an assistant coach, resulted in a 92.8 million dollar settlement. Perhaps more stunning than the number of boys and young men assaulted was the extensive and prolonged cover up by the university's administrators. As a result, the college president resigned and the contracts of the athletics director and head football coach were terminated. This case brought the topic to national prominence and forced a public discussion regarding who bears responsibility for such activities (Jenkins 2016).

Sexual assaults on women are much more prevalent, even viewed as "routine," and consequently garner less publicity, or even any attention. One in four women is subjected to an assault, or attempted assault on campus. In a recent radio program, it was noted that 45 percent of Stanford University's women students reported experiencing a sexual assault (Krasny 2016). Due to lax investigations of reported assaults, and a trend of retaining alleged perpetrators on campus, many women articulate feeling unsafe on campus. The false report of an alleged rape at the University of Virginia was more widely reported than the majority of verified cases of rape and assault, though it is estimated that only 2–8 percent of reports are falsified (Coronel et al. 2015). The negative press added to the reluctance women face in reporting abuse.

One recent case did focus national attention on the issue of rape and the tolerance or indifference accompanying discussions of the topic, especially when the alleged perpetrator is White and privileged. The case involved a Stanford University freshman who received a six-month sentence, to be served in the county jail, and three years of probation for a guilty verdict in the rape of an *unconscious* woman (see Chapter 6).

Sexual harassment is another significant campus issue which is often ignored or underplayed. It refers to offensive physical, verbal, or sexual behaviors towards a colleague, student, or employee. These behaviors are not necessarily overtly sexual but can contribute to a "hostile" environment. Such behaviors frequently permeate the campus culture and sometimes are dismissed as "normative" or "traditional." Sexual harassment complaints also risk being considered exaggerated but they likely are more pervasive than sexual assaults. National attention was first alerted to this issue in the televised hearings for the nomination of Clarence Thomas to the US Supreme Court. Law professor Anita Hill leveled harassment charges against

Figure 11.17 Sexual assaults on campus are pervasive and given insufficient attention Source: Rape, Abuse, & Incest National Network. Adapted from Department of Justice, Office of Justice Programs, Bureau of Justice Statistics, Rape and Sexual Victimization Among College-Aged Females, 1995–2013 (2014).

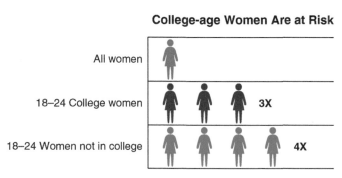

National Sexual Assault Hotline | 800.656.HOPE | online.rainn.org

Thomas, her former boss. She testified in front of an all-male, all-White Judiciary committee. Professor Hill's input had been solicited by the FBI in response to general allegations that Thomas had been harassing women. Hill did not initiate the interview leading to her testimony and other women were set to testify regarding Thomas's behaviors but were never called. Hill was vilified, particularly as an African American woman accusing an African American man of impropriety. She also was targeted as a puppet of the presidential campaign of Democrat Bill Clinton, though Hill was a registered Republican. Thomas was eventually confirmed by the narrowest vote in US history, 52:48 (Mock 2013). The publicity from the case made a significant impact on public awareness of sexual harassment and led to increased numbers of cases being filed with the Equal Economic Opportunity Commission (EEOC) (Kleiman 1992; Totenberg 2011). In recent years, Joe Biden, who chaired the Senate Judiciary hearings, has stated that he regrets his behavior (WITW Staff 2017).

Some recent high-profile cases have renewed attention on this issue and show that not much has changed. Charges against 19 employees of the Berkeley campus of the University of California, identified as violating sexual harassment policies, went largely ignored for years. Students and staff had filed complaints spanning years before the situation was investigated. The University ultimately took action resulting in the resignation of a vice chancellor and a renowned professor, and the demotion of the law school dean (Pauly 2016). None of the involved faculty were fired and the vice chancellor, after resigning, was initially given a position as an administrator at a satellite campus. Protests led to his removal from that job by system chancellor Janet Napolitano, though he remains on the chemistry faculty (Doumar 2016; McDermid 2016).

Collegiate athletes also have been seen as a group suffering from exploitation, though some reap rewards for their status. Universities have "utilized" women, sometimes called "hostesses," to entice athletes to accept the invitation to join a particular college's team. These practices have, from time to time, led to accusations of rape (Mulhere 2015; Trahan 2015; Kelleher 2009). Observers also suggest that the bodies of athletes are fodder for the college money-making sports, while the well-being of the athletes is unprotected. *The National Collegiate Athletic Association* (NCAA) boasts high graduation rates among its athletes, the highest being reported as 86 percent of division one athletes within six years of enrollment (Hosick 2014). There is evidence, however, that the graduation rate of African American athletes is 50 percent at best. African American males make up 3 percent of undergraduate enrollment in the US but comprise between 50–60 percent of athletes in revenue-generating sports (Montagne 2016). Athletes risk injury and loss of scholarships, putting their future livelihoods in jeopardy. These concerns have raised the question of whether they basically are hired professionals, rather than student athletes. Some athletes are agitating for "workers' rights," claiming that their work status is prioritized over any student status. Many athletes feel they are not getting the type of support they should for the revenue and notoriety they bring. Athletes at Northwestern University recently won the right to unionize (Williams 2014). Additional contested issues in college athletics include who should be responsible for medical expenses after injury; tuition after the athletes are no longer eligible to play;

Figure 11.18 African American males represent 50–60 percent of athletes in revenue-generating sports and are reported to have a graduation rate of less than 50 percent Source: AlpamayoPhoto / istockphoto.com

and expenses such as food and travel which are not covered by financial aid (Emmert 2014; Walsh 2013; Levin 2012).

Key Terms

Meritocracy   Cultural Capital   Hidden Curriculum   Standardized Tests   No Child Left Behind (NCLB)   Common Core Initiative   Brown v. the Board   Mendez v. Westminster Tracking   School to Prison Pipeline   AmeriCorps   Small Learning Community   Charter School Magnet School   School Vouchers   First-Generation Students   Undermatched Microaggressions   Trigger Warnings   Liberal Arts   Science, Technology, Engineering, and Math (STEM)

Concept Review

How Is Education Organized and Funded in the US?

Since its inception, the American public-school system has been dependent on local property taxes for its funding. Today the system is funded in relatively equal portions by the local district and state allotments, with the federal government contributing about 10 percent of the total school budget. This system has led to disparate standards of education across states and localities. Every state has had to address making educational opportunities comparable for all residents. The effort has resulted in persistent legal challenges to the funding mechanisms. In spite of recent modifications, the standards of education still vary by state, as well as within states.

Are the Schools Racially Integrated?

After major integration efforts brought about by both the Latino and African American populations in the 1940s and 1950s, there ensued a period of improved racial integration. The trend began to backslide in the late 1980s, increasing the portion of students attending schools with severe segregation. During the civil rights era, the racial integration of schools was viewed as the best route to obtaining equal education for all groups. Since that time, many students who were in school in the era of forced integration have been critical of the experience. They elaborate a sense of loss resulting from the scarcity of nonWhite teachers as well as the loss of community. Today, many localities are residentially segregated and, consequently, the schools reflect the demographics of the community.

How Can the Public School System Be Improved?

The surest route to improving schools is to provide more comprehensive teacher training since teacher excellence appears to have the most significant impact on student success. Another essential factor is parental support and involvement. Policies with regard to time off from work and other family-friendly interventions can be instrumental in enhancing parent involvement. The resources parents provide for students outside of school vary significantly. Differences in levels of expenditure are expanding, not only between wealthy and poor families but between the wealthy and the middle class as well, resulting in reinforcing inequalities characteristic of American education. The *Common Core Initiative* was developed to create a more uniform curriculum across the country and to promote more critical thinking, problem-solving, and life skills.

Has Testing Improved the Education in American Schools?

Following the passing of the *No Child Left Behind* Act, the time and money spent on student testing has grown exponentially. Many educators have questioned the efficacy of student testing, suggesting that the time spent on preparing students for tests, and the consequent restrictions on the classroom environment, are counterproductive to learning. It is also felt that the tests do not actually assess specific cognitive skills since scores can rise without a commensurate gain in specific skills. Teacher testing also has been widely instituted as a means of assuring adequate teacher training and skills, though there is no data to suggest a correlation between testing and teacher quality.

How Effective Is our System of Higher Education?

Decreases in state funding of public universities and commensurate increases in tuition place a heavy financial burden on students. Financial aid, particularly government programs for the low-income student, have not kept pace with the rising costs of higher education. Social class origin is the strongest predictor of the type of college a student will attend. Half of today's students are in community colleges and they are disproportionately culled from the lower levels of the socio-economic spectrum. The quality of the average American university is lower than in comparable countries. Student activism in the twenty-first century focuses on demands for more sensitivity to issues of nondominant statuses and "upsetting" topics. Some educators fear that student-led attempts to limit access to certain topics is infiltrating the integrity of the classroom and free speech. Additional campus concerns address issues of sexual assault, sexual harassment, college athletics, and policies with regard to undocumented students.

Review Questions

1. What is unique about the way that the US school system has been funded? What are the consequences of this approach to education? Do you feel it should be changed?

2. Compare and contrast the conflict and functionalist views of education. Are there points these views agree upon? What describes the basic points of divergence in these views?

3. Discuss three ways in which poverty affects children's ability to learn. What can be done to remedy these?

4. Is student testing promoting better achievement in children? Are there positive consequences to testing? Negative ones? Do you think testing helps to make teaching more effective?

5. How do you think teacher training should be conducted? What do you think about teacher testing? How can the effectiveness of good teaching be tested?

6. What is your view regarding the Common Core Initiative? What are its goals? Do you think it should be maintained?

7. Are the US colleges producing good students? Are the colleges equivalent to those in other countries?

8. What are microaggressions? How can they be addressed? Do you think students are being "coddled"? Should there be trigger warnings?

9. How should higher education be funded? Refer to state funding and its relationship to tuition in the public system.

10. What do you think should be done about the sexual assaults on students and staff in higher education? Should the alleged perpetrators be able to remain at schools while under investigation?

11. If students are being sexually harassed, what consequences should there be for the perpetrators? What can be done to protect students?

12. Should student athletes be considered "students" or professional athletes/workers?

References

2012–2013 Average Starting Teacher Salaries by State. (December, 2013) *National Education Association*. Retrieved from http://www.nea.org/home/2012-2013-average-starting-teacher-salary.html

AAPF. African American Policy Forum. (December 30, 2014) Black Girls Matter: Pushed Out, Overpoliced, and Underprotected. *AAPF*. Retrieved from http://www.aapf.org/recent/2014/12/coming-soon-blackgirlsmatter-pushed-out-overpoliced-and-underprotected

ADL. (2012) School Vouchers: The Wrong Choice for Public Education. *Anti-Defamation League*. Retrieved from https://www.adl.org/sites/default/files/documents/assets/pdf/civil-rights/religiousfreedom/religfreeres/School-Vouchers-docx.pdf

American Indian School Dropouts and Pushouts. (2016) *Northern Arizona University*. Retrieved from http://www2.nau.edu/~jar/AIE/Dropouts.html

Barmore, P. (April 4, 2016) Will Controversial New Tests for Teachers Make the Profession Even More Overwhelmingly White? *The Hechinger Report*. Retrieved from http://hechingerreport.org/will-controversial-new-tests-for-teachers-make-the-profession-even-more-overwhelmingly-white/

Bellafante, G. (December 19, 2014) Raising Ambitions: The Challenge in Teaching at Community Colleges. *The New York Times*. Retrieved from http://www.nytimes.com/2014/12/21/nyregion/raising-ambitions-the-challenge-in-teaching-at-community-colleges.html

Bidwell, A. (June 27, 2013a) Report: High School Students Have Made No Progress in 40 Years. *U.S. News*. Retrieved from http://www.usnews.com/news/articles/2013/06/27/report-high-school-students-have-made-no-progress-in-40-years

Bidwell, A. (November 7, 2013b) Racial Achievement Gaps Remain Largely Unchanged, Despite Higher Test Scores. *U.S. News*. Retrieved from http://www.usnews.com/news/articles/2013/11/07/racial-achievement-gaps-remain-largely-unchanged-despite-higher-test-scores

Bidwell, A. (December 3, 2013c) *American Students Fall in International Academic Tests*. Retrieved from http://www.usnews.com/news/articles/2013/12/03/american-students-fall-in-international-academic-tests-chinese-lead-the-pack

Bidwell, A. (March 16, 2015) *Racial Gaps in High School Graduation Rates Are Closing*. Retrieved from http://www.usnews.com/news/blogs/data-mine/2015/03/16/federal-data-show-racial-gap-in-high-school-graduation-rates-is-closing

Big Think Editors. (n.d.) #23: *Cut Special Education*. Retrieved from http://bigthink.com/dangerous-ideas/23-cut-special-education

Breslow, J.M., Wexler, E., Collins, R. (July 15, 2014) The Return of School Segregation in Eight Charts. *Frontline*. Retrieved from http://www.pbs.org/wgbh/frontline/article/the-return-of-school-segregation-in-eight-charts/

Brown, E. (October 20, 2016) These States Are Spending Less on Education Now than Before the Great Recession. *The Washington Post*. Retrieved from https://www.washingtonpost.com/news/education/wp/2016/10/20/these-states-are-spending-less-on-education-now-than-before-the-great-recession/?utm_term=.6666584c6bc9

Brown, E. (November 23, 2016a) Trump Picks Billionaire Betsy DeVos, School Voucher Advocate, as Education Secretary. *The Washington Post*. Retrieved from https://www.washingtonpost.com/local/education/trump-picks-billionaire-betsy-devos-school-voucher-advocate-as-education-secretary/2016/11/23/c3d66b94-af96-11e6-840f-e3ebab6bcdd3_story.html?utm_term=.86045fceb160

Bui, Q. (June 1, 2016) Hidden Side of the College Dream: Mediocre Graduation Rates. *The New York Times*. Retrieved from https://www.nytimes.com/2016/06/02/upshot/why-college-students-drop-out-follow-the-dollars.html

Caldwell, Patrick. (March/April, 2017) Who Moved My Teachers? *Mother Jones,* (42) 2: 36ff.

Camera, L. (November 6, 2015) Native American Students Left Behind. *U.S. News*. Retrieved from http://www.usnews.com/news/articles/2015/11/06/native-american-students-left-behind

Carey, K. (June 28, 2014) Americans Think We Have the World's Best Colleges. We Don't… *The New York Times*. Retrieved from https://www.nytimes.com/2014/06/29/upshot/americans-think-we-have-the-worlds-best-colleges-we-dont.html

Chen, G. (June 22, 2017) What Is a Magnet School? *Public School Review*. Retrieved from https://www.publicschoolreview.com/blog/what-is-a-magnet-school

Chiles, N. (November 25, 2014) 5 Special Things Black People Lost When Schools Were Integrated After Brown v Board of Education Decision. *Atlanta Black Star*. Retrieved from http://atlantablackstar.com/2014/11/25/5-special-things-black-people-lost-when-schools-were-integrated-after-brown-v-board-of-education-decision/5/

Coronel, S., Coll, S., Kravitz, D. (April 5, 2015) Rolling Stone & UVA: Columbia School of Journalism's Report. *Rolling Stone*. Retrieved from http://www.rollingstone.com/culture/features/a-rape-on-campus-what-went-wrong-20150405?page=4

Crockett, E. (June 6, 2016) This Letter from a Stanford Sexual Assault Victim Destroys 5 Bad Assumptions About Rape. *Vox*. Retrieved from http://www.vox.com/2016/6/6/11866756/brock-turner-stanford-letter-sexual-assault-rape-assumptions

Dell'Antonia, K.J. (June 5, 2016) The Families that Can't Afford Summer. *The New York Times*. Retrieved from https://www.nytimes.com/2016/06/05/sunday-review/the-families-that-cant-afford-summer.html

Doubek, J. NPR Staff. (April 17, 2016) Attention, Students: Put Your Laptops Away. *NPR*. Retrieved from http://www.npr.org/2016/04/17/474525392/attention-students-put-your-laptops-away

Doumar, K. (June 22, 2016) Former Campus Administrator Continues to Receive Executive Salary 1 Year After Resignation Amid Sex Harassment Allegations. *The Daily Californian*. Retrieved from http://www.dailycal.org/2016/06/22/former-campus-administrator-continues-receive-executive-salary-1-year-resignation-amid-sex-harassment-allegations/

Early Warning Confirmed Executive Summary. (2013) [PDF File] *Annie E. Casey Foundation*. Retrieved from http://www.aecf.org/m/resourcedoc/aecf-EarlyWarningConfirmedExecSummary-2013.pdf

Ebbert, S. (April 23, 2016) At Boston Latin, Little Outreach to City's Black, Latino Students. *The Boston Globe*. Retrieved from http://www.bostonglobe.com/metro/2016/04/23/boston-latin-little-outreach-city-black-latino-students/of6NlYrJhR8PvxMUYNi50L/story.html

Editorial Board. (June 24, 2016) Fueling the Fires of a Crisis at Boston Latin School. *The Boston Globe*. Retrieved from https://www.bostonglobe.com/opinion/editorials/2016/06/24/fueling-fires-crisis-boston-latin-school/yg2AVF92srMtiQb3ztxlkJ/story.html?p1=Article_Related_Box_Article_More

Edsall, T. (February 9, 2017) Integration Works. Can It Survive the Trump Era? *The New York Times*. Retrieved from https://www.nytimes.com/2017/02/09/opinion/integration-works-can-it-survive-the-trump-era.html

Emanuel, G. (March 10, 2016) America's High School Graduates Look Like Other Countries' High School Dropouts. *NPR*. Retrieved from http://www.npr.org/sections/ed/2016/03/10/469831485/americas-high-school-graduates-look-like-other-countries-high-school-dropouts

Emmert, M. (June 24, 2014) When College Athletes Get Hurt, Whose Wallet Should Feel the Pain? *Portland Press Herald*. Retrieved from http://www.pressherald.com/2014/06/22/when-college-athletes-get-hurt-whose-wallet-should-feel-the-pain/

Find Law. (n.d.) *Compulsory Education Laws: Background*. Retrieved from http://education.findlaw.com/education-options/compulsory-education-laws-background.html

Fischer, H. (February 22, 2016) Senate Approves Voucher Plan Decried as 'the End of Public Education in Arizona.' *Arizona Capitol Times*. Retrieved from http://azcapitoltimes.com/news/2016/02/22/arizona-senate-votes-for-vouchers-for-all-school-students/

Funding Gaps 2015 (March, 2015) [PDF File] *The Education Trust*. Retrieved from https://edtrust.org/wp-content/uploads/2014/09/FundingGaps2015_TheEducationTrust1.pdf

Gates, B. (June 3, 2015) Help Wanted: 11 Million College Grads. *Gatesnotes*. Retrieved from https://www.gatesnotes.com/Education/11-Million-College-Grads

Goldrick-Rab, S. (2016) *Paying the Price: College Costs, Financial Aid, and the Betrayal of the American Dream*. Chicago: The University of Chicago Press.

Gordon, J.R. (September 7, 2013) The Great Stagnation of American Education. *Opinionator*. Retrieved from http://opinionator.blogs.nytimes.com/2013/09/07/the-great-stagnation-of-american-education/?_r=0

Haidt, G. (September, 2015) How Trigger Warnings Are Hurting Mental Health on Campus. *The Atlantic*. Retrieved from http://www.theatlantic.com/magazine/archive/2015/09/the-coddling-of-the-american-mind/399356/

Hanford, E. (August 28, 2017) Why Are There So Few Black Male Teachers? *APMReports*. Retrieved from https://www.apmreports.org/story/2017/08/28/why-so-few-black-male-teachers

Harris, A.E. (June 17, 2015) Tough Tests for Teachers, With Question of Bias. *The New York Times*. Retrieved from https://www.nytimes.com/2015/06/18/nyregion/with-tougher-teacher-licensing-exams-a-question-of-racial-discrimination.html?_r=0

Hess, M.F. (September 8, 2015) The War on School Choice Comes to Washington State. *National Review*. Retrieved from http://www.nationalreview.com/article/423683/war-school-choice-comes-washington-state-frederick-m-hess

hooks, b. (Gloria Watkins) (1994) *Teaching To Transgress: Education as the Practice of Freedom*. London: Routledge.

Hosick, B.M. (November 4, 2014) Graduation Success Rate Continues to Climb. *NCAA*. Retrieved from http://www.ncaa.org/about/resources/media-center/news/graduation-success-rate-continues-climb

Jenkins, S. (May 10, 2016) Penn State Should Own its Role in the Sandusky Scandal. *The Washington Post*. Retrieved from https://www.washingtonpost.com/sports/colleges/penn-state-should-own-its-role-in-the-sandusky-scandal/2016/05/10/41eea4ce-16b3-11e6-924d-838753295f9a_story.html

Josephson, A. (May 15, 2018) The Average Salary by Education Level. *Smartasset*. Retrieved from https://smartasset.com/retirement/the-average-salary-by-education-level

Kamenetz, A. (December 28, 2015) School Testing 2016: Same Tests, Different Stakes. *Morning Edition NPR*. Retrieved from http://www.npr.org/sections/ed/2015/12/28/459068910/school-testing-2016-same-tests-different-stakes

Kamenetz, A. (September 17, 2016) How College Aid Is Like A Bad Coupon. *NPR*. Retrieved from http://www.npr.org/sections/ed/2016/09/17/492973995/how-college-aid-is-like-a-bad-coupon

Kelleher, K. (December 15, 2009) Sex Sells: "Hostess" Program Used To Recruit Players. *Jezebel*. Retrieved from http://jezebel.com/5426819/sex-sells-hostess-program-used-to-recruit-players

Kim, J. (August 18, 2016) Teachers Feel Undervalued—and They May Be Right. *Marketplace*. Retrieved from https://www.marketplace.org/2016/08/17/world/teachers-feel-undervalued-and-they-may-be-right

Kirp, D.L. (January 8, 2014) How to Help College Students Graduate. *The New York Times*. Retrieved from http://www.nytimes.com/2014/01/09/opinion/how-to-help-college-students-graduate.html?_r=0

Kirp, D.L. (December 27, 2014a) Opinion | Rage against the Common Core. *The New York Times*. Retrieved from http://www.nytimes.com/2014/12/28/opinion/sunday/rage-against-the-common-core.html

Kleiman, C. (March 3, 1992) Sexual Harassment Complaints on the Rise. *ChicagoTribune*. Retrieved from http://articles.chicagotribune.com/1992-03-07/news/9201210842_1_sexual-harassment-anita-hill-equal-employment-opportunity-commission

Klein, R. (September 14, 2015) Putting More Technology in Schools May Not Make Kids Smarter: OECD Report. *The Huffington Post*. Retrieved from http://www.huffingtonpost.com/entry/technology-in-schools-oecd report_us_55f32091e4b042295e362f19

Kolowich, S. (December 4, 2015) Many Community-College Students Struggle to Afford Food or Shelter, Study Finds. *The Chronicle of Higher Education*. Retrieved from http://chronicle.com/blogs/ticker/many-community-college-students-struggle-to-afford-food-or-shelter-study-finds/107140

Krasny, M. (June 7, 2016) Outrage Grows Over Jail Sentence for Stanford Sexual Assault. *Forum. KQED*. Retrieved from http://ww2.kqed.org/forum/2016/06/06/2010101855045/

Kristof, N. (November 9, 2013) Opinion | Oklahoma! Where the Kids Learn Early. *The New York Times*. Retrieved from http://www.nytimes.com/2013/11/10/opinion/sunday/kristof-oklahoma-where-the-kids-learn-early.html

Kristof, N. (October 10, 2015) The Asian Advantage. *The New York Times*. Retrieved from https://www.nytimes.com/2015/10/11/opinion/sunday/the-asian-advantage.html

Kurtzleben, D. (April 30, 2016) Why Are Highly Educated Americans Getting More Liberal? *Morning Edition*. Retrieved from http://www.npr.org/2016/04/30/475794063/why-are-highly-educated-americans-getting-more-liberal

Lee, F.R. (November 30, 2002) Why Are Black Students Lagging? *The New York Times*. Retrieved from http://www.nytimes.com/2002/11/30/arts/why-are-black-students-lagging.html

Leonhardt, D. (April 24, 2014) College for the Masses. *The New York Times*. Retrieved from http://www.nytimes.com/2015/04/26/upshot/college-for-the-masses.html

Leonhardt, D. (October 28, 2014a) A New Push to Get Low-Income Students Through College. *The New York Times*. Retrieved from https://www.nytimes.com/2014/10/28/upshot/a-new-push-to-get-low-income-students-through-college.html

Leonhardt, D. (November 4, 2016) Schools That Work. *The New York Times*. Retrieved from https://www.nytimes.com/2016/11/06/opinion/sunday/schools-that-work.html?emc=edit_ty_20161222&nl=opinion-today&nlid=56728292&te=1&_r=0

Levin, J. (May, 2012) The Most Evil Thing About College Sports. *Slate*. Retrieved from http://www.slate.com/articles/sports/sports_nut/2012/05/ncaa_scholarship_rules_it_s_morally_indefensible_that_athletic_scholarships_can_be_yanked_after_one_year_for_any_reason_.html

Lewin, T. (December 1, 2014) Most College Students Don't Earn a Degree in 4 Years, Study Finds. *The New York Times*. Retrieved from https://www.nytimes.com/2014/12/02/education/most-college-students-dont-earn-degree-in-4-years-study-finds.html?_r=0

Lukianoff, G., Haidt, J. (September, 2015) The Coddling of the American Mind. *The Atlantic*. Retrieved from http://www.theatlantic.com/magazine/archive/2015/09/the-coddling-of-the-american-mind/399356/

Madden, V. (September 21, 2014) Why Poor Students Struggle. *The New York Times*. Retrieved from https://www.nytimes.com/2014/09/22/opinion/why-poor-students-struggle.html

Mader, J. (February 3, 2016) California Faces a Dire Teacher Shortage. Should Other States Worry, Too? *The Hechinger Report*. Retrieved from http://hechingerreport.org/california-faces-a-dire-teacher-shortage-should-other-states-worry-too/

Mark-Viverito, M., (speaker) (2012) Committee on Education. *The New York City Council*. Retrieved from http://legistar.council.nyc.gov/LegislationDetail.aspx?ID=1143518&GUID=3CCE796B-E0A0-4816-9E70-DD93881A96C2&Options=ID%7cText%7c&Search=testing

Martinez, E. (November 23, 2015) Ticket to Success. *Perspectives, KQED*. Retrieved from https://www.kqed.org/perspectives/201511230643/ticket-to-success

McDermid, R. (March 14, 2016) *UC Berkeley Honcho Routed to Other Job After Harassment Case Now Ordered Removed*. Retrieved from http://www.bizjournals.com/sanfrancisco/blog/2016/03/uc-berkeley-removed-professor-sexual-harassment.html

McGuire, K. (October 10, 2016) Sara Goldrick-Rab on The Daily Show and NPR's Marketplace. *The Chicago Blog*. Retrieved from http://pressblog.uchicago.edu/2016/10/10/sara-goldrick-rab-on-the-daily-show-and-nprs-marketplace.html

Mead, S. (August 6, 2015) Be Prepared. *U.S. News*. Retrieved from http://www.usnews.com/opinion/knowledge-bank/2015/08/06/americas-approach-to-teacher-prep-is-broken

Meraji, M.S. (March 16, 2015) Why Many Smart, Low-Income Students Don't Apply To Elite Schools. *NPR*. Retrieved from http://www.npr.org/2015/03/16/393339590/why-many-smart-low-income-students-dont-apply-to-elite-schools

Mitchell, M., Leachman, M., Masterson, K. (August 15, 2016) Funding Down, Tuition Up: State Cuts to Higher Education Threaten Quality and Affordability at Public Colleges. *CBPP*. Retrieved from https://www.cbpp.org/research/state-budget-and-tax/funding-down-tuition-up.

Mock, F.L. (dir.) (2013) *Anita: Speaking Truth to Justice*. Samuel Goldwyn Films. Retrieved from http://www.imdb.com/title/tt2481202/companycredits?ref_=ttfc_ql_5

Montagne, R. (March 16, 2016) Low Graduation Rates Among Black Athletes. *Morning Edition NPR*. Retrieved from http://www.npr.org/2016/03/16/470635754/low-graduation-rates-among-black-athletes

Moraga, C. (2007) La Guera. In Andersen, M.L. and Collins, P.H. (2007) *Race, Class, and Gender,* 6th edn. Belmont, CA: Thomson Higher Education.

Morris, M.W. (2015) *Pushout: The Criminalization of Black Girls in Schools*. NY: The New Press.

Morrison, N. (April 27, 2015) If Teachers Feel Undervalued It's Because They Are. *Forbes*. Retrieved from https://www.forbes.com/sites/nickmorrison/2015/04/27/if-teachers-feel-undervalued-its-because-they-are/#2c95b78f412b

Mulhere, K. (January 27, 2015) Hostesses? In 2015? *Inside Higher ED*. Retrieved from https://www.insidehighered.com/news/2015/01/27/concerns-continue-about-role-hostesses-football-recruiting

Nasser, H.E. (December 3, 2014) Separate and Unequal: Racial Segregation Flourished in American Suburbs. *America Aljazeera*. Retrieved from http://america.aljazeera.com/articles/2014/12/3/racial-segregationamericansuburbs.html

Navarrette, Jr., R. (Mau 11, 2005) Parents Must Lead by Example. *The Union-Tribune*. Retrieved from http://legacy.sandiegouniontribune.com/uniontrib/20050511/news_lz1e11navarre.html

NCES. (May, 2016) *Racial/Ethnic Enrollment in Public Schools*. Retrieved from http://nces.ed.gov/programs/coe/indicator_cge.asp

NCLS. (October 29, 2015) Undocumented Student Tuition: Overview. *National Conference of State Legislatures*. Retrieved from http://www.ncsl.org/research/education/undocumented-student-tuition-overview.aspx

NEA. (n.d.) Charter Schools 101. *National Education Association*. Retrieved from http://www.nea.org/home/60831.htm

Neuhauser, A. (May 17, 2016) Foreign Students Outpacing Americans for STEM Graduate Degrees. *U.S. News*. Retrieved from https://www.usnews.com/news/articles/2016-05-17/more-stem-degrees-going-to-foreign-students

NPR Staff. (December 5, 2015) Simple Number, Complex Impact: How Many Words Has a Child Heard? *Weekend Edition Sunday*. Retrieved from http://www.npr.org/2015/12/05/458501823/simple-number-complex-impact-how-many-words-has-a-child-heard

Obama, B. (2016) *Barack Obama on Education*. Retrieved from www.ontheissues. org/2016/Barack_Obama_Education.htm

Pappano, L. (April 8, 2015) First-Generation Students Unite. *The New York Times*. Retrieved from https://www.nytimes.com/2015/04/12/education/edlife/first-generation-students-unite.html

Parker, K. (March 19, 2015) Trigger Warnings, Colleges, and the 'Swaddled Generation'. *The Washington Post*. Retrieved from https://www.washingtonpost. com/opinions/the-swaddled-generation/2015/05/19/162ea17a-fe6a-11e4-805c-c3f407e5a9e9_story.html

Paul, A.M. (September 12, 2015) Are College Lectures Unfair? *The New York Times*. Retrieved from https://www.nytimes.com/2015/09/13/opinion/sunday/are-college-lectures-unfair.html

Pauly, M. (April 20, 2016) America's Top Public University Has a Major Sexual-harassment Problem. *Mother Jones*. Retrieved from http://www.motherjones.com/ politics/2016/04/cal-berkeley-sexual-harassment-timeline

Pew Research Center. (February 11, 2014) The Rising Cost of Not Going to College. *Pew Research Center*. Retrieved from http://www.pewsocialtrends.org/2014/02/11/ the-rising-cost-of-not-going-to-college/

Phillips, O. (March 30, 2015) Revolving Door of Teachers Costs Schools Billions Every Year. *NPR*. Retrieved from http://www.npr.org/sections/ ed/2015/03/30/395322012/the-hidden-costs-of-teacher-turnover

Pinker, S. (January 30, 2015) Opinion | Can Students Have Too Much Tech? *The New York Times*. Retrieved from http://www.nytimes.com/2015/01/30/opinion/ can-students-have-too-much-tech.html

Polakow-Suransky, S. (January 13, 2016) Opinion | Teach Your Teachers Well. *The New York Times*. Retrieved from http://www.nytimes.com/2016/01/13/opinion/ teach-your-teachers-well.html

Quinton, S. (December 11, 2014) The Race Gap in High School Honors Classes. *The Atlantic*. Retrieved from http://www.theatlantic.com/politics/archive/2014/12/the-race-gap-in-high-school-honors-classes/431751/

Race Forward. (April 13, 2006) *Historical Timeline of Public Education in the US*. Retrieved from https://www.raceforward.org/research/reports/historical-timeline-public-education-us

Raphelson, S. (May 5, 2017) States Consider Legislation to Protect Free Speech. *All Things Considered*. Retrieved from http://www.npr.org/2017/05/05/527092506/ states-consider-legislation-to-protect-free-speech-on-campus

Reardon, S. (July, 2011) *The Widening Academic Achievement Gap Between the Rich and the Poor*. [PDF File] Retrieved from https://cepa.stanford.edu/sites/default/files/ reardon%20whither%20opportunity%20-%20chapter%205.pdf

Reardon, S. (April 27, 2013) No Rich Child Left Behind. *Opinionator*. Retrieved from http://opinionator.blogs.nytimes.com/2013/04/27/no-rich-child-left-behind/

Reyhner, J., Education Week Staff. (n.d.) 1819–2013: A History of American Indian Education. *Education Week*. Retrieved from http://www.edweek.org/ew/ projects/2013/native-american-education/history-of-american-indian-education. html

Rich, M. (April 11, 2015) Where Are the Teachers of Color? *The New York Times*. Retrieved from http://www.nytimes.com/2015/04/12/sunday-review/where-are-the-teachers-of-color.html?_r=0

Rich, M., Cox, A., Block, M. (April 29, 2016) Money, Race and Success: How Your School District Compares. *The New York Times*. Retrieved from http://www.nytimes.com/interactive/2016/04/29/upshot/money-race-and-success-how-your-school-district-compares.html

Rizga, K. (September/October, 2012) Everything You've Heard About Failing Schools Is Wrong. *Mother Jones*. Retrieved from http://www.motherjones.com/media/2012/08/mission-high-false-low-performing-school

Rizga, K., (September/October Issue, 2015) Sorry, I'm Not Taking This Test. *Mother Jones*. Retrieved from http://www.motherjones.com/politics/2015/08/opt-out-standardized-testing-overload

Rizga, K., Rizga, K., Rizga, K., Oh, I., Gross, A., Vicens, A. (August, 2015) America's Obsession with Standardized Tests Is Harming our Kids. There's a Better Way. *Mother Jones*. Retrieved from http://www.motherjones.com/politics/2015/08/opt-out-standardized-testing-overload

Russo, A. (n.d.) Teachers Unions and the Common Core: Standards Inspire Collaboration and Dissent. *Education Next*. Retrieved from http://educationnext.org/teachers-unions-common

Sanchez, C. (April 11, 2016) Gifted, But Still Learning English, Many Bright Students Get Overlooked. *NPR*. Retrieved from http://www.npr.org/sections/ed/2016/04/11/467653193/gifted-but-still-learning-english-overlooked-underserved

School Funding Fairness. (n.d.) Retrieved from http://www.schoolfundingfairness.org/

Schott Foundation for Public Education. (n.d.) *Black Lives Matter*. Retrieved from http://blackboysreport.org/national-summary/

Shulevitz, J. (March 21, 2015) In College and Hiding From Scary Ideas. *The New York Times*. Retrieved from https://www.nytimes.com/2015/03/22/opinion/sunday/judith-shulevitz-hiding-from-scary-ideas.html

Snyder, B.R. (1971) *The Hidden Curriculum*. New York: Knopf.

Standardized Tests (n.d.) Is the Use of Standardized Tests Improving Education in America? *Procon.org* Retrieved from http://standardizedtests.procon.org/

Strauss, V. (June 2, 2016) Gates Foundation Chief Admits Common Core Mistakes. *The Washington Post*. Retrieved from https://www.washingtonpost.com/news/answer-sheet/wp/2016/06/02/gates-foundation-chief-admits-common-core-mistakes/

Taylor, K. (April 24, 2016) Race and the Standardized Testing Wars. *The New York Times*. Retrieved from https://www.nytimes.com/2016/04/24/opinion/sunday/race-and-the-standardized-testing-wars.html

Teitelbaum, S.M. (March 19, 2014) The Myth of the Science and Engineering Shortage. *The Atlantic*. Retrieved from http://www.theatlantic.com/education/archive/2014/03/the-myth-of-the-science-and-engineering-shortage/284359/

Thompson, T. (n.d.) Fact Sheet: Outcomes for Young, Black Men. *Tavis Smiley Reports*. *PBS*. Retrieved from http://www.pbs.org/wnet/tavissmiley/tsr/too-important-to-fail/fact-sheet-outcomes-for-young-black-men/

Tintocalis, A. (November 25, 2015) Project-Based Learning on the Rise in California Public Schools. *KQED News*. Retrieved from http://ww2.kqed.org/news/2015/11/25/project-based-learning-on-the-rise-in-california-public-schools

Totenberg, N. (October 11, 2011) Thomas Hearings Had Ripple Effect. *Morning Edition*. Retrieved from http://www.npr.org/2011/10/11/141213260/thomas-confirmation-hearings-had-ripple-effect

Trafton, A. (December 11, 2013) Even When Test Scores Go Up, Some Cognitive Abilities Don't. *MIT News*. Retrieved from http://news.mit.edu/2013/even-when-test-scores-go-up-some-cognitive-abilities-dont-1211#.UqnNd5VX4TJ.twitter

Trahan, K. (December 3, 2015) Sex Sells: Louisville Isn't the Only School Using Women in Recruiting, and the NCAA Doesn't Seem to Care. *The Comeback*. Retrieved from http://thecomeback.com/ncaa/sex-sells-louisville-isnt-the-only-school-using-women-in-recruiting-and-the-ncaa-doesnt-seem-to-care.html

Turner, C., Khrais, R., Lloyd, T., Olgin, A., Isensee, L., Vevea, B., Carsen, D. (April 18, 2016) Why America's Schools Have a Money Problem. *School Money NPR*. Retrieved from http://www.npr.org/2016/04/18/474256366/why-americas-schools-have-a-money-problem

Turner, C., McCorry, K., Worf, L., Gonzalez, S., Carapezza, K., McInerny, C. (April 25, 2016a) Can More Money Fix America's Schools? *School Money NPR*. Retrieved from http://www.npr.org/sections/ed/2016/04/25/468157856/can-more-money-fix-americas-schools

Walsh, M. (May 1, 2013) 'I Trusted 'Em': When NCAA Schools Abandon Their Injured Athletes. *The Atlantic*. Retrieved from http://www.theatlantic.com/entertainment/archive/2013/05/i-trusted-em-when-ncaa-schools-abandon-their-injured-athletes/275407/

Weingarten, R. (April 18, 2016) How the Teacher Shortage Could Turn Into a Crisis. *The Huffington Post*. Retrieved from http://www.huffingtonpost.com/randi-weingarten/how-the-teacher-shortage_b_9712286.html

Weller, C. (July 18, 2017) There's an Epidemic of Grade Inflation and Unearned As in American High Schools. *Business Insider*. Retrieved from http://www.businessinsider.com/grade-inflation-us-high-schools-2017-7

White, K. (February 25, 2015) Racism Affects Black Girls as Much as Boys. So Why are Girls Being Ignored? *The Washington Post*. Retrieved from http://www.washingtonpost.com/posteverything/wp/2015/02/25/racism-in-schools-affects-black-girls-even-more-than-boys-so-why-dont-they-get-as-much-attention/

Wilde, M. (April 2, 2015) *Global Grade: How Do U.S. Students Compare? Parenting*. Retrieved from http://www.greatschools.org/gk/articles/u-s-students-compare/

Williams, A. (April 6, 2014) The Exploitation of College Athletes. *The Washington Times*. Retrieved from http://www.washingtontimes.com/news/2014/apr/6/williams-the-exploitation-of-college-athletes/

WITW Staff. (November 15, 2017) Joe Biden Apologizes for What Anita Hill "Went Through" in Senate Hearings 26 Years Ago. *Women in the World*. Retrieved from http://nytlive.nytimes.com/womenintheworld/2017/11/15/joe-biden-apologizes-for-what-anita-hill-went-through-in-senate-hearing-26-years-ago/

Woodcock, T. (June 24, 2015) The Death of Liberal Arts? Or the Reunion of Broken Parts. *The Huffington Post*. Retrieved from http://www.huffingtonpost.com/tony-woodcock/the-death-of-liberal-arts_b_7137538.html

Worstall, T. (November 11, 2012) Bill Gates On Why American Colleges Have To Change. *Forbes*. Retrieved from https://www.forbes.com/sites/timworstall/2012/11/11/bill-gates-on-why-american-colleges-have-to-change/#2a7dc0e9c73a

CHAPTER 12

Work and Political Economy

WHAT YOU WILL READ ABOUT IN THIS CHAPTER:

- The division of work into the ***primary labor market*** and the ***secondary labor market*** is discussed in terms of differences in wages, benefits and job security. The rise of the ***contingent labor force*** is presented, particularly with respect to its erratic hours, financial instability, and lack of workers' protections. The history of unionization is reviewed, and the current trends of decreased unionization are analyzed. Specific conditions of employment are discussed, especially with regard to service occupations.

- ***Economics*** is discussed with respect to *capitalist* elements such as the free market, transnational corporations, oligarchies, and shared monopolies. *Socialist* economies are contrasted to practices in capitalistic ones.

- American ***democracy*** is explained with consideration of pluralistic views and the power of special interests and it is briefly contrasted to other systems.

- The concept of ***political economy*** as interdependent concepts contributing to the shape of capitalism is traced to the works of Marx and Weber. Sociologists have a historical basis from these early theorists for combining the study of politics and economics into one cohesive analysis. Basic concepts in economics and politics are introduced.

- The analysis of the political economy begins with explanations of the influences of ***neoclassic***, ***Keynesian***, and ***neo-Marxist*** views. These theoretical approaches are utilized to understand contemporary political perspectives.

- The policies characteristic of major American ***political parties*** are analyzed. The Republican and Democratic parties generally represent divergent politics and demographics, with the former generally exhibiting more conservative platforms.

- Government and policy in the Trump era is discussed, especially with regard to its economic policies.

Introduction

The topic of work is integral to the study of sociology. Work directly affects income and the standard of living but it is just as significant in its impact on physical and mental health. The quantity and quality of personal and family time is partially a consequence of occupational incumbency. Many families persistently suffer stressors with respect to both time and money, despite the alleged economic recovery. Americans are exhibiting increased pessimism with regard to financial security and changes in the economic structure are likely to enhance these feelings, especially for people without specific technical skills (see Chapter 5). Workers, at both the lower and higher ends of the workforce, are experiencing anxieties regarding their incomes due to changing numbers of hours, rather than as a result of job loss. This is why some observers feel that a low jobless rate does not indicate confidence in the ability to obtain a secure standard of living (Cohen 2017).

How Is Work Organized?

Social scientists analyze the structure of work by distinguishing two sectors in the labor market. In the *primary labor market*, employment is relatively secure and the potential for mobility exists. Employees generally enjoy benefits such as healthcare, paid holidays and leave, and company-supported retirement options. Large corporations and government agencies are included in this sector. The *secondary labor market* is less secure, characterized by smaller businesses which are more vulnerable to layoffs or failure when the economy contracts. These companies have limited advancement for employees, especially if they are family owned, and often have weak or nonexistent benefits (Bonacich 1972).

Most of the jobs created since the recession are low-wage jobs which frequently are temporary or sub-contracted to save on employer costs. Consequently, some support workers, such as cleaning crews, may work in the primary sector but do not enjoy the workers' benefits since they are not employees of the company.

Box 12.1 – The Labor Market

The labor market is split into two. In the *primary labor market* employment is relatively secure; there is potential for advancement, benefits such as annual and sick leave, health insurance, and a retirement plan generally are available. This sector is characteristic of large corporations and government agencies. The *secondary labor market* is less secure and frequently offers only limited benefits and advancement. Smaller, newer, and family-owned business often are represented in the secondary labor market.

Of equal significance is the limited availability of jobs which have been affected by automation and globalization. Research suggests the impact of automation is more significant than job losses attributed to off-shore manufacturing or outsourcing. Productivity in manufacturing remains high but now requires fewer people and more machines (Wiseman 2016; Muro and Andes 2015). In 2015, 13 percent of factory jobs were lost to globalization while 88 percent of losses were due to automation and other factors reducing the need for human workers (Wiseman 2016).

Industries other than manufacturing also are losing employees, largely as a result of computer technology. Even such professions as physicians can be at risk. CT scan machines and advanced X-ray techniques, coupled with software programs, may make radiologists obsolete while protecting their human assistants, whose skills cannot be duplicated by technology. Computer programs will analyze the test results more accurately than physicians, though humans will be required to set a person correctly into the machines. Estimates regarding job losses as a consequence of automation range from 400–800 million jobs worldwide by 2030 (Meyer 2017), with the US suffering a 38 percent decrease (Glaser 2017). Technology has the potential to create new jobs, some not yet imagined. One study estimated that automation may wipe out 25 million jobs while creating 15 million, a net loss of 10 million (Brancaccio 2011). There are limitations to what robotic help can accomplish.

Human employment is still required, even to work in conjunction with automated "workers." These coordinated efforts have the potential to create many jobs, albeit with relatively low pay. In one large warehouse fulfilling consumer orders from Amazon, robots move shelves and retrieve packages but these must be picked up and packed in containers by humans. Human handling is still essential to differentiating the weight and fragility of items. In planning for their workforce, the company projected a need for 1000 workers but ultimately required 3000. The combination of skills, with the robots and humans, successfully achieved a huge reduction in time spent fulfilling orders and a consequent increase in the speed and volume of orders filled (Kim 2017). One reporter working at a warehouse "undercover," describes the experience, following a brief period of "training":

> That afternoon, we are turned loose in the warehouse, scanners in hand. And that's when I realize that for whatever relative youth and regular exercise and overachievement complexes I have brought to this job, I will never be able to keep up with the goals I've been given.
>
> The place is immense. Cold, cavernous. Silent, despite thousands of people quietly doing their picking, or standing along the conveyors quietly packing or box-taping, nothing noisy but the occasional whir of a passing forklift. My scanner tells me in what exact section—there are nine merchandise sections, so sprawling that there's a map attached to my ID badge—of vast shelving systems the item I'm supposed to find resides. It also tells me how many seconds it thinks I should take to get there. Dallas sector, section yellow, row H34, bin 22, level D: wearable blanket. Battery-operated flour sifter. Twenty seconds. I count how many steps it takes me to speed-walk to my destination: 20. At 5-foot-9, I've got a decently long stride, and I only cover the 20 steps *and* locate the exact shelving unit in the allotted time if I don't hesitate for one second or get lost or take a drink of water before heading in the right direction as fast as I can walk or even occasionally jog. Olive-oil mister. Male libido enhancement pills. Rifle strap. Who the f___ buys their paper towels off the internet? Fairy calendar. Neoprene lunch bag. Often as not, I miss my time target.
>
> (McClelland 2012)

Advancements in technologies are likely to increase the schism in the well-being of workers, creating many more low and high skill level jobs and few in the middle. Innovations can result in less routinization and more customer interactions requiring soft skills, which are growing weaker as a result of fewer social interactions in daily life (see Chapter 4). Whether job creation or disruption is salient, lifelong access to the development of new skills will be essential (Morgenstern 2016). An example can be seen in the decreases in the number of bank tellers as a consequence of ATMs and a corresponding increase in the tasks assigned to the remaining workers. Other industries with potentially shifting employee responsibilities include software development, administration, healthcare, graphic design, and artificial intelligence. Labor intensive work, unlikely to suffer replacement by machines because of the need for essential human contact, may be seen in certain types of teaching, care workers, healthcare workers, hairdressers, personal trainers, and other service occupations.

The American attitude towards workers is reflective of significant, if unstated, cultural attitudes regarding who is designated as a "worker" and how they are valued in society. Hatton (2011) suggests that the concept of a "regular" worker has been assigned exclusively to White males. All other categories, such as middle-class housewives, temporary workers, contractors and sub-contractors, "guest workers," incarcerated prisoners, immigrants, and interns fall short of the implicit designation of participation in the legitimate workforce. These people, considered "other" workers, are subjected to modified pay scales and working conditions. The pay scales for people of color; the hourly "pay" of prisoners; the lower hourly rates for food servers (in most states); and different wages for farm field workers all signify the "illegitimate" status of the incumbents.

Hatton demonstrates how various industries utilize ideologies of race, class, and gender to "sell" the concept of temp work. In the post-World War II era, women were able to join the labor force in support of the notion that "women's work" was more like a hobby to occupy the time women were not needed at home for childrearing or housework. She cites the title of a 1956 *Good Housekeeping* article, "Extra Money for Extra Work for Extra Women," as evidence that the category of "women's work" denied the fact that most women needed their earnings to support families. Temporary employment agencies, geared to women office workers, expanded beyond the traditionally female occupations of the "pink ghetto," promoting temporary work as a cost-effective way to gain staff without the ensuing "costly burdens" of "regular" workers. By the early 1960s the two largest temp agencies routinely placed a substantial number of men in industrial jobs and opened agencies specifically to facilitate their employment. Today, the widespread use of temporary workers remains steady with as many as 90 percent of employers reporting some annual use of temps. Three million people inhabit temp jobs every day. There are also people employed as casual or day laborers who are selected to work on a daily basis. Collectively, these workers are referred to as the ***contingent workforce***.

The flourishing contract and temporary labor market persists, in part due to government policies which discourage full-time work. Mulligan (2014) suggests that higher income taxes and payroll taxes defeat the purpose of full-time work because they ultimately fail to provide more income. Older Americans reject full employment since they will be penalized in their social security benefits if they earn more than the official income limit. Programs such as SNAP (food stamps) also limit the amount of income earned to be eligible for aid. Mortgage holders become ineligible for modification programs if they exceed a set income ceiling. The *Affordable Care Act* subsidies also are cut if a person earns too much and many cannot afford the loss of the subsidies (Mulligan 2014). Employers take advantage of these policies by establishing part-time jobs where the workers' low incomes can maintain their eligibility for assistance while, at the same time, enhancing corporate profit.

Additional ways that employers can obtain labor for low, or no, cost can be seen in unpaid and symbolic "stipends" for internships. Affluent youth frequently obtain these positions in order to gain experience leading to "regular," secure, and highly paid employment (Hatton 2014, 2015). The employer benefits from the skills of these graduates to fill gaps in the workforce. These positions are controversial because they advantage graduates who can afford them and can result in less privileged new workers accepting jobs which do not promote professional advancement (Hoder 2013).

The developing "gig" economy is another example of the changing structure of work. This refers to many variations in independent employment, ranging from verbal agreements for casual labor, to long-term contract work utilizing highly specialized skills. Desire to participate in the gig economy is characteristic of millennial workers who seek more autonomy in the work setting, more creativity in types of work and workplace, and greater utilization of their skill sets. The goal is to accomplish more independence and simultaneously to be responsive to the needs of "regular" workers in the twenty-first century, attempting to balance work and life pressures. Although some "gig" workers are successful entrepreneurs, many others are subjected to precarious incomes and substandard working conditions. As a consequence, much discussion has ensued regarding the labor conditions of the "gig" worker. Additionally, inequalities in this workforce have been noted, ranging from abilities to obtain basic needs to racial and class differences in treatment of workers and customers (Heller 2017; Editorial Board 2017). The nature of the gig economy, and its constituencies, both in terms of workers and customers, is complicated but there is growing concern that the effort to gain more control over the work environment may actually result in its opposite (Heller 2017) and that the target population, for both the workers and the consumers, may favor the usual privileged groups (Heller 2017).

Is the Gig Economy for You?

The gig economy represents a multitude of work opportunities with varying types of skills offered in a great range of settings. Casual and temporary labor, in the past, was often associated with low and unskilled physical labor. These opportunities were associated with the contingent workforce, because they were based on the need for labor in a specific project or context. The gig economy has expanded this concept to incorporate all types of work and cover any type of arrangement regarding the length and manner of service. In addition to traditional trades and crafts, gigs can be anything from dog walking, to software engineering, web design, theater, personal assistants, musicians, art, design, supporting a "start-up," Uber driver, or any job category imagined. A "gig" can be brief, amounting to just hours, or it can be long term; it can be ongoing or sporadic. A person can be "on-call" or make an explicit, finite contract. The term's origins are over 100 years old when it was used for a temporary musical gig, often lasting only one night. In the 1950s, it was commonly utilized to refer to temporary jobs for Beats, holding together body and soul. This latter definition is most relevant to today's gigs, though they may extend for months or even years (Nunberg 2016).

Today, many people, especially among millennials, choose to work in the gig economy for the flexibility it provides. These workers often attain opportunities through the internet. Sources can be as diverse as major websites listing all types of jobs, such as "Indeed" or Monster.com; or social media, or apps appealing to specific skills or personnel. In fact, many young people have elaborated a niche for themselves, based on their passions and skills, and market themselves accordingly. A "gig" work life can provide maximal freedom and allow for diverse experiences. It can be exciting and lucrative, and very satisfying, because the worker can create the terms of the gig. Alternatively, the gig economy can be frustrating and anxiety provoking. A person can never be sure that the terms will work out, either for the worker or the person receiving the services. Gig availability can be inconsistent and, consequently, income can be unpredictable. A gig worker also has to be dedicated and diligent or risk failing to obtain work, or to complete work in the time frame agreed upon. So, in choosing to be a gig worker, especially as a long-term option, a person must be willing to evaluate their personal characteristics to see if such a lifestyle will fit. Some people may venture into the gig world just temporarily, to tide them over in times of unemployment or coping with family responsibilities or decide that it is not for them. For those who feel the gig economy suits them, there is much to be gained (Torpey and Hogan 2016; Heller 2017).

Box 12.2 – The Contingent Workforce

The **contingent workforce** is comprised of workers in various capacities, such as contractors, subcontractors, freelancers, and day or casual workers whose employment is temporary and who do not have an employee/employer relationship on the job. This category increasingly applies to the "gig" economy where millennials, and others, work for themselves as entrepreneurs or in start-ups.

US Unionization

Labor history is often bypassed in the standard public-school education. The history of unionization represents sustained efforts to gain protective legislation and laws. Examples of this concentrated activism can be found in such diverse industries as mining, textiles, law enforcement, and farming. The conditions of work frequently entailed grave dangers with little, if any, protections against harm and no assistance for injury or death. The dangerous working conditions in mining prompted the *United Mineworkers of America*, founded in 1890, to stage work actions through

Figure 12.1 American work policies mitigate the availability of full-time work at a living wage. A better minimum wage, coupled with full time employment, will help some workers currently ineligible for subsidies but unable to make ends meet Source: a katz / Shutterstock.com

the first decades of the 1900s to unionize workers in the major coal states (UMWA n.d.). The *International Ladies' Garments Workers' Union* (ILGWU), founded in 1900, promoted textile workers' rights with massive strikes in the early decades of the 1900s. Tens of thousands of workers participated in actions in NYC in 1909, 1910, and in Lawrence, MA in 1912. The tragic Triangle Shirtwaist Factory Fire, resulting in the death of nearly 15 women workers, was one of the few incidents to incite public outrage. In law enforcement, a massive strike among Boston Police (1919) was initiated when union organizers were suspended from the force. At that time, the Boston Police commonly worked over 75 hours a week and made less than factory workers. It took until 1965, when the *Boston Patrolmen's Association* (PBA) was formed, to gain bargaining and union benefits. The PBA eventually affiliated with the AFL-CIO (Global Nonviolent Action Database n.d.).

The Struggle for California Farmworkers' Rights

One highly publicized movement to obtain unionization occurred among the California farmworkers. Although the union struggles, particularly in California, are fairly well-known, few people are aware of how far back the history extends. Initial struggles to obtain better working conditions were fragmented, especially by ethnicity. Sociologists often have suggested that corporate gain is made by promoting division and competition among labor, distracting workers from their common interests (Alexander 2016; Noble 2015/2017). Such a situation seems to have characterized farm laborers.

Filipino farmworkers had been organizing for decades, prior to the founding of the contemporary *United Farm Workers Union* (UFW). The Filipino workers had won a contract, after a sustained campaign in 1939, against asparagus growers by striking on *Good Friday*. This campaign was waged by Larry Itliong, the leader of their *Agricultural Workers Organizing Committee* (AWOC). The chief demand was to get paid $1.40 per hour (Morehouse 2015). The threat of loss to the asparagus farmers, coupled with the ire of citizens missing their Easter asparagus dish, proved a successful strategy and the strike was quickly settled.

After successfully organizing the workers in the Coachella Valley, the Filipino workers moved north to work in Delano. There, Itliong, along with Philip Vera Cruz and Pete Velasco, agitated to obtain the same wages as they had won further south. It was Itliong who first approached Chavez and Huerta, as they were organizing Mexican farmworkers in the *National Farmworkers Association* (NFA). The Mexican workers had no plans for a strike. In fact, they were targeted as strikebreakers by the growers. After Itliong made his appeal, the Mexican workers joined in striking with the AWOC. This was the first cooperative effort across cultural groups. The two groups stood unified against the growers in the Delano Grape Strike of 1965–1970, promoting an international boycott of table grapes. The effort led to the formation of the UFW.

Many Americans are familiar with the legend of Cesar Chavez, especially through their participation in the long-term boycott of table grapes. This action, along with media reporting such as Edward R. Murrow's 1960 classic documentary, *Harvest of Shame* (Friendly 1960), cast the plight of the workers into the national consciousness. What many Americans don't know is that the co-founder of the *National Farmworkers Association* (NFA), the Mexicans' precursor to the UFW, was a central California woman, Dolores Huerta. Huerta was a peer to Chavez, responsible for much of the political strategizing aimed at the state legislature. She also was a tireless fighter for women and myriad issues of social justice. For many decades she was largely unrecognized, although she was the sole woman involved with organizing or sitting on the executive board. Chavez considered Huerta an indispensable ally, providing perspectives that eluded him. When Chavez died suddenly in 1993, many believed Huerta would be named president of the union but she was passed over in favor of Arturo S. Rodriquez, who remains president (as of 2017). In many histories of the UFW and biographies of Chavez, Huerta is completely absent, a situation finally remedied in the 2017 film, *Dolores* (Bratt 2017). Huerta actually coined the phrase, *Si se puede*, the "yes we can" slogan that Obama utilized in his campaign and initially incorrectly attributed to Chavez. In 2012, President Obama awarded Huerta the *Congressional Medal of Freedom* (Bratt 2017).

In 2015, California Governor Jerry Brown established a state holiday in honor of Larry Itliong to honor his efforts in the same way he proclaimed a state holiday, in 2014, celebrating Cesar Chavez's birthday on March 31. Brown also mandated that California schools teach labor history as part of the standard curriculum (Morehouse 2015). Chavez Day is celebrated in seven additional states with school closings and state offices closed. In 2014, President Obama made Chavez Day a "federal commemorative holiday," which is not an official national holiday but marks the day for special observances and activities.

Box 12.3 – The United Farm Workers

The *United Farm Workers (the UFW)* was founded in the mid-1960s, during the Delano Grape Strike. The UFW actually represented a joining of forces between established groups of unionized Filipino farmworkers, led by Larry Itliong, and Mexican farmworkers' groups led by Cesar Chavez.

Although some of the poorest working conditions of American workers have been addressed by legislation resulting from unionization efforts, unionization is eroding, particularly in the private sector. Unionization among private sector workers is 6.4 percent while public sector employees are five times more likely to unionize, evidencing rates of 34.3 percent (Bureau of Labor Statistics 2017). The future of public unions is being severely challenged by legislation and court cases in states across the country, most notably in Wisconsin, Iowa, and CA (Masters 2017; Wolf 2016; Associated Press 2017). As a consequence of weakened worker bargaining, US workers average more work hours a week and more weeks a year, enjoy fewer paid holidays, and have less vacation time, than their European counterparts. Achievements obtained through unionization are not restricted to wages, benefits, and conditions of employment; unions also lobby for government programs

Figure 12.2 Pictured are the Filipino leaders of the Delano Grape Strike who sought the cooperation of Cesar Chavez, and the Mexican Farmworkers, to gain decent wages and conditions, ultimately resulting in the Delano grape boycott initiated in 1965
Source: UC San Diego Library and Archives

such as daycare and subsidized student loans (Kristof 2015). Unions can act as
one mechanism for accomplishing workers' rights, providing some constraint on
corporate interests.

Some corporations do better than others in establishing the conditions of
employment and the provision of benefits. Wal-Mart, for example, is notorious
for its stinginess considering it is the largest private employer in the US. Taxpayers
provide food stamps and healthcare subsidies for Wal-Mart employees (Egan 2014).
For example, the state of Wisconsin subsidizes Wal-Mart employees at the rate of
$5,000 per employee, or $904,000 for the average superstore (Egan 2014). The
magnitude of this subsidy is remarkable in consideration of the fact that the corporate
profits were $17 billion dollars in 2013. Estimates suggest that employee pay could
be raised by 50 percent without sacrificing shareholder profit (Egan 2014; Gandel
2013). Walmart consistently ranks as one of the world's largest corporations but
its employee and business policies have led to a constant stream of litigation, often
resulting in Wal-Mart making a payout (Samakow 2014; Laska n.d.).

Long work days, combined with the sparse government support of basic services,
such as healthcare and daycare, contribute to stressors regarding work and family
responsibilities. Sleep deprivation characterizes the majority of the American
population; estimates of workers who lack the recommended seven hours of sleep
range from 33–75 percent. Inadequate sleep causes irritability, accidents, and injuries.
Cumulative fatigue mimics the effects of blood alcohol levels of .1 percent, which
is over the legal limit of .08 percent. Sleep deprivation is implicated in diabetes,
depression, and brain functioning. Hazards stemming from sleep deprivation are
not limited to low wage workers but can be seen in tech companies whose salaried
workers frequently work through the night. Although research shows that short naps

Figure 12.3 Workers
grabbing a nap on the
job; an estimated 33–75
percent of Americans lack
sufficient sleep
Source: Ryan McGinnis /
Alamy Stock Photo

are effective in combating the effects of fatigue, most companies do not accommodate this simple intervention (Noguchi 2016a).

Lower paid workers are particularly vulnerable to job conditions which cause problems, particularly with respect to family concerns. Kantor (2014) wrote a story featuring a Starbucks barista who, as a single mother, struggled to support herself and her child on nine dollars an hour while dealing with fluctuating work hours, last minute scheduling, and transportation problems. The barista was trying hard to keep her job and stay off of public assistance. She sometimes had as little as five hours between shifts and, in addition to worrying about how to stay awake, relied on relatives to provide care for her four-year-old son. Erratic scheduling made her life nearly impossible and her family was growing weary of the shifting childcare needs. It brings up the question as to why the company could not give her a steadier schedule. Many major retail and restaurant businesses utilize computer software to schedule their staff. Some companies have policies which reward their managers for efficient staffing no matter how they choose to accomplish this. Employees frequently report having less than one day of notification to report for a shift, even though the official policy mandates a week's notice.

In response to publicity highlighting the above practices, *Starbucks* revised its policies to improve working conditions for its 130,000 baristas. The company agreed to provide at least a week's notification of schedules; revise scheduling software; and transfer workers with significant commutes to stores closer to their homes. The corporate executives reduced last minute notifications of hours; early releases from work; and significant modifications in shift times. Though *Starbucks* tries to maintain a good standard for its workers, some workers earn just the minimum wage and part-time workers suffer erratic hours (Kantor 2014a). *Starbucks* does offer benefits

Figure 12.4 Baristas and other food service workers are frequently subjected to changing schedules, erratic shifts, and last minute crew adjustments which can reduce their hours. They suffer from exhaustion and stressors, particularly with respect to childcare
Source: Sorbis / Shutterstock.com

lacking in other companies, by providing healthcare, retirement plans, stock options, and college tuition (Egan 2014). Starbucks is now ranked seventh in a list of the top ten companies offering benefits beyond the basic ones. The other companies in the ranking, starting with number one, are: Ikea, Reebok, Bain and Company, Goldman Sachs, Facebook, Scripps Health, (Starbucks), American Express, Eventbrite, and Whole Foods Market (Glassdoor Team 2017).[1]

Young workers, though theoretically protected by child labor laws are still vulnerable to hard work in dangerous conditions. Labor laws for **non-farm** work have a minimum age requirement of 14 years and limit children under 16 years old to an eight-hour day. Federal law allows youths, 12 and older, to have unlimited hours of **field work** as long as it does not conflict with school. Many immigrant children, and children of immigrants, work in the fields before or after school and in the summers. Frequently, the families depend on the incomes of the children to make ends meet. Youthful field labor persists. One recent article (Greenhouse 2014) highlighted the special dangers to child laborers in tobacco fields in the southeast. Youths working the fields suffer from "green tobacco sickness," or nicotine poisoning. These field workers experience skin irritations, dizziness, vomiting, irregular heartbeats, respiratory ailments, and other symptoms. They work up to 12-hour days without sufficient water breaks. Adolescents' immature neurological and reproductive development complicates long-term consequences to toxic exposure; the full impact of tobacco exposure is not known, though it mimics symptoms associated with tobacco smoking. Fifty-four groups, incorporating physicians, labor unions, and consumer groups, support a mandated fieldworker age of at least 18 years. Some tobacco companies, such as Philip Morris International, have voluntarily banned workers under 18. Yet, in spite of widespread recommendations and voluntary

Figure 12.5 A tobacco field worker. Working the tobacco fields is especially dangerous for youths whose neurological and reproductive growth is not complete. Youths legally employed in farm work can be as young as 12 years of age and can work unlimited hours when school is not in session
Source: andjic / istockphoto.com

support, the federal government withdrew legislation to increase the minimum age to 18 (Greenhouse 2014).

Undocumented and Poor

America's undocumented poor, particularly the children, confront a special set of problems. Children who were brought here as babies, or youths, have no legal status if their parents are undocumented. This situation makes it difficult for children to progress past a certain level in school, obtain jobs, or qualify for healthcare. The struggle of migrant farm families first came to command national attention through the documentary the *Harvest of Shame*, when CBS journalist Edward R. Murrow reported on the conditions of farmworkers (Friendly 1960). Although there have been some improvements in working conditions, a recent PBS documentary, *East of Salinas* (Pacheco and Mow 2015), highlights the difficult conditions of today's farmworkers, particularly when undocumented. In this movie, we become acquainted with Jose Ansaldo, a model third grader who is the undocumented eldest child of two undocumented farm workers. His two younger siblings were born in California and consequently have citizen status. We see his parents work back-breaking harvests from daybreak to sunset in the lettuce fields, his mother dropping her children at a babysitter's house before sunrise. During the winter the father journeys to the fields of southern Arizona, jeopardizing his residence in the US by working so close to the border, but struggling to make some income. The mother stays in the Salinas valley so as not to disrupt her children's education, though she has no work in winter and receives no aid. During the course of the documentary, the family moves to five different apartments, due to lack of rent money and to escape infestations of vermin and other substandard conditions. Jose is befriended by Oscar Ramos, his math teacher, who also grew up poor in the valley, and has chosen to return "home" to use his UC Berkeley degree to help his community. He is joined by a group of friends, also graduates of UC, who help the children by providing Christmas gifts and, more importantly, a sense of a future.

It is unrealistic to think that the young university graduates can solve this family's problems, especially those stemming from low pay and lack of documentation. We see a dedicated student in Jose, with goals to attend college and work in law enforcement or engineering. But, as the movie unfolds, he learns of his undocumented status, in contrast to his younger siblings, and he worries about what he can actually accomplish. Sustained debates surround the ultimate cost of undocumented immigration. Undocumented immigrants pay a higher income tax rate than American top earners, and 75 percent are estimated as paying into social security which they never can draw upon, so some believe that they pay for their costs to the systems they do use. Critics argue that these workers pose a net loss economically, since they receive education and other benefits which are not part of the means tested safety net. Typically, they are paid lower wages than their legal counterparts, saving businesses labor expenses. The assertion that undocumented workers cost more than they contribute is debatable, in light of extensive research (Soergel 2017).

East of Salinas portrays the harsh conditions of essential workers who put food on our tables. It might be incumbent upon all of us to think about our values as we shop the famers' markets and supermarkets loaded with fresh produce. Why do we want to make it so difficult for them just to survive or to help their children? How can these hardworking laborers go hungry while they feed America? Would we pay a quarter more for lettuce if it meant that Jose could eat better? Would we change our immigration laws if it meant that our crops would be produced with labor paid an equitable wage? The exploitation of our farm laborers is sustained by sentiments condemning the illegal status of the workers but we must also recognize that the loss of these workers, under new restrictive legislation passed in multiple states, has cost farmers their crops (McClatchy-Tribune 2014; McArdle 2011; Serrano 2012). The fear experienced by the workers as a consequence of new legislation have caused children to miss school and parents to fear familial separations. These farm workers are providing a service no one else really wants to do, or even can accomplish with the same efficiency. Our "American" values of fairness and rewarding hard work ought to lead to farmworkers being treated as assets, not liabilities, since we all literally depend on the fruits of their labor.

Poor labor practices persist, particularly with regard to unskilled labor. Groups of lower skilled non-farm workers have been organizing and gradually gaining improved conditions of employment. Domestic workers, drawn primarily from nonWhite groups, have been organizing for better pay, conditions, and respect since the 1930s. These efforts were initiated by African American household workers who endured long days with demanding tasks. These women organized for better pay and working conditions. Finally, in 1974, the Fair Labor Standards Act was amended to include household workers in federal minimum wage provisions (Nadasen 2016).

The subcontracting of janitors and security guards has been increasing, earning these workers 20 percent less in wages than people hired directly by a company. The companies that contract with these service workers sometimes do not pay minimum wage, overtime, or social security and even pocket unpaid government taxes. In the period of 2012–2014, 32 percent of security guards and 45 percent of janitors had no health insurance, in contrast to full-time unionized workers who are provided family health insurance. In 2015, the *National Labor Relations Board* ruled that companies hiring contracted workers are still liable for labor violations (Li 2016). Non-employee workers and independent contractors, proliferating in other occupations, are making efforts to organize and agitate for legal protections.

Overtime wages are frequently unpaid, not only to hourly workers but to lower level salaried workers. Employers have multiple ways to avoid paying overtime, such

Figure 12.6 Domestic workers have been organizing for minimum wage since the 1930s
Source: Jim West / Alamy Stock Photo

as forcing workers to complete tasks after signing out (CNN n.d.). Salaried workers are frequently denied access to overtime, since they are expected to work until the project is completed. Legislation passed in 2016 will almost double the amount of money a salaried worker can make and still be eligible for overtime pay (Morran 2016). These new provisions will increase the earnings of these workers but present potential risks of reduced hours to avoid significant increases in expenses (Noguchi 2016).

Sweatshop conditions, with their low pay, long hours, grueling work, and inadequate breaks pervade the trucking industry. The high level of skill that trucking requires fails to shield the workers from 14-hour days, with 11 of those hours spent behind the wheel (Balay and Shattell 2016). The driver can be subjected to being "micro-managed" by the company which frequently mandates where the driver has to get gas; when and where he can sleep; and what route he has to take. Experienced drivers are leaving the job as a consequence of low pay and poor conditions. As a result, the federal government is running a pilot program lowering the interstate driving age to 18 years, even though the accident rate for 18–21 year olds is considerably elevated. The experience and coordination required to drive 18-wheelers adds to the potential accident rates of inexperienced drivers (Smith 2016). Some companies address the dangers on the roads by imposing 24-hour driver surveillance, creating another element of stress for the drivers (Balay and Shattell 2016).

Professionals do not necessarily fare better than their less skilled counterparts. In the tech industry, where salaries can be high, so are rates of worker turnover and random firings. Heightened anxiety characterizes the experiences of workers in this sector as a consequence of erratic management (Lyons 2016). With smart phones and constant access to the internet, workers can be "on call 24/7," resulting in the elimination of any "down" time. Many workers sleep arm's reach from their cell phones. Workers are challenging this constant "on-call" requirement by filing lawsuits requesting pay for all the "home" overtime (Weber 2015). Some companies also are concerned with the potential for burnout, promoting relaxation on weekends by making business email unavailable for at least part of the weekend. In France, new labor laws prohibit companies from sending emails during non-business hours (Weber 2015; Glazer and Huang 2016).

Figure 12.7 Long days, rigid company mandates, and low pay create "sweatshop" conditions for long-haul drivers, discouraging them from sustaining the occupation and leading to hiring younger, inexperienced drivers to fill the vacancies
Source: Rick Lord / Shutterstock.com

Figure 12.8 Professional workers often take work home and some feel they have no "down time," with work intruding into domestic life
Source: HomeArt / Shutterstock.com

Does Money Buy Happiness?

It can; attaining an adequate salary is essential to well-being. Research shows that for people who make under $70,000, representing well over half of the working population, increased income has been shown to be significant in promoting happiness. Psychologist Daniel Kahneman asserts, "income above the threshold doesn't buy happiness, but a lack of money can deprive you of it" (Cohen 2015). Accordingly, one employer, Dan Price, CEO of Gravity Payments, decided to raise all his 120 employees' wages to $70,000 a year over a three-year period. He will accomplish this by reducing his own nearly one-million-dollar salary to the same amount and redistributing 75–80 percent of his annual profits from 2015. The average salary at his company at the onset of his program was $48,000.

Three months after this announcement, Mr. Price reported that he had sustained losses among both workers and customers. Some more highly skilled, experienced workers were unhappy with others getting such a big pay boost while they did not; some customers left as a result of fears that their fees would be increased to compensate for the higher wages. Mr. Price admitted he was undergoing personal financial stress, renting out his own home to make ends meet (Howell 2015). The example shows how one well-intentioned change can have dramatic ramifications if its *systemic* consequences are not considered, highlighting the need to consider systemic changes in policies affecting work and wages.

"I'm not asking for a raise, Mr Fuller, but would it be possible for you to treat me as a human being?"

Figure 12.9 Many workers are subjected to erratic schedules, unpaid overtime, and lack of vacation and paid leave
Source: Joseph Farris / Cartoon Stock

Incorporating more humane working conditions, coupled with better labor laws, wages, and benefits would improve work and family life, especially at the lower wage levels. Nevertheless, some problems arise as a result of long work weeks required in some jobs. A recent research study showed that that high-income people in the top 60–95 percent worked the most hours. For the people working longer hours, both women and men reported issues of work and family conflict. Women were more likely to address familial needs by taking advantage of "family friendly" policies allowing for flextime, job sharing and part-time work, or by switching to less demanding jobs. About one third of the men would leave work in order to attend children's activities but stayed connected to work with their smart phones. Attitudes towards workers' behaviors were biased; if a man left at 5:00pm, it was presumed he was going to meet a client while women were regarded as going home. Issues surrounding domestic responsibility were persistently applied to women. Company executives tended to view women as household managers and, in contrast to their responses to male workers, looked down on them if they put work first. Company family-friendly policies implicitly address women but generally do not incorporate the extra-work life of men. Domestic life remains culturally a "woman's issue," at least by policy and tradition. Women suffer from the dualities of work and home whichever way they lean; either they risk not being taken seriously in the workplace or are chastised as inattentive mothers. If these cultural biases are sustained, the issue regulating work policies will never adequately address family needs, and women will retain the brunt of the household responsibility and professional setbacks, making equity in the workplace elusive (Miller 2015).

Where Work Is Done Better

Michael Moore's movie, *Where to Invade Next* (2015), shows how both the laws and attitudes in other countries contribute to happier work situations. Virtually all the developed nations, other than the US, provide up to eight weeks of paid vacation and a dozen paid annual holidays, as well as paid parental leave; some even provide 15 paid days for a honeymoon. In Italy, workers enjoy a thirteenth month of salary at Christmas time; a two-hour lunch break to go home for lunch; high-quality meals in business cafeterias; and corporate support of unions. Moore features a "regular" Italian working couple talking about all the vacations they go on and how happy they are but they also admit they dream of moving to America. When Moore informs them of the short annual leave available to most workers, and the lack of other workers' benefits, they appear so stunned they actually are momentarily at a loss for words.

In Germany, Moore visits a pencil factory and finds that workers have a 36-hour week and get paid for 40 hours. Workers are out by 2:00 or 2:30 and do not have second jobs. The workers report socializing with friends, engaging in sports, going to cafes, and "relaxing" in their free time. Factories have windows which the owner says makes the workers "feel better." Workers can easily obtain a three-week "prescription" for a spa if they are feeling stressed. It is believed that taking care of workers ultimately saves the company money, especially by reducing worker turnover, an expense which can significantly impact the bottom line. Managers listen to workers' input, incorporating their ideas into policies to make work better and more productive. One half of the featured company's board of directors are workers. It is against the law to email vacationing employees or to send them emails after hours!

While it is true that Moore's movie is edited for a viewpoint and everyone he interviews in every country he visits positively glows with good feeling, it also is accurate that other countries treat their workers better. Not only are the job benefits more generous but companies provide training, exhibit higher wages, and maintain high levels of productivity. The US is one of only two countries that does not have paid parental leave. Americans protest the higher taxes characteristic of these countries, particularly in Northern and Western Europe, but Moore shows that they are not that much higher and the return is greater in overall security, especially with regard to healthcare, education, and retirement. Personal life expenses in the US, associated with healthcare, college tuition, retirement savings, and social security, make it difficult to persist in the assertion that Americans are "better off." The hours and pressures of work, particularly for lower paid American workers, impede the enjoyment of leisure time and contribute to the inability to pay for recreation and vacations. It is no wonder that Americans miss more work days, suffer more illnesses, and have lower longevity than workers in comparable countries (Moore 2015).

What Are Essential Concepts in Economics and Politics?

Economics

Economics refers to the ways in which a society produces and distributes goods and services. The final value of all the goods and services in a geographic boundary in a specific time period is referred to as the *Gross Domestic Product (GDP)* (Gross Domestic Product n.d.). It is utilized as a rough measure of the economic well-being of a nation. The US economy is post-industrial, characterized by the dominance of the *tertiary sector*, where most workers are in services and information occupations such as food service, sales, customer service, and software. In contrast, pre-industrial societies had populations engaged in the *primary sector*, referring to the extracting of raw materials and natural resources in farming, ranching, fishing, and mining. The *secondary sector*, characteristic of the industrial era, witnessed the salience of manufacturing in machines, clothing, appliances, automobiles, and any other tangible product.

Box 12.4 – Economics

Economics refers to all the goods and services produced and distributed in a country. The *Gross Domestic Product (GDP)* is the final value of these, usually given for a specific year. The GDP is often presumed to indicate the economic well-being of a nation. Economic activity is designated by "sector." The *primary sector* refers to the extracting of raw materials and natural resources seen in farming, ranching, fishing, and mining. The *secondary sector* is associated with manufacturing and the production of goods such as machines, appliances, furniture, clothing, automobiles, and other tangible items. The *tertiary sector* produces services and information incorporating such activities as food service, sales, customer service, software, and other professional activities. Work in post-industrial America is dominated by the tertiary sector.

Capitalism

Capitalism refers to an economic system based on private ownership, market freedoms in production and competition, and private profit (Capitalism n.d.). Capitalism is conceived as possessing a self-regulating, competitive *free market* that represents an ideal never fully realized. The government intervenes, in a variety of ways, to set wages, prices and competition, and control supply. In contemporary corporate capitalism, profits are dominated by a small sector of businesses controlling large global enterprises.

Box 12.5 – Capitalism

Capitalism refers to an economic system based on private ownership, private profit, a competitive "free market," and a neutral polity. Pure capitalism does not exist. Even in the advanced corporate capitalism of the US, government management of industry, market, and labor occurs.

Corporations are legal entities which conduct business as an individual would, but are comprised of owners and shareholders. Corporations dominated early American capitalism until around World War II. Subsequently, *transnational corporations* have become salient. In these corporations, also referred to as *multi-national corporations*, business is conducted across many countries but headquartered in one nation. Their interests typically represent a variety of goods and services, not necessarily inter-related. The magnitude of these corporations is vast and rankings of them vary, but some entities occur in all the lists, such as Wal-Mart, Apple, ExxonMobil, China National Petrol, and Toyota (Global 500; Biggest Transnational Companies 2012).

Box 12.6 – Corporations

Corporations are legal entities which conduct business. A *transnational or multinational corporation* conducts business across nations but is headquartered in one country.

Oligarchies are several companies which dominate an industry, such as in the publishing or food and beverage industries.

Shared monopolies occur when four, or fewer, companies control a large portion of an industry. Cereal companies and car manufacturers are often considered to be shared monopolies.

Because of the size, and power, of today's corporations, competition is neither fair nor open. *Oligarchies* refer to several companies which dominate an industry. An example would be the publishers of books and journals. Five companies, each representing multiple labels, dominate trade publishing (books for the general public) (Almossawi 2016) and five also dominate the textbook market (Dubay 2016). Ten companies dominate the food and beverage industry worldwide and influence diet, working conditions, and the environment (Hess 2014). A *shared monopoly* occurs when four, or fewer, companies account for half or more of a market. The *big three* American automobile companies (GM, Ford, and Chrysler) used to represent a shared monopoly but actually now control only 45 percent of the automobile market due to competition from foreign companies (Japanese-owned Toyota, Honda, and Nissan, and the Korean company Hyundai). No single company accounts for more than 18 percent of the American automobile market (Peterson 2014). The two largest cereal companies, General Mills and Kellogg's, also are facing increased competition from newer companies featuring healthier alternatives (Klara 2016; Ferdman 2015).

Market competition is limited by the consolidated interests of corporate boards made up of individuals who serve on the boards of multiple corporations. The government provides substantial support of their interests. The sociologist, William Domhoff, has been studying *Who Rules America?* with various colleagues, since the early 1980s. They report on:

> the American power structure based on the connections among 2,563 corporations, 6 business leadership and policy-discussion groups, 33 prominent think tanks, 82 major foundations, 47 private universities with large endowments, and 19 White House advisory committees for the years 2011–2012.
>
> (Domhoff et al. 2013)

The report says that 35.2 percent of the individuals in this power structure have connections in at least two of the reviewed organizations. The government also extends its hand into the market by setting prices of goods; levels in farm production; policies regulating labor; the imposition of tariffs; and the development of trade agreements.

Public participation in industry is limited through stock ownership which is skewed by a consolidated group who control the vast majority of stocks and virtually all the boards' policies. The top 5 percent of US households control around 70 percent of the stocks. While 35 percent of the population owns some stock, for most of the population, stock ownership is in retirement accounts and mutual funds (US Stock Ownership 2013). The stock market is dominated by five financial banking institutions (Martens and Martens 2014).

Socialism is a system which protects the "public good" over privatization of industry and profit. In socialism, the means of production are collectively owned by the citizens and the government makes policies based on promoting collective goals. Theoretically, such an economy would provide for all the basic needs of its citizenship through state-owned and controlled agencies. As is the case with capitalism, these ideals never are completely realized. The *Union of Soviet Socialist Republics* (USSR, 1917–1991), representing "state socialism," characteristically experienced shortages of basic consumer goods, including food, clothing, and personal products as well as housing. Luxury items were available only to the elite, which theoretically did not exist.

Box 12.7 – Socialism

Socialism is a system which prioritizes the "public good" over privatization of industry and private profit. The government owns and manages basic industries and services for the collective benefit of society, rather than for personal gain. There is no purely socialistic entity but the former Soviet Union and Cuba are two examples of nations identified with socialism.

What Was Life Like in the USSR?

There were plenty of stores in my hometown, but the shelves were never full of items. My parents often took a 5 hour trip to Moscow on a train to get some groceries and delicatessens like cured meats, bananas, oranges, etc. Now, when I go shopping at Costco or even a local grocery store I often come back with bags and bags of food, only to go back to a supermarket in a day or two, when my parents came back with less stuff from the capital of Russia back in 1980s. There was a dry cleaning store and a hair salon in the next building from us. My parents would visit the hair salon regularly, but dry cleaning was a luxury for us. Most people owned washing machines, as did we, and the clothes would dry in special fenced up areas next to the buildings. On a sunny day, women would hang their bedding and towels to dry up in the sun. Small items will dry up in apartments or on balconies. Nowadays these spaces are used for parking, but back in the day, you can find women hanging clothes in the sun, kids playing in the sandboxes, riding bikes around the building, trees, flowers, and bushes surrounding the neighborhood, cats taking their walks, dogs warming up in the sun, men playing dominoes and smoking.

I realize that this image is romanticized by the memories of my childhood, but this is how I remember my life in a small provincial town in a classless Soviet Union. It was more of a community then than it is now in Russia, where capitalism replaced group consciousness with individualism and competition for resources and jobs. People didn't have much, but enough to live a respectable life. And everyone was pretty much in the same boat. I believe that all these benefits are due to the fact that the workers and the Russian people had a great revolution and as a product of it, they achieved great conquests that today do not exist in the capitalist countries. For example, in the United States where education and health care are for a few.

At the same time and as I said at the beginning, there were social inequalities as well. It had a lot to do with who you knew and that often meant belonging to the Communist Party, which by the time I was born was corrupted as well. Once you were well connected, it provided you with additional income, often in terms of bribes, as well as opportunities to have access to luxurious items which gave you other options to make money or use them as bribes.

(Anna Malyukova 2017)

Politics

Democracy

Politics refers to the ways in which a society governs its citizens and protects the group. Democracy is "rule of the people." In a *direct* democracy, participants would gather to make decisions together, after discussion and debate. Such a practice is only possible with small numbers and today is seen in groups identifying as collectives. American democracy takes a *representational* form. Citizens express their positions by voting in leaders to represent their views at the local, state, and federal levels. These officials are expected to honor the views of their constituencies. At all government levels, elected officials are informed regarding public sentiment and expected to address these concerns. However, there are multiple intervening factors impeding this process. Voting has not always been available to all segments of the population with respect to age, race, and sex. The *Voting Rights Act of 1965* established protections for jurisdictions by setting restrictions on nine states with histories of racial discrimination. The Act established that these designated territories could make changes in voting procedures only with prior approval of the federal government. In a 2013 Supreme Court decision, the judges ruled this practice obsolete and rescinded it, transferring the burden of proof to the federal government which would have to show, after the fact, that changes in electoral practices were discriminatory. Since that decision, multiple states have challenged the ruling and blocked new rules which would restrict access to voting, particularly among African Americans, the elderly, and other nondominant groups. Other states have successfully instituted practices which are likely to impede voting. The death of Judge Alito (2016) and the retirement of Justice Anthony Kennedy (2018), changes the composition of the Supreme Court, affecting the balance of political affiliations among the judges and making the forecast of future decisions unpredictable (Hasen 2016).

Box 12.8 – Politics

Politics refers to the system of government in a society. *Democracy* is defined by "the rule of the people." The US system is considered a *representational democracy*, with the interests of the population being represented by elected and appointed officials. This is opposed to a **direct** democracy where all persons are involved in the consideration of an issue and agreement, or consensus, must be attained. The size of the US population makes a direct democracy untenable.

Box 12.9 – The Voting Rights Act of 1965

The Voting Rights Act of 1965 refers to the bill which made it impossible for jurisdictions with histories of racial exclusion to change their voting procedures without prior approval of the federal government. A 2013 Supreme court decision rescinded this provision, shifting the burden of proof to the federal government after a practice has been alleged to have a negative impact on a segment of potential voters.

Box 12.10 – The Electoral College

The electoral college is a representational process, mandated by the American *Constitution*, to elect the President of the United States by proportional delegates from each of the states. The electors from each state equal the number of the state's Congressional delegates. The citizenship does not directly elect the president by popular vote, though such a vote is taken.

Other issues with respect to the electoral process have been questioned in recent years. The 2016 election of Donald Trump, in spite of Hillary Clinton's winning margin in the popular vote, has led many to question the fundamental legitimacy of the *electoral college*. The electoral college was established as a compromise, ensuring citizen representation by a body of leaders judged to be qualified to represent the voters (What is the Electoral College? 2016). The average voter—the right to vote was limited to propertied White men at that time—was judged to be unable to make an informed assessment of candidates and issues but deemed qualified to choose delegates more suitable to the task. The inequities in the representational system were contentious and the electoral college was intended to compensate for that. The southerners wanted to bolster their representation by utilizing their slaveholdings as "discounted" constituencies, resulting in the three fifths rule applied to their slaves. Each state designates its electoral college representatives by its own design. Some states elect their delegates and others appoint them, and some states demonstrate a combination of processes of selection. The electoral college has been sustained for over 200 years (Amar 2016).

American elections are a **winner takes all** outcome. For example, the candidate for Congress with the most votes wins, even if by just a few votes. In many other countries, elections are governed by **proportional** outcomes, meaning that the people elected to the legislature will be chosen by the party in accordance with whatever proportion of the votes the party attains in the election. If three parties each won 33 percent of the vote, each would appoint one third of the legislature. This is why the notion of a *coalition* governing body is so crucial in other countries where, without party alliances, no effective government would be formed when no party has a clear majority of representatives. These countries represent *parliamentary democracies*, where the leader is designated as prime minister or chancellor.

American government often is described as a *pluralistic model* of democracy. This suggests the existence of neutral government entities protecting the rights of individuals and groups. A neutral balance of interests is assumed to be the government's goal. Lobbying by special interest groups make such a claim impossible. Although lobbying efforts occur in areas as diverse as civil rights, industry, finance, education, business, and farming, expenditures from corporate interests far exceed those of any other type of organization. In contrast, government by a *power elite*, a concept introduced by C.W. Mills (1956), suggests that power is in the control of a small, select, and closed group of people who control the corporations and academic and political institutions.

Box 12.11 – Models of Democracies

A *pluralistic model* of democracy supports the belief in the existence of neutral government entities which protect the citizens' rights and well-being. In contrast, the existence of lobbies and special interests has led some theorists to suggest the government is controlled by a small, consolidated *power elite* which promotes only its interests. The 2010 Supreme Court case, *Citizens United*, provides for virtually limitless corporate support of the political process. *Political Action Committees (PACs)* are organizations which collect funds from multiple sources to support a particular issue, also representing the dominance of special interests.

Losses in unionization contribute to losses in pluralism by intensifying the power of corporate interests since strong public unions can use their large membership to exert political influence through financial contributions to campaigns and organizations. Not only is decreased union membership contributing to diluted political input, but regulations supporting corporations have also strengthened their influence. In the 2010 *Citizens United* Supreme Court decision, the Court ruled it was unconstitutional to bar corporations, and unions, from buying advertising time, or utilizing other political means, to support or contest a particular candidate. Spending directly into a political candidate's campaign is still restricted but now these entities can contribute to Super PACs and other ad campaigns, which effectively support specific candidates (Bentley n.d.). Previous legislation had prohibited the use of financial support by corporations and unions to pay for any media outlet which mentioned specific candidates during election time. Many liberal organizations support the overturning of Citizens United, suggesting that it has permitted much greater imbalance in the contributions from large corporations and any other source.

Corporations spend a combined 2.6 billion dollars in lobbying efforts, a greater amount than the operating budget of Congress. Their relative influence is significant, amounting to 334 dollars for every dollar spent by unions and public interest groups (Drutman 2015). The power of corporate dollars has led multiple theorists to question the viability of the democratic system (Derber and Magrass 2014; Wright 2015; Reich 2015).

Political Action Committees (PACs) were established in the 1970s to combat restrictions on direct contributions to political campaigns. PACs garner money from multiple sources for a specific issue. PACs can represent industry or "public interest" groups ranging from disability rights to the National Rifle Association. Super PACs cannot contribute to particular parties or candidates but they can provide ads and other supporting information regarding candidates and they must make the list of donors available. The influence of the super PACs is significant.

Other political systems function in ways which are fundamentally opposed to democratic principles. In a *monarchy*, leadership is inherited, with power residing in an individual or family. In the past, monarchs often had absolute power to rule but today they are more likely to be *constitutional monarchies*, where power lies in elected government parliaments and the monarchy maintains a symbolic and ceremonial role. The UK, Sweden, Spain, and the Netherlands are examples of modern constitutional monarchies.

Box 12.12 – Other Political Forms of Governance

A *monarchy* represents the rule of inherited power through an individual or family.

Constitutional monarchies are largely symbolic monarchies which represent an elected parliamentary government, led by a prime minister or chancellor. Examples of these include Spain, the UK, Sweden, and the Netherlands.

Authoritarian regimes are political systems characterized by a ruling elite supported by business, the military or, infrequently, a monarchy. There are no personal freedoms or citizen representation incorporated in this model. Examples would be Cuba and the People's Republic of China. *Totalitarian* societies are extreme states which completely control the population into submission. Examples of this form would include Germany under the Nazi Party, Iraq under Saddam Hussein, and North Korea under Kim Jong-un.

Authoritarian regimes are political systems characterized by a small political elite supported by the military and business leaders, and in a few cases, a monarchy. In the case of military *juntas*, the military seizes leadership. The citizens are not incorporated into this model and are denied the right of free speech and free press. Cuba and the People's Republic of China are authoritarian regimes. A *totalitarian* regime represents an extreme case where all spheres of private and public life are controlled by the government and the population is coerced into submission by constant surveillance, secret police, and fear of being seized for any reason, or for no reason. The German *National Socialist Party*, or the Nazi Party; Iraq under Saddam Hussein; and North Korea under Kim Jong-un, represent totalitarian regimes.

The Political Economy Perspective

Derber and Magrass (2014) persuasively argue that the classic theorists, Weber and Marx, believed that sociology's unique contribution was in applying the dynamics of capitalism in a democratic context, marrying the study of economics and politics. Although their viewpoints diverged, each theorist believed that the mechanisms of the economy were dependent on the government and could not be analyzed separately. Weber saw the two spheres as interdependent whereas Marx perceived a more unilateral influence, with the economy as the determining factor in institutional relations and cultural development. Derber and Magrass suggest that C.W. Mills also understood the necessity of a *political economic* approach. Mills' analysis centered on the forces of the power elite which control the economy and cultural forces in such a way that no significant challenges can emerge.

The third major classical theorist, Emile Durkheim, diverged from the political economic viewpoint. Durkheim's scientific approach to the social world resulted in the fragmentation of politics and economics from sociology and treating capitalism as an independent legitimate system. The American functionalist viewpoint, following Durkheim, adheres to a neutral view of capitalism and the notion that it works for the greater good of society, rather than promoting the interests of a narrow elite (Derber and Magrass 2014). In contrast, political economist perspectives highlight the interdependence of the systems, offering a more realistic approach to the working of the advanced capitalism of today, with its widening social class inequalities.

Lack of attention to the inter-dependence of politics and the economy frequently results in confusion of what distinguishes each; economic systems are not synonymous with political ones. Often capitalism is associated with democracy and socialism with authoritarian regimes, though there can be various combinations of each. Illuminating the structural and cultural interweaving of economics and politics can lead to a more complex understanding of a particular society. Derber and Magrass (2014) examine *political economy* from the perspectives of neoclassicists, Keynesians, and neo-Marxists. These views roughly are associated with today's conceptualizations of conservative, liberal, and social democratic views.

Derber and Magrass present the neoclassicist belief that the market is an efficient construct which justly rewards talent and hard work resulting in disparities of income among workers. The functionalist perspective, represented by Davis and Moore (1945), reflects this viewpoint in its assertion that economic inequality derives from the value of the service or skills contributed to the marketplace. In this view, certain occupations command higher wages because their incumbents "deserve" it, due to the importance of their work or the specialized training required. The latter condition would apply to doctors, lawyers, entrepreneurs, and software engineers. Low-level, lower paid workers are "inessential" because they are dispensable, easily replaced at any time. Among this group would be unskilled workers, service workers, and field workers.

> ### Box 12.13 – Political Economy
>
> The *political economy* perspective suggests that the analysis of modern society can best be accomplished by joining the perspectives of political science and economics into a unified sociological approach. The theories of *neoclassicists*, *Keynesians*, and *neo-Marxists* represent views which are today associated with *conservative*, *liberal*, and *radical perspectives*. The conservative views the capitalist free market as efficient and fair and believes that a democracy provides the best motives for free enterprise. The liberal view suggests that capitalism must be modified by government regulation, or the majority of the population will become economically marginalized, compromising the viability of democracy. A radical view supports major institutional change moving away from capitalism towards socialism; no significant institutional change can occur without systemic economic change.

The Keynesian view opposes the idea that the economy is regulated by "fair" assessment of skill and intrinsic value attributed to labor. It is reflected in liberal economists' views represented by Paul Krugman, Robert Reich, and Joseph Stiglitz (see Chapter 5). They suggest that the extreme inequality of recent decades is neither inherent in capitalism nor culturally beneficial. They suggest that capitalism functions better when inequality is low, as seen in the immediate post-World War II era. These theorists believe that today's advanced capitalism can, with some "tweaking," revert to the greater equality between workers and executives seen in earlier decades. These theorists maintain that failure to revive a thriving middle class to consume and affiliate with the culture, not only compromises the economic well-being of the population, it ultimately threatens the viability of the democracy. This perspective advocates addressing the policies and wages which have eclipsed the middle class (Reich 2015; Stiglitz 2013, 2014; Krugman 2017) and creating a way for this group to sustain a middle-class lifestyle. Such a fix depends on the political will to regulate wages, the safety net, entitlement programs, education, and healthcare, all of which have been at risk (Edsall 2017; Fighting for Fair Trade n.d.). These theorists cannot imagine significant economic recovery without concomitant political forces supporting it.

The neo-Marxist perspective challenges the underlying premises of capitalism altogether. Unlike the Keynesian theorists, they see no salvation for the worker, or the culture, without deep structural changes. The dominance of a few mega corporations has deteriorated the capitalist enterprise, so that only the top "1 percent" thrives. The neo-Marxists believe there is no capitalistic remedy for this and the only way to assure the well-being of the population is by redistributing the wealth. The neo-Marxists believe the exploitation of labor to be crucial to virtually limitless profiteering and that disdain for labor has compromised the safety net. They point to the decreased value of "real" wages, even as productivity has soared, as evidence of the greed of the era and the impossibility of curbing it under the present system. Disinvestment in the infrastructure, outsourcing, and automation all show disregard for the viability of the workers. Although the Keynesians share some of these perceptions, they believe that redistribution can occur under present-day institutions while the neo-Marxists advocate transformations of the institutions. Neo-Marxists would support the "Occupy" movement, or any mass movement to create a different system, as the only means to accomplish change while the Keynesians support working through established institutional processes to increase economic well-being. Neo-Marxists are more likely to view the structure of social institutions as deliberately formed to consolidate the advantages of the corporate and government elite. They would point to the tax structure, government bailouts, business policies, financial policies, and ineffective labor protections as evidence that policies only protect the interests of the elite. They would also cite lucrative military contracts to select corporations with political affiliation as typical of the alliance of the government and the capitalist class.

Neoclassicists, in an opposing view, believe that a democratic system is dependent on capitalism. They believe in limited "big government" and promote minimal intervention in setting policies regarding minimum wage, social security, and regulation of business and finance. Freedom from government intrusion is considered fundamental to a free market and to supporting individual and business incentives to build the economy. In this perspective, government intervention would dissuade innovation and motivation, leading to systemic collapse. The *New Deal* programs and welfare states such as exist in Europe are deemed undesirable because they would chip away at personal drive and economic advances. In this perspective, the huge impact of corporate wealth on democracy is not considered a threat, although 80 percent of the public believes it to be (Derber and Magrass 2014).

The Keynesians, supporting the liberal views, also believe in the complementary relationship of capitalism and democracy but promote more citizen participation. They view the neoclassical position as too harsh for the average American's well-being. They believe government interventions should be scrutinized and implemented only as necessary to secure a solid functioning working and middle class. They declare that a large, economically vulnerable segment of the population threatens democratic stability (Derber and Magrass 2014; Reich 2015). In this view, government regulation is essential to protect the future of the worker and of the democracy:

> But small or "not-big" government is also a threat since government must be large enough not only to check huge corporations but also to provide everyone with the freedom to enter the market and get the education, health care, and jobs that guarantee a large middle class, one of the social bulwarks of democracy … Jobless people are not free and their desperation is a threat to the economy and to democratic stability.
>
> (Derber and Magrass 2014)

In this view, the absence of government programs such as the *New Deal* and the expansion of welfare in the "War on Poverty" threaten the maintenance of a democracy (Piven and Cloward 1993). Keynesian theorists believe that the government must do enough for the citizens to quell any potential protest movements and confirm the **legitimacy** of the system's effective support of the population. When a system is seen as legitimate, it is able to rule by *rational-legal authority*, in which written rules and regulations are established by the government. Force, or even its threat, generally is not required to maintain the smooth operation of the system. Social spending and public investments are integral to sustaining the system. This approach is reflected in support for entitlement programs, infrastructure renovation, and safety net programs (Brooks 2017).

Box 12.14 – Legitimacy

When a system is seen as **legitimate**, it is able to rule by **rational-legal authority**, where written rules and regulations are established by the government and supported by the citizens. Force is not generally required because the populace believes in the system.

The neo-Marxist view is that the advanced state of capitalism precludes any possibility of a working democracy. The theorists see the state as an arm of the bourgeoisie, or the "1 percent." The political system is controlled by capitalists no matter what democratic verbiage suggests. Political decisions favor the capitalists and divide the working class along demographic lines especially of race, ethnicity, and sex, diffusing the potential of labor to make effective demands on the system (Derber and Magrass 2014). Globalization operates as a unifying force in that demands for cheap labor, tariff relief, and subsidies are strengthened by the threat of corporate relocation. To support workers, globalization requires restrictive legislation across nations, or it will sustain exploitive practices around the world.

Box 12.15 – Democratic Socialism

Democratic socialism combines the economic protections of socialism with the personal freedoms guaranteed in a democracy. It has been characteristic of many developed countries, since the mid-twentieth century. Bernie Sanders brought it to the attention of Americans in his 2016 presidential campaign.

Democratic Socialism

The 2016 presidential candidacy of Bernie Sanders introduced the concept of *democratic socialism* to many Americans. Democratic socialism combines personal freedoms, associated with democracy, with greater regulation of the economy characteristic of a socialist approach. In this system, the government is responsible for providing essential goods and services but private property and enterprise would also be permissible under the regulations. Government would be by election among multiple parties. Essential institutions such as transportation, education, banking, utilities, and healthcare would be controlled by the government. Sanders exhibited these traits in his support of free tuition in public higher education and a government-supported single payer healthcare plan. Additional social benefits, such as daycare, parental leave, retirement, and income maintenance would be guaranteed by the government. The Scandinavian countries and much of Western Europe have adopted varying degrees of the Democratic Socialist approach though several European countries have sustained recent challenges from conservative parties. Current issues of economic decline, increased immigration, and automation appear to be contributing factors to the spread of conservative causes (Economist Online 2016; Shuster 2016).

Another alternative system, in contrast to democratic socialism, concerns government control of business and finance in *state capitalism:*

> In the 1990s most state-owned companies were little more than government departments in emerging markets; the assumption was that, as the economy matured, the government would close or privatise them. Yet they show no signs of relinquishing the commanding heights, whether in major industries (the world's ten biggest oil-and-gas firms, measured by reserves, are all state-owned) or major markets (state-backed companies account for 80% of the value of China's stock market and 62% of Russia's). And they are on the offensive. Look at almost any new industry and a giant is emerging: China Mobile, for example, has 600m customers. State-backed firms accounted for a third of the emerging world's foreign direct investment in 2003–2010.
>
> (Webb 2012)

State capitalism, previously considered a path leading to democratic capitalism, has emerged as a persistent form.

What Are Current Issues in Political Economy?

Recent decades have revealed the erosion of US democratic capitalism as can be seen in the modification of the *social contract* of the post-World War II era (Edsall 2014). A social contract refers to the agreements, both legal and tacit, between a nation's government and its citizens. After World War II, policies and legislations both were in support of the government's obligation to protect its working citizens. This took the form of providing for collective bargaining, workers' benefits such as health insurance and retirement supports, and subsidies for higher education through grants and loans. In the first several decades after World War II, a full-time working White man could expect a "return" on his commitment to his employer in a comfortable life and retirement. These are no longer assured for any employees, including the generally privileged group of White men. Erosion of the social contract has spread in terms of loss of income; minimal retirement supports; lack of benefits such as sick days, parental leaves, and healthcare payments; and general conditions of employment. Many "average" Americans anticipate working longer than planned, and longer than in previous generations, because they cannot afford to retire and do not have the funds to live without some earnings beyond the traditional retirement age.

> **Box 12.16 – The Social Contract**
>
> **The social contract** refers to the agreements, explicit and tacit, between a government and its citizens. In the post-World War II era, workers believed that the government would protect their well-being, both as workers and into retirement. Today, the social contract has been impacted by loss of income; minimal retirement supports; lack of benefits such as sick days, parental leaves, and healthcare payments; and general conditions of employment.

The "rewards" of workers were considered returns on hard work, financed in part by their wages. They were not viewed as unearned extras bestowed by generous employers. Corporations no longer see this as part of their obligation and the government has reneged on policies supporting the worker. Today the corporations are appropriating a greater portion of their profits through low wages, few benefits, anti-union activities, and frequent layoffs or "downsizing," maximizing their "bottom lines." Economists assert, however, that corporate profit can be sustained while providing better wages and benefits.

The frustration of American workers is often attributed to the difficulties of the current conditions of labor; the election of Donald Trump has been explained, in part, by this disaffection (Jones 2017; Thompson 2016; Tyson and Maniam 2016). The conservative journalist, David Brooks, discusses multiple factors contributing to the collapse of the working class. These include a mismatch between skills and the job market; declining marriage rates; increased substance abuse; and mistrust of the major social institutions. He diagnoses a widespread malaise: "The social fabric, the safety net and the human capital sources just aren't strong enough" (Brooks 2017). He maintains that the support of the capitalist market demands a pro-state approach. This approach would be characteristic of the Keynesian view.

The de-regulation of the banking industry in recent decades has led to enhancing profiteering while minimizing the risks to financial institutions. The economic collapse of 2008 revolved around a set of complex practices making it possible for banks to sell loans and investments appearing as solid, calculated risks but containing high risks passed on to other entities. They would be accomplished through selling the insuring of these investments as "low risk," with minimal probability of default, due to mixed risk levels in the loans (called *Collateral Debt Obligation*). Organizations such as pension funds, businesses, and savings funds became major investors in these enterprises which were backed by the banking insurance funds. Through a lack of transparency, the banks were passing on the risk to other entities (*Credit Default Risk*, in Lewis 2010). The financial institutions holding these credit insurances collapsed and a lending freeze ensued, businesses halted, and people's jobs, savings, and investments were lost (Lewis 2010; Ferguson 2010). The film, *The Inside Job* (Ferguson 2010), explains how professors at the most elite institutions of higher education failed to challenge the practices of Wall Street and even promoted "value neutral" theories which bolstered these practices. The process culminated in the insolvency of countless American households while rewarding most bankers, shifting the cost, through the government bailout of the banks, to the taxpayers and to future generations. While the banks have recuperated from the financial collapse of the "great recession," many American families have not, despite politicians' claims otherwise (Shaw 2015).

Political Parties

Political parties are formal organizations seeking participation in the government. The three branches of government—the executive, judicial, and legislative— represent an attempt to balance the power of any one party. America's two-party system is structured in such a way as to preclude contributions of entities lacking affiliation with either party. The Democratic Party generally supports more liberal social programs and greater regulation of social institutions, leading to a strong middle class. Its programs support higher minimum wages; public school systems; low or no cost public higher education; environmental protections; government subsidies for healthcare; reforms in the criminal justice system; the DREAM Act for undocumented immigrants; civil rights for all marginalized groups; reproductive rights; and gun control (2016 Democratic Party Platform). In contrast, the Republican Party policies are more conservative. They support smaller government; traditional marriage; repealing the ACA; strengthening the military; restrictions on abortions; independent energy; gun rights; inclusion of religion in education and of voucher programs; reduced safety nets; reducing but sustaining entitlement programs; and relaxing policies addressing environmental protections (We Believe in America n.d.).

Box 12.17 – Political Parties

A *political party* is a formal organization with a distinctive viewpoint, seeking representation in the government. The three branches of government—the executive, judicial, and legislative—are an attempt to balance the power of any one party. The US is a two-party system, with systemic elements limiting the influence of entities operating outside the parties.

The political affinities of the American population are demographically fragmented and increasingly unpredictable (Isenberg 2016). Generally, the Republicans have been older, more likely to be White, less educated, more religious, and more likely to be conservative. The Democrats characteristically have been younger, more educated, more secularly oriented, more likely to be immigrant and nonWhite, more supportive of LGBT rights, and more liberal. With respect to voting behavior, younger people are less likely to participate, particularly in non-presidential elections (Taylor 2016). The trend may be shifting since the 2016 election, which seems to have incited new interest in politics, especially among the young and women (Whelan and Panaritis 2017; Filipovic 2017; Hook 2017).

The last couple of decades have seen the rise of political factions disenchanted with the political parties. The *Tea Party*, originating during the 2007 Republican

Party campaign of Ron Paul, takes its name from an event that took place on the 234th anniversary of the Boston Tea Party. The adherents, most emanating from the Republican Party, support less government, less taxation, and less gun control. They are more likely to express beliefs limiting marriage to heterosexuals. They believe race issues are garnering too much attention and equal opportunity exists. They support individual rights, such as in the second amendment, and they are against government intruding in personal life. Demographically, they tend to be White, male, over 45 years old, and more educated than the general population (Montopoli 2012). They represent a split from more moderate Republican positions. The Tea Party has become diffused, with many of its politicians joining the newer *House Freedom Caucus* in the House of Representatives. This group represents the most conservative stances of the Republican Party. There are 36 confirmed members and likely several others. They are typically newer to the Congress than the average House members, a little younger, and almost exclusively White male; the caucus has one woman and one Latino (Desilver 2015). Legislation has been determined by the vote of the *House Freedom Caucus*, whose support is required by the Republicans to over-ride Democratic Party opposition (Bade et al. 2017; Shepherd 2017).

Box 12.18 – US Alternative Political Perspectives

The **Tea Party** and the **Alt-Right** have emerged as dissenting factions among the Republicans. Ideas supporting **Democratic Socialism**, influenced by the candidacy of Bernie Sanders, are the source of liberalizing influences within the Democratic Party.

The *Alt-Right* is a small, active citizen group promoting American isolationism, "cultural preservation," cultural homogeneity, support of the free market, White nationalism, anti-feminism, and anti-immigration positions. Sources of their influence are from websites, social media, and chat forums. *Breitbart News*, a syndicated news and opinion website, acts as "a platform for the alt-right" (Caldwell 2016).

The Democratic Party has not splintered into factions paralleling those emanating from the Republican Party. Bernie Sanders used support he garnered in the 2016 presidential campaign to liberalize the Democratic platform, especially with regard to issues of public higher education, healthcare, and trade agreements. Although Sanders gained a significant support base, he was ultimately unsuccessful in challenging the candidacy of Hillary Clinton. Following the election, the media exposed the Democratic leadership's manipulation of the party machinery to support Hillary Clinton and undermine Sanders. Subsequently, the Democratic National Committee (DNC) revealed a widening chasm in party factions. The position of DNC chairman, after a tight and contentious race, ultimately went to Tom Perez, former Secretary of Labor and Clinton supporter, narrowly beating Keith Ellison (Minnesota), a Sanders supporter. Perez quickly moved to appoint Ellison as the Vice Chairman in an effort to promote party unity and garner wider support among younger voters (Bradner 2017).

Politics in the Trump Era

Observers agree that many progressive policies are imperiled by the Trump presidency. The Trump administration represents "a profound retrenchment of domestic policy" (Edsall 2017). His healthcare and tax agendas promise to worsen the standard of living for many Americans, including those among his constituents, while cutting taxes for the wealthy (Horsley et al. 2017). His initial federal budget for fiscal year 2018 included cuts amounting to 54 billion dollars in education, housing and childcare assistance for low and moderate-income families, enforcement of environmental protections, worker and consumer protections, and arts and national park supports (Edsall 2017). Significant cuts were seen in the departments covering the Environmental Protection Agency, the Department of Labor, and the Department of Health and Human services while the Departments of Defense and Homeland Security would receive increases in their budgets. Experts on foreign policy, including former military leadership, predict negative impacts resulting from Trump's lack of knowledge regarding foreign affairs and its consequences for global relations (Edsall 2017). Trump's withdrawal from the Paris Climate Accord puts him in the company of only two other countries, and against 194 signers (Shear 2017). Trump's initial approval ratings, in his first 60 days, were the lowest in recorded history (Sheth 2017).

So far, Donald Trump has had the widest influence in the federal court system. He has appointed more federal judges in his first year than any other president. His nominees have faced severe opposition, even from members of his own party, and several have received a "not qualified" ranking from the *American Bar Association* (Ballesteros 2017). Even with such opposition, he has placed 12 federal circuit court judges and six in the district courts. The appointment of Neil M. Gorsuch to the

Figure 12.10 Political protesters during the 2016 campaign
Source: SGDPhotography / Shutterstock.com

US Supreme Court, secures the conservative Republican majority on the court. The Republicans followed by the nomination of Brett Kavanaugh, blocked Obama's nominee for ten months. Had Obama's nominee, Merrick Garland, been confirmed, the court would have had its first liberal majority in 50 years. If Trump appoints more judges, he will have the potential to solidify this dominance even further. Issues likely to be affected by the changing balance in the Court include threats to public unions; support for second amendment rights and against increased gun control; prolife supports; lack of campaign finance reforms; Affirmative Action policies; voting rights; religious freedom; and criminal and immigration law (Parlapiano and Yourish 2017).

In December 2017, the Congress passed a major tax reform without any bipartisan discussion and without a single Democrat voting for it. The bill is widely noted as the first major legislative accomplishment of the Trump administration. Representative Paul Ryan, the Republican Speaker of the House, declared regarding the passing of the bill: "Today, we are giving the people of this country their money back" (Kaplan and Rappeport 2017). The Democrats, represented by Democratic leader Representative Nancy Pelosi held an opposing view, saying the bill "is simple-theft – monumental, brazen theft from the American middle class and from every person who aspires to reach it." (Kaplan and Rappeport 2017). The 1.5 trillion-dollar bill will significantly increase the national debt, shifting payments to future generations in exchange for short-term reductions for most taxpayers. Corporate tax rates will be decreased from 35 percent to 21 percent, a move which was sold as essential to creating more jobs and supporting economic growth. The bill promises to lower taxes on most Americans though it is debatable to what extent all groups will sustain significant gains. The individual tax reduction is set to expire after 2025 (Kaplan and Rappeport 2017). The wealthy will see a substantial gain in the reduction of their tax rate from 39.6 percent to 37 percent, and an increased limit to inheritance before estate taxes kick in. Trump failed, in his first year, to make good on his promise to "repeal and replace Obamacare," but successfully included in the tax bill elimination of the individual mandate to obtain health insurance. As a result, premiums are expected to increase by 10 percent and as many as 13 million Americans will lack access to affordable healthcare (Martin 2017; Pear 2017). The bill will also likely violate aspects of the World Trade Organization agreements and set the stage for reductions on entitlement programs such as Medicare (Kysar and Sugin 2017). Debate persists regarding the ultimate long-term impact of the bill on the individual and the economy.

Key Terms

Primary Labor Market   Secondary Labor Market   Contingent Workforce   United Farm Workers   Political Economy   Economics   Capitalism   Capital Goods   Corporations   Transnational or Multi-National Corporations   Oligarchy   Shared Monopoly   Socialism   Democracy   Representative Democracy   Parliamentary Democracy   Voting Rights Act of 1965   Electoral College   Pluralistic Model   The Power Elite   Citizens United   Supreme Court Decision   Political Action Committee (PAC)   Legitimacy   Democratic Socialism   Social Contract   Republican Party   Democratic Party   Tea Party   Alt-Right

Concept Review

How Is Work Structured in the US?

The labor market is split into a primary and secondary labor market. The **primary labor market** is characterized by relatively secure positions with good benefits and opportunities for advancement. Large corporations and government agencies fall into this category. The **secondary labor market** is more tenuous since it is less likely to offer job security, benefits, and promotion. Companies in this market are smaller and more likely to be family owned. Today fewer workers are employed in any market sector, signifying the growth of a **contingent labor force** of casual workers, independent contractors, subcontractors, and "gig" workers with no benefits or job security.

What Is the History and Status of Unionization?

The struggle to create unions enhancing the conditions of employment was long and hard. Unions have achieved better pay, scheduling, overtime, and other condition of the workplace. Unions also lobby the government for legislation favorable to workers, further allowing for the participation of labor in the political process. Unionization of workers is decreasing, especially in the private sector and increasingly in the public sector. Although government workers are more likely to be unionized, some states have diminished the capacity for public unions to engage in collective bargaining.

What Type of Economy Does the US Have?

The US has an economy based in **corporate capitalism**. **Transnational corporations** have created a global market which has curtailed the ability of single nations to regulate their influences. Although capitalism is characterized by a free market ideal, the government exerts some control over market forces by setting minimum wages, trade policies, labor laws, and other legislation affecting the market. A **socialist economy**, by contrast, supports collective goals and is characterized by government control and policies promoting the public good over private profit. Most basic needs are met by government-operated agencies.

What Type of Political System Does the US Have?

The US has a **representative democracy**. The government represents the will of the population through voting. A **pluralistic model** of government suggests the ultimately neutral position of the government in its purported protection of the rights of the citizens. However, forces such as special interest groups, PACs, and lobbyists indicate the failure of the system to operate without bias. Some theorists suggest that the US is more accurately described as possessing a **power elite**, a small consolidated group of leaders who dominate industry, government, and academic institutions.

What Is the Political Economy Perspective?

The theory pertaining to a view of a **political economy** understands politics and economics as interdependent. Capitalism, as an economic system, is seen as crucial to sustaining a democratic political system, and vice versa. To the extent that the economy has become increasingly monopolistic, dominated by special interests, the political process of the democratic system is compromised. The views of these theorists represent varying political policies. **Neoclassicists** take a conservative approach associated with the programs supported by the Republican Party. **Keynesians** take a more liberal approach congruent with the Democratic Party viewpoint. **Neo-Marxists** would support the **Democratic Socialist** program characteristic of Northern European countries.

What Are the Political Beliefs Today?

Many theorists have suggested that the **social contract,** typifying the immediate post-World War II era, has been compromised. In that period, the profits from production were spread proportionately among all the social classes. Workers were rewarded for their labor through benefits offered by corporations. In recent decades these assets have been eroded by stagnant wages, decreased benefits, contingent labor practices, and loss of unionization. These changing circumstances have led to different approaches in politics. The **Republican Party** has become the party associated with more conservative views, resulting in greater support for corporations and less government regulation. The **Democratic Party** is considered as promoting more government regulation of business and more support for the workers. Working-class disaffection has surfaced in fringe parties such as the **Tea Party** and the **Alt-Right**. On the liberal side, disaffection with the major parties' positions was seen in the support of Bernie Sanders in the 2016 presidential campaign.

Review Questions

1. Would you prefer to work in the primary or secondary labor market? What factors would you consider in making your decision?

2. Do you think the gig economy would be a good place for you to work? Why or why not? Be specific in saying what factors you consider positive or negative.

3. How would you characterize your work experiences to date? What type of work is available to you? What limits your job choices?

4. What do you anticipate for your future jobs? What skill sets will you need? Are you concerned about your job becoming obsolete?

5. What characterizes the current labor practices in the US? In what way has the nature of work changed since the more immediate post-WWII era?

6. What is the purpose of unionization? Do you support unions? What factors influence your position?

7. Do you believe capitalism is viable in the context of transnational corporations? Is the free market possible with oligarchies and shared monopolies?

8. Is the US government more accurately described by a pluralist model or by a power elite? What factors contribute to your response?

9. What is the main tenet of the political economy approach? Which perspective among the neoclassicists, Keynesians, and neo-Marxists do you believe is most accurate? Why?

10. What positions and constituencies are associated with the major political parties? What gave rise to the Tea Party and the Alt-Right? Why was the Sanders campaign popular?

11. Do you think the election would have had a different outcome if the Democratic candidate had been Bernie Sanders? Why, or why not?

References

2016 Democratic Party Platform. (July, 2016) *Democrats*. Retrieved from https://www.democrats.org/party-platform

Alexander, A. (January 19, 2016) How Politicians Divide, Conquer, and Confuse American Workers Based on Race. *The Atlantic*. Retrieved from https://www.theatlantic.com/politics/archive/2016/01/how-politicians-divide-conquer-and-confuse-american-workers-based-on-race/458835/

Almossawi, A. (June 20, 2016) *The Big Five US Trade Book Publishers*. Retrieved from https://almossawi.com/big-five-publishers/

Amar, R.A. (November 10, 2016) The Troubling Reason the Electoral College Exists. *Time.com*. Retrieved from http://time.com/4558510/electoral-college-history-slavery/

Associated Press (February 6, 2017) *Scott Walker's Wisconsin Could Be a Model for Trump on Unions*. Retrieved from http://www.denverpost.com/2017/02/06/scott-walker-wisconsin-donald-trump-unions/

Bade, R., Dawsey, J., Haberkorn, J. (March 26, 2017) *Politico*. Retrieved from http://www.politico.com/story/2017/03/trump-freedom-caucus-obamacare-repeal-replace-secret-pact-236507

Balay, A., Shattell, M. (March 9, 2016) Long-Haul Sweatshops. *The New York Times*. Retrieved from https://www.nytimes.com/2016/03/09/opinion/long-haul-sweatshops.html

Ballesteros, C. (November 17, 2017) Trump is Nominating Unqualified Judges at an Unprecedented Rate. *Newsweek*. Retrieved from http://www.newsweek.com/trump-nominating-unqualified-judges-left-and-right-710263

Bentley, N. (n.d.) What is Citizens United? *Reclaim Democracy*. Retrieved from http://reclaimdemocracy.org/who-are-citizens-united/

Biggest Transnational Companies. (July 10, 2012) *The Economist*. Retrieved from http://www.economist.com/blogs/graphicdetail/2012/07/focus-1

Bonacich, E. (October, 1972) A Theory of Ethnic Antagonism: The Split Labor Market. *American Sociological Review*. 37(5): 547–559. Retrieved from http://majorsmatter.net/race/Readings/Bonacich%201972.pdf

Bradner, E. (February 26, 2017) Perez Wins DNC Chairmanship. *CNN*. Retrieved from http://www.cnn.com/2017/02/25/politics/dnc-chair-election/

Brancaccio, D. (November 16, 2011) The Future of U.S. Manufacturing. *NPR*. Retrieved from https://www.marketplace.org/2011/11/16/economy/economy-40/future-us-manufacturing

Bratt, P. (dir.) (2017) *Dolores*. 5 Stick Film.

Brooks, D. (March 10, 2017) The Republican Health Care Crackup. *The New York Times*. Retrieved from https://www.nytimes.com/2017/03/10/opinion/the-republican-health-care-crackup.html?_r=0

Bureau of Labor Statistics. US Department of Labor. (January 26, 2017) *News Release, Bureau of Labor Statistics*. [PDF File] Retrieved from https://www.bls.gov/news.release/pdf/union2.pdf Union Members.

Caldwell, C. (December 2, 2016) What the Alt-Right Really Means. *The New York Times*. Retrieved from https://www.nytimes.com/2017/03/10/opinion/the-republican-health-care-crackup.html?_r=0

Capitalism. (n.d.) *Investopedia*. Retrieved from http://www.investorwords.com/713/capitalism.html

CNN. (n.d.) *10 Big Overtime Pay Violators*. Retrieved from http://money.cnn.com/gallery/news/economy/2014/03/13/overtime-violations/2.html

Cohen, P. (April 13, 2015) One Company's New Minimum Wage: $70,000 a Year. *The New York Times*. Retrieved from https://www.nytimes.com/2015/04/14/business/owner-of-gravity-payments-a-credit-card-processor-is-setting-a-new-minimum-wage-70000-a-year.html

Cohen, P. (May 31, 2017) Steady Jobs, with Pay and Hours that are Anything but. *The New York Times*. Retrieved from https://www.nytimes.com/2017/05/31/business/economy/volatile-income-economy-jobs.html?_r=1

Davis, K., Moore, W. (1945) Some Principles of Stratification. *American Sociological Review,* 7 April: 242–249.

Derber, C., Magrass, Y. (2014) *Capitalism: Should You Buy It?* Boulder CO: Paradigm Publishers.

Desilver, D. (October 20, 2015) What Is the House Freedom Caucus, and Who's In It? *Pew Research Center*. Retrieved from http://www.pewresearch.org/fact-tank/2015/10/20/house-freedom-caucus-what-is-it-and-whos-in-it/.

Domhoff, G.W., Staples, C., Schneider, A. (August, 2013) *Interlocks and Interactions Among the Power Elite*. Retrieved from http://www2.ucsc.edu/whorulesamerica/power_elite/interlocks_and_interactions.html

Drutman, L. (April 20, 2015) How Corporate Lobbyists Conquered American Democracy. *The Atlantic*. Retrieved from https://www.theatlantic.com/business/archive/2015/04/how-corporate-lobbyists-conquered-american-democracy/390822/

Dubay, C. (June 28, 2016) The Biggest Educational Publishers. *BookScouter*. Retrieved from https://bookscouter.com/blog/2016/06/the-biggest-textbook-publishers/

Economist online. (May 24, 2016) The Rise of the Far Right in Europe. *The Economist*. Retrieved from http://www.economist.com/blogs/graphicdetail/2016/05/daily-chart-18

Editorial Board. (April 10, 2017) The Gig Economy's False Promise. *The New York Times*. Retrieved from https://www.nytimes.com/2017/04/10/opinion/the-gig-economys-false-promise.html

Edsall, T. (March 30, 2017) When the President Is Ignorant of his Own Ignorance. The *New York Times*. Retrieved from https://www.nytimes.com/2017/03/30/opinion/when-the-president-is-ignorant-of-his-own-ignorance.html?_r=0)

Egan, T. (April 24, 2014) How to Kill the Minimum Wage Movement. *The New York Times*. Retrieved from https://www.nytimes.com/2014/04/25/opinion/egan-how-to-kill-the-minimum-wage-movement.html

Ferdman, A.R. (March 18, 2015) The Most Popular Breakfast Cereals in America Today. *The Washington Post*. Retrieved from https://www.washingtonpost.com/news/wonk/wp/2015/03/18/the-most-popular-breakfast-cereals-in-america-today/?utm_term=.8f767ddd3088

Ferguson, C. (dir.) (2010) *The Inside Job* (video).

Fighting for Fair Trade and Good Jobs for American Workers. (n.d.) [PDF File]. Retrieved from https://my.ofa.us/page/-/pdf/Policy/Fact%20Sheet%20Trade%20 and%20Globalization%20021008%20FINAL%20IH.pdf

Filipovic, J. (February 15, 2017) Donald Trump Is Inspiring More Women to Run for Office Than Ever Before. *Marie Claire.* Retrieved from http://www.marieclaire.com/ culture/a24927/women-running-for-office-post-trump/

Friendly, F.W. (dir.) (1960) *Harvest of Shame.* CBS.

Gandel, S. (November 12, 2013) Why Wal-Mart Can Afford to Give its Workers a 50% Raise. *Fortune.* Retrieved from http://fortune.com/2013/11/12/why-wal-mart-can-afford-to-give-its-workers-a-50-raise/

Glaser, A. (May 25, 2017) The U.S. Will Be Hit Worse by Job Automation than Other Major Economies. *Recode.* Retrieved from https://www.recode. net/2017/3/25/15051308/us-uk-germany-japan-robot-job-automation

Glassdoor Team. (February 7, 2017) *Top 20 Employee Benefits and Perks for 2017.* Retrieved from https://www.glassdoor.com/blog/top-20-employee-benefits-perks-for-2017/

Glazer, E., Huang, D. (January 21, 2016) J.P. Morgan to Workaholics: Knock it Off. *The Wall Street Journal.* Retrieved from https://www.wsj.com/articles/j-p-morgan-chase-tells-investment-bankers-to-take-weekends-off-1453384738

Global 500. *Fortune* online. Retrieved from http://beta.fortune.com/global500

Global Nonviolent Action Database (GNAD) (n.d.) *Boston Police Strike for Better Working Conditions, 1919.* Retrieved from http://nvdatabase.swarthmore.edu/ content/boston-police-strike-better-working-conditions-1919

Greenhouse, S. (September 6, 2014) Just 13 and Working Risky 12-hour Shifts in the Tobacco Fields. *The New York Times.* Retrieved from https://www.nytimes. com/2014/09/07/business/just-13-and-working-risky-12-hour-shifts-in-the-tobacco-fields.html

Gross Domestic Product. (n.d.) *The Economic Times.* Retrieved from http:// economictimes.indiatimes.com/definition/Gross-Domestic-Product

Hasen, L.R. (August 2, 2016) Turning the Tide on Voting Rights. *The New York Times.* Retrieved from https://www.nytimes.com/2016/08/02/opinion/campaign-stops/turning-the-tide-on-voting-rights.html

Hatton, E. (2011) *The Temporary Economy: From Kelly Girls to Permatemps in Postwar America.* Philadelphia: Temple University Press.

Hatton, E. (2014) Mechanisms of Gendering: Gender Typing and the Ideal Worker Norm in the Temporary Help Industry, 1946–1979. *Journal of Gender Studies* 23(4): 440–456.

Hatton, E. (2015) Work Beyond the Bounds: A Boundary Analysis of the Fragmentation of Work. *Work, Employment and Society* 29(6): 1007–1018.

Heller, M. (May 15, 2017) Is the Gig Economy Working? *The New Yorker.* Retrieved from http://www.newyorker.com/magazine/2017/05/15/is-the-gig-economy-working

Hess, E.M.A. (August 16, 2014) Companies that Control the World's Food. *USA TODAY.* Retrieved from https://www.usatoday.com/story/money/ business/2014/08/16/companies-that-control-the-worlds-food/14056133/

Hoder, R. (June 19, 2013) The Privilege of the Unpaid Intern. *Motherlode Blog*. Retrieved from http://parenting.blogs.nytimes.com/2013/06/19/the-privilege-of-the-unpaid-intern/?_r=0

Hook, J. (February 2, 2017) *One Way or Another, Trump Is Engaging Young Voters in Politics, Poll Finds*. Retrieved from http://blogs.wsj.com/washwire/2017/02/02/one-way-or-another-trump-is-engaging-young-voters-in-politics-poll-finds/

Horsley, S., Davis, S., Noguchi, Y. (March 25, 2017) What Failure on Obamacare Repeal Means for Tax Reform. All Things Considered, *NPR*. Retrieved from http://www.npr.org/2017/03/25/521448581/what-failure-on-obamacare-repeal-means-for-tax-reform

Howell, K. (August 1, 2015) Dan Price, Seattle CEO Who Set Company Minimum Wage at $70K, Struggles to Make Ends Meet. *The Washington Times*. Retrieved from http://www.washingtontimes.com/news/2015/aug/1/dan-price-seattle-ceo-who-set-company-minimum-wage/

Isenberg, N. (2016) *White Trash: The 400-year History of Class in America*. New York: Penguin Books.

Jones, M.J. (March 13, 2017) Race, Education, Gender Key Factors in Trump Job Approval. *Gallup.com*. Retrieved from http://www.gallup.com/poll/205832/race-education-gender-key-factors-trump-job-approval.aspx?g_source=Politics&g_medium=lead&g_campaign=tiles

Kantor, J. (August 13, 2014) Working Anything but 9 to 5. *The New York Times*. Retrieved from https://www.nytimes.com/interactive/2014/08/13/us/starbucks-workers-scheduling-hours.html

Kantor, J. (August 14, 2014a) Starbucks to Revise Policies to End Irregular Schedules for its 130,000 Baristas. *The New York Times*. Retrieved from https://www.nytimes.com/2014/08/15/us/starbucks-to-revise-work-scheduling-policies.html

Kaplan, T., Rappeport, A. (December 19, 2017) Republican Tax Bill Passes Senate in 51–48 Vote. *The New York Times*. Retrieved from https://www.nytimes.com/2017/12/19/us/politics/tax-bill-vote-congress.html?_r=0

Kim, Q.S. (2017, June 7) Warehouses Promise Jobs, But What Happens When the Robots Come? *The California Report*. Retrieved from https://www.kqed.org/news/11491029/warehouses-promise-jobs-but-what-happens-when-the-robots-come

Klara, R. (June 20, 2016) How America's Top 2 Breakfast Cereal Makers Are Responding to Soggy Sales. *Adweek*. Retrieved from http://www.adweek.com/brand-marketing/how-americas-top-2-breakfast-cereal-makers-are-responding-soggy-sales-172020/

Kristof, N. (February 19, 2015) The Cost of a Decline in Unions. *The New York Times*. Retrieved from http://www.denverpost.com/2017/02/06/scott-walker-wisconsin-donald-trump-unions/

Krugman, P. (February 20, 2017) On Economic Arrogance. *The New York Times*. Retrieved from https://www.nytimes.com/2017/02/20/opinion/on-economic-arrogance.html

Kysar, R.M., Sugin, L. (December 19, 2017) The Built-in Instability of the GOP's Tax Bill. *The New York Times*. Retrieved from https://www.nytimes.com/2017/12/19/opinion/republican-tax-bill-unstable.html?ribbon-ad-idx=15&src=trending

Laska, L. (n.d.) The Wal-Mart Litigation Project – The Internet Resource for Wal-Mart Litigation. *Wal-martlitigation.com*. Retrieved from http://www.wal-martlitigation.com/

Lewis, M. (2010) *The Big Short*. New York: W.W. Norton and Company.

Li, S. (March 8, 2016) Janitors and Security Guards Are Paid 20% Less When They're Contractors, Report Says. *latimes.com*. Retrieved from http://www.latimes.com/business/la-fi-contract-janitors-story.html

Lyons, D. (April 9, 2016) Congratulations! You've Been Fired. *The New York Times*. Retrieved from https://www.nytimes.com/2016/04/10/opinion/sunday/congratulations-youve-been-fired.html

Malyukova, A. (February 27, 2017) Everyday Life in the Soviet Union. *Left Voice*. Retrieved from http://www.leftvoice.org/Everyday-Life-in-the-Soviet-Union

Martens, P., Martens, R. (July 8, 2014) *Wall Street on Parade: A Citizen Guide to Wall Street*. Retrieved from http://wallstreetonparade.com/2014/07/who-owns-the-u-s-stock-market/.

Martin, R. (December 4, 2017) What Will be the Impact of the GOP Tax Bill? *Morning Edition*. Retrieved from https://www.npr.org/2017/12/04/568261665/what-will-be-the-impact-of-the-gop-tax-bill

Masters, C. (February 14, 2017) Iowa Moves to Restrict Collective Bargaining for Public Sector Workers. *NPR.org*. Retrieved from http://www.npr.org/2017/02/14/515242288/iowa-moves-to-restrict-collective-bargaining-for-public-sector-workers

McArdle, M. (June 21, 2011) Georgia's Harsh Immigration Law Costs Millions in Unharvested Crops. *The Atlantic*. Retrieved from https://www.theatlantic.com/business/archive/2011/06/georgias-harsh-immigration-law-costs-millions-in-unharvested-crops/240774/

McClatchy-Tribune. (August 21, 2014) *U.S. Faces Shortage of Farmworkers Due to Fight over Immigration*. Retrieved from https://newsela.com/articles/immigration-harvest/id/4913/

McClelland, M. (March/April, 2012) I Was a Warehouse Wage Slave. *Mother Jones*. Retrieved from http://www.motherjones.com/politics/2012/02/mac-mcclelland-free-online-shipping-warehouses-labor

Meyer, D. (November 29, 2017) Robots May Steal as Many as 800 Million Jobs in the Next 13 Years. *Fortune*. Retrieved from http://fortune.com/2017/11/29/robots-automation-replace-jobs-mckinsey-report-800-million/

Miller, C. (May 28, 2015) The 24/7 Work Culture's Toll on Families and Gender Equality. *Nytimes.com*. Retrieved from http://www.nytimes.com/2015/05/31/upshot/the-24-7-work-cultures-toll-on-families-and-gender-equality.html

Mills, C.W. (1956) *The Power Elite*. London: Oxford University Press.

Montopoli, B. (December 14, 2012) *Tea Party Supporters: Who They Are and What They Believe*. Retrieved from http://www.cbsnews.com/news/tea-party-supporters-who-they-are-and-what-they-believe/

Moore, M. (2015) *Where to Invade Next*. Dog Eat Dog Films.

Morehouse, L. (September 7, 2015) The Forgotten Filipino-Americans Who Led the '65 Delano Grape Strike. *KQED radio*. Retrieved from https://ww2.kqed.org/news/2015/09/04/50-years-later-the-forgotten-origins-of-the-historic-delano-grape-strike/

Morgenstern, M. (November 2, 2016) Artificial Intelligence: The Impact on Jobs. Special Report. Automation and Anxiety. *The Economist*. Retrieved from http://www.economist.com/news/special-report/21700758-will-smarter-machines-cause-mass-unemployment-automation-and-anxiety

Morran, C. (April 4, 2016) 10 Years After Verdict, Walmart Must Pay $151 Million to Employees who Worked Off the Clock. *Consumerist*. Retrieved from https://consumerist.com/2016/04/04/10-years-after-verdict-walmart-must-pay-151-million-to-employees-who-worked-off-the-clock/

Mulligan, C. (January 8, 2014) Policies That Discourage Full-Time Work. *Economix Blog*. Retrieved from http://economix.blogs.nytimes.com/2014/01/08/policies-that-discourage-full-time-work/

Muro, M., Andes, S. (April 29, 2015) Don't Blame the Robots for the Lost Manufacturing Jobs. *Brookings*. Retrieved from https://www.brookings.edu/blog/the-avenue/2015/04/29/dont-blame-the-robots-for-lost-manufacturing-jobs/

Nadasen, P. (March 19, 2016) Unsung Black Heroines Launched a Modern Domestic Workers Movement—Powered by their Own Stories. *Public Radio International*. Retrieved from http://www.pri.org/stories/2016-03-19/unsung-black-heroines-launched-modern-domestic-workers-movement-powered-their-own

Noble, S. (2017, 2015) Plutocracy. *Metanoia Films*. Retrieved from http://www.nofrackingway.us/2017/01/08/how-we-got-here-the-history-of-divide-conquer-in-american-politics/

Noguchi, Y. (April 21, 2016) New Overtime Rules May Put Squeeze on Caregivers for Those With Disabilities. *NPR.org*. Retrieved from http://www.npr.org/sections/health-shots/2016/04/21/475159102/new-overtime-rules-may-put-squeeze-on-caregivers-for-those-with-disabilities

Noguchi, Y. (April 26, 2016a) Many Grouchy, Error-Prone Workers Just Need More Sleep. *NPR.org*. Retrieved from http://www.npr.org/sections/health-shots/2016/04/26/475287202/many-grouchy-error-prone-workers-just-need-more-sleep

Nunberg, G. (January 11, 2016) Goodbye Jobs, Hello Gigs. How One Word Sums Up a New Economic Reality. *NPR*. Retrieved from https://www.npr.org/2016/01/11/460698077/goodbye-jobs-hello-gigs-nunbergs-word-of-the-year-sums-up-a-new-economic-reality

Pacheco, L., Mow, J. (December 28, 2015) *East of Salinas*. PBS (documentary film).

Parlapiano, A., Yourish, K. (February 1, 2017) Where Neil Gorsuch Would Fit on the Supreme Court. *The New York Times*. Retrieved from https://www.nytimes.com/interactive/2017/01/31/us/politics/trump-supreme-court-nominee.html

Pear, R. (July 3, 2017) Congress Moves to Stop IRS from Enforcing Health Law Mandate. *The New York Times*. Retrieved from https://www.nytimes.com/2017/07/03/us/politics/congress-moves-to-stop-irs-from-enforcing-health-law-mandate.html

Peterson, K. (December 19, 2014) The Big Three Aren't so Big Anymore. *CBSnews.com*. Retrieved from http://www.cbsnews.com/news/the-big-three-arent-so-big-anymore/

Piven, F.F., Cloward, R. (1993) *Regulating the Poor: The Functions of Public Welfare*. New York: Penguin Random House LLC.

Reich, R. (2015) *Saving Capitalism: For the Many, Not the Few*. New York: Penguin Random House LLC.

Samakow, A.P. (December 21, 2014) Suing Wal-Mart: Bad Business Practices Lead to Litigation. *The Washington Times*. Retrieved from http://www.washingtontimes. com/news/2014/dec/31/suing-wal-mart-bad-business-practices-lead-litigat/

Serrano, A. (September 21, 2012) Bitter Harvest: U.S. Farmers Blame Billion-Dollar Losses on Immigration Laws. *TIME*. Retrieved from http://business. time.com/2012/09/21/bitter-harvest-u-s-farmers-blame-billion-dollar-losses-on-immigration-laws/

Shattell, A. (March 9, 2016) Long-Haul Sweatshops. *Nytimes.com*. Retrieved from http://www.nytimes.com/2016/03/09/opinion/long-haul-sweatshops.html

Shaw, D. (October 26, 2015) Who's Feeling the Most Financial Stress? *Marketplace*. Retrieved from https://www.marketplace.org/2015/10/26/world/anxiety-index/ who%E2%80%99s-feeling-most-financial-stress

Shear, M. (June 1, 2017) Trump Will Withdraw from the Paris Climate Agreement. *The New York Times*. Retrieved from https://www.nytimes.com/2017/06/01/ climate/trump-paris-climate-agreement.html

Shepherd, K. (March 28, 2017) Freedom Caucus: Do These 29 White Men Run America? *BBC News*. Retrieved from http://www.politico.com/story/2017/03/ trump-freedom-caucus-obamacare-repeal-replace-secret-pact-236507

Sheth, S. (March 19, 2017) Trump's Approval Rating Hit a New Low. *Business Insider*. Retrieved from http://www.businessinsider.com/trump-approval-rating-hits-new-low-2017-3.

Shuster, S. (September 22, 2016) European Politics Are Swinging to the Right. *Time. com*. Retrieved from http://time.com/4504010/europe-politics-swing-right/

Smith, A. (2010–2016) Trucking Companies Prepare for Possible Driver Union Battle. *Ask the Trucker*. Retrieved from http://askthetrucker.com/trucking-companies-prepare-for-possible-driver-union-battle/

Soergel, A. (April 18, 2017) Undocumented Immigrants Pay Billions in Taxes. *U.S. News*. Retrieved from https://www.aol.com/article/finance/2017/04/18/ undocumented-immigrants-pay-billions-in-taxes/22044564/

Stiglitz, J. (December 21, 2013) In No One We Trust. *The New York Times*.

Stiglitz, J. (June 27, 2014) Inequality Is Not Inevitable. *The New York Times*.

Taylor, P. (January 27, 2016) The Demographic Trends Shaping American Politics in 2016 and Beyond. *Pew Research Center*. Retrieved from http://www.pewresearch. org/fact-tank/2016/01/27/the-demographic-trends-shaping-american-politics-in-2016-and-beyond/

Thompson, D. (March 1, 2016) Who Are Donald Trump's Supporters, Really? *The Atlantic*. Retrieved from https://www.theatlantic.com/politics/archive/2016/03/who-are-donald-trumps-supporters-really/471714/

Torpey, E., Hogan, A. (May, 2016) Working in a Gig Economy. *Career Outlook*. *BLS*. Retrieved from https://www.bls.gov/careeroutlook/2016/article/what-is-the-gig-economy.htm

Tyson, A., Maniam, S. (November 9, 2016) Behind Trump's Victory: Divisions by Race, Gender, Education. *Pew Research Center*. Retrieved from http://www.

pewresearch.org/fact-tank/2016/11/09/behind-trumps-victory-divisions-by-race-gender-education/

UMWA. (n.d.) *United Mine Workers of America Website*. Retrieved from http://umwa.org/

US Stock Ownership: Who Owns? Who Benefits? (September 19, 2013) *The Globalist*. Retrieved from https://www.theglobalist.com/u-s-stock-ownership-owns-benefits/

Wage and Hour Division (WHD). (n.d.) *United States Department of Labor*. Retrieved from https://www.dol.gov/whd/overtime/final2016/

Webb, N. (January 21, 2012) The Rise of State Capitalism. *The Economist*. Retrieved from http://www.economist.com/node/21543160

Weber, L. (May 20, 2015) Can You Sue the Boss for Making You Answer Late-Night Email? *WSJ*. Retrieved from http://www.wsj.com/articles/can-you-sue-the-boss-for-making-you-answer-late-night-email-1432144188

What is the Electoral College? (2016) *Archives.gov*. Retrieved from https://www.archives.gov/federal-register/electoral-college/about.html

Whelan, A., Panaritis, M. (February 2, 2017) Trump Spurs a Flood of Political Newbies to Anger, then Action in Philadelphia. *Philly.com*. Retrieved from http://www.philly.com/philly/news/politics/presidential/Trump_spurs_a_flood_of_political_newbies_to_anger_then_action_in_Philadelphia.html

We Believe in America. (n.d.). Retrieved from https://gop.com/platform/

Wiseman, P. (November 2, 2016) Why Robots, Not Trade, Are Behind so Many Factory Job Losses. *AP News*. Retrieved from https://apnews.com/265cd8fb02fb44a69cf0eaa2063e11d9/mexico-taking-us-factory-jobs-blame-robots-instead

Wolf, R. (March 29, 2016) Public Employee Unions Dodge a Supreme Court Bullet. *USA Today*. Retrieved from http://www.usatoday.com/story/news/politics/2016/03/29/supreme-court-public-employee-unions-mandatory-fees-scalia/81123772/

Wright, E.O., Rogers, J. (2015) *American Society: How It Really Works*. 2nd edn. New York: W.W. Norton and Company.

Note

1. Rankings of companies with favorable employee policies vary according to what measures are utilized.

Religions in Society

Introduction

Religion means many things to different people and nothing at all to others. Some people have great difficulty personally imagining mystical experiences while others encounter them almost daily. "Religious" experiences have been described as occurring in a variety of circumstances, from religious revelation to feeling at one with nature, or in the experience of eating great food. Some people feel challenged by those who embrace atheism because they cannot imagine a way of being that does not include a religious base. Yet, what is meant by religion is somewhat amorphous. It is difficult for sociologists to define *religion* as a concept broad enough to incorporate all types of religion and yet remain specific enough to distinguish it from other conceptual frameworks. Other sociologists think that it does not require such distinctions because they focus on the social role religions play and believe that such a function can be accomplished by any system of thought impacting human behaviors. All sociologists are in agreement that the field concerns itself with the interplay between society and religions, rather than in evaluating the theological content. Some would agree with the historian Yuval N. Harari, that any belief system which is *commonly* held, and exerts some influence on behavior, can be seen as religion. This view is consonant with the functionalist view of religion, stemming from Durkheim's work, that religion affirms, and reaffirms, important ethos central to social life and reminds a society's members of what is valued in society. Other sociologists feel designation as a religion requires more specific elements. They believe that religions must contain elements which provide context beyond "human nature," relating to some "supernatural" features.

What Is Religion?

Religion can be defined as an organized set of *beliefs* and *rituals* which are socially recognized and represent a community of adherents. In its most basic element, religion can be defined by its social function rather than by the existence of deities. "Religion is any all-encompassing story that confers superhuman legitimacy on human laws, norms and values. It legitimizes human social structures by arguing that they reflect superhuman laws" (Harari 2017). Religions, according to the classic

Figure 13.1 Religions generally contain rituals and beliefs. Ceremonies accompany major life events. This picture portrays an Indian bride and bridegroom in a Hindu ceremony
Source: India Picture / Shutterstock.com

sociologist Emile Durkheim (Fields 1995), are characterized by differentiation of the culture into a *sacred* and *profane* realm. Sacred refers to anything which is special or out of the ordinary, while profane is applied to the routines of daily life. No matter what the specific content of a particular religion, there will be recognition of these separate domains. Rituals often are indicative of entry into the sacred realm. Durkheim's study of *The Elementary Forms of Religious Life* (1915) examined the belief in *animism* found in Australia's aboriginal cultures. Animism is the belief that every part of the natural world, such as plants and animals, has spirits which can influence human society. Durkheim described the social organization of the Indigenous groups into clans, each with its own totem, representing the group. Durkheim believed that religion expresses the power of the group within the religious theodicies making society seem to have the power of an "other" world. In worshiping the totem, in the form of an animal or some living being important to the group— simultaneously representing the group while also an object of sacred worship—the power of society is recognized as greater than the individual members. He believed that this essential religious form, which he saw as emblematic of an early culture, was instructive in understanding the elements of all religion. All clan members were under an obligation to treat anything associated with their totem as significant in guiding their own lives, whether that be protecting it from predators, not eating foods the totem depended upon, or using it in ceremonies. In the ritualistic homage paid to the totem, Durkheim believed that the authority of the group supported the individual. Bringing a person back to the protection of the community of believers will alleviate the crisis and save the sufferer from a loss of faith. This he believed to be incorporated into modern religions which can provide meaning when an individual might be most vulnerable, as in periods of illness or death. He felt this was the essence of religion, even if it has become obscured by complex scriptures and practices.

Box 13.1 – Religion Definitions

Sociologists define *religion* as a set of beliefs and rituals which are recognized in society. Typically, religions observe some separation between *sacred and profane* realms. Some functionalist oriented theorists accept that secular belief systems can act as religions.

Mysticism refers to feelings of unity with the universe or a sacred realm.

The *functionalist view* developed from Durkheim's work in its focus on how religion supports the social fabric of society, bringing the collectivity together in community. On a personal level, religion can provide meaning and support for situations which promote crisis, such as the death of a loved one or a financial or job loss. On a social level, religion promotes a sense of belonging and shared history, as well as offering consolation during difficult times through collective rituals, such as in the death rites of various religions. On a cultural level, religion promotes adherence to the values and "order" of society so that people feel invested in the established institutions, community, and culture (McGuire 2002). This collective aspect of religion appears to be the one currently most at risk in that that some 23 percent of the population is nonaffiliated (Pewforum 2015), meaning that they do not identify a particular church they belong to. Consequently, religion has lost much of its ability to affirm a cohesive community, but offers "meaning" in a more personalized manner. Many "New Age" religions are devoid of social practices and group rituals, adding to the fragmentation of American collective life, something which would be alarming in Durkheim's views since it provides no collectivistic interaction. Durkheim and the functionalists focus on the contributions of religion to social stability, tending to show a disregard for the times when religion may be divisive.

The classic theorist Max Weber also studied religion extensively, publishing monographs on specific religions as well as a theoretical treatise on the sociological import of religion (Weber 1963, 1976). Weber analyzed the consequences of "big" religious ideas on the social structure of society. He believed that the Protestant doctrine of predestination, establishing that God has determined the afterlife of every person prior to their birth, contributed to capitalism because it freed the individual from social obligations that prioritized helping others in order to earn a blessed afterlife. He also made a strong argument for the impact of the Protestant ethos on the development of personal habits. He suggested that the guiding principles of duty, social obligation, denial of bodily pleasures, and hard work were habits which would contribute to the expansion of capitalism. Additionally, people tended to see prosperity as a symbol of their inclusion in the select group, so they acquired a special motive for looking successful. Weber does not assert that Protestantism formed capitalism; he only proposed that its practices transferred nicely to the system of reinvestment of capital. In this way, religion could be a factor in promoting social change. Weber made these assertions by showing how the published writings of Protestant reformers promoted these ideas, and not by asking people if they were aware of such a relationship. It is likely that hard-working citizens would have been puzzled by a direct question on the relationship between the tenets of Protestantism and their social behaviors.

Karl Marx said:

> Religious suffering is, at one and the same time, the expression of real suffering and a protest against real suffering. Religion is the sigh of the oppressed creature, the heart of a heartless world, and the soul of soulless conditions. It is the opium of the people.
>
> (Marx 1844)

He felt religion made people oblivious to their exploitation, exhausted, struggling to survive, and lulled by the promise of a reward in the hereafter. This dynamic inhibits critical analysis of the social system. Think of the scene in the *Wizard of Oz* when Dorothy and her companions literally sleep in the field of poppies as a result of exposure to the narcotic effects of the flowers. Marx believed that religion created a sleep-like stupor which would lead to the acceptance of social inequalities to show faith in God's rewards in heaven. In the hands of the bourgeoisie, religion was a tool of oppression and subjugation, mitigating the likelihood of revolt. The *conflict theorists* believe that the dominant group uses religion to support the dehumanization and denigration of the proletariat. Critics of the conflict view suggest that these theorists underplay the role of the Church in providing actual aid and community to marginalized groups. Conflict theorists also tend to disregard the times when religion contributes to forces promoting social changes, as in the social movements of Latin America and Eastern Europe, where the Catholic church has been a major actor.

How Do Sociologists Describe Religions?

Every known human group has incorporated some type of belief system to explain the origins of life and other questions regarding human existence. Such consistency suggests that human nature "requires" a significant story to make meaning where no obvious ones exist. *Animism* is the oldest, and the most prevalent, form of religious belief in human history. *Animism* refers to the belief that all living organisms, and some inanimate objects, have spirits which can interact with and impact human life and must be treated with care and specific practices. Animism is characteristic of hunting and gathering cultures. *Monotheism*, the belief in one God, is characteristic of the Judaic/Christian/Islamic traditions representing only several thousand years of human society. *Polytheism*, or belief in multiple gods, was prevalent in the ancient worlds of the Greeks and Romans and persists today along with animistic beliefs, in many Eastern and African cultures, and in the Indigenous populations, of developed nations.

Box 13.2 – Religion and Churches

Animism, which is the belief in spirits, usually attributed to any living organism, has characterized most of human history, and is particularly associated with hunting and gathering cultures. *Polytheism*, the belief in multiple Gods, characterized the ancient worlds of the Greek and Roman empires. *Monotheism*, belief in one God as found in Judaism, Islam, and Christianity, is a relative newcomer, dating only to several thousands of years.

Ecclesia is an official religion incorporated into the governing body of a country.

Denominations refer to mainstream religious groups such as most Protestant, Jewish, and Islamic groups.

Sects refer to break-away groups from denominations which generally do not come into conflict with established religions. Mormon groups, which practice polygamy, can be viewed as sects.

Cults generally are relatively small groups which have beliefs and practices which conflict with elements of established religions or with society. One example would be the People's Temple, founded by Jim Jones, which began as a sect but transitioned to a cult when they moved to an isolated community in Guyana, eventually committing mass suicide.

Sociologists typically are not interested in evaluating the *content* of religious beliefs, preferring to focus on how these affect social issues such as politics, education, family life, and law. Religious group affiliations take different forms. In the United States, there is no recognized *ecclesia*, which refers to a society where one religion is integrated into the polity, eliminating the separation of religions and civil life. *Denominations* represent large groups of adherents to "mainstream" beliefs, as in most of the Protestant, Jewish, and Islamic subgroups. A *sect* "is a relatively small religious group that has broken away from another religious organization to renew what it views as the original version of the faith" (Kendall 2012). A *cult* is a religious group with "practices and teachings outside the dominant cultural and religious traditions of a society" (Kendall 2012).

Some major religions began as cults but today cults are mostly associated with charismatic leaders who win the devotion of their followers, as seen for example in the People's Temple led by Jim Jones. This cult began in the 1950s, moving to northern California in the 1960s. Temple membership reached an estimated 20,000. Initially, Jones aligned his activities with social causes serving the underprivileged by providing human service aid through food banks, drug rehab programs, and other related services. Jones required members to give up their private possessions in order to show their commitment to the group and its ideals and also to raise their kids communally. He was accused of financial, physical, and sexual abuse and ultimately took his group to Guyana to flee government scrutiny. In 1978, over 900 of his followers committed mass suicide and murder, since a third of the victims were children, by drinking poisoned Kool-Aid. A congressman was sent to investigate the charges and subsequently was killed with several others who accompanied him (NPR 2011).

Box 13.3 – Secularization and Pluralism

Pluralism refers to a society characterized by personal choice with regard to religion, where theoretically no religion is considered dominant or superior.

Secular society refers to the privatization of religion where religion is part of the personal life and there is no officially recognized religion; separation of church and state is mandated. Theoretically, the civil and political life of the culture is completely separate from the religious institutions.

Civil religion is when patriotism in a nation carries a religion-like weight. This is represented by the phrase, "God and country," indicating the association between the two.

The US exhibits a wide range of religious groups. Freedom of religion results in *pluralism*, or the co-existence of many religions. In theory, no one should suffer any discrimination as a result of religious affiliation. Research shows that Americans typically are assessed as more religious than people in comparable countries. For example, 60 percent of Americans report religion as "very important" as compared to just 21 percent of Western Europeans. Forty percent of Americans say they do something weekly with their religious institution (Holifield 2014). Religiosity in the US is undergoing modifications. There has been a reduction in the percentage of those identifying as Christian; an increase in non-Christian religious group membership; and a significant portion, 22.8 percent, who identify as "nonaffiliated" (Pewforum 2015). In the near future, Muslims will become the largest world religion (Lipka and Hackett 2017).

Officially, the United States is a *secular society*, which means that religious practice is a personal choice and theoretically no social institution should favor one religion over another. Education, politics, and the law should be free of any religious reference. This is not completely accomplished since there are areas in the public realm which reference Christianity. The ideal of separation of church and state is not complete in practice. For example, we swear people into office, and in court, on the Bible and we have "In God We Trust" on our money. One recent arena of intense controversy has been the phrase "under God" in our *Pledge of Allegiance*. The first version of the Pledge was adopted in 1892 and did not have the phrase "under God" added until 1954 with an Act of Congress. This was largely attributable to distinguishing the "American way" from the atheistic, communist threat to America represented by the Soviet Union in the Cold War era. Subsequently, there have been various challenges, in the courts and Congress, to the Pledge's incorporation of the "under God" phrase. Those seeking to eliminate the phrase object either to the monotheist allusion or to the inclusion of any mention referencing religion. Legal challenges have failed to eliminate the "under God" addition, though one third of Americans surveyed would like to see it removed (Somers 2014). A student has the right to opt out of recitation of the Pledge in the public schools (Kurlander 2013; FFRF n.d.).

Issues of separation of church and state were under scrutiny during the presidency of George W. Bush when he proposed a faith-based initiative to offer social services through religious institutions. The Pew Research Center survey of public opinion found that while 69 percent of those surveyed support providing faith-based services, such as employment counseling and drug treatment, 25 percent oppose it:

> More than eight years after former President George W. Bush unveiled his faith-based initiative to make it easier for religious groups to receive government funding to provide social services, the policy continues to draw broad public support. But as was the case when Bush first announced the initiative, many Americans express concerns about blurring the lines between church and state.
>
> (Pew Research Center 2009)

President Obama also supported faith-based initiatives though their future is now uncertain. The political mandates of the current administration are unclear, though it has been shown that millennials are much more likely to support faith-based operations (80 percent) than people over 65 (56 percent) (Pew Research Center 2009).

Although theoretically secular, the US has been described as having a *civil religion* where the symbolic representation of the country is assigned a religious status, and the concept of God is invoked to reflect a sacred devotion to country. Patriotism imbued with such religious fervor is indicated in the phrase "God and country."

Disrespect of civil symbols, as seen with respect to the national anthem or the flag, is considered unpatriotic and sacrilegious. Colin Kaepernick, as quarterback for the SF 49ers, instigated an intensive debate when he chose to kneel while the national anthem was played before the game. He sought to highlight the issue of social justice, or lack of it, in the US today. He especially strove to highlight the racial oppression of African Americans and police brutality towards that group. Since his first act of protest in the summer of 2016, many other players, managers, and owners have joined his protest by remaining seated or kneeling during the anthem. Others, including President Trump, have vilified the athletes, accusing them of lacking in patriotism and respect. He has been criticized as disrespecting "God and country." Nevertheless, many people believe that professional sports teams should not require athletes to stand for the anthem. This belief is strongest among Democrats, at 71 percent, with 18

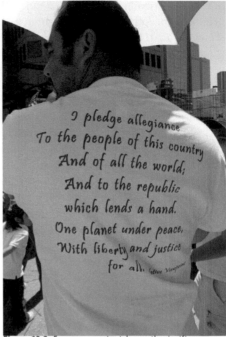

Figure 13.2 For some, country takes on the significance of religion, commanding the respect usually associated with religion. Sometimes it is incorporated into the view of a highly religious person while at other times nation can replace religion as the object of devotion
Source: Jacky Chapman / Alamy Stock Photo

percent of Republicans surveyed also agreeing that athletes should not have to stand for the anthem. This represents significant gains in support from the year before, when Kaepernick first refused to stand (Sides 2017).

Perhaps more dramatic than peacefully kneeling during the anthem is the issue of whether a person has the right to burn the American flag. In 1989, the Supreme Court reversed the conviction of a citizen who had burned the flag, establishing in a 5:4 vote that flag burning was protected speech under the first amendment right to free speech. Though many feel flag burning to be offensive, the court case was supported by two conservative judges who invoked the importance of protecting even offensive behaviors. A Constitutional amendment to ban flag burning was denied by Congress in 2006 (King and Sands 2016).

These examples notwithstanding, our cultural attitudes towards religion are mixed. We like our leaders to be Christian but not "too religious." Presidents are shown attending some kind of church service on major Christian holidays, such as Christmas and Easter. Yet Americans remain suspicious of persons belonging to non-mainstream Christian denominations and to non-Christian faiths. Obama was accused of being Muslim, and this belief persists and has been utilized to discredit him (Taylor 2016). Former President Carter underplayed his strong family ties to the Southern Baptist Church and to his own "born again" status. More recently Carter has withdrawn his membership in the Southern Baptist Church after more than six decades, largely due to its persistent denigration of women (Carter 2017; Sengupta 2000). Politicians fear alienating potential supporters with their religious affiliations; Gerald Ford also claimed "born again" status though he was unwilling to reveal this status during his campaign (Gibbs and Duffy 2007).

To date there has been only one president who was not affiliated with a Protestant denomination. President Kennedy's Catholic affiliation cast suspicion, especially with regard to the location of his primary loyalties as lying with the Vatican or with America. He won the popular vote by a slim margin. Many were relieved to see that he behaved independently of the Pope. Sentiments have been changing with regard to some aspects of religious affiliation. In 1958, 67 percent of people responding to a Gallup poll said they would vote for a Catholic president compared with 94 percent in 2012. In a less tolerant vein, consideration of 16 candidate traits showed that voters ranked atheism as the *least* desirable, preferring a philandering president to an atheist by an 18 percent margin (Ashtari 2014). In another study regarding the likelihood of a vote for an atheist president, the trait garnered the least support of any category included. In 1958, 18 percent responded favorably to voting for an atheist compared to 54 percent in a recent study. Atheism recently received a surprising endorsement when Pope Francis suggested that atheists should be accepted "as long as they did good," and that atheism was preferable to the double life led by Catholics who claimed the religion but committed "bad" acts (Suarez 2017).

Tolerance of nondominant candidates with other attributes has grown. In 2012, nine in ten respondents indicated that they would vote for an African American, Hispanic, female, or Jew. Other included groups evidenced less support; 80 percent would vote for a Mormon; 68 percent would vote for a gay or lesbian, and 58 percent would vote for a Muslim. For five of the nine religious groups in the survey, political party affiliation was not a significant factor in a person's willingness to vote for the candidate. A few party affiliations were identified; Republicans were more likely to vote for a Mormon, and Democrats were much more likely to vote for a Muslim, atheist, or gay/lesbian candidate (Jones 2012).

	Yes, would	No, would not
	%	%
Black	96	4
A woman	95	5
Catholic	94	5
Hispanic	92	7
Jewish	91	6
Mormon	80	18
Gay or lesbian	68	30
Muslim	58	40
An atheist	54	43

Gallup, June 7–10, 2012

Figure 13.3 In surveys of various demographic characteristics, people appear to be less likely to support an atheist than a woman, a person of color, or a non-Protestant

Figure 13.4 Americans are more religious than their counterparts in other developed countries. Generally, Americans want their politicians to be Protestant but not too religious. Presidents often are shown attending church services on major Christian holidays. Many Americans are reluctant to trust an atheist
Source: Steve Skjold / Alamy Stock Photo

What Interactions Are There Between Religion and Society?

Speculation regarding the relationship between religion and social trends has persisted in social science research since its inception. Research suggests that atheism is associated with intelligence and education, and that the correlation between intelligence and disbelief extends to the Greek and Roman empires (Goenka 2017). Ostensibly, intelligence is correlated with reasoning and problem-solving skills. Since education theoretically builds on these skills, obtaining higher education has notably been associated with trends towards liberal views. Graduates, and post-graduates, exhibited "consistently liberal" views on increasing multiple measures between 1995 and 2015. Political party affiliation remains consistent within the non-degreed population but has shifted for degreed groups who increasingly vote Democratic. College graduates also have more liberal social attitudes, especially in support of gender equity and gay and lesbian marriage. They also exhibit more overall value consistency. Between 1995 and 2015, there was a marked disparity in the sex ratio of college graduation with women outpacing men. The disparity is matched by a greater likelihood of liberal attitudes and Democratic party affiliation among women. Whether this is more a factor of gender or educational attainment is unclear, though the evidence points to the education differential. Additionally, liberals are taking stronger positions, a factor seemingly related to educational attainment. Political polarization is also seen in the more adamantly conservative positions of the past 20 years, a trend attributed to age as older conservatives have become even more so (Kurtzleben 2016).

Although education has generally been associated with liberalized views not all scholars agree with this appraisal. Robert Putnam, a Harvard Political Science professor, suggests that education has tremendous impact on its graduates in terms of life successes but is less convinced of its association with liberal views. He has studied the contribution of religious practices to education and values, ultimately realizing ambiguous results. Putnam suggests, after reviewing the relevant research, that youth involved with religion take harder classes, get better grades, earn higher test scores, and are less likely to drop out. When families attend church, youth have a better relationship to their parents, are more involved with sports, and with extracurricular activities. They also use less alcohol and drugs. When parents attend church, kids are 40–50 percent more likely to attend college. This may reflect some social class differences, since Putnam reports that church attendance is more characteristic of "rich" kids, whose parents have degrees, than "poor" kids whose parents do not have degrees. On the other hand, he suggests that college can have an "anti-religion" impact on youths due to an atmosphere which erodes faith, corrupts morals, and can inspire hostile attitudes towards religion (Horvat II 2015). As a consequence, although there appears to be an association between higher education achievement and liberal views, the family's religious practices can exert a mitigating influence, making religious practice significant even in less educated or affluent families.

The same assertion can be made with regard to other traits characteristic of more educated households. The college educated have widened the gap in many areas of life, including having a greater likelihood of bringing up children in a two-parent home; childrearing practices; access to good daycare; and involvement in more enrichment activities. Moreover, rich families are much more likely to eat family meals together and to help a child excel. Putnam's ultimate recommendations for strengthening family and community focus on increasing equality in society by most effective means (DeParle 2015).

Two controversial areas with respect to religion and education address school prayer and the teaching of creationism. Regulations regarding school prayer vary in different education settings. At the public university level, a prayer can be recited as long as the language omits "Jesus" and just says "God." It is thought that this can be considered a non-religious moment of reflection, as long as there is no reference to a particular religion. This is debatable, and some feel it is safer to just call for a moment of silence, because the God concept also limits the application of prayer to specific religions, omitting others. At the public high school level, a public prayer is construed as an endorsement of religion and is prohibited (DeParle 2015). Prayers are not permitted during a graduation ceremony since the activity is "coercive" and the prayer would indicate endorsement. However, students can pray before or after the event (ACLU n.d.). The presence of prayer in public school athletic events is confusing due to lack of clarity and consistency between jurisdictions. Generally, there seems to be legal provision for student athletes to voluntarily pray together in the locker room but it cannot be coach led (Smith 2015).

With respect to *human evolution and creationism*, the *National Science Teachers Association* (NSTA) strongly endorses teaching evolution as a necessary element of a science program preparing students for advanced studies. *Human evolution* suggests that *homo sapiens* emerged over the last 200,000 years from other hominids and shares ancestry with other primates (Homo sapiens n.d.; Homo sapiens A n.d.).

Creationism is the belief that all forms of life have a divine origin. The NSTA does not support the teaching of creationism in any form, including *intelligent design*. Theories of intelligent design acknowledge the highly complex elements comprising life forms but retain a belief in their cosmic origins (Milner and Maestro 2002); it is considered less specific to any one religion, reflecting a more sophisticated version of creationism (ncseadmin2 n.d.). Many science educators feel they should be protected from non- or anti-scientific approaches undermining the understanding of scientific process and critical thinking. Although 83 percent of Americans surveyed support the teaching of evolution, they are less adamant about the inclusion of creationism in non-science classes, with 17 percent supporting it as an element in a course such as philosophy. Additionally, 29 percent support evolution presented as a theory, combined with creationism introduced as a belief. With regard to legal statute, schools can teach about creationism as an element of religious belief in a descriptive rather than "devotional" fashion. Evolutionary thought is permitted as part of established science and the majority of teachers believe it should be required (Scott 2008).

Box 13.4 – Religion and the Education System

Creationism is the belief that the universe and all living organisms possess a divine origin.

Intelligent design is a modernized version of creationism, suggesting that even intelligent life emanates from a cosmic designer of supernatural, rather than human, origin.

Human evolution is the scientific belief, most notably associated with Charles Darwin, that human life evolved from other hominids and a shared ancestry with other primates.

Reproductive rights is another area impinging on the separation of church and state. Some religious groups support the teaching of "abstinence only" sex education, bypassing the discussion of related medical, health, and interpersonal issues associated with sexuality. The Guttmacher Institute is the oldest, and most comprehensive, organization studying issues of sex, sexuality, education, and reproductive issues. The following represents their summary findings regarding sex education, sexual activity, vulnerability to disease, and pregnancy (Guttmacher Institute 2016):

- Strong evidence suggests that comprehensive approaches to sex education help young people to delay sex and also to have healthy, responsible, and mutually protective relationships when they do become sexually active. Many of these programs resulted in delayed sexual debut, reduced frequency of sex and number of sexual partners, increased condom or contraceptive use, or reduced sexual risk-taking.
- Research suggests that strategies that promote abstinence-only outside of marriage while withholding information about contraceptives do not stop or even delay sex.

Moreover, abstinence-only programs can actually place young people at increased risk of pregnancy and STIs.

• No study of comprehensive programs to date has found evidence that providing young people with sexual and reproductive health information and education results in increased sexual risk-taking.

Sex education apparently contributes to positive outcomes for youths while an emphasis on abstinence can **increase** the risk of pregnancy, perhaps by leading to a lack of preparedness for any eventual sexual activity. Federal funds for abstinence-only programs are available, though they fail to address issues related to sex and health which can be considered fundamental education rights of youths (Guttmacher 2016; Stanger-Hall and Hall 2011).

More recently the *Affordable Care Act* (ACA) has been the source of religious debate, since it mandates insurance plans include free contraceptives, whether provided through private plans or as part of the ACA. The Obama administration exempted all houses of worship from this mandate but other institutions claiming religious affiliations—nonprofits, hospitals, and social service agencies—also wanted exemptions. The administration worked out a regulation establishing that the insurer, or government, would take over this responsibility if the agency submitted written notification requesting exclusion. A lawsuit, *Zubik v. Burwell*, was filed opposing this regulation. The lawsuit alleged that the policy was a violation of the Religious Freedom Restoration Act of 1993, established to protect minority religious groups from practices which might violate law. The plaintiffs claimed that compliance with the administration's written notification would result in their being complicit with contraception, against their practices and beliefs (Editorial Board 2016). The administration attempted a compromise solution but the plaintiffs were not appeased. The US Supreme Court said the government could find some other way to pay for the employees' contraception without written notification and passed the decision back to the lower courts which, in all cases but one, had ruled to accommodate the ACA mandate (Liptak 2016). This case illustrates how complicated the issues surrounding religion and the law can be and how difficult it can be to arrive at settlements to satisfy competing interests.

In the legal system, and elsewhere, religion can be a force of social stability or change. **The Religious Right**, a powerful and highly funded political entity wielding significant conservative influence since the 1980s, has been responsible for changing the political landscape. This segment of the conservative electorate represents a small minority even among the population identifying as "religious." The group's ascendancy was relatively short-lived but managed to raise significant funds to influence party politics. The organization developed in opposition to issues of reproductive rights, legalized abortion, and school desegregation. The promotion of "Christian" family values and religious-based education also were key elements in the group's efforts. Opposition to big government, taxes, LGBTQ rights, feminist demands, and other associated progressive causes also were addressed by the group. There is some disagreement about when the movement actually started but some date it to the inception of **the Moral Majority,** initiated by Jerry Falwell in 1979, while others date it from the inception of the Christian Coalition, founded by Pat Robertson in 1989. At its peak, in the mid-1990s, the Religious Right had a 26.5-million-dollar budget, two million members, and chapters in 30 states. It is credited with gaining a Republican Congress in both houses in the 1994 election. The Religious Right is credited with the rise of Republican Congressman Newt Gingrich as Speaker of the House from 1995–1998 and for many unsuccessful initiatives and legal cases to undo socially progressive changes. In 1999, it lost its 501 (c)(3) status as a tax free, nonprofit organization. The Religious Right, with its adherence to platforms of reduced taxes, a flat tax, and other platforms challenging the power of the government, contributed to the formation of the newer Tea Party faction of the Republican Party, which organized to support these initiatives. Both organizations gradually lost political clout and the divisions they incited within the Republican Party are credited with the faltering effectiveness of the party (see Chapter 12; Schlozman 2015; Murse 2017).

Box 13.5 – Religion and Politics

The Religious Right is an organization which promotes "Christian family values" and religiously based education. Generally, they are pro-life, anti-immigrant, and segregationist. The Religious Right has transitioned into the group known as the Tea Party, with a platform against raising taxes and "big government." The influence of the Religious Right peaked in the 1990s and frequently is associated with the rise of the dominance of the Republican Party in the mid-1990s.

Religion can also exert a progressive influence, as seen especially in the civil rights movement, particularly through the community activity of the southern African American churches. In addition to being places of worship and social support, the churches have been the seat of organizing efforts promoting progress in education, civil rights, and social services. Anyone interested in addressing the African American community over any issue is wise to align themselves with the churches. The centrality of the African American church as pivotal in organizing the community dates back to Reconstruction, when the churches emerged as the first African American led institutions (Building the Black Community 2003). A current example of the fortitude expressed by the African American church community can be seen by its response to the murder of eight congregants and a pastor of the Emanuel African Methodist Episcopal Church of Charleston SC in 2015 by a young White male. The community consciously chose to react with peaceful protests, promoting compassion and love and demanding changes in the racist attitudes and laws of the community. Amid national agitation regarding indifference to protecting the lives of Black Americans, the church community's response to the murders stands as an example of transcending tragedy and turning it into political action. The church leadership was successful in marshaling social activism in the removal of the confederate flag from the statehouse, retail stores, and other public places. They put principles into practice by modeling

Figure 13.5 Mourners embrace at the site of the Charleston church shooting Source: Joe Raedle / Getty Images

a nonviolent, restorative model advancing a non-racist agenda (Wertheimer 2016; Stanley 2015; Bauerlein 2015).

Nevertheless, hate crimes generally are on the rise, suggesting that religious intolerance persists. Which group do you think is most often targeted? It may be surprising to some; in 2015, 664 of the hate crimes targeted Jews, while 257 were against Muslims. However, though the portion of hate crimes against Jews is the largest, crimes against Muslims are multiplying at a faster rate, with a 67 percent increase from the incidents reported in the previous year (Ansari 2016). As a result of the terrorist world crisis and American political rhetoric, it can be predicted that the most public concerns for discrimination and violence address the Muslim population. Sentiment towards Muslims has deteriorated in the years since 9/11:

> The numbers tell a distressing tale. In October 2001, an ABC poll found that 47 percent of Americans had a favorable view of Islam. By 2010, that number had dropped to 37 percent.
>
> And today, alarmingly, only 27 percent of Americans have a favorable view of Muslim Americans. This last poll is the most concerning because it shows how my fellow Americans see my Muslim friends, colleagues and even me—because I'm Muslim.
>
> (Obeidallah 2014)

The incendiary aspects of the Muslim presence in America are pervasive. In 2016, for example, a high school in the city of Medford MA was planning to participate in "World Hijab Day" in order to encourage discussion and understanding of the Muslim faith and experience. The superintendent was enthusiastic in his support but the students, along with the superintendent, sorely misjudged community reactions. The district became deluged with complaints, fears relating to proselytizing, and a scathing *op ed* piece appeared against the celebration. Reluctantly, the Jewish superintendent, raised in Medford which is predominantly Catholic and Protestant, canceled the day. He said the organizers should have been more thoughtful in gaining community support prior to the announcement of the event. The Muslim students, though disappointed, felt that they had achieved their goal of promoting increased awareness of the Muslim American experience (Bell 2016).

Further evidence of the discomfort of American Muslims manifests in the fear of observant women regarding whether to wear the hijab in public. The hijab, a symbol of faith and values, readily identifies the women as Muslim and marks them as vulnerable to reprisals. Americans are likely to claim a non-discriminatory self-concept, identifying with a view of American culture as inclusive in the areas of race, religion, national origin, sexual orientation, and gender. Recent attacks on members of nondominant groups illuminate the gap between the ideal view of inclusion and the reality of persistent bigotry. Religious groups remain segregated. In a recent research study of diversity in religious organizations, in the majority of the 40 denominations studied about three quarters had a membership drawn from a single racial group (Lipka 2015).

What Issues Regarding Religion and Society Are Currently Emergent?

Contradictory trends have emerged with regard to religion in America. On the one hand, there is the assertion that atheism is ascendant. Some commentators have suggested that atheism will largely replace religion by 2041, as a consequence of increases in the educated and urban population and the rise of the welfare state (Sheets 2013). Other commentators suggest a different outcome, foreseeing a resurgence of religious beliefs. They cite increases in immigration and higher fertility rates among the more religiously observant. To support their view, they suggest that since religiosity is associated with higher fertility, regardless of education, income, or specific faith, the portion of the religiously affiliated is not on the decline (Sheets 2013). Proponents viewing atheism as ascendant emphasize the forecast suggesting that atheists will outnumber religious adherents, not that religion is dying (Barber 2012; Sheets 2013). Barber (2012) suggests the following factors contributing to this development: global changes in the quality of life; decreased infectious disease; increased longevity; the spread of the welfare state; and increased economic opportunities with concomitant decreases in inequality. Since the US has seen many of these changes in the post-World War II era, as well as dramatic increases in inequality in the past several decades, it is questionable whether these changes will be as significant domestically as in the developing world. What is apparent is that the religious landscape is being modified as the US becomes less Christian, less involved with organized religion, and more atheistic. American atheism is still limited, representing 3.1 percent of the population, while 4 percent report being agnostic. Atheists are more likely to be male, young, and Democratic. They also "are more likely than U.S. Christians to say they often feel a sense of wonder about the universe (54% v 45%)" (Lipka 2016). Millennials identifying as non-affiliated identify the perception that religious organizations are too involved in politics as part of the reason for their lack of affiliation (Bengston 2013). As in so many areas, there are countervailing forces, where some segments of the population appear to be moving towards being non-religious while other groups maintain a more traditional observant lifestyle.

Key Terms

Religion   Sacred/Profane   Animism   Mysticism   Monotheism   Polytheism   Ecclesia   Denomination   Sect   Cult   Pluralism   Atheism   Secular   Civil Religion   Evolution   Creationism   Intelligent Design   Religious Right   Moral Majority

---

Concept Review

What Is Religion?

Sociologists view religion as a system of beliefs and practice with distinct **sacred and profane** realms. Ritual practices generally mark entry into the sacred realm. Functionalists tend to see any system of beliefs guiding behavior as "religious," and are less likely to focus on the content. Secular beliefs can act as religions, with systems of rituals and beliefs. Theorists supporting a substantive view of religion are more likely to see inclusion of the supernatural as a necessary element of religion. The **functionalists** believe that religion is crucial to group identity and social stability. The **conflict** theorists believe that the dominant group uses religion to justify the dehumanization and denigration of the proletariat.

Animism is the belief that all life forms are imbued with spirits and can influence human society. It characterizes the beliefs in most hunting and gathering societies. Modern world religions include both **polytheistic** beliefs in many gods and **monotheistic** religions which recognize one, omniscient God. Monotheistic religions are the youngest religions.

What Types of Religious Organization Exist?

Ecclesia refers to a state religion, where civil society is organized by religion and presumed to represent all of the members. **Denominations** represent large groups of adherents to "mainstream" beliefs as in most of the Protestant, Jewish, and Islamic subgroups. A **sect** "is a relatively small religious group that has broken away from another religious organization to renew what it views as the original version of the faith" (Kendall 2012). A **cult** is a religious group with practices and teachings outside the dominant cultural and religious traditions of a society. Many current denominations originated as cults.

The US was founded on the concept of religious freedom and can be characterized as **secular** and **pluralistic**. In a **secular** society, there is no **ecclesia;** religion represents a personal choice and is not reflected in civil institutional practices. Consequently, there is a situation of *pluralism* in which no religion is salient. Some sociologists maintain that the US has a *civil religion* where the power of the society has taken on a religious fervor, providing ultimate meaning, as can be seen in the phrase, "God and country."

What Are Some of the Interactions Between Religion and Society?

Secularization is often associated with the expansion of liberal views, especially when accompanied by a college degree. Membership of the Democratic Party is often associated with education and liberalism. However, other research indicates that religiosity is correlated with higher achievement in education, and not necessarily indicative of more liberal views or political affiliation.

Religious beliefs have led to some contentious debates regarding education policies, especially in science. The teaching of scientific explanations of life based in *evolutionary* thought, as opposed to the teaching of *creationism* and *intelligent design* suggesting divine origins of life, is at the root of the controversy. Many science teachers feel that evolution should be mandated as part of the science curricula while other educators promote its inclusion as one of multiple theories.

Religious affiliation also plays a role in issues of *reproductive rights*, including access to sex education, birth control, and abortion. The ACA mandate to cover birth control and abortion has been contested by groups with religious affiliations.

What Is the Status of Religion Today?

The African American community historically has exhibited strong ties between church and community. These practices are sustained today, with the church remaining an integral organizing element in fighting for social justice causes and community unification. Observers feel that members of the general society are growing less tolerant of religious diversity, especially with respect to an increase in *hate crimes* and discrimination against Muslims. Some commentators predict an expansion in the influence of *atheism* while others predict a resurgence of *faith*. Contradictory tendencies are evident but it has been established that Americans are less likely than in the past to affiliate with a particular religious entity. How this trend will impact the social fabric is not yet understood.

Review Questions

1. Do you think religion should refer to any belief system a person adheres to, regardless of whether it is *religious* in content? Is a political belief a religion? Can nature, art, or music act as a religion?
2. Do you think animism is significantly different from modern world religions? If so, how? If not, why not?
3. Have you had a "religious" experience? Did it involve God? Can you describe it?
4. Do you think a pluralistic culture, such as we claim in the US, represents full religious inclusion of all the variations it contains?
5. Should the science curriculum teach evolution? Should it be taught as established knowledge or as theory?
6. Do you think religion should be part of the public-school curricula? Should schools address creationism? If so, in what context?
7. Should evolution be a mandated element of public school science programs?
8. Do you think that religion is an essential of American culture?
9. Do you think the government should remove the 'under God' phrase from the Pledge of Allegiance?
10. Do you think that politics should be completely independent of religious influence?

References

ACLU. (n.d.) *Religious Freedom in Public Schools*. Retrieved from http://www.aclu-tn.org/religious-freedom-in-public-schools/

Ansari, A. (November 15, 2016) FBI: Hate Crimes Spike, Most Sharply Against Muslims. *CNN*. Retrieved from http://www.cnn.com/2016/11/14/us/fbi-hate-crime-report-muslims/index.html

Ashtari, S. (May 19, 2014) Americans Would Rather Vote for a Philandering, Pot-Smoking President than an Atheist One. *Huffpost*. Retrieved from http://www.huffingtonpost.com/2014/05/19/presidential-poll-atheists_n_5353524.html

Barber, N. (April 25, 2012) Atheism to Defeat Religion by 2023. *Psychology Today*. Retrieved from https://www.psychologytoday.com/intl/comment/226062

Bauerlein, V. (July 10, 2015) Confederate Flag Removed from South Carolina Statehouse. *The Wall Street Journal*. Retrieved from https://www.wsj.com/articles/confederate-flag-removed-from-south-carolina-statehouse-1436538782

Bell, M. (May 25, 2016) 'Hijab Day' at this Boston Area High School Was Canceled, but it Got People Talking. *PRI*. Retrieved from https://www.pri.org/stories/2016-05-25/hijab-day-boston-area-high-school-was-canceled-it-got-people-talking

Bengston, V.L. (November 4, 2013) Generation Atheist! Millennials to Religion—Get out of Politics. *Salon*. Retrieved from http://www.salon.com/2013/11/04/were_raising_a_generation_of_atheists/

Building the Black Community: The Church. (2003) Retrieved from http://www.digitalhistory.uh.edu/exhibits/reconstruction/section2/section2_church.html

Carter, J. (April 27, 2017) Losing My Religion for Equality. *Theage.com*. Retrieved from http://www.theage.com.au/federal-politics/losing-my-religion-for-equality-20090714-dk0v.html

DeParle, J. (March 4, 2015) "Our Kids," by Robert D. Putnam. *The New York Times*. Retrieved from https://www.nytimes.com/2015/03/08/books/review/our-kids-by-robert-d-putnam.html?_r=0

Editorial Board (March 21, 2016) Religion and Birth Control at the Supreme Court. *The New York Times*. Retrieved from https://www.nytimes.com/2016/03/21/opinion/religion-and-birth-control-at-the-supreme-court.html

FFRF. Freedom From Religion Foundation. (n.d.) *Pledge of Allegiance*. Retrieved from https://ffrf.org/outreach/item/14030-pledge-of-allegiance

Fields, K.E. (translator/introduction) (1995) To Emile Durkheim's *The Elementary forms of Religious Life*. (Original 1912.) NY: The Free Press.

Gibbs, N., Duffy, M. (November 21, 2007) The Other Born-again President. *Time*. Retrieved from http://content.time.com/time/nation/article/0,8599,1573304,00.html

Goenka, H. (May 18, 2017) Why Do More Intelligent People Tend to be Atheist? *International Business Times*. Retrieved from http://www.ibtimes.com/why-do-more-intelligent-people-tend-be-atheist-2540302

Guttmacher Institute. (April, 2016) *American Adolescents' Sources of Information About Sex*. Retrieved from https://www.guttmacher.org/fact-sheet/facts-american-teens-sources-information-about-sex

Harari, Y.N. (2017) *Homo Deus: A Brief History of Tomorrow*. NY: Harper Collins Publishers.

Holifield, E.B. (February 15, 2014) Understanding Why Americans Seem More Religious than Other Western Powers. *Huffpost*. Retrieved from http://www.huffingtonpost.com/2014/02/15/americans-more-religious_n_4780594.html

Homo Sapiens (n.d.) Retrieved from http://www.thefreedictionary.com/Homo+sapiens

Homo Sapiens A (n.d.) Retrieved from https://www.britannica.com/topic/Homo-sapiens

Horvat II, J. (April 17, 2015) The Impact that Religion Has on Education that Teachers Are Ignoring. *TheBlaze*. Retrieved from http://www.theblaze.com/contributions/educators-ignore-the-part-religion-can-play-in-education/

Jones, J. (June 21, 2012) Atheists, Muslims See Most Bias as Presidential Candidates. *Gallup.com*. Retrieved from http://www.gallup.com/poll/155285/atheists-muslims-bias-presidential-candidates.aspx

Kendall, D. (2012) *Sociology in Our Times: the Essentials*, 8th edn. Belmont CA: Wadsworth, Cengage Learning.

King, J., Sands, G. (November 30, 2016) How the Law Protects Flag Burning in the United States. *ABC News*. Retrieved from http://abcnews.go.com/Politics/law-protects-flag-burning-united-states/story?id=43855624

Kurlander, S. (December 6, 2013) Make Recitation of Pledge of Allegiance Mandatory as an Educational Tool. *Huffpost*. Retrieved from http://www.huffingtonpost.com/steven-kurlander/american-patriotism-make-_b_4305825.html

Kurtzleben, D. (April 30, 2016) Why Are Highly Educated Americans Getting More Liberal? *NPR*. Retrieved from http://www.npr.org/2016/04/30/475794063/why-are-highly-educated-americans-getting-more-liberal

Lipka, M. (July 27, 2015) The Most and Least Racially Diverse U.S. Religious Groups. *Pew Research Center*. Retrieved from http://www.pewresearch.org/fact-tank/2015/07/27/the-most-and-least-racially-diverse-u-s-religious-groups/

Lipka, M. (June 1, 2016) 10 Facts About Atheists. *Pew Research Center*. Retrieved from http://www.pewresearch.org/fact-tank/2016/06/01/10-facts-about-atheists/

Lipka, M., Hackett, C. (April 6, 2017) Why Muslims Are the World's Fastest Growing Religious Group. *Pew Research Center*. Retrieved from http://www.pewresearch.org/fact-tank/2017/04/06/why-muslims-are-the-worlds-fastest-growing-religious-group/

Liptak, A. (May 17, 2016) Justices, Seeking Compromise, Return Contraceptive Case to Lower Courts. *New York Times*. Retrieved from https://www.nytimes.com/2016/05/17/us/supreme-court-contraception-religious-groups.html?_r=0

Marx, K. (1844) A Contribution to the Critique of Hegel's Philosophy of Right. *Deutsch-Französische Jahrbücher, 7 & 10*. Retrieved from https://www.marxists.org/archive/marx/works/1843/critique-hpr/intro.htm

McGuire, M.B. (2002) *Religion: The Social Context*, 5th edn. Belmont CA: Wadsworth.

Milner, R., Maestro, V. (eds) (April, 2002) Intelligent Design? *Natural History Magazine*. Retrieved from http://www.actionbioscience.org/evolution/nhmag.html

Murse, T. (May 26, 2017) Election Day 2016. *Thoughtco*. Retrieved from https://www.thoughtco.com/when-is-election-day-2016-3367482

Ncseadmin2. (n.d.) What Is "Intelligent Design" Creationism? *National Center for Science Education*. Retrieved from https://ncse.com/creationism/general/what-is-intelligent-design-creationism

NPR staff. (January 14, 2011) Representative Leo Ryan's Daughter Recalls his 1978 Murder. *Morning Edition*. Retrieved from http://www.npr.org/2011/01/14/132869886/rep-leo-ryans-daughter-recalls-his-1978-murder

Obeidallah, D. (September 11, 2014) 13 Years After 9/11, Anti-Muslim Bigotry Is Worse Than Ever. *Daily Beast*. Retrieved from http://www.thedailybeast.com/13-years-after-911-anti-muslim-bigotry-is-worse-than-ever

Pewforum. (May 12, 2015) America's Changing Religious Landscape. *Pew Research Council*. Retrieved from http://www.pewforum.org/2015/05/12/americas-changing-religious-landscape/

Pew Research Center. (November 16, 2009) Faith-based Programs Still Popular, Less Visible. *Pew Research Center*. Retrieved from http://www.pewforum.org/2009/11/16/faith-based-programs-still-popular-less-visible/

Schlozman, D. (August 15, 2015) How the Christian Right Ended Up Transforming American Politics. *TPM*. Retrieved from http://talkingpointsmemo.com/cafe/brief-history-of-the-christian-right

Scott, E. (2008) Cans and Can'ts of Teaching Evolution. *National Center for Science Education*. Retrieved from https://ncse.com/library-resource/cans-cants-teaching-evolution

Sengupta, S. (November 21, 2000) Carter Sadly Turns Back on National Baptist Body. *Nytimes.com*. Retrieved from http://www.nytimes.com/2000/10/21/us/

carter-sadly-turns-back-on-national-baptist-body.html?scp=6&sq=%22jimmy%20
carter%22%20baptist%20church&st=cse

Sheets, C.A. (July 24, 2013) Author Claims 'Atheism will Replace Religion' by 2041. *International Business Times*. Retrieved from http://www.ibtimes.com/author-claims-atheism-will-replace-religion-2041-1359487

Sides, J. (October 25, 2017) National Anthem Protests are Becoming More Popular. You Can Thank Donald Trump. *The Washington Post*. Retrieved from https://www.washingtonpost.com/news/monkey-cage/wp/2017/10/25/national-anthem-protests-are-becoming-more-popular-you-can-thank-donald-trump/

Smith, K. (December 11, 2015) Naperville Central Coach Told He Can't Lead Players in Prayer. *Dailyherald*. Retrieved from http://football.dailyherald.com/article/20151210/news/151219899/

Somers, M. (September 4, 2014) Under What? Poll: One Third of Americans Want God Out of the Pledge. *The Washington Times*. http://www.washingtontimes.com/news/2014/sep/4/under-what-poll-one-third-of-americans-want-god-ou/

Stanger-Hall, K.F., Hall, D.W. (2011) Abstinence-Only Education and Teen Pregnancy Rates: Why We Need Comprehensive Sex Education in the U.S. *PLoS One* 6(10): e24658. Retrieved from https://www.ncbi.nlm.nih.gov/pmc/articles/PMC3194801/

Stanley, T. (June 20, 2015) Charleston Church Massacre: Love Not Politics Will Triumph Over this Evil. *The Telegraph*. Retrieved from http://www.telegraph.co.uk/news/worldnews/northamerica/usa/11688365/Charleston-Church-massacre-love-not-politics-will-triumph-over-this-evil.html

Suarez, A. (February 23, 2017) Pope Francis News: Pontiff Slams Hypocritical Catholics, Suggests Atheism Is Better than Living Immoral Christian Life. *International Business Times*. Retrieved from http://www.ibtimes.com/pope-francis-news-pontiff-slams-hypocritical-catholics-suggests-atheism-better-living-2496887

Taylor, A. (January 21, 2016) The 'Obama is a Muslim' Conspiracy Theory Is Still Reverberating in the Middle East. *Washington Post*. Retrieved from https://www.washingtonpost.com/news/worldviews/wp/2016/01/21/the-obama-is-a-muslim-conspiracy-theory-is-still-reverberating-in-the-middle-east/?utm_term=.1e80d7690a73

Weber, M. (1963) *The Sociology of Religion*. Boston: Beacon Press, originally published 1922.

Weber, M. (1976) *The Protestant Ethic and the Spirit of Capitalism*. New York: Scribner, originally published 1904–1905.

Wertheimer, L. (June 12, 2016) 1 Year After Church Shooting, Compassion Carries Charleston Forward. *Morning Edition Sunday, NPR*. Retrieved from http://www.npr.org/2016/06/12/481750692/1-year-after-church-shooting-compassion-carries-charleston-forward.

Note

1. Definitions of sect and cult vary by sources; the one utilized here is more concise than others.

CHAPTER 14

Population,
the Environment,
and Technology

WHAT YOU WILL READ ABOUT IN THIS CHAPTER

- The developed countries have undergone a **demographic transition** characterized by both low birth and death rates. The current American birthrate is not sufficient to replace the population making the nation dependent on immigration to sustain an adequate labor force. Additionally, the characteristics of the population are shifting with more racial, ethnic, and religious diversity and an increase in the religiously "non-affiliated."

- The **immigrant** population and the children of immigrants will be a significant portion of the population and compensate for lower Native-born US fertility rates. Policies regarding immigration need to be assessed, particularly in regard to undocumented persons who arrived as children. The **DREAM** act is still a possible means for granting a path to citizenship for undocumented immigrants. Currently, childhood arrivals are protected by **DACA**, a program instituted by President Obama, currently threatened by the Republican administration.

- The **millennial generation** is now the largest group in the workforce and differs behaviorally from their parental generation. The millennials are personally liberal, generally accepting of such issues as gay marriage, transgender rights, and environmental concerns. As workers, the millennials seem to be showing a predilection for "meaningful" work or for the opportunity to bring their social concerns and personal values into the workplace. The generation, as a group, is not as financially well off, at their current ages, as their parents' generation was at the same age.

- The US will experience an increase in the elderly population as the baby boomers reach 65 and over. The **elderly** are projected to be 21.7 percent of the population by 2040. They are less likely to be poor than the elderly of previous generations and less likely to be poor when compared to the general population. The **social security** system is more stable than many people believe but the growing portion of the elderly and the shrinking portion of active workers will strain the system over the next several decades. Estimates suggest it will remain solvent for another 30 years and subsequently sustain about 75 percent of the current payout.

- The influx of immigrants from Latin America and Asia, as well as non-Christians, has highlighted issues of **race**, **ethnicity**, **diversity**, **and inclusion**. Policies pertaining to the deportation of undocumented residents, particularly those who arrived as youths, are especially urgent, considering the failure of the Congress to pass any legislation addressing immigrant reform.

- **Environmental issues**, with respect to protecting the earth's resources, requires policies to minimize the impact of modern trends. Renewable energy resources and the reduction of carbon emissions necessitate international cooperation and policy. Our manner of living, especially our dependence on fossil fuels, can be modified to minimize its environmental impact. More deliberate environmentally friendly policies can reduce carbon emissions while promoting healthier lifestyles.

- Difficult issues emerge as technology develops. The role of the automobile, especially with respect to the development of *self-driving cars* and the use of space for storage of autos, is predicted to undergo a transition. *Artificial intelligence*, or the ability of computers to think beyond what humans program them to do, is an area of concern impacting future social issues. Innovations such as *genetically modified organisms*, which are involved in food production, are an area of contention with regard to their long-term consequences. The possibility of *superbugs*, antibiotic resistant bacteria, is another development that has led to policy debates in the area of public health.

Introduction

In the coming decades, the US will undergo significant changes resulting from the changing demographics of the population, especially with respect to age, race and ethnicity, and immigration. Environmental degradation appears to be accelerating, as is the political debate surrounding it. The repercussions of varied technological innovations are also the subject of speculation, especially regarding their impact on work, the environment, and social life. These topics are the subjects addressed in this chapter.

What Demographic, or Population, Shifts are Occurring?

Many countries have undergone a *demographic transition* where both birthrates and death rates are low. This situation results in the maintenance of a stable population. Advanced societies generally have reached this stage and many developing countries are moving towards it. At the end of the eighteenth century, political economist Thomas Malthus developed a theory regarding the potential negative impact of the rapid population growth brought about by improved health conditions. He feared that population growth would far outpace food production and the water supply, posing hazards for the population. Since then, theorists have debated his thesis and it has been suggested that Malthus was incorrect in his predictions of widespread shortages, since he failed to foresee the reduced fertility made possible by birth control. Advanced industrial societies exhibit a low fertility rate; in the US the rate was 62.5 births per 1000 women of childbearing age in 2013 and 62.9 percent in 2014 (Livingston 2015). The 2015 data showed a reverse trend. Lifetime births to women today average 1.862. To sustain the population, the birthrate would have to be 2.1. The 2015 death rate increased for the first time in a decade. It is not yet clear whether this represents a new trend or an anomaly. Life expectancy decreased, with these new data, for the first time since 1993. Women live, on the average, about five years longer than men (Stein 2016). With a shrinking but aging population, the US will have to depend on immigration to maintain an adequate labor force (Adamy 2016; Shah 2015).

Figure 14.1 US Population 2015 by sex. This pattern is typical for developed countries. Previously, the population distribution was more triangular, with a wide bottom base indicating high fertility rates and lower average longevity Source: US Census Bureau, Vintage 2015 Population Estimates

The demographic profile of the US population is undergoing significant transformations which will impact the economy and social life. In the next several decades the proportion of US residents who are immigrants, or children of immigrants, will grow. The religious composition of the society will change with the proportion of people identifying as Christian decreasing, with more claiming "non"

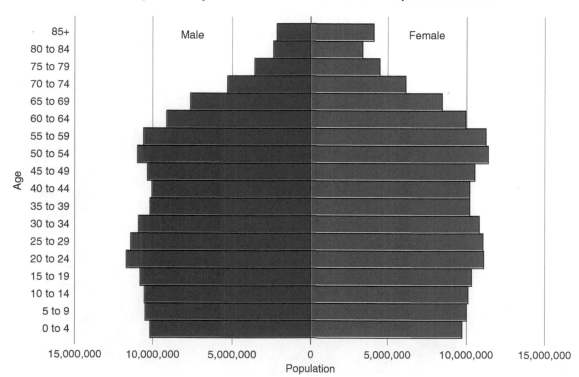

Population Pyramid of the US Total Resident Population in 2015

affiliated status. No racial or ethnic group will represent a numerical majority of the society. The proportion of elderly in the population will grow. The baby boomers are being supplanted by millennials, as the largest cohort (Cohn and Caumont 2016; Cohn 2015). Consequently, more people will join the ranks of the retired while society undergoes a decrease in workers to support them. The population will be more diverse though significant patterns of racial, ethnic, and social class segregation remain.

Immigration

American society will appear substantially changed over the next several decades. By 2044 non-Hispanic Whites will no longer be a majority of the population (Yoshinaga 2016). The foreign-born population is 14 percent but by 2065 it is projected to be 18 percent. The labor force will become increasingly dependent on immigration, and the children of immigrants. By 2055, it is predicted that the US population will be 36 percent Asian and 34 percent Hispanic (Cohn and Caumont 2016; Cohn 2015; Gonzales 2015). Currently, racial and ethnic *minorities* account for more than half of the population under the age of five and more than half of newborn babies. The US median age was 37.8 in 2015 but 28 for Hispanics. Hispanics will have a higher fertility rate than non-Hispanic Whites, because the group is younger, with one third under 18 years old (Statista n.d.; Patten 2016). Hispanic birthrates will outpace their death rates while the converse will occur among non-Hispanic Whites. While no longer a numerical majority of the population, non-Hispanic Whites will remain the dominant group since it will take some time for the shifting demographics to result in significant changes in positions of power in finance, government, business, media, and arts.

Figure 14.2 The immigrant population, and their children, will be essential to replace the population and sustain the workforce
Source: Ryan Rodrick Beiler / Shutterstock.com

Distribution of US Population by Race/Ethnicity, 2010 and 2050

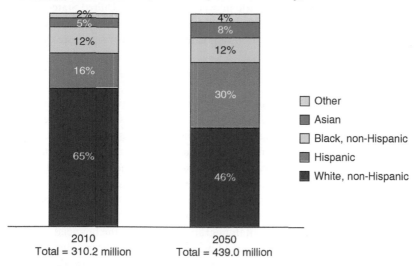

Figure 14.3 US population 2010 and 2050 by race and ethnicity, showing that by 2050 non-Hispanic Whites will no longer be a numerical majority
Source: US Census Bureau, 2008, Projected Population by Single Year of Age, Sex, Race, and Hispanic Origin for the United States: July 1, 2000 to July 1, 2050

NOTES: All racial groups non-Hispanic. Other includes Native Hawaiians and Pacific Islanders, Native Americans/Alaska Native, and individuals with two or more races. Data does not include residents of Puerto Rico, Guam, the US Virgin Islands, or the Northern Marina Islands.

SOURCE: US Census Bureau, 2008, Projected Population by Single Year of Age, Sex, Race, and Hispanic Origin for the United States: Jully 1, 2000 to July 1, 2050. http://www.census.gov/population/www/projections/downloadablefiles.html.

Assertions that today's immigration rates are extraordinary fail to consider the broader historical context. Today's rate of immigration is similar to the immigrant influx in the first half of the twentieth century. The second half of the twentieth century evidenced a lull in immigration. A significant difference concerns the regional origins of today's immigrants rather than the volume of arrivals. In the twentieth century, the majority of foreign-born persons were White, and mostly from European countries. Today's immigrant groups are much more diverse, emanating from Latin American, Asian, and African countries. Current immigration is associated with the Latino population, with substantial movement from Mexico and Latin America, though the Asian population surpassed the Latino groups as new immigrants in 2012. Currently the rate of Mexican immigration is a net zero, since as many Mexican people are returning to Mexico as are leaving it (Garcia-Navarro 2015).

As a result of changing policies in the twentieth century, 30 percent of those who are foreign born, about 11 million people, are in the US illegally:

> it is easy to forget how sudden and extraordinary our ethnic makeover has been. Americans middle-aged or older were born into a country where immigrants seemed to have vanished. As recently as 1970, the immigrant share of the population was at its lowest level on record, and the foreign-born were mostly old and white. Now the immigrant share of the population is nearing Ellis Island–era highs, and the African, Asian, and Latin American

newcomers are easily recognized as minorities. They hail from every corner
of the developing world and settle in every corner of the United States,
making new gateways out of places with no memory of huddled masses. Since
1970, the foreign-born population of greater Atlanta has risen more than
3,000 percent.

(DeParle 2013)

Debate regarding the legalization of undocumented arrivals stems from economic
and cultural fears. On the economic front, the question posed often addresses
whether immigrants pose a net gain or loss. The more compelling evidence shows,
all things being considered, the net domestic gain from immigration is small but
positive (Pro/con 2017). Immigrants contribute to the economy through labor
and property taxes, social security taxes, and purchases of goods and services.
They also are *less* likely to draw on government benefits. Other factors suggest
that the costs of public education and healthcare yield a net loss, but not a
substantial one. The highest cost of immigration may lie in the financial burden
of government pursuit of undocumented people. Expenditures for *Immigration
and Customs Enforcement* (ICE) and *Customs and Border Protection* are
18 billion dollars annually, accounting for more than the 14.4 billion dollars
spent on the combined budgets of the other four federal law enforcement agencies
(Beadle 2013). Given these costs, there are practical reasons to address policies
regarding undocumented residents. US immigrants also feed foreign economies
by annual contributions of over 400 billion dollars to their countries of origin,
representing three times the amount those countries receive in foreign aid
(DeParle 2013).

The human costs to the quality of life of non-documented residents are staggering.
Obama attempted to limit their deportations, especially in families where members'
legal statuses were mixed, by proposing the ***Development, Relief, and Education of
Alien Minors*** (or ***DREAM***) ***Act***, which would have provided a road to citizenship.
The DREAM act failed to pass because the houses of Congress could not come to
terms on a bill. Obama enacted the ***Deferred Action for Childhood Arrivals (DACA)***
in 2012 by an executive order, providing temporary protection to youths by allowing
them to continue their studies and to obtain work permits of two years' duration. The
order impacts about 1.8 million persons (AIC 2012).

Many DACA youths still live in fear of deportation, particularly in states which
have passed severe immigrant legislation. Many of the DACA youths attended
public school in the US and have no context to return to in their "homeland." Some
institutions have tried to assuage these fears. Ninety college and university presidents
called for the continuation and expansion of the DACA program, citing benefits
to the education system and to the community (Marshall 2016). The University
of California (UC) pledged to protect the educational opportunities of the DACA
students (Latimer 2016), and leaders of the UC, California State University System
(CSU) and the Community Colleges of California (CCC) have joined together to
pressure Donald Trump to allow their students to finish their studies free from
deportation (May 2016). An extension of the program, enacted by Obama in 2014,

was halted by court injunction and eventually prohibited by a 2016 Supreme Court decision (Liptak and Shear 2016).

The people who registered under the DACA program feel especially vulnerable to deportation since their information is now a part of official records (Marshall 2016). Although Obama issued executive orders to aid undocumented residents, his administration's activities were mixed since deportation reached a record number of 2.4 million immigrants during his tenure (NumbersUSA 2016; Editorial Board 2016). With his imminent departure from the presidency, Congresswoman Judy Chu asked President Obama to protect the information pertaining to the DACA registrants (Editorial Board 2016), though he did not make any mandate. In September 2017, President Trump rescinded the DACA program but added a six-month grace period to see if Congress could come to terms on an immigration policy. By suspending the revocation of the program, Trump was considered to be hedging his bets, both supporting and failing to support the *DREAMER* cohort. Although he stated that he hoped Congress would arrive at an acceptable policy, if they didn't he could extend his suspension beyond the original March 5, 2018 deadline (McManus 2017; Nakamura 2017). As of the summer of 2018, as a consequence of federal court rulings, DACA enrollees can apply for renewal but multiple cases are still pending and the Supreme Court may ultimately be the source of policy (Breisblatt 2018).

Box 14.2 – DREAM Act

The *Development, Relief, and Education of Alien Minors (DREAM)* is an initiative introduced by the Obama administration to help undocumented residents gain access to legal residence and ultimately a path to citizenship. The *DREAM* Act failed to pass because the houses of Congress could not agree upon a bill. In the meantime, the *Deferred Action for Childhood Arrivals (DACA)* was enacted by executive order of President Obama in 2012, to reduce the deportation of those who arrived here as children. This impacts about 1.8 million persons. In September 2017 Trump rescinded DACA but delayed it by suspending the revocation for six months.

One recent trend in undocumented immigrants concerns the influx of minor children and young people fleeing from Honduras, El Salvador, and Guatemala due to drug trafficking, violence, and death threats. These countries are referred to as Central America's Northern Triangle and many, as young as eight years old, have made dangerous journeys, to reach the US, unaccompanied by an adult (WOLA 2016). Due to circumstances at home, many of these youths face death or imprisonment and require refugee status. Most should be eligible for protection under the *Trafficking and Victims Protection Reauthorization Act* but fail to be screened for the program or transferred to the Office of Refugee Resettlement (AIC 2014). In 2012, only 4 percent of the people granted asylum status were youths from the three countries (Stinchcomb and Hershberg 2014). Their numbers swelled in

Figure 14.4 Bakersfield CA – March 24, 2013: Enthusiastic participants wave signs and gather to get ready to march at a rally for a new immigration law on Cesar Chavez Day
Source: Richard Thornton / Shutterstock.com

Figure 14.5 Many younger immigrants have no identity outside of being American
Source: Ryan Rodrick Beiler / Shutterstock.com

2014, dropped in 2015 and increased again in 2016. As newly arrived youths, with no attorney, these young people have a high priority status for deportation. It has been suggested that the most humane thing for the 730,000 youths in this situation would be to grant them refugee status and resettle them, rather than warehouse and

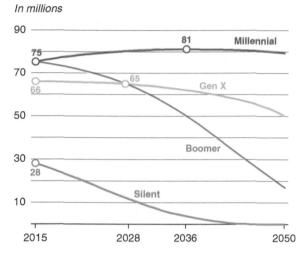

Projected Population by Generation

In millions

Note: Millennials refers to the population ages 18 to 34 as of 2015.

Source: Pew Research Center tabulations of US Census Bureau population projections released December 2014 and 2015 population estimates.

Figure 14.6 Current portions of the population by generational designation
Source: "Millennials projected to overtake Baby Boomers as America's largest generation," Pew Research Center, Washington DC (March 1, 2018), http://www.pewresearch.org/fact-tank/2018/03/01/millennials-overtake-baby-boomers/

deport them (Editorial Board 2016). Obama has been accused of abandoning the plight of the Northern Triangle youths, even as he appealed to world leaders to aid in the world refugee crises (Ordonez 2016).

Millennials

The millennial generation, born between 1981 and 1997,[1] now makes up the single largest group, representing more than one quarter of the population (Fry 2016). The millennials have overtaken the baby boomers (born between 1946 and 1964) as the largest cohort. Among the millennials, 44.2 percent identify as being something other than non-Hispanic White, as opposed to 37.9 percent of the general population. (US Census Bureau 2015). Other characteristics associated with the millennial generation include fewer two-parent families; more women who are the sole or primary family breadwinner; shifts in political party affiliation; decreased numbers identifying as Christian; fewer middle-class households; and Asians comprising the largest immigrant group (Cohn and Caumont 2016).

Box 14.3 – Millennials

The *millennial* generation refers to the generation born between 1980–2000 (though researchers utilize varying dates). This generation is now the largest cohort in the population overtaking the baby boomers, born between 1946–1964. They also comprise the biggest portion of the labor force. They tend to be progressive, especially with regard to personal issues such as gay marriage and transgender rights. They seek to find personal meaning in their work and look for employment consonant with their values. Millennials appear to be encompassing life events such as marriage, childbearing, and homebuying later in life than the boomers.

The millennials' trends are predictive of future trends in diversity and other characteristics. Millennials are less religious than previous generations and become less observant as they grow older. They are less likely to attend religious services weekly and less likely to say that religion is important in their life. As a group, they are more liberal on social and political views and more politically independent. Fifty percent of millennials do not affiliate with any political party though they are more likely to vote for Democratic Party candidates and represented a large source of support for Bernie Sanders in the 2016 campaign (Skurie and Green 2016). They are the largest group in the workforce, representing one in three workers (Fry 2015). They are less likely to be married than previous generations and more likely to marry at older ages than their parents. Cohabitation, though more common, has not replaced marriage. Surveys show that millennial women seek a husband with a secure job and similar views on childrearing as a priority. Millennial men report similar childrearing views as the most important trait in mate selection. Median hourly wages of millennials aged 25–34 are depressed, representing one fifth less than median hourly wages of their 1980 counterparts. Single women are more likely than single men to be employed; the ratio of single men with jobs to single women is 91:100. The millennials acknowledge the potential for downward mobility since 80 percent believe they will be worse off financially than their parents (Luscombe 2014; Gandel 2016).

The dominant post-World War II suburban culture was possible through the proliferation of public initiatives to build the interstate highway system, providing easy access to the city and promising a more rustic family-centered lifestyle (Schlosser 2001). Relatively inexpensive cars and gasoline, coupled with cheap housing loans, promoted the access to suburban living which became an integral part of the American Dream. Schlosser (2001) demonstrates how this phenomenon changed American family life due to easy access to fast foods. Today's suburbs are not the idyllic haven they once promised since they now exhibit the problems of poverty and housing previously associated with urban environments (Semuels 2015). Factories and businesses have relocated to the suburbs, especially as the cost of desirable urban real estate has become prohibitive.

The millennials initially appeared to prefer an urban lifestyle but recent research indicates that the search for affordable housing and quality of life has modified their earlier tendencies. Good suburban jobs, and supporting businesses and housing, have created vibrant suburban alternatives for the millennials, as major urban cities have become so gentrified as to be prohibitive for most workers. Even the most depressed areas are being taken over by youthful professionals, displacing the poor and the middle class (Pogash 2015; Garofoli and Said 2017; Rogers 2016; Wood et al. 2016; Warerkar 2016; Abbey-Lambertz 2016).

The millennials have been slower to buy cars and move to the suburbs, doing so at later ages than the boomers. They also are waiting until their thirties to have children, whether due to economics, work, or personal preference remains unclear. One third of today's homebuyers are millennials, making them the largest group of buyers, followed closely by the boomers. The millennials make up two thirds of the first-time homebuyers. A substantial group, 49 percent, are moving to the suburbs, where most grew up. Many will live a short commute to their hometowns so their parents can help with babysitting their children. They are purchasing "average" three bedrooms, two bath homes but they are buying older ones and remodeling them. They also are modifying the traditional suburb by favoring areas with a retail hub, better public transportation, more green space, good schools, and more walking potential (Safo 2016; Berger 2017).

Future technology is predicted to enhance these suburban modifications, changing the contours of suburbia. Driverless cars and drone-delivered goods, coupled with fewer commuters, are likely to result in more self-contained suburbs. Houses will be smaller, cars will be located on the periphery, since they will be utilized less often, allowing for smaller plots and less pavement. Parks and recreation, increasingly identified as a factor in home-buying decisions, will become more prevalent, along with environmental protections built into the energy use and structure of the neighborhoods (Berger 2017).

Millennials have shown some differences in leisure activities, giving more priority to international travel than previous generations and choosing different means of travel. Twenty percent of today's international tourists are young people, generating more than 180 billion dollars in annual revenues. This figure rose 30 percent between 2007 and 2015. Their travel tends to be less formal, more active, and more focused on learning about other cultures. They are more likely to camp or stay in youth hostels. They are reluctant to postpone travel until retirement since they appear skeptical about having the means to do so later in life. Less than one third of private employers are offering defined benefit coverage for retirement. One half of the millennials believe that social security will be unavailable to them and an additional 39 percent believe it will be significantly reduced. Only 6 percent believe that they will have the financial benefits of social security at the same level as their parents (Machado 2014). The focus on early travel appears to indicate the generation's attitudes towards future well-being. They do not see employment as securing their futures and they also believe that travel can help define future career paths and goals.

Other trends in leisure and recreation also are undergoing a transition, albeit one which is more worrisome. Research shows that of the 300 million people who visit national parks and recreation areas, the participation of older people and of non-Hispanic Whites is disproportionately high while the visits of nondominant group members are disproportionately low (Rott 2016; AP 2015). This brings up concerns about the future political pressures to preserve these spaces, as the portion in the population representing these non-users is growing. President Trump ordered a review of protected federal land which he asserted represented "land grabs" by previous presidents (AP 2017). In December of 2017, Trump announced that he will cut the Bears Ears monument in Utah by 85 percent, and the Grand Staircase

Figure 14.7 Bryce
Canyon National Park
Source: silky /
Shutterstock.com

Escalante National Monument by almost half. These acts are likely to be contested by environmentalist and Native Nations. He also is promoting other changes which will allow for logging and commercial fishing in previously protected areas (Turkewitz 2017).

The national parks are typically underutilized by youths and members of nondominant groups. Park policies are constructing programs to engage more groups, recognizing that park maintenance depends on such engagement (McClurg 2016). One program offers internships to high school students to get them involved in outdoor activities they might not otherwise be exposed to. Park personnel are actively recruiting nondominant youths to these programs which emphasize recreational use. Another example is the free park buses running from SF to the Golden Gate National Park Recreation Area.

In 2015, the millennials became the largest group in the labor force, though participation dropped for the youngest group, aged 20–24. There is no clear-cut explanation for this but it could be that the older workers are prolonging work life rather than retiring, so there are fewer openings available. It also has been suggested that increased minimum wages affect young and inexperienced workers more than others by reducing available jobs (Gandel 2016). Today's jobs earn millennials less than their counterparts earned ten years earlier. In the past several decades, the age at which a person obtained the median wage increased from 26 to 30. Full time employment of high school graduates declined 13 percent in this time period while it declined 8 percent for college graduates. The average student loan debt is $33,000 though the debt is not spread evenly among the young since the affluent can emerge from college without debt and make the debt load seem distributed more widely than it actually is (Goodman 2015).

With regard to work, the millennials are oriented towards community service and bringing their values to the workplace. They express a strong desire to find "happiness and fulfillment" and consequently are not committed to following a traditional career trajectory. The millennials view work as a significant contributor to self-concept. Eighty-eight percent said that a positive culture at work was essential to their dream job and 58 percent said they would accept a 15 percent pay cut to work in a company with values like their own. The millennials seek a strong work–life balance and suggest that the *American Dream* for them is not only about alleviating constraints of sex, race, and class but about promoting lifestyle options. The educated millennials value ethical companies and the ability to contribute to decision making at work and are more likely to seek this type of employment (Solomon 2016; Millennials at work... 2011). Money alone is not enough to motivate millennials when personal values are at stake. Sixty percent of millennials age 22–32 changed jobs in the period 2010–2015, sometimes looking for a more satisfying situation, even at the cost of lost income or security (Fortune 2016). Situations where choices and personal values are pre-eminent are more characteristic of the affluent or the well-educated, since lower level workers have fewer opportunities to apply these options. The unemployment level of the millennial cohort is 8 percent while young people with bachelor's degrees have only a 3.8 percent unemployment rate (Pew Research Center 2014). Nevertheless, against the backdrop of reduced economic resources, the generation has maintained optimism and shows liberal attitudes towards personal life choices, such as sexual orientation and marriage (Foley 2014).

Figure 14.8 The national and state parks need to attract more diverse youth to participate in the park utilization and provide for activists to assure the continuity of the parks Source: Jacob Lund / Shutterstock.com

Millennial Work Ethos

The Millennial Impact Project, begun in 2009, studied millennials working at nonprofits:

- Millennials engage with causes to help other people, not institutions.
- Millennials support issues rather than organizations.
- Millennials prefer to perform smaller actions before fully committing to a cause.
- Millennials are influenced by the decisions and behaviors of their peers.
- Millennials treat all their assets (time, money, network, etc.) as having equal value.
- Millennials need to experience an organization's work without having to be on site.

(Feldman et al. 2014)

In the fifth year, the Project switched from studying millennials in nonprofits to looking at work in the private sector. Using an online survey, the researchers received 1514 completed surveys from young workers in 300 different companies. The researchers were satisfied that they had a representative sample ("99% confidence interval with a 3.3% error rate"). Fifty-six percent of the respondents were women and 44 percent were men. The researchers report that the millennials' interests and service orientation extended to private companies. The primary motivations for initial job applications concerned what a company did or what product it offered, coupled with salary and benefits. An additional consideration was the corporate culture of the company. After these, the millennials articulated company concern for causes and social issues. Ninety-two percent of millennials felt that they were contributing to a company which was making a positive impact on the world. Eighty-seven percent of respondents felt encouraged to volunteer or participate in the company's cause. Women and men respondents each donated to a nonprofit, though women were somewhat more likely than men to do so, 91 percent to 84 percent respectively. Forty-four percent of the respondents joined a companywide service project and 44 percent volunteered their skills to help a cause; 47 percent of these volunteered with a team or department from work. When asked what they would like to see more of, more than half, 57 percent, of respondents wanted to increase volunteer days. The second type of initiative Millennials wanted more of was a company-sponsored sabbatical, or a temporary (paid) break from work to volunteer or serve with a cause, suggesting a one- to two-month sabbatical after five years at the company. The third type of cause programming Millennials identified as desirable were projects they could do with their department, or team, to benefit a cause (Feldman et al. 2014).

The Elderly Population

As the boomers become overtaken by the millennials in the workforce, they will swell the portion of the elderly population, defined as 65 and older. The elderly are 14.5 percent of the population and are estimated to be 21.7 percent by 2040 (ACL n.d.). Issues of aging are becoming more prominent. Even as people are living healthier longer, how to help aging persons, especially as they become frail, is one area largely unaddressed by social policy. Often a family is left to make decisions for themselves with very little institutional support. Institutionalization is relatively uncommon, with 1 percent of young elderly (65–75), 3 percent of middle elderly (75–84), and 10 percent of older elderly (85+) in some kind of group setting. The increasing number of families with independent elderly members has focused attention on how to support the elderly in their homes, especially for those who live alone. Most elderly desire to remain at home which is more satisfying, and cost effective, than the alternatives (IOA 2014).

Box 14.4 – The Elderly

The baby boomers are swelling the portion of the elderly in the population, currently at 14.5 percent. On the whole, the boomers are healthier and living longer than in previous generations. Their longevity has led to more questions regarding issues of older old age, especially with respect to long-term illness and end of life care. As a group, the elderly are less likely to live under the official poverty level than other groups. The **supplemental poverty measure**, which utilizes the actual cost of living including medication, healthcare expenses, housing, and utilities, doubles the official figure for the impoverished elderly.

The well-being of the elderly over the past 35 years has improved but problems remain. The elderly poverty rate is 12 percent, making them less likely to be poor than in previous generations as well as less likely to be officially poor than people in other age groups (KFF 2015). The poverty rates of the elderly become more significant if the *supplemental poverty measure* (SPM) is utilized rather than the official *federal poverty level*. The supplemental level addresses the actual costs of living, such as medication, medical treatments, and housing. The following examples illustrate different rates of poverty utilizing each method:

- John, age 70, lives alone and owns a home with a mortgage in Louisville, Kentucky. In 2013, John's sole source of income was $17,500 in Social Security benefits and he incurred $8,000 in out-of-pocket medical expenses that year. **Under the official measure of poverty**, John is not counted as living in poverty because his $17,500 income in 2013 was higher than the nationwide official poverty threshold of about $11,200 for an elderly individual who lives alone. **Under the SPM**, however, John IS counted as being in poverty, because his high medical expenses are deducted from his income, leaving resources of $9,500.

Figure 14.9 The hands of an older person; the aging population is increasing as boomers reach 65 and older
Source: Gitanna / Shutterstock.com

This amount is less than the SPM poverty threshold for a homeowner with a mortgage living alone in Louisville (about $10,700).

• Doris, age 85, is a widow and rents an apartment in Miami, Florida. In 2013, her sole source of income was $12,000 in Social Security benefits, and she spent $500 on out-of-pocket medical expenses. **Under the official measure,** Doris is not counted as living in poverty because her $12,000 income is higher than the $11,200 official poverty threshold for an elderly person living alone. **Under the SPM,** Doris IS counted as being in poverty because she lives in an area with a high cost of living. Doris's resources under the SPM are $11,500 (deducting her medical expenses from her income), which is less than the SPM poverty threshold for single renters living in Miami (about $13,400) (KFF 2015).

Nine states have SPMs that are twice as high as the official poverty level (Cubanski et al. 2015). If the SPM is double the official poverty rate, 45 percent of the elderly fall below the figure. This figure more nearly represents individuals functionally at risk of failing to meet basic needs. By either measure, women are more likely to be counted as poor, as are people over 80, who also are more likely to be women. The poverty rate for elderly Hispanics is three times that for Whites and the level for elderly Blacks is two and half times that of Whites.

Many elderly persons depend on the social security system to support their old age, though there are significant segments of the elderly who have retirement plans or pensions through their jobs. The financial reality for those who depend solely on social security is tenuous:

Consider that nine out of ten Americans 65 and older are receiving Social Security. And the average monthly Social Security benefit for those 65 and older is $1,262. Many receive much less than that.

According to the Social Security Administration, 53% of married couples and 74% of those unmarried receive 50% or more of their income from Social Security.

Further, 23% of married couples and about 46% of unmarried seniors rely on Social Security for 90% or more of their income.

The median income for seniors 65–74 is $36,320; if you're over 74 that drops to $25,417 according to the U.S. Census Bureau. And 12% of those 65 and older are living at the poverty level.

(Hawkins 2013)

The social security system has been the subject of much speculation concerning its viability as the baby boomers retire and the ratio of working adults to retirees falls. Even with the estimate that 40 percent of all workers will work beyond the age of 65, by the year 2030 it is projected that there will be three workers for each retiree, down from about five workers presently (Ezrati 2014; Solman 2013).

Analysis indicates that the viability of the Social Security system is not as precarious as is sometimes portrayed. The social security trust, the invested funds that the government utilizes to cover any shortfall in the money collected and paid out annually, will last until 2034. At that time, it is estimated that annual contributions will permit people to receive social security at a level of about 75 percent of the current payout, according to the Social Security Administration. The Congressional Budget Office, in contrast, estimated that the shortfall might be seen as early as in 2025 and predicts the trust fund to be dry by 2033 (Vernon 2013). Whichever estimate is more accurate, the American population must conduct accurate needs assessments and plan accordingly. Most jobs are cutting pension contributions at a

Figure 14.10 Older women are more likely to be poor than older men
Source: michaelheim / Shutterstock.com

time when employers, and the government, would be wise to incentivize retirement savings. The political parties are divided on this issue. The Republicans are more likely than the Democrats to support cutbacks in social security (Waldman 2015). The private sector generally is less likely than the public sector to support pension funds though these also are facing reductions and even elimination.

Housing is frequently the most significant obstacle to well-being for the elderly. In large cities, such as San Francisco and New York, it is especially difficult to find affordable housing. The rising cost of housing, however, has spread to areas formerly more accessible. Those who are eligible for subsidized housing often find that wait lists are extensive. Former President Jimmy Carter, an active participant in *Habitat for Humanity*, has said that the housing crisis is worse now than at any time in recent history (Rivero 2016). A person is considered cost burdened if they pay more than 30 percent of their income for housing, since that level of expenditure makes it uncertain whether they will be able to meet other basic needs. The US Department of Housing and Urban Development's website states: "A family with one full-time worker earning the minimum wage cannot afford the local fair-market rent for a two-bedroom apartment anywhere in the United States" (HUD n.d.).

The health expenses of the elderly represent the other major area of financial stress. Many older people are living into their 70s and 80s, making the group larger and healthier than in previous generations of seniors. Nevertheless, two thirds of the over age 65 population will experience multiple chronic conditions (Editorial Board n.d.).

Keeping Older Americans at Home

It costs an average of $6700 per month to maintain a person in a nursing facility. For low-income people, much of the cost is absorbed by Medicaid. Many people prefer to remain at home for as long as possible, especially if they feel safe. A federally funded pilot project with low-income elderly in Baltimore facilitated remaining in the home by modifying the physical environment and providing access to supportive services. The highly successful project, *Community Aging in Place, Advancing Better Living for Elders* (CAPABLE), provided each participant a budget of $4000 to employ nurses, occupational therapists, and handymen. Working on the assumption that many of the problems older people face are not really caused by disease but by the consequences of disease, such as shakiness associated with Parkinson's disease, the project sought to address the ensuing problems. Adjustments can be made to limit the potential harm of these conditions. For example, a weighted drinking cup can help a person to drink without fear of spilling or dropping the drink. Fixing ripples in linoleum can provide stability in walking. Monitoring a person's medication use and setting up ways of assuring compliance with scheduling can be determined for each case and supervised by a visiting nurse. Simple exercises can be practiced to support balance and mobility, resulting in a greater likelihood that a person can stand in the kitchen to boil water or prepare a simple meal. Improvements in the bathroom, which along with the kitchen is considered a problem area, can be accomplished by providing a seat in a shower or modifying a toilet. In an analysis of the program's success, the outcomes suggest that implementing these types of interventions can reduce facility admissions by 40 percent. It was also suggested that the *Affordable Care Act* can financially support these programs since programs using federal money to improve medical outcomes and save money fall under the Act and do not require Congressional approval (Drevitch 2013).

End of life care is the healthcare segment representing the greatest financial burden. Twenty-five percent of annual Medicare spending is distributed among the 5 percent of patients in the last year of life, concentrated mostly in the last few months (Gawande 2010). As the baby boomers age, the demand on the Medicare budget may become impossible to sustain. It will become crucial to examine a person's desire to undergo treatments to prolong life, especially if they are to be accompanied by decreased life quality and minimal gains. A majority of Americans, 57 percent, support stopping treatment if they would be in a lot of pain and their condition would be considered incurable, while 35 percent surveyed reported wanting intervention to stay alive as long as possible. White Americans are less likely to prolong life under these conditions than other race and ethnic groups.

There is evidence that many patients want to have a more informed say regarding treatment. Surveys of terminal patients indicate that their top priorities are to avoid suffering, to spend time with family, to be touched, to be mentally aware, and to not be a burden. Facilitating these goals might be the best way to help the dying; many

Figure 14.11 An older woman and her nurse
Source: Alexander Raths / Shutterstock.com

interventions, including newly "improved" treatments, have very modest impact on the time gained from their use and frequently severely compromise the quality of life (Dubner 2016). Many people might elect to skip these and just enjoy their remaining time. Hospice services help the terminally ill to live the fullest life possible for that remaining time. Hospice does not facilitate death, as some people think, but provides support around healthcare decisions by offering palliative measures to enhance quality of life. Sometimes helping dying persons to live better for the time thought to remain actually has prolonged their life beyond the prognosis (Gawande 2010). The majority of Americans, 62 percent, favor the right to suicide and this group is more likely to identify as "religiously unaffiliated." The population is more evenly split on the issue of doctor-assisted suicide, with 47 percent approving of it and 49 percent disapproving (Hafiz 2011). Five states (in 2016) legally permit physician-assisted suicide (Livio 2016). More comprehensive policies will likely be developed as the elderly population expands.

What Are the Environmental Threats to Human Society?

Recognized threats to the environment include air and water pollution; global warming and climate change; depletion of natural resources; waste disposal; loss of biodiversity; deforestation; ocean acidification; urban sprawl; chemical toxins; and genetic engineering. Proposals for conservation measures to assure the sustenance of public lands, water, and forests for public use began in the early twentieth century. Early proponents of environmental preservation included such activists as John Muir, Gifford Pinchot, and President Teddy Roosevelt. Organizations such as the Sierra Club (1892) and the National Parks (1916) were developed in this period (Shabecoff 1989). They were able to accomplish significant legislation regarding issues of population, energy, pollution, and climate. It took several more decades for these concerns to be expressed in popular consciousness.

The 1960s initiated a period of greater attention to environmental threats and the need to respond to these with national and international policies. Programs addressing these issues were initiated in the post-World War II era, when the first water quality legislation was passed (1948). Attention was also focused on the disappearance of butterflies in NJ and illnesses stemming from industrial smog emissions (1949), all leading to the first air pollution conference in 1950. By the 1960s concerns over automobile emissions, endangered species, pollution, population pressures, energy issues, and oil spills promoted a more active movement and initial widespread public awareness of the dangers posed to the environment and the *ecosystem*. The ecosystem is defined as "all humans, plant life, mountains, glaciers, atmosphere, rocks, galaxy, massive oceans and seas. It also includes natural resources such as water, electric charge, fire, magnetism, air and climate" (Ecosystem n.d.). In April 1970, the first *Earth Day* was held and the Nixon administration established the US Environmental Protection Agency, ratified by Congress. The energy crisis, initiated by the Arab Oil Embargo of 1973–1974, highlighted the urgency of reducing the use of oil and gas and the need to be more self-sufficient. **Global warming** refers to the increased temperature of the earth's surface as a result of greenhouse gasses.

Carbon dioxide, and other compounds contributing to air pollutants, trap the heat from solar radiation in the earth's atmosphere, raising the average temperatures. The resulting climate changes cause disruption in the production of food by changing temperatures and weather patterns and by melting icecaps and raising the sea levels (MacMillan 2016). These trends highlight the need to limit emissions from fossil fuels such as coal, natural gas, and oil. Early attention to these environmental threats resulted in President Jimmy Carter (1977) promoting an energy plan to reduce consumption of fossil fuels and to establish the goal of achieving 20 percent of the energy supply from renewable sources. In 1977, President Carter established the US Department of Energy as a cabinet-level department.

Major crises occurring in this earlier period brought media attention to environmental issues. In 1978 the plight of residents of *Love Canal* in upstate NY directed attention to the harmful potential of chemical dumping. With government approval, the Hooker Chemical Company had dumped some 21,000 tons of chemical waste into a partially dug canal from 1942–1953. In the late 1970s, heavy rains caused flooding of basements and playgrounds and resulted in a proliferation of illnesses, birth defects, and miscarriages in the resident population. By 1978, President Carter declared a state of emergency and 239 families were evacuated; another 700 were deemed not at sufficient risk to justify evacuation though they likely suffered some consequences from the exposure (Geneseo n.d.).

Another major environmental incident, promoting popular awareness of environmental threats, concerned the 1979 meltdown at the *Three Mile Island* nuclear plant in Pennsylvania, leading to the evacuation of 140,000 people and taking ten years to "clean up." The fear resulting from the accident led to massive demonstrations in New York City and to the reduction, and ultimate elimination, of nuclear power plant construction (History.com n.d.).

Figure 14.12 Three Mile Island nuclear plant sustained a meltdown in 1979
Source: A.L. Spangler / Shutterstock.com

Figure 14.13 Environmental activism has highlighted concerns for the future
Source: Rena Schild / Shutterstock.com

Box 14.5 – The Environment

The ecosystem refers to all the living things in an environment and all the processes and resources which support these. This would include mountains, oceans, animals, plant life, glaciers, the atmosphere, and other natural resources.

Global warming refers to the significant rise in earth's surface temperatures and the need to reduce fossil fuels which promote air pollution, trapping heat into the earth's atmosphere. Policies limiting the emission of carbons emanating from fossil fuels are necessary to arrest and reduce global warming.

Environmental racism is the disproportionate exposure to hazards suffered by nondominant groups, particularly communities of color and poor communities.

With the 1980 election of President Ronald Reagan, fear spread that he would sell off public land and resources to private enterprises, thus further adding to environmental deterioration. The worst fears regarding President Reagan's environmental policies did not emerge. He did not sell off public land nor did he impose deregulations regarding energy use, as some had predicted. Early in his administration he did slash budgets and seemed to be attacking environmental protective legislation but personnel changes resulted in the eventual "moderation" of his administration's activities. Although his administration did not dismantle protective measures previously enacted, it was characterized by a disregard for attacking problems of pollution, acid rain, toxic waste, and the water supply (Shabecoff 1989). By the end of his administration, heightened concerns regarding the severity and sources of environmental threats incited new activist groups and encouraged more media focus on these (Shabecoff 1989).

By the 1990s, awareness of environmental dangers had become more prominent in the public sector, accompanied by demands for personal and policy changes. The extent of global warming and climate change was gaining recognition, as was the possibility of catastrophic accidents resulting from lack of regulation and safety measures, as seen for example in the *Exxon Valdez* oil spill of 1989. The Valdez accident resulted in the release of 11 million gallons of oil, killing a quarter of a million birds and covering 1300 square miles in Prince William Sound in Alaska. More than 25 years later, the beaches are still polluted and there is oil just below the surface (Taylor 2014).

The 2010 *British Petroleum* oil spill was even worse, with some 130 million gallons leaking from an oil rig into the Gulf of Mexico, and killing 11 people. The ultimate extent of the damages to the ecology of the Gulf is impossible to calculate. The effects of erosion along 1000 miles of shoreline are long term and the consequent decimation to local livelihoods severe (Gallucci 2015). After this era, environmental activism gained steam and became more integrated into political discourse (see below).

What is Environmental Racism?

Environmental racism refers to the disproportionate exposure to hazards suffered by nondominant groups, particularly in communities of color and poor communities. These dangers include exposure to chemical toxins, radiation, pesticides, and other agents which harm the health of the community through air pollution, water contamination, or ingestion in products of local farming. The issue of environmental racism is intimately tied to combatting climate change since it is frequently the nondominant groups whose access to food, water, and jobs is most at risk (Espinosa 2016). The 134 million Americans who live closest to chemical facilities are 75 percent more likely to be Black, 60 percent more likely to be Latino, and 50 percent more likely to be poor than the general population (Atkin 2014). Native Americans are also disproportionately at risk. Just a few examples can illustrate the exposure suffered by these communities. One example, against Native Americans, concerns the mining of uranium on the 27,000 square mile Navajo reservation from 1944 to 1986. This land covers territories in Utah, New Mexico, and Arizona and was home to over 500 mines owned by multiple companies which supplied the government with the mineral. Many miners died from respiratory ailments, cancer, and kidney failure, all conditions which have been linked to uranium contamination. The fallout can still be seen in babies today and is likely due to water and livestock contamination and other consequences from *tailings*, referring to the residue resulting from mines that were never sealed. In a recent study, well after the departure of the mining companies, 27 percent of the participants showed uranium in their urine, compared to a national average of 5 percent (Morales 2016; Frosch 2009).

Another long-term exposure, affecting a large population, was discovered in an investigation into a breast cancer cluster of 77 men, all of whom had been at Camp Lejeune, a former military base active in North Carolina from the 1950s to the 1980s (Williams 2012). Typically, there might be one case of male breast cancer for every 100 women diagnosed with it, which is why this localized cluster, inadvertently discovered, ultimately drew the attention of researchers. One person with the diagnosis went public wondering if there was also a link with his disease, after seeing a television report linking toxic chemicals used at the military base to rates of leukemia and birth defects. Accounting for military personnel, their families, and local civilians, over 750,000 people were exposed to the water supply at the camp, which was used for drinking, bathing, swimming, and cooking. The hazardous chemicals included the degreaser *benzene*, a known carcinogenic agent, which was found in the well water; in one case, it registered 76 times the federal limit. Other chemicals identified were *chlorinated solvents*, also known to be carcinogenic, which are implicated in birth defects in the offspring of people exposed to them. The chemical agents *trichlorethylene* (TCE) and *perchloroethylene* (PCE) were used as degreasers before being dumped at a nearby site. These substances had a history of utilization in pet food, decaffeination of coffee, wound disinfection, and obstetrical anesthesia but were discontinued. TCE is thought to contaminate between 9–34 percent of local water supplies today. The military was slow to respond. It is engaged in epidemiologic research to determine if there are significant health differences when comparing Camp Lejeune residents with a control group who lived in, or near, California's Camp Pendleton. Even if differences are documented, it is difficult to definitively attribute them to any specific cause. Though the military is a government agency, its enlisted ranks tend to be among lower social classes and nondominant groups and have been utilized in studies testing the effects of various substances. Experimental exposure to toxins has been conducted without the informed consent of the participants. Some experiments were completely unrevealed to the participants, who sometimes were selected on the basis of race. Other experiments were voluntary but crucial information was withheld from the participants (Dickerson 2015; 2015a):

> The armed forces, of course, have a long history of making their uniformed ranks sick. There was ionizing radiation from various nuclear detonations, Agent Orange in Vietnam, Gulf War Syndrome, and, most recently, burn pits spewing dioxin and other toxins in the Iraqi outback. In each case, Congress has had to compel the Department of Defense to study the resulting illnesses and offer redress to the troops. At Lejeune, Partain and Ensminger fault the military for shutting down its tainted wells too late, failing to disclose the full extent of the pollution, and denying benefits to sick Marines. To date, Lejeune vets have filed more than 2,100 medical claims, many for illnesses like non-Hodgkin's lymphoma, kidney and bladder cancer, and cirrhosis of the liver, which have known or suspected links to the solvents found in Lejeune's wells. The Veterans Administration has approved only 25 percent of the claims it has reviewed.
>
> (Williams 2012)

Other government entities, outside the military, also have been a source of abusive practices. A highly publicized recent case of negligent exposure to harm concerns the city water supply of Flint Michigan. The news that the Flint water supply, having been diverted from Lake Huron to the Flint River to save money, was sickening the largely African American population of the city through lead poisoning was made even more dramatic by revelation of its apparent cover up by state officials (McCoy and Connor 2016). Residents reported that the water had a bad smell, taste, and color. There is sufficient evidence to show that knowledge regarding the dangers in the water had been covered up for 18 months while the citizens were still being exposed. The first alert was from a local pediatrician who noticed an increase in rashes and hair loss. She examined records of blood lead levels in local toddlers, which are required by federal laws, and found that they were doubled and, in some cases, tripled. In response to her alarm, she initially was labeled as causing "near hysteria," though several weeks after her findings were made public the city was returned to water supplied by Lake Huron. The change to the Flint River had been a cost-cutting strategy after the city had been declared, in 2011, to be in a financial state of emergency. Even so, at that time a report indicated that the pipes were corrosive and that they could be fixed by an additive at the cost of $100 a day which would have avoided 90 percent of the water-related problems (Ganim and Tran 2016). Long-term effects of lead exposure cause lowered mental faculties, projected to cost over 400 million dollars to support the estimated 8000 Flint children affected (Sanburn 2016). This situation, perpetrated on the citizens of Flint, has been attributed to "viewing people in Flint as expendable" (McCoy and Connor 2016).

Another recent project which received much media attention concerns the proposed route of the Dakota Access Pipeline. The Dakota Access Pipeline is a project of a large energy company based in Texas. The 3.7-billion-dollar project will transport 470,000 barrels of crude oil a day across 1200 miles from North Dakota to Illinois. The intended route would run close to the water sources on the Standing Rock Sioux reservation. The Sioux protested the route, asserting the health threat to their community from potential leaks which would contaminate their water supply. In the last days of the Obama administration, fears regarding the Dakota Pipeline were made more real when another pipeline in North Dakota, the Belle Fourche, was discovered by a local landowner to have leaked 180,000 gallons of crude oil. Authorities have maintained that this older pipeline was riskier than the newer pipeline which will contain technological safeguards not incorporated into the Belle Fourche facility, though the Sioux remain unconvinced (Paterson 2016).

Additionally, the pipeline would disturb burial sites sacred to the Sioux, adding to the cultural disregard of the group. The company asserted the overall safety of the project, citing minimal risk of a leak, but the Sioux remain committed to stopping the pipeline. The course of the pipeline was redesigned from its original route, north of Bismarck, due to resident protests regarding fears of water contamination (Amy Dalrymple Forum News Service 2016). The company's alternate route, along the reservation, was allegedly chosen to minimize the risk as it is less densely populated. In December 2016, after five months of intensive protest, President Obama ordered the U.S Army Corps of Engineers to suspend construction and conduct a more thorough environmental review, and to consider rerouting it (McKenna 2017; BBC 2017). Even with continued protests, permission to finish that area of the pipeline was mandated by an executive order signed by Donald Trump (McKenna 2017; Eilperin and Dennis 2017). Despite continuing protests by the Sioux and a pending federal lawsuit, oil began flowing through the pipeline in June 2017 (Kennedy 2017).

Activist protests regarding the pipeline have incited the largest Indigenous organizing effort in over 100 years. Eighteen months of activity, with thousands living in collective camps representing Native and non-Native communities, led to the protest being considered the largest contemporary action for sovereign rights and environmental justice (McKenna 2017). Demonstrators were met with dozens of arrests leading to accusations of excessive force by the authorities (BBC 2017). The Native groups remain adamant in their opposition but the Standing Rock Sioux suffered financial devastation as a result of the protest, and with the pipeline in operation they are trying to move on (McKenna 2017).

What Measures Can Be Taken to Address Environmental Issues?

Carbon emissions are the major contributor to **global warming** and are a result of burning gas, oil, and coal. Historically, carbon dioxide is naturally absorbed by plants and trees but the rate of burning of fossil fuels has caused the carbon dioxide to be trapped in the earth's surface atmosphere, creating a greenhouse effect and raising the temperature of the earth. The US has the third highest per capita rate of carbon dioxide emissions and accounts for 16 percent of world emissions, much greater than our 5 percent of the world population (Statista 2017; UCS n.d.). Fossil fuels have accounted for 80 percent of the US energy source since 1900 (EIA 2015). The reduction in these sources and replacement with renewable energy sources is the best tactic for reducing global warming. State and federal governments frequently have been blocked from passing more aggressive bills to limit carbon emissions or to impede developments in *"dirty" energy*.

The Paris Climate Change Conference (December 2015) was the most progressive international initiative to address the intensifying threat of climate change. It was the first instance of a universal, legally binding agreement involving 195 countries. General principles agreed upon during the conference included a commitment to reduce global warming and sustaining conditions supporting that goal; a plan to meet every five years to review and innovate programs; international support of developing countries; and a commitment to dedicate 100 billion US dollars to aid in supporting climate stabilization (European Commission n.d.). In June 2017 President Trump reaffirmed his commitment to withdraw from the Paris Agreement. The US is the only developed country which will fail to participate. In June 2017 Trump withdrew the US support of the climate accord (Mooney 2018).

On the domestic front, the Obama administration developed programs promoting environmental goals. One bill established increased fuel efficiency for automobiles and trucks. Obama also successfully passed the Clean Power Plan to cut emissions from power plants. His 2009 energy loan program increased the funding for projects developing innovation in renewable energy. This was supported by extension of the administration's Energy Policy Act of 2005 with funding from the American Recovery Act. Out of these programs the largest solar farm in the world opened in Arizona in 2014, with 5.2 million solar panels. The programs have facilitated development of *renewable energy* projects, using energy from the sun, earth's heat, wind, and biofuels from food that can be replaced without limit. Obama's loan program, even with some projects' failures, has turned a profit and led to the development of improved energy-efficient automobile engines and completely electric-powered cars. The alternative of electric cars is gaining a foothold in mainstream America (Editorial Board 2017).

Figure 14.14 Harnessing the energy of the wind represents a renewable energy
Source: pedrosala / Shutterstock.com

Figure 14.15 A solar oven
Source: M Cornelius / Shutterstock.com

Many more of these programs are required to reach the goal of 80 percent reduction of greenhouse gas pollution by 2050 (Biello 2015).

Box 14.6 – Energy Resources

Renewable energy refers to biofuels that can be replaced without limits, such as energy from wind or the sun. These sources are not only infinite but produce clean energy.

Dirty energy is energy that produces carbon emissions which pollute the air and contribute to *global warming*, or the increased temperatures which will change the ecology so that growing seasons and geography will alter, as will the sea levels.

Hydraulic fracturing/fracking occurs with deep drilling to release natural gas. It is accomplished by the utilization of highly pressurized combinations of water, sand, and chemicals to break apart the shale and release the gas. Fracking is thought to be cleaner than coal production but not as environmentally beneficial as renewable energy. Potential dangers, especially to the groundwater, associated with fracking are the source of opposition to the process.

Cap and trade programs limit the carbon emissions from one source. The program allows companies with reductions in emissions to sell their carbon emission "surplus" to other entities. Federal efforts to pass *cap and trade* have so far been unsuccessful.

The *environmental justice movement* refers to grassroots, or community-based efforts, to promote policies of environmental protection, with particular focus on the consequences of pollution or toxins sustained within a community. The efforts generally incorporate multiple local agencies to create better living and environmental conditions.

The use of *fracking*, referring to *hydraulic fracturing*, which has proliferated in some areas since the 1990s and currently is used in 21 states, has been considered a means to reducing carbon dioxide emissions. Intensive debates have erupted over its implementation (Hirji and Song 2015). The process, developed 65 years ago, entails deep drilling into the earth utilizing a highly pressurized mix of water, sand, and chemicals to break apart shale and release natural gas. This process allows for access to deeply embedded reserves of oil and gas. Support for fracking stems from the ability of fracking to reduce carbon dioxide emission levels associated with coal burning, and to the creation of more jobs and more energy. Proponents of fracking have pointed out that the water used is significantly less than amounts for other uses such as in livestock, industry, and mining. They assert that it is cleaner than other current methods of fossil fuel development and that there is no evidence of groundwater contamination from the fluids injected in the process and no evidence of radioactive waste water being leaked. Proponents counter opponents by highlighting the increased production and decreased costs of the fracking process; the ability of fracking to reduce dependency on other countries for energy sources; and increased job opportunities and community development resulting from fracking.

Opposition to fracking is motivated by fears of environmental dangers, especially to the groundwater reserves. The opposing forces promote greater explorations into renewable energy. These naturally limitless energy sources provide a cleaner alternative and are viewed as potentially more economically sound (McGraw 2016). Opponents of fracking highlight the large amount of water utilized, transportation costs, and the potential harm of toxic chemicals as dangerous and short sighted. They suggest that resulting reductions in carbon dioxide are not enough to justify the increase in methane gases emitted in the process, which also contribute to greenhouse gases. They point to occurrence of surface spills leaking into groundwater as indicating potential contamination. So far, spills have been limited to leaks at the surface and proponents maintain that leaks in the drilling process can be avoided in construction by adequately sealing the drilling housing. However, recent research shows that surface leaks are more common than previously acknowledged (Pierre-Louis 2017). Opponents strongly assert that potential environmental harm is not worth the minimal gain in resources, especially when there are better alternatives to be developed.

A federal bill to reduce carbon dioxide emissions, through **"cap and trade,"** failed in 2010. Cap and trade initiatives limit how much carbon emission can be tolerated from one source. The proposal permits companies reducing their emissions to sell their carbon emission "surplus" to other entities. The ensuing reduction in emissions, when compared to 1990 data, is not considered significant. Critics advance the alternative of halting the development of coal-fired power plants which would stop

Figure 14.16 Citizen protest concerning efforts to promote coal production by claiming it can be done "cleaner" than in the past
Source: Nick Hanna / Alamy Stock Photo

tons of carbon from entering the atmosphere at all. The results would be far more effective than "cap and trade," though neither of these policies has been pursued by state or federal government. The most successful source of environmental protection has occurred in grassroots organizations, local nonprofits, and community groups. Local groups have barred the establishment of 166 coal-powered plants and pressured others to plan closure. Localized efforts are part of the *Environmental Justice Movement*, incorporating grassroots organizations to affect progress at local levels. The *Beyond Coal* campaign, for example, successfully organized people around tangible targets, stopping the construction of coal-fired power plants at the local level. This enabled the campaign to appeal to a constellation of allies, such as public health advocates and unions, reaching beyond the usual environmental activists. These local community efforts generally have been more effective than government agencies, which are more vulnerable to political trends and powerful lobbies (Hertsgaard 2012).

What Is in the Future of Technology?

Cultural habits need to be considered when determining routes to environmental protection and innovative technology can be garnered to achieve these ends. Personal automobile use accounts for one fifth of all US carbon dioxide emissions. There was a steady decline in automobile usage from its peak in 2007 until 2014. This trend is apparently reversing as gas consumption rose in 2015 to approximate 2007 levels and appears on track to surpass that in 2016. In 2016, American drivers put in 280 billion road miles in just half a year. The increasing usage is attributed to reduced gas prices. The purchase of bigger vehicles also has had a resurgence (Brady

Figure 14.17 LA traffic
Source: egd /
Shutterstock.com

2016). When gas taxes, vehicle taxes, and use taxes are accounted for it is apparent that the American cost of automobile use is significantly less than in European countries. The American government-subsidized highway system encouraged the use of automobiles as convenient and relatively cheap transportation. The growth of suburbs followed, with the development of their dependency on driving and their lack of pedestrian-friendly alternatives. The American system of public transportation, in many cities and towns, suffers from inefficiencies and lack of funding. Increased fare rates and reduced service in scheduling and access make public transportation inconvenient or even impractical. In Europe, there are policies to dissuade car use such as reduced parking in highly congested areas, car-free zones, and tolls (Buehler 2014). Consequently, Americans are more likely to depend on their cars than their European counterparts, even for short trips of less than a mile. Americans use cars for 70 percent of their short trips while 70 percent of Europeans would walk, bicycle, or use public transportation, supporting a healthier habit.

Americans typically do not consider walking or cycling which, in some areas, is very dangerous. There is a growing movement to make cities more bicycle friendly by making more bike lanes, though many localities still have little to offer in the way of safety measures for cycling. Recreational walking is even discouraged due to laws protecting private property and to the lack of "right to roam" laws permitting walking on private property. In other countries, public access to private property is protected. The lack of passage on private property, and the contraction of public lands, contributes to the American sedentary lifestyle where more than 40 percent of the population do not get the minimal level of exercise recommended for health (Ilgunas 2016). Promoting walking and cycling would not only cut pollution but potentially increase health through physical activity and interaction with "real" human beings.

Figure 14.18 Restaurant sign in San Rafael, CA
Source: Photography by Rosalind Gottfried

Americans' social interaction appears to be reaching an all-time low. Smart phones have changed the social landscape, especially for the post-millennial generation who never have been without them (Twenge 2017). Many people would be lost, both literally and figuratively, without their smart phones. A significant number of people would not know what they were supposed to be doing or even how to contact their friends or family. Technology has made positive contributions to modern life but it appears to be increasing obesity, laziness, lower academic skills, and lack of connectedness. For some people, participating in social media and texting has become a substitute for activities such as meeting for coffee or a meal (Twenge 2017). People seem to have little motivation, or patience, for incorporating physical sociability into their lives. Additionally, attentiveness is truncated. A Microsoft survey determined that the average attention span is now eight seconds (Egan 2016)! Distraction has been implicated in many accidents. People fly through activities, whether online or in person, with very little focus on what they are engaging in. In fact, one recent *New York Times* article talked about young urban professionals whose main purpose in getting together was to send Instagram and Snapchat images to others (Rosman 2016). Remember that research shows that *Facebook* images of gatherings of people which don't include ourselves are alienating and can contribute to feelings of exclusion and depression (Chapter 4). Finally, access to the internet is in jeopardy due to the 2017 Federal Communications Commission's (FCC) reversal of regulations protecting net neutrality. These regulations ensured that no company, or any other business or government entity, would have priority allowing them to get faster service, or "jump ahead" of other service providers. This change was made in anticipation of promoting innovation but it may also lead to slower internet access and more costly services to get a faster speed. Members of Congress have stated their goal to rescind the FCC reversal of net neutrality. The FCC also ruled that high-speed internet is no longer to be treated as a utility and is not to be subjected to regulations governing use and costs (Kang 2017).

In capitalist society, what may be even more insidious than the effects of technology on social life is the use of information to sell us everything from products, to services, to political causes. Many companies, such as Facebook and Google, track internet histories to target users for sales and other purposes. These companies utilize computer algorithms gained from data programmed into their computer base. All of the major tech companies are devoting substantial resources to the development of *artificial intelligence (AI)*, which would create computers with the ability to think beyond what the human brain can conceive. For example, Google purchased a British tech company, "DeepMind," for at least a half of a billion dollars, reportedly beating out Facebook (Shu 2014). "DeepMind" apparently had not yet developed a specific product, though it did have 75 employees working on algorithms and related research considered "cutting edge." Google has purchased other startups in its pursuit of artificial intelligence and a master algorithm.

The possibility of a *master algorithm* carries the potential to tell a computer *how* to learn, not just *what* to learn. It would have the capacity to "think" beyond its programmed data, producing information not in any data base. This "intelligent" machine could have beneficial effects such as being utilized to tailor drugs specifically to an individual's biology, using information regarding genotype, medical history, tissue composition. It could help with personal life by analyzing aspects of job decisions, marital decisions, anything that a person needs to do or think about—a phenomenon horrifying to some and welcomed by others. The information could also be the end of human volition, a specter very real to some of the experts working on AI.

Domingos, a leading computer scientist in AI, points out that we need to treat any future "master algorithm" as a tool and not let it control humans. He suggests there is a difference between intelligence and being human, as machines do not possess "free will," emotions, or consciousness. He addresses the desirability of artificial intelligence with a focus on the concept of *singularity*. Singularity is when computers will move into artificial intelligence to such an extent that their ability to "self-improve" will become exponential and they will quickly surpass human intelligence. In the worst-case predictions regarding singularity, the machines would control, and possibly destroy, human society. On the positive side, such super-intelligent machines could potentially lead society to a utopian future containing no human suffering. Some believe the doomsday prophecies to be unfounded while others feel we should pay attention to potentially destructive outcomes (Khatchadourian 2015; Goodell 2016). Each side believes it is more insightful. Google, for example, has established an in-house ethics board to guard against potential abuses of technological innovation, though many fear that nothing can guarantee the consequences of the next stage of intelligent machines (Shu 2014; Domingos 2015).

Box 14.7 – Technology

Smart phones are changing the way people interact. Although they have positive uses, socially they are associated with fewer face to face interactions, which have been shown to have positive health effects.

The development of *artificial intelligence*, where computers can think beyond their programming, raises the potential for *singularity*, where computers will quickly gain extraordinary powers, leaving human intelligence behind. The relative benefits of this potential development are highly contested.

Antibiotic resistant bacteria have resulted in the fear of *superbugs*, or infections that will be uncontrollable and potentially lead to pandemics. The prophylactic use of antibiotics in animals for human consumption is highly contested and outlawed in other countries.

Genetically modified organisms (GMOs), which transfer genes from one organism to another, are utilized in farming and food production. Their utility and safety, for the human population as well as the whole ecosystem, are debatable. More research is needed to convince critics of their safety. The labeling of foods containing GMOs is voluntary in the US.

Smart technology, with the ability to accomplish independent "learning" has progressed from just a few years ago. Experimental "driverless" cars are not only programmed to drive without a human but can incorporate changes from experiences occurring on the road. But many difficult issues arise which can yield contradictory responses. A driverless car can be more environmentally sound, decrease traffic, and reduce accidents due to human error. But one study asking respondents if a driverless car should be utilitarian came up with contradictory results. Respondents were asked, if faced with sacrificing one or two people to save more, should a driverless car do so? Theoretically people responded affirmatively. But, when asked if they would sacrifice themselves, or purchase a self-protecting car primarily concerned with the passengers' safety, 81 percent opted for self-protection even though that figure was just a little higher than the response to the first scenario (Howard 2016).

Other technical innovations pose threats to our health, potentially promoting the spread of disease. The development of antibiotic resistant bacteria has public health officials worried about future pandemics. Newly developed bacteria, referred to as *superbugs*, immune to treatment with known medications, are proliferating worldwide. It is suggested that one essential contributing factor is the over prescribing of antibiotics when they are not medically indicated. Inappropriate prescriptions can stem from a medical provider's decision to err on the side of caution, treating a patient for a condition which has not yet been positively identified. The over prescribing of antibiotics, without actual evidence of a bacterial infection, can also result from patients' pressures for treatment to alleviate pain or discomfort.

Superbugs are not the only fallout from the proliferation of antibiotics. There are over 100 antibiotics. As a result, antibiotic residue has been found in the water supply of many localities (Chuanwu et al. 2009). Humans also ingest antibiotics from meat and dairy products from animals treated for infections or potential infections. Animals account for 80 percent of antibiotic use. Prophylactic use of antibiotics for animals is considered "therapeutic." In other words, the use of antibiotics PRIOR to any infection or disease is considered a legitimate intervention. When a label says that there are no antibiotics given to the animal for growth it does not necessarily mean that the animal is drug free since providing a drug for *therapeutic* purposes is distinct from utilizing it for growth. Ranchers say it is necessary for them to use antibiotics to assure the health and growth of the herd but in other countries, where the use of antibiotics without identified infection is prohibited, herd growth and profit have been sustained. Serious health concerns, and death, can result when bacteria become antibiotic resistant, so practices should carefully regulate antibiotic usage. Although it cannot be determined how much of the increase in resistant bacteria is due to animal use, surely there is some effect since it accounts for 80 percent of the drugs' prevalence (Flatow 2016; Moyer 2016; Sun and Davis 2016).

Another area of controversy in food production concerns the use of *Genetically Modified Organisms* (*GMOs*). Genetic modification refers to an organism that has been altered by the addition of genes not normally found in that organism (ARW 2017). Currently the *Food and Drug Administration* (FDA) requires labels for content and nutrition but not for the *process* of production, which would result in identifying a food as a GMO. The ensuing debate focuses on whether food that is genetically modified, or contains such ingredients, should say so on the label. The FDA still permits the sale of GMOs to consumers without labeling, in the belief that the products do not differ substantially from other foods, though the claim is not universally agreed upon. GMO supporters contend that genetic modification is simply an extension of the human history of manipulating the food supply and they suggest that, ultimately, GMOs can enhance the level of production and ensure adequate reserves. They also suggest that GMOs can reduce the environmental damage from insecticides while still increasing the yield and nutritional value of the food.

Opposing views suggest that GMOs differ from past developments in farming and food production which did not actually cross *biological barriers* by moving genes from one species to another as GMOs can. They argue that many studies regarding the safety of GMOs are industry sponsored, rather than independently funded, suggesting potential bias. A study in Scotland, for example, established the presence of internal structural damage in genetically modified potatoes. Fears concerning damage to the product are not the only source of controversies surrounding GMOs. Another potential hazard concerns the consequences of producing insect-resistant crops. Although these can reduce the need for pesticides, they can potentially harm other species, ironically creating the need for more and stronger insecticides. They also raise the fear that genetically modified crops can potentially threaten non-genetically modified crops and reduce crop diversity. Further, opponents of GMOs contend that the most significant threat to the food supply is not food shortages but the lack of equitable food distribution and affordability, rendering the urgent need to protect plants through GMOs inconsequential. They demand the labeling of GMO products as a "right to know" so that consumers can make an informed choice (Viewpoints n.d.). Currently, there only are guidelines for voluntary labeling and some companies deliberately state their products are not made with GMOs so that cautious consumers will continue to buy them (Misko 2016).

Key Terms

Demographic Transition   Birthrate   Death Rate   Fertility Rate   Development, Relief, and Education of Alien Minors (DREAM) Act   Deferred Action for Childhood Arrivals (DACA)   Millennials   Supplemental Poverty Measure   Environmental Racism   Dirty Energy   Global Warming   Renewable Energy   Hydraulic Fracturing (Fracking)   Cap and Trade   Artificial Intelligence   Singularity   Superbugs   GMOs

Concept Review

What Are Essential Demographic Shifts in the Population?

The developed countries have undergone a **demographic transition**, characterized by low birth and death rates, resulting in a stable population. Some advanced developed countries may be at, or near, a negative population growth. In the US, the influx of immigrants will assure a stable population, even with a decreasing birthrate. The fate of undocumented residents, even those who arrived as children, is in limbo. The **DREAM Act** would have provided undocumented residents a path to permanent residency and citizenship but it failed to be passed. President Obama enacted **DACA**, providing temporary protection from deportation for about 800,000 youthful undocumented residents. Donald Trump has revoked the order, as of March 5, 2018, apparently in the hope that his action will provoke Congress to address immigration reform but court actions have stalled the revocation.

Who Are the Millennials and What Do They Represent?

The **millennials** are the people born between 1980 and 2000, though dates vary in specific studies; they are currently the largest group in society and the biggest portion of workers. Generally, they exhibit liberal attitudes with respect to personal issues such as sexuality, reproductive rights, and work. Financially, they are projected to be less well-off than their parents' generation. They desire a workplace consonant with their personal values and seek the opportunity to bring these values into the community through the workplace. As very young adults, they seemed set on a course different from the boomer generation, but as they have reached their 30s it appears that most of their differences were ones of delay rather than substitution. They are buying cars, moving to the suburbs, and having children, albeit at a later age than in their parents' cohort.

What Issues Will Emerge as the Population Ages?

The general population is getting older, with an average age of almost 38, indicating fewer women of childbearing age. The Latino population is younger, and therefore predicted to have a higher fertility rate than Anglo women. Births to Latinos already outnumber those to Anglos. The **elderly** population, 65 and older, is increasing and will continue to do so as the boomers hit that mark. As the boomers retire, there will be fewer workers to support the increase in Social Security recipients. Controversies surround projected shortfalls in the ability of the system to sustain payouts at the current levels. Although the elderly are less likely to be poor than in the past, and less likely to be poor than other cohorts, their functional poverty can be high when considering the costs of healthcare and housing. The future affordability of healthcare is in jeopardy.

How Will Immigration Impact Society?

Immigration currently represents 14 percent of the population and is predicted to reach 18 percent in the next several decades. The high levels of immigration have promoted intolerance, particularly towards non-Christian groups and undocumented persons. The immigrant population and their children are predicted to be crucial to the viability of the economy, supplying workers as the population ages and fertility rates decrease. The Latino population is the largest racial or ethnic group but it is not the largest group immigrating today. Asians comprise the largest groups of immigrants and they will overtake the Latino population as the largest non-Anglo group.

What Environmental Issues Are Salient?

Climate change is the most challenging problem humanity faces, particularly with respect to altering the eco-system. The 2015 *Paris Climate Agreement* represents the first legally binding attempt to reduce global warming and to return the temperature to pre-industrial levels. The Trump administration has vowed to withdraw from the Agreement, making the US the only developed country to refuse to sign on. Environmentally conscious groups promote improving the development of renewable energy sources and limiting the expansion of "dirty energy." The past 20 years have been a period of environmental activism, where most successes have been at the local levels. Environmental hazards are disproportionately severe among people of color and in poor communities. The proliferation of hydraulic fracturing, or "**fracking**," is a practice which has stirred much controversy, especially due to its potential to contaminate water supplies.

What Are Future Issues with Regard to Technology?

The advent of the "driverless" car has the potential to reduce automobile usage, change the shape of communities, and promote more walking. The "smart" car, capable of learning from its experiences, also poses dangers since accidents are unlikely to be eliminated, though they can potentially eliminate those due to driver errors. The ability of intelligent computers to move beyond the intellectual capabilities of humans is anticipated as leading to either destructive or utopian outcomes, though there is little agreement on which outcome will be salient. Another technical development garnering debate concerns the over use of antibiotics leading to antibiotic resistant bacteria considered **superbugs**, which could lead to global pandemics. Also controversial are the uses of **GMOs** in the food chain. Some believe that the potential gains associated with them are not worth the potential risks to plant, animal, and human health.

Review Questions

1. What is the demographic transition? Which countries exemplify this concept and what features distinguish them? What future trends may occur in countries which have undergone the transition?

2. What are the current demographic trends in US population? Address issues of age, employment, race, religion, and immigration.

3. What are the contributions of the immigrant population to the well-being and future of the US?

4. What programs have been proposed to address the undocumented population and what is their current status? How do you think they will be resolved?

5. Who are the *millennials* and what traits do they reveal? Are the millennials similar to the boomers, when the boomers were younger?

6. Who are the *baby boomers* and what societal issues emerge as they age?

7. What are the major environmental concerns and how does the US address these?

8. What is *environmental racism*? Who are the primary targets?

9. What is *fracking* and why is it controversial? What is your position on it?

10. Explain the concepts of artificial intelligence and singularity. Are you optimistic with regard to the development of these?

11. What do you think of GMOs? Should they be regulated and should food require labeling? Why or why not?

References

Abbey-Lambertz, K. (May 12, 2016) How Sky-High Rents Are Radically Changing New York Neighborhoods. *The Huffington Post*. Retrieved from http://www.huffingtonpost.com/entry/new-york-city-gentrification-rent_us_57333863e4b0bc9cb048a8f6

A Changing Mission. (2017) *San Francisco Chronicle*. Retrieved from http://www.sfchronicle.com/the-mission/

ACL. (n.d.) *Administration for Community Living. Aging Statistics*. Retrieved from https://aoa.acl.gov/Aging_Statistics/index.aspx

Adamy, J. (June 2, 2016) U.S. Birthrate Falls Slightly While Death Rate Rises. *The Wall Street Journal*. Retrieved from http://www.wsj.com/articles/u-s-birthrate-falls-slightly-while-death-rate-rises-1464840003

AIC. American Immigration Council. (June 5, 2012) *A Comparison of the DREAM Act and Other Proposals for Undocumented Youth*. Retrieved from https://www.americanimmigrationcouncil.org/topics/legislation

AIC. American Immigrant Council. (July 1, 2014) No Childhood Here: Why Central American Children are Fleeing Their Homes. *American Immigration Council*. Retrieved from https://www.americanimmigrationcouncil.org/research/no-childhood-here-why-central-american-children-are-fleeing-their-homes

Amy Dalrymple Forum News Service (August 18, 2016) Pipeline Route Plan First Called for Crossing North of Bismarck. *BismarckTribune*. Retrieved from http://bismarcktribune.com/news/state-and-regional/pipeline-route-plan-first-called-for-crossing-north-of-bismarck/article_64d053e4-8a1a-5198-a1dd-498d386c933c.html

ARW. (2017) GMO crops: The Arguments Pro and Con. *American Radio Works*. Retrieved from http://americanradioworks.publicradio.org/features/gmos_india/pro_con.html

AP. The Associated Press. (March 30, 2015) The Campaign to Make National Parks Relevant to Millennials. *Mashable*. Retrieved from http://mashable.com/2015/03/30/find-your-national-park/#A4v8_HyoTiqg

AP. The Associated Press. (September 18, 2017) Interior Secretary Recommends Shrinking Six National Monuments. Retrieved from https://www.nbcnews.com/news/us-news/interior-secretary-recommends-shrinking-six-national-monuments-n802236

Atkin, E. (May 2, 2014) Low-income, Black, and Latino Americans Face Highest Risk of Chemical Spills. *ThinkProgress*. Retrieved from https://thinkprogress.org/low-income-black-and-latino-americans-face-highest-risk-of-chemical-spills-da1e85c4d76c#.iuly7wpu2

BBC News. (February 7, 2017) Dakota Pipeline: What's Behind the Controversy? Retrieved from http://www.bbc.com/news/world-us-canada-37863955

Beadle, P.A. (January 8, 2013) Cost of a Broken System: U.S. Spent More on Immigration than all Other Federal Enforcement Agencies Combined. *ThinkProgress*. Retrieved from https://thinkprogress.org/cost-of-a-broken-system-u-s-spent-more-on-immigration-than-all-other-federal-enforcement-agencies-3b38581733e2

Berger, A.M. (September 15, 2017) The Suburb of the Future, Almost Here. *The New York Times*. Retrieved from https://www.nytimes.com/2017/09/15/sunday-review/future-suburb-millennials.html

Biello, D. (September 8, 2015) Obama Has Done More for Clean Energy than You Think. *Scientific American*. Retrieved from https://www.scientificamerican.com/article/obama-has-done-more-for-clean-energy-than-you-think/

Brady, J. (August 29, 2016) Cheaper Gas Means More Americans Are on the Road. *NPR*. Retrieved from http://www.npr.org/2016/08/29/491770316/cheaper-gas-means-more-americans-are-on-the-road

Breisblatt, J. (May 16, 2018) Confused About the Current Status of DACA? Here Is What You Need to Know. *American Immigration Council*. Retrieved from http://immigrationimpact.com/2018/05/16/daca-what-you-need-to-know/

Buehler, R. (February 4, 2014) Nine Reasons the U.S. Ended so Much More Car-dependent than Europe. *Citylab*. Retrieved from https://www.citylab.com/transportation/2014/02/9-reasons-us-ended-so-much-more-car-dependent-europe/8226/

Chuanwu, X., Zhang, Y., Marrs, C.F., We, W., Simon, C., Foxman, B., Nriagu, J. (June 29, 2009) Prevalence of Antibiotic Resistance in Drinking Water Treatment and Distribution Systems. *AEM.ASM.org*. Retrieved from http://aem.asm.org/content/75/17/5714.full

Cohn, D. (October 5, 2015) Future Immigration Will Change the Face of America by 2065. *Pew Research Center*. Retrieved from http://www.pewresearch.org/fact-tank/2015/10/05/future-immigration-will-change-the-face-of-america-by-2065/

Cohn, D., Caumont, A. (March 31, 2016) 10 Demographic Trends that Are Shaping the U.S. and the World. *Pew Research Center*. Retrieved from http://www.pewresearch.org/fact-tank/2016/03/31/10-demographic-trends-that-are-shaping-the-u-s-and-the-world/

Cubanski, J., Casillas, G., Damico, A. (June 10, 2015) Poverty Among Seniors: An Updated Analysis of National and State Level Poverty Rates Under the Official and Supplemental Poverty Measures. *Kaiser Family Foundation*. Retrieved from http://kff.org/medicare/issue-brief/poverty-among-seniors-an-updated-analysis-of-national-and-state-level-poverty-rates-under-the-official-and-supplemental-poverty-measures/

DeParle, J. (November, 2013) Why the U.S. Is So Good at Turning Immigrants into Americans. *The Atlantic*. Retrieved from http://www.theatlantic.com/magazine/archive/2013/11/assimilation-nation/309518/

Dickerson, C. (June 22, 2015) Secret World War II Chemical Experiments Tested Troops by Race. *Morning Edition*. Retrieved from http://www.npr.org/2015/06/22/415194765/u-s-troops-tested-by-race-in-secret-world-war-ii-chemical-experiments

Dickerson, C. (September 5, 2015a) Veterans Used in Secret Experiments Sue Military for Answers. *Morning Edition*. Retrieved from http://www.npr.org/2015/09/05/437555125/veterans-used-in-secret-experiments-sue-military-for-answers

Domingos, P. (2015) *The Master Algorithm*. New York: Basic Books.

Drevitch, G. (September 13, 2013) How Can We Keep Seniors in their Homes as Long as Possible? *Forbes.com*. Retrieved from http://www.forbes.com/sites/nextavenue/2013/09/13/how-can-we-keep-seniors-in-their-homes-as-long-as-possible/2/#73d8d47c45a8

Dubner, S. (November 8, 2016) Bad Medicine, Part 2: (Drug) Trials and Tribulations. *Freakonomics Radio*. Retrieved from https://www.podcastchart.com/podcasts/freakonomics-radio/episodes/bad-medicine-part-2-drug-trials-and-tribulations

EIA. (July 2, 2015) Fossil Fuels Have Made Up at least 80% of U.S. Fuel Mix Since 1900. *U.S. Energy Information Administration (EIA)*. Retrieved from http://www.eia.gov/todayinenergy/detail.cfm?id=21912

Ecosystem (n.d.) Retrieved from https://www.vocabulary.com/dictionary/ecosystem

Editorial Board (n.d.) Healthy Living in Your 70s and Older. *Healthcommunities.com*. Retrieved from http://www.healthcommunities.com/healthy-aging/healthy-living-tips-70s-older-elderly.shtml

Editorial Board. (July 4, 2016) An Exodus in our Own Backyard. *The New York Times*. Retrieved from https://www.nytimes.com/2016/07/04/opinion/an-exodus-in-our-own-backyard.html

Editorial Board. (July 18, 2017) A Brighter Future for Electric Cars and the Planet. *New York Times*. Retrieved from https://www.nytimes.com/2017/07/18/opinion/a-brighter-future-for-electric-cars-and-the-planet.html?mcubz=3&_r=0

Eilperin, J., Dennis, B. (February, 2017) Trump Administration to Approve Final Permit for Dakota Access Pipeline. *Washington Post*. Retrieved from https://www.washingtonpost.com/news/energy-environment/wp/2017/02/07/trump-administration-to-approve-final-permit-for-dakota-access-pipeline/?utm_term=.1948e0045532

Egan, T. (January 22, 2016) The Eight Second Attention Span. *The New York Times*. Retrieved from https://www.nytimes.com/2016/01/22/opinion/the-eight-second-attention-span.html?action=click&contentCollection=opinion&module=NextInCollection&region=Footer&pgtype=article&version=column&rref=collection%2Fcolumn%2Ftimothy-egan&_r=1

Espinosa, C. (January 26, 2016) Environmental Justice Is a Latino Issue and Will Influence Our Vote. *Latino Rebels*. Retrieved from http://www.latinorebels.com/2016/01/26/environmental-justice-is-a-latino-issue-and-will-influence-our-vote/

European Commission. (n.d.) *Climate Action*. Retrieved from https://ec.europa.eu/clima/policies/international/negotiations/paris_en

Ezrati, M. (June 18, 2014) How America Can Overcome the Challenges of an Aging Population. *PBS*. Retrieved from http://www.pbs.org/newshour/making-sense/how-america-can-overcome-the-challenges-of-an-aging-population/

Feldman, D., Dashnaw, C., Hosea J., Banker, L, Wall, M., Ponce, J. (2014) *The 2014 Millennial Impact Report*. Retrieved from http://cdn.trustedpartner.com/docs/library/AchieveMCON2013/MIR_2014.pdf

Flatow, I. (June 3, 2016) Old Ideas Might Help Us Fight New Superbugs. *Science Friday PRI*. Retrieved from https://www.sciencefriday.com/segments/old-ideas-may-help-us-fight-new-superbugs/

Foley, M. (March 16, 2014) Millennials Indebted but Optimistic About the Future. *The Cheat Sheet*. Retrieved from http://www.cheatsheet.com/business/economy/millennials-indebted-independent-but-optimistic-about-the-future.html/?a=viewall

Fortune. (January 29, 2016) Why Millennials Have no Problem Quitting Their Jobs. *Fortune*. Retrieved from http://fortune.com/2016/01/29/millennials-quit-jobs/

Frosch, D. (July 26, 2009) Uranium Contamination Haunts Navajo Country. *The New York Times*. Retrieved from http://www.nytimes.com/2009/07/27/us/27navajo.html

Fry, R. (May 11, 2015) Millennials Surpass Gen Xers as the Largest Generation in U.S. Labor Force. *Pew Research Center*. Retrieved from http://www.pewresearch.org/fact-tank/2015/05/11/millennials-surpass-gen-xers-as-the-largest-generation-in-u-s-labor-force/

Fry, R. (April 25, 2016) Millennials Overtake Baby Boomers as America's Largest Generation. *Pew Research Center*. Retrieved from http://www.pewresearch.org/fact-tank/2016/04/25/millennials-overtake-baby-boomers/

Gallucci, M. (April 16, 2015) BP Oil Spill Has Lasting Economic Toll Five Years After Deepwater Horizon Explosion. *International Business Times*. Retrieved from http://www.ibtimes.com/bp-oil-spill-has-lasting-economic-toll-five-years-after-deepwater-horizon-explosion-1883832

Gandel, S. (March 4, 2016) OMG, Young Millennials Are the Job Market's Biggest Losers. *Fortune*. Retrieved from http://fortune.com/2016/03/04/young-millennials-job-market-losers/

Ganim, S., Tran, L. (January 13, 2016) How Tap Water Became Toxic in Flint, Michigan. *CNN*. Retrieved from http://www.cnn.com/2016/01/11/health/toxic-tap-water-flint-michigan/

Garcia-Navarro, L. (October 11, 2015) America's Immigration Rhetoric Out of Touch with the Numbers. *Weekend Edition Sunday*. NPR. Retrieved from http://www.npr.org/2015/10/11/447688060/america-s-immigration-rhetoric-out-of-touch-with-the-numbers

Garofoli, J., Said, C. (2017) To Whom Does San Francisco's Oldest Neighborhood Belong? *SF Chronicle*. Retrieved from http://www.sfchronicle.com/the-mission/a-changing-mission/

Gawande, A. (August 2, 2010) Letting Go: What Should Medicine Do When it Can't Save Your Life? *The New Yorker*. Retrieved from http://www.newyorker.com/magazine/2010/08/02/letting-go-2

Geneseo. (n.d.) *Love Canal: A Brief History*. Retrieved from https://www.geneseo.edu/history/love_canal_history

Gonzales, S. (September 28, 2015) Immigrants Will Drive U.S. Population Growth in Next Five Decades: Pew. *Reuters*. Retrieved from http://www.reuters.com/article/us-usa-immigration-study-idUSKCN0RS08V20150928

Goodell, J. (March 9, 2016) Inside the Artificial Intelligence Revolution: A Special Report, Part 2. *Rolling Stone*. Retrieved from http://www.rollingstone.com/culture/features/inside-the-artificial-intelligence-revolution-a-special-report-pt-2-20160309

Goodman, M.L. (May 27, 2015) Millennial College Graduates: Young, Educated, Jobless. *Newsweek*. Retrieved from http://www.newsweek.com/2015/06/05/millennial-college-graduates-young-educated-jobless-335821.html

HUD. (n.d.) U.S. Department of Housing and Urban Development. *Affordable Housing*. Retrieved from http://portal.hud.gov/hudportal/HUD?src=/program_offices/comm_planning/affordablehousing/

Hafiz, Y. (November 21, 2011) Facts About American Attitudes Towards Death. *The Huffington Post*. Retrieved from http://www.huffingtonpost.com/2013/11/21/death-america-pew-research_n_4312321.html

Haglage, A. (December 9, 2016) Water Is Life: Four Months at Standing Rock. *Lenny Letter*. Retrieved from http://www.lennyletter.com/politics/interviews/a646/water-is-life-four-months-at-standing-rock/

Hawkins, C. (March 17, 2013) Resources for Seniors Surviving on Social Security. *Seniorliving*. Retrieved from http://www.seniorliving.org/retirement/resources-surviving-social-security/

Hertsgaard, M. (April 2, 2012) How a Grassroots Rebellion Won the Nation's Biggest Climate Victory. *Mother Jones*. Retrieved from http://www.motherjones.com/environment/2012/04/beyond-coal-plant-activism

Hirji, Z., Song, L. (January 20, 2015) Map: The Fracking Boom, State by State. *Insideclimatenews.org*. Retrieved from https://insideclimatenews.org/news/20150120/map-fracking-boom-state-state

History.com. (n.d.) *Three Mile Island*. Retrieved from http://www.history.com/topics/three-mile-island

Howard, J. (June 23, 2016) Driverless Cars Create a Safety 'Dilemma': Passengers vs. Pedestrians. *CNN*. Retrieved from http://www.cnn.com/2016/06/23/health/driverless-cars-safety-public-opinion/index.html

IOA. Institute on Aging. (August 29, 2014) Hourly Care for Your Senior: You Won't Believe Why It's the Cheapest Option. *Institute on Aging*. Retrieved from https://blog.ioaging.org/caregiving/hourly-care-senior-wont-believe-cheapest-option/

Ilgunas, K. (April 23, 2016) This Is Our Country. Let's Walk It. *The New York Times*. Retrieved from http://www.nytimes.com/2016/04/24/opinion/sunday/this-is-our-country-lets-walk-it.html?partner=rss&emc=rss

Kaiser Family Foundation (KFF). (2015) *Poverty Rate by Age*. Retrieved from http://kff.org/other/state-indicator/poverty-rate-by-age/

Kang, C. (December 14, 2017) FCC Repeals Net Neutrality Rules. *The New York Times*. Retrieved from https://www.nytimes.com/2017/12/14/technology/net-neutrality-repeal-vote.html?_r=0

Kennedy, M. (June 1, 2017) Crude Oil Begins to Flow Through Controversial Dakota Access Pipeline. *The Two-way*. Retrieved from http://www.npr.org/sections/thetwo-way/2017/06/01/531097758/crude-oil-begins-to-flow-through-controversial-dakota-access-pipeline

Khatchadourian, R. (November 23, 2015) The Doomsday Invention. *New Yorker*. Retrieved from http://www.newyorker.com/magazine/2015/11/23/doomsday-invention-artificial-intelligence-nick-bostrom

Latimer, B. (December 1, 2016) Univ. of California Announces Plan to Protect Undocumented Students. *NBC News*. Retrieved from http://www.nbcnews.com/news/latino/univ-california-announces-plan-protect-undocumented-students-n690766

Liptak, A. and Shear M.D. (2016, June 23) Supreme court tie blocks Obama's immigration plan. *The New York Times*. Retrieved from https://www.nytimes.com/2016/06/24/us/supreme-court-immigration-obama-dapa.html.

Liptak, A. (September 18, 2017) Cohn: Trump Still Planning to Withdraw from Paris Climate Accord. Retrieved from http://www.cnn.com/2017/09/18/politics/gary-cohn-climate-paris-trump/index.html

Livingston, G. (February 24, 2015) Is U.S. Fertility at an All-time Low? It Depends. *Pew Research Center*. http://www.pewresearch.org/fact-tank/2015/02/24/is-u-s-fertility-at-an-all-time-low-it-depends/

Livio, K.S. (August 2, 2016) *Only 5 States Allow Physician-assisted Suicide. Could N.J. Be the 6th?* Retrieved from http://www.nj.com/healthfit/index.ssf/2016/08/nj_lawmakers_try_again_to_pass_assisted_suicide_bi.html

Luscombe, B. (September 24, 2014) Why 25% of Millennials Will Never Get Married. *Time*. Retrieved from http://time.com/3422624/report-millennials-marriage/

Machado, A. (June 18, 2014) How Millennials Are Changing Travel. *The Atlantic*. Retrieved from https://www.theatlantic.com/international/archive/2014/06/how-millennials-are-changing-international-travel/373007/

MacMillan, A. (March 2, 2016) Global Warming 101. *NRDC*. Retrieved from https://www.nrdc.org/stories/global-warming-101

Marshall, S. (November 16, 2016) What Could Happen to DACA Recipients Under Donald Trump. *ABC News*. Retrieved from http://abcnews.go.com/Politics/happen-daca-recipients-donald-trump/story?id=43546706

May, P. (November 29, 2016) California College Leaders to Trump: Let Our Students Stay. *The Mercury News*. Retrieved from http://www.mercurynews.com/2016/11/29/california-college-leaders-to-trump-let-our-students-stay/

McClurg, L. (August 8, 2016) National Parks Have Some Work to Do to Become 'Parks for All'. *KQED*. Retrieved from http://ww2.kqed.org/science/2016/08/08/national-parks-have-some-work-to-do-to-become-parks-for-all/

McCoy, B., Connor, T. (July 29, 2016) Six More Officials Charged in Flint Water Crisis for Alleged Cover-Up. *NBC News*. Retrieved from http://www.nbcnews.com/storyline/flint-water-crisis/six-more-offcials-charged-flint-water-crisis-alleged-coverup-n619811

McGraw, S. (May 1, 2016) Is Fracking Safe? The 10 Most Controversial Claims About Natural Gas Drilling. *PM*. Retrieved from http://www.popularmechanics.com/science/energy/g161/top-10-myths-about-natural-gas-drilling-6386593/

McKenna, P. (November 13, 2017) Ousted Standing Rock Leader on the Pipeline Protest that Almost Succeeded. *Inside Climate New*. Retrieved from https://insideclimatenews.org/news/13112017/dakota-access-pipeline-protests-standing-rock-chairman-dave-archambault-interview

McManus, D. (September 6, 2017) Trump's DACA Decision Passes the Buck to Congress—for now. *The L.A. Times*. Retrieved from http://www.latimes.com/opinion/op-ed/la-oe-mcmanus-daca-trump-20170906-story.html

Millennials at Work Reshaping the Workplace. (2011) [PDF File]. Retrieved from https://www.pwc.com/m1/en/services/consulting/documents/millennials-at-work.pdf

Misko, G. (January 4, 2016) FDA Denies Petition for GMO Labeling. *PackagingDigest.* Retrieved from http://www.packagingdigest.com/labeling/fda-denies-petition-for-gmo-labeling-2016-01-04

Mooney, C. (June 1, 2018) Trump Withdrew from the Paris Climate Plan a Year Ago. Here's What Has Changed. *The Washington Post.* Retrieved from https://www.washingtonpost.com/news/energy-environment/wp/2018/06/01/trump-withdrew-from-the-paris-climate-plan-a-year-ago-heres-what-has-changed/?utm_term=.f2ee0f9ea284

Morales, L. (April 10, 2016) For the Navajo Nation, Uranium Mining's Deadly Legacy Lingers. *NPR.* Retrieved from http://www.npr.org/sections/health-shots/2016/04/10/473547227/for-the-navajo-nation-uranium-minings-deadly-legacy-lingers

Moyer, M.W. (May 27, 2016) Dangerous New Antibiotic Resistant Bacteria Reach U.S. *Scientific American.* Retrieved from https://www.scientificamerican.com/article/dangerous-new-antibiotic-resistant-bacteria-reach-u-s/

Nakamura, D. (September 5, 2017) Trump Administration Announces End of Immigration Protection Program for 'Dreamers.' *The Washington Post.* Retrieved from https://www.washingtonpost.com/news/post-politics/wp/2017/09/05/trump-administration-announces-end-of-immigration-protection-program-for-dreamers/

NumbersUSA. (May 3, 2016) Supreme Court Divided on DAPA Case. *NumbersUSA.* Retrieved from https://www.numbersusa.com/news/supreme-court-divided-dapa-case

Ordoñez, F. (September 19, 2016) Has Obama Forsaken Central America's refugees? *McClatchy Washington Bureau.* Retrieved from http://www.mcclatchydc.com/news/nation-world/national/article102339862.html

Paris Climate Agreement (n.d.) *European Commission.* Retrieved from http://ec.europa.eu/clima/policies/international/negotiations/paris_en

Paterson, L. (December 15, 2016) Pipeline Spill Adds to Concerns About Dakota Access Pipeline. *Morning Edition NPR.* Retrieved from http://www.npr.org/2016/12/15/505658553/pipeline-spill-adds-to-concerns-about-dakota-access-pipeline

Patten, E. (April 20, 2016) The Nation's Latino Population Is Defined by Its Youth. *Pew Research Center.* Retrieved from http://www.pewhispanic.org/2016/04/20/the-nations-latino-population-is-defined-by-its-youth/

Pew Research Center. (February 11, 2014) *The Rising Cost of Not Going to College.* Retrieved from http://www.pewsocialtrends.org/2014/02/11/the-rising-cost-of-not-going-to-college/

Pierre-Louis, K. (February 24, 2017) Fracking Fluid Is Leaking More Often than We Thought. *Popular Science.* Retrieved from https://www.popsci.com/fracking-fluid-hydraulic-fracturing-spill

Pogash, C. (May 22, 2015) Gentrification Spreads an Upheaval in San Francisco's Mission District. *The New York Times.* Retrieved from http://www.nytimes.

com/2015/05/23/us/high-rents-elbow-latinos-from-san-franciscos-mission-district. html

Pro/con. (2017) Should the Government Allow Immigrants Who Are Here Illegally to Become US Citizens? *Procon.* Retrieved from http://immigration. procon.org/

Rivero, T. (August 27, 2016) President Jimmy Carter on Election, Affordable Housing, and More. *WSP Video.* Retrieved from http://www.wsj.com/video/pres-jimmy-carter-on-election-affordable-housing-and-more/2B17AEC8-0DB1-4A19-91F6-57F32FA2C267.html

Rogers, R.M. (May 18, 2016) Gentrification in Bayview Hunters Point. *Medium.* Retrieved from https://medium.com/@romemackrogers/gentrification-in-bayview-hunters-point-2637d2bc4b0#.jwu7dhp5v

Rosman, K. (April 7, 2016) *Move Over, Rat Pack and Brat Pack: Here Comes the Snap Pack.* Retrieved from https://www.nytimes.com/2016/04/07/fashion/rat-pack-brat-pack-snapchat.html?contentCollection=weekendreads&action=click&pgtype=Homepage&clickSource=story-heading&module=c-column-middle-span-region&region=c-column-middle-span-region&WT.nav=c-column-middle-span-region

Rott, N. (March 9, 2016) Don't Care About National Parks? The Park Service Needs You To. All Things Considered. *NPR.* Retrieved from http://www.npr. org/2016/03/09/463851006/dont-care-about-national-parks-the-park-service-needs-you-to

Safo, N. (February 25, 2016) A Move Toward Three Bedrooms and Two Baths. *Marketplace.* Retrieved from http://www.marketplace.org/2016/02/22/business/ real-estate

Sanburn, J. (August 8, 2016) Flint Water Crisis May Cost the City $400 Million. *Time.* Retrieved from http://time.com/4441471/flint-water-lead-poisoning-costs/

Schlosser, E. (2001) *Fast Food Nation: The Dark Side of the All-American Meal.* New York: Houghton Mifflin Company.

Semuels, A. (January 7, 2015) Suburbs and the New American Poverty. *The Atlantic.* Retrieved from https://www.theatlantic.com/business/archive/2015/01/suburbs-and-the-new-american-poverty/384259/

Shabecoff, P. (January 2, 1989) Reagan and Environment: To Many, a Stalemate. *The New York Times.* Retrieved from http://www.nytimes.com/1989/01/02/us/reagan-and-environment-to-many-a-stalemate.html?pagewanted=all

Shah, N. (June 17, 2015) U.S. Birthrate Hits Turning Point. *The Wall Street Journal.* Retrieved from http://www.wsj.com/articles/u-s-birthrate-hits-turning-point-1434513662

Shu, C. (January 26, 2014) Google Acquires Artificial Intelligence Startup DeepMind For More Than $500M. *TC.* Retrieved from https://techcrunch.com/2014/01/26/ google-deepmind/

Skurie, J., Green, C. (February 23, 2016) Why Do Millennials Love Bernie? *The Atlantic.* Retrieved from https://www.theatlantic.com/video/index/470469/why-do-millennials-love-bernie/

Smialek, J., Giroux, G. (June 25, 2015) The Majority of American Babies Are Now Minorities. *Bloomberg*. Retrieved from http://www.bloomberg.com/news/articles/2015-06-25/american-babies-are-no-longer-mostly-non-hispanic-white

Solman, P. (2013) Colleges and Universities See Graying Workforce Holding on to Coveted Positions. *PBS Newshour*. Retrieved from http://www.pbs.org/newshour/bb/business-jan-june13-makingsense_03-18/

Solomon, M. (January 26, 2016) You've Got Millennial Employees All Wrong; Here Are the Four Things You Need to Know Now. *Forbes*. Retrieved from https://www.forbes.com/sites/micahsolomon/2016/01/26/everything-youve-heard-about-millennial-employees-is-baloney-heres-the-truth-and-how-to-use-it/#4efeb8354904

Statista. (n.d.) Median Age of the U.S. Population 1960–2015. Retrieved from https://www.statista.com/statistics/241494/median-age-of-the-us-population/

Statista. (2017) *Largest Producers of CO2 Emissions Worldwide in 2016, Based on their Share of Global CO2 Emissions*. Retrieved from https://www.statista.com/statistics/271748/the-largest-emitters-of-co2-in-the-world/

Stein, R. (December 8, 2016) Life Expectancy in U.S. Drops for First Time in Decades, Report Finds. *NPR*. Retrieved from http://www.npr.org/sections/health-shots/2016/12/08/504667607/life-expectancy-in-u-s-drops-for-first-time-in-decades-report-finds

Stinchcomb, D., Hershberg, E. (2014) Unaccompanied Migrant Children from Central America: Context, Causes, and Responses. *SSRN*. Retrieved from http://dx.doi.org/10.2139/ssrn.2524001

Sun, L.H., Davis, B. (May 27, 2016) The Superbug that Doctors Have Been Dreading Just Reached the U.S. *Washington Post*. Retrieved from https://www.washingtonpost.com/news/to-your-health/wp/2016/05/26/the-superbug-that-doctors-have-been-dreading-just-reached-the-u-s/?utm_term=.76a81f908aaf

Taylor, A. (March 24, 2014) The Exxon Valdez Oil Spill: 25 Years Ago Today. *The Atlantic*. Retrieved from http://www.theatlantic.com/photo/2014/03/the-exxon-valdez-oil-spill-25-years-ago-today/100703/

Turkewitz, J. (December 4, 2017) Trump Slashes Size of Bears Ears and Grand Staircase Monuments. *The New York Times*. Retrieved from https://www.nytimes.com/2017/12/04/us/trump-bears-ears.html

Twenge, J.M. (September, 2017) Has the Smartphone Destroyed a Generation? *The Atlantic*, 320(2): 59–65.

UCS. (n.d.) Each Country's Share of CO2 Emissions. *Union of Concerned Scientists*. USA. Retrieved from http://www.ucsusa.org/global_warming/science_and_impacts/science/each-countrys-share-of-co2.html#.WZsvciiGOUk

US Census Bureau. (June 25, 2015) Millennials Outnumber Baby Boomers and Are Far More Diverse. *The United States Census Bureau*. Retrieved from http://www.census.gov/newsroom/press-releases/2015/cb15-113.html

Vernon, S. (November 4, 2013) Will Social Security Run Out of Money? *CBS News*. Retrieved from https://www.cbsnews.com/news/will-social-security-run-out-of-money/

Viewpoints (n.d.) Is Genetically Modified Food Safe to Eat? *PBS*. Retrieved from http://www.pbs.org/wgbh/harvest/viewpoints/issafe.html

WOLA. (January 15, 2016) Washington Office on Latin America. Five Facts about Migration from Central America's Northern Triangle. *WOLA*. Retrieved from https://www.wola.org/analysis/five-facts-about-migration-from-central-americas-northern-triangle

Waldman, P. (January 26, 2015) Opinion: Why is GOP Going After Social Security? *CNN*. Retrieved from http://www.cnn.com/2015/01/26/opinion/waldman-social-security/

Warerkar, T. (May 19, 2016) Behold, NYC's 15 Most Rapidly Gentrifying Neighborhoods. *Curbed New York*. Retrieved from http://ny.curbed.com/2016/5/9/11641588/nyc-top-15-gentrifying-neighborhoods-williamsburg-harlem-bushwick

Williams, F. (May/June, 2012) How a Bunch of Scrappy Marines Could Help Vanquish Breast Cancer. *Mother Jones*. Retrieved from https://www.motherjones.com/environment/2012/05/camp-lejeune-marines-breast-cancer-florence-williams/

Wood, M., Hershman, H., Castle, C. (August 19, 2016) Oakland, California, Might Be the Center of Gentrification. *Marketplace*. Retrieved from https://www.marketplace.org/2016/08/19/life/oakland-ca-might-be-center-gentrification

Yoshinaga, K. (July 1, 2016) Babies of Color Are Now the Majority, Census Says. *NPR*. Retrieved from http://www.npr.org/sections/ed/2016/07/01/484325664/babies-of-color-are-now-the-majority-census-says

Note

1. This Pew research date designates the millennials as being born between 1981–1997 though researchers vary on the dates with some including 1980–2000, or 1982–2000, or 1982–2004.

CHAPTER 15

Social Change and the Twenty-first Century

WHAT YOU WILL READ ABOUT IN THIS CHAPTER:

- Manifesting a *humane society* is more complicated in an age of advanced technology. *Durkheim's* theory regarding the influence of *social integration* on personal well-being becomes more problematic with the changing nature of community. The increased dependency on social media and the decreases in church affiliations and other civic activities enhances feelings of fragmentation. Apart from dramatic natural disasters, there seems to be minimal cultural support for active compassion.

- *Social movements*, organized efforts to promote social change, do not arise overnight and often take time to be embraced as reflecting a "just" cause. Many people resist efforts to secure full rights for nondominant groups. Major movements for social changes have occurred with regard to issues of gender, race, ethnicity, sexual orientation, immigration, and poverty. The *Black Lives Matter* movement is the most recent manifestation of civil rights activity, particularly with regard to the death of African Americans at the hands of law enforcement and criminal justice personnel.

- As society becomes more diverse, issues of racial and religious *inclusion* become more pronounced. The question of how to embrace and incorporate *institutional* diversity remains problematic. These concerns apply to all marginalized groups.

- There is some evidence that the millennials are more likely to embrace inclusion of marginalized groups and support social mechanisms to accomplish such goals.

- The biggest issue in the near future will be employment and wages, as more work becomes automated and less labor intensive. How to provide a decent standard of living, especially for less skilled workers, is likely going to be a major social issue. *Basic Income Grants*, guaranteeing a minimal income, are proposed as a means to compensate for unemployment and low wages. Successful experiments have been accomplished with these decades ago in Canada. Such a program was recently defeated in a Swiss referendum but has been implemented in several settings, both domestically and internationally.

Introduction

How can we form a society which would be more compassionate and promote a high quality of life for all its inhabitants? In this last chapter, we return to the discussion (see Chapter 1) linking suicide to the lack of social integration or, in Durkheim's term, *anomie*. We know that feeling a part of the civil life of society is a protection against suicide. The isolation of people in private residences, the loss of physical community to technology, and the lack of protecting Americans' well-being with regard to health and familial supports, have all taken a toll. Harari (2017) shows that greater [cultural] prosperity does not bring commensurate gains in life satisfaction since significant increases in suicide rates often characterize the transitioning of a society from traditional to developed. As Junger suggests (Woodruff 2016), modern society has brought the human species some wonderful benefits, both in the ease of living conditions and in the treatment of ailments, but at what price to our humanity, especially in the care of less fortunate groups.

Modern life, with all its technological advancements and advantages, has brought psychological and emotional despair of a kind apparently absent in earlier societies. Suicide in the US has increased dramatically in recent years. Some research has suggested it is a consequence of economic struggles, particularly among unemployed White males. But increases in suicide among women have outpaced those of men and the research indicates that all people born after 1945 are experiencing increased vulnerability to suicide. This cohort represents the baby boomers, the most affluent generation in American society to date. Suicide is the leading cause of death in persons aged 18–49. The explanation appears to lie in the pervasive loneliness and social isolation of recent decades (Tavernise 2016): "Sociologists in general believe that when society robs people of self-control, individual dignity, or a connection to something larger than themselves, suicide rates rise" (Dokoupil 2013). Or as one author studying suicide remarks, "the absence of social connection triggers the same, primal alarm bells as hunger, thirst and physical pain" (Cacioppo in Entis 2016). Respecting the humanity of our neighbors and caring for them, whether through assuring healthcare, financial security, or basic neighborliness, may be much more crucial than a matter of mere courtesy; our life may literally depend on it (see Chapters 4 and 9). This lawn poster reminds us that we should affirm the value of human connection. As the African proverb states, "It takes a village to raise a child."

Figure 15.1 Lawn sign, Sacramento CA. "It takes a village to raise a child," but in many regions in contemporary society, the local village has been subsumed by the virtual community, which does not have the same impact on daily life and has been shown to increase feelings of isolation and depression

Source: Photography by Rosalind Gottfried

How Can We Develop a More Humane Society?

Societal well-being depends not only on individuals but on social policies supporting basic life needs, such as housing, nutrition, healthcare, education, and employment. Our nation has ample resources to provide for these but appears increasingly less inclined to do so. Institutional forces, political greed, and special interests frequently supersede the interests of the public. Documentarian Sebastian Junger defines tribe and its modern-day loss:

> The real and ancient meaning of tribe is the community that you live in that you share resources with that you would risk your life to defend.
>
> And, actually, I would say the Internet is doubly dangerous for all — and, again, for all of its miraculous capacity, not only does it not provide real community and real human connection. It gives you the illusion that it does, right?
>
> So, oh, I have got lots of friends on Facebook, so I'm good. You're actually not good. And I'm not an expert in this, but from what I studied for my book "Tribe," what you need is to feel people, smell them, hear them, feel them around you.
>
> I mean, that's the human connection that we evolved for, for hundreds of thousands of years. The Internet doesn't provide that.
>
> (Sebastian Junger, author of *Tribe* (2016),
> interview excerpts in Woodruff 2016)

Box 15.1 – Humane Society

A *humane society* would be one based on compassion for all, providing for the basic human needs of food, clothing, and shelter in a manner respecting human dignity for all citizens and residents.

Junger cites his experiences living with US military troops in Restrepo, Afghanistan, where 20 men slept in small spaces shoulder to shoulder, as illuminating the essential social nature of the human animal. Despite the horrors of war, he noticed that the men were reluctant to go home and he came to understand that returning to their "real" lives represented a particular kind of loss. The urgency of caring deeply for another when your life depended on it was a life-changing experience. Totally apart from the actual war service, the soldiers did not want to lose the intensity of the affiliations they felt for each other. Life at home, in contrast, frequently is characterized by impersonal experiences, disconnection, and lack of purpose. Junger observes that it takes a crisis such as 9/11, dramatically severe hurricanes, wild fires, or the death of another African American youth, to bring the community into common cause. Daily routines keep most people invested only in their immediate relationships. Supporting evidence can be seen in the fact that suicide and depression decrease in times of crisis, as does violent crime and murder (Woodruff 2016).

Suicide, as noted above, has been on the rise since 1945. Junger maintains that his "privileged" suburban childhood amounted to "the loneliest place in the world." Suburbia is the legacy of the post-World War II era, made possible by cheap housing and gas and decent working- and middle-class wages. The idyllic childhood based on neighborhood and stay at home mothers was a short-lived lifestyle, restricted to a couple of decades and specific to certain regions and groups of people. Today, life is further complicated by easy "virtual" access to others, which may provide the illusion of connection while actually impeding it. Technological connections are unfulfilling, in many ways, compromising the content of discourse and even influencing the tenor and frequency of face to face interactions. Junger's solution, echoed in many commentaries on modern life, suggests it is imperative to reconnect with our basic *human-being-ness*, highlighting our interdependence and social nature. Multiple experiments show that mutual relationships of care and reciprocity are what most people, and many animals, crave (Harari 2017, Chapter 3). Research shows that people value experience more than things (Hamblin 2014). Throughout American history, from the Revolution to the *Black Lives Matter* movement, some people have sought to improve the quality of life for all.

What Are Social Movements?

Social movements are sustained mass movements to effect changes addressing forces negatively impacting a segment of society. Most social movements in the US have been in the tradition of *reform movements*. *Reform movements* are social movements which advocate for significant change by expanding or modifying current institutions. Movements which promote the destruction of existing institutions and their replacement with institutions representing deep social structural changes are considered *revolutionary movements*. Social movements differ from *collective action*, where a group spontaneously protests an event or unfavorable condition but lacks an organizational structure and articulated long-term goals. If collective actions generate leadership and clearly articulated platforms, they can transform into social movements. The collective efforts of soldiers and citizens during World War II resulted in an era of activism by groups working to extend societal ideals to a wider range of society's members. The experiences of soldiers, fighting for democracy abroad, inspired the extension to seeking equal treatment at home. This activity culminated in legislation extending military benefits to all groups who served. The activism also infiltrated the culture through the civil rights movement, the women's movement, and the anti-Vietnam war movement. The "Occupy" movement, highlighting the dominance of the "1 percent," over a period of several weeks, became a national phenomenon reverberating in the public consciousness, referred to by politicians and celebrities, prominent in social media, and incorporated into the fabric of business. However, it failed to emerge as a coordinated social movement, due in part to its lack of leadership and its failure to articulate a specific strategy to accomplish vaguely formulated social changes (Gautney 2011). Later analyses suggest it did make an impact, especially with regard to the content of the 2016 presidential campaigns, in which each party gave central play to issues of economic inequality (Levitin 2015). The prevalence of the "1 percent," as a common term referring to the very wealthy, attests to its impact.

The use of social media as a tool contributing to social movements plays a part in coordinating social activism, though its long-term impact requires further study (Tufekci 2011). E-petitions have become commonplace and research shows they either proliferate quickly or "die" in hours (Matias 2016). The seemingly constant flow of petitions generated by the actions of President Trump may not be successful in influencing his behaviors but it is suggested that they are significant in recruiting people to organizations with political agendas (Carpenter 2017). These groups represent the extension of full civil and human rights regardless of sex, gender identification, sexual orientation, immigrant status, race, religion, or ethnicity.

Box 15.2 – Social Movements

Social movements are organized mass movements to create significant social changes in the social institutions, laws, or practices of society. Modern social movements of the post-World War II era include demands for women's rights, civil rights, environmental rights, gay and transgender rights, social justice, and peace.

Reform movements are social movements which promote change by expanding, or modifying, current institutions. Movements which seek the destruction of existing institutions would be considered *revolutionary movement*s.

Feminist (Women's) Movements

The *first wave of a feminist movement* grew out of the abolitionist movement. As women participated in the anti-slavery movement, they grew more conscious of the ways in which they were maintained in positions of subservience. They also learned practical matters, such as how to strategize to make social and legal changes. Collective action for the initial women's movement is often attributed to the *1848 Seneca Fall Women's Rights Convention* calling for the inclusion of women in all citizen rights. After this two-day program, attended by 200 women, a subsequent meeting convened in Rochester NY and became an annual event. Attendees were drawn from the abolition movement and the nascent women's suffrage movement. The movement's concerns were temporarily derailed by the Civil War. Seventy years of arduous strategizing, often resulting in conflicting priorities, preceded the states' ratification of the 19th amendment in 1920. Frequently, the divisiveness fell along the lines of race and class interests, causing alienation between groups of women, some of whom formed their own associations or withdrew from the movement. The general public, largely unsympathetic to the demands of the women, frequently responded to activism with derision and hostility. Women eventually took up more dramatic activities, adding to demonstrations by getting arrested and going on hunger strikes.

Figure 15.2 The American suffragette movement was almost exclusively composed of White women of affluence. It took 70 years of concerted effort to accomplish the enfranchisement of women Source: Everett Historical / Shutterstock.com

A period of relative dormancy was sustained after the vote was won, extending to the early 1960s.

Box 15.3 – Feminist Movements

The modern *feminist movements* are comprised of at least three distinctive phases. The *first wave* refers to the feminist movement originating in the abolitionist movement of the nineteenth century. This effort was derailed by the Civil War but regained momentum by the 1870s. Chief among its concerns was the passage of women's suffrage, accomplished by the 19th amendment to the American Constitution, ratified in 1920.

The *second wave* of feminism generally is considered as emerging from the anti-Vietnam War, student, and civil rights movements of the 1960s. Its chief concerns were reproductive rights, work and pay equity, equal education opportunity, sports funding in education, and political representation and participation. Often criticized as elitist, it failed to incorporate the participation and concerns of poor and working women, and women of color.

The *third wave* of the feminist movement, generally attributed to women of the millennial generation, especially focuses on issues of support for working parents, such as paid sick and family leave, flexible work schedules, job sharing and part-time work, pay equity, healthcare, and daycare supports. This group is more apt to highlight issues of *intersectionality* and inclusion of women of color, the disabled, and the gender fluid.

The cultural antipathy to the movement, even at times among women, was reflected again in the *second wave of the women's movement* where issues ranged from work opportunities, to equal pay, to reproductive rights, to civil rights for married women. It is difficult to pinpoint a specific date as the origin of the *second wave.* Some consider 1963 pivotal since that is the year Betty Friedan published *The Feminine Mystique* and John F. Kennedy established the *Presidential Commission on the Status of Women.* The president's mandate actually was a concession to women in compensation for the failure to include the *Equal Rights Amendment* in the 1960 Democratic Party platform. The Democrats feared abandonment by women voters.

Another contributing factor in the development of the second wave concerns women's participation in the civil rights, student, and anti-war movements of the sixties. Women frequently were relegated to limited roles in these movements and ultimately this led to applying a gender analysis to the groups' dynamics. The mainstream feminist movement of this era has accurately been criticized as representing the interests of White middle-class women, especially with regard to the emphasis on goals leading to equality in education, employment, wages, reproductive rights, and politics. Many working-class and nonWhite women felt their life experiences were disparate from the movement's concerns and that their needs were omitted from the feminist agenda. They were especially sensitive to the necessity of building alliances with the men in their communities, believing that gender issues could not be segregated from race and class. The intersectionality of race, class, and gender isolated them from their affluent White associates. The contours of their lives already looked more "feminist" in that they worked, raised families, and were active in community organizations; they did not adopt the housewife role as a primary identifying role, as did many middle-class women of the era. They were more focused on conditions of employment such as wages and hours, which strained their ability to provide adequately for their families' needs. Their feminism was "active" rather than theoretical, and expressed in grassroots organizing, "from the bottom up" (Steinem 2015). African American and Native American women engaged in activism, predating the second wave, while Latina and Asian American women's activism generally occurred with the onset of the second wave.

The organizations and activities of the mainstream movement nevertheless had a significant impact in the culture. Privileged women had more choices, leisure, and resources to participate in "consciousness raising" groups and develop political organizations to advance their interests. One phrase associated with the second wave movement, "the personal is political," highlighted issues believed to be "personal" but which actually needed to be addressed by social policy. Women rejected the idea that issues of reproductive rights, abortion rights, equal pay, healthcare, maternity leave, subsidized daycare, changes in clothing, credit and financial issues, and sufficient safety nets were merely personal and the responsibility of women. Legal and structural changes were necessary to accomplish these and men also had to change their concepts of gender, regarding both women's roles and their own. Organizations supporting these concerns developed and enjoy wider membership today, since many of these goals have not yet been fully realized. Some of these groups include the *National Organization for Women* (NOW), *Emily's List,* and the *National Abortion and Reproductive Rights Action League.* There are also women's and Black caucuses in the Houses of Congress and in state political entities.

TV's *Mad Men:* Women at Work at the Cusp of the Second Wave

Higher education for women expanded in the 1950s but jobs available to these women were not commensurate with their education and skills. Many women worked only while they were single or if they made an "unfortunate" marriage. It was not unusual for women to have male supervisors who possessed less education, credentials, and experience. Women with years of experience were even required to train men to be their bosses and not contest the situation. This lack of access to better jobs cost women literally millions of dollars over their lifetime (see Chapter 7).

For some affluent women, working was not typically a viable option once they were married. Even if they desired to work, frequently their husbands would not support them in this goal and the cultural milieu also dissuaded them from labor force participation (Friedan 1963). The television series *Mad Men* (Weiner 2007–15) captures the attitudes of that era towards women in the workforce. The objectification of attractive women working in support staff positions is portrayed by the character of Joan Holloway whose intelligence and drive is subjugated to her being treated as a sex object. The character's business acumen is shown over years of deliberate machinations, punctuated by many incidents of humiliation as the recipient of snide and patronizing commentary. Her character ultimately triumphs by obtaining some leverage, culminating in a small portion of company ownership. But at what cost? Though a proud woman, there is no mistaking that her ascendance cost her dearly.

The role of Peggy Olson, who ultimately becomes an ad writer, reveals the arduous and circuitous route to gain professional level no matter how much intelligence and wit is brought into the workplace. The Olson character sees a chance to contribute a "woman's view" to ad campaigns and peddles her ideas. At first, she is expected to be content with having her ideas adopted rather than having her title changed. Eventually, through the "generosity" of her boss as benefactor, she advances in her career, in many ways surpassing her male colleagues, though she also pays a high price. Still, these women are strong characters in that they prevail against multiple odds and countless hurdles (Chval 2015). Each of these women undergoes multiple transformations as they learn how to manipulate their situations to accomplish their goals. Smart, focused, insightful, and motivated, we are left to ponder what would have been accomplished if they had been born 50 years later, or born male.

The third wave of feminism starts with the post baby boom generation, born after 1964. These women seek to extend initial gains in politics, education, and culture (Straus 2000). Policies promoting work and family balance for all domestic partners, regardless of gender or sexual orientation, are especially highlighted in demands for paid family leave, sick days, daycare subsidies, and family-friendly work policies such as flexible scheduling, working remotely, job sharing, and part-time employment. The millennial women are more attentive to issues of *intersectionality*, highlighting inclusion of women of color and women with nontraditional sexualities or gender identities (Lueptow 2014; Jacob, n.d.). Nevertheless, the feminist movement still reverts to the biases of White, professional women. The organizers of the January 2017 *Women's March on Washington* failed to incorporate diverse groups until called out regarding their omission, though their response to the criticism was rapid (Rand 2017). The California state women's march in January 2017 also was charged with lacking diversity and ultimately separated into two separate rallies outside the Sacramento State Capitol (Eventbrite 2017).

Third wave women are more likely to view men as allies for change than as the oppressors. So far, many more women have embraced "male" roles to be sole, or primary, breadwinners while a much smaller group of men have taken on traditional domestic roles of full-time homemakers or single parents. In light of the changing economy, and the swelling ranks of full-time working women, it is suggested that men need to make commensurate modifications in their roles, especially in the home, if a nonsexist society is to become a reality. Cultural and legal reforms have a long way to go before the sexes can be said to have achieved societal equality. Legislative changes have been won, and lost, and remain contentious as can be seen in the areas of reproductive rights, violence against women, parental leave, wages, and other workplace issues. The recent barrage of media reports of sexual harassment incidents, ranging from assault and rape to verbal denigration, further points to the long road ahead.

A Men's Movement?

By the mid-1970s, men were organizing for a "men's movement" to free themselves from traditional mandates of *masculinity*. The men's movement expressed concerns ranging from gaining legal rights to inter- and intrapersonal challenges to develop more "emotional intelligence." The question of whether men need a *social movement*, similar to the women's movement, is debatable. Men's groups developed in the 1970s, chiefly concerned with exploring issues regarding psychological well-being and masculinity, though some strongly promoted the need to address laws which favor women, as in divorce and child custody. By the 1980s, segments of the men's movement had morphed into an anti-feminist movement (Blake 2015) and even created a backlash against the women's movement (Faludi 1991). Some proponents of the men's movement, partially due to pressure to be more like women, chose to celebrate the unique male energy and embrace it (Bly 2015).

Some women believe that a men's movement calling for policy and legal changes unfairly equates the oppression of men with that of women. Others believe that as women gain equality men will necessarily be liberated from core demands of the traditional male role, making a separate movement unnecessary. But gender is not just a matter of social roles; there are issues of socialization, intimacy, cultural symbolism, appearance, and much more. Although women may have an interest in promoting men's consciousness raising, which could lead to better personal relationships, some feel that shedding traditional male roles is more appropriately dealt with among men. Nevertheless, in spite of recent media attention regarding the stagnation of working men's wages, men are still the dominant sex in terms of economics, government, business, and leadership (Coontz 2012).

> ## Box 15.4 – Men's Movement
>
> A **men's movement** developed in the 1970s, largely in response to changes in women's roles. The men's movement focuses less on issues of economic justice and more on the nature of the masculine role, especially with respect to relationships, family, and legal issues associated with these. Some key figures in the movement have become associated with a backlash against women.

Gay Rights

Many young people are unaware of the extent to which gay people were persecuted in the twentieth century. Gay persons lived in fear of losing jobs, social status, housing, and even their freedom if they were identified as gay, since homosexuality violated the sodomy laws. Activism dates back to the early decades of the twentieth century. Sporadic actions characterized the earlier movement. The first Gay Rights organization was founded in Chicago in 1924 by Henry Gerber. The Mattachine Society was established in 1950 by activist Harry Hay to promote social support for gay people. In 1952 the American Psychiatric Association (APA) listed homosexuality as a sociopathic personality disturbance (LGBT Rights 2017). In 1953, President Dwight Eisenhower barred homosexuals from federal employment, establishing them as "security risks." In 1961, the state of Illinois became the first state to decriminalize homosexuality by repealing its sodomy laws. The APA removed homosexuality from its list of "psychiatric disorders" in 1973, partially in response to organized protests.

The gay rights movement transitioned to a more mass movement with the *Stonewall Riots* of 1969 (PBS 2011), generally regarded as the initiating event of the movement. In 1969, police raided the Stonewall Inn, a gay bar in Greenwich village in New York City. They were attempting to enforce a law which denied the service of alcoholic beverages to homosexuals. The patrons fought back and they persisted for days, garnering support from friends, relatives, and concerned allies. In the 1970s, the gay rights movement adopted the pink triangle as a symbol of gay pride, appropriating the design which previously had been utilized as a symbol of homosexual "perversion and deviance" (LGBT Rights 2017). The first rainbow flag, adopted as a symbol of the gay rights movement, was sewn in 1978 by Gilbert Baker.

> ### Box 15.5 – Gay Rights
>
> *Gay rights*, as a social movement, was initiated in the street protests of 1969, arising from police attacks against the patrons of a gay bar, *The Stonewall Inn*, in NYC. Decades of social action to obtain legal rights and social acceptance for homosexuality followed that uprising. A 2015 Supreme Court decision prohibits discrimination in marriage with respect to gender identity or sexual orientation. Agitation for full civil rights in areas of work, housing, and law persists.

In the ensuing years, following the Stonewall "riots," the gay rights movement accomplished new rights and underwent numerous setbacks (LGBT Rights 2017). The first National March for gay rights occurred in 1979. In 1993, Clinton established the "Don't Ask, Don't Tell" mandate which allowed for gay persons to serve in the military, from which they were previously barred, as long as they were *closeted*. This policy was reversed during the Obama administration in 2011. In 2015, the *Military Equal Opportunity Act* was extended to protect gay and lesbian military personnel.

In recognition of homophobia, in 1995 sexual orientation was included in the *Hate Crimes Sentencing Enhancement Act*, allowing for harsher sentences in acts which constitute *hate crimes*, defined as those stemming from categorical membership in protected groups with respect to race, color, religion, national origin, ethnicity, gender, and disability. Homosexual couples still faced discrimination and violence and were denied the legal benefits which are protected under marriage. Many long-term couples lived as "housemates," even to their friends and relatives. Gay activists fought for the right to marry. Initially granted under state laws in various states, the right was won and lost multiple times before gaining permanent legal status. Gay marriage suffered a setback in 1996, when the Clinton administration passed the *Defense of Marriage Act* (DOMA) officially recognizing legal marriage *only* between heterosexual partners. That same year, the state of Hawaii established an opposing precedent stating that there was no legal provision to deprive gay persons of the right to marry. In 2000, Vermont became the first state to recognize the civil unions of gay couples. Massachusetts become the first state to permit legal marriage of gays in 2004, followed by New Jersey in 2006. Then, in 2008, California voters passed a proposition outlawing gay marriage, which was overturned in the federal courts in 2010. Finally, the right to marry, regardless of gender identity or sexual orientation, was upheld by a 5:4 vote of the US Supreme Court in 2015 (Liebelson and Terkel 2015). However, state and county initiatives to prohibit gay marriage persist, even after the 2015 Supreme Court ruling, but ultimately are defeated in the courts (Binder 2015; Binder and Perez-Pena 2015).

The right to marry does not ensure full civil rights for gay and lesbian people. Social and cultural discrimination persists, as does organized resistance to it. In 2015, for example, the Boy Scouts of America rescinded its prohibition of gay leaders and gay employees. In 2016, President Obama established the Stonewall

Figure 15.3 The site of the NY Stonewall riots (2017), initiating the gay rights movement in 1969. The federal government now ensures the rights of gay and lesbians to legally marry and to seek all civil and employment rights guaranteed by the Civil Rights Act of 1964
Source: Photography by Rosalind Gottfried

Inn and the surrounding neighborhood as the first national monument to gay rights (Rosenberg 2016). This national recognition places the struggle for gay rights as a "legitimate" social movement, central to accomplishing civil rights for all Americans. The right of gay persons to file for protection from discrimination, as guaranteed by the 1964 Civil Rights Act, was definitively established in a federal appeals court in 2017 (Phillips 2017).

Gay Rights as Civil Rights

The term civil rights is most closely associated with the struggle for racial equality but it pertains equally to any group suffering discrimination and denied basic Constitutional rights and protections. The following is an excerpt from a gay man's letter to President Barack Obama:

> I brought my twins to D.C. to witness your second inauguration in 2013; they turned four that very day. While they innocently thought that everyone had gathered at the Capitol for their birthday, our family did receive a present on that bitter cold morning just the same. I was floored by your mention of Stonewall in the same breath as Seneca Falls and Selma – incredulously asking everyone around me "Did he really just say that?" Yes, the President of the United States just gave legitimacy to my struggle as a gay man, and you're damn right I shed a tear or two in appreciation. Our family returned to D.C. later that winter to be part of a rally at the Supreme Court when the Windsor case was being heard. This was more of a pilgrimage than a road trip. When I was a young man, I couldn't fathom being comfortable enough with my sexuality to bring a boyfriend home, let alone think about marriage, the most "normal" of American institutions. Now I was a grown partnered man, bringing his kids to the site where history was being made. Your administration's decision to no longer defend the indefensible DOMA, paved the way for the court's eventual decision. I just had to be in the room where it happened.
>
> (Bua 2017)

Transgender Rights

There are an estimated 700,000 transgendered people in the US. A transgender identity does not connote anything about sexual orientation; trans individuals possess any sexual orientation including straight, gay or bisexuality (see Chapter 7; Parvini and Anderson 2015). The social movement for transgender rights is a more recent development since there was previously little recognition of the legitimacy of a trans identity. Issues affecting the transgender population have received specific attention since the post-World War II era when a San Francisco doctor, Harry Benjamin, pioneered hormone therapy in treating patients (Head 2017). In 1959, the first recorded request for a marriage license for a transgendered woman and a cisgendered man was denied in New York. In 1976, the state of New Jersey decided, in a Superior Court case, to allow people to marry according to their current gender identity (Head 2017). The National Center for Transgender Equality was established in 2003 to advocate for equal protections for transgendered persons (NCTE n.d.).

> **Box 15.6 – Transgender Movement**
>
> The *transgender movement* is a more recently developed social movement. The first recorded act demanding transgender rights occurred in New York in 1959, when a trans woman was denied a license to marry a cisgendered man. The transgender movement promotes equal rights for all transgendered persons in all avenues of social life, from work and wages to marriage and parenthood.

Transgendered persons suffer discrimination in virtually all aspects of society—work, housing, domestic life, education, the military, healthcare, physical and mental health, and access to bathrooms. Unemployment rates are twice as high as in the general population (Parvini and Anderson 2015). As of 2015, only 16 states, and the District of Columbia, prohibit job discrimination based on gender identity, despite a 1989 US Supreme Court case establishing that transgendered persons are included in Title 7 protections regarding sex stereotyping in employment (Head 2017). In 2009, the Employment Non-Discrimination Act incorporated protection for transgendered persons, who were formerly excluded from the Act (Head 2017).

Young people suffer discrimination in the education system, not only in peer assaults but through school policies. In May 2016, the Obama administration mandated protection for transgendered youths in school bathrooms and locker rooms, suggesting that this access was protected under Title IX of the Civil Rights Act. Some states challenged the Obama order. North Carolina passed a "bathroom bill," establishing the use of bathrooms by *birth* gender, leading to significant financial losses when entertainment, athletic events, and businesses boycotted its venues in protest (Abadi 2016; Jurney 2016). In March 2017, the state instituted a partial repeal of the bill, making allowances for the use of facilities aligning with a person's *chosen* gender identity but leaving intact another portion of the bill prohibiting mandatory protection of transgendered persons by local law enforcement (Jurney 2016). Assessment of lost revenues, along with negative press brought about by the agitation by activists, influenced the partial repeal (Hanna et al. 2017).

Challenges to the hard-won rights of transgendered persons are in process as part of the Trump administration's policies. In February 2017, the federal departments of Education and Justice rescinded the Obama order protecting the transgender rights of students to utilize facilities by their chosen gender identity (Hersher and Johnson 2017). Trump's Attorney General, Jeff Sessions, opposes expanding the civil rights of gay, lesbian, and transgender persons (Peters et al. 2017). In December 2017, the US Court of Appeals in Washington DC upheld the right of transgendered persons to enlist in the military, denying a Trump administration initiative to halt this policy change. The case likely will be taken to the Supreme Court (AP 2017).

In December 2017, it was reported that the Trump administration was prohibiting the CDC from incorporating seven words in their annual budget. These words reportedly included: transgender, fetus, diversity, entitlement, science-based, evidence-based, and vulnerable. The story, published in the *Washington Post*, garnered much media attention. Protests erupted with the seven words, and the phrase "We will not be erased," projected onto the façade of the Trump International Hotel in Washington. The CDC, a part of the Department of Health and Human Services, has denied the report and affirmed its commitment to "evidence-based science" (Domonoske 2017). The alleged ban has raised the fears of the community, especially with respect to other Trump administration initiatives.

Because of the cultural attitudes, and discrimination suffered by transgendered persons, 41 percent of that population has attempted suicide, compared with 1.6 percent of the general population (Parvini and Anderson 2015). Transgendered individuals, often subjected to targeted violence, are protected by the *Matthew Shephard and James Byrd Jr. Hate Crimes Act of 2009*. The International Trans Day of Visibility (TDOV), March 31, was established in 2009 to bring attention to the discrimination suffered by the transgendered population.

The Civil Rights Movement for Racial Equality

The US history of slavery, indentured servitude, and Jim Crow laws reflects the long history of suffering among the African American population. Efforts to gain full legal and human rights for the African American population predate the Civil War and remain a concern today. Legal changes occurring in the nineteenth century were largely ineffective in establishing equal civil rights. Legislation freeing the Confederate slaves (1863; 1865); the 14th amendment (1868) ensuring "due process and equal protection" to African Americans; and the 15th amendment (1870) granting African Americans and former slaves the legal right to vote (America's Civil Rights Timeline n.d.) failed in accomplishing their stated goals.

In 1905, W.E.B. Du Bois and other African American leaders established the *Niagara Movement* to fight against racial segregation and discrimination. By 1909 they joined with White activists to establish the *National Association for the Advancement of Colored People* (NAACP) to promote the civil and political rights of African Americans. The period 1910–1920, referred to as "the great migration," witnessed the mass movement of African Americans to the industrial north in search of better work and life opportunities. Although African Americans were discriminated against in jobs and housing, there were more opportunities in the north. Franklin D. Roosevelt (FDR) provided some aid in *the New Deal*, though racial discrimination persisted. By 1941, as the country's enhanced production for the war effort progressed, FDR issued *Executive Order 8802*, banning discrimination in the defense industry with regard to "race, creed, color, or national origin" (Executive Order 8802). The Fair Employment Practices Commission was initiated to ensure the law's enactment.

The era most often associated with the term, the *civil rights movement*, occurred as an outgrowth of World War II. In 1948, partially in recognition of the contributions of African Americans to the war effort, President Truman issued *Executive Orders 9980 and 9981* establishing fair practices in federal government agencies and the armed services. African American soldiers returning from war were inspired to fight for their own rights and found support in churches and other local groups. Subsequently, social actions became focused on issues of equal opportunity in education, employment, housing, and voting. The 1954 US Supreme Court Case *Brown v. The Board of*

Education of Topeka Kansas mandated the integration of public schools, with its declaration that separation of the races was inherently unequal. It took decades to integrate the schools in both the north and south and the implementation of the Court's order was met with widespread resistance and violence.

Many organizations participated in the national movement for racial rights, staging events illuminating inequalities and discrimination. The 1955 Montgomery bus boycott, initiated when Rosa Parks refused to relinquish her seat to a White person, lasted over a year and ended "colored sections" of city buses. The city ultimately capitulated when businesses became weary of lost revenues due to the Black boycott of downtown. In 1957, the *Southern Christian Leadership Conference* (SCLC) was established to promote **civil disobedience**, the deliberate breaking of unjust laws, to incite change. In 1960, after a "sit in" to integrate a Greensboro North Carolina lunch counter, college students organized the *Student Nonviolent Coordinating Committee* (SNCC) to establish racial equality. The freedom riders were groups of White and African Americans who boarded buses together in the mid-1960s to test new laws mandating integrated public transportation between states. They were frequently met with angry mobs and subjected to incidents of violence.

As the 1960s progressed, the national campaign for racial equality gained media and legal prominence. In 1963, M.L. King delivered his *I Have a Dream speech*, during the *March on Washington*, which famously advocated racial reconciliation and integration, and imagined a time when his own children would "not be judged by the color of their skin but by the content of their character" (King Jr 1963). In 1964, the 24th Constitutional amendment abolished poll taxes and in 1965, *The Voting Rights Act* was passed prohibiting measures common in the south which impeded African

Figure 15.4 To protect the safety of the Little Rock 9, as they integrated into Central High, the national guard escorted them to school to protect them from violent and angry mobs
Source: Library of Congress

Americans from voting (see Chapter 8). *Freedom Summer* commenced as a national effort to register people, especially in the south, to vote. It would take decades to accomplish the registration of African American voters. Partially in response to the civil rights activities in the south, President Johnson signed the *Civil Rights Act of 1964*. The bill represents a comprehensive piece of legislation addressing racial discrimination which would, in ensuing years, be amended to include categories beyond race, color, creed, and national origin. In 1967, Thurgood Marshall was appointed by President Johnson as the first African American US Supreme Court justice. *The Civil Rights Act* of 1968, often referred to as the Fair Housing Act, was established by President Johnson to prohibit discrimination in the sale, renting, and financing of housing. In 1988, the law was extended to include disabilities and family status (International Civil Right Center and Museum n.d.; Hud.gov n.d.).

> ## Box 15.7 – The Civil Rights Movement for Racial Equality
>
> The fight for racial equality dates back to the abolitionist movement of the pre-Civil War era and is reflected in the 14th and 15th Amendments to the Constitution. ***The civil rights movement*** is most commonly associated with the activism of the period from the 1940s to the 1970s, highlighting equal access to education, housing, voting, and public transportation.

The struggle for racial equality and rights for all marginalized groups persists in contemporary organizations and activities. The era commonly associated with phrase, *the civil rights movement*, is generally considered the period of activism following World War II to the assassination of M.L. King, Jr. in 1968. Acts challenging unfair practices were met with violence, arrests, and setbacks. In addition to the assassination of King, there was the murder of Medgar Evers, the Mississippi NAACP field secretary (1963) and the murder of Malcolm X, the leader of the Black nationalist movement (1965). Countless activists, protestors, and bystanders were injured, killed, or arrested. Other episodes of violence garnered major media attention. These included such events as the brutal Mississippi murder of the 14-year-old Emmett Till (1955) for allegedly whistling at a White woman; the 1963 deaths of four African American girls at the 16th Street Baptist Church in Birmingham; and the 1964 murders of three *Freedom Summer* activists in Mississippi. Two of the three young people killed in that episode were White and, as a consequence of their deaths, the civil rights movement became more widely reported. Many documentaries, feature films, and books commemorate the most notorious battles over school desegregation at Little Rock High School (1957), William Frantz Elementary School in New Orleans (1960), and the University of Mississippi (1962). The Selma, Alabama marches of 1965 and Freedom Summer also have been the subject of documentary and feature films. Images of these episodes of violence have become icons of the movement. To commemorate the contributions, and struggles, of the African American population, the Smithsonian Institution planned its nineteenth museum to be a National Museum of African American History and Culture in

Figure 15.5 To provide for her safety, Ruby Bridges was escorted to her first-grade classroom at William Frantz Elementary School in New Orleans (LA). The White parents kept their children home in protest; by the end of the year, there were no White children at the school. This painting was made by American artist Normal Rockwell. The national guard escorted Ruby to school on a daily basis
Source: White House Photo / Alamy Stock Photo

Washington, DC. It opened in September 2016 and is the only museum devoted solely to African American culture and history. It provides both permanent and special exhibits (NMAAHC n.d.). Despite the national recognition of the arduous struggle for racial equality, some commentators believe that true inclusion will not occur until the government officially recognizes the incalculable contributions of the African American population by establishing some system of reparations (Coates 2014).

Black Lives Matter

In recent years, the African American community has risen up to counter the disregard for Black lives as evidenced by the physical brutality exercised by law enforcement personnel. The national focus was incited by the case of the unarmed 17-year-old Trayvon Martin (2012), shot for "walking while being Black" in a predominantly White neighborhood. African Americans have been dealing with their physical vulnerability, just for being in public, for decades. The circumstances surrounding the Martin case catapulted the issue into national prominence when George Zimmerman, a neighborhood watch captain, fatally shot Martin after being told by a neighborhood watch dispatcher not to pursue the young man. When Zimmerman was acquitted of the murder, the African American community reacted by launching the *Black Lives Matter* movement to protest the persistent acts of violence; the lack of legal accountability of law enforcement; and societal indifference to the plight of the Black population (*Black Lives Matter*). President Obama made the following comments regarding Trayvon Martin's death:

> And for those who resist that idea that we should think about something like these "stand your ground" laws, I'd just ask people to consider, if Trayvon Martin was of age and armed, could he have stood his ground on

that sidewalk? And do we actually think that he would have been justified in shooting Mr. Zimmerman who had followed him in a car because he felt threatened? And if the answer to that question is at least ambiguous, then it seems to me that we might want to examine those kinds of laws.

... we need to spend some time in thinking about how do we bolster and reinforce our African American boys. And this is something that Michelle and I talk a lot about. There are a lot of kids out there who need help who are getting a lot of negative reinforcement. And is there more that we can do to give them the sense that their country cares about them and values them and is willing to invest in them?

... And for us to be able to gather together business leaders and local elected officials and clergy and celebrities and athletes, and figure out how are we doing a better job helping young African American men feel that they're a full part of this society and that they've got pathways and avenues to succeed – I think that would be a pretty good outcome from what was obviously a tragic situation. And we're going to spend some time working on that and thinking about that.

And then, finally, I think it's going to be important for all of us to do some soul-searching. There has been talk about should we convene a conversation on race ...

And let me just leave you with a final thought that, as difficult and challenging as this whole episode has been for a lot of people, I don't want us to lose sight that things are getting better. Each successive generation seems to be making progress in changing attitudes when it comes to race. It doesn't mean we're in a post-racial society. It doesn't mean that racism is eliminated. But when I talk to Malia and Sasha, and I listen to their friends and I see them interact,

Figure 15.6 Protests followed the acquittal of neighborhood watch volunteer George Zimmerman for the killing of 17-year-old Trayvon Martin, who was simply walking in a Florida neighborhood. African American families have been facing fears with regard to their sons and law enforcement for decades
Source: Janine Wiedel Photolibrary / Alamy Stock Photo

Figure 15.7 *Black Lives Matter* billboard, Sacramento CA
Source: Photography by Rosalind Gottfried

they're better than we are – they're better than we were – on these issues. And that's true in every community that I've visited all across the country.

(Obama 2013)

In 2016, 258 Black people were killed by police, many unarmed and/or in non-threatening positions of compliance (Craven 2017). In July 2016, gunfire erupted

Figure 15.8 African American parents have always recognized the need to discuss issues of safety with their children but events of police shootings of African American youths have catapulted this need into public awareness with the *Black Lives Matter* movement. This sign asserts the persistent anxiety among the African American population
Source: Mark Kerrison / Alamy Stock Photo

during a peaceful *Black Lives Matter* demonstration in Dallas, Texas, resulting in the death of five police officers and the wounding of another seven officers and two demonstrators (Fernandez et al. 2016). Media images of the Dallas demonstration instigated national reflection regarding issues surrounding violence, race, law enforcement, and gun control.

> ### Box 15.8 – *Black Lives Matter*
>
> **#*Black Lives Matter*** is a national movement of Black activists seeking justice for Black Americans, particularly in the use of deadly force by law enforcement; the lack of legal accountability for consequent injury and death; and societal indifference to the plight of the Black community.

As a result of increased scrutiny, there have been resignations and firings of law enforcement personnel but very few criminal convictions. In thousands of cases of police killings since 2005, only 54 resulted in charges. Most of these cases ended in acquittal and very few of those convicted spent any time in detention. The absence of a weapon on an alleged suspect is not sufficient to obtain a conviction. Exceptional circumstances, such as being shot in the back, must be proven (Kindy and Kelly 2015). Some observers feel that despite the media attention on the *Black Lives Matter* campaign, the cultural disregard for Black life persists unabated. Activists in the movement suggest that the dominant groups just do not "get it." They point to conversion of the phrase to, "#AllLivesMatter," in some speeches and publications as testament to the inability of American culture to focus on the persistent plight specifically accruing to the Black population (Victor 2016).

The Chicano Movement

The Chicano movement also has its roots in the post-World War II era. Early actions addressed issues of equal access and full integration. A 1947 ruling from southern California in the US 9th Circuit Court of Appeals, *Mendez v Westminster* (Macias 2014), prohibited segregation of Latinos and Anglos in public schools. In 1954, in *Hernandez v Texas* (Macias 2014), the Supreme Court established that the 14th amendment protected *all* racial groups against discrimination. These cases, and the increased size and visibility of the Latino population, brought issues of ethnic discrimination into cultural relief. The political weight of the Hispanic population, as it was referred to then, was first recognized during the presidential campaign of J.F. Kennedy. The *Mexican American Political Association* came out in support of his candidacy, establishing its base as a significant voting bloc. In recognition of the group's contribution to his successful run, Kennedy appointed Hispanics to his administration and addressed community concerns (Nittle 2016).

In the later 1960s, the *Mexican American Legal Defense and Education Fund* was established to address ongoing issues of access and discrimination. Latino community activists created actions to garner national attention for equal rights for Latinos. In 1966, Reies Lopez Tijerina led a march from Albuquerque NM to the state capital

Figure 15.9 A mural honoring the farm workers' unionization efforts
Source: Pineros y Campesinos Unidos del Noroeste

in Santa Fe, protesting the illegal annexing of Mexican land to the US southwest. Activist Poet Rodolfo "Corky" Gonzalez agitated for a separate Mexican American state (Nittle 2016). The first National Chicano Conference convened in 1969. Mexican California farm laborers, joining with the Filipino workers, established the United Farm Workers Union from 1965–1970 (see Chapter 12). In the 1970s, the Supreme Court made it illegal to deny a public education to non-English speaking persons and the *Equal Opportunity Act* of 1974 led to the implementation of bilingual education.

Box 15.9 – The Chicano Movement

The Chicano movement has its origins in the activism of the post-World War II era. The late 1960s and 1970s saw the development of organizations to protect the legal, educational, and cultural rights and values of Chicanos, a word first used to politicize the formerly more "neutral" term of Hispanic. The *M.E.Ch.A.* student organization developed to promote Chicano/a Studies and integration into the education curricula. *UnidosUS*, with roots in the civil rights era, is the largest Latino advocacy group today.

The political activism of the 1960s spread to college campuses with protests highlighting the male, Euro-centric curricula. Latino groups established demands to make the curricula inclusive; address the high dropout rate of Latinos; and end the ban on speaking Spanish at school (Nittle 2016). In 1969, multiple student organizations, led by Rodolfo Gonzalez, combined into *El Movimiento Estudiantil Chicano de Aztlan,* or *M.E.Ch.A.* as it is known today (Castaneda 2006). The group created a plan, originating at the University of California, Santa Barbara, to reclaim cultural and historical identities and promote self-determination. The group's ethos is reflected in its name: The word Chicanx, formerly considered an ethnic slur, was redefined to stand as a source of pride, symbolizing the social movement against the group's oppression:

> The Mexican-American (Hispanic) is a person who lacks respect for his/her cultural and ethnic heritage. Unsure of her/himself, she/he seeks assimilation as a way out of her/his "degraded" social status. Consequently, she/he remains politically ineffective. In contrast, Chicanismo reflects self-respect and pride in one's ethnic and cultural background. Thus, the (Chicanx) acts with confidence and with a range of alternatives in the political world. She/he is capable of developing an effective ideology through action – *El Plan de Santa Barbara*.
>
> (M.E.Ch.A. n.d.)

> Today we understand Aztlán not as a defined territory. Instead, it is an idea that unifies all Raza as a sacred place of origin, to which Raza espouse a physical connection. Aztlán is the common homeland and is the place of the collective experience and social praxis.
>
> (M.E.Ch.A. n.d.)

M.E.Ch.A. helped to establish courses, and departments, in Chicano/a studies. There are active chapters in high schools and institutions of higher education across the country.

As the largest nondominant group in the US today, the Latino population is a group with the potential to exert a great impact on the shape of the future. The Latino population represents 12 percent of all voters, accounting for 37 percent of the new voters between the 2012 and 2016 elections. The Latinos constitute a significant voting bloc, courted by both major political parties. The Latino population has generally affiliated with the Democratic Party, suggesting that they feel that party will better represent their concerns. As Latinos become more established and diversified, the portion of Latinos stating that the Democrats are more concerned than the Republican with Latino issues has declined slightly between 2012 and 2016, with one quarter of Latinos reported as perceiving no essential differences between the parties. Consequently, the group is no longer considered to be more aligned with the Democrats. In some states, the group is not as pivotal as it could be since the majority of Latino voters are in states which have a clear political party preference; only three of the seven strongly contested states have a significant portion of Latino voters (Krogstad 2016). Ideally, the community should act with unity to achieve its maximum influence, but differences in immigration trends and socio-economic status potentially dilute the group's impact.

Multiple organizations operate today to promote the interests of the Latino population. *The National Council of La Raza*, NCLR, initially called the *Southwest Council of La Raza*, established in 1968, became a national organization in

1972 and is currently the largest Latino advocacy group. The term *la raza*, literally defined as *race*, was selected for its associated meaning referring to "the people," or "community." In 2017, the group changed its name to *UnidosUS*, to more accurately reflect the position of the community today. The new name was chosen to reduce criticism, largely from the Republicans, that the organization was promoting a racist, separatist, agenda. *Unidos*, Spanish for *united*, used in conjunction with *US*, is meant to convey the activity of the Latino community as embedded in US culture, suggesting a dual identity combining ethnic pride with full participation in the dominant culture (Gamboa 2017). This national advocacy group, representing the community's interests in a wide range of cultural issues, is supported by many other Latino organizations with more specific areas of focus in politics, education, law, journalism, medicine, science, finance, and social services—covering virtually all areas of civic and political life (Diversity Best Practices 2014).

The Native American Rights Movement

Native Americans have lived in North America for over 10,000 years. Since the time of the Europeans' arrival, they have been subjected to forced relocations, disease, servitude, and cultural annihilation. With the establishment of the US government, the Indigenous peoples have suffered broken treaties, family separations, forced assimilation, theft of natural resources on their lands, and loss of sites relating to their cultural heritages. At the time of the European arrival, over 500 years ago, the Native American population is estimated to have been between 10 and 16 million (Faville n.d.), while presently it is estimated at 2.5 million. The Native Americans were not granted citizenship until 1924, after many had served in the US military during World War I. State laws effectively barred many from voting, even after the enactment of the *Voters Rights Act of 1965* (Native Americans n.d.).

In the post-World War II era, the US government instituted a policy of urban relocation of Indigenous peoples, imposing cultural assimilation, with catastrophic consequences for the integrity of the communities. Many of the Indigenous urban residents suffered impoverished conditions and failed to "adjust." In 1961, the policy was discontinued but it was an unwelcome reminder of all the times that Indigenous families were separated and subjected to government plans to "better" their conditions while actually destroying and violating their *cultural continuity* (The Native American Movement n.d.). An Indigenous group must prove cultural maintenance to gain official tribal recognition by the US government, despite a situation where that very entity made it impossible for the Indigenous groups to remain intact. Currently, there are 566 "official" tribes; official status is necessary to qualify for government programs; and some groups have been denied this status even after presenting proof of their sustenance as a culture. The affairs of the Native Americans are still regulated by federal government agencies, despite the government's official declaration of their "sovereign status" and civil rights (Indian Civil Rights Act of 1968 n.d.; NCSL 2016). Each group retains the right to establish what constitutes membership eligibility (NCSL 2016).

> ### Box 15.10 – The Native American Rights/American Indian Movement
>
> The movement to establish the rights of the Indigenous peoples of the US has a long history, escalating in the activist period of the 1960s. The movement addresses issues relating to Indigenous land rights, money, and property stemming from agreements violated by the US government. An Indigenous group must prove cultural continuity to gain federal recognition but, ironically, the government's policies have impeded this process.

The 1960s incited an era of Indigenous political activism, inspired by other movements of the era. The first successful case, regarding land and water rights, was in 1967. In the next year, the *American Indian Movement* (AIM) was established to provide the government with Indian-run organizations to support development programs. In 1969, a group of Native Americans occupied Alcatraz Island in the SF Bay to draw attention to the unlawful European American "occupation" of lands stolen from the original inhabitants. In 1971, federal officials forcibly removed the protestors. In 1970, activists also occupied Mt Rushmore to draw attention to an 1868 treaty which promised the land to the Sioux (Zinn Education Project 2016). In 1972, AIM organized a march to draw attention to the persistent violation of Native rights. The march followed the *Trail of Broken Treaties* to commemorate the forcible removal of the Cherokee Nation in the nineteenth century (American Indian Rights n.d.). The group occupied the buildings of the *Bureau of Indian Affairs* to highlight the continued government intrusion into Indigenous affairs. Protests occurred for several more years, notably in the 1973 reclaiming of the Sioux village of *Wounded*

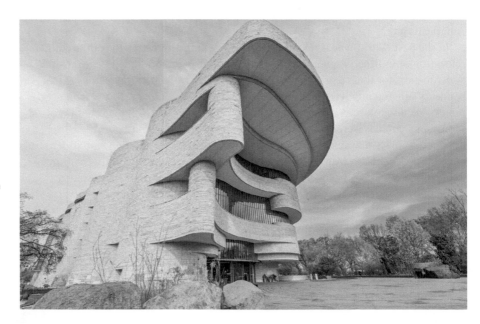

Figure 15.10 The National Museum of the American Indian opened in Washington DC in 2004. It is the only museum dedicated exclusively to Indigenous peoples and it was constructed in collaboration with tribes and communities across the Americas
Source: Orhan Cam / Shutterstock.com

Knee, which suffered a massacre in the late nineteenth century. The protestors sought to highlight the plight of the community, where half of the residents were poor and alcoholism rates were high. After the death of a protestor and the injury of another, the government pledged to re-examine treaty rights, though nothing ever came of the agreement, further perpetuating a history of broken agreements (The Native American Movement n.d.).

Despite consistent activism, Indigenous communities remain among the poorest groups in the US, with little access to educational opportunities, healthcare, and economic opportunities. Only recently have efforts been successful in protecting Native languages from becoming extinct, by supporting the creation of a written form to ensure they will not die with their last speakers (Fitzgerald 2014; Andrews n.d.; Braun 2009). In response to Indigenous pressures, more sports and business organizations have agreed to remove offensive, denigrating language and emblems from their teams (Fitzgerald 2014; Brady 2016). Violations of Native lands and well-being persist, as we saw in the last chapter regarding the opening of the Dakota Pipeline on Native lands (see Chapter 14), a chilling echo of the historical treatment of the Indigenous peoples. In working with the Indigenous peoples of the US, sensitivity to the obliteration of much of their culture, and the subsequent trivialization of what has remained, must be honored. One activist in the Dakota Pipeline protests remarks:

> I'm conflicted. I think a lot of the people that show up are good intentioned and they aim to be here to work and to assist us. To take a seat at our table. [They] realize that it's an indigenous movement and that they are here as allies and as nothing more. Then there are people who show up and feel like [they have] earned the right to wear red face or earned the right to put a feather in [their] hair. [Some white celebrities are] going to serve turkey to the Indians on Thanksgiving and apologize for white people ... I feel like that detracts a lot from what it is we're trying to do. This is an indigenous movement, and we appreciate our allies, but a lot of people show up, I think, with their own agendas and their Instagrams. Ally-ship is appreciated, you know, but we don't need people to come and save us. We're saving ourselves.
>
> (Eryn Wise, in Haglage 2016)

Will a More Diverse Society Promote Inclusion of Nondominant Groups?

An increasingly diverse population will lead to greater interaction between group members, but will it bring the cultural respect and balance so many nondominant groups have tried to establish? There is evidence that increased interaction does reduce stereotyping, especially if it establishes meaningful exchanges. Research shows that when people are simply reminded of stereotypes, whether positive or negative ones, they likely will reinforce them (Grant and Sandberg 2014; Vedantam 2016). However, the inclusion of a simple statement highlighting the desirability of avoiding stereotypic thinking actually *reduces* it (Grant and Sandberg 2014). Greater social engagement can break down stereotypes, so promoting diversity in institutional settings is crucial to countering prejudice (Pew Research Center 2016). Changes occurring between individuals eventually lead to institutional changes; as veteran activist Gloria Steinem (2015) has remarked: "Change grows from the bottom." The need to integrate neighborhoods, workplaces, religious institutions, and schools is central to accomplishing inclusion.

In spite of such optimistic theories, a *New York Times/CBS* poll shows attitudes towards race relations are generally negative, in 2016 dropping to their lowest level since President Obama took office (Russonello 2016). Between 2015 and 2016, 60 percent of those surveyed said that race relations were getting worse, a figure that increased by 38 percent in that period. White and African Americans exhibit disparate beliefs regarding the role of race. Three quarters of African Americans believe that the police are more likely to use deadly force against a Black person than a White person. This perception is two times more common among African Americans than among White people. Regarding the job performance of police, 80 percent of White people judge it to be good or excellent, while the majority of African Americans assess it as fair or poor. Two fifths of African Americans report that police make them feel anxious rather than safe while White and Hispanic populations are more likely to express feeling safe around police. Seventy percent of African Americans are sympathetic to the *Black Lives Matter* movement while only 37 percent of White respondents feel the same. Young people are also more likely to support the sentiments of the *Black Lives Matter* movement. Fifty percent of people under 30 sympathize with the movement, in contrast to 36 percent who are 45 and older. Eighty-four percent of survey respondents had read or heard about the police violence

Figure 15.11 The Pew Research Center 2016 study of race attitudes shows correlations with specific events
Source: "On Views of Race and Inequality, Blacks and Whites Are Worlds Apart," Pew Research Center, Washington DC (June 27, 2016), http://www.pewsocialtrends.org/2016/06/27/on-views-of-race-and-inequality-blacks-and-whites-are-worlds-apart/

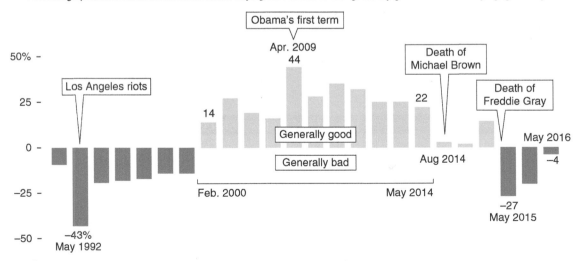

Views of Race Relations Are More Negative Now Than They Have Been for Much of the 2000s

Percentage point difference between all adults saying race relations are "generally good" and those saying "generally bad"

Note: Trend data from CBS News and CBS News/NewYork Times surveys.

Source: Survey of US adults conducted Feb. 29–May 8, 2016. Q5F1. "On Views of Race and Inequality, Blacks and Whites are Worlds Apart"

of the previous week in response to unrest over the death of a Black man, Freddy Gray, in police custody in Baltimore (Pew Research Center 2016).

Race relations appear to have suffered a backlash in the twenty-first century. Current attitudes are as low as they were in 1992 after the Los Angeles race riots. In 2016, 48 percent of survey respondents reported feeling race relations were bad, while 44 percent viewed them as good. Survey respondents were balanced between feeling race is getting too much attention (36 percent) or too little attention (35 percent). Only 19 percent felt race relations to be improving, with 41 percent identifying them as stable, and 38 percent reporting that they were getting worse. African Americans and Hispanics (61 percent and 58 percent respectively) were more likely than White people (45 percent) to say race relations were bad. Registered Democrats were more likely than Republicans to see race relations as bad (59 percent and 46 percent respectively) and less likely to respond that they were good (34 percent and 48 percent). African Americans and Hispanics were more likely than White people to talk of race-related topics with their friends. White people were more likely than African Americans to characterize their interactions with African Americans as "very friendly" (70 percent compared to 50 percent) (Pew Research Center 2016).

Sentiments regarding the future of race relations also vary by group. Eighty-eight percent of African Americans believe more change is needed for racial equity to occur, while only 53 percent of Whites feel that way. African Americans express perceptions of sustained discrimination, feeling they are treated unfairly in the workplace; in obtaining loans or mortgages; by the police and courts; and when voting. Additionally,

When asked about the underlying reasons that blacks may be having a harder time getting ahead than whites, large majorities of black adults point to societal factors. Two-thirds or more blacks say failing schools (75%), racial

For Whites, Too Much Attention Paid to Race; for Blacks and Hispanics, Not Enough

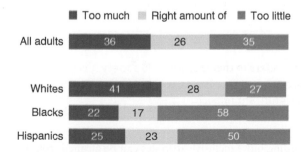

% saying there is ___ attention paid to race and racial issues in our country these days

■ Too much   ■ Right amount of   ■ Too little

	Too much	Right amount of	Too little
All adults	36	26	35
Whites	41	28	27
Blacks	22	17	58
Hispanics	25	23	50

Note: "All adults" includes adults of all races. Whites and Blacks include only non-Hispanics. Hispanics are of any race. "Don't know/Refused" responses not shown.

Source: Survey of US adults conducted Feb. 29–May 8, 2016. Q16. "On Views of Race and Inequality, Blacks and Whites are Worlds Apart"

Figure 15.12 Pew Research Center 2016 survey shows significant differences between Whites and Blacks/ Hispanics with regard to cultural attention to race issues
Source: "On Views of Race and Inequality, Blacks and Whites Are Worlds Apart," Pew Research Center, Washington DC (June 27, 2016), http:// www.pewsocialtrends. org/2016/06/27/ on-views-of-race-and- inequality-blacks-and- whites-are-worlds-apart/

discrimination (70%) and a lack of jobs (66%) are major reasons that black people may have a harder time getting ahead these days.

(Pew Research Center 2016)

Diversity and race relations issues are not confined to Black and White relations, though there is a tendency to focus on African Americans. The portion of the population identified as Latino now surpasses that of the African Americans but frequently receives less media and policy attention. Some observers believe the absence of media coverage results from the perception of the "foreign" status of American Latinos and the devaluation of their communities (Fountain, Jr. 2016). Forty percent of Latinos identify anti-Hispanic and anti-immigrant sentiment, while an additional 38 percent perceive it to exist "somewhat" (Lilley 2015). Excessive force and police shootings also have been documented in the Latino community, extending back to the nineteenth century when Mexicans were lynched by law enforcement in the west and southwest (Garcia 2015). The Latino population suffers the second highest rate of killing by police after African Americans. Overall, Latinos are 2.6 times more likely to be incarcerated than Whites and in 14 states that figure is much higher (Morin n.d.). Latino children are also three times more likely than White children to have an incarcerated parent.

Religious affiliation also contributes to social tensions. Many American Muslims fear discrimination and violence. Hate crimes against Muslims saw increases of 300 percent in the months following the Paris terrorist attacks of November 2015 (Stack 2016). Fears regarding the likelihood of a *jihadist* incident in the US are exaggerated. Religious attitudes expressed by a few extremist individuals are falsely attributed to the group. Over the 40 years from 1975–2015, there have been no lethal attacks on any person that were associated with any of the seven countries in Trump's proposed ban of Muslim-dominated countries (Friedman 2017). Neither have any Syrian refugees been implicated in any death in the US. Every jihadist who attempted, or committed, a lethal act since 2001 was a citizen or legal resident (Friedman 2017). In fact, Americans face a greater risk of being killed by right-wing extremists than by jihadists (Eichenwald 2016). Nevertheless, more Americans today (40 percent) fear outsider terrorist attacks than in the immediate aftermath of the 2001 tragedies, with Republicans showing a significantly higher rate than Democrats (McGill 2016).

Box 15.11 – Post-racial Era

"Post-racial era" refers to the belief that US society has moved beyond the need for consideration of race issues, ostensibly because they no longer demonstrate a significant impact.

Optimism regarding more inclusive attitudes can be gleaned from polls of younger Americans. Higher education is related to more liberal ideas and the educated population is becoming more diverse. The belief that US society has moved beyond the need for consideration of race issues, referred to as a *"post-racial era,"* is not yet a reality. Students of color, as well as low-income students, maintain that the campus is not "user-friendly" (Post-racial n.d.). Racism persists on campuses, as does discrimination against all nondominant groups. To successfully address these issues, activists recognize the need for collaboration between nondominant and dominant groups. A good example of this type of activity occurred at the University of Missouri. African American students brought national attention to the university administration's failure to respond to their efforts to highlight racism on the campus. One graduate student, Jonathan Butler, initiated a hunger strike to be carried out until the university president resigned. His position statement listed racial episodes where student leaders were called the "N word." He also protested the discontinuation of graduate student health insurance; the loss of Planned Parenthood services; and the appearance of a swastika in a residence hall. Students supported Butler's hunger strike and utilized the phrase "concerned student 1950," in commemoration of the first African American student admitted to the university, to symbolize their support. The university's football team was largely African American. Football generates a huge portion of university revenue and is integral to campus culture. The football team refused to play, at a cost of one million dollars per game, until the university president resigned. A photo of 30 African American football players was circulated, quoting Martin Luther King, Jr. "Injustice Anywhere is a threat to Justice Everywhere" (Goodman et al. 2016). White players, the coach, and the athletic department supported the African American student protest. Concerned faculty voted to walk out in support of the students' demands and the *Missouri Students Association* also called for the resignation of the president. The president resigned and an interim president, Michael Middleton, was appointed. Middleton, a civil rights attorney, also had been one of the first African Americans graduated from the University's law school and formerly had held the position of Vice-Chancellor. When he was asked if he ever felt marginalized while at the University he responded with "Every day" (Pearce 2015). He said he would work to address the systemic racism at the university. The Missouri case incited other universities to explore race issues, resulting in other actions and resignations (Goodman et al. 2016), though not all campaigns were successful (Sinclair 2016).

Eliminating racist symbolism impinges upon deeply entrenched campus cultures. Because the symbolic references of cultural icons often are unexamined by the privileged groups, demands for change are often met with intransigence. Yale University, in spite of student protests, initially decided to maintain the name John C. Calhoun for one of their residential colleges, even though Calhoun was an avid slave owner and avowed White supremacist (Rosenberg 2016). Shortly after the decision to retain the Calhoun identity, a frustrated African American employee broke the college's stained-glass window depicting two slaves picking cotton, saying he was "tired of seeing the image" (Neary 2016). In 2017, the University trustees reversed their stance and voted to change the college's name to the Grace Murray Hopper College, in honor of a graduate (MA 1930, PhD 1934) who had been a Navy rear admiral and an early computer scientist (Yale News 2017). As noted earlier (see Chapters 2 and 7), permanent references and monuments to women and other nondominant group members are rare.

Efforts to create greater inclusion have extended to the public-school system. In Oakland CA, the school district has 20 schools offering a fully credited course, modified for grades 3–12, on the African American Male Image. The program highlights the achievement of Black males and fosters student success with mentoring, leadership training, conferences, and Afro-centric courses which fulfill University of California entrance requirements. The program is incorporating a job center. As a newer program, its long-term efficacy is difficult to assess but so far it has reduced school absenteeism and suspensions. More than half of the program's initial graduates earned college scholarships (Brown 2016).

Another progressive California initiative will integrate gay and lesbian history into the public-school curriculum, starting in 2016–2017. Guidelines for inclusive curricula are to be initiated in the second grade. Inclusion of people with disabilities will also be added. No one protested the LGBT guidelines when they were announced at a meeting of the state's Board of Education on history and social science curriculum, though there was resistance to addressing religious minorities such as Jews, Hindus, and Muslims, and Native Americans (Associated Press 2016).

Where Do We Go from Here?

Since the 1960s, American social cohesion has been experiencing a downward trend, after rising steadily in the early part of the century. American *social trust*, indicative of social alienation, is hovering at 30 percent, an unhealthy low exacerbated by the divisiveness of the 2016 presidential campaign (Dubner 2017). Societies where people are happiest reveal much higher levels of social trust. A society facilitating social trust benefits in two dimensions. One concerns alliances of what is called *bonding social capital*, stemming from likeness found in close friends and relatives networks. These persons can be relied upon to offer the emotional comfort essential in supporting the physical and mental health of network members. But social scientists suggest that we especially need to cultivate affiliations referring to *bridging social capital*, where meaningful interactions between people with different backgrounds occur. These experiences have been shown to result in greater comfort with people possessing different characteristics from ourselves, crucial in contributing to the health of the greater society. The current trends towards greater diversity make it unlikely that people can complacently remain in their cocoon of exclusively bonding with those like themselves. US schools have incorporated *service learning* (community volunteerism) as an element required for high school graduation in some locales. Such activities compel people to "walk in another's shoes," at least temporarily. The UK government is similarly promoting national citizen service for its youths, involving residential periods with mixed groups as a means of advancing social trust (Dubner 2017).

There are other avenues to travel in promoting meaningful connectivity between diverse persons. Technology, as noted throughout the book, is an inescapable element of contemporary life, with post-millennials never having lived without *smart* technology and suffering some social deficits as a result. But commentators have mourned the ill effects of technological "progress" since the dissemination of household televisions 70 years ago. With the introduction of television, people stayed home rather than gathering outside, on the porch, in the pub, or on the streets. It has been noted that face to face interaction is more satisfying than screen face. In myriad ways, technology can act to disassociate us from our humanity, no matter what the intentions or potential. As the British psychologist, David Halpern, has remarked:

we've often used our wealth to buy technology and other experiences that mean we don't have to deal with other people: the inconveniences of having to go to a concert where I have to listen to music I really like, I can just stay at home and just watch what I want and so on and choose it.

Even in the level of if I think about my kids versus me growing up, when I was growing up we had one TV and there were five kids in the household, I mean, we had to really negotiate pretty hard about what we were going to watch. My kids don't have to do that and probably not yours either. There are more screens in the house than there are people. They can all go off and do their own thing. To some extent, that is us using our wealth to escape from having to negotiate with other people, but that isn't necessarily the case.

Some people and some countries seem to use their wealth more to find ways of connecting more to other people. And the technology has both these capabilities and we can't just blame it. It's the choices we're making and how we use it and the technology which we're, kind of, asking and bringing forth.

(Dubner 2017)

In partial response to the insecurities emanating from loss of trust, mixed with an economy seemingly unresponsive to many individuals' needs, multiple countries with advanced economies have been showing a marked trend towards conservative political positions. This platform often leads to cuts to the safety net for the poor, and near poor. One contrasting proposal involves the provision of a *guaranteed minimum income*, sometimes referred to as a *Basic Income Grant* (BIG). It would constitute a stipend enabling a person to secure basic needs such as food, housing, and utilities. Healthcare would be universal and financed by the government, administered by one agency. The BIG stems from the suggestion that providing a minimal income can enhance the quality of life of both the individual and society, while also supporting dedicated workers. Such an innovation would eliminate the need for multiple government bureaucracies overseeing the safety net, saving money and time. People who wish to pursue non-commercial work, such as art, music, theater or dance, can do so knowing that their healthcare and other basic needs will be sustained. A person can also choose to work on community projects, entrepreneurial pursuits, or take care of a family member without fearing catastrophic fallout. The wealthy would not actually benefit from the **BIG** as taxation would be restructured so that it would be repaid by those who did not need it (Wright 2015).

On the surface, this proposal may seem illogical but it represents multiple potential benefits. Switzerland has considered implementing such a program (Lowrey 2013) but the initiative, called the *unconditional basic income*, was voted down by a wide margin (Lowrey 2013). Proponents argued the BIG was necessary in lieu of the availability of good jobs with decent wages. Opponents claimed it would threaten the work ethic. Supporters challenged this assertion and cited its efficacy in cutting overall welfare costs, but ultimately the electorate were not convinced (Aljazeera 2016). In contrast, Finland has instituted a Basic Income Grant, saying that it will help with displaced workers; replace unemployment benefits; and encourage work by supplementing part-time or free-lance employment (Sodha 2017). After two years the government failed to renew the program, though one expert suggests that the program's trial was insufficient in time and funds (Henley 2018). Kenya also instituted a similar program (Dörrie 2017). In the US, Silicon Valley corporations, mindful of the employment effects of automation, are proposing new policies to support a growing contingent of obsolete workers. This could reduce stress associated with retraining or entry into the "gig" economy. They are promoting a "universal basic income" to benefit individuals, businesses, families, and society and instituting pilot programs (Brancaccio 2017).

> ## Box 15.12 – Basic Income Grant (BIG) or Guaranteed Minimum Income
>
> A BIG would be a government program providing a minimal income to all citizens. The potential for massive unemployment, largely resulting from automation, has been garnering much attention in social science and journalism. It is believed that providing citizens with a minimal income would save money, by reducing government bureaucracies serving populations in need with just one department. The relief experienced by knowing basic needs are met could enhance the development of arts, entrepreneurship, and family life.

A Basic Income Grants program actually was accomplished in Canada in the mid-1970s. One study, from the village of Dauphin in Manitoba province, showed beneficial effects of the project, especially with respect to long-term savings. The village was selected because the strong ethnic ties in the community made it unlikely that even unemployed members would leave the area. A family of four would get the equivalent of 16000 dollars in today's Canadian currency. Income generated by work would result in a deduction from the grant but with a favorable rate so that work would still be rewarded (dollars earned would be deducted at a 50 percent rate, rather than dollar for dollar). Most participants had some work. A few people refused to participate in the program but most people took advantage of it. The project showed multiple favorable outcomes. Women took longer maternity leaves; teenaged boys were more likely to prolong their educations since their contributions to the household income were not as crucial; and people saved money to cushion against emergencies. Other gains were seen in overall well-being; hospitalizations were reduced, especially in mental health; small businesses were improved upon; families sent kids to the dentist; and people had more flexibility to work on special projects or care for family members. Though costs of a societal wide program would likely increase taxes, these could be minimized through the suspension of existing social benefits programs which would become extraneous (Gardner 2016). Promoting a guaranteed income would require a different cultural attitude towards aid, especially if the program contained no specific work or skill development component. Proponents suggest that the flexibility of the program would yield a net gain.

The means to make society more equitable and cooperative exist; there are plenty of models available. As Robert Reich and other economists have pointed out (see Chapter 5), the 1950s–1960s provide an example of a thriving middle class with modest levels of social class inequality. Most of the benefits in the ensuing decades accrued only to the wealthy, who perpetuate the belief that they earned their privileges (Reeves 2017). We can replicate the more equitable model of the immediate post-war decades but it will require a will to do so. Any attitudinal changes must be coupled with changes in our wage structure, business models, education system, and political environment. These modifications are not only humanitarian but financially expedient. Implementing more expansive and affordable healthcare options; better wage scales; more equitable public education; more affordable higher education; less protection for the banks and finance institutions; more protections for consumers; restrictions on money in lobbying and elections; and a more secure safety net makes both sense and cents. We should keep in mind that all people ultimately want the same thing—to express our full humanity in the collective life of society.

Key Terms

Social Movements   *Collective Action*   *Feminist (Women's) Rights Movements (First, Second, and Third Waves)*   *Men's Rights Movement*   *Stonewall Inn Uprising*   *Gay Rights Movement*   *Transgender Rights Movement*   *Civil Rights Movement for Racial Equality*   *Black Lives Matter*   *Civil Disobedience*   *Chicano Rights Movement*   *Native American (American Indian) Movements*   *Post-racial Era*   *Basic Income Grant*

Concept Review

What Type of Society Do We Want to Create?

In this sociology text, we have focused on critical issues in our social institutions. The question of how to make our society more **humane** brings us full circle to Emile Durkheim (see Chapter 1) and his discussion of social integration as a means of assessing a person's feelings of inclusion in society. Many nondominant group members experience significant stress, largely as a result of marginalization. If we want a society which respects the dignity of all human life, many of our social policies need to be reformulated to address all members' basic human needs.

What Is a Social Movement?

Social movements represent organized group actions geared to changing conditions that are problematic for some, or all, of the population. Frequently, issues identified as social problems have been in existence for a substantial period of time before actions address them. Often, a specific event acts as a catalyst to the recognition of the social issue, culminating in the formation of a group to address the problem. The media, enhanced now by social media, play a significant role in enhancing cultural awareness of the problem.

What Are Major Social Movements?

Social movements are a consistent feature of modern society, with histories as far back as the American revolution and the pre-Civil War era. Contemporary **social movements** represent the concerns of marginalized groups such as in women's rights; men's rights; gay rights; transgender rights; and civil rights as represented by the African American movement, the #BlackLivesMatter movement, the Chicano movement, and the Native American/American Indian movement; disability rights (see Chapter 9); and the environmental movement (see Chapter 14).

What Is the Current Status of Race Relations?

The suggestion that the US now represents a **post-racial** society, where race is no longer a defining feature of civil life, is more an ideal than a reality. In the coming decades, America will become increasingly diverse, with increases in the portion of the population identifying as nonWhite and non-Christian. Although the demographics are shifting, the question of how inclusive the society will become, in terms of truly integrating nondominant groups, remains ambiguous. The majority group expresses more optimism regarding the current and future state of the nondominant groups than those who represent these groups. People of color are likely to view racial discrimination and related issues as significant factors in their life achievements while White people are increasingly likely to suggest they are not a factor. Millennials as a group appear more likely to hold inclusive attitudes with regard to race and other dimensions of exclusion, and can be seen as a presenting the potential for real changes.

What Can Be Done to Ensure Better Participation and Inclusion in Society?

With the spread of automation and the low wages associated with most un- and semi-skilled jobs, many social scientists are suggesting that issues of widespread unemployment must be addressed on a social policy level. One proposal supports the availability of a **Basic Income Grant**, guaranteeing all residents access to a minimal income. Such a program would eliminate the need for unemployment and welfare benefits and accompanying stigmas. It could augment the income of workers who must rely upon part-time and temporary work. Entrepreneurship, volunteerism, arts, and family life could be enhanced if basic needs are met. The consolidation of government bureaucracies into one agency could fund this initiative and provide a more humane, less stigmatized program.

Review Questions

1. What can Emile Durkheim's work show us about building a more humane society? Be specific about what aspects of social life he highlighted as contributing to social integration.

2. What is a social movement and what are major social movements in US history? What factors led to the development of the social movements of the 1960s?

3. What are some current social movements and can you predict any emerging movements? Where do you think the most significant problems will lie in the near future? What factors will contribute to these problems being exacerbated?

4. What characterizes the current attitudes toward race in America? Do views vary between races and ethnicities? Do nondominant groups share the same expectations with White groups?

5. What is the Basic Income Grant? What are the pros and cons of establishing such a grant? Would you support it? Why or why not?

6. If you were president, how would you go about improving all people's well-being? If you could pick only one area to begin, what would it be? Why? How would you approach making a change in it?

7. What defining features make us "human"? What do you think it would take to make social policies more responsive to all individuals' needs?

References

Abadi, M. (September 21, 2016) North Carolina Has Lost a Staggering Amount of Money Over its Controversial 'Bathroom Law.' *Business Insider*. Retrieved from http://www.businessinsider.com/north-carolina-hb2-economic-impact-2016-9

Aljazeera. (2016) Swiss Voters 'Reject Basic Income Grant for All.' *Aljazeera*. Retrieved from http://www.aljazeera.com/news/2016/06/switzerland-referendum-basic-income-grant-160605061102498.html

America's Civil Rights Timeline. (n.d.) Retrieved from https://www.sitinmovement.org/history/america-civil-rights-timeline.asp

American Indian Rights (n.d.) *Boundless*. Retrieved from https://www.boundless.com/u-s-history/textbooks/boundless-u-s-history-textbook/the-sixties-1960-1969-29/expanding-the-civil-rights-movement-1464/american-indian-rights-1227-9763/

Andrews, J. (n.d.) Saving Their Language. *South Dakota Magazine*. Retrieved from http://www.southdakotamagazine.com/lakota-saving-their-language

AP (2017) Appeals Court Denies Trump Admin's Stay of Transgender Military Ban. *The New York Daily News*. Retrieved from http://www.nydailynews.com/news/national/appeals-court-denies-trump-stay-transgender-military-ban-article-1.3716189

Associated Press. (July 14, 2016) California Approves LGBT History Lessons for Classrooms. *The Wall Street Journal*. Retrieved from https://www.wsj.com/articles/california-approves-lgbt-history-lessons-for-classrooms-1468538937

Binder, A. (February 8, 2015) Alabama Judge Defies Gay Marriage Law. *The New York Times*. Retrieved from https://www.nytimes.com/2015/02/09/us/gay-marriage-set-to-begin-in-alabama-amid-protest.html

Binder, A., Perez-Pena, R. (September 1, 2015) Kentucky Clerk Denies Same-sex Married Licenses, Defying Court. *The New York Times*. Retrieved from https://www.nytimes.com/2015/09/02/us/same-sex-marriage-kentucky-kim-davis.html

Black Lives Matter. Retrieved from http://blacklivesmatter.com/

Blake, M. (January/February, 2015) Mad Men: Inside the Men's Rights Movement—and the Army of Misogynists and Trolls it Spawned. *Mother Jones*. Retrieved from http://www.motherjones.com/politics/2015/01/warren-farrell-mens-rights-movement-feminism-misogyny-trolls

Bly, R. (2015), *Iron John: A Book About Men*. (25th anniversary edition) Boston MA: Da Capo Press.

Brady, E. (August 25, 2016) The Real History of Native American Team Names. *USA Today*. Retrieved from https://www.usatoday.com/story/sports/2016/08/24/real-history-native-american-team-names/89259596/

Brancaccio, D. (April 18, 2017) What Universal Basic Income Could Mean for the Future of Work. *Marketplace*. NPR. Retrieved from https://www.marketplace.org/2017/04/18/economy/robot-proof-jobs/basic-income-y-combinator-oakland-krisiloff

Braun, M.D. (November 15, 2009) Preserving Native America's Vanishing Languages. *National Geographic*. Retrieved from http://voices.nationalgeographic.com/2009/11/15/0005_native_american_vanishing_languages/

Brown, L.P. (February 4, 2016) Lessons in Manhood for African-American Boys. *The New York Times*. Retrieved from http://www.nytimes.com/2016/02/07/education/edlife/in-oakland-building-boys-into-men.html

Bua, F. (September 1, 2017) Thanks, Obama: A Gay Dad's Love Letter to POTUS. *The Huffington Post*. Retrieved from http://www.huffingtonpost.com/entry/thanks-obama-a-gay-dads-love-letter-to-potus_us_587259ede4b0eb9e49bfbc8f

Carpenter, D. (February 3, 2017) Yes, Signing Those Petitions Makes a Difference—Even if they Don't Change Trump's Mind. *The Washington Post*. Retrieved from https://www.washingtonpost.com/news/monkey-cage/wp/2017/02/03/yes-signing-those-petitions-makes-a-difference-even-if-they-dont-change-trumps-mind/?utm_term=.ad52ab1abd90

Castañeda, R.O. (2006) The Chicano Movement in Washington State 1967–2006 Part 2 Chicano Cultural Awakening. *University of Washington*. Retrieved from http://depts.washington.edu/civilr/Chicanomovement_part2.htm

Chval, L. (May 14, 2015) The Transformation of Peggy Olson in 'Mad Men'. *Chicago Tribune*. Retrieved from http://www.chicagotribune.com/redeye/redeye-mad-men-peggy-olson-transformation-20150514-column.html.

Coates, T. (June, 2014) The Case for Reparations. *The Atlantic*. Retrieved from https://www.theatlantic.com/magazine/archive/2014/06/the-case-for-reparations/361631/

Coontz, S. (September 29, 2012) The Myth of Male Decline. *The New York Times*. Retrieved from http://www.nytimes.com/2012/09/30/opinion/sunday/the-myth-of-male-decline.html

Craven, J. (January 1, 2017) More than 250 Black People Were Killed by Police in 2016 [updated]. *Huffingtonpost*. Retrieved from https://www.huffingtonpost.com/entry/black-people-killed-by-police-america_us_577da633e4b0c590f7e7fb17

Diversity Best Practices. (2014) *21 Latino Organizations You Need to Know*. Retrieved from https://www.diversitybestpractices.com/news-articles/21-latino-organizations-you-need-know

Dokoupil, T. (May 23, 2013) Why Suicide Has Become Epidemic and What We Can Do to Help. *Newsweek*. Retrieved from http://www.newsweek.com/2013/05/22/why-suicide-has-become-epidemic-and-what-we-can-do-help-237434.html

Domonoske, C. (December 20, 2017) CDC Denies Banning Words; Rights Group Projects Disputed Terms onto Trump D.C. Hotel. *NPR News*. Retrieved from https://www.npr.org/sections/thetwo-way/2017/12/20/572242449/as-cdc-denies-banning-words-hrc-projects-disputed-terms-on-trumps-d-c-hotel

Dörrie, P. (December 5, 2017) The Promise of Kenya's Experiment with Universal Basic Income. *World Politics Review*. Retrieved from https://www.worldpoliticsreview.com/articles/23750/the-promise-of-kenya-s-experiment-with-universal-basic-income

Dubner, S.J. (January 18, 2017) Is the American Dream Really Dead? *Freakonomics Radio*. Retrieved from http://freakonomics.com/podcast/american-dream-really-dead/.

Eichenwald, K. (February 4, 2016) Right-wing Extremists Are a Bigger Threat to America than ISIS. *Newsweek*. Retrieved from http://www.newsweek.com/2016/02/12/right-wing-extremists-militants-bigger-threat-america-isis-jihadists-422743.html.

Entis, L. (June 22, 2016) Chronic Loneliness Is a Modern-day Epidemic. *Fortune*. Retrieved from http://fortune.com/2016/06/22/loneliness-is-a-modern-day-epidemic/

Eventbrite. (2017) *Women's March in Sacramento Changefest. Message from Host*. Retrieved from https://www.eventbrite.com/?utm_source=eb_email&utm_medium=email&utm_campaign=event_reminder&utm_term=eb_logo

Executive Order 8802: Prohibition of Discrimination in the Defense Industry (1941). (n.d.) *Our Documents*. Retrieved from https://www.ourdocuments.gov/doc.php?flash=true&doc=72

Faludi, S. (1991) *Backlash*. New York: Anchor Books.

Faville, A. (n.d.) A Civil Rights History: Native Americans. *The Knight Chair in Political Reporting*. Retrieved from http://knightpoliticalreporting.syr.edu/?civilhistoryessays=a-civil-rights-history-native-americans

Fernandez, M., Perez-Pena, R., Bromwich, E.J. (July 8, 2016) Five Dallas Officers Were Killed as Payback, Police Chief Says. *The New York Times*. Retrieved from https://www.nytimes.com/2016/07/09/us/dallas-police-shooting.html

Fitzgerald, M.C. (October 28, 2014) Saving Native American Languages. *The Huffington Post*. Retrieved from http://www.huffingtonpost.com/colleen-m-fitzgerald/saving-native-american-la_b_5732850.html

Fountain, Jr. G.A. (February 7, 2016) Stop Ignoring the Police Killings of Latinos. *Aljazeera America*. Retrieved from http://america.aljazeera.com/opinions/2016/2/stop-ignoring-the-police-killings-of-latinos.html

Friedan, B. (1963) *The Feminine Mystique.* New York: W.W. Norton and Company.

Friedman, U. (January 30, 2017) Where America's Terrorists Actually Come From. *The Atlantic.* Retrieved from https://www.theatlantic.com/international/archive/2017/01/trump-immigration-ban-terrorism/514361/

Gamboa, S. (July 10, 2017) *The National Council of La Raza Changes Name to UnidosUS.* Retrieved from https://www.nbcnews.com/news/latino/national-council-la-raza-changes-name-unidosus-n781261

García, M. (July 31, 2015) Why Isn't Anyone Talking About Police Brutality in the Latino Community? *Cosmopolitan.* Retrieved from http://www.cosmopolitan.com/politics/news/a43905/latinas-open-up-disturbing-effects-of-police-brutality/

Gardner, S. (December 20, 2016) On the Canadian Prairie, a Basic Income Experiment. *Marketplace.* Retrieved from https://www.marketplace.org/2016/12/20/world/dauphin

Gautney, H. (October 10, 2011) What Is Occupy Wall Street? The History of Leaderless Movements. *The Washington Post.* Retrieved from https://www.washingtonpost.com/national/on-leadership/what-is-occupy-wall-street-the-history-of-leaderless-movements/2011/10/10/gIQAwkFjaL_story.html?utm_term=.bd517877671b

Goodman, A., Goodman, D., Moynihan, D. (2016) *Democracy Now: Twenty Years Covering the Movements Changing America.* New York: Simon and Schuster.

Grant, A., Sandberg, S. (December 6, 2014) When Talking About Bias Backfires. *The New York Times.* Retrieved from http://www.nytimes.com/2014/12/07/opinion/sunday/adam-grant-and-sheryl-sandberg-on-discrimination-at-work.html

Haglage, A. (December 9, 2016) Water Is Life: Four Months at Standing Rock. *Lenny.* Retrieved from http://www.lennyletter.com/politics/interviews/a646/water-is-life-four-months-at-standing-rock/

Hamblin, J. (October, 2014) Buy Experiences, Not Things. *The Atlantic.* Retrieved from https://www.theatlantic.com/business/archive/2014/10/buy-experiences/381132/

Hanna, J., Park, M., McLaughlin, E.C. (March 30, 2017) North Carolina Repeals 'Bathroom Bill'. *CNN Politics.* Retrieved from http://www.cnn.com/2017/03/30/politics/north-carolina-hb2-agreement/

Harari, Y.N. (2017) *Homo Deus.* New York: HarperCollins Publishers.

Head, T. (2017) History of Transgender Rights in the United States. *ThoughtCo.* Retrieved from https://www.thoughtco.com/transgender-rights-in-the-united-states-721319

Henley, J. (April 23, 2018) Finland to End Basic Income Trial After Two Years. *The Guardian.* Retrieved from https://www.theguardian.com/world/2018/apr/23/finland-to-end-basic-income-trial-after-two-years

Hersher, R., Johnson, C. (February 22, 2017) Trump Administration Rescinds Obama Rule on Transgender Students' Bathroom Use. *NPR.* Retrieved from http://www.npr.org/sections/thetwo-way/2017/02/22/516664633/trump-administration-rescinds-obama-rule-on-transgender-students-bathroom-use

Hud.gov. (n.d.) *Disability Rights in Housing.* Retrieved from https://portal.hud.gov/hudportal/HUD?src=/program_offices/fair_housing_equal_opp/disabilities/inhousing

Indian Civil Rights Act of 1968. (n.d.) [PDF File]. Retrieved from http://www.courts. ca.gov/documents/Indian-Civil-Rights-Act-of-1968.pdf

International Civil Rights Center and Museum. (n.d.) *American Civil Rights Timeline.* Retrieved from https://www.sitinmovement.org/history/america-civil-rights-timeline.asp

Jacob, K. (n.d.) Engendering Change: What's Up With Third Wave Feminism? *The Feminist eZine.* Retrieved from http://www.feministezine.com/feminist/historical/ Third-Wave-Feminism.html

Jurney, C. (November 3, 2016) North Carolina's 'Bathroom Bill' Has Flushed Away $600 Million in Business and Could Dash Governor's Re-election Hopes. *Forbes.* Retrieved from https://www.forbes.com/sites/corinnejurney/2016/11/03/north-carolinas-bathroom-bill-flushes-away-nearly-1-billion-in-business-and-governor-mccrorys-re-election-hopes/#1d2645e5682a

Kindy, K., Kelly, K. (April 11, 2015) Thousands Dead, Few Prosecuted. *The Washington Post.* Retrieved from http://www.washingtonpost.com/sf/ investigative/2015/04/11/thousands-dead-few-prosecuted/

King, Jr., M.L. (1963) I Had a Dream Speech Text. *Huffingtonpost.* Retrieved from https:// www.huffingtonpost.com/2011/01/17/i-have-a-dream-speech-text_n_809993.html

Krogstad, M.J. (October 14, 2016) Key Facts About the Latino Vote in 2016. *Pew Research Center.* Retrieved from http://www.pewresearch.org/fact-tank/2016/10/14/key-facts-about-the-latino-vote-in-2016/

Levitin, M. (June 10, 2015) The Triumph of Occupy Wall Street. *The Atlantic.* Retrieved from https://www.theatlantic.com/politics/archive/2015/06/the-triumph-of-occupy-wall-street/395408/

LGBT Rights Milestones Fast Facts. (April 8, 2017) *CNN Library.* Retrieved from http://www.cnn.com/2015/06/19/us/lgbt-rights-milestones-fast-facts/

Liebelson, D., Terkel, A. (June 26, 2015) Supreme Court Legalizes Gay Marriage Nationwide. *The Huffington Post.* Retrieved from http://www.huffingtonpost. com/2015/06/26/supreme-court-gay-marriage_n_7470036.html

Lilley, S. (March 24, 2015) Latinos Talk Health, Discrimination, Immigration in New Poll. *NBC News.* Retrieved from http://www.nbcnews.com/news/latino/poll-latinos-talk-health-discrimination-immigration-n329211

Lowrey, A. (November 12, 2013) Switzerland's Proposal to Pay People for Being Alive. *The New York Times.* Retrieved from https://www.nytimes.com/2013/11/17/ magazine/switzerlands-proposal-to-pay-people-for-being-alive.html

Lueptow, K. (January 10, 2014) Feminism Now: What the Third Wave is Really About. *Everyday Feminism.* Retrieved from http://everydayfeminism.com/2014/01/ feminism-now/

Macias, F. (May 16, 2014) Before Brown v. Board of Education There Was Méndez v. Westminster. *Library of Congress.* Retrieved from https://blogs.loc.gov/ law/2014/05/before-brown-v-board-of-education-there-was-mendez-v-westminster/

Matias, J.N. (May 3, 2016) How Do Social Media Shape Collective Action? Helen Margetts at the *MIT Media Lab.* Retrieved from https://civic.mit.edu/blog/natematias/ how-do-social-media-shape-collective-action-helen-margetts-at-the-mit-media-lab

McGill, A. (September 9, 2016) Americans Are More Worried About Terrorism than they Were After 9/11. *The Atlantic.* Retrieved from https://www.the atlantic.com/politics/archive/2016/09/american-terrorism-fears-september-11/ 499004/

M.E.Ch.A. *Movimiento Estudiantil Chcanx de Aztlan.* Retrieved from http://www. chicanxdeaztlan.org/p/about-us.html

M.E.Ch.A. (2017) *About Us.* Retrieved from http://www.chicanxdeaztlan.org/p/ about-us.html

Morin, L.J. (n.d.) Inequities for Latinos in Criminal Justice. *The Walter Cronkite School of Journalism and Mass Communication.* Retrieved from http://cronkitezine. asu.edu/latinomales/criminal.html

Native Americans. (n.d.) *The Leadership Conference.* Retrieved from http://www. civilrights.org/resources/civilrights101/native.html?referrer=http://search.tb.ask. com/search/GGmain.jhtml?searchfor=natie%20american%20rights%20movem ent&st=sb&tpr=omni&p2=%5EY6%5Exdm459%5ES17547%5Eus&ptb=154 7EC31-DA13-4922-A886-43C55143AD58&n=782b6fe0&si

NCSL. National Conference of State Legislatures. (October, 2016) *Federally Recognized Tribes.* Retrieved from http://www.ncsl.org/research/state-tribal-institute/list-of-federal-and-state-recognized-tribes.aspx

NCTE. (n.d.) *National Center for Transgender Equality.* Retrieved from https:// transequality.org/about

Neary, L. (host). (July 17, 2016) Yale Dishwasher Broke Window Depicting Slaves: 'No One Has to Be Exposed to That Anymore.' *Weekend Edition Sunday, NPR.* Retrieved from http://www.npr.org/2016/07/17/486359454/yale-dishwasher-broke-window-depicting-slaves-no-one-has-to-be-exposed-to-that-a

Nittle, K.N. (August 1, 2016) The Chicano Movement: Brown and Proud. *ThoughtCo.* Retrieved from https://www.thoughtco.com/chicano-movement-brown-and-proud-2834583

NMAAHC. National Museum of African American History and Culture. (n.d.) *A People's Journey, A Nation's Story.* Retrieved from https://nmaahc.si.edu/

Obama, B. (July 19, 2013) *Remarks by the President on Trayvon Martin.* Retrieved from https://obamawhitehouse.archives.gov/the-press-office/2013/07/19/remarks-president-trayvon-martin

Parvini, S., Anderson, T. (May 12, 2015) Transgender Issues: 7 Things to Know about LGBT Movement's Next Frontier. *Los Angeles Times.* Retrieved from http://www. latimes.com/nation/la-na-transgender-20150512-story.html

PBS. (April 25, 2011) Stonewall Uprising. *American Experience.* Retrieved from http://www.pbs.org/wgbh/americanexperience/films/stonewall/

Pearce, M. (November 12, 2015) Black Administrator Named Interim President of University of Missouri. *Los Angeles Times.* Retrieved from http://www.latimes.com/ nation/la-na-missouri-race-20151113-story.html

Peters, W.J., Becker, J., Davis, H.J. (February 22, 2017) Trump Rescinds Rules on Bathrooms for Transgender Students. *The New York Times.* Retrieved from https:// www.nytimes.com/2017/02/22/us/politics/devos-sessions-transgender-students-rights.html?_r=0

Pew Research Center (June 27, 2016) 2 Views of Race Relations. Retrieved from http://www.pewsocialtrends.org/2016/06/27/2-views-of-race-relations/

Phillips, A. (April 6, 2017) How a Federal Court Ruling Could Be a 'Big Moment' for LGBT Rights. *The Boston Globe*. Retrieved from http://www.bostonglobe.com/news/nation/2017/04/05/how-federal-court-ruling-could-big-moment-for-lgbt-rights/I6ruzIyh6WKnP5ynICdkCM/story.html?event=event25

Post-racial. (n.d.) *Urban Dictionary*. Retrieved from http://www.urbandictionary.com/define.php?term=post-racial

Rand, J. (January 4, 2017) The Third Wave of Feminism Is Now, and It Is Intersectional. *The Huffington Post*. Retrieved from http://www.huffingtonpost.com/entry/the-third-wave-of-feminism-is-now-and-it-is-intersectional_us_586ac501e4b04d7df167d6a8

Reeves, R. (June 10, 2017) Stop Pretending You're Not Rich. *The New York Times*. Retrieved from https://www.nytimes.com/2017/06/10/opinion/sunday/stop-pretending-youre-not-rich.html?ref=opinion

Rosenberg, A. (May 3, 2016a) Yale Doesn't Need Calhoun College. It Needs a Real Slavery Memorial. *The Washington Post*. Retrieved from https://www.washingtonpost.com/news/act-four/wp/2016/05/03/yale-doesnt-need-calhoun-college-it-needs-a-real-slavery-memorial/

Rosenberg, E. (June 26, 2016b) Stonewall Inn Named National Monument, a First for the Gay Rights Movement. *The New York Times*. Retrieved from https://www.nytimes.com/2016/06/25/nyregion/stonewall-inn-named-national-monument-a-first-for-gay-rights-movement.html?_r=0

Russonello, G. (July 13, 2016) Race Relations Are at Lowest Point in Obama Presidency, Poll Finds. *The New York Times*. Retrieved from https://www.nytimes.com/2016/07/14/us/most-americans-hold-grim-view-of-race-relations-poll-finds.html

Shoichet, C., Berlinger, J., Almasy, S. (July 6, 2016) Alton Sterling Shooting: Second Video of Deadly Encounter Emerges. *CNN*. Retrieved from http://www.cnn.com/2016/07/06/us/baton-rouge-shooting-alton-sterling

Sinclair, K. (February 3, 2016) Student Demands: Who's Resigned, What's Renamed. *The New York Times*. Retrieved from https://www.nytimes.com/2016/02/07/education/edlife/student-demands-an-update.html?_r=0

Sodha, S. (February 2, 2017) Is Finland's Basic Universal Income a Solution to Automation, Fewer Jobs and Lower Wages? *The Guardian*. Retrieved from https://www.theguardian.com/society/2017/feb/19/basic-income-finland-low-wages-fewer-jobs

Stack, L. (February 15, 2016) American Muslims Under Attack. *The New York Times*. Retrieved from https://www.nytimes.com/interactive/2015/12/22/us/Crimes-Against-Muslim-Americans.html

Steinem, G. (2015) *My Life on the Road*. New York: Random House.

Straus, T. (October 23, 2000) A Manifesto for Third Wave Feminism. *AlterNet*. Retrieved from http://www.alternet.org/story/9986/a_manifesto_for_third_wave_feminism

Tavernise, S. (April 22, 2016) U.S. Suicide Rate Surges to a 30-year High. *The Telegraph*. Retrieved from https://www.nytimes.com/2016/04/22/health/us-suicide-rate-surges-to-a-30-year-high.html?_r=0

The Legacy of La Raza Unida. (October 11, 2012) *Southwestern*. Retrieved from http://www.southwestern.edu/live/news/7306-the-legacy-of-la-raza-unida

The Native American Movement. (n.d.) Retrieved from http://www.let.rug.nl/usa/outlines/history-1994/decades-of-change/the-native-american-movement.php

Tufekci, Z. (August 30, 2011) New Media and the People-powered Uprisings. *MIT Technology Review*. Retrieved from https://www.technologyreview.com/s/425280/new-media-and-the-people-powered-uprisings/

Vedantam, S. (January 14, 2016) Researchers Probe Stereotype: Christians and Science Don't Get Along. *NPR*. Retrieved from http://www.npr.org/2016/01/14/463010075/researchers-probe-stereotype-christians-and-science-dont-get-a-long

Victor, D. (July 15, 2016) Why 'All Lives Matter' Is Such a Perilous Phrase. *The New York Times*. Retrieved from https://www.nytimes.com/2016/07/16/us/all-lives-matter-black-lives-matter.html?module=WatchingPortal&region=c-column-middle-span-region&pgType=Homepage&action=click&mediaId=wide&state=standard&contentPlacement=5&version=internal&contentCollection=www.nytimes.com&contentId=http%3A%2F%2Fwww.nytimes.com%2F2016%2F07%2F16%2Fus%2Fall-lives-matter-black-lives-matter.html&eventName=Watching-article-click

Weiner, M. (2007–2015) *Mad Men*. Television series Lionsgate Television. Retrieved from http://www.imdb.com/title/tt0804503/

Woodruff, J. (host). (June 29, 2016) Sebastian Junger's 'Tribe' Examines Loyalty, Belonging and the Quest for Meaning. *PBS*. Retrieved from http://www.pbs.org/newshour/bb/sebastian-jungers-tribe-examines-loyalty-belonging-and-the-quest-for-meaning/

Wright, E.O., Rogers, J. (2015) *American Society: How it Really Works*. (2nd edn) New York W. W. Norton and Company.

Yale News. (February 11, 2017) *Yale to Change Calhoun College's Name to Honor Grace Murray Hopper*. Retrieved from http://news.yale.edu/2017/02/11/yale-change-calhoun-college-s-name-honor-grace-murray-hopper-0

Zinn Education Project (2016) Native American Activism: 1960s to Present. *Teaching a People's History*. Retrieved from https://zinnedproject.org/materials/native-american-activism-1960s-to-present/

Index

Note: Page numbers in *italic* type refer to figures.